P9-CBP-126

# BERNARD SHAW

## VOLUME I

1856–1898

Books by the same author

*Hugh Kingsmill*
*Lytton Strachey*
*Unreceived Opinions*
*Augustus John*

Edited by the same author

*The Best of Hugh Kingsmill*
*Lytton Strachey by Himself*
*The Art of Augustus John*
(with Malcolm Easton)
*The Genius of Shaw*
*The Shorter Strachey* (with Paul Levy)
William Gerhardie's *God's Fifth Column*
(with Robert Skidelsky)

# Bernard Shaw

## MICHAEL HOLROYD

---

## Volume I · 1856–1898
### *The Search for Love*

---

**VINTAGE BOOKS**
A DIVISION OF RANDOM HOUSE, INC.
NEW YORK

FIRST VINTAGE BOOKS EDITION, JULY 1990

Copyright © 1988 by Michael Holroyd

All rights reserved under International and Pan-American Copyright
Conventions. Published in the United States by Vintage Books, a
division of Random House, Inc., New York, and simultaneously in
Canada by Random House of Canada Limited, Toronto. Originally published
in Great Britain by Chatto & Windus Ltd. and in the United States by Random House,
Inc., in 1988.

Grateful acknowledgment is made to New Directions Publishing Corp. and Faber
and Faber Ltd. (London) for permission to reprint lines from "Portrait d'une
Femme" by Ezra Pound, published in *Collected Shorter Poems* (British ed.) and
in *Personae* (U.S. ed.) Copyright 1926 by Ezra Pound.

Library of Congress Cataloging-in-Publication Data
Holroyd, Michael.
Bernard Shaw / Michael Holroyd.
p. cm.
Includes bibliographical references.
Contents: v. 1. 1856–1898, The search for love.
ISBN 0-679-72505-9 (v. 1)
1. Shaw, Bernard, 1856–1950—Biography. 2. Dramatists,
Irish—19th century—Biography. 3. Dramatists, Irish—20th century—
Biography. I. Title.
[PR5366.H56 1990]
822'.912—dc20 89-40603
[B] CIP

Manufactured in the United States of America
10 9 8 7 6 5 4 3 2 1

# CONTENTS

v

# ILLUSTRATIONS

## NOTE FOR THE AMERICAN EDITION

Shaw's spelling, based soundly on phonetic principles, still seems idiosyncratic today. He was reacting against the caprices of 'Dr Johnson's alfabet' or what American readers would now call 'British English'. For this American edition of my biography, I have decided not to translate British English into American English so that American readers may have the advantage of sharing Shaw's irritation at its irregularities, and experience with amusement or relief his reaction against them in the authentic Shavian English quotations.

MICHAEL HOLROYD

# BERNARD SHAW

## 1856-1898

Once and for all, we are not born free; and we never can be free. When all the human tyrants are slain or deposed there will still be the supreme tyrant that can never be slain or deposed, and that tyrant is Nature.

*The Intelligent Woman's Guide to Socialism, Capitalism, Sovietism & Fascism.*

# CHAPTER I

## [ o ]

*Eternal is the fact that the human creature born in Ireland and brought up in its air is Irish.* 'Ireland Eternal and External'
(1948)

Bernard Shaw died on 2 November 1950 aged one week, three months and ninety-four years. For almost a decade interviewers had been recording his emphatic farewells: 'Goodbye ... *Goodbye* ... *Goodbye!*' They had departed. But next summer he would again greet them with his paradoxes, and their obituaries were copy-edited once more into birthday salutations. Everyone was over-rehearsed for the time when G.B.S. could no longer have the last word, and when it arrived there was babel. Actors appeared nostalgically on new-fangled television sets; writers spoke without interruption on the wireless; statesmen round the world – Clement Attlee, Pandit Nehru, Harry S Truman – uttered their prepared tributes. The world seemed dense with old Shavian sayings and stories.

This extraordinary outpouring, spreading over the front pages of newspapers and into their leaders, was a recognition of someone who, to produce the maximum influence on English-speaking culture, had made himself a publicity phenomenon. From America an offer of a million dollars had reached him for exclusive rights to a final message. 'There is nothing more to be said,' he had answered. One newspaper had gained possession of the village of Ayot St Lawrence and was able to advise its readers that 'just before dawn the mist cleared, and as Shaw was dying the stars were looking down'. Another had signed up his nurse, who reported that her patient had happily willed himself to die. A photographer nipped in and snapped him dead: 'he preserved the same puckish expression he had borne throughout life. His beard still stuck out at the same perkily, truculent angle.'

Perhaps to embrace this obituary mood, the critic Eric Bentley had bought several magazines and papers, but 'what I was reading made me sick,' he recorded. 'It was praise of Shaw, but what praise, and from whom! ... Such mourning for Shaw was a mockery of Shaw ... Grasping the first occasion when Shaw was powerless to come back at them, the bourgeoisie brayed and Broadway dimmed its lights.' To Bentley's mind it was the final acceptance of Shaw at the expense of all Shaw stood for – a process that had begun when he had given them 'G.B.S. the irresponsible clown', and advanced when, in old age, he grew perverse. 'You have an old man pretty much where you want him.'

Eric Bentley's *Bernard Shaw*, which marked the birth of a new Shaw, had been written without the collaboration of G.B.S., ghostwriter of so many previous volumes about himself, and was published shortly before the old man's death which, Bentley now hoped, might liberate his writing for the future.

Every text belongs to the future and is re-created by the reader, guided by his 'minder', the critic. But it is diminished if renewed in ignorance of the past or at the expense of the creative bringing-to-birth by the writer. This book aims to further the work of Bentley and subsequent resurrectionary critics, but by a method some Shavians suspect of being hostile to what Shaw stood for, the biographical method. Biographies of writers are written in collaboration with the posthumous subject of the biography. What is seen or overlooked, known and forgotten, comes to be shared between them. It is, like the process of reading itself, an 'intimacy between strangers'. The literary biographer must use, but may rearrange, the biographee's experiences, sometimes making heard what is unspoken or showing what has been hidden. But he may not go outside this pact. The line he tries to follow points towards empathy without veering off into sentimentality and maintains a detachment that stops short of incompatibility.

The irresponsible clown G.B.S. is present in this Life in company with the values that he advertised. They are part of a general human narrative that includes child and adult, magic and actuality, literature and living, chronology and time regained – blends and clashes that exercised G.B.S.'s ingenious powers of synthesis and became the dramatic focus of his work.

\*

He had asked that his ashes should be mixed inseparably with those of his wife, which had been kept at Golders Green Crematorium, and then scattered in their garden. 'I prefer the garden to the cloister.' Before this was done there was talk of burying his ashes in some religious national shrine such as Westminster Abbey. In the Dáil a proposal was made to convey them back to Ireland and place them beside Swift's at St Patrick's Cathedral in Dublin. The Irish Ambassador had turned up at Golders Green; and the Taoiseach, John Costello, tried to persuade his countrymen that Shaw had 'demonstrated many times his goodwill towards his native country and his fundamental sympathy with her national aspirations'. It was true that, having lived his first twenty years in Ireland, Shaw felt 'a foreigner in every other country'. Intermittently, all his life, he busied himself on Irish matters, married an Irishwoman, was given the Freedom of the City of Dublin, and left much of his money and property to Eire. But though he pronounced himself to be 'a XVII century Irishman', it was only outside Ireland that he was recognized as Irish. 'Being born in a stable does not make a man a horse.' He enjoyed exercising what the English believed to be his ineradicable Irishness, explaining that it was principally a matter of the weather which, having worked on his ancestors over a couple of centuries, had left its mark on him 'in greater flexibility and humorous power of resisting sentimental illusions'. As John Costello said, 'Bernard Shaw never forgot his Irish birth', but he often must have wished to do so and he set out in his writings to give himself a new birth: a re-creation. He claimed to be at least as indigenous as the half-American Winston Churchill or a half-Spaniard such as Éamon de Valera, both excellent examples of advantageous cross-breeding. 'I am a typical Irishman; my family come from Yorkshire,' he assured G. K. Chesterton who, typically English, confirmed that 'scarcely anyone but a typical Irishman could have made the remark'.

## [ I ]

*I am pure Dublin . . . We are a family of Pooh Bahs – snobs to the backbone. Drink and lunacy are minor specialities. (1912)*

*I forget exactly how many centuries you have to go back to reach a period at which every living person was an ancestor of every person now living; but the number is surprisingly small. We must be content with the bond of our common humanity. (1916)*

The Shaws made no secret of being aristocrats. They knew nothing of the middle class. Their aristocracy was a fact of natural history and the unpromiscuous social order of Ireland. No Shaw could form a social acquaintance with a Roman Catholic or tradesman. They lifted up their powerful Wellingtonian noses and spoke of themselves, however querulously, in a collective spirit (as people mentioning the Bourbons or Habsburgs) using the third person: 'the Shaws'.

These Shaws, being of respectable garrison stock, took their morality, politics and religion from Dublin Castle. They were ladies and gentlemen of the Danish, Norman and Cromwellian invasions. The family had come from Scotland, then moved to England. In 1689 Captain William Shaw slipped from Hampshire into Ireland to fight in the Battle of the Boyne. He was rewarded for rescuing his wounded commander with a large grant of land in Kilkenny. There, as landed gentry, the Shaws lived out lives of unexceptionable ease, hunting, shooting, fishing.

So prolific were they that some of the younger sons were obliged to follow their fortunes to Dublin. Most successful was Robert Shaw, who entered the Irish Parliament, refused to be bribed in support of the Union, founded the Royal Bank and in 1821 was made a baronet. His cousin Bernard (grandfather of G.B.S.) also seemed set for success. He practised law and, as a combination of notary public and stockbroker, became a prosperous Dublin businessman. On 1 April 1802, aged thirty, he married the daughter of a clergyman, Frances Carr, who over the next twenty-three years gave birth to fifteen children. As High Sheriff of Kilkenny, Bernard spent much of his time in the country and neglected his Dublin business, with the result that his partner absconded with £50,000 of his money. Bernard woke up to find himself penniless, collapsed, and died in his sleep. He had made no provision for his eleven surviving children, and his widow had to apply for help to Sir Robert. The banker-baronet was a wealthy man. 'Unlike the typical Shaw, he was plumpish and had the appearance somewhat of a truculent bear disturbed out of a doze.' He was hopelessly in love with Frances who, though disdaining his offers of marriage, accepted rent free 'a quaint cottage, with Gothically pointed windows' at Terenure. Her sole inheritance was a measure of the Shaw clan's extra-special gentility which she asserted through all vicissitudes. Appearances were kept up – the widow hanging, by way of escutcheon, her husband's brass helmet and sword (he had performed in the Yeomanry as an amateur soldier) in the hall. Though these were lean years, she launched her sons and daughters on the world 'in an unshaken and unshakeable consciousness of their own aristocracy'.

Like most large families, these Shaws were not exclusively teetotallers; nor did they all maintain until death the tolerant Irish standards of sanity. We see them through the eyes of G.B.S. Of his four aunts, Cecilia ('Aunt Sis'), the eldest, was a temperate maiden lady. She had been pronounced dead when a child and placed in a coffin; but, climbing out, lived on into her nineties, 'a big, rather imposing woman, with the family pride written all over her'. Aunt Frances, a gently nurtured lady, drank secretly over many years before, submitting to it openly, she passed away. Charlotte Jane ('Aunt Shah') married an irreproachable man connected with a cemetery. Aunt Emily, exceeding in nothing but snuff, married a scholastic clergyman, William George Carroll, who, but for his temper (it was said), would have been a bishop – though he poisoned one of his daughters when mistaking a bottle of liniment for medicine.

'I know as much about drink as anybody outside a hospital of inebriates,' G.B.S. later wrote. His knowledge had come largely from his father and some uncles. Two of his uncles were unknown to him, having emigrated to the Antipodes and 'like Mr Micawber, made history there'. A third, Robert, was blinded in his youth; he married and 'never had an opportunity of drinking'. Uncle Henry was the rich man of the family, able to afford two wives and fifteen children. Trained as a corn-merchant, he invested his money in a collapsing coal mine. Having lost £60,000, he fell into a severe nervous prostration and before his death became mentally unstable.

The other three brothers, including Shaw's father, were alcoholics. It was a solitary neurosis they shared. 'They avoided observation whilst drinking,' G.B.S. noted, '. . . [but] their excesses rendered them wretched. They appreciated music, books and acting, but had not the energy to cultivate these tastes and never took the initiative in visiting any place of entertainment. They all, when well-advanced in life and apparently confirmed beyond hope in their habits, gave up drinking at once and for ever.'

Uncle Barney (William Bernard) and Uncle Fred (Richard Frederick) both died in the family mental retreat, Dr Eustace's, in the north of Dublin. The youngest, Uncle Fred, didn't drink until he married a girl named Waters, several of whose family were insane. His drinking bouts then grew excessive and he suffered from delirium tremens, but gave up alcohol altogether once his wife, a bad-tempered lady whom he used to beat, had left him to live in London. He was reputed to be ungenerous (he worked in the Valuation Office) and, in retirement, 'harmlessly dotty'.

Uncle Barney was an inordinate smoker as well as a drunkard. Frequently drunk by dawn, he lived a largely fuddled life until he was past fifty. Then, relinquishing alcohol and tobacco simultaneously, he passed the next ten years of his life as a teetotaller, playing an obsolete wind instrument called an ophicleide. Towards the end of this period, renouncing the ophicleide and all its works, he married a lady of great piety, took off his boots and fell completely silent. He was carried off to the family asylum where, 'impatient for heaven', he discovered an absolutely original method of committing suicide. It was simple and irresistibly amusing; even so, no human being had yet thought of it, involving as it did an empty carpet bag. However, in the act of placing this bag on his head, Uncle Barney jammed the mechanism of his heart in a paroxysm of laughter, which the merest hint of his suicidal technique never failed to provoke among the Shaws – and the result was that he died a second before he succeeded in killing himself. The coroner's court described his death as being 'from natural causes'.

'The least suggestion of drink, however jocular, is deadly to a Shaw,' G.B.S. told one of his cousins. 'Drink is the biggest skeleton in the family cupboard.' But G.B.S. did not leave this skeleton in its cupboard. He had a choice of making the Shaw drunkenness into 'either a family tragedy or a family joke', and he decided on the joke, hauling out the dancing skeletons and making their bones rattle. So, in the crowded bookshop window of his works, we may see a cabaret of Shavian aunts and uncles with a chorus of inebriate cousins, accompanied by brass bugles, tambourines and harp; and at the centre, a wonderfully hopeless chap, second cousin to a baronet, George Carr Shaw, G.B.S.'s father.

[ 2 ]

*Fortunately I have a heart of stone: else my relations would have broken it long ago.* (1939)

The story of George Carr Shaw's life was simple. He would tell you it had evolved as the retribution for an injury he had once done a cat. He had found this cat, brought it home with him, fed it. But next day he had let his dog chase it and kill it. In his imagination this cat now had its revenge, seeing to it that he would have neither luck nor money. He was permanently unsuccessful because of this cat; unskilled, unsober, and unserious too. It was no less than natural justice: he knew that. His genius for poverty established this lesson beyond doubt. His fate was to become 'a futile person'.

Between the ages of twenty-three and thirty he had been a clerk at Todhunter's, the Dublin ironworks, but in 1845 he lost this job. He had nothing to fall back on but his pretensions – the social pretensions of landed gentry without land. What employment could there be for a Protestant poor relation with no inheritance, no profession, no manual skill, no qualifications of any sort? By means of family influence he landed up with a tailor-made superfluous post at the Four Courts in a sinecure without duties and responsibilities. Unfortunately, it was one of the first of such positions to be abolished in the legal reforms of the early 1850s, for which 'outrage' George Shaw received a pension of £44 a year. During 1851 he essayed a clerkship or two with some corn-merchants until his brother Henry gave him temporary employment in his firm. There were opportunities in Dublin for a wholesale corn-merchant (retail trade was impossible for a Shaw). But George Shaw needed money. Until now he had walked by himself, a gentleman who was no gentleman, and all places were alike to him. He was in his thirty-eighth year and had recently come in contact with a twenty-one-year-old girl, Lucinda Elizabeth Gurly, called 'Bessie'. She was short, thin-lipped, with the jaw of a prizefighter and a head like a football; but she had an attractive inheritance and was of an apparently innocent nature. Her financial expectations and his own new business hopes emboldened George Carr Shaw. He felt drawn to her. 'It was at this moment,' G.B.S. records, 'that some devil, perhaps commissioned by the Life Force to bring me into the world, prompted my father to propose marriage to Miss Bessie Gurly.'

\*

'My mother's maiden name was Gurly, which is so ugly that I think it must be a corruption of the French Gourlay,' G.B.S. wrote to a correspondent. 'Possibly the Gourlays were Huguenots driven to Ireland by persecution. My maternal grandfather was a ferocious Protestant.'

The mysterious master-spirit among Bessie's forebears had been her maternal grandfather, a country gentleman of imposing presence whose origin was so obscure that he was understood to have had no legal parents. But he was rich and lived *en grand seigneur* on his property of over two thousand acres in Kilkenny and at a place called Whitechurch to the south of Dublin. Each week he would drive in to a little pawnshop in Winetavern Street, one of the poorest quarters of the city. The name on the door, it was said, was Cullen, an employee, under cover of whose identity John Whitcroft made his money. The opulent squire of Whitechurch and of Kilsee House, County Kilkenny, was the pawnbroker of Winetavern Street.

The squire-pawnbroker had married well and saw to it that the alliances made by his children were limited to county families. He wanted respectability by blood: they wanted money. On 29 December 1829 his daughter Lucinda married a ginger-whiskered squire from Carlow named Walter Bagnall Gurly, who was then living nearby at Rathfarnham. 'He was a wiry, tight, smallish handknit open-air man,' G.B.S. remembered, able to make his own boats and to ride the most ungovernable horses; an ingenious carpenter, dead shot, indefatigable fisher of fish: in short, 'able to do anything,' G.B.S. summed up, 'except manage his affairs, keep his estate from slipping through his fingers, or refrain from backing bills for neighbours as thriftless as himself'.

In ten years of marriage they had one daughter and a son. Then, on 14 January 1839, Mrs Gurly died. Bessie was nine. 'I was promptly taken in hand,' she later wrote, 'and educated within an inch of my life.' She had been placed under the care of her great-aunt, Ellen Whitcroft, a terrible hump-backed lady. This spidery creature brought her up to be a paragon of good breeding. Bessie was taught how to dress correctly, to sit motionless and straight; how to breathe, pronounce French, convey orders to servants. At Logier's Academy in Sackville Street she was schooled in harmony and counterpoint, playing the piano 'with various coins of the realm on the backs of my hands, also with my hair which I wore in two long plaits down my back tied to the back of my chair, also with a square of pasteboard hung on my neck by a string pretty much as pictures are hung ... in order to prevent me looking at my hands ... I had quite a reputation as a splendid "*performer*".' By these methods, her son observed, she was taught 'how *not* to play the pianoforte with such entire success that she has never been able to play since with any freedom or skill'.

By a programme of constraints and browbeatings, scoldings and punishments, she was 'educated up to the highest standard of Irish "carriage ladies"'. As such she maintained an unquenchable dignity, never sang, said, or did anything coarse, loved flowers more than human beings and walked through the streets seeing nobody. Her aunt, who had left her fortune to Bessie as a dowry, intended a great destiny for her – something that because of her deformity she had never achieved herself: marriage into the nobility. With these superior expectations, and in a state of extreme cultivation, Bessie was floated into Dublin Society where she encountered the sinking George Carr Shaw.

About this time something dreadful happened, involving a pair of gloves. After thirteen years as a widower, Bessie's father made a shotgun decision to remarry, this time to the daughter of his thriftless neighbour. It was a disastrous project and certain to be opposed by the Whitcroft family. Gurly had managed to retard his relapse into near-bankruptcy by substituting for mortgages (his usual notion of procuring money) the obtaining of loans from Aunt Ellen and her brother, John Hamilton Whitcroft, son and heir of the pawnbroker. He therefore 'tried to conceal from him the fact and date of his marriage,' G.B.S. wrote. 'Unfortunately my mother, who also, under the influence of her aunt, thought the marriage very improper, let out the secret to her uncle. The consequence was that my grandfather on going out on his wedding morning to buy a pair of gloves for the ceremony, was arrested for debt at the suit of his brother-in-law and was torn from his nuptials to a spunging house.'

The wedding was postponed and Gurly, who was furious, believing that his daughter had deliberately betrayed him so as to prevent the marriage, attempted to cut Bessie out of his first marriage settlement. He was prevented by a solicitor, and had to be content with forbidding her his house. Her only refuge was Aunt Ellen. But secretly Bessie detested her aunt and everything that, masquerading as education and religion, had made her childhood miserable. It was now that George Carr Shaw drifted forward to make his bid for Aunt Ellen's property by proposing marriage to her niece. What was she to do? Bessie's choice was unenviable. On one side was a vindictive father and indignant stepmother-to-be, some intermittent relatives and her loathsome aunt who, between them, reduced her life to domestic slavery. Opposite them hovered George Carr Shaw.

Shaw was not a romantic figure. It seems possible that even then he was an advanced alcoholic, and with steady diarrhoea. Almost twice her age, he had a weak mouth, one squinting eye and a number of epileptic ways. 'If any unpleasant reflection occurred to him, he, if in a room, rubbed his hands rapidly together and ground his teeth. If in a street, he took a short run.' He was an unconvivial man, with disconcerting quirks of humour and little interest in women. Drink and money were his world.

Though her choice was unenviable, Bessie appears to have shown no hesitation. In her son's opinion, she carried, like blinkers, the stamp of her Spartan childhood to the grave. 'Misfortunes that would have crushed ten untrained women broke on her like waves on granite.' Strength lay in her character and ignorance in her schooling: this was the Shavian version. But, in fact, whenever she found herself in unpleasant circumstances, she bolted. With one of his most subtle paradoxes, G.B.S. reversed the entrance and exit so that his mother often appears to be boldly pushing forward to some positive goal. Frantically anxious to escape from her family, she overlooked the squinting eyes, grinding teeth, mists of drink and all George Carr Shaw's peculiarities, and took stock only of the social acceptability that made his proposal open the doorway to some better life. It seemed a simple way out. 'I see no difficulty about my father falling in love as much as usual with my mother,' G.B.S. wrote.

'It was my mother who, not knowing what it all meant, made a convenience of his offer, and got tragically caught.' It was, he concluded, 'impossible to doubt her good faith and innocence'. Yet this was to be a marriage of two blind people, each treating the other as guide dog. 'Money in marriage is the first and, frequently, the only passion,' wrote St John Ervine of nineteenth-century Irish marriages. In this sense G.B.S.'s father may be said 'as much as usual' to have married for love: love of money and the independence it would bring them both – after which, like so many of their forebears, they were to live impecuniously ever after.

The Whitcrofts were again horrified. Bessie's marriage would be even worse than her father's. Aunt Ellen had tolerated George Carr Shaw as Bessie's chaperon because of his well-connected harmlessness. To be with Shaw was an alibi for almost anything; never before had he been known to take an initiative. Aunt Ellen explained that the marriage was impossible – a scandalous throw-away on someone whose income was wholly inadequate to the social rank he claimed. Finally, when none of her objections prevailed, she revealed that Shaw was a known drunkard – in any event it was notorious in the family. Bessie knew how to deal with this. She went round to Shaw and asked him; and he confessed that all his life he had been a bigoted teetotaller. But he did not give her to understand that he was a teetotaller who drank. 'In fact,' explained G.B.S., 'he was so horribly ashamed of his dipsomania that he had to deny it just as Rousseau had to deny stealing the ribbon. There are things that we cannot bring ourselves to confess.'

So the marriage went ahead. Aunt Ellen had one more card to play: she disinherited her niece. This was undeniably a more serious blow to Shaw than to Bessie. Needing money to take advantage of a business opportunity from his brother Henry, he sold his pension for £500 (to a man named O'Brien who immediately insured his life for £600), and used this capital to buy a partnership in a corn-merchant business with his brother's ex-partner, George Clibborn. It was a start – to be supported after his marriage by his wife's own money (over a thousand pounds) and whatever could be regained of Aunt Ellen's inheritance. It could have been worse.

This was a good summer for Walter Bagnall Gurly. On 25 May 1852 he finally married his second wife who, two months before, had given birth to their first daughter; and twenty-three days later, at the same church, St Peter's in Aungier Street, he attended the wedding of his daughter and George Carr Shaw. As a wedding gift, Aunt Ellen had sent the couple a bundle of IOUs signed by Gurly – which he seized and burnt. Better still was the marriage settlement he had insisted on their signing a few hours before the ceremony. Bessie's personal assets were listed as 'one thousand two hundred and fifty-six pounds Nine shillings and two pence Government three and a quarter per cent Stock'. All this, together with income to be derived from her father's first marriage settlement and from the Will of her pawnbroker grandfather, was transferred by deed to two trustees. The effect of this, in those days before the Married Woman's Property Laws, was to ensure that the inheritance would remain Gurly-money, never the Shaw-money it would otherwise have become. So George Carr Shaw had gained a wife and lost a fortune. There was nothing to be done – it was enough to make one weep with laughter.

When they drove off after the wedding, George Carr Shaw turned to kiss his bride. She felt so disgusted that she was still protesting more than thirty years later. 'The rebuff must have opened his eyes a little too late,' their son judged, 'to her want of any really mately feeling for him.'

# [ 3 ]

*William Morris used to say that it is very difficult to judge who are the best people to take charge of children, but it is certain that the parents are the very worst.* (1943)

They had chosen Liverpool for their honeymoon, and here their first child was conceived. It was nearly the end of their marriage. Years later, Mrs Shaw told her son that, opening her husband's wardrobe, she had 'found it full of empty bottles'. The truth had tumbled out. Bessie's one thought being to escape, she determined to run away to sea. She would be a stewardess. But on reaching the docks she discovered that the men there were even drunker than her husband. She fled back. 'I leave you to imagine,' wrote G.B.S., 'the hell into which my mother descended when she found out what shabby-genteel poverty with a drunken husband is like.'

They returned to Dublin and moved into 'an awful little kennel with "primitive sanitary arrangements"', 3 Upper Synge Street – an unpretending road of eleven small squat houses which runs round the corner from Harrington Street. Here their three children were born: Lucinda Frances, called Lucy, on 26 March 1853, Elinor Agnes, nicknamed 'Yuppy', two years later; and, on 26 July 1856, their son George Bernard, 'fifty years too soon', he calculated. He was baptized by

13

his clergyman uncle, William George Carroll, Rector of St Bride's in the then Established Protestant Episcopal Church of Ireland, 'on which occasion my sponsor arrived drunk and incapable, and the sexton was ordered to take his place exactly as he might have been ordered to put coal on the fire'.

In his nursery days he was called Bob; by the time he had grown into his holland tunic and knickerbockers he had become 'Sonny'; it was not until he had orphaned himself and was reborn the child of his own writings in England that he developed the full intellectual plumage of 'G.B.S.'.

We first see Bob at the age of one. 'The young beggar is getting quite outrageous,' his father writes proudly to Bessie who was staying with her family. 'I left him this morning roaring and tearing like a bull.' These passions, which encompassed eating his hat, vomiting up currants, annoying his teeth or making a jigsaw of unread newspapers, were chiefly concentrated on marvellous walking expeditions from Papa to Nurse (who was threatening a breakdown) and back again. From his bed he plunged head-first onto the floor; and from the kitchen table he cascaded through a pane of glass without 'even a *pane* in his head'.

This bull of a boy was soon domesticated into the sedate Sonny, a very correct young gentleman ('sometimes a tussle but never a fight'), separated from the others, especially from his mother. His bedroom also served as his father's dressing-room, and the most affectionate sound in Synge Street in those early days was his father's puns. He had the good manners never to argue with his father or to ask him the *why* of anything. *What* was his question, and it allowed George Carr Shaw to edge round many things unknown to them both. From their talks, Sonny learnt that Unitarians were people who believed that Christ had not been crucified, since he had been seen scuttling down the far side of the hill of Calvary; he was let in on the secret of how his father had saved the life of Uncle Robert – 'and, to tell you the truth, I was never so sorry for anything in my life afterwards'. It became a game between them, almost an intimacy, that the son should provoke his father to such exhibitions. Sometimes George Carr Shaw would tell him adventure stories, holding the Bible before him as he improvised. But when Sonny began to scoff at this divine masterpiece, George Carr Shaw was shocked, rebuking him for such ignorance and concluding, with a convulsion of chuckling, that 'even the worst enemy of religion could say no worse of the Bible than that it was the damnedest parcel of lies ever written'.

In a letter to his wife, George Carr Shaw had written of 'a Mill which Clibborn & I are thinking of taking at Dolphin's Barn . . . Wont it be great fun and grandeur to find yourself when you come back the wife of a dusty Miller, so be prepared to have the very life ground out of you . . .' Bessie was not amused: besides, it was all talk, he never did anything positive. 'You are out for once in your life,' he told her. 'We *have* taken the Mill.'

Dolphin's Barn Mill was on the country side of the canal. Sonny, who sometimes walked there with his father and sisters before breakfast, liked to play under the waterwheel by the millpond and in the big field adjoining the building. 'The field had one tree in it, at the foot of which I buried our dead dog. It was quite wild. I never saw a human soul in it.' On the front of Rutland Avenue was a Clibborn & Shaw warehouse, one corner of which had been made into a shop where corn, wheat, flour and locust beans were surreptitiously retailed to the villagers. This humiliating side of the business was the only one to make money. Milling in Ireland was declining, and the sole profits came, not from the grinding of corn, but from the selling of imported corn on commission. Clibborn & Shaw knew nothing of this. George Clibborn, who had been apprenticed as a draper, was a rough-mannered man whose bluntness Shaw liked to mitigate by small gestures of geniality. They did not prosper. Once, when the firm was almost ruined by the bankruptcy of one of its debtors, both of them burst simultaneously into tears. Clibborn (who nevertheless had some private income) wept openly in their office; Shaw (whose entire capital was imperilled) retreated to an empty corner of the warehouse and, until exhaustion overtook him, cried with laughter at the colossal mischief of it all.

It was this sense of mischief that Sonny responded to, and that G.B.S. believed he inherited. But planted in so many of Papa's comedies were seeds of disaster. When pretending to fling his son into the canal, he almost succeeded; and a monstrous suspicion began to crawl into Sonny's mind. On arriving home he went to his mother and whispered his awful discovery, 'Mama: I think Papa's drunk.' This was too much for Bessie who retorted with disgust, 'When is he ever anything else?' Recalling this incident many years later, G.B.S. wrote to Ellen Terry: 'I have never believed in anything since: then the scoffer began.'

*

G.B.S. subsequently conceded this to have been a 'rhetorical exaggeration', yet 'the wrench from my childish faith in my father as perfect and omniscient to the discovery that he was a hypocrite and a dipsomaniac was so sudden and violent that it must have left its mark on me'.

Though he transferred the responsibility for his desolate childhood to his father, the central character in this scene had been his mother. The mark it left on him was one of incredulous disillusion: 'I shall carry traces of that disillusion to my grave.' Bessie was a grievously disappointed woman, embittered (so G.B.S. privately felt) by their ridiculous poverty: 'We all suffered for it.' She believed, and persuaded her son to believe, that 'everybody had disappointed her, or betrayed her, or tyrannized over her'. From this time onwards Sonny began to see his father through his mother's eyes, as a man to imitate in as much detail as possible, but in reverse. It suited George Carr Shaw's temperament to play along. When he caught Sonny pretending to smoke a toy pipe, he entreated him with dreadful earnestness never to follow his example. The eventual outcome was that G.B.S. neither smoked nor drank. In this special Shavian sense, George Carr Shaw became a model father.

Of his mother, G.B.S. once admitted, 'I knew very little about her.' This was partly because she did not concern herself with him. Her own childhood had been made miserable by bullying, but Bessie never bullied; she made her son miserable by neglect. 'She was simply not a wife or mother at all.' Nor was Synge Street a home: 'neither our hearts nor our imaginations were in it.'

'Dublin is a city of derision at best,' G.B.S. wrote many years later; 'but in our house reverence did not exist.' He tried to reverence his mother. Needing her attention, he found with dismay that he could do nothing to interest her. In her eyes he was an inferior little male animal tainted with all the potential weaknesses of her husband. She turned away and, exercising one of the first planchette boards to be imported into Ireland, concentrated on life elsewhere.

'Poverty, ostracism, disgust, three children, a house rented at £30 a year or thereabouts, a drunken husband obviously incapable of improving the situation . . .' In the circumstances, G.B.S. concluded, 'it says a great deal for my mother's humanity that she did not hate her children'. In his books and letters, he gives a picture of his mother based on her recollections, his own selected observations, and some hard-headed sentiment. He places her on a carpet of filial loyalty, which he invites every potential biographer to pull from beneath her feet. His American biographer, Archibald Henderson, scrupulously overlooking this invitation, received in red ink a brusque rebuff: 'This sympathy with the mother is utterly false. Damn your American sentimentality!'

In the Shavian version Bessie becomes a monument to Stoicism. 'She never made scenes, never complained, never nagged, never punished nor retaliated nor lost her self-control nor her superiority to spites and tantrums and tempers. She was neither weak nor submissive; but as she never revenged, so she never forgave. There were no quarrels and consequently no reconciliations. You did a wrong; and you were classed by her as a person who did such wrongs, and tolerated indulgently up to a point. But if at last you drove her to break with you, the breach was permanent: you did not get back again . . . She did not hate anybody, nor love anybody.'

From the first unpublished draft of this passage one sentence has been dropped: 'She had a high inertia in practical matters: was unenterprising and long-suffering.' What she lacked was the vitality of a positive religion. Shaw presents her record as a primer for 'astonishing and admirable' conduct under the appalling conditions of a moribund capitalist society: a guide to be followed by her son until the birth of moral passion had grown into the creed of Creative Evolution.

In a rare moment of emotion, G.B.S. wrote to Ellen Terry of his 'devil of a childhood, Ellen, rich only in dreams, frightful & loveless in realities'. But looking directly at such bleakness was too painful. Usually he put on the spectacles of paradox. This paradox became his 'criticism of life', the technique by which he turned lack of love inside out and, by attracting from the world some of the attention he had been denied by his mother, conjured optimism out of deprivation.

The fact that neither of his parents cared for him was, he perceived, of enormous advantage. What else could have taught him the frightful value of independence and self-sufficiency? He was spared, too, by their unconcealed disappointment in each other, from lingering illusions about the family. It was remarkable how these paradoxical privileges began to multiply once he became skilled at the game. His father and mother were so wonderfully uncoercive that Sonny never suffered from the meddlesomeness of morbidly conscientious parents. They acted as if education were a natural attribute, like breathing or digestion; and since no one took malevolent pleasure in indoctrinating him, he was left with very little to unlearn – almost nothing, for example, in the way of moral or religious instruction. No obstacle was put in the path of taking his lessons from actual experience and finding out what he must never expect from life. 'I had to learn everything by breaking my shins over it,' he wrote, 'and to become wise by making a fool of myself from the very beginning.' From his observations he soon deduced the wonderful impersonality of sex, and the kindness and good sense of distancing yourself from people you loved. Though he abhorred any ill-treatment of children, it was not long before he realized that love was wasted on them. Nobody was capable of love until he had earned it. To sail out into adult life demanding it as a natural inheritance invited shipwreck. He kept afloat where others sank.

'The fact that I am still alive at 78½ I probably owe largely to her [Bessie's] complete neglect of me during my infancy,' G.B.S. confided to Marie Stopes, 'because if she had attempted to take care of me her stupendous ladylike ignorance would certainly have killed me. It used to be a common saying among Dublin doctors in my youth that most women killed their first child by their maternal care . . . motherhood is not every woman's vocation.' G.B.S. believed that his mother preferred her daughters, in particular the red-haired Yuppy, lavishing her full indifference on himself. Yuppy had wilted under her slight attentions. As a child she developed goitre; only the fortunate absence of medical aid enabled Nature to perform a cure. Then at the age of twenty-one, assisted by a sanatorium of doctors, she died of tuberculosis. It could be no accident either that Lucy, Bessie's second favourite, was to die next, following a long period of ill-health, seven years after her mother's death. She 'suffered far more by the process than I did,' G.B.S. wrote of their upbringing, 'for she wanted to be trained, and was not immune, as I and my mother were, from conventional vanities: in fact the process that was the making of me was the wrecking, if not of her, at least of all her chances in life'.

This was a Shavian version of the survival of the fittest. When you unravel the paradox you discover a truism. Bessie had been fortified by emotional privation that, in a different form, she handed down to Sonny and both, benefiting from this stern preservative, lived long. What did it matter if 'my people knew me very well on my worst side and not at all on my best?' What better preparation could there be for reviewers?

There was no feuding at Synge Street. The house was small, but so far as possible they treated one another like furniture. 'We as children,' G.B.S. explained, 'had to find our own way in a household where there was neither hate nor love.' Sonny's own way within this frigidly neutral climate eventually led him to the conclusion that Nature had intended an element of antipathy in consanguinity as a defence against incest. Happily his family had been well dosed with this preventative. 'Kinship unites only when it is distant,' he wrote later '(a dog being a dearer friend than a man) and sunders when it is close.' Many well-meaning people, believing the propaganda of clannish sentimentality, became so tortured by their healthy repugnance to fathers, mothers, daughters, sons, wives, husbands that battery and bloody murder had largely been taken over as family business. That such were the fruits of blood relationship made domestic failure a cause of laughter and celebration for the Shaws. 'I have not yet found real homes except in very stupid families to whom a house is a world,' he wrote.

The cult of generous impersonality became for G.B.S. a means of resolving discord. 'A family without good manners is impossible,' he judged. '[It] can only be kept intact if all the parties behave with the most scrupulous consideration for one another.' He believed that he had inherited from his parents genetic qualities that they had found incompatible but which it was his duty, in expiation, to reconcile within himself. Only by marrying opposites, through paradox or a dialectical process of synthesis, did he feel that he could fulfil his moral obligation to optimism and a better future.

He was careful not to recommend the impossible. We cannot remain unaffected by wrongdoing, pain, disappointment. But if, as everyone said, we cannot change the way human nature responds to circumstances, then change the circumstances. Most of us have drugged ourselves in order to live in hell. We fear change-for-the-better as something that may deprive us of these sweet drugs that make our hell voluptuous, so we resist to the point of suicide almost any serious attempt at improvement, even for our children.

Yet, despite our record of self-destruction, we are, G.B.S. believed, all one with another; there is no *us* and *them*, and in the end no necessary conflict. Which one of us can claim that, given another's background and upbringing, he would have done better? We should therefore seek to improve people's upbringing and to make the circumstances of their background uniform. Only after such levelling up to a uniformity of conditions could individuality of talent flourish without bitterness. In place of the warring of envy and class, G.B.S. was to substitute a Hegelian policy of inclusiveness. But to include everything in his sights he was obliged to fly his balloon of words higher and higher, into the stratosphere of hypothesis where, in all its thin remoteness, his vision became complete.

He writes of a strangeness 'which made me all my life a sojourner on this planet rather than a native of it. Whether it be that I was born mad or a little too sane, my kingdom was not of this world: I was at home only in the realm of my imagination, and at my ease only with the mighty dead.' It is this voice from the living dead that, despite the marvellous Shavian cadence, chilled his audience. In the lost childhood of Sonny the philosophy of G.B.S. was conceived. 'What else can I do?' he had asked. He strove to bring the world into harmony with his lonely nature, but the world reacted subconsciously to what was suppressed rather than to what he proclaimed. His vision was complete in all but substance: he could see everything but touch little. For what he had done was not (as he claimed) to change dreaming for reality, but to replace the first loveless reality with one dream and then another. 'I very seldom dream of my mother,' he told Gilbert Murray; 'but when I do, she is my wife as well as my mother. When this first occurred to me (well on in my life), what surprised me when I awoke was that the notion of incest had not entered into the dream: I had taken it as a matter of course that the maternal function included the wifely one; and so did she. What is more, the sexual relation acquired all the innocence of the filial one, and the filial one all the completeness of the sexual one ... if circumstances tricked me into marrying my mother before I knew she was my mother, I should be fonder of her than I could ever be of a mother who was not my wife, or a wife who was not my mother.' Only in his imagination was such completeness possible. Below the elevation of the dream lay a meagreness of experience.

Most of the time Sonny and his sisters were abandoned to Providence and the servants – 'and *such* servants, Good God!' The exception was 'my excellent Nurse Williams' who left while Sonny was still very young. But what could you expect on £8 a year? 'I had my meals in the kitchen,' G.B.S. recalled, 'mostly of stewed beef, which I loathed, badly cooked potatoes, sound or diseased as the case might be, and much too much tea out of brown delft teapots left to "draw" on the hob until it was pure tannin. Sugar I stole ... When I was troublesome a servant thumped me on the head until one day, greatly daring, I rebelled, and, on finding her collapse abjectly, became thenceforth uncontrollable. I hated the servants and liked my mother because, on one or two rare and delightful occasions when she buttered my bread for me, she buttered it thickly instead of merely wiping a knife on it ... I could idolize her to the utmost pitch of my imagination and had no sordid or disillusioning contacts with her. It was a privilege to be taken for a walk or a visit with her, or on an excursion.'

Occasionally Bessie would take him to see Aunt Ellen, hoping that the old lady would feel sufficiently attracted to leave him her property. She wasn't, but Sonny seemed mesmerized by her. This strange little humpbacked lady, fastidious, refined, with her pretty face and magical deformity, appeared like a beneficent fairy. One Sunday morning Papa announced that she was dead, and Sonny ran off to the solitude of the garden to cry, terrified that his awful grief would last for ever. When he 'discovered that it lasted only an hour,' wrote G.B.S., 'and then passed completely away', he had his first taste of realism.

Shaw was unable to tolerate feelings of sadness; any indulgence in tragedy could be endured, he thought, only by those with limited emotions. 'People who cry and grieve never remember,' he wrote. 'I never grieve and never forget.' Sadness was a poison to his system and before absorption it had to be instantly converted into something else. His attitude to death was perhaps the most extreme example of this manufacture of cheerfulness.

Owing to his unreasonably large stock of relatives there was a steady supply of Irish funerals from which Sonny could amuse himself. Papa, he saw, 'found something in a funeral, or even in a death, which tickled his sense of humor.' Dublin

'buried its dead in two great cemeteries, each of which was held by the opposite faction to be the antechamber of perdition, and by its own patrons to be the gate of paradise . . . Now the sorest bereavement does not cause men to forget wholly that time is money. Hence, though we used to proceed slowly and sadly enough through the streets or terraces at the early stages of our progress, when we got into the open a change came over the spirit in which the coachmen drove. Encouraging words were addressed to the horses; whips were flicked; a jerk all along the line warned us to slip our arms through the broad elbow-straps of the mourning-coaches, which were balanced on longitudinal poles by enormous and totally unelastic springs; and then the funeral began in earnest. Many a clinking run have I had through that bit of country at the heels of some deceased uncle who had himself many a time enjoyed the same sport. But in the immediate neighbourhood of the cemetery the houses recommenced; and at that point our grief returned upon us with overwhelming force: we were able barely to crawl along to the great iron gates where a demoniacal black pony was waiting with a sort of primitive gun-carriage and a pall to convey our burden up the avenue to the mortuary chapel, looking as if he might be expected at every step to snort fire, spread a pair of gigantic bat's wings, and vanish, coffin and all, in thunder and brimstone'.

In this way, replacing mordant sentimentality by 'eternal derision', Sonny began to laugh pain out of existence. He seldom exercised the mechanism of grief over the dead. Detachment from the fear of death was a step towards Shavian invulnerability in life. Although G.B.S. claimed to have no opinion of death ('it is a fact like the rising of the sun and has simply to be faced, not argued about'), he barricaded the subject round with an elaborate philosophical construction. His death-anxiety was transferred into a fear of poverty (which, with a little courage and thought, we could eliminate), and any sediment of apprehension was done away with by a hygienic campaign against earth burial. Freed from emotion and escapist fables of personal immortality, death became an intensely democratic process. We began to die when more people wished us dead than wished us alive.

Sonny spent much of his solitary time in tears, though G.B.S. liked being alone. He had stories for company. His stories formed his philosophy and they always had a happy end. He did not brood superstitiously on the vacant corpse. Many a colleague, on the death of a wife, son or mother, was to find himself in receipt of Shaw's feeling congratulations. 'Dont order any black things,' he instructed Edith Lyttelton after the death of her husband. 'Rejoice in his memory; and be radiant: leave grief to the children. Wear violet and purple. Dying is a troublesome business: there is pain to be suffered, and it wrings one's heart; but death is a splendid thing – a warfare accomplished, a beginning all over again, a triumph. You can always see that in their faces.'

## [ 4 ]

*I am an Irishman without a birth certificate.*

Sometime after her marriage Bessie was raised up into a new world of 'imagination, idealization, the charm of music, the charm of lovely seas and sunsets' by a mysterious intruder, called Lee, one of the originals of George du Maurier's Svengali. He was a 'mesmeric conductor and daringly original teacher of singing,' G.B.S. records. It was the extraordinary effect he produced on Bessie that impressed her son. Sonny watched him closely.

There was something gypsy-like about his appearance. Though his upper lip and chin were close-shaven, his face 'was framed with pirate-black whiskers.' In the fashion of poets and pirates, he wore his luxuriant black hair long, but he was a fastidious man and dressed sharply. He had a deformed foot and limped with peculiar elegance. But it was the volubility of his language, the confidence and zest with which he asserted his heterodox opinions, that Sonny noticed more than any physical adroitness. He noticed too the way his mother listened, the way she came alive under Lee's spell.

Sonny did not like Lee, but he could not help admiring him. He was, it seems, about six years old when his mother first introduced this stranger to him at Synge Street. But, 'as his notion of play was to decorate my face with moustaches and whiskers in burnt cork in spite of the most furious resistance I could put up, our encounter was not a success; and the defensive attitude in which it left me lasted, though without the least bitterness, until the decay of his energies and the growth of mine put us on more than equal terms'.

G.B.S. never knew when Lee and his mother met. He assumed, sometimes in trenchant terms, that in the early 1860s and some nine or ten years after her marriage, Bessie had gone to have her voice trained by the singing instructor who lived nearby. It was difficult to know, for Bessie seldom spoke about herself to her son, and Lee made a legend of his past. He claimed to have been born in Kilrush, County Clare, the natural son of Colonel Crofton Moore Vandeleur, MP, JP, DL. When he was a boy he had fallen down a flight of stairs. His wound was badly dressed, and though he wore his lameness 'as if it were a quality instead of a defect', he was left with a lifelong animosity towards orthodox medical science. He had never been to school and had 'nothing good to say of any academic institution'. Instead he became self-taught, provided himself with the title 'Professor of Music' and went on to pioneer a revolutionary discipline of voice-training which he called 'the Method'. He was more than a singing teacher: he was a philosopher of voice. He had made an elaborate study of the physiology of the vocal organs, experimenting on himself and on his pupils; he had dissected birds and (with the connivance of medical friends) examined human corpses in his search for the secret of *bel canto*. Every conventional teacher of the day knew that there were three voices located in the head, throat and chest. But Lee denounced this trinity as fabulous, and held that the voice proceeded from a single instrument called the larynx. Guided by his anatomical adventures, by a journey to Italy, and by the sound in London of a perfectly preserved baritone voice belonging to an ageing Italian (who could drink a glass of wine while uttering a sustained note), he had patented his 'Method'. Music, he would tell Sonny, was his religion. He was an inspirational teacher.

But there were some facts of Lee's career that Sonny never heard and that G.B.S., whatever his suspicions, did not know. He had been born in 1830, the elder of two sons of Robert Lee, coalman, and his wife Eliza. At the age of eight he was living at 4 Caroline Row in Dublin and attending the Christian Brothers' O'Connell School nearby. In the school records his name is given as George Lee, and his brother's as William. This was a Catholic school, and it was here he took violin lessons and instruction in singing and music generally. On 9 January 1843, Robert Lee died. The family moved from Caroline Row and, by 1851, was living at 2 Portobello Place. Less than two years later they had moved again, this time to 16 Harrington Street. This was the beginning of Lee's musical career. Between 1851 and 1853 the family must have found some money – possibly from Colonel Vandeleur on the coming of age of George and William. The rateable value of 2 Portobello Place had been £5 10s., that of 16 Harrington Street was £34. It was in 1852 also that Lee founded his Amateur Musical Society, taking some sort of professional rooms for a year or two at 11 Harrington Street on the opposite side of the road. From nowhere in the published writings or letters of G.B.S. can it be inferred that Lee started his musical society and set up as singing teacher within a few months of Bessie's marriage to George Carr Shaw; nor is it clear that 2 Portobello Place was about two hundred yards from the Shaws in Synge Street, that 16 Harrington Street was some one hundred and twenty-five paces distant, and that two houses only separate Sonny's future birthplace from Lee's professional chambers.

In such circumstances it seems unlikely that Bessie, with her pure mezzo-soprano voice, and Lee, roaming the streets in search of singers for his society, should not have met between 1852 and 1860. There is no proof that they did, simply no information at all. G.B.S., often in the most positive fashion, knew nothing and appears almost to have taken pains to remain unknowing. There is little doubt that more than once Sonny speculated as to whether he might have been Lee's natural son; and there is no doubt that G.B.S. was aware of other people's speculations. 'About G.B.S.'s parentage,' wrote Beatrice Webb in her diary for 12 May 1911. 'The photograph published in the Henderson Biography makes it quite clear to me that he was the child of G. J. V. Lee – that vain, witty and distinguished musical genius who lived with them. The expression on Lee's face is quite amazingly like G.B.S. when I first knew him. One wonders whether G.B.S. meant this fact to be communicated to the public.'

That Shaw may have had an unconscious wish to be the son of the remarkable George Lee and not of the miserable George Carr Shaw is possible. His campaign to demonstrate that he was George Carr Shaw's son was conducted primarily in defence of his mother. He was to model himself on Lee because of the extraordinary effect Lee had produced on Bessie and, in a number of three-cornered relationships, he was to play out the asexuality of their liaison by means of his own chastity. The themes of consanguinity and illegitimacy recur obsessively in his plays, but it is the emotional independence of the woman that is virtuously stressed. Eliza's parting from Professor Higgins in *Pygmalion* to marry Freddy Eynsford-Hill is Shaw's restatement of Bessie's unromantic attachment to Lee who is seen as a means to her self-sufficiency. In logic, Sonny should have been Lee's son. But the Life Force (particularly when coated with sexual attraction) did not bend to logic, and heredity itself was whimsical. As Shaw demonstrated in his most deliberately pleasant play, *You Never Can Tell*, remarkable children were frequently born to incompatible parents.

But G.B.S. had to be certain. His prose reeks of certainty. He took a line, perhaps the only practicable line, over the Lee connection, and he stuck to it. He wanted to give his socialism legitimacy. So he obliterated the ambiguous Christian name he shared with George Lee and George Shaw, using only the initial G. 'Professionally I drop the George,' he told an editor. 'Personally I dislike it.' 'Don't George me,' he would growl at people who made this mistake. 'I loathe being called George.' He would remain George only to his family and the name does not appear on his title pages.

In his fashion G.B.S. was a truth-teller. He shared frankly with the world whatever he decided to believe. But facts belonged to the past and had to be brought up-to-date to serve the living impulse of the future. The path along which his own impulse led him was paved with facts; but there were others that had misleadingly tumbled elsewhere and which he ignored. Though often charged with inconsistency he was deviously inflexible. For to be wrong over one such serious matter might invalidate the truth-communicating equipment that gave him his philosophy of life. As a polemicist he is marvellously convincing, but since he is fleeing from uncertainties his writings are studded with many brilliant evasions, and eventually, as doubt was beaten back, something human in Shaw diminished.

Lee had returned from London in 1859 with, he believed, the secret of beautiful singing. The following year, this technique had become Lee's 'Method' and the effective chaperon between him and Bessie. By finding a use for the knowledge of harmony and counterpoint hammered into her by Logier, Lee gave Bessie 'a Cause and a Creed to live for'. She became the chorus leader and general factotum of his musical society.

Lee's life had changed in those years. On 6 March 1860 his mother died. The two brothers were looked after by Mrs Margaret Leigh who was their servant of all trades. G.B.S. recalls that she was 'a terrible old woman', but gets her name wrong in a way ('Old Ellen' – a confusion perhaps with his aunt Ellen Whitcroft) suggesting that Sonny's terror may partly have been provoked by Bessie. Then, on 7 May 1862, William Lee, who was an invalid, died, aged twenty-seven, and was buried near Robert and Eliza Lee in the Roman Catholic Glasnevin Cemetery. His death brought Lee 'to the verge of suicide'. Since life outside music seemed, in the Shavian version, to offer little to either Lee or Bessie, they became wedded to 'the Method', with Lee an increasingly dominant factor in the Shaw household.

In his Preface to *London Music* G.B.S. touches on a peculiar aspect of this story. 'Lee soon found his way into our house, first by giving my mother lessons there, and then by using our drawing-room for rehearsals. I can only guess that the inadequacies of old Ellen in the Harrington-street house, and perhaps the incompatibilities of the brother, outweighed the comparative smallness of our house in Synge-street.'

Another guess might have involved a personal attachment between Lee and his mother. It is in ignoring this so decisively as he does that G.B.S. begins to make errors. He presents Lee as a man apart, 'too excessively unlike us, too completely a phenomenon, to rouse any primitive feelings in us'. Because he was a cripple 'marriage and gallantry were tacitly ruled out of his possibilities, by himself, I fancy, as much as by other people. There was simply no room in his life for anything of the sort . . .' At all events he never married and was 'somehow unthinkable' as a married man. Aside from what G.B.S. tells us we know very little about Lee, but everything we do know contradicts this view of the man. We know that his Byronic limp was a focus of romantic interest; we know that at least two women in his musical society, and possibly Sonny's sister, Yuppy, fell in love with him; we may see from the famous photograph of Lee how he basked in female adoration. We also know that later in life he made advances to Lucy Shaw and ended his days running a sort of night-club in London where he carried on an affair with his housekeeper. G.B.S. does not conceal this. But he presents it as a late-flowering sentimentalism that bloomed when, having been seduced by the capitalist atmosphere of 'overfed, monied London', he proved unfaithful to 'the Method' and had been dropped by Bessie. In its arrest of Lee's sexual development till almost the age of fifty this argument is implausible.

To disinfect the relationship from all sexual implication, he built up Bessie into an implacable fortress. 'My mother,' he explained, 'was one of those women who could act as matron of a cavalry barracks from eighteen to forty and emerge without a stain on her character.' 'To the closest observation' she was 'so sexless' that it was a wonder to him how she could so far have forgotten herself as to have conceived three children. He could only guess that George Carr Shaw, when drunk, had forced himself on her and that to this disgusting operation he owed his existence. 'I was just something that had happened to them,' he bleakly concluded. Such a beginning, which explained his mother's neglect, was preferable to having the Lee-Bessie association 'unpleasantly misunderstood'. George Carr Shaw 'was Papa in the fullest sense always,' he wrote, 'and the dynamic Lee got none of the affection Papa inspired'. There was one point to add. A photograph of himself, which reminded him of his father, gave him special pleasure, he claimed. For the likeness between himself and George Carr Shaw was so remarkable that 'I gave a severe shock to a friend of his shortly after his death . . . [who] saw me from some distance and supposed I was my father's ghost'. Of this incident, which cannot have taken place less than twenty years after his father's death, 'Inspector Maigret would make short work,' concludes the writer John O'Donovan. Such dubious arguments reflect the urgency Shaw felt to make his case as strong as possible: for the case had to be strong because of what was soon to happen between Lee and his mother.

# [ 5 ]

*We must reform society before we can reform ourselves . . . personal*
*righteousness is impossible in an unrighteous environment.*
Shaw to H. G. Wells (1917)

Two experiences, both visual, dominate Sonny's early years. The first was his sight of the Dublin slums. 'I saw it and smelt it and loathed it.' Instead of exercising him in the open-air, his nurse would go with him to the squalid tenements of her friends. They were poor people, and Sonny detested them. Sometimes she would take him to a public house and (it is suggested) add to her £8 a year by picking up soldiers at the barracks. Shaw's lifelong hatred of poverty was born of these lonely days of slumming. Poverty became a crime responsible not only for prostitution, but lovelessness.

On being asked, at the age of seventy-five, to name the happiest hour of his life, Shaw was to answer decisively: 'When my mother told me we were going to live on Dalkey Hill'. In 1864, two years after his brother's death, Lee had moved from Harrington Street to 1 Hatch Street. After this he proposed a new arrangement: to lease a cottage on Dalkey Hill, nine miles south of Dublin, and to share it with the Shaws. Torca Cottage, into which they all moved in 1866, had four reasonably-sized rooms, a back room for Sonny, and a kitchen and pantry into which they squeezed the servant's bed. There was nothing extraordinary about it except its position. The front garden overlooked Killiney Bay, and the back garden Dublin Bay. 'I owe more than I can express to the natural beauty of that enchanting situation commanding the two great bays between Howth and Bray Head,' Shaw remembered towards the end of his life, 'and its canopied skies such as I have never seen elsewhere in the world.' In the miserable Synge Street house, opposite a big field blotted out by hoardings and behind 'the bare dark walls, much too high . . . too high to be climbed over', Sonny had felt a prisoner. At Torca he became 'a prince in a world of my own imagination'. The beauty, blue like the Mediterranean, enchanted the boy. His playground was Killiney Hill, a wonderland of goat-paths and gorse slopes down which he would run to the sandy shore and into the sea. Here he learnt to 'love Nature when I was a half-grown nobody'. During his metamorphosis into a fully-fledged somebody in urban England, G.B.S. would point to his remembrance of Dalkey. 'I am a product of Dalkey's outlook,' he declared. The beauty of Dalkey evoked a happiness that 'takes you out, far out, of this time and this world'; but such 'imaginative feasts' starved him of reality, he later claimed, and delayed his development. 'With a little more courage & a little more energy I could have done much more; and I lacked these because in my boyhood I lived on my imagination instead of on my work.'

The work of G.B.S., which was to aim his artillery of words at the realities of his own time and make the world less frightful, was a product not only of his joyous memories of Dalkey but of his visits to the Dublin slums which, 'with their shocking vital statistics and the perpetual gabble of its inhabitants', reflected the unhappiness Sonny seldom escaped. 'An Irishman has two eyes,' Shaw told G. K. Chesterton. One was for poetry, the other reality. But as Sonny grew into an adult the Dalkey eye closed. This is why, at his most serious, G.B.S. always seems to be winking.

After a year at Dalkey, Lee and the Shaws agreed to extend the *ménage à trois* to Hatch Street, while they continued to occupy Torca Cottage for most summer holidays. 'The arrangement was economical,' G.B.S. explained, 'for we could not afford to live in a fashionable house, and Lee could not afford to give lessons in an unfashionable one.' He may not have realized that Lee was already living at Hatch Street and that the Shaws were moving into rooms there recently vacated by other tenants. Lee, G.B.S. tells us, paid the rent for all of them – the rateable value being £35 – in addition to the costs at Dalkey. The amalgamation, which G.B.S. described as 'the economical and sensible thing', had the advantage of giving the Shaws a well-appointed, three-storied house in a smart part of Dublin. 'Being a corner house it had no garden,' Shaw told Frank Harris; 'but it had two areas and a leads. It had eight rooms besides the spacious basement and pantry accommodation as against five in Synge St.' It was a peculiar house in that the hall door was in one street and the windows (with one exception) were in another. The exception, a window over the hall door and near the roof, was Sonny's bedroom where, his friend Edward McNulty remembered, 'there was barely room for anything but his bed'.

For Lee, the advantage of this ménage was having Bessie, and perhaps her daughters, nearer at hand. Though, in the context of Synge Street, G.B.S. tells us that his mother 'could not housekeep' and had 'absolutely no notion of the value of money', he represents her management of Hatch Street as being of great benefit to Lee.

For Sonny too the new régime was an improvement. Like his mother he was dazzled by Lee and adopted many of his startling ideas – everything from sleeping with the windows open, to eating brown bread instead of white and parading his disdain for all professional men: doctors, lawyers, academics and the like. Lee filled the house with music and banished family prayers. In the early Synge Street days, George Carr Shaw, as sole head of the household, used to conduct family prayers which were reinforced for Sonny and his sisters by attendance at a Sunday School where genteel Protestants aged five to twelve, well-soaped and best-dressed, mouthed religious texts and were rewarded with inscribed cards. After this they would be marched to the Molyneux Church in Upper Leeson Street to fidget interminably round the altar rails. 'To sit motionless and speechless in your best suit in a dark stuffy church on a morning that is fine outside the building, with your young limbs aching with unnatural quiet . . . hating the clergyman as a sanctimonious bore, and dreading the sexton . . . is enough to lead any sensitive youth to resolve that when he grows up and can do as he likes, the first use he will make of his liberty will be to stay away from church.' Shaw suffered this because 'my father's respectability demanded it'. When they went to live at Dalkey they broke with the observance and never resumed it.

Respectability, Shaw tells us, had been largely exploded by Bessie's dissolute brother Walter Gurly, a ship's surgeon who visited them between transatlantic voyages. He was an artist in obscenity. His limericks, profanities, scatological tales of sea and school were fastidiously wrought and delivered with terrific gusto. 'He was a most exhilarating person,' G.B.S. remembered, '. . . always in high spirits, and full of a humor that was barbarous in its blasphemous indecency, but Shakespearian in the elaboration and fantasy of its literary expression. He was not untrained: he was a trained man broken loose. He was full of the Bible, which became in his hands a masterpiece of comic literature; and he quoted the sayings of Jesus as models of facetious repartee.' Such exuberance had the effect, Shaw wrote, 'of destroying all my inculcated childish reverence for the verbiage of religion, for its legends and personifications and parables'.

G.B.S. uses the entertaining figure of Uncle Walter as a comet, shimmering across the skies, to distract our attention from a more significant feature in the religious firmament of the Shaws. Though strange to Sonny's ears, there was nothing in Walter Gurly's irreverent jokes that quarrelled with the tradition of Protestant gentry – a tradition that, Shaw acknowledges, made Protestant Ireland 'the most irreligious country in the world'. Irish Protestantism, he explains, 'was not then a religion: it was a side in political faction, a class prejudice, a conviction that Roman Catholics are socially inferior persons who will go to hell when they die and leave Heaven in the exclusive possession of Protestant ladies and gentlemen'.

It is evident from what he wrote that G.B.S. knew that Lee was a Catholic, but he prevaricated by converting religion in Ireland into a matter of belief rather than of caste. To Stephen Winston he proclaimed that 'music was the only religion he [Lee] ever professed'; to Frank Harris he wrote: 'The Method was my mother's religion. It was the bond between her and Lee. A bond of sex could not have lasted a year'; to Demetrius O'Bolger he revealed that Lee was 'sceptical' about religion, and added, 'the religion of our house was the religion of singing the right way'. By such means he directed his biographers along what he saw as the path leading to truth at the expense of a few out-of-the-way facts. But although he claimed to be 'in intense reaction against the Shaw snobbery', his own snob-tragedy was to be G.B.S.'s disappointment with Sonny for having felt ashamed among his school friends at sharing a house with someone no Shaw should rightly know – except in the person of a servant. The most he would admit to years later was having grown up in a Catholic atmosphere because, God being no respecter of voices, so many of the singers who joined the Amateur Musical Society and came to the house for practice, happened to be Roman Catholics. But he told St John Ervine: 'Lee had no creed: I never heard him mention religion: he conducted Mendelssohn's Protestant Music and the Catholic masses with impartial perfection.'

The only person for whom there seemed no special advantages at Hatch Street was George Carr Shaw. Reduced to 'nullity' by Lee, he became 'full of self-reproaches and humiliations when he was not full of secret jokes, and was either biting his moustache and whispering deep-drawn Damns, or shaking with paroxysms of laughter'. Lee's well-placed musical patrons made him particularly sensitive to social tremors. So if, in a fit of suicidal irritation, George Carr Shaw decided to bring down scandal on the house, he might ruin them all. It was better to keep him mildly placated. In a private note, written for a medical friend in 1879, Shaw described the pattern of his father's drinking:

'In society he drank porter, champagne, whisky, anything he could get, sometimes swallowing stout enough to make him sick. Subsequently, when he had no opportunity of drinking except in taverns, he only took brandy. He smoked regularly and moderately. His appetite was good; but he suffered from diarrhea at intervals. Although he was never sober, he was seldom utterly drunk. He made efforts to reform himself, and on one occasion succeeded in abstaining for sixteen months; but these efforts always ended in a relapse. On one or two occasions he disappeared for a few days and returned with his watch broken, clothes damaged and every symptom of uncontrolled excess; but ordinarily he came home in the evening fuddled, eat [sic] his dinner, had a nap, and then kept going out for drams until he went to bed. He never drank or kept drink in the house ... I have seen him when drunk, seize a small article on the mantelpiece and dash it upon the hearthstone, or kick a newspaper into the air; but, though he was very irritable, he never used the slightest violence to any person ... his timidity probably made forbearance habitual to him.'

After his father was dead, G.B.S. eliminated much of the sordidness of this alcoholism by giving to his published descriptions of it a hilarious Shavian gloss.

'A boy who has seen "the governor", with an imperfectly wrapped-up goose under one arm and a ham in the same condition under the other (both purchased under heaven knows what delusion of festivity), butting at the garden wall of our Dalkey Cottage in the belief that he was pushing open the gate, and transforming his tall hat to a concertina in the process, and who, instead of being overwhelmed with shame and anxiety at the spectacle, has been so disabled by merriment (uproariously shared by the maternal uncle) that he has hardly been able to rush to the rescue of the hat and pilot its wearer to safety, is clearly not a boy who will make tragedies of trifles instead of making trifles of tragedies.'

After two or three years at Hatch Street, George Carr Shaw was felled on the doorstep by a mild fit. Shortly afterwards he stopped drinking altogether and became so rigid a teetotaller that those who knew him found it 'difficult to realize what he formerly was'.

G.B.S. was to represent his father as having been an habitual drunkard at the time of his marriage. His authority for this lay in tales his mother taught him. But there must have been a considerable change between the man whose drinking went undetected by his fiancée and the husband who was 'never sober'. From this period the only surviving letters from George Carr Shaw to his wife were written in the summer of 1857, the year after Sonny's birth. They show someone apologetically giving more affection than he receives. 'My dear one, . . . my Honey,' he calls her. 'You *are* my own Bessie and may you long continue so to be.' She had gone, with Lucy, to see her father in Galway, hoping to improve their relationship and the Shaws' finances. '. . . if I were to let another day pass without dropping you a line you would begin to think I had made off with myself,' her husband writes, 'but there is no such luck in store for you . . . I was surprised to hear that you & Mr Lynch had not yet become acquainted. I thought you would have been lovers by this time.' She suffers from nervous attacks ('face ache') and he knowledgeably prescribes 'the Gin again if you get bad,' adding sanctimoniously: 'There are some people with whom such a remedy might prove worse than the disease, but I am not afraid of you . . .' Yet he seems to have apprehensions of a different kind: 'Farewell my I was going to say my darling but you are, ah well I believe you are G.C.S.'

In a letter to a prospective biographer, G.B.S. wrote: 'You ask whether my father liked Lee. He certainly did not, and would not have tolerated the arrangement if he could have afforded a decent house without it, or if he could have asserted himself against my mother, who probably never consulted him in the matter. There was never any quarrelling in the house: my mother went her own way, which happened to be the musical way of Lee, just as Lee went his; and my father could only look on helplessly . . . He cannot have liked it; but he could do nothing to alter it.'

It was this impotence that appears to have driven George Carr Shaw to greater drinking excesses. All that G.B.S. personally observed took place when Lee was already part of the Shaw family life. 'When his children had grown too big for him to play with, and the suspense as to whether he would come home drunk or sober never ceased,' G.B.S. told a cousin, 'he got practically no comfortable society from them. His relatives did not want to see him; and my mother did not want to see his relatives: she was interested only in people who could sing, and they were mostly Catholics, not proper company for the Protestant caste of Shaw.'

Before his marriage, and during its early years, George Carr Shaw had been on visiting terms with his smart Protestant relatives. By the 1860s their doors were shut to him and his family. 'My immediate family and the Shaw clan,' G.B.S. recalled, '. . . were barely on speaking terms when we met which we did only accidentally, never intentionally.' But Sir Frederick

Shaw, the baronet, described by Macaulay as 'a bigoted Protestant', would never have received at Bushy Park the Catholic-infested Shaws of Hatch Street. G.B.S. uses his father's drunkenness to blur other factors leading to their social excommunication. But finally, no one was to blame. Social conditions, which had helped to drive his father to drink, would also one day pervert Lee. In so far as they embodied these social conditions, both men grievously disappointed his mother. So Society became the dragon against which the fabulous G.B.S., armoured with tracts and speeches, would lead his campaign of lifelong knight-errantry.

## [ 6 ]

*It is a ghastly business, quite beyond words, this schooling.* Preface to *Misalliance*

*If I had not returned to the house, I don't think they would, any of them, have missed me.* Preface to *London Music*

At Synge Street Sonny and his sisters had been provided with a day governess. Caroline Hill was an impoverished gentlewoman who puzzled the children by her attempts to teach them the alphabet and mathematical tables. She also supplied recitation from the poets and would punish her pupils when their laughter grew too outrageous by 'little strokes with her fingers that would not have discomposed a fly'. For grounding in Latin, Sonny called on his clerical uncle at St Bride's who took him through the declensions, conjugations and added to his vocabulary.

At the beginning of the summer term of 1865, when he was almost ten, Sonny was sent to his first school, the Wesleyan Connexional, less than half a mile away at 79 St Stephen's Green. He hated this school. 'I have not a good word to say for it,' he wrote in 1928 to another old Wesleyan. 'It could not even teach Latin; and it never seriously tried to teach anything else. A more futile boy prison could not be imagined. I was a day-boy: what a boarder's life was like I shudder to conjecture.'

The chief reason for his dislike of this and later schools appears to have been that they took him further away from his mother. This, he came to believe, had been their real purpose – that of 'preventing my being a nuisance to my mother at home for at least half the day'. 'In these crèches – for that is exactly what they were – I learnt nothing.'

The Wesleyan Connexional School occupied an old private house next door to the mansion of Sir Benjamin Lee Guinness. Its big school-room

33

stood at the end of a yard at the rear where the stables had been and which by the 1860s served as a playground. It was the cheapest of those Dublin schools patronized by the Protestants. The dwelling-house was over-crowded with boarders; the classes overcrowded by day-boys. Boarders and day-boys were reciprocally contemptuous and called each other 'skinnies'. The sanitation was primitive and the lessons meagre – there were no explanations, no apparatus of any kind. The teachers were mostly young men waiting for a ministry and they restricted their instruction to Caesar, Virgil and Homer. 'In the large classes,' Shaw recalled, 'the utmost examination possible in the lessons meant one question for each boy in alphabetical order, or at most two. If you could answer the questions or do the sums, or construe the few lines that fell to your lot, you passed unscathed: if not, or if you talked in class or misbehaved, you were marked in your judgement book for caning by the headmaster.'

The headmaster when Sonny first went there was Robert Cook, a young Methodist Minister for whom nothing educational existed except Greek and Latin verse. He was much feared for his terrible lectures, and would prepare boys for flogging with spasms of copious weeping. He was briefly succeeded by a man named Macintosh and then, the most distinguished of the lot, by Parker who conducted his classes with a ferocious cane in hand.

'When Parker appeared armed with a long lithe chestnut colored oriental cane, which had evidently cost much more than a penny, and slashed our hand with it mercilessly, he established an unprecedented terrorism. He was young (really too young), darkly handsome: apparently a perfect Murdstone. But he soon found that he was carrying his youthful terroristic logic too far ... he had what no schoolmaster should allow himself to indulge: a dislike of stupid boys as such.'

Sonny seemed to have no power of learning anything that did not interest him. Except in English composition – and an unexpected burst of knowledge in scripture – he did not do well, holding his place at or near the bottom of his class. To his biographers, particularly Archibald Henderson, Shaw represented Sonny at school as 'rampant, voluble, impudent ... a most obstreperous player of rough games ... [who] avoided his school tasks ... and was soon given up as incorrigible.' It was a good example of G.B.S. turning things inside out. That was how he had felt: it was not how he appeared to others. He was remembered as a quiet boy; he was not caned and on two occasions was awarded good conduct certificates. The other boys liked him for his comic stories about a character called Lobjort borrowed from *Household Words*, but otherwise his remote and rather priggish personality, designed to protect him from unhappiness at home, did not make him popular. There is a story of how, as a scientific experiment, he and a friend set fire to the gorse on Dalkey Hill, and another boy who had not been involved was put in custody by the police. 'It was outside my code of honor to let another bear the burden of my guilt,' Shaw told Hesketh Pearson, 'so I put on my best jacket and called on the landlord of the hill, Mr Hercules Macdonnell, who received me on the terrace of his villa with a gravity equal to my own. I orated . . . with an eloquence beyond my years, and finally received a letter to the police inspector to say that the matter could be let drop.' His command of long words and precocious literary style gave him an air of maturity that appealed more to adults than to other children. He was unfitted for boy society. 'I think my treatment as an adult at home (like the Micawbers' treatment of David Copperfield) made school very difficult for me.'

Some of this difficulty must have arisen from his irregular comings and goings. The roll books at Wesley show that after only three months in 1865 he was taken away and did not return there until August 1867. After another three months he left again, then came back in February 1868 for nine months. During one or more of these intervals he attended a preparatory school at 23-24 Sandycove Road, Glasthule, near Dalkey.

'My parents,' Shaw wrote, '. . . acted as if . . . I would come out as an educated gentleman if I wore the usual clothes, ate the usual food, and went to the same school or other every day.' But by the end of 1868 he had done so badly in examinations and fallen so far behind that he was withdrawn altogether from the Wesleyan Connexional. 'I may add that I was incorrigibly idle & worthless as a schoolboy, & am proud of the fact.' Incompetent as a teaching institution, the Wesleyan seemed to him everything a school ought not to be: 'My curse on it. Forget it.'

It was Lee, rather than Sonny's parents, who took the initiative. He had got to know the drawing-master at the Central Model Boys' School in Marlborough Street, Joseph Smeeth, who persuaded him that the teaching there was better than at the Wesleyan Connexional or any other of the cheaper genteel schools in Dublin. At the beginning of February 1869, Sonny was sent to Marlborough Street, where he remained a little over seven months. He was to focus on this school almost all the unhappiness of his boyhood. Under the heading 'A Secret kept for 80 years', he described the effect of his incarceration at this place in a chapter, 'Shame and Wounded Snobbery', of his *Sixteen Self Sketches*. The Central Model Boys' School, he revealed, was 'undenominational and classless in theory but in fact Roman Catholic . . . It was an enormous place, with huge unscaleable railings and gates on which for me might well have been inscribed "All hope abandon, ye who enter here"; for that the

35

son of a Protestant merchant-gentleman and feudal downstart should pass those bars or associate in any way with its hosts of lower middle class Catholic children, sons of petty shopkeepers and tradesmen, was inconceivable from the Shaw point of view . . . I lost caste outside it and became a boy with whom no protestant young gentleman would speak or play.'

However, the enrolment books of the Central Model show that Sonny's form contained eight members of the Established Protestant Church, only five Roman Catholics and one 'Other Denomination'. Fathers' occupations included a hotel porter, two carpenters, a farmer, butcher, solicitor, bricklayer, shopkeeper, hatter, sergeant and gaol warder. It was, in fact as well as theoretically, what Shaw denied it to have been: non-sectarian – an experimental school for persons of modest means, retailer and wholesaler, Protestant and Catholic. What Shaw did, eighty years afterwards, was to transfer to this place the 'shame and wounded snobbery' arising from his Catholic-infested home at Hatch Street. He gives us the symptoms but not a diagnosis of his condition.

Marlborough Street exacerbated the embarrassment and unorthodoxy of his life at Hatch Street. His mother 'was utterly indifferent to public opinion and private gossip, taking her course as if such forces did not exist, leaving scandal dead of being hopelessly ignored'. But his father felt acutely ashamed, and when Sonny demanded to be taken away from school, George Carr Shaw, relishing perhaps the defeat of Lee's programme, supported him. Sonny left the Central Model on 11 September 1869 and was restored to Protestant conservatism in the last of his boy prisons, the Dublin English Scientific and Commercial Day School. This school was lodged in a large building with broad staircases and stately rooms, formerly Lord Aungier's town house, on the corner of Aungier and Whitefriars Streets, and was sponsored by the Incorporated Society for Promoting English Protestant Schools in Ireland. Its social standing was as good as that of the Wesleyan Connexional, and so were its teaching methods, though it dispensed with Latin and Greek and trained pupils for business. Sonny remained here almost two years and became joint head boy. But his repugnance for all his schools was implacable. In an interview he gave in his eighties he said that he regretted having gone to school at all; that he valued nothing he had experienced there, and that the teachers, who came to hate their children as 'instruments of torture', were merely turnkeys hired 'to keep the little devils locked up where they cannot drive their mothers mad'.

*

Sonny made his one close friend at the Dublin Commercial School. Matthew Edward McNulty, later to become a novelist, bank manager and playwright, was 'a corpulent youth with curly black hair' – and 'a genius'. His first sight of Sonny, at the age of thirteen, was of 'a tallish, slender youngster with straw-colored hair, light greyish-blue eyes, a skin like that of a baby and lips like those of a beautiful girl. There was a faint smile over his face as he listened to his companions and looked around the strange class room . . . We were, in fact, friends at first glance.'

McNulty was the only person with whom Sonny could share his dreams and ideas. It was a curious relationship, unique in Shaw's life, and soon to be solemnized by a declaration of 'Eternal Friendship' in which they pledged to share each other's prosperity or adversity, pricking their arms with a pin to sign the agreement with authentic blood. When apart they entered into tremendous correspondence, sending off long letters to each other, sometimes twice a day, full of drawings and dramas. These unpreserved soul histories 'were to be destroyed as soon as answered', Shaw maintained, though according to McNulty, Shaw's request for reciprocal destruction was made after Sonny had sprouted into G.B.S.

'Except in my secret self I was not happy in Dublin,' Shaw wrote. In his secret self he wanted to be a great man, probably a great artist like Michelangelo. His first passion was for drawing – not landscape but the human figure. He borrowed Duchesne's outlines of the old masters, bought the Bohn translation of Vasari, prowled for hours through Dublin's deserted National Gallery dragging McNulty with him – two schoolboys, one short and dark, the other tall and fair, going from picture to picture, full of argument, until they knew every work there and could recognize at sight the style of many Flemish and Italian painters. They also enrolled together for late afternoon courses at the Royal Dublin Society's School of Art and passed examinations in perspective, practical geometry and freehand drawing. But Sonny was not satisfied with copying Laocoöns and Sleeping Fauns and, taking McNulty back to his room in Hatch Street, he announced a bolder plan for studying the nude. 'I was to be his naked model,' McNulty remembered, 'and, in return, he was to be mine. This study was to continue from day to day as convenient until we had both become masters of the human figure . . . We argued the point for some time but I was adamant and Shaw's long-cherished dream of an inexpensive model was rudely shattered. I was very sorry for him at the time but I would have been more sorry for myself if I had had another attack of bronchitis.'

37

Sonny eventually renounced the artist's life because 'I could not draw' – though McNulty recalled a rather different explanation: 'My people cannot afford to send me to Italy and it is necessary for an artist to study there.' He had decided instead, he told his friend, to found a new religion.

At an early age Sonny had tried to build from religion a fanciful world in which to forget the miseries of the real one. But like all amateur architects he had invented an uninhabitable place – 'a sort of pale blue satin place', as Broadbent describes it at the end of *John Bull's Other Island*, 'with all the pious old ladies in our congregation sitting as if they were at a service; and . . . some awful person in the study at the other side of the hall.' Sonny did not enjoy this dream of heaven which presented itself as a small square apartment in which he was sitting with his ankles dangling, poorly dressed and filled with fears because

'I knew that I should presently be brought up for judgment by the recording angel before some awful person in the next room; and I had good private reasons for anticipating that my career would not be found up to the mark . . . on the only occasion on which I ever dreamt myself in heaven, I was glad when I woke. I also dreamt once that I was in hell; but I remember nothing about that except that two of my uncles were there and that it did not hurt. In my waking hours I thought of heaven as a part of the sky where people were dressed in white, had golden harps, did not eat or drink or learn lessons, and were wholly preoccupied in being intensely good.'

Such dreams, in which may be seen the genesis of the hell scene in *Man and Superman* and the Utopia of *Back to Methuselah*, were empty because they had been plastered together from borrowed images. His rebellion against conventional religious training, following the same course, he believed, as that of his mother, had begun in church. Churchgoing and family prayers satisfied none of his spiritual needs, and he did not miss them when they were given up. His heterodox upbringing had helped to clear away the crushing lumber of 'isms' and creeds. When he was very young his Roman Catholic nurse had sprinkled him with holy water without giving him a sense of sin or of redemption from sin. The overheard conversations of his Uncle Walter and Lee, and the sound of good Roman Catholic voices singing Masses as well as Mendelssohn, had opened up his imagination to a truly catholic Church.

When very young he had used the Lord's Prayer as a protective spell against thunderstorms and reinforced this by composing, in the manner of a sonata, more luxurious devotions of his own. But one evening on Torca Hill 'I suddenly asked myself why I went on repeating my prayer every night when, as I put it, I did not believe in it. Being thus brought to book by my intellectual conscience I felt obliged in common honesty to refrain from superstitious practices.' By the third night, he tells us, his discomfiture had vanished: 'I had forgotten all about my prayers as completely as if I had been born a heathen . . . this sacrifice of the grace of God, as I had been taught it, to intellectual integrity synchronized with the dawning of moral passion in me which I have described in the first act of *Man and Superman*.'

What Sonny had done was to transfer his religious energy from daydreaming to his actual life. He had come to recognize that, as an unlovable boy, he could expect no help or happiness from other people. His 'moral passion' was conceived as a source of strength in accepting this and as a means of producing, independently of other people, the self-respect he lacked. Though he might not make himself into the sort of person his mother loved, he could become the sort of person she was: insensible to public opinion and a Bohemian without Bohemian vices. Before this he had thought of himself as a boastful coward. 'I was such a ridiculously sensitive child,' he wrote, 'that almost any sort of rebuff that did not enrage me hurt my feelings and made me cry.' From his 'moral passion' he gained the Stoicism he imagined his mother to have had, lifting him above tears and rage. This religion, created in opposition to the Irish religious climate, reached its heretical peak in 1875 with a letter he wrote to *Public Opinion*. It took the form of a literary-political attack on the Moody and Sankey revivalist meetings then being celebrated in Dublin. He ridiculed the vanity of their 'awakenings' as creating 'highly objectionable members of society', and announced, to the horror of several uncles, that he personally had renounced religion.

He was by this time a committed Shelleyan. 'I read him, prose and verse, from beginning to end.' Shelley, who was to make Shaw into a momentary anarchist and lifetime vegetarian, completed the job of clearing away the refuse of those religions repugnant to his constitution, ready for the planting of Creative Evolution. Sonny was a voluminous reader. Before he was ten he was saturated in Shakespeare and the Bible which, from a vainglorious desire to do what no one else had done, he attempted to read straight through, breaking down only at St Paul's Epistles 'in disgust at what seemed to me their inveterate crookedness of mind'.

Since he learnt aesthetically, never pedagogically, Sonny absorbed almost everything except his schoolbooks. He had no access to a library and no money with which to buy books. Nobody at Hatch Street read. Lee, who made a habit of falling asleep at night over Tyndall on Sound, was not a literary man. He had been perplexed at hearing that Carlyle was an author and not Dublin's Lord Lieutenant, the Earl of Carlisle; and he was puzzled by his failure to find, even in the large-print edition of Shakespeare, *The School for Scandal*. But his pupils often presented him with books – anything from Byron's works to Lord Derby's translation of Homer's *Iliad* – and to these were added pirated editions of novels brought back from America by Sonny's Rabelaisian uncle. Sonny read all of these without direction or interference: 'all normal people require both classics and trash,' he later recommended. He particularly relished romance – *The Arabian Nights, The Pilgrim's Progress, The Ancient Mariner, John Gilpin*. He fled from his own life into the adventures of Scott and Dumas. 'The falsifications of romance are absolutely necessary to enable people to bear or even to apprehend the terrors of life. Only the very strongest characters can look the facts of life in the face.' But his Damascene conversion on Torca Hill had made him determined to become one of this band of 'strongest characters' and he started choosing his books accordingly. 'At twelve or thereabouts,' he remembered, 'I began to disapprove of highwaymen on moral grounds and to read Macaulay, George Eliot, Shakespeare, Dickens and so on in the ordinary sophisticated attitude.' On the understanding that the author was an atheist, he went through John Stuart Mill's autobiography; he studied Lewes' *Life of Goethe* and every translation of *Faust* he could lay his hands on. 'No child,' he was to write, 'should be shielded from mischief and danger, either physical or moral, in the library or out of it. Such protection leaves them incapable of resistance when they are exposed, as they finally must be, to all the mischief and danger of the world.'

Shaw's ingenious form of self-protection is best seen from his use of two favourite writers, Dickens and Shakespeare. At Hatch Street, where there were bound volumes of *Household Words* and *All the Year Round*, he first read *Great Expectations* and *A Tale of Two Cities*, and records: 'they affected me strongly.' Beginning as a Dickensian disciple, he went on to convert Dickens, as the unconscious prophet of revolution, into an early attempt by the Life Force to produce an authentic Shavian. Behind this intellectual process lay a deep fellow-feeling and the need to keep Dickens closely allied to him. This sympathetic feeling sprang from the comparison he made between their early unhappiness, and the theatrical methods by which they later superimposed success upon unhappiness. Shaw wrote of his time at the Central Model School as being equivalent to 'what the blacking warehouse was to Dickens'; and his description of Dickens' outward life as 'a feat of acting from beginning to end' is a variation only of his self-portrait: 'the real Shaw is the actor, the imaginary Shaw the real one.' By converting his schooldays into a Dickensian episode he gave them a sense of drama and a context in which, though otherwise too pessimistic for words, they could be treated with humorous detachment. In recommending Mr Pickwick as the 'safest saint for us in our nonage' he was also advocating the power of comedy to dispel the mischief from which strong characters should not seek artificial protection through censorship. Dickens, he wrote, 'saturated the whole English-speaking world with his humor.'

For a time he replaced his own life with the fictional worlds of Dickens and Shakespeare. 'I was living in an imaginary world,' he remembered. The characters of Dickens were 'more real than reality and more vivid than life'. He knew some of Shakespeare's plays by heart and the characters from Shakespeare more intimately than he knew his living contemporaries: 'Hamlet and Falstaff were more alive to me than any living politician or even any relative.'

'I pity the man who cannot enjoy Shakespeare,' he wrote. In his teens Sonny relished Shakespeare. For in the reading of Shakespeare there was all life except the actual presence of the body from which, as a vehicle of emotion, Sonny had become alienated. In separating the word-music from the meaning he was to become like Ulysses, tied to the mast and listening to the sirens. For Shaw's prejudice was optimism. He accepted, modified, rejected aspects of experience according to the hypothetical opportunities they offered for improvement. Shakespeare's plays offered few such opportunities. To follow the tragedies of Shakespeare and expose yourself to feel what wretches feel, could lead to the 'barren pessimism' that Shakespeare himself might survive, but Shaw could not. Shakespeare's celebration of the splendours and miseries of sexual love paralysed Shaw who described it as 'folly gone mad erotically', and used all his wit and critical intelligence to reduce it to 'platitudinous fudge'. He could allow himself to respond to the passion of the language only by insisting that it swept literature 'to a plane on which sense is drowned in sound'. Here, in 'his enormous command of word-music', Shakespeare was safe. So, like Caliban, Sonny listened and was comforted by the sounds that filled the place of his captivity.

*Without music we shall surely perish of drink, morphia, and all sorts of artificial exaggerations of the cruder delights of the senses.*
'The Religion of the Pianoforte' (1894)

'My university has three colleges', Shaw used to say. They were Dalkey Hill, the National Gallery, and Lee's Amateur Musical Society. The atmosphere at Hatch Street was full of the ozone of music, the performance of learned music beginning with Handel and of the dramatic music that began with Gluck and Mozart. 'I was within earshot of a string of musical masterpieces,' Shaw wrote, 'which were rehearsed in our house right up to the point of the full choral & orchestral rehearsals.' Before he was fifteen he knew Beethoven's Mass in C, Mozart's Twelfth Mass, Mendelssohn's *Athalie*, Handel's *Messiah*, Verdi's *Trovatore*, Donizetti's *Lucrezia* and above all Mozart's *Don Giovanni* from cover to cover, besides many separate numbers from other works, so that he could sing and whistle their themes to himself as other boys whistled music hall songs. After seeing Gounod's *Faust*, he decorated the walls of his room at Dalkey with watercolour heads of Mephistopheles. 'We made of Mephistopheles a familiar, almost living character,' McNulty recalled. This veneration for the patron saint of sceptics was, he believed, forced into activity 'by the miserable atmosphere of snobbery & state superstition which debased & stultified everything except the scepticism and derision that were its natural antidote'.

In music Sonny's senses came alive, and he found the living presence of those feelings that literature described. Romance flourished without ridicule in the world of music – he felt he was experiencing all manner of impossible emotions: the 'candour and gallant impulse of the hero, the grace and trouble of the heroine, and the extracted quintessence of their love'. Once he had grown out of his earlier impulse towards piracy and highway robbery, he felt inclined to be a wicked baritone. 'In my attempts to reproduce the frenzies of the Count di Luna, the sardonic accents of Gounod's Mephistopheles, the noble charm of Don Giovanni, and the supernatural menace of the Commendatore, not to mention all the women's parts and the tenor . . .,' he wrote, 'I thought of nothing but the dramatic characters.' But he could neither play nor read a note of music, for 'nobody dreamt of teaching me anything'.

Irish gentlemen at that time were fashionably attracted to brass instruments, while ladies found themselves drawn to the refinements of strings and the pianoforte. As part of their social accomplishments, the

Shaws had been in the habit of meeting for musical evenings round the ottoman at Bushy Park where they would harmonize popular melodies with three chords (tonic, dominant and subdominant) on a variety of instruments. Aunt Emily sawed tunes from the cello; Aunt Shah, who had pretty fingers, showed them off upon the harp and with the tambourine. Uncle Barney puffed at his giant-keyed brass bugle; and George Carr Shaw, besides fingering the flute and penny whistle, would vamp a bass on the trombone in congregation with colleagues of ascertained gentility along the banks of the Dodder. But their musical tastes were primitive. They knew nothing of opera, had no use for oratorio or symphony and (except for Uncle Barney) they were ineligible for Lee's orchestra, playing only by ear.

It was with this musical *hoi polloi* that Sonny found himself classed. When an amateur player named Phipps offered to teach him the oboe, George Carr Shaw, horrified by the notion of his son becoming a professional musician, objected that the price of an oboe and tuition fees put it out of the question. Sonny did what he could. Presented by one of his uncles with an ancient cornet-à-piston ('absolutely the very worst and oldest cornet then in existence'), he took lessons twice a week from an English Guardsman, walking to his house in Mount Pleasant Street with the obsolete instrument wrapped up in a brown paper under his arm. This phase lasted only a few months. 'I was told,' Shaw explained, 'that it would spoil my voice . . .'

But it was Lucy who sang. 'My elder sister had a beautiful voice,' Shaw wrote. '. . . Unfortunately her musical endowment was so complete that it cost her no effort to sing or play anything she had once heard, or to read any music at sight. She simply could not associate the idea of real work with music . . .' This irksome contrast to himself goaded Shaw into describing her as having no conscience, happy to 'spend her life in artistic self-murder . . . without a pang of remorse, provided she be praised and paid regularly'. The result was that she 'sang without the slightest effort and without the slightest point, and was all the more desperately vapid because she suggested artistic gifts wasting in complacent abeyance'.

Although, partly because of her frail health, it was Agnes of the hazel eyes and gorgeous curtain of red hair who received most attention within Hatch Street, the star among the neighbours was Lucy. She was not beautiful, but had an expression that charmed and interested, and a faint resemblance to Ellen Terry to which she drew attention by wearing Lyceum-style clothes and shapeless feather hats. She had a reputation as an entertainer and mimic, keeping her heart afloat by turning everything to gaiety and music. 'It is thus that I love to remember her,' wrote one of the neighbours, 'leading the fun and raillery with my two young Aunts – her satellites – dazzling and enchanting the various ineligible swains current at the time.' One of her admirers was Sonny's friend McNulty who later 'asked her to marry me: but she refused on the grounds that she was five years older: and that when I was forty-five she would be "a white haired old woman of fifty". So, that little romance faded.' Lucy was not happy with any man on whom she could not amiably look down. 'Away from home,' her brother wrote, '[she] was everybody's darling: she broke many hearts, but never her own.' She longed not for a man, but for a mother and father: a family. Not having one, she affected a passionate independence and did not exclude George from her defensively low opinion of men. 'Brothers don't matter to their sisters,' Shaw commented; 'at least I didn't matter to mine: it is the stranger who is loved. The natural dislike for near relatives is ordained to save frightful complications. So presto vivace . . . and away with melancholy!'

Shaw appears to have come to terms with their hare-and-tortoise relationship early on. In his second novel, *The Irrational Knot*, written at the age of twenty-four, he gives a strangely confident forecast of the end of their race, when the dying Suzannah (Lucy) speaks of her life and Ned's (G.B.S.): 'I wish I had my life to live over again: you wouldn't catch me playing burlesque. If I had got the chance, I know I could have played tragedy or real Italian opera . . . My cleverness was my ruin. Ned was not half so quick. It used to take him months to learn things that I picked up offhand, and yet you see how much better he has done than I.'

Italian opera seemed what Lucy was heading for even before she sang Amina in Lee's production at the Theatre Royal, Dublin, of that most conciliatory of operas, Bellini's *La Somnambula*. The whirlpool of Lee's musical activities was by then spinning fast. He had begun to organize musical evenings in the Ancient Concert Room at 42½ Great Brunswick Street. These were often in aid of hospitals and would include a popular overture, some ballads and choruses, and the strengthening contribution from a regimental band. For the Shakespeare Tercentenary of 1864, having worked up a programme of Purcell and Schubert together with local odes and songs, Lee emerged at the head of his Amateur Musical Society as an orchestral conductor. He had no scholarship but, conducting from a first violin or vocal score, gave the right time to the band. 'There was practically no music in Dublin except the music he manufactured,' Shaw wrote. 'He kept giving concerts . . . and he had to provide all the singers for them. If he heard a flute mourning or a fiddle scraping in a house as he walked along the street, he knocked at the door & said "You come along & play in my orchestra." If a respectable citizen came for twelve lessons to entertain small tea parties, he presently had that amazed gentleman, scandalous in tights & tunic, singing as "il rio di Luna" to my mother's Azucena, or Alfonso to her Lucrezia, as the case might be. He coached them into doing things utterly beyond their natural powers. They got through when they stuck to "the method": . . . when they funked it or tried to be luscious according to their own taste, they exploded in a disastrous *couac*, and were good-naturedly encored to give them another chance. They took off their wigs with their hats, and fenced poker & tongs fashion; but in spite of all contretemps the thing got done: he taught them *for use* and not for guineas.'

It seemed to George that Lee pulled them through all emergencies by sheer mesmerism. 'This favourite Society', reported *The Irish Times* on 30 May 1865, '. . . includes many of the most distinguished amateur vocalists in the city . . . On few occasions has the Ancient Concert's Music Hall contained a larger and more fashionable attendance . . . and the concert was in every respect most judiciously carried out.' This was typical of the notices that the Amateur Musical Society received in the late 1860s. But Lee was not content. He wanted to conduct oratorio festivals and operas; and his ambitions focused upon London.

*

It was probably in 1869 that Lee first began to dream of a conquest of London and he appears to have taken Bessie Shaw into his confidence. On 30 October that year Bessie and her brother made an agreement with their father whereby the son received £2,500 and Bessie £1,500 paid to her at the rate of £100 a year 'for her own sole and separate use and free from the debts control or engagements of her husband'. This was in addition to £400 settled on Agnes either through the estate of Ellen Whitcroft or Mrs Shaw's own trust of 1852. Bessie now had the maximum financial independence it was in her power to command.

Six weeks later, Lee published a book entitled *The Voice: Its Artistic Production, Development, and Preservation.* Encased between heavy dark green boards elaborately stamped in gold, with a woodcut on its cover from Maclise's *Origins of the Harp* and anatomical illustrations in the text from a manual of physiology, this volume of 130 pages of 'agreeably tinted' paper was a business advertisement and represented Lee's passport to a larger musical world. It appears to have been successful, but had been ghosted, Shaw tells us, 'by a scamp of a derelict doctor whom he entertained for that purpose' – probably Malachi J. Kilgarriff, Demonstrator at the Ledwich School of Anatomy, a Catholic and one-time neighbour of Lee's in Harrington Street.

Not long after this, while still thirteen, Sonny was sent off to a firm of cloth merchants, Scott, Spain and Rooney, on one of Dublin's quays. He was interviewed by Scott, a smart young man with mustachios, for a job in the warehouse loading bales. After a few perfunctory words, his employment was on the point of being settled when the senior partner, Mr Rooney, walked in and, having spoken to Sonny for a few minutes, declared that 'I was too young, and that the work was not suitable to me. He evidently considered that my introducer, my parents, and his young partner, had been inconsiderate, and I presently descended the stairs, reprieved and unemployed . . . I have not forgotten his sympathy.'

Unable to convert him from an expenditure at school to a source of income in the warehouse, they had failed to get him off their hands. He returned for another year to the Dublin English and Scientific Commercial Day School. Then, through the influence of his Uncle Frederick (Chief of the Land Valuation Office) he was found employment as office boy in a 'leading and terribly respectable' firm of land agents, Uniacke Townshend and Co. He started work there on 26 October 1871 with an annual salary of £18. He was no longer Sonny to his family, but the name he most loathed: George.

Six weeks later an odd, apparently insignificant thing happened: Lee changed his name. In all press notices, legal documents and registers he had been George J. Lee, the J. sometimes appearing as John. After 2 December 1871 the J. is replaced for the rest of his life by a V. which is often lengthened to Vandeleur. This flowering of his new name coincided with a fresh thrust of his musical ambitions. So long as he had confined his activities to the usual amateur limits, giving a few charitable concerts for the ill, the old and the poor each year, he could be condescended to by the professionals as one of Dublin's more extravagant eccentrics. But since the publication of *The Voice*, Lee had been extending his Society beyond these limits – increasing his advertisements in the press together with the number and glory of his patrons which, by 1871, included His Excellency the Lord Lieutenant and other nobility, a Commander of the Cavalry in Ireland, and the Garrison Commander. He had by now begun producing Italian Opera (mixed into the menu with burlesque and miscellaneous band music) at the Theatre Royal and the newly opened Gaiety Theatre – taking these productions on tour to Limerick and Cork, and making a reconnaissance himself to London.

The opposition to Lee was led by Sir Robert Prescott Stewart, an ambitious academic who had won many prizes for his glees and who rose to become the most highly regarded Irish musician of his day. Stewart made his first move in the summer of 1871 – persuading the more eminent members of Lee's committee to resign. At a meeting on 11 November, following the congratulations on increased membership and money, *The Irish Times* reported that 'some misunderstanding has arisen as to members of the Society performing in English or other operas at the theatre [the Theatre Royal], and in consequence of which a considerable number of the committee refused to offer themselves for re-election'. It was regrettable, *The Irish Times* correspondent concluded, if the existence of the Society should be endangered by this 'little misunderstanding'.

Lee acted immediately. By the time another meeting had been called on 30 November, he had reconstituted his Society into the Amateur Musical, Operatic and Dramatic Society, replaced the various Lords and Generals with a sixteen-man Committee that included a Colonel, two Majors and ten Captains, and announced that the following month A GRAND MILITARY, DRAMATIC AND OPERATIC PERFORMANCE WILL BE GIVEN AT THE NEW GAIETY THEATRE.

Throughout 1872 Lee was climbing towards the summit of his Dublin career. In January he had transformed his amateurs into the New Philharmonic Society – a title that signalled his ambition to replace the almost fifty-year-old Philharmonic – and, under one title or another, led them indefatigably through concerts, oratorio festivals and truncated operas. In all this activity Bessie, as his musical adjutant, was indispensable to him, arranging orchestral accompaniments, copying out band parts, composing songs ('The Parting Hour', 'The Night is Closing Round, Mother') under the *nom de plume* 'Hilda' and singing with what *The Irish Times* described as 'artistic grace and expression'. Though she played Lucrezia Borgia in Donizetti's opera and 'staggered under bouquets' as Azucena in *Il Trovatore*, her voice, which 'never expressed eroticism', was particularly thrilling in the interpretation of songs about bereaved lovers seeking reunion in the next world and won for her a reputation 'in connection with this society as a most accomplished artiste'.

Lee endeavoured at first to treat Stewart cautiously. Having organized a series of musical events for the sumptuous International Exhibition that year, he invited Stewart to compose the music for J. F. Waller's Inaugural Ode. Stewart not only supplied the music but took the baton from Lee, mounted the rostrum and, before an audience that included the Duke of Edinburgh, conducted his own work. When the Exhibition closed on 30 November, Lee gave another concert, commissioned another ode from Dr Waller but set the words to an old tune.

So successful had Lee become that on 19 September he bought the lease of Torca Cottage (which up to then he had merely rented). Though many of his concerts were advertised as being in aid of charity, only what was termed 'the Surplus' found its way to various hospitals. This usually amounted to about £25 – whereas Lee himself, so John O'Donovan has calculated, 'would have pocketed a sum not far off £200 for each concert'.

Early in 1873 Lee fulfilled one of his major ambitions by conducting the Dublin Musical Festival which featured many of the greatest singers of the day. 'The crowds of persons who besieged each portion of the hall soon filled to its utmost capacity, every particle of available space obtainable . . . the large doors leading into the building at the end of the Hall had to be thrown open and numbers were content to obtain standing room in the outer galleries,' reported *The Irish Times*. After congratulating Lee on his splendid results, the reviewer predicted that with patience he would surely 'reap the rewards his energies and abilities deserve'.

Eager for these rewards, Lee prominently advertised two benefit concerts of 'Amateur Italian Opera' for himself and the leader of his orchestra, the violinist R. M. Levey, in late March or early April. But Stewart was already at work in a most ingenious way, with the result that the debenture holders availed themselves of their right to one free ticket and crowded into the theatre. On 5 April, Lee and Levey published a sarcastic announcement in *The Irish Times* in which they begged 'to return their grateful thanks (?) to the many debenture holders who honoured their BENEFIT on Monday and Friday Evenings, either by making use of their FREE admissions, or transferring them to others'.

The deciding battle was fought over the 1873 Exhibition the following month. In his opening concert, Lee, having assembled a combined chorus and orchestra of over five hundred, gave a performance of Mendelssohn's *Athalie*. Rehearsals had been rocky. The contralto, Madame Demeric Lablache, declined to sing until Lee asked Bessie Shaw to take her place 'which she did to such good purpose that Madame Lablache took care not to give her another such chance'. Three thousand or more people attended the Concert Hall which presented a very bright appearance and, reported *The Irish Times*, 'the five hundred voices blended most harmoniously'. But there was no ode. Stewart, however, was in the audience and next day in the *Daily Express* he published a politely scathing criticism of the performance, anonymously. Although Mr Lee had been 'heartily applauded' by his own chorus, Stewart concluded: 'Indiscriminate praise is worthless, and e'er long, heartily despised, even by those who are the objects of it'. In private Stewart was more outspoken. On page fifty of his copy of *The Annuals of the Theatre Royal, Dublin*, he noted in the margin next to Lee's name: 'an impostor, who traded successfully on the vanity of amateur singers: he had a few aliases; now Mr Geo. Lee; again Mr Geo. J. Lee: and also J. [sic] Vandeleur Lee; at last he was Vandeleur

Lee simply'. In a letter to Joseph Robinson, he admitted: 'I did in my time one good work in Dublin. I unmasked one arrant impostor and drove him away.'

The details of this 'unmasking' are unknown. There seems to have been a row at which Levey, and probably other members of the New Philharmonic were present. On 26 May Lee gave his last concert in Dublin. Despite the presence of the Lord Lieutenant, *The Irish Times* reported, attendance was disappointing. At the beginning of June, having abruptly cancelled another concert, he left Dublin for ever and his place as conductor of the New Philharmonic was taken by Sir Robert Prescott Stewart.

Lee had gone to London. A few days later, on 17 June, her twenty-first wedding anniversary, Bessie Shaw followed him taking Agnes on the boat with her. And at Hatch Street 'all musical activity ceased'.

## [ 8 ]

*The worst sin towards our fellow creatures is not to hate them, but to be indifferent to them; thats the essence of inhumanity. The Devil's Disciple*

'We did not realize, nor did she, that she was never coming back.' But there was much that George must have realized, and Shaw misremembered. In his musical criticisms, as Corno di Bassetto in *The Star* and G.B.S. in *The World*, he never mentioned Stewart, though he singled out the 'scholarly trivialities' of Stewart's Irish protégé, Charles Villiers Stanford, for particular disdain. The only suggestion that he had known of Lee's losing battle with Stewart is an acknowledgement in the 1935 Preface to *London Music* that 'Lee became the enemy of every teacher of singing in Dublin; and they reciprocated heartily'. But a few pages later he gave as the reason for Lee's departure from Ireland his having reached the Dublin limit of excellence. The Superman is still intact. Nothing remained but London because 'Dublin in those days seemed a hopeless place for an artist; for no success counted except a London success'.

In the Shavian version, therefore, 'Lee did not depart suddenly from Dublin ... there was nothing whatever sudden or unexpected about it.' George obviously knew that his mother had left within a fortnight of Lee but in answer to one of his biographers Shaw wrote: 'As to your question whether Lee's move to London and my mother's were simultaneous, they could not have been. Lee had to make his position in London before he could provide the musical setting for my mother and sister. But the break-up of the family was an economic necessity anyhow, because without Lee we could not afford to keep up the house.'

Shaw's fullest explanation of what he wanted his biographers to believe was provoked by the son of an Irish police Inspector, Professor Demetrius O'Bolger, whose book Shaw refused to sanction for publication. Hatch Street, he wrote,

'was beyond my father's means: it was the economic combination with Lee (who had to have a good professional address) that had made it possible. My father's business was not prospering: it was slowly dying. Then there was my eldest sister Lucy. She was attractive; had abundant musical faculty and a beautiful voice . . . She seemed to have a future as a prima donna; and this was about the only future that presented itself as an alternative to a relapse into squalid poverty, and the abandonment of the musical activity which had come to be my mother's whole life.

'There was only one solution possible, granting that my mother and father could be quite as happy apart as together, to say the least. Lee was soon able to report a success: all the West End clamoring for lessons at a guinea, and his house in Park Lane a fashionable musical centre. This was clearly the opening for Lucy. It did not take very long for my mother to make up her mind. She sold up Hatch St., after a reconnaissance in London; settled my father and myself in furnished lodgings; and took a house for herself and her two daughters in Victoria Grove, Fulham Road . . . a couple of miles from Park Lane.'

To this account G.B.S. added a Shavian flourish: his father began to find himself much happier. 'I should think it was the happiest time of his life.'

Shaw's deft rearrangement of the facts avoids the appearance of his mother having made a fool of herself. But it is now possible to put some of these facts back in their original places. When Lee arrived in London he put up in lodgings at Ebury Street where he remained a year. A mile away, at 13 Victoria Grove, Bessie and Agnes were presently joined by Lucy. Though Bessie continued to sing and work for Lee, who was in and out of Victoria Grove very much in the old fashion, it was probably important that they lived apart since George Carr Shaw had initiated Court Proceedings citing Lee 'not as a criminal offender against the sacredness of Holy Matrimony but rather as an object of jealousy to the Petitioner'. Their 'reconnaissance' as Shaw calls it, lasted nine months during which time they were paying the rent for two separate premises in addition to the rent at Hatch Street which must largely invalidate the argument of 'economic necessity'. It was not until the beginning of March 1874 that, George Carr Shaw having apparently abandoned his Court Proceedings, Bessie returned to Dublin to sell up the furniture in Hatch Street, raise what money she could, and move her husband and son into rooms at 61 Harcourt Street. Then for the last time she left Dublin with her two daughters and returned to London. Perhaps because of some out-of-court arrangement with George Carr Shaw who agreed to pay her one pound a week, she still did not in the interests of economic necessity live at the same address as Lee. In April he was to cut his last connection with Ireland by selling the lease of Torca Cottage to a musical colleague, Julian Marshall, from whom he afterwards rented 13 Park Lane in London.

The departure of his mother and Lee was a tragedy for George. From the pictures in the National Gallery, the hills and bays of Dalkey and Killiney, the music that filled Hatch Street he had woven 'a sort of heaven which made the material squalor of my existence as nothing'. Shaw represents this daydream world as having been exhausted when he was ten, but the evidence suggests that, especially in his ambitions to be a great artist or musician, they persisted until his mother finally left him at the age of sixteen. Instead of an artist, he was a clerk; he would enjoy no more summers at Torca; and 'I heard no more music'. From now on (as his reaction to Joyce's *Ulysses* later illustrated), an emotional revulsion infuses all his feelings for Dublin. The drastic change in his circumstances left him with one passion: a passion for improvement. 'I recognized my own youth in Peer Gynt's,' he wrote, 'with painting and music and poetry added. My struggle afterwards was to become efficient in real life.'

*

It was now that George taught himself to do something other than feast on daydreams. His mother had not sold the piano. Though aware that 'the effect of ordinary amateur playing on other people is to drive them almost mad', George's musical starvation drove him recklessly to disregard the convenience of other lodgers. He bought a technical handbook and taught himself the alphabet of musical notation; he learnt the keyboard from a diagram; then he got out his mother's vocal score of *Don Giovanni* and arranged his fingers on the notes of the first chord. This took ten minutes, 'but when it sounded right at last, it was worth all the trouble it cost'. What he suffered, 'what everybody in the house suffered, whilst I struggled on . . . will never be told'. But though he gave no pleasure to anyone except himself, sometimes driving other people away in tears, he acquired what he wanted: 'the power to take a vocal score and learn its contents as if I had heard it rehearsed by my mother and her colleagues'. From this practice and his reading of academic textbooks, he also mastered the technical knowledge of what he would need to become a music critic in London. It was a wonderful example of the advantages of deprivation.

He was helped by his imprisonment in the 'highly exclusive gentlemanly estate office'. For although he had no interest in land agency and hated the duties of his clerkship as barren drudgery, his desk and cash box 'gave me the habit of daily work'. For fifteen months, during which his salary was increased from £18 to £24, he had filed, found and manufactured copies of the firm's business letters, kept a postage account, bought penny rolls for the staff's lunch and combined the duties of Office with Errand Boy. In these duties he sulkily distinguished himself to such effect that, when in February 1873 the cashier absconded, George was employed as a temporary substitute. The work gave him no difficulty. 'Immediately the machine worked again quite smoothly. I, who never knew how much money I had of my own (except when the figure was zero), proved a model of accuracy as to the money of others.' He was so conscientious an accountant that the engagement of a cashier of appropriate age and responsibility was dropped and his salary doubled to £48. He bought himself a tailed coat, remodelled his sloped and straggled handwriting into an imitation of his predecessor's compact script and 'in short, I made good in spite of myself'.

He was now in a very bustling post and a position of trust, the most active and responsible chap in the office, equal to any of the staff. He met people of all conditions. In the daily paying and receiving of insurance premiums, annuities, mortgage interests, private debts and allowances he became a private bank, accustomed to handling large sums of money, and to collecting weekly rents by tram each Tuesday, tiny sums from slum dwellers in Terenure – an experience he had not forgotten when he came to write *Widowers' Houses*. But though he picked up business discipline, he disliked his work as cordially as he had detested school, for 'my heart was not in the thing'. He was never uncivil, never happy. He felt orphaned. Thirty-five years later he poured out his bitterness through the nameless clerk in *Misalliance* who seeks to avenge his mother's shame of bearing him out of wedlock:

'Do you know what my life is? I spend my days from nine to six – nine hours of daylight and fresh air – in a stuffy little den counting another man's money. Ive an intellect: a mind and a brain and a soul; and the use he makes of them is to fix them on his tuppences and his eighteenpences and his two pound seventeen and tenpences and see how much they come to at the end of the day and take care that noone steals them. I enter and enter, and add and add, and take money and give change, and fill cheques and stamp receipts; and not a penny of that money is my own: not one of those transactions has the smallest interest for me or anyone else in the world but him; and even he couldnt stand it if he had to do it all himself. And I'm envied: aye, envied for the variety and liveliness of my job . . . Of all the damnable waste of human life that ever was invented, clerking is the very worst.'

George knew he did not belong there and could not remain long. Land agency in Ireland being a socially pretentious business, Uniacke Townshend 'was saturated with class feeling which I loathed'. The office was overstaffed with gentleman apprentices, mostly University men, who had paid their principal large premiums for the privilege of learning a genteel profession and who were called Mister while George was plain Shaw. It was his involuntary feeling of inferiority among these colleagues that drove him to excel in this 'dutiful tomfoolery', for he was convinced, despite the Dublin atmosphere of derision, that 'nothing but technical skill, practice, efficiency: in short, mastery, could be of any use to me'. By proving himself superior to them might he feel their equal. Though he did not possess their rank, he 'was not precluded from giving myself certain airs of being in the same position'. Part of his job was to pay the Dublin bills of country clients. He began by calling at shops on his way back from the bank, and settling them across the counter. But because he could not 'bear the indignity of tips from shopkeepers' he stopped calling and obliged them to come to the office for their money.

Art was the great solvent of bigotries and snobberies. George found he was most popular with the apprentices in his role as *maestro di cappella*. In his imagination he had become a Lee-like presence, replacing Townshend, and providing the young men there with operatic tuition as value for their premiums. 'I recall one occasion,' he wrote, 'when an apprentice, perched on the washstand with his face shewing above the screen . . . sang *Ah, che la morte* so passionately that he was unconscious of the sudden entry of the senior partner, Charles Uniacke Townshend, who stared stupended at the bleating countenance above the screen, and finally fled upstairs, completely beaten by the situation.'

This represented a victory for George over Townshend whom, McNulty recalled, he disliked 'chiefly because he put an "H" in his name, flagrant evidence, in Shaw's opinion, of middle class snobbery'. Townshend, who was 'a pillar of the Church, of the Royal Dublin Society, and of everything else pillarable in Dublin', considered George an 'Infidel' and extracted from him a promise never to discuss religion in the office. 'Against my conscience I gave him my word, and kept it,' Shaw recorded, '. . . [but] I did not intend to live under such limitations permanently.' He remained ashamed of his promise and waited for a time to revenge himself on his employer, *de haut en bas*.

In his need for someone to look up to and learn from he had fastened at Harcourt Street on another Superman. Chichester Bell was a cousin of Graham Bell (who invented the telephone), a nephew of Melville Bell (the inventor of phonetic script) and son of Alexander Bell (an imposing professor of elocution at the Wesleyan Connexional). He took the place of Lee in George's life and helped him to emerge from Lee's phenomenal influence. He was a far more sophisticated man: physician, chemist, amateur boxer and accomplished pianist. Where other boys collected stamps or trailed girls, George lusted after information. The multitudinous knowledge of Chichester Bell became his vade-mecum. The two of them studied Italian together and though George never spoke the language he learnt almost everything else, from physics to pathology, universal alphabetics and 'Visible Speech'. With Bell, who was also responsible for converting him to Wagner, George started many of his lifelong interests and completed his education in Ireland.

There was almost no one else he saw, for he was intensely shy. 'I had no love affairs,' he confessed to Frank Harris. 'Sometimes women got interested in me; and I was gallant in the old-fashioned Irish way, implying as a matter of course that I adored them; but there was nothing in it on my side . . .' More probably there was nothing in it on theirs. Late in 1877 Shaw came across a letter he had written to Agnes, describing what he was to call 'The Calypso Infatuation', and referring to a girl he had first met in 1871. He does not seem to have fallen in love with her until the beginning of May 1875 when he was almost nineteen. A retrospective diary note he made under the heading 'The LXXX [Love] Episode', in which he records burning his letter to Agnes two days after finding it, ends with 'The Catastrophe, or the indiscretion of No. 2', and is dated at 'about the beginning of August'. He celebrated this aborted romance with a hymn to stupidity:

> Hail, Folly! and flourish, Delusion
>> Continue whilst man remains brute
> Of Passion, and Dreams & Confusion
>> To bring forth your fruit
> All the fiends take each black-eyed enslaver
>> Calypso, Queen Mab & Yolande
> Love philtres tempting of savour
>> In the mouth turn to sand . . .

The 'indiscretion of No. 2' may have been her scheme to engage him to a sister after her own marriage to another man, for the poem tells that 'she succumbed to the cruel old fashion' and went to live with her husband not far from Torca Cottage in

> . . . an exquisite gaol by the sea
>> To her weary sense stagnant and rotten
>> But Elysium to me
> Four years of my childhood I spent there
>> Their danger was veiled to me then
> Four more years elapsed, and I went there
>> And saw her again . . .
> And she proved a too perilous plaything . . .

The poem ends with a tribute to the spell she had laid on him.

> I thought her of women the rarest
>> With strange power to seduce and alarm
> One beside whose black tresses the fairest
>> Seemed barren of charm
> The wisest men sometimes get smitten
>> And I fear I was so in those days
> But my fate brought me shortly to Britain
>> Away from her gaze
> Then farewell, oh bewitching Calypso
>> Thou didst shake my philosophy well
> But believe me, the next time I trip so
>> No poem shall tell.

These lines were unusual for Shaw's verses to women, most of which were 'gallant' and rather jaunty. He felt most when he was rejected, because that was the only love he knew. But he recoiled from searching for happiness in others because their rejection of him carried behind it the annihilating force of his mother's initial rejection. He was too frightened not to stand alone. So he conceived a system of behaviour that required us to love one another less (no difficulty there) and respect ourselves by virtue of our work. Throughout his life he persistently ridiculed redemption by love and exposed the Christian folly of urging unlovable people to love each other. 'I preach Justice instead,' he declared, 'even to those we hate.' He eliminated personal feeling as a guide to conduct, insisting that men must 'learn to be just to people whom they very properly loathe, and not to consider their loathing an excuse for injuring them'. Sexual attraction, which so often thrived on hostility, was something other than love: it was the evolutionary call of the future – which could also be served by solitary endeavour.

55

Work became his mistress. He kept no other company. McNulty, who was employed by a bank, had been sent to Newry. 'I found no sympathetic companions,' he remembered. 'Shaw wrote to me every day. Otherwise I was absolutely alone.' Though George insisted that he never dreamed of taking up writing as he dreamed of being an artist and musician, the written word was threaded into his friendship with McNulty, and he worked off much incipient literary energy in their duel of correspondence. At school some of their favourite reading together had been a boys' paper called *Young Men of Great Britain*, describing itself as 'A Journal of Amusing and Instructive Literature'. McNulty recalled that 'it was meat and drink to us and almost as vital to our existence as the air. We awaited each weekly instalment with feverish impatience'. Here Shaw sent a dramatic short story, involving piracy and highway robbery, that had as its main character a wicked baritone with a gun. He also wrote, in September 1868, asking a question, to which the answer was: 'Write to Mr Lacey, theatrical publisher, Strand, London W. C.' A neighbour remembered him sitting alone 'absorbed in the construction of a toy theatre'. He had a play (perhaps part of *Henry VI*) for this theatre about the fifteenth-century Irish rebel Jack Cade, for which he would cut out scenes and characters bought at a shop opposite the Queen's Theatre. Among his own early works was a gory verse drama, 'Strawberrinos: or, the Haunted Winebin', well-illustrated and full of extravagant adventures in which our hero Strawberrinos is constantly bested by a Mephistophelean demon.

Shaw's first ten years' experience as a playgoer lay in Dublin. At the Theatre Royal he had been used to seeing the splendours of serious pantomime, farces and melodramas involving villainous disguises and the convolutions of dense intrigue. In 1870 the great touring actor, Barry Sullivan, had arrived in Dublin and soon became so popular an entertainer there that he returned almost every season afterwards. George, for whom Sullivan was a hero, joined the crowds, emerging from the theatre with 'all my front buttons down the middle of my back'. Of all the stars and travelling attractions, Sullivan seemed to him incomparably the grandest. A man of gigantic personality, then in his prime, he was the last of a dynasty of rhetorical and hyperbolical actors that had begun with Burbage and, in Shaw's opinion, he was 'among the greatest of them'. The style of work at which he aimed, its blatant force mixed up with Shavian good manners, stayed with G.B.S. all his life:

'His stage fights in Richard III and Macbeth appealed irresistibly to a boy spectator like myself: I remember one delightful evening when two inches of Macbeth's sword, a special fighting sword carried in that scene only, broke off and whizzed over the heads of the cowering pit (there were no

1 George Carr Shaw (previous page)  2 Lucinda Elizabeth Shaw

3 Lucinda Frances ('Lucy') Shaw

4 Elinor Agnes ('Yuppy') Shaw

5 Vandeleur Lee, Shaw's mother on his right and
Shaw's father behind on his left

6 Matthew Edward McNulty and Shaw, 1874

7 Shaw in his early twenties

8 The Reading Room in the British Museum, circa 1876

stalls then) to bury itself deep in the front of the dress circle after giving those who sat near its trajectory more of a thrill than they had bargained for. Barry Sullivan was a tall powerful man with a cultivated resonant voice: his stage walk was the perfection of grace and dignity; and his lightning swiftness of action, as when in the last scene of Hamlet he shot up the stage and stabbed the king four times before you could wink, all provided a physical exhibition which attracted audiences quite independently of the play ... He was as proud as Lucifer, and as imposing; but he was the only actor I ever heard come before the curtain at the end of a play to apologize for having acted badly ... With an unanswerable dignity he informed the applauding Dublin playgoers that he had done justice neither to them nor to himself, and begged their indulgence. They were awestruck; and then their applause had a note of bewilderment; for most of them had thought it all very splendid.'

The Theatre Royal became a particular place of excitement for George. The company of actors playing round a star such as Barry Sullivan was not a spectacle to him, but an experience. It was as if they were his family, and the theatre his home. He could feel his blood quickening during the performance, his mind beating, hurrying. This was vicarious living at its most vigorous, eclipsing anything actual at Harcourt Street or Uniacke Townshend. It was romance without risk. Dublin's theatrical enchanters conjured up a region where 'existence touches you delicately to the very heart, and where mysteriously thrilling people, secretly known to you in dreams of your childhood, enact a life in which terrors are as fascinating as delights; so that ghosts and death, agony and sin, became, like love and victory, phases of an unaccountable ecstasy'. He forgot loneliness in this palace of dreams and began to form his theatrical mind so that, when he came to write plays himself, he instinctively went back to the grand manner and heroic stage business he had imbibed from the pit of the Theatre Royal.

Like music, the theatre carried the passions alive into his heart as life would never be allowed to do. 'Much as I have learnt from music,' he was to write, 'and frankly as I abandon romance to the musician, there is a music of words as well as of tones.' The Theatre Royal was Dublin's opera house as well as its playhouse, opera and drama supplying each other with many conventions and materials. Early in his career Barry Sullivan had sung in opera, and Shaw likened his acting to that of the great Russian singer Chaliapin. This connection between the two arts was part of Shaw's artistic heritage and stood at the centre of his operatic technique as a dramatist. 'My method, my system, my tradition, is founded upon music,' he declared in 1939. '... If you study operas and symphonies, you will find a useful clue to my particular type of writing.'

In 1874 George spent his summer holidays at Newry with his friend McNulty. McNulty had developed what he called 'a morbid condition of nerves'. He was so sensitive to the earth's rotation that he could not trust himself to lie down on a sofa without falling off. 'I fancied I could see the sap circulating in plants and trees,' he wrote. Sometimes he would open his eyes to discover himself looking down at his own body in bed. He had taken to psycho-analysing buildings and trees and with the aid of some Scottish metaphysics, to sitting out at night 'realizing the stars'. George's scepticism and humour, though not always comfortable, helped to reduce this tension. There was a new authority and tact about him. On their second day the two of them had their photographs taken and George pretended that he looked a nonentity beside his friend. They talked of the future, of the inevitability of fame either through buying a cottage together 'in seclusion with G. B. Shaw & E. McNulty recluses, book-worms and philosophers alone', or by striding out and taking the world by the scruff of its neck. Every evening they wrote and every evening it had to be something different – 'a short story, a comedy, a tragedy, a burlesque and so forth,' McNulty remembered, 'and the real joy of the event lay in reading and forcefully criticizing each other's work. This series we called: "The Newry Nights' Entertainment".'

The following year McNulty was transferred back to Dublin and the two of them saw a good deal of each other. They went for long walks together at night, and McNulty would call round at Harcourt Street to stagger through duets on the grand piano. George, he observed, 'took little or no notice of his father who still spent his evenings poring miserably over his account books'. Otherwise, his glasses low on his nose, his head tilted back, he browsed before a newspaper or smoked his one clay pipe a day, breaking it when he had finished and throwing the fragments in the grate: 'a lonely, sad little man', McNulty concluded.

George had resolved never to allow the diffidence he shared with his father similarly to cripple him. He looked to his father only as a warning; otherwise, like Lee, he looked to London. He had two ideas: learning to do something, and then getting out of Ireland to have the chance of doing it.

His opportunity came early 1876. Agnes, suffering from consumption, had been taken down to Balmoral House, a sanatorium on the Isle of Wight. As soon as he realized that she was dying, George acted. Though he was now getting £84 a year at Uniacke Townshend, he felt more than ever unsatisfied by his drudgery there. One of his colleagues had been an ancient book-keeper who confided that he 'suffered so much from cold feet that his life was miserable,' Shaw recorded. 'I, full of the fantastic mischievousness of youth, told him that if he would keep his feet in ice-cold water every morning when he got up for two or three minutes, he would be completely cured.' This prescription proved efficacious: and shortly afterwards the man died. To his horror George was then offered his job. If there was one person who envied the cashier it was the book-keeper who had to repeat all the cashier's entries knowing that almost none of them would be looked at again. But Charles Townshend wanted to place a relative as cashier and boot George upstairs to make room for him. To his embarrassment, George refused and had to be moved, with an increased salary, to the position of general clerk. On 29 February 1876 he gave a month's notice. 'My reason is, that I object to receive a salary for which I give no adequate value,' he wrote. 'Not having enough to do, it follows that the little I have is not well done. When I ceased to act as Cashier I anticipated this, and have since become satisfied that I was right.'

This letter shows the paradoxical device of his new authority. In much the same way in which his correspondence to his mother had begun to take on a parental tone, so this letter has the regretful air of an employer dismissing an employee. Its succinct moral and intellectual superiority must have been particularly galling to the man who had taken such high ground with him on matters of religion. Anxious not to offend George's harmless Uncle Frederick at the Valuation Office, Charles Townshend quickly backed down and offered him his job back as cashier. But George was adamant. He thanked him – however 'I prefer to discontinue my services'.

In retrospect G.B.S. applied a blinding Shavian polish to his arrival in England. Armed with the English language he proposed to advance on London, as the centre of literature, art and music, and crown himself 'king' there. He had decided to become 'a professional man of genius'. Dublin had been a filthy city – the waste ground from a discouraging phase of civilization whose young men drivelled their lives away in slack-jawed obscenities. 'Thus,' he wrote, 'when I left Dublin I left (a few private friendships apart) no society that did not disgust me. To this day my sentimental regard for Ireland does not include the capital. I am not enamored of failure, of poverty, of obscurity, and of the ostracism and contempt which these imply; and these were all that Dublin offered to the enormity of my unconscious ambition.'

He did not feel ambitious in a vulgar sense. 'Like Hamlet I lack ambition and its push,' he wrote, 'and suffered from the delusion that everybody had my gifts.' Yet it was not ambition he lacked: it was (like Hamlet) advancement. Lest his need for expression be interpreted as a desire for success, he insisted that he never struggled, never consulted anyone or made a resolution in his life. He was pushed slowly up by the force of his ability. 'It is not possible to escape from the inexorable obligation to succeed on your own merits,' he confessed. Like most Irishmen he claimed that he disliked most Irishmen, but he did not cross the Channel for love of the English. 'Emigration was practically compulsory,' he told St John Ervine. He came to plunder the invader who had made Dublin hopeless for him; or, as G.B.S. was to express it, 'England had conquered Ireland; so there was nothing for it but to come over and conquer England.'

Agnes died of phthisis on 27 March. Between the two opportunities offered by her death and that of the book-keeper, George had never hesitated. Looking back on his twenty years in Ireland he summed up: 'My home in Dublin was a torture and my school was a prison and I had to go through a treadmill of an office'. London represented hope.

He worked out his full month at Uniacke Townshend, then packed a carpet bag, boarded the North Wall boat and arrived in London. It was a fine spring day and he solemnly drove in a 'growler' from Euston to Victoria Grove. With his mother and Lucy, he then travelled down to Ventnor on the Isle of Wight to attend Agnes's funeral, returning to London on 30 April. They selected a headstone and an epitaph to be cut on it: 'TO BE WITH CHRIST WHICH IS FAR BETTER' – from a passage in Paul's Epistle to the Philippians where Paul compares the folly of living with the wisdom of dying. It was a theme that was often at the back of George's mind. Nearly sixty years later he was to write to Margaret Mackail, exposing what he felt about his own childhood: 'as the world is not at present fit for children to live in why not give the little invalids a gorgeous party, and when they have eaten and danced themselves to sleep, turn on the gas and let them all wake up in heaven?'

# CHAPTER II

## [ 1 ]

*I am afraid you will find London a drearily slow place to make a beginning in. Every opening is an accident; and waiting for accidents is rather discouraging.* (1894)

'Unoccupied': this was the word Shaw used to describe his first summer in London. With introductions from his Aunt Georgina and from Lee, he applied for a couple of jobs, but 'without result'. He was determined not to land himself back in the Dublin treadmill of employment and he gave everyone to understand that 'on no account will I enter an office again'. But there seemed no opening in the stone wall that confronted him and by September, at a fee of three and a half guineas, he submitted to a crammer's course for admission to the Civil Service. His mother and Lucy breathed out with relief – then in with alarm as, less than two months later, he gave up this 'tutelage of a grinder' and accepted the occupation of Lee's amanuensis.

Lee's credit with the Shaws had fallen dramatically since they came to London. In one of his letters to O'Bolger, G.B.S. writes that when he rejoined his mother he found Lee using Victoria Grove in the same way as he had used Synge Street, not sleeping there, but regarded 'as much a matter of course to us as the hatstand'. But from some correspondence between the Shaws the previous year it appears that Lee, having grown so infatuated that 'he wanted to marry her', was bullying Lucy into acting as the principal singer in a musical society he had started at his house called the Troubadours. Though she did take the part for him of Queen of Spain in Marchetti's *Ruy Blas*, Lucy intensely disliked working under Lee's direction, and wrote to her brother telling him of the huge rumpus that had ballooned up between them all. George, at his most paternal, diagnosed hot air: 'As to Lee, I would decline to listen to him. We all know what his tirades are worth, and I think his coming to Victoria Grove and launching out at you as he did, simply outrageous.'

Whether or not Bessie realized that Lee was in love with her daughter, she appears to have felt angered by Lucy's unwillingness to co-operate with Lee, since this could only reduce all their chances of success. In a letter to Dublin written early in 1875, Bessie had declared that Lee was ruined. 'Let Lee then confine himself as much as possible to the music, in that department he is unsurpassed, and he will not be ruined half so often,' George had replied. And in a letter to Lucy posted the same day (24 February 1875) he recommended: 'If Mamma argues, call things by their proper names, be excessively polite to her, and she will see that there is not the smallest use in it.' During the next year matters between them had deteriorated and, before George arrived in London, Lucy wrote to explain that 'Lee and I are bitter enemies now; we are frostily civil to each other's faces, and horribly abusive behind backs'.

The advice that George had so confidently fathered on his family he was unable to adopt himself. Lee was no writer, 'and when he was offered an appointment as musical critic to a paper called *The Hornet* . . . or had occasion to obtain very reasonable hotel bills or no bills at all in consideration of his praising the neighbourhood in the newspapers, I had the job of writing the criticisms and the articles,' Shaw explained. 'It was to some extent on my account that he undertook such pretences of authorship.'

Shaw provided *The Hornet* with careful criticism, carefully phrased and threaded with careful jokes that do not carry the generosity of the mature G.B.S. His mind focused on faults, on the obligation to spot them in performers and the necessity of avoiding them himself. The concert hall becomes a blackboard on which he scrupulously chalks up his remarks. Aware of the 'ignorant nonsense' of much musical journalism, he is self-consciously on guard against the nauseous eulogies he reads in some of his colleagues' columns. If his own work is a little priggish, it still achieves wonderful confidence for someone aged twenty-one. He is not afraid, on a first hearing, to dismiss Sir Frederic Cowen's new opera *Pauline* as possessing 'little originality' and displaying 'an utter absence of dramatic faculty'. Carl Rosa's first violin is accused of having played flat 'from beginning to end'; Herr Behrens is spotted frequently substituting 'semiquaver passages for the triplets' and betraying his ignorance of English by selecting the middle of a phrase as a suitable opportunity to take breath. Shaw castigates the timidity of other music critics twice or three times his age who 'can only judge one performance by reference to another', and shows off his own independence most fiercely when attacking 'the extremely low degree of excellence exhibited in operatic performances in England'.

Although there is only the ghost of Shaw in these apprentice buzzings, some Shavian acrobatics start to tumble out towards the end of his *Hornet* life. Wagner's overture to *Tannhäuser* holds the audience seated 'despite the loss of the express at 5.15'. Signor Rota is complimented as 'a master of the art of shouting'; and Madame Goddard is recorded as fascinating her hearers 'with a strikingly unpleasant imitation of a bagpipes'. In place of military drum and cymbals, Shaw advises the management of Her Majesty's 'to employ a stage carpenter to bang the orchestra door at a pre-arranged signal'. And after a performance of Donizetti's *Lucia* he deplored the Master of Ravenswood's habit of flinging his cloak and hat on the ground as 'ridiculous in the first act, impolite in the second, and only justified by the prospect of suicide in the third'. In his last buzz for *The Hornet*, he emphasizes the need, keenly felt by himself after observing Lee, to toil laboriously in pursuit of excellence, and the obligation to wait for success instead of maiming your talent in the pursuit of popularity.

Shaw felt tainted by this work. He would hand Lee the criticisms and Lee would hand him, without deduction, the fees, 'contenting himself with the consciousness of doing generously by a young and forlorn literary adventurer, and with the honor and glory accruing from the reputed authorship of my articles'. In later years G.B.S. exaggerated the 'vulgarities, follies, and ineptitudes, publicly and disgracefully committed, [that] have raised me wincing to such skills as I possess'. To these 'indescribably asinine musical criticisms', he declared, he owed all his knowledge of the characteristics of bad criticism: 'I did not know even enough to understand that what was torturing me was the guilt and shame which attend ignorance and incompetence.'

Never being shown proofs, he was unable to prevent what he called 'venal interpolations by other hands'. But his 'critical crimes' for *The Hornet* never warrant the hostility he turns on them. His shame proceeded less from their demerits than from the deception of ghost writing. In the words of George Russell, Shaw was 'the last saint sent out from Ireland to save the world'. He had arrived in London determined never to act on second-hand principles or submit to external circumstances. But in his first encounter he found himself in a conspiracy that formed part of the polite fraud he was attempting to demolish. It felt like a step back into cowardice.

The only honourable course open to him was to unmask himself. Almost he succeeded. By May 1877 the editor of *The Hornet* believed he had uncovered the truth. 'I have frequently rec'd "copy" palpably not your style,' he complained to Lee, 'but that in composition, idea and writing of a Lady.' The plot thinned. Knowing, perhaps, something of Lee's character, he suspected a squadron of these ladies, and 'they can't write'. By September, all was over. 'I must tell you candidly that *our* agreement is not being kept by you,' the editor told Lee. 'I stipulated for *your*

63

production and not that of a Substitute. I can't insert the class of writing I have rec'd the last 2 weeks . . . Please send word to your man to send no more copy.' Shaw's last sting was delivered on 26 September 1877 when Lee was in Scotland. Two years later (shortly before *The Hornet* closed) he reviewed the episode that had made him so miserable: 'I threw up my studies, and set to work to reform the musical profession. At the end of a year my friend [Lee] was one of the most unpopular men in London, the paper was getting into difficulties, and complications were arising from the proprietor's doubts as to a critic who was not only very severe, but capable of being in two places at the same time. I gave up that too (making a virtue of necessity), and the proprietor presently retired, ruined.'

*

The pressure that had affected Shaw so unhappily during his year at *The Hornet* he also attributed to Lee. His failure, he wrote, 'disguised as it was by a few years of fashionable success, was due wholly to the social conditions which compelled him to be a humbug or to starve'. In a land where the majority of educated ladies and gentlemen could say with genial pride that they did not know one note from the next, where they were awed by such mystic words as 'subdominant' and 'diminished seventh', Lee might have expected to be more than a teacher, perhaps an oracle. But popular ignorance degraded him. He was no longer able to teach honestly. In order to stay alive, he advertised himself as being able to make fashionable ladies sing like Patti in twelve lessons – at (a fee undreamed of in Dublin) a guinea a lesson. To Bessie, Lee had been, besides a great conductor, 'the sole apostle of The Method: the only true and perfect method of singing: the method that had made her a singer and preserved the purity of her voice in defiance of time'. She knew that the Method required two years of patient practice and that his Patti promise was a swindle. The 'moment she found that he had abandoned "the method",' Shaw told O'Bolger, '. . . she gave him up'.

Shaw gave as the particular cause for breaking with Lee, a sexual sentimentality which, ripening in the coarse atmosphere of London, had turned towards Lucy. 'My sister, to whom this new attitude was as odious as it was surprising, immediately dropped him completely, and thus gave him the possibly very disheartening shock of making him aware that she had not even liked him. He came no more to our house; and as far as I can recollect neither my mother nor my sister ever saw him again.'

To G.B.S., this sexual sentimentality and the economic perversion of his musical talent were symptoms of the same disease. 'I do not know at what moment he began to deteriorate,' he wrote. He then went on to invent a new Lee, an English Hyde who emerged from the Irish Jekyll. Lee was, he tells us, 'no longer the same man'. He was unrecognizable. 'G. J. Lee, with the black whiskers and the clean shaven resolute lip and chin, became Vandeleur Lee, whiskerless, but with a waxed and pointed moustache and an obsequious attitude.' So the volcano, so active in Ireland, becomes extinct in England, and the Dublin genius collapses into a London humbug. Such an end Shaw described as 'a tragedy'. It was tragedy with a moral: Lee is the victim of a pantomime with Capitalism its bad fairy.

Lucy quickly escaped. She left the tottering Troubadours, turned professional in 1879 and five years later joined the Carl Rosa Opera Company. For her mother, now nearing fifty, it was less easy. Though she 'despised' Lee, it is impossible to know in what measure her contempt was emotional, financial or moral. Perhaps, while preparing to abandon this wrecked vessel, she did not differentiate. Her son makes it exclusively a matter of musical principle. But the language he uses carries other overtones. His mother was left, he writes, with one passion – 'and that was for flowers. Her husband disappointed and disgusted her; Lee rescued her through his musical genius from that disappointment and disgust, but finally collapsed and disappointed her too ... The result was almost a worse disillusion than her marriage ... that Lee should be unfaithful! unfaithful to the Method! ... with all the virtue gone out of him: this was the end of all things; and she never forgave it.'

But she continued apparently to 'tolerate' him. Though 'my mother made no allowance for social pressure', this was the economic force that for a time still held them together. But whereas Lee exploited social hypocrisy and added to it by his ambitions, the Shaws made of it only a passing convenience. To G.B.S. this difference was crucial: it was the difference between the old Mrs Warren and young Vivie Warren in the last of his *Plays Unpleasant*. Mrs Warren lost Vivie: Lee lost Mrs Shaw.

A symbol of Lee's days of vanity in London was his smart Park Lane house. 'He had always said that he would take a house in Park Lane; and he did,' Shaw told Frank Harris. 'No 13, it was: a narrow house, but with one fine music room.'

Number 13 Park Lane lay at the less fashionable end of the street Shaw described as 'sacred to peers and millionaires'. It was half-a-house (part of number 14) and, because of a murder committed there two years before Lee moved in, less expensive than Shaw imagined. Here, for the benefit of encumbered gentlefolk and other honourable personnel, Lee organized a few charity concerts and performances of amateur opera. But there was no tide of publicity to buoy him up; his nerve began to fail and in panic he filled his music room with the raised voices of elevated Englishwomen and let them yell. Bessie, who sang an elderly Donna Anna for him at a performance of *Don Giovanni*, assisted with a number of his soirées, and it was at one of these that the *Punch* cartoonist George du Maurier, making some sketches of the Shaws and what G.B.S. was to describe as their 'damaged Svengali', conceived his idea for *Trilby*. When, in 1895, du Maurier's novel was adapted for the stage, Shaw was to write: 'Svengali is *not* a villain, but only a poor egotistical wretch who provokes people to pull his nose . . . Imagine, above all, Svengali taken seriously at his own foolish valuation, blazed upon with limelights, spreading himself intolerably over the whole play with nothing fresh to add to the first five minutes of him – Svengali defying heaven, declaring that henceforth he is his own God, and then tumbling down in a paroxysm of heart disease (the blasphemer rebuked, you see), and having to be revived by draughts of brandy. I derived much cynical amusement from this most absurd scene . . . But surely even the public would just as soon – nay, rather – have the original Svengali, the luckless artist-cad (a very deplorable type of cad, whom Mr du Maurier has hit off to the life).' Shaw was to try his own hand at creating such a figure in *The Doctor's Dilemma*.

By the time Shaw had finished with *The Hornet*, his mother had left Park Lane and, appropriating 'the Method' (in something of the same way Eliza Doolittle threatens to make off with Professor Higgins' speech methods), set herself up as a private singing teacher. She had no further need of Lee. But Shaw 'remained on friendly terms' with him, playing the piano at some of his rehearsals and saving him the cost of a professional accompanist. Once or twice he even sang. The *dégringolade* was by now pretty far advanced. Those furiously smart people who had taken Lee up on his arrival in London had moved on to newer sensations, and his later recruits were socially less exalted. Shaw, who began by playing Mozart and ended rehearsing the Solicitor in Gilbert and Sullivan's *Patience*, later described the deterioration:

'One day at one of the At Homes a young lady who, like the rest, had come to regard me as in some sense responsible for Lee's proceedings, came to me with a resolute and wrathful countenance, and, pointing to a chair near the door, asked me who that lady was, and whether she was a member of the society. And I recognized in the young woman who occupied the chair very uneasily, unsuccessfully dressed and with her complexion still more unsuccessfully touched up, the housemaid! After that, the end was inevitable . . . The Troubadours disbanded; and after a phase with a different set of musical people who simply came to the house in Park Lane and sang a lot of old opera music without any pretence of conducting, I being the "maestro", we came to the end of a season which was never resumed.'

After that it was a matter of living with 'the young lady who had rescued him from entire loneliness', renting his rooms to bachelors and the music chamber for dubious supper parties. He continued to keep in touch with Shaw, offering him introductions to men with 'good press influence' and odd jobs as *répétiteur* for an occasional lady who wished 'to try over her songs'. There were also miscellaneous commissions: one for 'a few short squibs relating to the Amateur Opera performance to be given this season [May 1882] for the benefit of the distressed ladies of Ireland'; another for drawing up a Prospectus on 'How to Cure Clergyman's Sore Throat'; and a third, begun but never completed by Shaw, that involved drafting a third edition of *The Voice*.

On the evening of 27 November 1886, while putting his arm through the sleeve of his nightshirt, Lee dropped dead.

On the morning of the inquest, three days later, one of Lee's musical group told Lucy the news and she passed it on to her brother. Next day, 1 December, he called at 13 Park Lane to verify the report. 'Heard from servant,' he noted in his diary, 'that he was found dead of heart disease on Sunday morning. Went back home to tell Mother . . .' At the inquest on 30 November it had been established that Lee was suffering from extensive heart disease and the jury returned a verdict of death by natural causes. Shaw, who (as his diary makes clear) had not gone to this inquest, adds that it 'revealed the fact that his brain was diseased and had been so for a long time'. Neither the newspaper reports nor the death certificate ('Angina Pectoris. Found dead on floor.') corroborate this statement which nevertheless enabled Shaw to reason that the mischief converting Lee from Jekyll to Hyde had begun to do its work years before. 'I was glad to learn that his decay was pathological as well as ecological,' he concluded, 'and that the old efficient and honest Lee had been real after all.'

Besides a feeling of strangeness that she should be leaving other people to bury him, Lee's death (her son tells us) produced no effect on Bessie at all. For her he had already been dead some years. As for Shaw, he put away *The Voice* with relief, 'and my career as a pseudo-Lee closed for ever'.

*What inexpensive pleasure can be greater than that of strolling through London of an evening, and reconstructing it in imagination? Just think of it! To begin with, you make a fine straight boulevard from your house (or perhaps your lodging) to your office, and establish a commodious omnibus service along it. Abolishing St Pancras, Victoria, Waterloo, and the rest, you bring all the great railways to a common terminus within five minutes' walk of your door. Then, your own modest needs being satisfied, you indulge in architectural meditation, fancy free. You burst the bonds and bars of the Duke of Bedford; you make Notting hill low and exalt Maida-vale by carting the one into the other; you make Southwark Bridge a less formidable obstacle to traffic than Primrose-hill; you extend the Embankment from Blackfriars to the Tower as an eligible nocturnal promenade from which to commit holders of portable property to the deep; you rescue the unfortunate persons who, having at one time or another ventured into the labyrinth between Bond-street and Park-lane, are still wandering, lost in Mayfair; you turn the mountainous tract south of Pentonville into a deer forest for urban sportsmen; you lead stray churches from the middle of the Strand into the courtyard of Somerset House; you build an underground London in the bowels of the metropolis, and an overhead London piercing the fog curtain above on viaducts, with another and another atop of these, until you have piled up, six cities deep, to Alpine altitudes with a different climate at each level. Sanitary arrangements amid which disease cannot exist; smokeless fires that will gently lull us to permanent repose with carbolic oxide; spotless statues and shirt-fronts; common kitchens in all the squares; phalanstères, familistères, reading rooms, museums, baths, gymnasia, laundries, and open spaces, with all such items as water, fuel, gas, and oil, guaranteed not to cost more than a farthing for sixteen hours – all these will ensue spontaneously from your arrangements. For purposes of transit you will devise a system of pneumatic tubes, through which passengers, previously treated by experienced dentists with nitrous oxide, can be blown from Kensington to Mile-end in a breath; or, as an ingenious gentleman at the Colonial Office has already suggested, endless bands might be let into the pavement and kept in perpetual motion by steam drums at each street corner. Upon these the pedestrian might step and be borne away to his destination, where he would simply spring aside to the stationary part of the pavement, leaving the long line of tradesmen's boys, solicitors, statesmen, and who not, mass and class, streaming by on the bosom of the band. What a London that would be!* 'Ideal London' (1886)

The drinking, racegoing, whoring, the blasphemous religion and politics that made up Dublin social life in the 1860s and early 1870s had nauseated Shaw. Unless intoxicated with music or books, he had found no comfortable place there except the theatre, which was a kind of intoxication too. And when he came out of the theatre he was again engulfed, polluted, by that cynical and impoverished atmosphere. What could anyone find amusing in all that 'foul mouthed, foul minded derision and obscenity?'

Having escaped from Dublin, he expected to find things ordered differently in London. Oscar Wilde who, though he had visited London before, came to live there two years later than Shaw, was to inhale an air 'full of the heavy odour of roses . . . the heavy scent of the lilac, or the more delectable perfume of the pink flowering thorn'. The parks and gardens, squares and palisades sprouted their green between the seasoned brick and wedding-cake stucco of the West End where Wilde elegantly sauntered. But Wilde had come from respectable Merrion Square via Oxford to Mayfair and did not see the stagnant and ill-smelling London Shaw was getting to know – a London of primitive streets with clinging red mud, miserably treated animals, dark unventilated basements and an atmosphere malodorous with soot and dust. Even Dostoevsky, on a visit in the 1850s, had been shocked by the sullen population of 'white Negroes' storming the pubs at nightfall. By the 1880s London was 'not only the largest and richest, but also the dirtiest and meanest, capital in the world'. Below the prim pattern of bourgeois life that Wilde was so delightfully to shock lay a vast reservoir of squalor and brutality, full of appalling slums inhabited by the 'lower classes'. 'It was when these dreadful drunken or savage creatures broke out for a moment from their lairs into the life of a small middle-class child that he first knew the paralysing anguish of fear,' wrote Leonard Woolf. '. . . They were human beings, but they made me sick with terror and disgust in the pit of my small stomach . . .' Drury Lane, the charming ambience of *Pygmalion*, was a derelict area until 1900, the territory of men and women in tatters, who crawled the streets like animals.

'London, when you have once seen it, is inconceivable, and the more you have seen of it the less you can believe in it,' Shaw wrote after he had lived there a dozen years:

'Shelley, whose brain was big enough to take a great deal of it in, described Hell as "a city much like London". Dickens, who knew London, depicted it as full of strange monsters, Merdles, Veneerings, Finches of the Grove, Barnacles, Marshalseas indigenous to the Borough but cropping up sporadically among the monuments of Rome and Venice: all dreadfully answering to things that we know to be there, and yet cannot believe in without confusion and terror. How pleasant it is to shrink back to the genial Thackeray, who knew comparatively nothing about London, but just saw the fun of the little sets of ideas current in Russell and Bryanston-squares, Pall-mall, Fleet-street, and the art academies in Newman-street.'

The dirt, drink and economics of London were to turn both Shaw and Leonard Woolf into socialists. No new planning, they believed, could be achieved without a change of attitude in the country similar to one that had taken place in themselves. 'The problem, unfortunately, is not one of realignment and patent dwellings,' Shaw wrote in 1886:

'It is one of the development of individual greed into civic spirit; of the extension of the *laissez-faire* principle to public as well as private enterprise; of bringing all the citizens to a common date in civilization instead of maintaining a savage class, a mediaeval class, a renaissance class, and an Augustan class, with a few nineteenth-century superior persons to fix high-water mark, all jostling one another in the same streets, so that we never know where we are, or whether, on any advanced measure, the tenth century will not be too strong for us . . . we must be content with the new streets through St Giles's, and the periodical washing of the Albert Memorial . . . until London belongs to, and is governed by, the people who use it.'

\*

Number 13 Victoria Grove stood on the east side of a cul-de-sac off the Brompton Road. The houses were semi-detached, with tiny gardens, and they occupied, along with those in a number of parallel groves, a countrified area, still with plenty of orchard and market garden, between Fulham and Putney. Here, for two years after *The Hornet*, Shaw did little but write short stories, literary reviews, articles, treatises, essays in philosophy. He wrote in order, he later said, to teach himself to write. It was 'mere brute practice with the pen . . . as a laborer digs or a carpenter planes'. There was a mountain of stuff to be got rid of, and he cleared his system by writing it out of himself. It was the sort of material he could turn out 'at sixpence a mile', only no one wanted it at any price.

By February 1878 he was at work on a profane Passion Play in blank verse 'with the mother of the hero represented as a termagant'. Judas and Jesus in this play represent two sides of Shaw. Judas is

<blockquote>
a man unblinded<br>
And trained to shun the snare of self delusion
</blockquote>

who sees in his corrupt surroundings a 'beastly world'. Jesus, the dreamer, poet and prophet, who looks towards an invisible future, embodies hope. In the combination of the two, Shaw argues, the observer and the man of imagination, we reach reality. Judas's advice to the young Jesus is the lesson Shaw himself was endeavouring to master:

<blockquote>
Then must thou<br>
Learn to stand absolutely by thyself,<br>
Leaning on nothing, satisfied that thou<br>
Can'st nothing know, responsible to nothing,<br>
Fearing no power and being within thyself<br>
A little independent universe.
</blockquote>

Both Judas and Jesus are susceptible to beautiful women. Judas, for example, when remembering his love for Mary, recalls Shaw's infatuation in Ireland with the 'bewitching Calypso'.

<blockquote>
I was too young<br>
To shun the bait, although I saw the snare.<br>
I freed myself at last, and felt as though<br>
I had left half my soul behind. At present<br>
I am none the worse, and almost think the dream<br>
Was worth the waking.
</blockquote>

Jesus discovers that, though otherwise he may soar above common things, when beguiled by the peasant girl Rahab 'I am a weak creature'. Her displeasure can turn 'the sky black'. But until he clears his mind of the illusion that he can find in her

<blockquote>
unimaginable things:<br>
Sympathy, purity, kinship into heaven,<br>
A divine something far beyond the scope<br>
Of sordid man –
</blockquote>

he cannot escape the horrors of family life in Nazareth and pursue his 'seeming wintry goal undaunted.'

After forty-nine pages – 1260 lines – the play breaks off in the second scene of Act II. 'I havent burnt it,' Shaw told Karl Pearson fifteen years later, '. . . and should perhaps have finished & published it if I had not been too poor to dream of such luxuries.' It was, he admitted, 'the sort of thing we have all done. We hardly know what blank verse is; and of the nature of an "act" we are utterly ignorant: yet we do it to give expression to the Shakspare in us. Nobody reads it when it is done . . . Yet there were some fine lines in it . . .' There were reasons other than poverty for not completing it. He had discovered how easy it was to produce streams of unsubtle rhythm achieving 'the true blank manner'. But the lines do give evidence of his reading of nineteenth-century poets and his ability to imitate them – particularly Wordsworth. Across one abandoned passage he wrote: 'Vile Stuff.' Not having planned the play in advance he began to foresee insuperable difficulties ahead. Fifty-five years later, in his Preface to *On the Rocks*, he explained that a modern Passion Play was impossible because 'the trial of a dumb prisoner, at which the judge who puts the crucial question to him remains unanswered, cannot be dramatized unless the judge is to be the hero of the play . . . Jesus would not defend himself . . . If ever there was a full dress debate for the forensic championship to be looked forward to with excited confidence by the disciples of the challenged expert it was his trial of Christ. Yet their champion put up no fight: he went like a lamb to the slaughter, dumb.' Nor could Shaw invent the words because, without Judas, Jesus had become unbalanced in an absurdly un-Shavian way. 'Jesus comes out as an arrogant lunatic, dull, speechless, and too intolerable to be pitiable until they torture him,' he later wrote of Masefield's *The Trial of Jesus*. 'Pilate and Annas carry off all the honors. No doubt that is the truth of the matter; but a real madman with a ridiculous delusion cannot be a hero of tragedy (Lear and Ajax [in *Troilus and Cressida*] have no delusion of their own greatness) and a passion play without Jesus as the hero is impossible.'

Also finished in February 1878 was *My Dear Dorothea*, a didactic pamphlet modelled on George Augustus Sala's rather damp squib *Lady Chesterfield's Letters to Her Daughter*, which Shaw had read the previous year. He was evidently attracted by pastiche. Lady Chesterfield's correspondence being 'a code of manners and morals for the nursery', Shaw subtitled his work: 'A Practical System of Moral Education for Females Embodied in a Letter to a Young Person of that Sex.' Much of the advice (including a warning against taking advice) would later become familiar furniture of Shavian philosophy: act, though in a sensible way, selfishly (that is, with self-control) and do not be peevishly self-sacrificing; arm yourself with politeness which is a mark of superiority over unpleasant people; cultivate hypocrisy with others for kindness' sake, but never with yourself; read anything except what bores you; leave religion alone until you've grown up; get into mischief, but do not look for pity; neither ask anything as a favour, nor expect more than you've deserved by your conduct. Finally: 'Always strive to find out what to do by thinking, without asking anybody.' It is the creed, charmingly presented, of the man who was to argue passionately for that experiment of the Life Force we call children to develop in a 'society of equals'.

*My Dear Dorothea* is the most paradoxical of anarchist tracts in that it advises children how to abolish the authority of adults by becoming more parental than their parents. The most closely autobiographical passages refer to Dorothea's mother:

'If your mother is always kind to you, love her more than you love anything except your doll ... If you had indeed such a mother, my dear Dorothea, you would not need my advice at all. But I must not forget how seldom little girls have such guardians; and I will therefore take it for granted that your mother ... thinks of you only as a troublesome and inquisitive little creature ...

'For such a parent, you must be particularly careful not to form any warm affection. Be very friendly with her, because you are in the same house as she, and it is unpleasant to live with one whom you dislike. If you have any griefs, do not tell her of them. Keep them to yourself if possible ... Other people have too many cares of their own to think much about yours.

'If you observe this rule, you will not need to trouble your mother at all; and you will find that she will seldom trouble you, except by complaining when you make a noise ... These complaints you must bear patiently ... You will soon be sent to school, and so get rid of her.'

Shaw's advice was a prescription against suffering, yet there is the danger that Dorothea will grow up a monster of reticence and calculation. 'It is a most illuminating and sorrowful self-portrait,' Stevie Smith was to write. '... Because it shows that Shaw was as proud as the devil and put pride in the place of love. And why should a bright creature of such mercurial wits and fighting frenzies so limit himself if not for fear? ... every now and then the heart limps in, but he is ashamed of it and begins to bluster.'

In the autumn of 1878, Shaw started his first novel – and abandoned it almost at once. The surviving notes show that it was to have been called *The Legg Papers* and that he may have transferred his original idea to 'The Miraculous Revenge', his story of a peripatetic graveyard which W. B. Yeats was to include in the first number of his Irish miscellany, *The Shanachie*.

In March 1879 he began again, this time on a novel called, 'with merciless fitness', *Immaturity*. Much of the manuscript is filled with corrections. 'As I could not afford a typewriter nor a secretary, I had to write directly and legibly for the printer with my own hand.' Five novels and part of a sixth he got through in this way. His handwriting, neat and spindly, sloping slightly backwards, in dark brown ink on demy paper that has been sliced into quarto, is that of the chief cashier of Uniacke Townshend who had absorbed business habits 'without being infected by the business spirit'. Shaw condemned himself to a daily reckoning of five pages – and so scrupulously that if his fifth page ended in the middle of a sentence 'I did not finish it until the next day'. The strain of this apprenticeship may be sensed in *Immaturity*: 'I have drudged year after year until I have very little patience left for anything but work,' says one of the characters, '. . . it is the holding on day after day only a hair's breadth from failure.'

Shaw was to describe this novel as his 'first attempt at a big book' – nearly two hundred thousand words with one main and three subsidiary plots. The main interest is autobiographical. The character of Robert Smith is Shaw himself at twenty. In a passage that was eventually omitted, Smith is described as being 'too serious to be a trifler, and too young to have acquired the habit of supporting institutions for the sake of conventional propriety. Besides, he had the culture that is given by loneliness and literature.'

This culture is at the centre of Smith's moral sense, and his difficulty in preserving it becomes one of the main themes of *Immaturity*. 'Smith began to crave for a female friend who would encourage him to persevere in the struggle for truth and human perfection, during those moments when its exhilaration gave place to despair. Happily, he found none such. The power to stand alone is worth acquiring at the expense of much sorrowful solitude.' This is the voice of Shaw. Unable to make contact with other people, he polished his isolation to a virtue. Smith's prim visual infatuation with a ballet dancer, releasing energy to be used for work, illustrates Shaw's susceptibility to women and his determination not to let them occupy his mind to the exclusion of everything else. Mlle Bernadina de Sangallo, as she is called in this first draft, takes her dreamlike existence from Ermina Pertoldi, a dancer whom Shaw used to see at the Alhambra and who filled his night-time fantasies. '*Immaturity* is a work to be proud of,' wrote a friend, Elinor Huddart. 'There is enough thought in it for a dozen novels, and not enough emotion in it for half a one . . . these people how they talk! . . . I don't like any of your women . . . Can no one have self-control and independence without a demeanour of ice and insolence? . . . The love which you depict is chilling . . . Their amatory sayings fall like snow-flakes.'

Like Smith, Shaw sometimes 'relapsed into that painful yearning which men cherish gloomily at eighteen, and systematically stave off as a nuisance by excitement or occupation in later years'. Work, with which Shaw began to stave off this nuisance, becomes the hero of *Immaturity* once the discovery is made that all work is pleasant once the habit is formed. 'There is no such thing really as idleness; for the idle people are often the busiest; but they are unsatisfied,' Smith explains. 'I suppose work in the sense we mean is sustained and intelligently directed effort resulting in the production or attainment of some worthy end . . . ' Cyril Scott, an artist modelled on the landscape painter Cecil Lawson, agrees with Smith, and finds salvation. 'What is there to live for but work?' asks Scott. 'Everything else ends in disappointment. It's the only thing that you never get tired of, and that always comes to good.'

Shaw allows another worthy end: marriage. People should marry, not to stave off that 'painful yearning', but to have children. 'There is no gratification which a woman can afford you, that will not be sweeter when that woman is not your wife, except the possession of boys and girls to continue the record when you are in your coffin. Therefore marry the woman who will bring you the finest children, and who will be the best mother to them; and you will never find out that you might have done better elsewhere.'

Since hereditary factors are incalculable, Shaw places his bet on instinct. In the debate he sets up between common sense and romance, it is common sense that is seen to lack courage, evade experience, shut its eyes to biological selection; and it is romance, arguing against 'the folly of prudent marriages', that triumphs. 'The chief objection to fictitious romance,' he writes elsewhere in *Immaturity*, 'is that it is seldom so romantic as the truth.' Shaw originally intended calling the last section of the book 'The fate of sentimentalism', and it is against sentimentality not against the romantic sex instinct that his chief objection lies. 'The design was, to write a novel scrupulously true to nature,' he told Macmillan, '. . . a constant irony on sentimentalism, at which the whole work is mainly directed.'

Smith is repeatedly accused, as Shaw was to be, of remorseless matter-of-factness. 'You are really very matter-of-fact, Mr Smith. You rub the gloss off everything.' It is this artificial gloss, embodied by the fashionable poet Hawksmith (a sort of Smith gone wrong) that Shaw dislikes. 'Matter-of-fact people are a great nuisance,' Smith concedes, 'and always will be, so long as they are in the minority.' The implication is that the days of Hawksmith (who owes something to Oscar Wilde) are numbered, and the day of Smith (who writes poems in private, not for public performance) will come. Hawksmith has not strength enough to resist the applause of a society that is, below its glossy surface, uncaring and uncomprehending. It is society, making so difficult the attainment of a worthy end whether in the arts, politics or a good marriage, that is the villain of the novel.

In the end, those characters who resist the pretexts and proprieties of Victorianism marry successfully. But Smith does not marry, nor does his work (which is vaguely defined) apparently lead to a worthy end. 'You are not a boy; and you are not grown-up,' one of the characters tells him. 'Some day you will get away from your books and come to know the world and get properly set. But just now there is no doing anything with you. You are just a bad case of immaturity.' In the final paragraph of 'provoking barrenness' Smith stands meditating on his immaturity: 'At last he shook his head negatively, and went home.'

In a Preface, written during the summer of 1921, Shaw describes his intelligence as a piece of machinery that needed a 'religion' to switch it on – 'a clear comprehension of life in the light of an intelligible theory . . . to set it in triumphant operation.' His sequence of novels became the search for that religion. In *Immaturity*, 'the book of a raw youth', there is the outline of a pale, private Shaw who existed before his conversion by that religion into the fantastic personality of G.B.S. But by admitting this phenomenon, 'fit and apt for dealing with men', to have been an imposture, and owning that 'I succeeded only too well', Shaw acknowledges having set aside something of his integrity. Like Hawksmith, he took on a public gloss. But whereas Hawksmith acquired his gloss from the caressing of society, the brilliant Shavian creature that emerged and flew away from the dull chrysalis of Smith wanted to outshine society and lead us all to another place ruled over by 'one of my most successful fictions'. Like the 'Vandeleur Lee' who developed from G. J. Lee, 'G.B.S.' was a manufactured identity: not a victim of capitalist society – a weapon to be used against it.

*

Shaw finished *Immaturity* on 28 September 1879 and completed his revisions six weeks later on 5 November. It was now a question, in the words of his father, of 'thrusting it down the throats of some of the publishers and so getting it into the hands of the mob'. On 7 November Shaw called on Hurst and Blackett and the following day sent them the manuscript. Next week they declined it.

Of his disappointment, which was deep, he showed nothing. 'A man who has no office to go to – I don't care who he is – is a trial of which you can have no conception,' he was to write many years later. At Victoria Grove he was being more and more frequently reproached with laziness – his father in Dublin adding to the chorus of complaint and, to George's exasperation, obtaining a testimonial from Uniacke Townshend. Now and then he had gone half-heartedly out to look for work – once to the East India Docks ('not worth anything', he noted in his diary) and later, after an introduction by the poet Richard Hengist Horne, to the Imperial Bank at South Kensington. 'Your son must *not* talk about religion or give his views thereon,' Horne warned Mrs Shaw, '& he must make up his mind to work

& do what he is told – if not there is no use his calling.' In such circumstances it was not difficult for Shaw scrupulously to avoid employment. But as the pressure from his family tightened he was driven to more elaborate means of escape, and eventually these failed him. From his cousin Mrs Cashel Hoey he had received an introduction to the manager of the Edison Telephone Company, Arnold White, to whom on 5 October 1879, while still revising *Immaturity*, he wrote the sort of devastatingly honest letter he could usually rely on to extricate himself:

'In the last two years I have not filled any post, nor have I been doing anything specially calculated to qualify me for a business one . . .

'My only reason for seeking commercial employment is a pecuniary one. I know how to wait for success in literature, but I do not know how to live on air in the interim. My family are in difficulties. I may be deceived as to my literary capacity, and in any case, it is as well to be independent of a fine art if clean work is to be made . . . However, I should be loth to press you for a place in which I might not be the right man. If you can give me any hints as to what I might do with myself elsewhere, I shall be well satisfied, for I know you will be able [to] understand my position. Hitherto I have disregarded so much advice from well intentioned friends, that I am reputed almost as impracticable as another member of the family with whom you are acquainted.'

Arnold White, who had liked Shaw, was not put off by this letter and offered him employment in the Way-Leave Department of the Edison Telephone Company. Shaw began working there on 14 November, immediately following the rejection of *Immaturity*. After six weeks he amassed a gross income of two shillings and sixpence, and forfeited by way of expenses two guineas. The trouble was that he had agreed to be paid on a generous commission basis. His job was to persuade all sorts of people in the East End of London to allow insulators, poles, derricks and other impedimenta of telephoning to bristle about their roofs and gardens. 'I liked the exploration involved,' he remembered, 'but my shyness made the business of calling on strangers frightfully uncongenial; and my sensitiveness, which was extreme, in spite of the brazen fortitude which I simulated, made the impatient rebuffs I had to endure . . . ridiculously painful to me.'

Nearly twenty years later, in a passage celebrating English pigheadedness, he reviewed some of his experiences in this job: 'electric telegraphy, telephony, and traction are invented, and establish themselves as necessities of civilized life. The unpractical foreigner recognizes the fact, and takes the obvious step of putting up poles in his streets to carry wires.

This expedient never occurs to the Briton. He wastes leagues of wire and does unheard-of damage to property by tying his wires and posts to such chimney stacks as he can beguile householders into letting him have access to. Finally, when it comes to electric traction, and the housetops are out of the question, he suddenly comes out in the novel character of an amateur in urban picturesqueness, and declares that the necessary cable apparatus would spoil the appearance of our streets. The streets of Nuremberg, the heights of Fiesole, may not be perceptibly worse for these contrivances; but the beauty of Tottenham Court Road is too sacred to be so profaned: to its loveliness the strained bus-horse and his offal are the only accessories endurable by the beauty-loving Cockney eye. This is your common-sense Englishman. His helplessness in the face of electricity is typical of his helplessness in the face of everything else that lies outside the set of habits he calls his opinions and capacities.' In such memories lived real anger.

By the end of 1879 he had obtained one consent. The truth appeared to be that he could not afford regular employment: 'I am under an absolute necessity to discontinue my services forthwith,' he told the head of his department. As a result of this threatened resignation he was given a basic wage of £48 a year and, two months later, promoted at a salary of £80 to be head of the department and 'organize the work of more thick-skinned adventurers instead of doing it myself'. He was now stationed in one of the basement offices of a building in Queen Victoria Street, loud with Americans singing sentimental songs and swearing as lyrically as any Irishman. They all adored Mr Edison, nauseated his rival Mr Bell, worked with a terrible energy out of all proportion to the results achieved, and dreamed emotionally of telephone transmitters patented to their own formula. Shaw watched them carefully, noting with some shade of satisfaction (since he had got his knowledge, Shavian style, from a member of the Bell family) that none of them knew the scientific explanation of telephoning – unlike himself:

'They were free-souled creatures, excellent company: sensitive, cheer-ful, and profane; liars, braggarts, and hustlers; with an air of making slow old England hum which never left them even when, as often happened, they were wrestling with difficulties of their own making, or struggling in no-thoroughfares from which they had to be retrieved like strayed sheep by Englishmen without imagination enough to go wrong.'

Shaw waited patiently for his novel to rescue him. But *Immaturity* was rejected by every British and American publisher to whom it was sent. Sampson Low begged to be spared the pleasure of reading it; other publishers, when returning the manuscript to him, urged him to send them something else. 'No', wrote George Meredith for Chapman and Hall; 'unattractive', decided John Morley at Macmillan. Shaw had produced on them the impression 'that I was a young man with more cleverness than was good for me and that what I needed was snubbing and not encouraging'.

To encourage himself he eventually hit on a defensive parody of these publishers' opinions: 'I feel I'd rather die than read it.' But to gain his ease with the public and especially with his family he had wanted it published and spent some time investigating whether he should borrow money and publish it at his own expense – a policy he later warned authors never to give in to.

'The characters are certainly not drawn after the conventional patterns of fiction,' John Morley had reported. But Shaw, describing it as 'a museum specimen of the Victorian novel' which had been written at precisely the wrong time, submerged his personal feelings in a smooth historical narrative that explained his failure as unawareness of a new reading public with the tastes of schoolboys and *grisettes*:

'The Education Act of 1871 was producing readers who had never before bought books, nor could have read them if they had; and publishers were finding that these people wanted not George Eliot and the excessively literary novice Bernard Shaw, but such crude tales of impossible adventures published in penny numbers only for schoolboys. The success of Stevenson's *Treasure Island* and Jekyll and Hyde fairy tale, forced this change on the attention of the publishers; and I, as a belated intellectual, went under completely . . . Had I understood this situation at the time I should have been a happier novice instead of an apparently hopeless failure.'

## [ 3 ]

*. . . the progress of the world depends on the people who refuse to accept facts and insist on the satisfaction of their instincts.*
*Back to Methuselah*

Something was wrong with the Edison telephone: it liked speaking in American – that is, with 'such stentorian efficiency that it bellowed your most private communications all over the house instead of whispering them with some sort of discretion,' Shaw wrote. 'This was not what the

British stockbroker wanted ...' On 5 June 1880 the Company amalgamated with the Bell Telephone Company and gave its employees one month's notice. Shaw, turning down an invitation to apply for a job with the new United Telephone Company of London, flung himself back into the literary world.

*Immaturity* was to lie 'dumb and forgotten' for fifty years; the *Passion Play* and *My Dear Dorothea* remained unpublished during Shaw's life; a short story he had written, 'The Brand of Cain', was steadily rejected by magazines over five years until his one copy disappeared in the post. Of more than a dozen other stories and articles he had written in 1879 on 'subjects ranging from orchestral conducting to oakum picking' most were rejected, some were lost. The two that were eventually published (the first, 'Opera in Italian', being unsigned and unpaid for; the second, on 'Christian Names', appearing anonymously in *One and All*) earned him fifteen shillings. In the summer of 1880, attempting another assault on critical journalism, he approached John Morley, the new editor of the *Pall Mall Gazette*, enclosing some examples of his work and asking whether he might make a music or theatre critic. 'I cannot hesitate to say,' Morley answered, 'that in my opinion you would do well to get out of journalism.' For a long time following this rebuff, Shaw was to remain the complete professional failure – 'nobody would pay a farthing for a stroke of my pen'. To John Morley, revealing his self-dislike, he replied: 'I fear I am incorrigible ... Should you ever require anything particularly disagreeable written about anybody, pray remember, yours faithfully, G. B. Shaw.'

Describing this period later on, G.B.S. fashioned it into a retro-spectively painless experience. Though the most foreign of all foreigners – an Irishman – he was no peasant lad setting his foot courageously on the lowest rung of the social ladder – and he advised his biographers to put all such romantic notions out of their heads. 'I never climbed any ladder: I have achieved eminence by sheer gravitation.' It was a matter of waiting in line for the rather overcrowded career of professional man of genius. Had he been capable of gratitude, he would have inflicted it on his parents. He sponged off them without shame and they, in their poverty, tolerated him as a burden they could not dislodge. 'I did not throw myself into the struggle for life: I threw my mother into it. I was not a staff to my father's old age: I hung on to his coat tails ... People wondered at my heartlessness ... My mother worked for my living instead of preaching that it was my duty to work for hers: therefore take off your hat to her, and blush.'

The facts were grimmer. He had been warned off journalism and, despite the failure of *Immaturity*, a career in novels seemed the only one open to him. Everyone wrote novels in the 1880s. Lucrative literature meant the novel – drama, economics, philosophy were unsaleable. But his family was mortified that George should feel it necessary to humiliate publishers again by 'exposing them to the stupidity of failing to see any merit in me'. Apparently without a gleam of talent, he was making himself into an over-industrious good-for-nothing. He had tried to accustom himself to French and Italian, learning neither; he began to teach himself shorthand; he silently studied harmony and counterpoint; he experimented as a baritone, persuading his mother to train his voice by 'the Method' until he could sing 'as well as a man without twopennorth of physical endowment can be made to sing'; he persisted in playing the piano; he read greedily and, worst of all, he wrote.

He started on his second novel that summer, marching through it at the rate of a thousand words a day. 'I never advise anyone to choose an artistic profession,' he was to write many years later: 'People must force their way into them in spite of the advice of all their friends, and the threats and entreaties of their distracted parents. You dont adopt literature as a profession: it adopts you if you can deliver the goods. There are no academies to confer degrees ... The only test of competence is acceptance for publication: friendly opinions are of no use.'

Every opinion seemed unfriendly. His father was constantly fretting at him to find 'something to do to earn some money. It is much wanted by all of us.' Mrs Shaw unsuccessfully sought interviews for him; and Lucy, having failed to get their mother to turn George out of the house, had persuaded McNulty (as the only person likely to have influence) to write imploring him to take a job. Though sweet on Lucy, McNulty felt uneasy over this commission (which put an end to their correspondence for nine months) and it was only from his elder sister Mary that Shaw was shown a glint of encouragement. 'I dont mind your report about your failure,' she wrote. 'Why you have only tried with your first book and I am certain your next wont fail.' But Mary McNulty had died before his second novel was finished.

Shaw deafened himself to everything, wrote steadily, using some of his experiences at the Edison Telephone Company and some retaliatory observations of Lucy, and finished the novel which he called *The Irrational Knot* on 1 December 1880.

The inventor-engineer hero of this book, Ned Conolly, is not a self-portrait in the sense that Smith had been, but he embodies much that Shaw had learnt to admire since coming to London, and expresses many of his newest ideas. As a workman, a man of talent and integrity, Conolly opposes the perpetual falsehood of London society. 'You seem to see

81

everything reversed,' one character tells him; and another, a clergyman, describes his opinions as being 'exactly upside down'. In sympathy with this upside-down view, Shaw inverts the conventional plot of the Victorian novel by having his heroine marry Conolly near the start and lose him at the end of the book.

Conolly is one of Nature's gentlemen, recognizing excellence by achievement, never by rank. He will not 'suffer any man to speak of my class as inferior. Take us all,' he says, 'professions and trades together, and you will find by actual measurement round the head and round the chest, and round our manners and characters, if you like, that we are the only genuine aristocracy at present in existence.'

The story throws up almost every situation, from illegitimacy and alcoholic marriages to adultery and death, that society encircled with its moated attitude. In place of this entrenchment, the moral basis of which is shown to be little more than the good opinion of 'every club in London', Shaw proposes a more rational line of morality – 'original and not ready-made' – against which the publishers' readers were to write words such as 'disagreeable' and 'perverse'.

Aiming his attack on the 'villainous institution' of marriage, Shaw was later able to recognize *The Irrational Knot* as having been 'an early attempt on the part of the Life Force to write *A Doll's House* in English'. When shown the last scene of Ibsen's play he remarked that he had done the same thing himself years ago – and 'they laughed. Do you wonder at my being as hard as nails . . .' But he was to revise it extensively after becoming familiar with *A Doll's House*. There is a tingling sense of excitement as the novelist creates his strong-minded women, Susannah and Marion, takes them on and sees them defeated.

In a deceitfully-conducted world, it is the half-dead who flourish: men converted into tailors' models, and women into ornaments to be gaped at in glass cages. It is with the rejection of all these dolls and dummies that the novel ends. Conolly will not accept any of such fashionable deception even if it means giving up a woman who attracts him and whom otherwise he could love. The process of rediscovering truth may be bitter, but it is also invigorating. The novel carries an individualist philosophy – the need to rely on oneself, and the courage to win independence through isolation. At the end Conolly calls for 'an end to hypocrisy! No unrealities now: I cannot bear them.' And he concludes: 'I am for the fullest attainable life.'

But Shaw was to learn that Conolly would be 'as incompatible with the public as with his wife'. In fact he was not introduced to the public for a long time. Shaw spent a fortnight revising the 641 'prodigiously long' pages of the novel, and afterwards added a confidently eccentric note for the printer: 'Please punctuate & divide the paragraphs exactly as in copy, and set up such words as dont, didnt, wouldnt &c without the usual apostrophe.' On 15 December 1880 he sent the manuscript to Macmillan whose reader reported that it was 'a novel of the most disagreeable kind ... There is nothing conventional either about the structure or the style ... the thought of the book is all wrong; the whole idea of it is odd, perverse and crude ... So far as your publication is concerned, it is out of the question. There is too much of adultery and the like matters.'

'The better I wrote,' Shaw concluded, 'the less chance I had.' The better he wrote the more emphasis he appeared to place on the enormous social importance of getting rid of bad institutions. He then forwarded this writing to Macmillan, Longman, Bentley and other publishers who, as the most powerful figures in the Victorian book world, were examples of these institutions. 'To make my hero a working electrical engineer, a Rationalist and Materialist, going like a steam roller through a little crowd of futile ladies and gentlemen, and reducing by his superior dexterity even their amateur attempts at drawingroom music, was too much. These pages were returned by the publishers sans phrase.'

As an extreme measure, Shaw eventually sent *The Irrational Knot* to an American publisher 'who refused it on the ground of its immorality'. Provoked to mild sarcasm, he warned a London publishing house that 'there is an elopement in it, which would perhaps shock a nation that recoils from damns'. But British publishers took a more sophisticated line. Smith Elder regretted that a book 'possessing considerable literary merit' was 'too conversational'; William Heinemann not only declined to publish it but advised the author not to submit it to anyone else: 'it is too crude and unripe.' Sidney Pawling, publisher's reader, complained: 'some of it is clever, most of it is dull ... the hero is a machine like working man without any attractive qualities – an absolutely impossible person too.' Shaw agreed, in his fashion. Reviewing his novels himself in 1892 – a need arising 'through the extreme difficulty of finding anyone else who has read them' – he wrote not entirely truthfully of *The Irrational Knot*: 'This was really an extraordinary book for a youth of twenty-four to write; but, from the point of view of the people who think that an author has nothing better to do than to amuse them, it was a failure, because the characters, though life-like, were a dreary company, all undesirable as personal acquaintances; whilst the scenes and incidents were of the most commonplace and sordid kind.'

*What people call health – appetite, weight, beefiness – is a mistake.*
*Fragility is the only endurable condition.* (1898)

*I am a species of savage and cannot be entertained like a civilized*
*man. In short, I am a vegetarian.* (1884)

On 23 December 1880, a week after *The Irrational Knot* had been sent to
Macmillan, the Shaws moved out of Victoria Grove to an unfurnished
apartment on the second floor of 37 Fitzroy Street.

The advantage for George was the proximity to the British Museum.
He had recently started to use the Reading Room, and now began going
there regularly. The difference this made to him was fundamental.
Though almost penniless, he had round the corner in Bloomsbury a
magnificent library, without any servants to look after or rent to pay and
'with all the advantages of communal heating, lavatory accommodation
and electric light, with a comfortable seat, unlimited books, and ink and
blotting-paper all for nothing . . .' Here, in what Gissing called 'the Valley
of the Shadow of Books', he found a home. It became his club, his
university, a refuge, and the centre of his life for almost a decade. He felt
closer to strangers in this place than to his own family and their friends.
He worked here daily for some eight years, applying for more than three
hundred books each year, advancing through the entire *Encyclopaedia
Britannica* (though skirting some of the scientific articles), conquering
Himalayas of medical and municipal statistics for future articles, lectures
and letters to the press, adding to his musical knowledge by the study of
treatises and works on elocution, and completing his long literary
apprenticeship. 'My debt to that great institution . . . is inestimable.'

It was partly as a result of his reading that in January 1881 he became a
vegetarian. Shelley had first 'opened my eyes to the savagery of my diet,'
he recorded.

> Never again may blood of bird or beast
> Stain with its venomous stream a human feast!

While investigating the art of eating out cheaply, Shaw came across a
number of the inexpensive vegetarian restaurants that had recently opened
in London: the Cyprus overlooking Cheapside, the Orange Grove in St
Martin's Lane, the Alpha in Oxford Street and the Pine Apple near
Oxford Circus, Gatti and Rosedano's in the Strand, the Porridge Bowl in
Holborn, various Aerated Bread Shops and, most popular of all, the

Wheatsheaf off Rathbone Place. During his first five years in London he had 'cultivated literature, not on a little oatmeal, but on beef and mutton,' he explained. '. . . Pork I loathed; rabbits were as repugnant to me as jugged cat; fowls were too expensive and unsubstantial to be more than occasional luxuries . . . I dined at a restaurant as well as I could for one and sixpence, which is a perfectly sufficient sum for a decent dinner in London, incredible as that may seem to many West-enders. But I grew tired of beef and mutton, the steam and grease, the waiter looking as though he had been caught in a shower of gravy and not properly dried, the beer, the prevailing redness of nose, and the reek of the slaughter-house that convicted us all of being beasts of prey. I fled to the purer air of the vegetarian restaurant.' But because people submitted to monotonous meals of macaroni, rice pudding and waterlogged cabbage, he sometimes saw 'more suffering there than ever came under my observation in the worst of the dens of butchery I had formerly frequented'. Such sights soon stirred him to advice:

'Don't mistake for hunger the disquietude caused by the change of habit; if you gave up beer or potatoes only you would feel just the same. Don't eat too much. To find the proper quantity without actual measurement of nitrogen, guess at the equivalent of a beefsteak in brown bread, peas, beans, or haricots, and you will get an approximately correct result by dividing your guess by six. Do not expect to like porridge and lentils in their naked simplicity. Boil oatmeal porridge for twenty minutes; and if you think the result mere oatmeal and water, try boiling it for two hours. If you still think it as unpalatable as dry bread, treat it as you treat the bread; stir up a bounteous lump of butter in it, and do not forget the salt. In eating wheatmeal porridge, remember that there's nothing so becomes a man as moderation and an admixture of stewed fruit. If you want fancy dishes make them for yourself out of plainly cooked vegetables, with the help of rice and the cruet stand; and do not be seduced by messy pies, entrées, or such weak concessions to the enemy as "vegetable rabbit", "vegetable sausage", and the like. "Vegetable goose" is, however, to be commended when in season. It is simply a vegetable marrow with sage stuffing and apple sauce. Remember that brown bread is a good familiar creature, and worth more than its weight in flesh. Don't attribute every qualm you feel to a breakdown of your constitution for want of meat.'

Shaw's experiments encouraged in him the belief that vegetarian food might improve his general health – in particular remove the severe headaches that had started to attack him each month and that he attributed, not to anxiety or overwork, but to unscientific eating habits.

There must be benefits, he reasoned, in studying food a little instead of going on with the old unthinking habits imposed on him in childhood. In one sense, vegetarianism came easily to Shaw. A symptom of his neglect in Ireland had been the poor diet; the only food he had liked was the stoneground bread which his mother had occasionally buttered for him. To reject all this – the evidence of his own rejection – was no hardship for Shaw. 'I am no gourmet,' he wrote: 'eating is not a pleasure to me, only a troublesome necessity, like dressing or undressing.' He looked forward to a time when people would complete the digestion of their food in their own bodies, and when, with no more need for sanitation, they would evolve themselves into an ethereal state superior to the creatures (encased in their gross envelopes of bodies) they were at present. In the fourth of his *Farfetched Fables*, he was to imagine such a race subsisting on an ecstatic diet of air and water; this was Shaw's ambrosia, and the food of his gods.

Our habits of eating impressed Shaw as unhygienic, but the vegetarian was slightly less unhygienic than the meat-eater. 'If I were to eat it [meat], my evacuations would stink; and I should give myself up for dead,' he wrote in the last year of his life. Too little, he felt, was made of the fact that a frightened animal, terrified by smelling blood and seeing other animals killed in the slaughterhouse, stank. The flesh of such an animal, Shaw suggested, was tainted with poison and to eat it involved abusing the adaptiveness of the human digestion.

Shaw maintained his vegetarianism (with tiny inevitable lapses) for seventy years until his death. The sense of being a living grave for murdered animals filled him with repugnance: 'No one should live off dead things.' Part of this horror arose from the kinship he felt for animals. This fellow-feeling was confirmed by the systematic argument of science with which Darwin and other naturalists had established man's connection with animals. After which the practice of meat-eating became a lingering habit of superstition which he defined as 'restricted cannibalism' or, in his most striking phrase, 'cannibalism with its heroic dish omitted'.

G.B.S. was not only a vegetarian, but a living advertisement for vegetarianism and, to other vegetarians, its propaganda idol. Having found from his experiments in the side-street restaurants round Bloomsbury that he could make a financial saving from putting his principles into practice, he went on to recommend vegetarianism not only as a step forward in civilization but as a means of world economy. 'My objection to meat is that it costs too much,' he wrote many years later, 'and involves the slavery of men and women to edible animals that is undesirable.' He conducted his campaign with an astonishing evenness of temper. Many of his statements on vegetarianism were vivid examples of his dialectical skill.

'To-day people are brought up to believe that they cannot live without eating meat, and associate the lack of it with poverty. Henry Salt, a champion vegetarian, said that what was needed in London were vegetarian restaurants so expensive that only the very rich could afford to dine in them habitually, and people of moderate means only once a year, as a very special treat, as in Paris, where British tourists brag of having dined at So and So's with a European reputation for high prices and exquisite cookery.

'What you have to rub in is that it is never cheap to live otherwise than as everybody else does; and that the so-called simple life is beyond the means of the poor.'

Shaw guarded himself against giving the conventional vegetarian diet an unqualified recommendation: 'I dont believe the vegetarians have solved the food problem any more than the carnivorous people,' he admitted. He described as a 'blazing lie' the claims of some front-line vegetarians to be secure from cancer, tooth decay, rheumatism and so on: 'I know of no disease from which vegetarians are exempt.' Abstinence from dead bodies did not necessarily produce longevity, but affected the quality of living. He himself had more energy and he exploited it less (indeed hardly at all) on empty anger. He reminded those Englishmen in whom the superstition persisted that 'by eating a beefsteak he can acquire the strength and courage of the bull', that the bull (like an elephant) was vegetarian. Some vegetarians, he added, were bulls. Though believing that his tonic diet 'conserves temper; and temper is life', he was sensitive to a need for scotching the popular myth that vegetarians were effeminate. He warned readers of the dangerous invigoration released by such vital foods as macaroni, raisins, nuts, rice, tomatoes and breadcrumbs. Abstention from meat eating 'seems to produce a peculiar ferocity,' he noted. '. . . And it is the worst form of ferocity: that is, virtuous indignation.' All his life he promoted vegetarians as the most pugnacious of people: 'Hitler, they say, was a vegetarian; and I can well believe it.'

G.B.S. often tampered with his private feelings before speaking publicly. He had an air of knowing what was best for people, like an omniscient head waiter. He calculated that, when the unappetizing truth was coated with Shavian sauce, his clientele would gobble up more than they had realized. So we often get from Shaw fewer statements of truth than statements designed to hoodwink us into the truth. In private he could write: 'I am a vegetarian purely on humanitarian and mystical grounds; and I have never killed a flea or a mouse vindictively or without remorse.' This was the essential Shaw. But because he felt that most people were vulgar, he made G.B.S. into the most 'unsympathetic' of

87

vegetarians. 'He has no objection to the slaughter of animals as such,' Shaw's printed card on Vegetarian Diet reads. 'He knows that if we do not kill animals they will kill us. Squirrels, foxes, rabbits, tigers, cobras, locusts, white ants, rats, mosquitoes, fleas and deer must be continually slain even to extermination by vegetarians as ruthlessly as by meat eaters. But he urges humane killing and does not enjoy it as a sport.'

Shaw took the same unsentimental attitude to animals as towards people. From the nitrogenous point of view, and in line with Swift's modest proposal for the Irish, he saw no objection to a diet of tender babies, carefully selected, cleanly killed and gently roasted. Eaten with sugar, or a little beer, such a dish would, he estimated, leave nothing to be desired in the way of carbon, but: 'I prefer bread and butter.' If eating people was wrong, so was eating pigs: for reasons of health and economics. Bringing millions of disagreeable animals into existence expressly to kill, scorch and ingest their bodies was a monstrous practice which made our children callous to butchery and bloodshed. Those whose life's work it was to be constantly acting valet to a cow, playing the part of its nurse and midwife, tending it at shows, sweeping up after it and then finally (and understandably) slaughtering it, were coarsened to such a degree that their faces actually came to resemble the animals with which they associated. The enormous expense of this slavery of men to beasts became exorbitant once we knew that any given acreage could produce a greater quantity of grown food than food arising from stock-raising. Vegetarianism therefore had greater long-term value than the present habit of corpse-eating.

Such arguments (which affronted some vegetarians) borrowed the language of the businessman in the interests of appealing to the stockbroker. But by suppressing his fastidious instinct Shaw revealed a misanthropy that moved few people to act on his words even when they could find no words of their own to do battle for them.

Though his diet caused him no epicurean deprivation – 'like Thoreau (who said he could live on tenpenny nails) I would eat anything' – he needed courage to insist on it in these early years. 'Do not kill anything for me, because I simply won't eat it,' he would warn people. But most often it was wiser not to tell anyone he was vegetarian; otherwise he would be confronted with alarming quantities of breadcrumb preparations. At home no special arrangements were made. He ate those vegetables the others took with their fish or meat, and would call on his most provocative platform powers to prevent the cook from using meat fat, cubes or essence in their preparation. Some mornings a housemaid deposited among his books and papers a bowl of glue-like porridge and this often remained there for days while Shaw occasionally spooned a sticky mouthful or two.

When travelling, he liked to carry lunch with him, diving his hands into his pockets and coming up with a fistful of almonds and raisins. He enjoyed advising vegetarians to avoid as much as possible all vegetables – particularly asparagus – which gave one's urine a disagreeable smell, but he ate potatoes and brussels sprouts because he said no one could avoid doing so in England. The vegetarian foods, with names ending in -ose, which resolved themselves into variously disguised forms of oil cake, revolted him; but he was mildly pleased with cheese and fruit, tolerated omelettes for many years, and developed an increasingly sweet tooth for chocolate biscuits, fruit cake, honey, jelly babies, even spoonfuls of sugar and, though they were not puritanically vegetarian, concoctions from the horns and hoofs of defunct cattle that appeared on the plate as violently coloured jellies.

He drank water, soda-water, barley-water, an innocent beverage named Instant Postum, ginger beer, milk ('I have a doglike habit of taking as much of it as I can get'), cocoa, and 'I dont refuse chocolate in the afternoon when I can get it'. But no tea, 'however mediocre', very little coffee and never alcohol. With his father's example behind him, Shaw had been watching the effect of alcohol with the eye of an expert. 'My father drank too much. I have worked too much.' It was probably as much a weakness in his character, he later acknowledged, as a strength that compelled him to be such a strenuous teetotaller, but that was not the point. Reviewing his first nine years in London – 'years of unbroken failure and rebuff, with crises of broken boots and desperate clothes ... penniless, loveless, and hard as nails' – he concluded that 'I am quite certain that if I had drunk as much as a single glass of beer a day ... my powers of endurance would have been enormously diminished.'

To most people, he argued, a little alcohol made little difference. The routine of their work never called on them to do their best: 'only the leaders and geniuses need do their utmost.' It was among this company that Shaw was wrestling for a place.

Characteristically, he was to dismay members of the Church and Nonconformist Temperance Societies while coveting support from licensed victuallers. He went on to ridicule prohibition, assert that 'tea does more harm in the world than beer', buy shares in a municipal public house and eventually advocate the Russian method of piping vodka ('a comparatively mild poison') into society under efficient government control.

Shaw's attitude to drink recalls Dr Johnson's dictum that 'Life is a pill which none of us can bear to swallow without gilding.' In his copy of Bunyan's *The Life and Death of Mr Badman*, Shaw wrote: 'Living is so painful for the poor that it cannot be endured without an anaesthetic.' He used writing as a narcotic to be rid of himself on paper. What Johnson meant by life is translated in Shaw's vocabulary to living conditions.

> How small, of all that human hearts endure,
> That part which laws or kings can cause or cure.
> Still to ourselves in every place consigned,
> Our own felicity we make or find:
> With secret course, which no loud storms annoy,
> Glides the smooth current of domestic joy.

Johnson's dark terrain, ringed with sentiment, is suddenly switched alight by the Shavian dawn to reveal a municipal landscape where loneliness is dissolved in the financial and medical co-operation of collectivism:

> How small, of all that human hearts endure
> That part that private man can cause or cure!
> For who on independent action bent
> Can ease his taxes or reduce his rent?
> Who that is heedless of his neighbor's drain
> Can save his children from a bed of pain?

The reality he distilled from Johnson's verse was one in which drunkenness could be recognized as a symptom of the malignant disease called poverty. For most people the sham happiness it provided was the only happiness available in our dishonourable commercial civilization. In his printed card on Temperance, Shaw wrote: 'We must first get rid of poverty, and make reasonable happiness possible without anaesthetics.' To his mind alcohol was a trick, a depressant in the disguise of a stimulant, falsely associated (like corpse-eating) with virility, and used by people with low vitality 'of which they should be ashamed instead of glorying in it'. Drink seldom propelled us into melodramatic ruin and madness; it was a chloroform that lowered our self-criticism and self-respect.

Shaw needed self-respect to withstand the low esteem in which he was held among publishers and at home. One of his vegetarian jokes took the form of reassuring an anxious population that, by adopting the diet of Bernard Shaw, they would not themselves turn into Bernard Shaws. Yet there was an element of transubstantiation in his belief that the new diet he shared with saints and sages would help to change him into a different person. Partly it was the alteration in habits and disciplines from the first quarter of his life. But he was conscious of another factor in what was almost a mystical resurrection: 'The odd thing about being a vegetarian is, not that the things that happen to other people don't happen to me – they all do – but that they happen differently: pain is different, pleasure different, fever different, cold different, even love different.'

*Think of my circumstances and prospects getting worse and worse
until they culminated in smallpox next year (81) when I forced 'Love
Among the Artists' out of myself . . .*

The year 1881 was particularly discouraging. Shaw's novels came back
regularly from the publishers; magazines rejected all his articles, essays
and short stories. Each day he read at the British Museum and as an extra
form of language tuition sang in French three nights a week to an Alsatian
*basso profundo* called Richard Deck. Deck was an atheist with a mad wife
and a couple of pupils whom he taught emoting in his single room off the
Camden Road. He arranged for Shaw simultaneously to teach him English
while learning French, for although he had been in London a dozen years
he was unable to carry on any intelligible conversation. Having forgotten
his Alsatian dialect of German, he had fallen back on appallingly fluent
unacademic French, which had absorbed all manner of slang from the
other countries he had visited. Despite a fine voice and considerable
artistic gifts, Deck's extreme thin-skinnedness and infirmity of will had
left him a mere builder of castles in the air. Yet Shaw felt peculiarly fond
of him and, following his death from fever in the autumn of 1882,
remembered him as 'a remarkable man, offering me advice concerning
pronunciation, directing my attention to the aim of gymnastics . . . and
introducing me to the ideas of Proudhon'. In many respects he was the
sort of father George would have loved.

On 19 May he started a new novel. He had been at work on this for
about a week when he began to feel ill. The new vegetarian diet had not
cured his headaches and, in the belief that he was spending too much time
indoors, he prescribed for himself a number of rides round London on the
top of omnibuses. A few days later he discovered he had smallpox, and
speculated over how many people he might have infected.

Smallpox was then one of the most dreaded diseases in Western Europe
partly because, Shaw was later to explain, 'the bad cases were so
disfiguring, and partly because the increase of population produced by the
industrial revolution, and the insanitary conditions in which the new
proletariat lived, had made it much commoner and more virulent'. In 1853
Parliament had made compulsory the vaccination of every child in Britain
within three months of birth. Sonny had been vaccinated in infancy and
the vaccination had taken well. This form of vaccination (which in 1898
was to be banned) meant the injection of cowpox matter from the pustule

of a diseased cow or the disease substance from the inflamed arm of a recently vaccinated person. Shaw makes little reference to his illness except to say that he emerged from it a convinced anti-vaccinationist. Having studied the literature and statistics of smallpox he concluded that the case for fortifying the blood against the disease by inoculations was unproven.

The strength of his feelings arising from this illness reveals itself in the language he used to attack the practice of vaccination – 'really nothing short of attempted murder,' he wrote in 1906. 'I know all about vaccination,' he claimed when in his seventies; 'and if other people knew as much it would be declared a criminal practice.'

Once, when his mother had been seriously ill in Dublin, Shaw recounts, Lee had taken 'her case in hand unhesitatingly and at the end of a week or so gave my trembling father leave to call in a leading Dublin doctor, who simply said "My work is done" and took his hat'. This daring lack of faith in doctors appealed to Shaw who learnt from it the lesson that we all have more authority over our lives and the lives of those close to us than the credulity induced by mechanistic science allows. Lee's prescription had been fresh air, extreme cleanliness and a good diet, and these, translated into socialism, became the ingredients of political good health promoted by Shaw: 'it is now as plain as the sun in the heavens,' he wrote towards the end of his life, 'that pathogenic microbes are products of the zymotic diseases; and that these diseases are products of ugliness, dirt and stink offending every aesthetic instinct, . . . that dirt and squalor and ugliness are products of poverty; and that . . . zymotic diseases can be abolished by abolishing poverty, the practical problem being one of economic distribution.'

Shaw's campaign against vaccination formed part of his objection to the rising superstition of science that reduced human beings to robots under the control of an engineer-priesthood of doctors. 'I am glad your case is a slight one,' a friend wrote, '. . . you have been vaccinated in your infancy, so ought if the doctors are to be believed, to have nothing to fear.' But were they to be believed? Or were they to be feared? It was less his helplessness as a smallpox patient that Shaw hated than the revoltingness of the disease itself into which, he felt, he had been medically tricked.

Shaw externalized Evil. In his world there were no evil men except the insane; but there were evil circumstances which he could identify, attack and eliminate. Vaccination let the enemy in and allowed evil to circulate within our bodies. The method of inoculating children with casual dirt moistened with an undefined pathogenic substance obtained from calves was a proceeding so grossly reckless and unclean as to impress Shaw as being morally insane. His sense of contamination became part of his socialist dogma and a warning against substituting faith in a dangerous experimental prophylaxis for a full-scale sanitation programme ensuring minimum conditions of public health: isolation not vaccination.

After three weeks confined to his room in Fitzroy Street, Shaw went down to recuperate at Leyton in Essex with his Rabelaisian uncle Walter Gurly, who, having married an English widow during one of his trips to America, had removed to a life of precarious respectability as country physician on the borders of Epping Forest.

Shaw's convalescence here, which lasted till October, was made worse by the resumption of meat-eating. A number of his friends had been alarmed by his devotion to what Chichester Bell's sister Aileen called 'these wretched vegetables'. 'Do give it up,' she wrote him, '– & live like other people.' 'I consider that you are keeping yourself alive out of pure contrariness,' wrote another girl. In later years it became the sport of doctors and friends to attribute Shaw's infrequent illnesses to vegetarian decay; while he himself enjoyed pointing to intense vegetable vitality as the cause of his remarkable recoveries. Never again, however much people fretted at him, would he abandon his diet because of illness.

He had a scar on his right cheek. Whether the disfigurement was slight or Shaw merely made slight of it, he felt extremely sensitive. 'I was sorry to hear of your illness,' Aileen Bell wrote to him, 'and the idea of your telling Mrs Horne not to describe your personal appearance – as if I should like you the less . . .'

Shaw never claimed to have grown a beard; it grew of its own accord. 'I have a rather remarkable chin and would like to let the public see it; but I never had time to shave.' This joke, and several others on similar lines, covered up the initial motive for the beard which was to camouflage his sensitivity. He grew into it so that it became exactly the right beard, part of the substance of G.B.S. – a good red socialist affair and vastly conspicuous. Few people who had their attention arrested by this flagwaving at the head of the Shavian talking-machine would have known that Shaw was publicly concealing something.

Shaw represented himself as the passive partner to his beard: he simply followed it wherever it went. So bewitched had he been with the figure of Mephistopheles, he was to explain, that 'when Nature completed my countenance in 1880 or thereabouts (I had only the tenderest sprouting of hair on my face until I was 24), I found myself equipped with the upgrowing moustaches and eyebrows, and the sarcastic nostrils of the operatic fiend whose airs (by Gounod) I had sung as a child, and whose attitudes I had affected in my boyhood'. There could be few better examples of G.B.S.'s beard doing the talking. In fact he practised upon his appearance during this smallpox convalescence and for some time afterwards. Richard Deck, for example, drew his attention to the method by which, in Greek statues, the hair is always brushed up from the brow so as to form a 'natural coronet'. 'Like a Victorian matron I experimented with my brushes and comb, and found that the Greek plan was feasible and picturesque,' Shaw later told Charles McEvoy; 'so I adopted it.'

The face that he designed for himself was startling. 'It is the face of an outlaw, of one at war with life, customs,' wrote one woman; 'it is full of protest: wild and determined, a very brigand of a face.' Another woman, observing him among the socialists at William Morris's converted coach-house in Hammersmith, noted: 'His face came out very distinctly in the unshaded light of the stable-room, and as he listened it seemed to me to be lit up not only by that outside light but also, and in a particular way, by some inner lamp, as if Morris's words had lighted a candle of great and incandescent power within him. Shaw's face that night burned itself in on me; I have never seen any face like it since . . . His pale skin, his hair that the light above it turned to gold, and his strong, gleaming teeth, made a picture that no one, I think, could ever forget . . .'

Shaw was a good six feet, and his taut body seemed wound up with energy. His looks and movements were rapid; he walked with long springy strides, and at tremendous speed, on the front of his feet, as if gravity had little authority over him. When seated he seemed to relax all over, huddling and stretching, sticking out his long legs and then pulling them up to his chest as if embracing himself. In this position he chattered and swayed with laughter. Then he stood up, thin, erect, well-pleased with himself it appeared, the head upraised, body tilted back, beard pointed. The impression of this figure, combative and audacious, was often invaded by irresistible comedy. It was this comic spirit that, for all the Satanic red twirls and flourishes, encouraged a friend to describe his face as an 'unskilfully-poached egg', and enabled Shaw himself to write: 'My own beard is so like a tuft of blanched grass that pet animals have nibbled at it.'

The private face was as yet only partially eclipsed and shows itself in the novel, *Love Among the Artists*, he forced out of himself while at Leyton. Love among artists is different from love among other people, for artists love their work more than they love other people. Shaw's novel plots social against artistic values. 'I am in a worldly sense an unfortunate man,' says Owen Jack, the hero-composer of the book, 'though in my real life, heaven knows, a most happy and fortunate one.' Jack defines worldly success as 'the compensation of the man who has no genius'. Some men, he says, 'begin by aiming high, and they have to wait till the world comes up to their level'. With such *obiter dicta* Shaw, with a backward look at Lee's failure, kept his confidence afloat. He had begun to suspect that, like Jack, 'my talent and originality have been my chief obstacles here'; and, again like Jack, he hardened himself 'into a stone statue of dogged patience'.

Jack (who Shaw asks us to believe was based partly on Beethoven but who reflects something of Richard Deck and something of Vandeleur Lee), and the pianist Aurelie Szczymplica, are the two geniuses of *Love Among the Artists*, and they inhabit the classless world of music in which Shaw felt happiest. Both of them are ill-adapted to domestic purposes. The point is made by (among others) Ned Conolly, the genius-engineer imported as a minor character from *The Irrational Knot*, who explains how he too achieved self-sufficiency to become – as Shaw was studying to be – 'a man who had learned to stand alone in the world – a hard lesson, but one that is ruthlessly forced on every sensitive but unlovable boy who has his own way to make, and who knows that, outside himself, there is no God to help him'.

No woman either to help him. Conolly's marriage had ended badly; Aurelie Szczymplica, who 'had given up the whole world of Mrs Grundy and found her own soul', condescends to a marriage that makes her husband ecstatically unhappy, dismays her mother and promises a bleak future for her child. But were she to give energy and attention to all this, she would diminish her work. Jack escapes marriage. Once, he explains, he had begun 'to languish in my solitude; to pine for a partner; and, in short, suffer . . . I selected a lady; fell in love as hard as I could; and made my proposals in due form. I was luckier than I deserved to be. Her admiration of me was strictly impersonal; and she nearly had a fit at the idea of marrying me . . . I sometimes shudder when I think that I was once within an ace of getting a wife and family.'

Since marriage 'kills the heart and keeps it dead', it is better, Jack concludes, to 'starve the heart than overfeed it. Better still to feed it on fine food, like music.' One benefit of living alone is that you escape the politics of family affection which Jack defines as 'half sense of property, and half sense of superiority'. Another character, Mrs Herbert, who owes something to Shaw's mother, wonders if there is 'any use in caring for one's children? I really dont believe there is.' The effect of such a mother on her children is described by her son (the blissfully unhappy husband of Aurelie Szczymplica) in a speech that directly reflects Shaw's feelings about himself and Lucinda Elizabeth:

'Can you understand that a mother and a son may be so different in their dispositions that neither can sympathize with the other? It is my great misfortune to be such a son . . . she felt nothing for me but a contemptuous fondness which I did not care to accept. She is a clever woman, impatient of sentiment, and fond in her own way. My father, like myself, was too diffident to push himself arrogantly through the world; and she despised him for it, thinking him a fool. When she saw that I was like him, she concluded that I, too, was a fool, and that she must arrange my life for me in some easy, lucrative, genteel, brainless conventional way. I hardly ever dared to express the most modest aspirations, or assert the most ordinary claims to respect, for fear of exciting her quiet ridicule. She did not know how much her indifference tortured me, because she had no idea of any keener sensitiveness than her own ... She taught me to do without her consideration; and I learned the lesson.'

He blames her for rejecting his love; but she, though despising her son's attempts at painting, as Mrs Shaw must have despised the writing of *Love Among the Artists*, is given the motto of the novel when she says: 'the common notions of parental and filial relations are more impractical than even those of love and marriage.'

Shaw came to believe that *Love Among the Artists* marked 'a crisis in my progress as a thinker'. Whether or not his share in the smallpox epidemic had 'enfeebled my intellectual convictions,' he suggested, 'I found that I had come to the end of my Rationalism and Materialism.' This conversion, of a man who vigorously cultivated his power of reasoning in the cause of socialism, into 'a most vehement anti-Rationalist' has an air of paradox. But his belief in the factitious character of logic was genuine. 'I could prove anything,' he once told Archibald Henderson. At this level it was chess-playing. On a religious level, for such a nature as his wherein the pain always exceeded pleasure, it led to pessimism. 'Make a note,' says the hero of his last novel, *An Unsocial Socialist*, 'that wishes for the destruction of the human race, however rational and sincere, are contrary to nature.' He disbelieved in Reason as it appeared to operate in human history. Far from being a ratiocinative process in which the discovery of knowledge came at the end of the reasoning and as a result of it, knowledge occurred to us by instalments in the form of fiction, hypotheses or jokes – after which we set about finding reasons for it. Though intellect should be a passion, reason was no more than a necessary machinery, he believed, producing a scepticism that helped to keep any fixed body of opinion up to date. The difference between Shaw's interpretation of Rationalism and that of philosophical text-books is best explained in one of his letters:

'A man has his beliefs: his arguments are only his excuses for them. Granted that we both want to get to Waterloo Station: the question whether we shall drive across Westminster Bridge or Waterloo, or whether we shall walk across the Hungerford foot bridge, is a matter for our logic; but the destination is dogmatic. The province of reason is the discovery of the means to fulfil our wills; but our wills are beyond reason: we all will to live . . . we only see what we look at: our attention to our temperamental convictions produces complete oversight as to all the facts that tell against us.'

Shaw had returned to 37 Fitzroy Street in October and finished *Love Among the Artists* on 10 January 1882. 'I have a much higher opinion of this work than is as yet generally entertained,' he admitted. But to the publishers he again listened in vain for the faintest encouragement. He had ostracized society, and society ostracized him. 'My composer was even less understood by the publishers' readers than my mechanic,' he concluded. 'He was, it seemed, simply no gentleman.' The most famous publishers' reader, Edward Garnett, in a report for Fisher Unwin, advised against publishing the book if they could 'get something else from the author'. *Love Among the Artists*, he wrote, *deserved* publication, but would probably fall flat with the general reader. 'The literary art is sound, the people in it are real people, and the fresh unconventionality is pleasing after the ordinary work of the common novelist: but all the same – *few people would understand it, & few papers would praise it.*'

Shaw did not read this report but he knew the argument. 'I am not without a hope that the point of my work, obscure though it seems to be,' he wrote to the publisher Richard Bentley, 'will yet strike your reader, who (if you will excuse my saying so) either underrates the capacity of "the general reader", or applies the term to a class of persons who – like himself – read little else but newspapers, and whom therefore a novelist is not concerned to please.' Garnett classed Shaw as a good literary workman, clever, but no artist. 'It is interesting to compare the novel with Yeats's little work [*The Wanderings of Oisin*], which with certain faults shows a sense of *colour* & *softness* that betrays the artistic mind,' Garnett concluded. 'There is a little genius in Yeats: there is an individuality of mind in Shaw's work, but neither are likely to command much attention.'

While at Leyton, Shaw had finally taught himself Pitman's Shorthand. This, 'probably the worst system of shorthand ever invented', suited him best, he decided, because Greg's was known only in America and Sweet's Current Shorthand had been made 'illegible by anyone except himself'. In fact he probably chose Pitman's because he had begun learning it before he knew of Sweet. In any event, Pitman himself was everything a man should be – a teetotaller, vegetarian, radical, key man-of-business with whiskers. 'Tears of admiration come to my eyes when I think of him,' wrote Gilbert Murray.

Shorthand enabled Shaw to intensify his programme of self-education at the British Museum and to write at a speed that kept pace with his thoughts. It also raised the family's hopes of his employment. While *Love Among the Artists* was being returned to him by the London publishers, Shaw proposed himself for the job of preparing the work of another unpublished novelist, Ethel Southam, who had advertised for a simple copyist. From Shaw she received many hundreds of words of advice about punctuation, and against tautology, on the use of dialogue and prepositions, and the avoidance of adjectives – after which the partnership collapsed and G.B.S. was deprived of the amusement of pointing to a ghost-written collaboration as his first book.

This was only one of the many jobs that he succeeded in not obtaining over the next two years. Pressed again by his family, he read the advertisement columns, answering those few offers that accorded with his principles or talent. He applied for employment as secretary to the Smoke Abatement Institute and as secretary to the Thames Subway Committee; he tried for everything from staff member to 'Descriptive, Satirical, and Critical Paragraphist' on a number of papers. He was dutiful, where duty alone prompted him to apply, in not concealing his politics ('those of an atheistic radical'), his lack of university education, mathematical and linguistic inabilities ('no German whatsoever'), and experience as secretary or shorthand clerk ('I can write longhand rapidly – in fact more rapidly than I can yet write shorthand'). But for all literary work he tried his utmost and failed almost completely.

> For shame for shame, you naughty dog
> Youre putting out your tongue
> At that poor pelican whose heart
> By your contempt is wrung
> It often gives its own heart's blood
> To feed its thirsty young.

This was one of several rhymes Shaw showed a publisher who had bought up some old blocks and, by adding explanatory verses, hoped to manufacture a school prize book. Shaw's verses, written as parodies of what was needed and sent as a joke, were accepted for a fee of five shillings. 'I was touched, and wrote him a serious verse for another picture,' Shaw remembered. 'He took it as a joke in questionable taste, and my career as a versifier ended.' But he could not break the habit of work. Though apparently leading nowhere it had become one of the necessities of life to him. On 12 April 1882 he had begun his fourth novel.

# [ 6 ]

*Which yet my soul seeketh, but I find not: one man in a thousand
have I found; but a woman among all these have I not found.*
Ecclesiastes vii.28

*Why is my pain perpetual, and my wound incurable, which refuseth
to be healed? Wilt thou be altogether unto me as a liar, and as waters
that fail?* Jeremiah xv.18

In a notebook he kept during his first six or seven years in London, Shaw
copied down these two passages. He described himself at this period as 'a
complete outsider'. He was outside literary and social life; and not yet
inside politics. During his convalescence from smallpox, he had even
thought of emigrating to America where Chichester Bell was going – but
later destroyed a letter in which some allusion to this had been made. He
prowled solitary. The bleakness of these years grew so unbearably intense
that he afterwards translated it into a hatred of his novels.

The senior literary club in London was then the Athenaeum, and its
junior the Savile. Shaw had been invited to lunch at the Savile shortly after
his arrival in London, 'and swore I would avoid literary society like the
plague all the rest of my life as Wellington avoided military society'. The
intimate gossipy conversation, connected with nothing outside itself,
dismayed him. From this cautionary experience, Shaw formulated a creed.
Men of letters should join their professional association (the Society of
Authors) to defend their financial concerns, but avoid literary introductions and recommendations as they would snakes. There was enough to do
making headway against your natural enemies without adding to them the
enemies of others. 'Literary men,' he told John Galsworthy, 'should never
associate with one another, not only because of their cliques and hatreds
and envies, but because their minds inbreed and produce abortions.'

Part of his discomfort at the Savile Club arose from social awkwardness.
London had many surprises that put him off balance. He had thought to
reach the centre of literature and art, but it seemed as if a mighty harvest
had left the soil sterile. Though the place was full of culture, London
society contrived to get along on an intellectual diet of sport, party politics,
and the helter-skelter of fashion and travel. In Dublin the professions had
formed the aristocracy and, without any great income and no experience of
horses or guns, one could enjoy the best company untainted by suspicions
of social inferiority. In London there were different rules, and far greater

importance was staked to money. 'The real superiority of the English to the Irish,' Shaw was to write, 'lies in the fact that an Englishman will do anything for money and an Irishman will do nothing for it.' But this was a later discovery to which, since for the time being he had no money, 'I had to blind myself'. There were times – weak moments – when he longed for people to blind themselves to him. He was a scarecrow catapulting himself along the streets with a light step and a professional habit of cheerfulness, but in broken boots, a tall hat so limp he wore it back to front to avoid doubling the brim when raising it, cuffs whose margins had been refined with his mother's scissors, trousers whose holes were hidden by a tailed coat fading from black to green. He was an example of poverty: 'I got nothing for nothing and very little for a halfpenny. I was abused and vilified.' But he converted it into a joke: 'it is my practice to make a suit of clothes last me six years,' he explained. 'The result is that my clothes acquire individuality, and become characteristic of me. The sleeves and legs cease to be mere tailor-made tubes; they take human shape with knees and elbows recognizably mine. When my friends catch sight of one of my suits hanging on a nail, they pull out their penknives and rush forward, exclaiming, "Good Heavens! he has done it at last".'

His plight was so glaring that people hinted they were good for loans and sometimes pressed money on him. But he never borrowed, having no reason for believing he could repay them. While not exaggerating the joys of strict conscientiousness, or its wide acceptance, he was conscious of its superiority and the charm of his conversation if it never led to a request for five shillings. 'When you borrow money, you sell a friend,' he wrote – which was one reason why, when rich himself and extraordinarily generous, he was left with so few friends.

He went to the National Gallery on its free days and, when he had a shilling in his pocket, to the theatre. Almost the only social gatherings in which he was included had been Lee's *soirées musicales*, where he came in contact with that unathletic section of society which had replaced sport and politics with singing, amateur acting and sketching in water colours. But by the 1880s, largely through his sister Lucy, he also began to receive invitations to the 'At Homes' of Lady Wilde and of Elizabeth Lawson, mother of the landscape painter Cecil Lawson on whom he had modelled the artist Cyril Scott in *Immaturity*. They were the sort of engagements that make a man long for death. To equip himself for such ordeals he sought out from the catalogue at the British Museum volumes on polite behaviour, poring over *Manners and Tone of Good Society, or, Solecisms to be Avoided* by 'A Member of the Aristocracy', and learning to avoid sipping the contents of the finger-bowl.

Morbidly self-conscious, he was nevertheless determined not to be overlooked. He liked the Lawsons, and the artistic atmosphere of their house in Cheyne Walk was congenial, but he had not mastered the art of pleasing, could not dance, spoke hesitantly though usually to disagree, and sometimes made a jarring exhibition of himself. His shyness was overwhelming. 'I sometimes walked up and down the Embankment for twenty minutes or more before venturing to knock at the door,' he remembered; 'indeed I should have funked it altogether . . . if I had not been instinctively aware that I must never let myself off in this manner if I meant ever to do anything in the world . . . The worst of it was that when I appeared in the Lawsons' drawingroom I did not appeal to the goodnature of the company as a pardonably and even becomingly bashful novice. I had not then tuned the Shavian note to any sort of harmony: and I have no doubt the Lawsons found me discordant, crudely self-assertive, and insufferable.'

Already by the early 1880s Shaw was turning from Society to societies – debating societies, socialist societies, societies that questioned and attacked the laws of society against which his nature ineffectually rebelled. He had been mortified to discover how much he cared for the good opinion of people of whom he had no good opinion. In Victorian society men could acquire social training and liberal culture only at the cost of acquiring class prejudices and incurring anti-social obligations, losing moral courage in the process. Having too little conceit in his nature, he depended too much on vanity, and recognized the need to raise his self-esteem outside the artificial atmosphere of the drawing-room. As literature continued to fail him he began moving towards politics. In the novel he was presently writing he described English polite society as 'in the main a temple for the worship of riches and a market for the sale of virgins'. And the hero of his next novel, *An Unsocial Socialist*, was to declare: 'I deny, it is true, that what is now called "society" is society in any real sense; and my best wish for it is that it may dissolve too rapidly to make it worth the while of those who are "not in society" to facilitate its dissolution by violently pounding it into small pieces.'

For some time he continued intermittently to paddle in polite society, but by 1903 could write that 'I believe I have not been at an at-home for fifteen years; and as far as I can see, the next social engagement in which I am likely to take part is my funeral'. When asked for the reason for this abstention he gave a political answer: 'Property, property, property, is the real secret of my withdrawal from all human intercourse except with the people I have actually to work with.'

Shaw saw very little of anyone with whom he did not work. Politics provided him with colleagues. Otherwise he had few companionships. Among these were an officious minor poet Richard Hengist Horne and his wife Sophie; a person of mild exterior, Edwin Habgood, from the Edison Telephone Company; James Lecky, an exchequer clerk from Ireland privately interested in phonetics, keyboard temperament and Gaelic, who was also a big noise in the English Spelling Reform Association (signing himself 'jeemz leki'), whom Shaw had met through Chichester Bell and who was to introduce him to the philologists Alexander John Ellis and Henry Sweet; and J. Kingston Barton, a doctor (living with his brother William) with whom Shaw passed many of his Saturday evenings. On Sundays he saw the Beattys.

Pakenham Beatty – Irish playboy, amateur pugilist, minor poet in the Swinburne flight – was a moustachioed perpetual boy of a man. Born in Brazil, he had spent part of his childhood in Dalkey, been educated somewhere between Harrow and Bonn, and got to know Shaw as a fellow-exile in London. He belonged to a breed of troubadour-entertainers that was to include Frank Harris and Gabriel Pascal, for whom Shaw had a special fondness planted in him by his Rabelaisian Uncle Walter. Beatty was so many of the things Shaw was not and he enabled him, if not to live, at least to enter a life very different from his own. He was not 'sensible' about money. He spent it in the Irish manner, generously, spontaneously, without thought, until everything was gone and he was left with nothing but the settled habit of spending. He had no profession, and his source of money was a small inheritance that, before it ran dry, allowed him to flirt with fine art. At the end of 1878, he published – in an edition disposed of with review copies and presentations to Shaw and other friends – a volume of verse entitled *To My Lady and Other Poems*. One of his ladies, Edith Dowling, married him early the following year and became known as 'Ida' Beatty. They had two daughters and a son christened Pakenham William Albert Hengist Mazzini Beatty whom Shaw nicknamed 'Bismarck'.

Shaw and the Beattys invaded one another's lives extensively. In this company Shaw was no longer his mother's unloved son, wilting in his father's shadow: he became a figure of attention and authority, someone to be relied on for his generosity and fun. While he had no money, he spent all his advice on them, giving freely nuggets of the information laboriously quarried out at the British Museum – information about the children's books, boots, careers, clothing, diet, education, illnesses, pianos and so on; and later, when he was earning money, he gave it to them in sums ranging between £10 and £200 and underwrote a good part of the children's schooling. 'Old grandfather Shaw', as Ida Beatty called him, was a father and a friend to them all.

In this muddle of Beattys, Shaw made his appearance as a practical man of business and know-how – a part invested by his imagination with much glamour. He judged them to be *hopeless*, in which condition they *needed* him. But he also had need of them, since, for all their hopelessness, they had something almost entirely lacking in the Shaws: an atmosphere of family affection. This affection in its abundance overflowed into remoter vessels of the family – and on to other families. Pakenham Beatty was extravagantly fond of his two sisters-in-law and even went on to shower his attentions jointly on Shaw's sister Lucy and a friend of their mother, Jane Patterson. But Shaw refused to be shocked. 'You and Lucy have about as much reason to be frightened as a pair of vigorous and experienced cats have to recoil before an exceptionally nervous mouse,' he told the indignant Jane. Once Don Juan had been unmasked he fell back into drink. But again Shaw experienced no moral outrage. One afternoon he came across his friend recovering from delirium tremens and surrounded by whispering relatives who, having bullied him into making a will, were assembled as if for a funeral. 'I dispersed them with roars of laughter and inquiries after pink snakes &c, an exhibition of bad taste which at last converted the poor devil's wandering apprehensive look into a settled grin. I then took him out for a walk, and endeavored to relieve his mind of the strong illusion that nothing can ever tempt him to taste liquor more. Tomorrow he goes to a retreat at Rickmansworth, to be reformed.'

Shaw was a rock in this Bohemian whirlpool, splashed, invigorated and unchanged. The Beattys added to his education outside the British Museum. He loved Beatty for his bad verses ('something too awful') and for presenting such an attractive disincentive to the romantic life. 'Lord bless you,' he was to write to him, 'my plays are full of your jokes.' He had re-christened him 'Paquito', a name that would serve as an alias for the eponymous hero of *Captain Brassbound's Conversion*, while his son Mazzini's name was to receive a jocular commentary from Hesione Hushabye in *Heartbreak House*. Paquito, who in 1884 published an unperformed verse tragedy, *Marcia*, that was pilloried by Shaw, also saw himself satirized as Chichester Erskine in Shaw's last novel, *An Unsocial Socialist*.

'Since then Erskine had been bent on writing another drama, without regard to the exigencies of the stage, but he had not yet begun it, in consequence of his inspiration coming upon him at inconvenient hours, chiefly late at night, when he had been drinking, and had leisure for sonnets only. The morning air and bicycle riding were fatal to the vein in which his poetry struck him as being worth writing.'

Paquito's letters to Shaw were mostly in high-flown and facetious verse. His non-poetic intervals were devoured by the ambition to be an amateur light-weight rough-and-tumble champion. 'I am about to take boxing lessons from the scientific Ned Donnelly, a very amiable though powerful person in appearance ... If you wish,' he invited Shaw, 'these lessons which I learn from Donnelly I will teach unto you.' Shaw couldn't resist and, 'articles of agreement' as to the lessons having been drawn up, the experiment began in December 1881. The comedy of all this was serious business for Shaw. He did his training at the British Museum, battling with Pierce Egan's *Boxiana* and other devoted expositions. Paquito had presented him with a copy of Donnelly's *Self-Defence* ('the best book of its kind ever published') and 'insisted on my accompanying him to all the boxing exhibitions'. The result was that, while becoming a scholar of the ring and expert spectator, Shaw gained among his new political acquaintances the imaginary reputation as an athlete – 'a tall man with a straight left' whose knowledge of pugilism might prove valuable if it came to revolution.

There were times when Shaw himself seemed to accept such fantasies. He left off training at the British Museum and showed up at a school-of-arms in Panton Street called the London Athletic Club. Here he obtained polite tuition on how to conduct himself from 'the scientific Ned Donnelly' himself who, as Professor of Boxing, had instructed the most brilliant light-weight of his day Jack Burke, on whom Shaw now based the hero of the novel he was writing. A month after finishing this book, on 17 March 1883, he entered the Queensberry Amateur Boxing Championships on the turf at Lillie Bridge. At a weight of ten stone (140 lbs) he applied to take part in both Middle and Heavyweight Classes, and was given a place for both categories in the programme, but not in the ring. It was the climax of his prize-fighting career, a paper apotheosis, after which he found he 'had exhausted the comedy of the subject', and turned his interest into journalism.

Shaw's long affair with boxing was to worry some of his admirers. How could this ascetic, humanitarian, anti-vivisectionist champion of the vegetable world involve himself in brute pugilism? 'Paradoxing is a useful rhyme to boxing,' he once thanked a journalist. 'I will make a note of it.' He saw at once the great publicity in pugilism and he used it to draw attention to himself, not just personally, but as a vehicle for his developing ideas. Newspapers, he believed, were 'fearfully mischievous' but unfortunately indispensable. They were mischievous because, under capitalism, they tempted journalists to promote ignorance as if it were 'news'; yet they were indispensable as creators of public opinion. So it became essential to use this 'illiterate profession' – and what could be more natural than to marry one such brute profession to another? Since the public were more interested in sport than serious politics, Shaw was to spread his political views through the sports pages as he would the music and art columns. Under his treatment boxing was to become an allegory of capitalism, the prize-ring a place where he could exhibit Shavian theories on Distribution of Income and award a points decision to the Life Force over muscle-bound man. 'Boxing is only pardonable when it is very well done,' he was to write. This was also his attitude to life: otherwise better dead.

Shaw's knowledge of boxing formed part of an armoury that, by the end of the 1880s, was to make him, in Max Beerbohm's opinion, 'the most brilliant and remarkable journalist in London'. At first, it was principally a method of improving the machine that was his body, as bicycling and swimming were to be. Unlike bicycling, it didn't get you anywhere, and it was not as pleasant as swimming which, with its cleansing effect and the sensation of rendering the body weightless, almost non-existent, became 'the only exercise I have ever taken for its own sake'. But his shadow boxing, even before it was converted wholly into words, was the essence of Shavianism, less a reaction to life than a response to other people's reaction to it.

For almost six years he visited the Beattys most Sundays, sparred several platonic rounds with Paquito the poet, then sat at the feet of his wife Ida (a pupil of Gounod), practising French. This was the first of numerous triangular relationships where he recreated his mesmeric but chaste version of Vandeleur Lee with Lucinda and George Carr Shaw, and kept those ghosts at peace. Though Ida Beatty had nicknamed him 'old grandfather Shaw', the connection between them was not, in Shaw's imagination, incapable of dangerous romance. 'Dont talk to me of romances: I was sent into the world expressly to dance on them with thick boots – to shatter, stab, and murder them,' he challenged her. 'I defy you to be romantic about me . . . and if you attempt it, I will go straight to Paquito; tell him you are being drawn into the whirlpool of fascination which has engulfed all the brunettes I know; express my opinion that it serves him right for having made an unmitigated ass of himself . . .' This was shadow boxing from which Shaw emerged very much in control of a situation that did not exist. In part, he was being paradoxical about his own susceptibility to women: for he could not exclude dreams of more orthodox affairs. 'All these foolish fancies only want daylight and fresh air to scatter them,' he instructed Ida, as if the fancies had been hers and not his. 'Once or twice, or three times at most, I may have allowed myself a moment's weakness out of sheer good nature, but only to spring upright again with added resilience.'

Shaw made himself attractive to women by informing them he was attractive – then warning them against this damnable attractiveness. He converted the neglected Sonny into a besieged G.B.S., who would have fainted with surprise 'if a woman came up to me in the street and said "I DONT adore you".'

'You are often exasperating,' Eleanor Marx informed him. Being in love with Shaw could be a bewildering and an exasperating business. 'I cannot say whether you write in earnest or not,' Aileen Bell complained. 'You are very contradictory . . . What am I to do?' He teased and tested; he loved you and he loved you not. He achieved an air of confidence by taking away your own confidence. He could fascinate – but was also intensely irritating: 'when we did fight in the old days,' Aileen Bell wrote to him, 'I used to go upstairs afterwards, & stamp about my room & abuse you, saying "I hate George Shaw".' His talent was to disconcert. He charmed you, then made you too angry for words and (since the affair was one of words) impotent. On paper, where he held absolute authority, he was promiscuous. He attributed to you the romantic daydreams he suppressed in himself, and encircled you in fantastical webs of designs, jealousies and misunderstandings. It was difficult to know sometimes what to feel, or what to think, or what was a joke and whether it concealed some truth: and as soon as you made up your mind, everything changed again.

Little of Shaw's relations with women during his first four or five years in London can be reconstructed. They appear to have been romances of the mind and are cryptically recorded in his early diary notebooks. At the end of 1876, he noted: 'Inauguration during the year of the Terpsichore episode. Also La Carbonaja.' Terpsichore was his codename for Ermina Pertoldi, the ballerina of the Alhambra Theatre and a character in *Immaturity*. La Carbonaja was the daughter of a London hostess who gave him a medal of the Virgin Mary, hoping to convert him to Catholicism within six weeks. Against 24 December 1877 appear the words: 'La follia della Carbonaja', and the year ends with: 'Eclipse of Calypso... Terpsichore in repose.' The following year La Carbonaja is 'in the ascendant' and in 1879 'La C flickers until 11th [January] When the star of Leonora gains the ascendant (Terpsichore evaporated)...Made the acquaintance of the Lawson family on 5th [January], and met Leonora on the 11th'. From 'Leonora', he preserved a pressed flower together with an odd note: 'These flowers were plucked from the garden of a millionaire by one of his would-be brides as a memento of a sweet prelude to a "might have been".'

Unable to come to terms with women except in a make-believe world, Shaw conducted his most successful affairs either from the galleries of theatres or his gymnasium in the British Museum, and worked himself eventually to sleep at night. But there were intervals when physical longings awoke in him and all work stopped.

> Violet Beverley
> No matter how cleverly
> I try to work when you sit beside me
> At set of sun
> There is nothing done
> Only the unwritten page to chide me
> Only your empty chair to deride me...

> I came to write, and I stayed to look
> I dared not offend, yet could not refrain
> And so, whilst you sat there deep in your book
> I studied your face again and again
> And thus, Miss Beverly
> No matter how cleverly...

Under these verses, composed on 11 April 1882 at his desk in the Reading Room, Shaw wrote: 'Subsequently there is reason to believe that her name, after all, is not Violet Beverly, but Mabel Crofton. Consequently ... "Mabel Crofton, no matter how often..." &c &c.'

Confusion began when this make-believe came in contact with the actual world. Between 1878 and 1894 he kept a correspondence in play with Elinor Huddart, author of some fervidly imaginative novels (*My Heart and I, Commonplace Sinners*) that would have won her notoriety 'if I could have persuaded her to make her name public, or at least use the same pen name, instead of changing it for every book'. She had been impressed at first by his kindness and good sense. 'How you manage to pick my work to pieces form end to end,' she wrote to him on 16 September 1878, 'and yet never hurt me (and I am rather easily hurt) I cannot conceive.' One reason she was not hurt was that Shaw had invented an Elinor of his own prescription who was to be possessed by his spirit and made into a new creature. 'You are the only man friend I have ever made,' she told him. '...I am content to be your friend and no man's wife.' For someone who appeared so frivolous it was astonishing how persistent he could be. He beat down on her like a sun, warming her, blistering her, trying to blow a new climate round her and imbue her with new life, as a writer. But 'I can put forth no new leaves,' she objected. 'I am not a beech tree...If you have thought me dying for years past you might as well consider me dead now . . . Leave my ashes in peace, they can do you no good.' But he would not leave her, altogether. He wanted to pour his will-power into women so that their achievements became the children of the union. 'Your interest in me is dead, that is all,' Elinor pleaded. 'Do not attempt to revive it.' Eventually she took refuge in a lunatic mysticism, praying to the moon – a safe distance at last from Shaw's orbit. 'Now I vanish into my mist again,' she wrote to him on the last day of 1892, 'glad to have heard a voice I know cry out in the fog: cry from a height above me, out of the fog. "Here I am all right." Hear me say in answer "All right".'

It had been a triumph of Shaw's authority that he, a writer of rejected novels, could advise and dominate a successful novelist. But he could not impregnate her with new talent. In his exertions to work his will vicariously through women his flirtations became those of a schoolmaster. 'I beg of you,' Aileen Bell once wrote to him, 'not to lecture me quite so much'. However much he did lecture, urge, flatter and coax, he could not make the worlds of fantasy and actuality coalesce: 'Many vices appear seductive to me in imagination that in reality revolt me by their coarseness.'

In his relationships with women Shaw was seeking a second childhood in which he could receive all the attention and happiness he had been denied by his mother. But since it was impossible for him literally to achieve this, he shifted his desires into his literary life. Sexual excitement produced in him an ejaculation of words from which letters were conceived, novels and plays born. Any sexual relationship that could not provide an alternative world, partly made out of words, tended to disgust him. 'If you hurt your friends' bodies the way you hurt their feelings,' Elinor Huddart wrote to him, 'you would be voted bloodthirsty.'

Shaw's love eliminated many things to which women were accustomed. He did not idealize them. In his plays he was to create a stereotype, Woman-the-Huntress, whom he sent into battle against the Victorian Woman-on-a-pedestal. Debarred by his childhood from being able to form close emotional attachments, he gave his passionate allegiance to ideas – but saw women as vehicles for those ideas. His Dublin homes had been ruled by Lucinda Elizabeth, not George Carr Shaw, and this, he believed, was how the adult world was administered. Though the reconnaissance work towards social change was often done by men, society changed only when women wanted it to do so. Revolution came from men, evolution through women. Shaw took the body away from women and addressed their minds. His own mind was astonishingly fast, but emotionally he was lame. The result was that women found themselves continually out of step with him. When Shaw looked at a woman, he appeared to turn his back on her and raise a mirror. It was a disconcerting stare, positive, remote, and appearing so bold while actually in retreat.

*

Sonny had yearned for love; G.B.S. soared wittily above it; and Shaw was pulled between the two. The tug-of-war moved critically backwards and forwards over his first serious girl friend, Alice Lockett. He had met her sister Jane while he was recovering from smallpox at Leyton in 1881. In February the following year he returned to Leyton and, while recuperating from scarlet fever, was introduced to Alice. She was twenty-three and robustly good-looking. He fell violently in love at once – that is to say, he felt himself strongly attracted to her. After his convalescence he managed to return to Leyton by the uncharacteristic means of getting temporary employment there, earning six guineas in as many days counting votes during the election of Poor Law guardians. For a week he saw her, walked in the moonlight, talked, flirted. By 17 April, he felt able to report to Elinor Huddart that 'Alice thinks I am in love with her'. The honeymoon was almost over and the contest between them ready to begin.

Jane and Alice had been conventionally brought up in a fortified middle-class family and educated at a Victorian Ladies' College. Their future seemed rigidly assured until a succession of disasters had overtaken the family. In 1879 their father had died and the next year their elder brother, now head of the family, also died. Their mother suffered a paralytic stroke, and her two daughters, transferred to the care of their grandmother, prepared to take up professions. Jane, who was experimenting with a novel called *Yeast* (exorbitantly condemned by Shaw) studied for a career in education; Alice, who enrolled in a nursing course at St Mary's Hospital in Paddington, engaged herself for a series of singing lessons from Mrs Shaw.

The affair was uncomfortably carried on between the railway station and piano stool ('Oh the infinite mischief that a woman may do by stooping forward to turn over a sheet of music!'). Neither had much money and both of them were dissatisfied with their place in society. Alice felt she had been relegated in the social order by her family misfortunes, and nursed dreams of a dramatic ascent up the ladder of society; Shaw was determined to kick that ladder away. Alice sensed a power in Shaw that might lead him many places, but he was always disappointing her by his misuse of it. In place of the manly leadership she expected of him, he presented her with exhibitions of clever indecisiveness. Quarrelling between them was inevitable. 'I hate people to hesitate,' she chided him.

In one of his early notebooks Shaw had jotted down his observations on the typical society woman. 'Clever, frivolous, vain, egotistic,' he wrote. 'Pretty & knows it. Sits silent and affects the scornful. This characteristic the keynote of her character . . . The scornful observer equally an object of scorn to a second observer of the same type supposed to be in the opposite corner. Such a frame of mind when habitual, absolutely incompatible with improvement. Contraction of sympathy and distorted view of things revolting. Also a morbid sensitiveness and a consequent pleasure in inflicting hurts on others. Effect of this type of egotist in making others seem intolerably egotistical . . .'

It was to save Alice from becoming this woman that Shaw exerted all his powers. He saw himself as playing on her dissatisfaction so as to redirect the course of her life and reclaim her soul from social petrifaction. Normally he had no close access to such people, being cut off from them by his poverty. But this time there was no barrier of money; Alice could be substantially within his power. He re-created her as a figure in his novels and she became someone through whom he attacked the London society that had lured Lee and Lucinda away from him and, when he followed, rejected him.

Shaw divided Alice into two people. Miss Lockett was formal and false. She had been stiffened by the starch of society and was full of protective scorn and attempted sarcasm. Towards men she bore herself tyrannically, having no notion that any interest of men in women might exist apart from a desire to marry. Humourless, incessantly pretending, she had equipped herself with the habits and prejudices of her class, and presented this absurd baggage of second-hand notions to the world as perfect gentility. But sometimes Miss Lockett forgot to be offended, scornful, pretentious – and Alice emerged. Alice was the child in her, sympathetic, unspoilt, spontaneously generous, someone capable of considering her own instinctive judgement a safer guide than the formulated rules of society. Alice was capable too of Shavian improvement; the proud and foolish Miss Lockett had gone too far down the hackneyed road of her own dignity to be brought back. Between these two beings Shaw enacted a perpetual drama. Miss Lockett 'is the dragon that preys upon Alice,' he told her, 'and I will rescue Alice from her'.

Shaw dramatized in Miss Alice Lockett a division he knew to exist within himself. In one corner there was G.B.S., that model of the righteous rescuer, 'resolved . . . to be an example to others, to tread the path of duty, to respect himself, to walk with the ears of his conscience strained on the alert, to do everything as perfectly as it could be done, and – oh – monstrous! – to improve all those with whom he came in contact.' In the opposite corner stood Sonny, the Irish contender, who was not afraid to become 'as a little child again and was not ashamed to fall in love with Alice'.

But the voice that lectured Miss Lockett on the importance of becoming Alice was that of G.B.S., not Sonny who could seldom 'snatch a few moments from his withering power' to warn her not to listen to the 'detestable, hardhearted, heartless, cynical, cool devil seated in my chair telling me that all this is insincere lying affection. But I defy him – it is he who lies.' But G.B.S. worked day and night; he was seldom out of love with his work – in which condition he accused Alice of taking advantage 'of the weakest side of my character', and warned her to believe nothing that Sonny whispered to her: 'I have a wicked tongue, a deadly pen, and a cold heart.' At times it seemed as if Alice was little more than the spectator to a Shavian-contained melodrama. But the crisis in Shaw was real. Before a caress with Alice had time to cool, a strenuous revulsion seized him. He longed to return to his ascetic life, to his books, his developing socialism. But then the memory of her beauty could prevent him going to bed in peace, and gave him a thrill that could last 'through a political meeting and four hours of private debate on dry questions of economy'.

When we speak I say 'Miss Lockett';
Now my courtesy I'll pocket
And indulge myself when spelling
'Alice,' and not hear her telling
Me to check my mad presumption,
With an exquisite assumption
Of offended dignity
Which endears her more to me.

Shaw's appeals to Alice were often the means by which he tried to offend her so as to save himself from falling in love. But sometimes he did not have the heart to succeed – and then Sonny would whisper things that G.B.S. would have to shatter with his laughter.

Shaw had hit on the device of pretending to be what he was – but with a comic exaggeration that prompted disbelief. He pretended, for example, to be vain, and people saw it was a pretence. He pretended to be 'in love' with Alice and she, congratulating herself on not being taken in, accused him of insincerity. But it was infuriating to know that long before the accusations she hurled had reached him he admitted them all – boasted of them. Sometimes it seemed as if she were only speaking the vigorous lines he had prepared for her. It was oddly unreal – though her feelings could be genuinely agitated, usually towards indignation. 'You know very well you have the power of paining me,' she wrote to him, 'and you are not very careful in exercising it.' And he wrote to her: 'We are too cautious, too calculating, too selfish, too heartless, to venture head over heels in love. And yet there is something – ' Both tried to limit their vulnerability to the other. But Alice did not understand where her power lay – she never realized into what extraordinary suspense her beauty put him. In attempting to hurt him with deliberate cruelty, she merely became the stubborn and timid Miss Lockett of his hostile imagination, squaring up to her impregnable enemy G.B.S.

'George Shaw, I consider you an object to be pitied – but the truth is I might just as well speak to a stone. Nothing affects you: you are a machine, and perfectly incapable of feeling of any kind whatever. Now your book has failed – for which I am truly sorry for your sake, although it is perhaps better for other people. I suppose you mean to begin another and be another year dependent on your mother. Why on earth don't you work?'

Different things were important to them. She had been in the marriage market since leaving school and looked on 'love-making' as the most serious business in life. It was because Shaw believed that Sonny was incapable of inspiring love in women that he invented G.B.S., a machine-made superman who, with a shadow of regret that it could not mean more, treated sex as for recreation in both meanings of the word. 'You [don't] even give me the benefit of a serious mood,' Alice complained. 'I could be serious,' he told her, 'only you would not understand me then . . .'

A strain of gallantry which was incorrigible in Shaw, to which his humour and his tenderness to women he liked gave variety and charm, would supervene upon his seriousness with a rapidity that Alice's far less flexible temperament could not follow. She tried to understand him – but he took care that she should not. In serious moments he could make her see with his eyes, flattering her ('Must I eternally flatter flatter flatter flatter?') by his apparent conviction – which she shared – that she was capable of a higher life. But the higher life for which G.B.S. was being constructed lay outside her knowledge. His political dreams had no meaning for her so 'it is my small troubles that I go to you with,' he told her, ' – what do you know of my larger needs, or how could you sympathize with them? I have spoken of them to you once or twice just to try you, and you never suspected that there was anything serious in question.' Nothing short of her being born again – 'a thing that sometimes happens' – could have brought her back into his life after that.

Alice Lockett's challenge to Shaw had been to make him feel his loneliness most painfully. At moments his self-command wavered. 'Write to me,' he asked her, 'and I will make love to you – to relieve the enormous solitude which I carry about with me. I do not like myself, and sometimes I do not like you; but there are moments when our two unfortunate souls seem to cling to the same spar in a gleam of sunshine, free of the other wreckage for a moment.'

Miss Lockett's social ambitions would not allow her to be stranded in this way; she wanted to travel first class. As for Shaw, it was Sonny who was left senseless and G.B.S., hurling 'truth about like destroying lightning', who ascended from that wreckage into the sky. 'I am too strong for you. I snap your chains like Samson.'

On two occasions they returned each other's letters; several times they decided never to see each other. The affair lasted until 1885 when all love had gone out of it and they drifted apart. In 1890 Alice married a former house-surgeon at St Mary's, William Salisbury Sharpe. Obliged during the First World War to borrow some money from Shaw, she lived on to witness the halo of world renown encircle G.B.S. But in many criticisms of his books and plays she would have been able to read of an absent quality – and to have recognized in this absence the departure of Sonny over which she had helplessly watched.

## [7]

*It was lonely to be myself; but not to be myself was death in life.*
*Cashel Byron's Profession*

*Love cannot keep possession of me: all my strongest powers rise up*
*against it and will not endure it. An Unsocial Socialist*

On 22 April 1882, ten days after starting his fourth novel, Shaw moved with his mother to 36 Osnaburgh Street, on the east side of Regent's Park. This 'highly respectable house' was at least an improvement on the insalubrious rooms in Fitzroy Street where he had so often been ill.

They saw little of Lucy. She had replaced her family by the troupes of actors and singers with whom she travelled the country. She seldom came to Osnaburgh Street, preferring lodging-houses. From the Carl Rosa Opera Company she transferred to a D'Oyly Carte group and in 1884 went off with them on tour.

Lucinda Elizabeth Shaw continued methodically to give private tuition in singing. In 1885 she suddenly struck a new vein of work as music instructor at Clapham High School, and the following year became choir-mistress and teacher of class singing at the North London Collegiate School for Ladies where she remained until her retirement in 1906.

Shaw went his own way – to the British Museum. Like Lucy he was soon to find a new family, but in the meantime went on working alone. His fourth novel – 324 pages of neat manuscript – was finished on 6 February 1883. *Cashel Byron's Profession*, as he called it, was later so much enjoyed by R. L. Stevenson, W. E. Henley and others that Shaw came to marvel at his escape from becoming, at the age of twenty-six, a successful novelist. The book is a fairy-tale about power. Its hero, Cashel Byron, a prize-fighter as clever with his fists as Shaw was with words, embodies Shaw's fantasy about action. To him is given the first Shavian speech (which goes the distance of three thousand words) – on the superiority, as a means of reforming society, of 'executive power' over 'good example'. It is a dialectic on the philosophy of winning, and a hymn to skill and science over incoherent strength. Written ostensibly to offset the 'abominable vein of retaliatory violence' that flowed through the literature of the nineteenth century, Shaw's real object was to force his book into print.

The contest was billed as between 'the visionary prizefighter as romantic warrior hero and the matter-of-fact trader in fisticuffs at certain weights and prices and odds'. Taking a profession that society officially repudiated, Shaw uses it as a metaphor for the way people unofficially live their lives within society – a formula he was to try again in *Mrs Warren's Profession* and *Major Barbara* (which he thought of calling 'Andrew Undershaft's Profession'). He drops an unclassifiable stranger into the select pool of English hypocrisy – and enjoys the awkward splash. Vanity, lack of courage, empty ambition flourish and spread dishonesty in such profusion that honest men in England must go about alone. The hero and heroine, lady and prize-fighter, are both honest and alone but Shaw's make-believe leads them from love at first sight through all supposed social barriers to marriage in the last chapter – a conventional happy-ever-after ending or, in the heroine's words, 'a plain proposition in eugenics' that is to be ironically upset by the irrationalism of heredity. The Lady is Cashel's prize – in a way that Ida Beatty or any of the other women with whose husbands G.B.S. sparred would never be Shaw's. In the book, romance had won by a knock-out and 'my self-respect took alarm'.

'The lower I go, the better I seem to please,' Shaw wrote hopefully to the publisher Richard Bentley. But though in later years *Cashel Byron's Profession* was 'to serve my turn as an advertisement' far more than his other novels, it was turned down in similar terms by all the same London publishing houses – principally, Shaw came to believe, because of the formidable reputation he had won as a writer of unpublishable books. 'It flies too decidedly in the face of people's prejudices to make it likely that it will be a popular book,' advised the reader for Macmillan, the fifth publisher to refuse it, in January 1884. '. . . well and brightly written, but the subject is not likely to commend itself to any considerable public. The plot is too whimsical to please many readers.'

Reviewing the book himself, Shaw established that one of the fights in the novel was a reproduction of the wrestling match in *As You Like It*. Under cover of this parody of academic literary criticism he hints at his effort to write a book as the public liked it. His reaction to what he called his 'shilling shocker' became studded with the glittering and apparent contradictions which formed part of his insulation against failure. In a letter to another novelist, Tighe Hopkins, he wrote: 'Cashel Byron was but a sermon, after all'. But his real opinion was that the book carried too little sermonizing. Many of the 'little bits of socialism that were daubed in' he had deleted during his revisions in order to make the book more readable – and this became his reason for preferring his next novel, *An Unsocial Socialist*. People who could read that, he boasted, 'will read anything'. *Cashel Byron's* readability and *Boy's Own* charm were a half-exploited opportunity that comprised the 'fundamental folly' of the thing. In 1886, following at least seven rejections, he recommended it as 'one of the cleverest books I know'. But in 1905 he told Archibald Henderson that he had 'always' considered admiration of *Cashel Byron* 'the mark of a fool'. In the interval, and as early as 1887, Shaw had been converted from the principle of Individualism to Collectivism. *Cashel Byron's Profession* was an individualist novel, which was why, when eventually published, its author found himself exposed to the humiliation of favourable reviewing 'by a detestable individualist press'.

Shaw liked to 'confess' that he had written *Cashel Byron* 'mainly to amuse myself'. But in 1888, when welcoming another publisher's repudiation of it, he burst out: 'I hate the book from my soul.' He hated the conditions in which he had written it and the London publishers for whom he had written it: he hated the person who had written it; he hated failure. He had sailed as near compromise as he dared – too near and to no effect. Next time (for he was not ready to give up) there should be no compromise.

He called his fifth novel *The Heartless Man* – later changing the title to *An Unsocial Socialist*. As with the two previous novels he drafted most if it in shorthand at the British Museum, and then transcribed it in longhand. The plot revolves round Sidney Trefusis, the heartless socialist of both titles. At the beginning of the book, Trefusis shocks everyone by running away from his newly married wife for the serious reason that he is in love with her and, even worse, she is beautiful and loves him. By accepted standards it has been a brilliant match, full of money and romance. But accepted standards have made women into a class of person fit only for the company of children and flowers. With a man like Trefusis they can have no connection, except sex. Unfortunately the sexual attraction between them was far too strong – so strong, Trefusis gravely complains to his bemused wife Henrietta, that 'our intercourse hinders our usefulness. The first condition of work with me is your absence. When you are with me I can do nothing but make love to you. You bewitch me.'

Trefusis's work is the promotion of socialism, though 'whether I am advancing the cause is more than I can say'. As Shaw's mouthpiece for neo-Marxism, he has a simple message that no one understands. He does not preach equality. He recognizes the natural inequality of man but condemns England's social inequality for failing to correspond to it. This artificial inequality strangling the human spirit – and particularly in women – will vanish, he claims, once 'England is made the property of its inhabitants collectively'. All economic roads led to socialism, though few economists saw their destination. The choice was 'Socialism or Smash'.

Most people preferred Smash because it looked safer. To open their eyes, British socialists needed to study the romantic aspect of the movement, for it was women who, by giving a cause respectability, could make it grow. Shaw's women are sympathetically drawn but, as custodians of Society's standards, they embellish the capitalist philosophy of Smash. Trefusis's aim, whether through sermonizing, flirtation or romantic insincerity, is to head them off from this course. He tries to fortify the instinctive part of them (their 'souls') against their formal and affected selves. It is the old struggle to release natural vitality from a maimed and unnatural system of morality. The most attractive of these girls, for whose socialist souls he wrestles, is Gertrude Lindsay – Shaw's portrait of Alice Lockett. It is a hostile portrait, done in the colours of revenge, depicting a discontented girl, contemptuous by nature, who is 'more afraid of the criticisms of those with whom you dance and dine than of your own conscience', who counts 'the proposals of marriage she received as a Red Indian counts the scalps he takes', and who treats her dog (a St Bernard) with more kindness than 'any human being'.

Gertrude's father, Trefusis discovers, suffers from what country people call 'the Evil'. ' "Scrofulous ulcers!" he exclaimed, recoiling. "The father of that beautiful girl!" He turned homeward, and trudged along with his head bent, muttering, "All rotten to the bone. Oh, civilization! civilization! civilization!" '

From such disgust springs his passion for curing mankind. Prudently, it is not Gertrude with her capitalist blight who becomes Trefusis's second wife, but Agatha Wylie – a Shavian Becky Sharp whose description had been inspired by a glimpse of 'a young lady with an attractive and arresting expression, bold, vivid, and very clever, working at one of the desks' in the British Museum Reading Room. Within the novel she has two advantages: she is not in love with Trefusis and she retains in her nature more of the uncorrupted child. She is a symbol of the future, and (as the critic Arnold Silver has pointed out) less a separate woman than Shaw himself in female form. His marriage to her is a form of self-sufficiency in place of involvement with a pain-producing creature such as Gertrude.

Agatha is incorruptible, but everyone is to some extent corrupted. In a letter to Alice Lockett, Shaw regretted that they had not met in Ireland where she could have seen 'the round towers of other days in the wave beneath you shining there'. Though pretty and green, 'England is a vile country,' he wrote. 'I speak not of the men and women – they are vile everywhere; but of the scenery.' Shaw deliberately picked up the vulgarities of his enemies and came to the battle as well-armoured as they were. Trefusis is similarly affected by the society in which he lives. 'I can only say that Trefusis was none of my making,' Shaw wrote to one of his correspondents.

'He came out of me a liar, just as I came out of the womb of Nature what I am and not otherwise: I assure you his actions raise the whole insoluble problem (or unsolved problem, let us say) of free will as formidably as any actual deed of my own ... Trefusis is only a liar as the novelist or the comedian is a liar. His bad side is the side on which he is an incorrigible mountebank; but his burlesques are burlesques of shams, intentionally satirical and destructive – burlesques of the sham laborer and the sham lover of middle class romance. Have you noted, too, that it is always his terrible truth telling, and never his lying, that gets him into trouble.

'As to making my hero repellent, that was inevitable. Our social conditions do not produce attractive characters in the fighting ranks of the great class war. Injustice and scorn in one camp; degradation and ignorance in the other; cupidity, fear and mistrust in both: the struggle with these leaves its mark on all who engage in it – and indeed the qualities that enable a man to engage in it are not exclusively the amiable qualities. There are splendid compensations for the fighter on the right side; but the evil remains.'

By separating his socialist hero into two people, Shaw reflected the division he felt existed in his own character. Trefusis, the son of a millionaire, wishes to break all connection with his class and the system of exploitation that has made him rich. Some of the most entertaining pages of the novel are those where he becomes an insufferably talkative, low comedian of a labourer – a Dickensian character called Smilash (a compound of the words smile and eyelash). In this partnership, Shaw the comedian and Shaw the reformer are brought together for the same ends. The character of Smilash appeals to the 'vagabond impulse' in Trefusis, and the actor in Shaw. 'I am just mad enough to be a mountebank,' Trefusis explains. 'If I were a little madder, I should perhaps really believe myself Smilash instead of merely acting him ... With my egotism, my charlatanry, my tongue, and my habit of having my own way, I am fit for no calling but that of saviour of mankind ...'

Trefusis is the great man who had lain asleep in Smith (the tentative hero of *Immaturity*), and wakes up by the light of Marxist economics. Shaw's novels had been experiments to find a political framework in which to spin his thought and personality. Conolly, the engineer of *The Irrational Knot*, had been 'a monster of the mind' embodying rationalism; Owen Jack, the composer from *Love Among the Artists*, was 'a monster of the body' representing unconscious instinct; in *Cashel Byron's Profession* Shaw had toyed with a romantic fusion of mind and body in the marriage of his prize-fighter and educated lady. In *An Unsocial Socialist* the union takes place not between two people but within one. Trefusis is Shaw's first socialist hero and Don Juan figure in whom he attempts to reconcile his sexual and political attitudes. The novel foreshadows *Man and Superman*, with Trefusis a prototype of Tanner. Shaw was to speak of socialism as having given him a 'religion'. From the hour of his conversion, he wrote, 'I became a man with some business in the world.' He used this business like a magnet to shift his various contradictory impulses into new shapes, and line them up towards a political end. Within himself this achieved some harmony, but as a saviour of mankind Trefusis is largely unemployable. His ineffectiveness, like that of Tanner, is fixed in the futility of 'Talking!' and the '*Universal laughter*', rather than action that it prompts.

Shaw had planned a novel of much greater length and larger scope 'depicting capitalist society in dissolution, with its downfall as the final grand catastrophe'. But having completed the first section, two monstrous chapters long, he found himself 'too young for the job' and submitted the 336 manuscript pages of *An Unsocial Socialist* as a complete novel.

It was an extraordinary book to have produced in the early 1880s – 'the first English novel written under the influence of Karl Marx with a hero whose character and opinions forecast those of Lenin,' Shaw later declared. He finished his revisions on 15 December 1883 and sent it five days later to Kegan Paul, Trench & Co. 'It appears to us written in good style and language,' they replied in their letter of rejection, 'but it suffers, in our opinion, from the fatal effect on a novel, of not being interesting.'

Smith Elder & Co., the second publisher to read it, agreed: 'We are afraid that the subscribers to the circulating libraries are not much interested in Socialism.' David Douglas of Edinburgh and Chatto & Windus in London excused themselves from looking at it. For Macmillan, John Morley (not realizing that he had previously advised the author to give up writing) reported that it was a Ruskinian '*jeu d'esprit*, or satire, with a good stroke of socialist meaning in it . . . The story is designedly paradoxical, absurd and impossible, as if it were one of Peacock's. But whoever he may be, the author knows how to write; he is pointed, rapid, forcible, sometimes witty, often powerful and occasionally eloquent.' But, Morley concluded, the socialistic irony would not be attractive to many readers and it was 'too clever' for the general public: 'they would not know whether the writer was serious or was laughing at them.' In refusing the book, Macmillan wrote that they would be glad to look at anything else he might write 'of a more substantial kind' – a request that, Shaw replied, 'takes my breath away'. In his correspondence with Macmillan, he came as near making an exasperated appeal for sympathy as he could.

'All my readers, as far as I know them, like the book; but they tell me that although they relish it they dont think the general public would. Which is the more discouraging, as this tendency of each man to consider himself unique is one of the main themes of the novel. Surely out of thirty millions of copyright persons (so to speak) there must be a few thousand who would keep me in bread and cheese for the sake of my story-telling, if you would only let me get at them.'

It was not the publisher but new political friends who were to give Shaw his chance of getting at the public. *An Unsocial Socialist*, he claimed, 'finished me with the publishers'.

'A clerk for a hero (my first) was not a recommendation but at least he accepted the world as it was and wore a white linen collar in its social eddies. I was perhaps to be encouraged. But my second, a working electrical engineer crashing through the castes and mastering them: that was distasteful and incorrect. I was going wrong. Then a British Beethoven, careless of his clothes, ungovernable, incomprehensible, poor, living in mean lodgings at an unfashionable address: this was absurd. The next, a prizefighter, wooing and marrying a priggishly refined lady of property, made a bit of a romance, without a dying child in it but with a fight or two. But a Socialist! A Red, an enemy of civilization, a universal thief, atheist, adulterer, anarchist, and apostle of the Satan he disbelieved in!! And presented as a rich young gentleman, eccentric but not socially unpresentable. Too bad.'

But for socialists it was almost too good to be true. Where else could they find so able a story incorporating so much of their point of view? What other novelist, for example, would allow his hero, pursued by an angry headmistress, two parsons and a posse of policemen, to stop and lecture his wife for some fifteen pages on Marx's theory of surplus value?

Instead of adding it to the pile of four others that all the publishers had refused, Shaw sent off his aborted *magnum opus* to J. L. Joynes, one of the editors of *To-Day*, a new 'Monthly Magazine of Scientific Socialism'. Joynes recommended the serialization of the novel to his fellow-editor, the non-Fabian philosopher E. Belfort Bax, who replied: 'Go on and prosper with Shaw . . .'

*An Unsocial Socialist* appeared in serial form between March and December 1884. Shaw was not paid, but for the first time he had an audience. 'William Morris spotted it and made my acquaintance on account of it. That took me into print and started me.' Between April 1885 and March 1886 *Cashel Byron's Profession* was also serialized, due largely to the enthusiasm of the magazine's printer, H. H. Champion, a restless, clever, epileptic man who had left the army to take part in the socialist movement of the 1880s, and who was later to become Shaw's dramatic agent in Australia. Champion had a taste for pugilism, and liked the novel so much that he stereotyped the pages from *To-Day* and published them in a misshapen 'Modern Press' edition of two thousand five hundred copies in March 1886. This was Shaw's first published book, costing a shilling and carrying a royalty of one penny a copy. Two of his other novels, *The Irrational Knot* (April 1885-February 1887) and *Love Among the Artists* (November 1887-December 1888), were also to be published serially in another socialist magazine, Annie Besant's *Our Corner*. Only *Immaturity* failed to reach publication on the tide of the socialist revival, and was not printed until 1930 in Shaw's Collected Edition.

Once the novels started to be printed, publishers woke up to them. America produced a number of enterprising pirated editions, while in Britain publication was handled more traditionally. 'Your book has definitely been published some time,' the firm of Swan Sonnenschein (nicknamed Moonschein) hazarded. In fact they had published *An Unsocial Socialist* in 1887, two years after acceptance and in an edition the early copies of which misspelt the publisher's own name and, on the title page, recommended Shaw as 'Author of "The Confessions of Byron Cashel's Profession," etc., etc.' – an excellent reason, Shaw warned collectors, 'for pitching it into the fire'. As for *Cashel Byron's Profession* itself, 'I have never seen an advertisement,' he informed the British publisher Grant Richards, 'never met a human being who had ever seen one, never expect to meet one.'

Shaw's political interests soon devoured his ambitions as a novelist, but though he took only a remote interest in these works, claiming that they had sprung to life despite all his efforts to suppress them, he couldn't resist improving them a little and he extensively revised and augmented *An Unsocial Socialist* for its publication in book form. These revisions, amounting to several thousand words, were designed not to change its meaning but to make that meaning more clear.

By 1888 he decided that his 'book-writing days are over, unluckily . . . I should not know how to write a novel now'. The previous year he had abandoned an attempt at a sixth novel because 'I could not stand the form: it is too clumsy and unreal. Sometimes I write dialogues; and these are working up to a certain end . . .' This disenchantment with the novel is already apparent in *An Unsocial Socialist*. In the 1887 appendix to this book, which takes the form of a letter to the author from Trefusis, Shaw writes: 'I cannot help feeling that, in presenting the facts in the guise of fiction, you have, in spite of yourself, shewn them in a false light. Actions described in novels are judged by a romantic system of morals as fictitious as the actions themselves.' This puritan hatred of fiction he shared with Defoe who, in *Serious Reflections*, had described the 'supplying of a story by invention' as 'a sort of lying that makes a great hole in the heart, at which by degrees, a habit of lying enters in'. Like Defoe, he resolved to make his fiction as much like fact as possible.

Now that it was too late, publishers were urging him to go on. His books would work into a good circulation, Swan Sonnenschein encouraged him, providing he 'stick to novels, or go in for plays (which are even more suited to you, in my opinion) . . .' Shaw acknowledged that he might 'descend as low as that one day', but five failures had been 'enough to satisfy my appetite for enterprise in fiction' and it was not surprising that 'I found nothing new for me to do in that direction'. He was sick of the world of literature, fiction, publishers. The novelist was a 'voluptuary in labor', he wrote in *An Unsocial Socialist*. 'Nine out of ten of them are diseased creatures, just sane enough to trade on their own neuroses. The only quality of theirs which exhorts my respect is a certain sublime selfishness which makes them willing to starve and let their families starve sooner than do any work they dont like.'

Since he could not marry his story-telling to his socialism, Shaw relinquished story-telling. Socialism relieved his loneliness and grew into a weapon to be used against the society that had all but emasculated him. From his socialist philosophy he harvested optimism, while the novels, representing his first nine years in London, remained like dead fruit on the bough. 'They are all jejune and rotten,' he declared. 'I shant write any more of them.' Over fifty years later he wrote that his 'complete failure to find a publisher for any of them was for me a hardening process from which I have never quite recovered'.

Hesketh Pearson, adapting a remark of Oscar Wilde's, wrote that 'there are two ways of disliking the works of Bernard Shaw: one way is to dislike them, the other is to like his novels' – the truth of which was to be demonstrated by George Orwell's criticism of Shaw: 'he has squandered what talents he may have had back in the '80s . . . Shaw's best work was one or two early novels . . .' But his career as a novelist, as he himself said, 'ended before it had begun'. Although they carry many ideas that were to be developed in his plays, these novels seemed to Shaw to have been written by someone else – someone with his roots in Ireland who once dreamed of some grand literary conquest in London. That Shaw was almost dead, and the journalist who was about to be born in his place would write anonymously, under many pseudonyms, and eventually as G.B.S.

*

One final tie with his past was cut when on 19 April 1885 George Carr Shaw died. They had had little communication over the last five years. 'I have nothing else to say that you would care about,' his father had written on 2 September 1880; and again, on 4 December 1882: 'I have nothing else particular to say.' Of his son's published works he read only *An Unsocial Socialist*, liked it, but warned him: 'dont get yourself into Holloway Jail.' Though he often asked for letters, 'whether you have anything to say or not', he seldom heard from George who he felt did not 'have anything sentimental left in you'. Years later, Shaw wrote: 'When I recall certain occasions on which I was inconsiderate to him I understand how Dr Johnson stood in the rain in Lichfield to expiate the same remorse.' But he had never fought his father, so all the battles of his adult life would seem bloodless.

George Carr Shaw died suddenly of congestion of the lungs while recovering from pneumonia in a bed-and-breakfast lodging house in Leeson Park Avenue. 'I hastened there, and was ushered upstairs into a bedroom,' McNulty recorded. '. . . He had died in his sleep: and his lips wore a smile, proving, as the landlady sympathetically remarked, that he had, at all events, died without suffering.' He had not been wanted, dead or alive, and he was not missed. Lucy was in Ireland at the time, but she did not go to the funeral. When the news reached Shaw, he sent a note, with two staves of music headed 'Grave', to his friend Kingston Barton:

'Telegram just received to say that the governor has left the universe on rather particular business and set me up as
                              An Orphan.'

From the insurance on his father's life, Shaw was able to buy that summer his first new clothes for years – including an all-wool Jaeger suit, a black coat, vest, collar, cravat and pants, all for £11 1s. 'In short, I had become, for better for worse, a different man.'

# CHAPTER III

## [ 1 ]

*I was a man with some business in the world . . . my main business*
*was Socialism.*

The London in which Shaw had been living was like a City of Revelation.
Among the philosophical ruins wandered pedants and prophets offering
miracles that were shortly to come to pass. From agnostics, anarchists and
atheists; dress- and diet-reformers; from economists, feminists, philanth-
ropists, rationalists, spiritualists, all striving to destroy or replace
Christianity, was the socialist revival of the late nineteenth century to be
drawn. Squabbles between and within these heterodox groups were
continuous, puffing up clouds of polemical literature. This was the last age
of the religious and political tract. One, by a clergyman of the Established
Church, proved that Jehovah was a small red venomous snake; a second,
by a German, replaced this snake with a fish; yet a third, by a Methodist
professor, abolished both snake and fish, and explained that Jehovah was a
widower. Such scholarly confusion was intensified by the crumbling of
known structures: clergymen pursued new sexual mores and political
creeds; high-minded unbelievers, relying on ritual, were beset by spiritual
cares. Science, like a great steam engine, having crashed through the
infallibility of the Bible, was being garlanded with the dogmas and symbols
of mythology and made the Idol of a new religion.

After Albert's death in 1861, Victorianism, still symbolized by the
black-dressed Queen, had been kept alive by artificial aids. In reaction to
this moribund moralism, a new urgency had entered the progressive
movement, reinforced by those who, in the aftermath of Darwinism, had
merged personal sin with social guilt and transferred their service to God
into a duty to the community. The revolt of the 1880s and 1890s grew into
a collectivist movement of social reconstruction with many interconnected
aesthetic, moral and political themes. New clubs and societies sprang up in
London, catering for all talents and temperaments. Many working-class
socialists joined the street parades of the Social Democratic Federation;
anarchical socialists with a taste for sexual radicalism were attracted to the
glamorous Socialist League; while the Fabian Society was filled by
quietists and scholars of the middle class who wanted to use their literary

and sociological skills to rewrite the economy and rearrange the social patterns of the country without a shot fired. All were agreed that there was a crisis in the land. Thirty per cent of the population of London – the richest city in the world – were living in poverty. Such was the magnitude of capitalism's failure.

After the fetid atmosphere of the drawing-room which had closed its doors to all this ferment, Shaw felt relief at entering such honest turmoil. There was work to do and a use, far beyond the lighting-up of pretty epigrams, for the lamp that was his mind. What made him part of this outside world was a factor common to almost all these little bands of prophets: the search for self-esteem that had perished after the Darwinian earthquake. Shaw's personal need coincided with the need of the age. For the first time he began to feel at one with other people. If he could not disperse his solitude through brute affection, he might at least link it to the solitude of others by giving up the burden of individualism and submerging himself in the austere comforts of collectivism. The 'power to stand alone', which Smith had acquired in *Immaturity*, 'at the expense of much sorrowful solitude', was no longer necessary. G.B.S. stood shoulder to shoulder.

The man who, in 1885, could admit that 'I hate all fraternity mongering just as heartily as any other variety of cant' and go on to declare himself the 'member of an individualist state, and therefore nobody's comrade', had decided at the beginning of 1887 that 'it is time for us to abandon the principle of Individualism, and to substitute that of Socialism, on pain of national decay'. There was one more somersault to go through. By 1891 he had reconciled his instinct with his practice by discovering that 'the way to Communism lies through the most resolute and uncompromising Individualism'. In practice Shaw meant that we should pursue our individual talent for non-egocentric purposes – 'pragmatic' individualism, but not *laissez-faire* 'economic' individualism. Though his public energies were diverted from the old individualist channel by the socialist movement of the 1880s, he could still reassure a friend: 'Believe me, I always was, & am, an intense Individualist.'

His occupation had arrived. Having inherited qualities that were never reconciled in his own nature, he turned them inside out and tried to unify all the heretics of London – atheists, economists, salvationists – in one socialist bloc. He had embarked on a political odyssey that turned into a religious quest wherein he sought to harmonize two discordant attitudes towards the universe: the scientific conception of an evolutionary system, and the divine vision of life emanating from religious faith. He was driven on this quest by his passion to discover some ingenious synthesis between knowledge and belief, thought and action, the fact and the ideal.

What Shaw sacrificed by turning himself into a factory for the production of this synthetic formula was everything he wanted to be rid of – to which he gave the provocative label 'happiness'. His first manoeuvres towards self-fulfilment by shedding his earlier neglected self aimed at substituting his family with a community of his own choosing. 'I haunted public meetings,' he remembered, 'like an officer afflicted with cowardice, who takes every opportunity of going under fire to get over it and learn his business.' Towards the end of 1880 he had joined the Zetetical Society, which met weekly in the rooms of The Women's Protective & Provident League in Long Acre. Though 'nervous & self-conscious to a heartbreaking degree . . . I could not hold my tongue. I started up and said something in the debate, and then felt that I had made such a fool of myself . . . I vowed I would . . . become a speaker or perish in the attempt. And I carried out this resolution. I suffered agonies that no one suspected. During the speech of the debate I resolved to follow, my heart used to beat as painfully as a recruit's, going under fire for the first time. I could not use notes: when I looked at the paper in my hand I could not collect myself enough to decipher a word.' Yet he persisted, keeping his terror so well hidden that to many of the members he appeared completely self-possessed. At his third meeting he was invited to take the chair, and the following year could confidently write to the secretary: 'My readiness to consider and decide questions of metaphysics, Logic, Psychology, Political Economy, Jurisprudence and Ethics, and indeed all questions whatever, is not, I trust, unknown to the Committee of the Z. S.'

The Zetetical Society was a junior copy of the London Dialectical Society, which Shaw joined in 1881, reading his first paper there (on the virtues of Capital Punishment over Life Imprisonment) early the following year. Women took an important part in the debates of both societies and helped to insist upon uncensored speech on all social, political and philosophical subjects. From the practice of examining each speaker with questions at the conclusion of his paper (heckling was also part of the menu), Shaw began to sense his own formidable debating powers.

He also experimented with some literary groups, passing calm evenings with the New Shakespere Society, and more breezy ones with the Browning Society, to which in 1883 he had been elected by mistake. The members of this group were 'a terror to Browning'. Equally terrible was the Shelley Society, for whose private production in 1886 of *The Cenci* Shaw acted as apologetic press officer. As an example of Shelley 'groping for the scientific drama which is yet in the future, and which alone could have reconciled his philosophic craving for truth to the unrealities of the stage', this five-act blank-verse tragedy was, Shaw wrote, '. . . a strenuous but futile and never-to-be-repeated attempt to bottle the new wine in the old skins.'

As a 'Republican, a Leveller, a Radical of the most extreme type', Shelley had cleared Shaw's mind of old-fashioned moralities in politics and religion and made room for the planting of Creative Evolution. Shaw was surprised, therefore, to find that the Shelley Society presented the poet 'as a Church of England country gentleman whose pastime was writing sermons in verse'. When he announced to the Society that, as an out-and-out Shelleyan, 'I am a Socialist, an Atheist and a Vegetarian', two pious ladies resigned.

The late-Victorian literary world took its tone from the poets and men of letters who, finding themselves imprisoned in a world of machines and morality, dreamed luxuriously of ampler ages and of magic lands to which, perhaps, death might release them. But Shaw had done with dreaming. Having begun to submerge his self-consciousness into a social conscience, he wanted, like Shelley, to pierce the illusions that made the present order seem eternal, and show the world its great future; he wanted 'a cause and a creed to live for'.

He found them on the evening of 5 September 1882 at the nonconformist Memorial Hall in Farringdon Street where the American economist, Henry George, was speaking on Land Nationalization. George had come to Britain the previous autumn after ten years of successful evangelizing in America. But his *Progress and Poverty*, which had rapidly sold 100,000 copies at home, was described by Karl Marx as 'the capitalist's last ditch'. It seemed impossible that this should be the man to transform radical politics in Britain. But in August 1882 George had had a stroke of luck: he was arrested in Ireland by a gang of Galway policemen who took him to be a revolutionary Fenian. He was doubly fortunate in that the man arrested with him was J. L. Joynes, vegetarian and master at Eton, whose full account of these happenings appeared as *The Adventures of a Tourist in Ireland*. This far-off incident was to have consequences crucial to Shaw. 'Now Eton expects, among other things, that every master shall keep out of the hands of the police.' Joynes, having been given the choice of his mastership or the book, published and was damned by the college. He turned his back on respectability, 'renounced the substantial mammon of Eton', and became editor of the magazine *To-Day*, which published *An Unsocial Socialist*. His first report of these Irish adventures had appeared as a dispatch – 'A Political Tour of Ireland' – in *The Times* on 4 September. It was the furore created by this account that persuaded

Shaw, with so many others, to attend George's crowded lecture the following day.

George, who spoke with an appealing American intonation, holding the emphasis back to the last syllable of each word, was a deliberate orator. He was simple, he was sentimental; and, like the best avant-garde Americans, he was fifty years behind the times in most of Europe. But he was not a shy man, had no scruples about appealing to his friend The Creator, or calling on the eternal verities, Liberty, Justice and Truth. He gave to politics the powerful orchestration of religion.

George's *Progress and Poverty*, which Shaw bought that evening for sixpence, and which was reported as being eagerly read by the working class, offered an explanation as to why increasing economic progress brought increasing poverty. The ownership of land had always been a precondition of power in Britain. Parliament had been dominated by the opinions of landed interests to an extent where 'aristocracy' became another word for the great owners of land. These few landowners monopolized the birthright of the people, but the nationalization of this land would give the people back their birthright and eliminate the social inequalities of the past.

For the first time it flashed on Shaw that all this controversy between Science and Religion, Darwin and the Bible, was barren ground occupied only by the middle class. 'The importance of the economic basis dawned on me.' By shifting his attention to the economic root of our civilization, George's book enabled Shaw to come to terms with his own past. He had been betrayed into his one exhibition of feeling (seizing and kissing his mother's hand) over the ownership of Torca Cottage – and that, being false, had led to disillusion. He could also find a single impersonal reason, bleached of all grievance, for his loveless home and miserable years in the estate office of Uniacke Townshend. All had been part of an inhuman system on which at last he had the correct perspective.

But it was an extraordinary paradox that the man who swept Shaw and five-sixths of his colleagues into the great socialist revival of the 1880s was so far from being a socialist himself that he actually attacked the socialism he had inspired. His overall land remedy created great complications for future socialists, who had to abolish the naïve distinctions between agriculture and industry, rent on land and interest on capital. George, moreover, went on to reduce Land Nationalization to the new solution of a single tax on the value of land – a casting back to the eighteenth century and the *Impôt Unique* of Honoré Mirabeau. Shaw, who played Voltaire to George's Mirabeau, set out to show that even if George's single tax were levied on the rents of capital and ability as well as on land, the socialization of these rents by means of the single tax would involve the socialization of industry, for which there was no provision in George's scheme.

To George, who had witnessed the parcelling out of the American West to railway interests, everything in Britain seemed dynamically stationary. He did not realize that the land had begun to decline rapidly as a source of employment, that the life of the field was in retreat before the life of the City. A different group of men, who would not be absorbed by the landed rulers, had started making their way to fortunes from the new industries. Some of these plutocrats actually advocated George's Single Tax because they saw the advantage to themselves of diverting attention, and taxation, from their own enormous gains to those of the landlord. They helped to persuade some entrenched Liberals, such as the elder Joseph Chamberlain and John Morley, of the radical value of George's proposal as an alternative to socialism. But for Shaw the problem of the plutocrats was to become not one of single tax but single income.

George had his place in the history of British socialism, but almost from the start this place was in the past. By altering the way in which British socialists came to look at their past, he changed the direction in which they would proceed. His Single Tax was a stepping stone to socialism, and socialists stepping over it did not take it with them. They were converted by George, but not to him. He was their John the Baptist. Shaw had no sooner read *Progress and Poverty* than he went on to Karl Marx, and finally 'devoted about four years to the study of abstract economics so as to get my foundations sound for my work as a socialist in devising practicable methods of industrial and political reconstruction'.

He spoke at clubs; he read in the British Museum. He searched among a number of new organizations for a political headquarters. The Dialectical and Zetetical Societies, which had had their origin in John Stuart Mill, were now failing, Shaw believed, to rise to the Henry George movement. He began therefore to replace them in his syllabus with a number of other groups. He tried out his voice at the Bedford Debating Society organized by an Irish Unitarian preacher, Stopford Brooke (on whom Shaw partly modelled the Revd James Morrell in *Candida*); he attached himself to the Land Reform Union which had been formed to propagate George's nationalization theories and which fossilized into The English Land Restoration League; he joined two discussion groups in Hampstead, which were later to enable him to 'overtake' Marx; and he went to meetings of the Democratic Federation, the first socialist political organization in Britain.

This was led, with Jove-like force of beard and brow, by H. M. Hyndman, whose majestic head teemed with insurrectionary dreams. He saw himself, in his immaculate frock-coat, fine gloves, silk hat and other grand insignia of the class he fiercely denounced, as leading his rough proletarian army through a revolutionary dawn into the clear light of national regeneration. But it was ballet rather than revolution. Many of his political tactics, which were to include drilling the unemployed and rousing the working class to parade in the streets, seemed to be rehearsals for the Apocalypse – which was fixed for 1889, the anniversary of the French Revolution. With snorting nostrils, restless blue eyes, an important high-chested carriage, he already looked like a prime minister. His Federation, which scorned the middle-class intellectual and attempted to make communists of the workers, followed the Marxist party line. For Hyndman had known Marx and, when leaving his house one day, put on his hat by mistake and found that it fitted. In 1881 he had published a book, *England for All*, that, while introducing Marxist doctrines to English readers, did so without mentioning Marx's name – except (a point that failed to satisfy Marx) in a Preface. Hyndman's excuse was, as Marx bitterly told Engels, 'that the English don't like to be taught by foreigners [and] . . . my name was so much detested'.

But it was Hyndman's connection with Henry George, another foreigner whose ideas he was testing for appropriation, that had attracted Shaw to what became known as the Social Democratic Federation. At his first meeting, during question time, he mentioned George and, being patronized as a novice, was told to go off and read Marx. There was no English version available so, Shaw's German not being up to deciphering an original text, he studied the first volume of *Das Kapital* in Deville's French translation, working during the autumn of 1883 at the British Museum. 'That was the turning point in my career,' he told Hesketh Pearson. 'Marx was a revelation . . . He opened my eyes to the facts of history and civilization, gave me an entirely fresh conception of the universe, provided me with a purpose and a mission in life.' *Das Kapital*, he wrote, 'achieved the greatest feat of which a book is capable – that of changing the minds of the people who read it.' It was, he admitted, 'the only book that ever turned me upside down' – a position, Max Beerbohm observed, he maintained for the rest of his life.

During those early days, before he took on the conversion of idolatrous Marxists into international bourgeois Shavians, it seemed to him that Marx was 'a giant and a genius', who was to change the world more fundamentally than Jesus or Mahomet – and certainly more than Darwin. But when, brimming with Marxism, he returned to the SDF, he found that Hyndman's lieutenants had not read him themselves. Though *Das Kapital* had completed his conversion to socialism, he still did not have a political home. He was now a 'candidate member' of the SDF, but for two reasons decided not to join. The first was Hyndman's own incapacity for teamwork – he would not have shared the leadership with God Almighty. His famous temper was responsible for driving away many socialists – among them Edward Aveling, Belfort Bax, Walter Crane, Eleanor Marx and William Morris, who formed themselves into an anti-parliamentary group called the Socialist League, soon to be infiltrated by the anarchists.

But there was a second reason why Shaw turned his back on Hyndman. Socialism had not caught on with the working classes in the early 1880s and Hyndman's scheme of concentrating the power of their immense numbers into one irresistible body (his own) seemed impossible. Social change looked as if it was being gradually brought about by the very bourgeoisie whom Marx had so bitterly blasted. 'I was in doubt about throwing in my lot with the Social Democratic Federation,' Shaw explained, ' – not because of snobbery, but because I wanted to work with men of my own mental training.' It was then that he came across the first tract, *Why are the Many Poor?*, of the newly formed Fabian Society. Here was an interesting name that suggested an educated body appealing to middle-class intelligentsia: 'my own class in fact'. From this tract he discovered the Society's address and on 16 May 1884 turned up for its next meeting.

*

The nominal founder of the Fabian Society had been Thomas Davidson, the illegitimate son of a Scottish shepherd. He was a puritan romantic, omnipresent yet elusive. 'You met him, talked to him, were inspired by him,' said one of his disciples, 'and the next day you found he had fled.' He would drop in on Pope Leo XIII in Rome, turn up in Paris or New York, appear on the site of Troy or among the Italian Alps, picking up new threads for his patchwork metaphysics. As the Evangelical movement disintegrated before the advance of Darwinism, a great call had gone up for such missionaries, dedicated to plain living and high thinking, from whom those left with the habit of belief without its substance could recharge their hopes.

Davidson was an inspired talker and very strong on immortality. In 1881 he had blazed through London, inflaming miscellaneous agitators and idealists with what William James called his 'inward glory'. On his next visit two years later some of these acolytes – a journalist, an architect, medical student, some Government clerks and ladies of advanced opinions – held a meeting at the lodgings of one of them, a stockbroker and water-diviner. There was an atmosphere of awkwardness. They listened to a paper on 'The New Life', exchanged some words about a Utopian colony in Southern California, and formed 'a sort of club'.

There was no programme, only (as with the Apostles at Cambridge) a state of mind. Members were of two conditions: those whose impulse was primarily religious; and others, more politically minded, who wished to undertake the reconstruction of society. Soon the club split up into two branches – 'The Fellowship of the New Life' attracting the aspiring saints, and the Fabian Society, the world-betterers whose religion became socialism.

'What does the name mean? Why Fabian?' asked Edward Pease, the first secretary of the Society. There was once an African general-in-chief, the story went, who swore a great oath that he would destroy Rome. He beat the Romans in battle whenever he met them and would have accomplished his oath had not the Roman General, Fabius (afterwards named 'the Waiter'), invented a policy of spontaneous inactivity. The Fabian Society's motto, concocted by a post office clerk called Podmore, who by night turned into a ghost-hunter for the Society of Psychical Research, was printed as an epigraph to the Fabian Tract that Shaw read in the spring of 1884.

'For the right moment you must wait, as Fabius did, most patiently, when warring against Hannibal, though many censured his delays; but when the time comes you must strike hard, as Fabius did, or your waiting will be vain and fruitless.'

When critics asked the name of the history from which this quotation came, Pease answered gleefully that the work of the Fabian Society was not to repeat history, but to make it. Since the instincts of the early Fabians were literary as well as political, their business – chiefly under Shaw's influence – was to alter history by rewriting it.

To Shaw, the beauty of the Fabian title was that it could be used to mean anything. He saw at once an opportunity for dominating this group with his ideas. The Minutes of the meeting of 16 May had a famous mauve-ink side-note in unmistakably Shavian hand and style – the careful signature with its incongruous flourish of defiance: 'This meeting was made memorable by the first appearance of Bernard Shaw.' On 5 September he formally enrolled and before the end of the year had published what amounted to his first address to them – an unsigned two-page leaflet entitled *A Manifesto*, which is listed as Fabian Tract No. 2. Never again was Shaw so succinct. In a thousand words he tabulated seventeen propositions that, though debated clause by clause by the

Fabians, remained (in Pease's words) 'unqualified "Shaw"'. The Manifesto had a trenchancy and wit, giving it a different sound from all other socialist documents. Under present circumstances, it stated, 'wealth cannot be enjoyed without dishonour or foregone without misery'; the most striking result of nineteenth-century capitalism in Britain had been to divide society 'into hostile classes, with large appetites and no dinners at one extreme and large dinners and no appetites at the other'; nationalization of the land 'is a public duty'; under *laissez-faire*, competition 'has the effect of rendering adulteration, dishonest dealing and inhumanity compulsory'; instead of leaving National Industry to organize itself, the State should therefore compete 'with all its might in every department of production', and also with private individuals, ' – especially with parents – in providing happy homes for children, so that every child may have a refuge from the tyranny or neglect of its own custodians'; there should be equal political rights for the sexes, since 'Men no longer need special political privileges to protect them against Women'. The Manifesto ended with two quintessential statements:

'That the established Government has no more right to call itself the State than the smoke of London has to call itself the weather.
'That we had rather face a Civil War than such another century of suffering as the present one has been.'

When Pease nervously demurred at this last proposition, Shaw at once reassured him: the Fabians were only committed to *discussing the practical consequences* of such an opinion – no such revolutionary alternative would be offered in practice.

By the beginning of 1885 two things had been achieved. The Fabians had found a programme – and Shaw a platform.

## [ 2 ]

*I found that I had only to say with perfect simplicity what I seriously*
*meant just as it struck me, to make everybody laugh. My method is to*
*take the utmost trouble to find the right thing to say, and then say it*
*with the utmost levity. And all the time the real joke is*
*that I am in earnest.*

During 1884, Shaw had taken on two gruelling jobs that were to hang round him well into the following year. Between November and April he edited for H. H. Champion's Modern Press a British edition of Laurence

133

Gronlund's *The Cooperative Commonwealth*, an exposition of socialism that had recently appeared in America. 'By God, I never read [such] English!' he exclaimed to Champion. Shaw's editing gave the book a sparkling tone. He polished it with optimism. 'I have practically to rewrite [it] as it goes through the press,' he admitted. Gronland, for example, had written: 'It is, of course, to the discontented that they [Socialists] address themselves; they have nothing to say to such as think that the world is good enough as it is.' Shaw substituted for this: 'Socialism has the advantage of appealing to the interests as well as to the enthusiasm of all except the few who think the world good enough as it is.' Shaw's payment for this editing was to be £5, 'if the book ever produces anything over the costs & advts' – a figure that became more remote once Gronland, repudiating Shaw's version, published his American 'authorized' edition, with a preface addressed 'To the British Reader'.

Even less profitable was a commission Shaw had accepted as early as January 1884 to provide a glossary and index for the Hunterian Club's edition of Thomas Lodge's Works. 'I wasted the year deplorably,' he noted in his diary. For technical reasons it proved a far more troublesome job than he had anticipated. 'I am very anxious to get it over and off my mind,' he assured the Hunterian secretary after six months. At intervals over the following year he would receive imploring letters from the Club, and these would result in desperate resolutions to buy an alarm clock – but then: 'Sat at home playing and thinking uselessly about the Lodge Index' and wishing Lodge 'had never been born'. In July he transferred the commission to Thomas Tyler, a 'rectangular, waistless, neckless, ankleless . . . man of letters of an uncommercial kind' who had previously made a translation of Ecclesiastes 'of which eight copies a year were sold'. Tyler completed the job but not long afterwards died, 'sinking unnoted like a stone in the sea' – though remaining for the grateful Shaw 'a vivid spot of memory in the void of my forgetfulness'.

Shaw, whose name was removed from the title page, had transferred to Tyler the gross fee of five guineas for which he had agreed to do the job 'at my leisure'. The trouble was that, though industrious, he had had no interest in the work, and he had no leisure. Besides his increasing activity in socialism, which kept him well-exercised, writing unpaid pamphlets and making unpaid speeches, he had also during 1885 'slipped into paid journalism'.

This had come about through his friendship with William Archer who, two months younger than Shaw, had already made his name with a charming series of articles on theatre in the *London Figaro*. Working at the British Museum Reading Room in 1883, Archer's attention had been drawn to what appeared as a damaged brown paper parcel on the next seat. This was Shaw. 'There I used to sit day by day,' Archer recalled, 'beside a pallid young man with red hair and beard, dressed in Jaeger all-wool clothing which rather harmonized with his complexion. My interest was excited not only by his appearance, but by the literature to which he devoted himself day after day. It consisted of Karl Marx's *Das Kapital* in French, and a full orchestral score of Wagner's *Tristan und Isolde*.' Before long they were introduced. 'We had many interests in common,' Archer recalled, 'and soon became intimate friends.'

Shaw loved Archer and Archer reciprocated this love. To many of their acquaintances both men seemed dry and remote. But they shared the intimacy of humour, and neither mistook the other's emotional reticence for lack of feeling. Archer's humour, like Shaw's, was a passion often exercised by his own misfortunes. His dour exterior, producing an impression of rigid puritanism, was deceptive. When emotional he grew so wooden that, on the point of tears, he looked like a piece of mahogany. Shaw admired him for his honesty – his unpretentiousness and unbribable integrity. There was no room in their friendship for reciprocal civilities. Equally matched, they teased and chided and fathered monstrous advice on each other freely. The candour of their exchanges, often trenchant in disagreement, was a relief to them both, for they inflicted no malice and received no wounds. They published nothing that they were not prepared to write in their correspondence together; they said nothing to others that they had not argued over together.

But their candour had its frontiers. Both were puritanically dedicated men, not without emotion but without the faculty for expressing this openly in late Victorian England. The generous advice they urged on each other was a tragi-comic reflection of their own inability to change. They teased, goaded, celebrated and admonished each other, and under the device of open disagreement made a secret code of their affection.

They disagreed most on whatever interested them most – particularly the theatre. As dual champions of Ibsen they each regretted that the other was not an Ibsenite, Archer (in Shaw's view) being blinded to Ibsenism by his innocence, Shaw's judgement of Ibsen (Archer saw clearly) being warped by all sorts of extraneous moral considerations. Their mutual criticism was played in the same key and in marvellous counterpoint, for, as Archer put it, 'I think you're doing precisely what you think I'm doing.' Each wanted the other to succeed – and felt that he alone knew how this vicarious quality of success was to be come by. Archer might not be able to combat his high cheek-bones or the outline of his jaw, but he could unbutton the collar that gave 'his head the appearance of being wedged by the neck into a jampot' – and, in doing so, Shaw counselled, strip off his skin of sobriety 'and consent to make an ass of yourself publicly . . .' Shaw, on the other hand, had to do the opposite thing: quell all that reckless extravaganza, grow up, and cease from making an ass of himself in public. 'He loses influence by being such an incorrigible jester,' Archer lamented, 'by wearing the cap and bells in and out of season.' After thirty-five years of advice, Archer was still struggling to redeem him: 'I doubt if there is any case of a man so widely read, heard, seen & known as yourself,' he confided to Shaw in 1921, 'who has produced so little practical effect on his generation . . . The wisdom is *in* you, right enough; it has only to be liberated from the tyrannous, irrepressible idiosyncrasy . . . [this] isn't a sermon – it's an appeal.'

Both had made one awful error: Shaw in writing plays, and Archer in not writing plays. Shaw was the more successful in repairing such absurdity. By accusing his friend of meddling 'in all sorts of controversies in a dilettante way', of loafing 'about the field throwing stones', of failing to give his 'strength to anyone or any cause', he hoped to scold him into shouldering his proper business: 'Why the devil dont you write a play instead of perpetually talking about it?' Goaded by the perpetual stings, when just short of his sixty-fifth birthday, Archer woke up one morning from a dream of a Rajah in the depths of the Himalayas accompanied by his valet – obviously a 'complete scheme for a romantic melodrama,' he revealed to Shaw, 'which only needs your co-operation to be infallibly THE PLAY OF THE CENTURY.' But Shaw collaborated only to the extent of discussing the play with Archer and helping him to transform the dream into a lurid plot 'about an Asiatic Rajah made cynical by a western education, and a Green Goddess who had to be propitiated by blood sacrifices'. *The Green Goddess* became a melodramatic success, partly, Shaw felt, because 'collaboration between us was impossible'. He had learned this when, in the late summer of 1884, he set to work on an earlier theatrical notion of Archer's, which successfully postponed Shaw's outbreak as playwright for another eight years.

With our knowledge of Shaw's practical success in the theatre, it is easy to ridicule the persistence of Archer's cordial discouragement. '. . . Let him cease to recall Mr Shaw from the pond of farcical comedy,' admonished Max Beerbohm in 1898. 'The critic's aim should be to encourage every writer to do what he can do best, what is most natural to him; not to implore him to persist in tasks which (be they never so superior) he will never accomplish.' This was true, but Archer held a higher opinion than Beerbohm of the essential Shaw. In time, however, he came to modify his tactics. He abandoned all attempts either to make

Shaw renounce the stage or 'to make a serious playwright of him'. His plays were *not* plays; Archer had no trouble in spotting this. His friend had dispensed with plot, with character, with drama and with the red corpuscles of life, to demonstrate that argument squeezed into a well-built dramatic machine was as good as any play. So: 'Let us be grateful for him as he is, and . . . enjoy and applaud him. He is not, and he never will be, a great dramatist; but he is something rarer, if not better – a philosophic humorist, with the art of expressing himself in dramatic form.'

Archer was one of Shaw's most percipient critics, but his criticism, presented as friendly and despairing advice, required Shaw to change into someone else (or to reverse the change into G.B.S.). 'Archer knows me so well personally,' Shaw explained, 'that he cannot understand how anybody can read my books without seeing that it is "only Shaw talking," and not literature.' But Archer appreciated his friend's multifarious talent: 'I doubt whether there has ever been a more extraordinary and fascinating combination of gifts in one single human brain,' he acknowledged. He saw through Shaw's optimism; he did not see Shaw's need for optimism. It was the urgency of this need that was driving Shaw to hammer together, like a magical raft, his synthetic philosophy and float lightly upon it over the sea around him. Archer wanted him to abandon this whimsical craft and plunge into the water. But that ran against Shaw's instinct; he could not do it – if he tried he would drown. His nourishment came not from reality as Archer witnessed and experienced it, but from a fantasy that, for all its hard businesslike style, slid along a slice of invisible air. His word-addiction kept him incredibly suspended, and he seldom allowed himself to fall victim to events. But Archer believed this limited his appeal. He would never get a ducking. His audiences might not be able to ignore him but, resenting his superiority, they were resolved never to take him seriously. He was a light creature. '. . . he does not live in the real world,' Archer observed, 'but in an *a priori* world of his own construction.'

'He sees things not as they are, but as it suits him to think they are. His vision is warped by his craving for the unexpected, for the startling, for the paradoxical. He constructs a system, or various systems, and then he fits things into them.

'. . . this subordination of accuracy to preconception and effect is, I believe, what has chiefly prevented Shaw from making himself a real force in the world . . . In philosophical language, the subject obscures the object. The result is that the name George Bernard Shaw suggests to us an erratic, a brilliant – often a really illuminating – meteor, not one of the great fixed stars of thought.'

Archer would occasionally slip along to Shaw's little room on the second floor of 36 Osnaburgh Street, and watch his friend making his cold porridge tepid over a gas fire. Troubled by what he saw, he 'took my affairs in hand,' Shaw recorded, by obliging him to earn some money by journalism. 'It was the easiest thing in the world to get him work, because whatever he did was brilliant,' Archer later wrote, pleased at having diverted Shaw so long from playwriting. He planted him among the reviewing staff of the *Pall Mall Gazette*, where he contributed book reviews from May 1885 to December 1888; he procured him a place on the *Magazine of Music*, which applied to Shaw for articles pretty regularly during the later months of 1884; and he introduced him to an Irishman named Edwin Palmer who, in February 1885, started the *Dramatic Review* and employed Shaw as his music critic. 'My first article appeared in the second number (8/2/-),' Shaw noted in the extended shorthand diary he began keeping that year. 'At first I contributed only signed articles, but later in the year I wrote a set of paragraphs every week for the musical column. The paper ceased to pay in the autumn, and I am now keeping up the paragraphs without any hope of getting paid for them.'

But Shaw was not an easy man to help: the only help he would accept was aid to self-help. 'If Palmer's bankruptcy puts you for the moment in a tight place,' Archer appealed to him, 'I am making more money than I have any present need for, and shall always be glad to help you to keep going until one or other of your argosies comes home. I hope you will not hesitate to let me know if (or when) I can be of any service to you in that way. I shall charge you the same interest as I get at the bank – viz *nil*.' Such help, which Shaw was frequently to offer others in a similar manner, he could never receive himself. Archer, however, had hit on a more delicate ruse. He had been prevailed upon by Edmund Yates, editor of *The World*, through whose columns he had recently begun what Shaw called 'his victorious career' as theatre critic, to double as a critic of art. Knowing nothing about pictures, yet knowing Shaw, Archer invited his friend to accompany him round the galleries. Shaw agreed and, as Archer had anticipated, poured forth a stream of comment and suggestion. Archer listened, then wrote the article and forwarded to Shaw a cheque for £1 6s. 8d., being half his fee. But Shaw, recommending more exercise and earlier hours, at once sent it back. 'My moral ground is this,' he wrote. 'If you are a competent critic, you do not need my assistance. If you are not competent, you are imposing on Yates, and I cannot share the proceeds of a fraud. This, I hope, is conclusive. If it is not, I can easily find a fresh position equally elevated and inexpugnable.' Archer, exasperated by his friend's stubbornness, told him he was a 'damned fool not to accept the money,' adding, 'I certainly should in your position.' Since Archer's incorruptibility was notorious (he even refused to accept performing fees for his translations of Ibsen lest he should compromise his disinterestedness as a critic), this should have been a telling argument when sending the cheque back to Shaw:

'Yates does not want a competent critic of art; what he wants is a man competent to write about art in a particular fashion, and that, with your help, I apparently am. Therefore I am not imposing upon Yates ...

'If you took the trouble to read what I do write you would see that every second idea is yours, while I can assure you that even the ideas which are my own would not occur to me if you were not there ...

'I utterly shrink from going alone to these confounded shows – besides making my writing about them poor & pointless it will make my life a burden to me; and I utterly decline to take you with me except on sharing terms. So be a good fellow & stow your logic.'

But Shaw was proof against this plea: 'Were you to be placed naked in a blast furnace, my decision would be the same.' He re-returned the cheque, 'and if you re-re-return it,' he warned, 'I will re-re-re-return it ...' He then treated Archer to an outpouring of Shavian economics that, by way of Ricardo's Law of rent and Lassalle's Law of wages, concluded that it paid him famously to go without remuneration: 'I have the advantage of seeing the galleries for nothing without the drudgery of writing the articles.' Archer was providing him, to add to his schooling in the National Gallery of Ireland, with a free education and: 'we all grow stupid and mad to just the extent to which we have not been artistically educated.'

The episode is illuminating in that Shaw does not show his friend the crucial reason for his refusal. He offers nothing that can be felt. Archer was bewildered. He had no way of telling that the arrangement he was proposing reproduced for Shaw those ghost-writing days with Lee on *The Hornet*, and threatened to bring back all their misery. It was as if Shaw believed he had been put in the way of a Biblical temptation – and he welcomed it. For he was also being given a second chance and an opportunity to scrub away that tainted year when he had submitted to polite fraud. It was particularly ingenious that he should be tempted by his closest and most honourable friend, and from the worthiest motives. As an admirer of *The Pilgrim's Progress*, Shaw would not have had it differently. It was a soft and amiable corruption to which he was being beckoned, and the first major test of whether his religion of socialism was making a new man of him. Archer, the innocent implement of this trial, is a siren voice: everything he says is reasonable, well-intentioned and brimful of common sense. But Shaw steadfastly refuses, exhilarating in his new strength and knowing that never again will he be seriously assailed by second-hand principles to submit to external circumstances. He is impoverished and free.

Archer, however, was not free. For some weeks he continued to work laboriously as art critic for *The World* 'until my conscience could endure it no longer'. He then persuaded Shaw to do a specimen article which he sent to Yates and which easily secured him the post. In Shavian language, Archer had 'rescued me by a stratagem', having deliberately planned to resign his post as soon as Shaw got a firm hold on it. This, so Archer held, was a lovely essay in *a priori* Shavianism, where true belief becomes a matter of will over chronology.

\*

Shaw held the post of art critic on *The World* from the spring of 1886 to the autumn of 1889. He had in June 1885 started to contribute an 'Art Corner' (covering all the arts) to Annie Besant's *Our Corner*, having met Annie Besant at the Dialectical Society in January 1885, and he continued this column until September 1886. According to Archer, Shaw (who was slightly colour-blind as regards blues and greens) 'didn't know much more about painting than I, but he thought he did, and that was the main point'. Shaw believed that 'my strong point as a critic was my power of analysis'. He was assisted by a critical formula. 'I was capable of looking at a picture then,' he admitted,

'and, if it displeased me, immediately considering whether the figures formed a pyramid, so that, if they did not, I could prove the picture defective because the composition was wrong. And if I saw a picture of a man foreshortened at me in such a way that I could see nothing but the soles of his feet and his eyes looking out between the toes, I marveled at it and almost revered the painter, though veneration was at no time one of my strong points.'

In fact Shaw's column galloped over so many tedious wallfuls of undistinguished work that there was little occasion for analysis. He provided a flow of description along which bobbed much amiable disparagement. 'I have thought once or twice of following Ruskin's example with an "Arrows of the Chace" volume,' he told Holbrook Jackson in 1909. But this was never done and once his art criticism ended, it remained buried. Spaded up a hundred years later, it still glints with his wit and dexterity. 'On art I am prepared to dogmatize; on traffic, ask a pleeceman,' he wrote. It was his comic dogmatism that made these catalogues of pictures so entertaining to readers of *Our Corner* and *The World*:

'In the "Scene from Measure for Measure", Ferdinand [*sic*] undeniably looks bothered; but the tame little nun beside him is not the terrible Isabella of Shakespeare. As Ferdinand's [*sic*] cell has such a pretty look-out, and as he is allowed to keep a dainty mandoline – the pianoforte of the period – he is presumably a first-class misdemeanant. Yet great stress is laid on the unclean condition of his thick hair. To allow a prisoner a mandoline, and deny him a wash, seems inconsistent enough to justify the introduction, in the painter's favourite vein of symbolism, of a bundle of red tape . . .'

'. . . even Mr Watts's "Cain", though attended by a beauteous angel, conveys little more than a disagreeable impression of a very ugly old man with apish hands and an inscrutable problem in artistic anatomy in his supra-clavicular region . . . *"Mariage de Convenance*: After!" is hung in the pet place on the north wall of the second room. A haggard, elderly gentleman in evening-dress sits as nearly supine as a man can stretch himself in a straight-backed chair staring into the dining room fireplace like one conscious of having made a very paltry job of his own affairs. On the wall, dimly visible in the fading daylight, is the portrait of the lady of the house, at sight of whose proud face the sympathetic feminine spectator will exclaim, "Poor fellow!" and the stern masculine moralist, "Serve him right!" . . .'

'Concerning Mr Poynter's "Difference of Opinion", with its expanse of closely-clipped grass glittering in the sun, one can only suggest, not disrespectfully, that it would make a capital advertisement for a lawn-mower . . .'

'Hero's right arm, mathematically a right angle, is artistically a wrong one; and the rock which supports her is too obviously a mere piece of furniture to kneel on. Sir James Linton has painted, with the hand of an artist and the sympathies of a costumier . . . Has the President no feeling for his fellow-men, that he persistently treats them as mere clothes-horses to pile armour and fur upon?'

'Mr Phil Morris's "Storm on Albion's Coast" contains a raging ocean made of what I think is called "tulle" . . . Mr Kennedy has spent much careful work to doubtful advantage on something resembling an East End starveling stuffed into the tail of a stale salmon, and called a mermaid. Miss Dorothy Tennant is reviving the traditional "brown tree" with a vengeance, as a background to her dainty little nude figures. The humorous picture of the year is Mr C. Shannon's "Will he come in?" a group of primeval men in a pond, where they have taken refuge from a red-haired mammoth . . .'

'"Disaster" is the title given by Mr Walter Langley to his scene in a Cornish fishing-village; and, on the whole, I agree . . . The tiger in "Alert" is sitting for its portrait with immense self-satisfaction, and is quite an example to the primeval beasts who used to prowl about Mr Nettleship's canvasses . . .'

'. . . The President's [Walter Crane's] design, in which Mr Gladstone, axe in hand, cuts down a serpent a thousand feet high, is allegory reduced to the desperation of mixed metaphor . . .'

Shaw's two gods in matters of art were Ruskin and Morris. He treated them as models for his own life. Of Ruskin, 'a really great artist-philosopher,' he was to write: 'He begins as a painter, a lover of music, a poet and rhetorician, and presently becomes an economist and sociologist, finally developing sociology and economics into a religion . . . to an almost divine condition.' Even in a small way for *The World*, Shaw considered himself as carrying on Ruskin's business. 'Of course the dilettanti objected,' he told his biographer Archibald Henderson, 'as they objected against Ruskin, that this was not art criticism but moralizing.' But you might as soon divorce mathematics from astronomy, he added, as art from morality. Or from economics. For so long as artists continued to live by the sale of their pictures they had to paint to please the buyer. 'In a society in which we are all striving after the thief's ideal of living well and doing nothing,' Shaw said, '. . . and in which the only people who can afford to buy valuable pictures are those who have attained to this ideal, a great artist with anything short of compulsory powers of attraction must either be a hypocrite . . . or starve.' We looked for no valuable advance in art, he argued, until we looked for an improvement in the beauty of our lives – that is 'until we redistribute our immense Wealth and our immense Leisure so as to secure to every honest man his due share of both in return for his share of the national labour'.

In his role as business expert Shaw enjoyed affronting picture-gallery conventions. 'Did they never teach you that the frame is the most important part of the picture, and a good "trade finish" (like Van Eyck's) its most indispensable quality?' he innocently asked Austin Spare. He advised artists to sell their paintings 'by the foot' and it was for their economics rather than their aesthetics that he praised the members of the New English Art Club: 'These impressionables render us the inestimable service of doing those things which the buyers do not want to be done, and leaving undone those things which the buyers want to be done: consequently there are no commissions in them.' To the painter and potter Phelan Gibb he later explained: 'I can only plead that as I am an economist and not a painter, the criticism is the only one I can offer without impertinence.'

Shaw made what opportunities he could in *The World* and *Our Corner* for tracing the influence of socialism on the grammar of picture dealing. He followed Ruskin's taste as well as his example. 'I went into the National Gallery and spent more than an hour over the Turner drawings in the basement with deep pleasure in them,' he noted in his diary. A roomful of Turner's watercolours, he declared, 'will convince any sceptic that Mr Ruskin's praise of Turner was not excessive'. But he claimed to be as much a politician at the press-view as a Member of Parliament on the hustings: 'I am always electioneering.' Recalling his work as art critic half a dozen years later, he wrote: 'When I was more among pictures than I am at present, certain reforms in painting which I desired were advocated by the Impressionist party, and resisted by the Academic party. Until these reforms had been effectually wrought I fought for the Impressionists – backed up by men who could not draw a nose differently from an elbow against Leighton and Bouguereau – did everything I could to make the public conscious of the ugly unreality of studio-lit landscape and the inanity of second-hand classicism.'

Shaw objected to the 'insistently mundane' exhibitions at Burlington House. The Royal Academy, he wrote, 'has spurned the canvases which its rivals have been glad to hang; and it has selected and conspicuously exhibited the very largest and worst attainable specimens of the picture-shop refuse of 1889, carefully placing these wherever the frames would fit, and wherever the colours would not. It has, indeed, done indescribable things – things that overstrain and paralyse the objurgatory centres, leaving the spectator limply querulous, and the unmoved Council masters of the situation.' In assailing the 'elderly school' of matronly British artists, Shaw claimed to be revenging himself on those who 'for many years outraged my taste for nature until I positively hated the sight of an ordinary picture'. Sometimes he has the air of campaigning vigorously in an election that was already won. By the end of the 1880s the Academy was 'getting a tremendous lesson from the men who are trying to paint no more and no less than they see,' he reported; 'and I am . . . disposed to help to rub that lesson in'.

These men from the rival Society of British Artists were led by Whistler, whom Shaw consequently found himself championing and who 'must be at least as well satisfied as any propagandist in London,' he commented. 'The defeat of his opponents at the [1887] winter exhibitions is decisive. It is not so much that the new school . . . displays the best pictures, as that it puts the old school so hopelessly out of countenance.' This was an example of Shavian electioneering by a critic who privately believed Whistler to be a gentleman painter clever enough to make a merit of not being able to paint a large range of pictures. For even Whistler would have had to recognize that 'there is not half-a-crown's worth of successful or even honest effort in some of the works conspicuously hung in the vinegar and brown paper bower he has made for his followers in Suffolk Street.' Yet their taste was still preferable to the arts of the future President of the Royal Academy, Sir Frederick Leighton, which were 'the arts of the toilet as practised by rich ladies', and when Whistler was ousted from the Presidency of the Society of British Artists by the conservative Wyke Bayliss, Shaw told his readers that 'the public do not gain by the derangement; for this exhibition shows a deplorable falling-off from the standard of the last two'.

One quality that Shaw welcomed in painting was perseverance – the quality on which he was relying as a writer, and which distinguished an artist such as Holman Hunt. But he was ideologically committed to progress and sensed that the notations of Whistler's 'symphonies' and 'harmonies', dashed off in an hour or two, were shorthand messages from the future. At the same time Whistler was Ruskin's enemy, and had declared in his famous *Ten O'Clock* lecture that art was 'selfishly preoccupied with her own perfection only . . . having no desire to teach'. Shaw's art criticism is impressive in its political dexterity. He treats Whistler more as a campaigner-artist than an artist-philosopher.

Closer to his natural taste were the Pre-Raphaelites. 'In surveying the works of a Pre-Raphaelite painter,' his first column of *The World* had opened, 'attitude – mental attitude – is everything. The normal Bond Street attitude would not do: you must become as a little child with a Ruskinised nurse if you wish to enjoy yourself genially, or to utter criticism sympathetic to the painter.' In Shaw's eyes, the merit of Millais's work lay in its colouring; that of Holman Hunt in the laborious perfection of his workmanship. But the prize painter of the Brotherhood was Burne-Jones, who 'has the power to change the character of an entire exhibition by contributing or withholding his work'.

Shaw became critical of some later Pre-Raphaelite work. He could not resist making fun of Holman Hunt ('the facial expression of Mr Holman Hunt's men and women is not so intelligible as that of his goats and sheep') whose imagination 'never takes the British public out of its depth'; he found some difficulty in recognizing as the same man Millais the baronet and the man 'whose aims and motives were of the highest when he was a Pre-Raphaelite brother'; and he stayed to criticize Rossetti, whose 'want of thoroughness as a draughtsman, and the extent to which his favorite types of beauty at last began to reappear as mere Rossettian conventions, with impossible lips and mechanically designed eyebrows, came with something of a shock upon many who had previously fancied him almost flawless'.

The artificial world of the galleries constantly baulked the painter so that, to shake his soul free from false standards, a complete artist and great man such as William Morris stepped naturally 'from the Pre-Raphaelite circle down into the streets'. Shaw despised the art world as he had the circles of society which surrounded it, and he thought most critics were 'babies at their job, and very corrupt and petulant ones at that'.

His advantage over these critics was that, in seeking to encourage art that was nourished by the facts of life without idealistic falsification, he never 'lost sight of my serious relation to a serious public'. This was what he had in common with Ruskin and Morris. At least three times every week he would abscond from literature and art, go down among the Fabians and, like a man bathing himself, 'talk seriously on serious subjects to serious people. For this reason – because I persisted in socialistic propaganda – I never once lost touch with the real world.' The real world without art was deeply unsatisfying to Shaw, but the art world without reality seemed worse. As a compromise he supported the Arts and Crafts movement:

'It has been for a long time past evident that the first step towards making our picture-galleries endurable is to get rid of the pictures – the detestable pictures – the silly British pictures, the vicious foreign pictures, the venal popular pictures, the pigheaded academic pictures, signboards all of them of the wasted talent and perverted ambition of men who might have been passably useful as architects, engineers, potters, cabinet-makers, smiths, or bookbinders. But there comes an end to all things; and perhaps the beginning of the end of the easel-picture despotism is the appearance in the New Gallery of the handicraftsman with his pots and pans, textiles and fictiles, and things in general that have some other use than to hang on a nail and collect bacteria. Here, for instance, is Mr Cobden Sanderson, a gentleman of artistic instincts. Does Mr Cobden Sanderson paint wooden portraits of his female-relatives, and label them Juliet or Ophelia, according to the colour of their hair? No: he binds books, and makes them pleasant to look at, pleasant to handle, pleasant to open and shut, pleasant to possess, and as much of a delight as the outside of a book can be.'

Shaw advertised artists as people who, while apparently providing something that no one wanted, anticipated a demand. That was the ground on which the real value of art to human society must stand. But the real value of art was obscured by its commercial value. If art was to win privileges it must do so by its 'usefulness'. In the utilitarian sense the artist did not answer a need. He was, in the Whistlerian style, satisfying a desire in his own nature and gaining a unique satisfaction in doing so. Yet there was no higher mission and no work more valuable, Shaw maintained, than that of the artist. 'I make no distinction between literature and art,' he said. He saw art and literature as great educators. 'I say that all art at the fountainhead is didactic, and that nothing can produce art except the necessity of being didactic.' Whether it preached or argued, exposed, assured, revealed, consoled, art was a magic and, like Prospero's Ariel, it commanded kings. Through new combinations of sound, new bridges of feeling and rhythms of colour, people absorbed, often instinctively and unknowingly, information that, presented merely as information, they would reject from prejudice or boredom. This was the penetrating power of art, and when Shaw spoke of it he turned naturally to music. 'And great artists, in order to get a hearing, have to fascinate their hearers; they have to provide a garment of almost supernatural beauty for the message they have to deliver. Therefore, when a man has a message to deliver in literature, with great effort and toil he masters words until he can turn them into music.'

This formed part of Shaw's case against Whistler's concept of art. We must not limit art, he argued, to the satisfaction of our desire for beauty. People cannot endure beauty any more than they can endure love. The paradoxical triumph of romanticism was to have drugged us into believing that we worshipped love and beauty even as we struggled to avoid their demands.

'The man who draws to please himself is a wretched – well, what do you call a man who makes love to himself?' Shaw asked the artist Austin Spare, '. . . he who makes revelations and interpretations for other people is quite a useful person.' This distinction was important for Shaw, and he was ingenious in his method of absolving good art from sterile self-love. In an article on the pictures of Holman Hunt, he makes the point that their quality depends not on the efficacy of these canvases as propaganda, but on the earnestness of the artist's intentions. Most of these paintings, Shaw wrote:

'are elaborated beyond the point at which elaboration ceases to be improvement in the eyes of the normal Londoner; but even he must admit the apparent solidity, the convincing power, and the vital glow of these

146

pictures in comparison with the works which artists like M. Bouguereau manage to finish so highly in half as many months as Mr Holman Hunt would spend years. The difference in the result is a tremendous practical rebuke to the doctrine of art for art's sake. Mr Holman Hunt, the catalogue tells us ... painted 'The Hireling Shepherd' 'in rebuke of the sectarian vanities and vital negligences of the nation.' The seriousness of the painter's aim probably did not bring a single Sandemanian into the fold of the Established Church, or induce one woman of fashion to give up tight-lacing (the most familiar form of 'vital negligence'); but it is the secret of the perseverance and conscientiousness which has made this small picture one of the most extraordinary units of a collection that does not contain one square inch of commonplace handiwork.'

Self-respect curdled into self-love, in Shaw's prescription, unless preserved by seriousness: the dilettante was *always* narcissistic. Shaw's hostility to 'art for art's sake' arose from its exclusivity – he could not stir it into his philosophical mixing-bowl. Oscar Wilde appeared the pre-eminent dilettante; the best example of the serious man was William Morris. There was much in Morris to appeal to Shaw. The child lived on in him, and his love of the mediaeval world sprang from his longing to re-achieve those happy years 'when I was a little chap'. He summoned up a vision of the long past, a garden of happiness where nature, in the pattern of leaves and flowers, invaded the rooms: 'it was a positive satisfaction to be in his houses,' Shaw later remembered.

In his pilgrimage through the world, Morris had set his heart on founding a brotherhood that, by seeking mediaeval cures for the malaise of capitalism, would crusade against the squalid confusion of industrial Victorian society and replace it with a regenerated Britain – a green-tree land of gardens, fields and forests. Rossetti had started him off on his career as artist-craftsman; Burne-Jones had provided him with a sympathetic group in which he could feel a sense of fellowship. But 'if Morris's quarrel with society had been no deeper than his friends',' Shaw wrote, 'he would have succeeded Tennyson as Poet Laureate.' In his young days, he had deliberately pursued beauty as part of the Pre-Raphaelite campaign against Britain's proliferating ugliness. Morris thought 'that he had only to produce something beautiful and to force people's attention to it to make them recognise its beauty'. But in later life, art 'ceased to be a commodity which people could find in Burne-Jones's pictures or his own carpets'. His revolutionary politics followed a revolution in his own life to which Shaw's attitude is revealing.

Like Shaw, Morris had an extreme fear of emotional suffering; like Shaw, he identified schools as prisons, locking him out of Eden. But he

147

returned to Eden when, in 1859, he married 'an apparition of fearful and wonderful beauty', Janey Burden, the daughter of a groom. She was given the place of his magical sister Emma, and he dreamed of their inhabiting an enchanted enclosure in the dark adult world. But Janey, after giving birth to two daughters, retired into elegant illness. For her, as for Augustus John's Dorelia, beauty had been a means of emancipation. She looked like a 'figure cut out of a missal,' Henry James said, and had been raised from her simple working-class life to be Queen of the Pre-Raphaelite kingdom, a Blessed Damozel, tragic, imposing, silent – instead of the bright, chatty little woman she naturally was. The insidious adoration of Rossetti made this illusion real, whereas Morris's dream of a re-created childhood focused on his daughters. Besides, his rough temperament and developing interest in the working class seemed to threaten her with a return to the mean conditions of her past. With the loss of her love, a creative joy faded from Morris's life. But Shaw, who always insisted that there was nothing 'discordant' connected with Morris, observed no unhappiness. Janey, he wrote, 'was beautiful, and knew that to be so was part of her household business. His was to do all the talking. Their harmony seemed to me to be perfect. In his set, beauty in women was a cult: Morris had no more reason to be jealous of Rossetti than Mrs Morris of the gloriously beautiful Mrs Spartali, or of Lady Burne-Jones . . .' When Morris, in old age, covered the forests of his wallpapers with whitewash, Shaw did not recognize the extinction of something essential, but signalled a hygienic advance in 'his need for the clean, the wholesome, & the sensible'.

To Shaw, it was as if Morris had woken up from an impossible dream of fair women, opened his eyes on a Ruskinian landscape and strode out over it to reach the communism that 'was part of his commonsense'. He had transferred his hopes from an individual to a collective sphere, achieving fulfilment through the integration of politics and art. No matter that he had little natural aptitude for politics, that he was, in Hyndman's words, 'never satisfied unless he was doing things which, to say the truth, he was little fitted for'. Shaw acknowledged his position as head of the Socialist League to be 'absurdly false', recommending that he be treated with marked consideration as 'a privileged eccentric and in no way an authority as to socialist policy' – almost exactly in the same manner as the Labour Party was later to regard G.B.S. himself. What Shaw celebrated in Morris was the move from poetry into prophecy. Contrasting Morris with Keats, he pictures Keats, the purely 'literary poet' who pens his lines on fauns and nymphs and dryads and swains, as the sort of writer he himself might have become had he stayed daydreaming in Ireland. Instead he had followed the way of Morris, 'for whom poetry is only a means to an end, the end being to deliver a message which clamors to be revealed through him. So he secures a hearing for it by clothing it with world-garments of such beauty, authority, and eternal memorableness, that the world must needs listen to it. These are prophets rather than poets; and for the sake of being poets alone would not take the trouble to rhyme love and dove or bliss and kiss.'

Morris was the clearest case of a hero in the Shavian iconoclastic world. Shaw recognized him as a natural leader – someone in whom child and man coexisted, who combined individual genius with collectivist principles, who gave inspiration and example. Shaw was a natural hero-worshipper, determinedly on guard against this tendency in himself. But he trusted Morris and felt wonderfully at home at his house on Hammersmith Terrace. Here he met many kindred spirits – men such as Sydney Cockerell and Walter Crane – and in this sympathetic and exciting atmosphere the exhilarating enjoyableness of his own personality bloomed.

Instead of Wilde's aesthetics for the élite, here was a man who worked with others on behalf of everyone – a man who wanted to bring applied arts and the perspective of beauty into all life. The 'idle singer of an empty day' had grown into the busy singer of a bursting day. Morris was a visionary who, like Keats, wanted to reveal 'the principle of beauty in all things'. But was he also a practical man? Shaw believed that the artist's wares had to be marketed in the knowledge that most customers hated beauty because, as a reflection of love, it could hurt them. The secret in his poet's heart is the knowledge of how to live without love. But though his capacity for loving was undeveloped, Shaw did not lack emotion. Cunningly fenced off behind some of the most brilliantly unsentimental prose in the language, is plenty of feeling. His criticism is never embittered or cynical; and his generosity, whether in protest or sermon, argument or flight of nonsense, is directed at rallying us to spectacular improvement. Everywhere implied is Shaw's faith in the employment of the arts, which eventually expressed itself in a puritan encyclical:

'The claim of art to our respect must stand or fall with the validity of its pretension to cultivate and refine our senses and faculties until seeing, hearing, feeling, smelling and tasting become highly conscious and critical acts with us, protesting vehemently against ugliness, noise, discordant speech, frowsy clothing, and re-breathed air, and taking keen interest and pleasure in beauty, in music and in nature, besides making us insist, as necessary for comfort and decency, on clean, wholesome, handsome fabrics to wear and utensils of fine material and elegant workmanship to handle. Further, art should refine our sense of character and conduct, of justice and sympathy, greatly heightening our self-knowledge, self-control, precision of action, and considerateness, and making us intolerant of baseness, cruelty, injustice and intellectual superficiality or vulgarity. The worthy artist or craftsman is he who serves the physical and moral senses by feeding them with pictures, musical compositions, pleasant houses and gardens, good clothes and fine implements, poems, fictions, essays and dramas which call the heightened senses and ennobled faculties into pleasurable activity. The great artist is he who goes a step beyond the demand, and, by supplying works of a higher beauty and a higher interest than have yet been perceived, succeeds after a brief struggle with its strangeness, in adding this fresh extension of sense to the heritage of the race.'

# [ 3 ]

*. . . experience has taught me that people who are much admired often get wheedled or persecuted into love affairs with persons whom they would have let alone if they themselves had been let alone.*

These words appear in a short story, 'Don Giovanni Explains', that Shaw wrote in the summer of 1887. He makes use in this story of his experiences with women over the past three years to find the best truth available to him. Don Giovanni's ghostly narrative explains away his reputation. Like Shaw, he had been born a shy man, but

'. . . my indifference to conventional opinions, and a humorously cynical touch in conversation, gained me from censorious people the names atheist and libertine; but I was in fact no worse than a studious and rather romantic freethinker. On rare occasions, some woman would strike my young fancy; and I would worship her at a distance for a long time, never venturing to seek her acquaintance. If by accident I was thrown into her company, I was too timid, too credulous, too chivalrously respectful, to presume on what bystanders could plainly perceive to be the strongest encouragement; and in the end some more experienced cavalier would bear off the prize without a word of protest from me. At last a widow lady at whose house I sometimes visited, and of whose sentiments towards me I had not the least suspicion, grew desperate at my stupidity, and one evening threw herself into my arms and confessed her passion for me. The surprise, the flattery, my inexperience, and her pretty distress, overwhelmed me. I was incapable of the brutality of repulsing her; and indeed for nearly a month I enjoyed without scruple the pleasure she gave me, and sought her company whenever I could find nothing better to do. It was my first consummated love affair; and though for nearly two years the lady had no reason to complain of my fidelity, I found the romantic side of our intercourse, which seemed never to pall on her, tedious, unreasonable, and even forced and insincere except at rare moments, when the power of love made her beautiful, body and soul.'

There were three categories of relationship in Shaw's life: flirtations with single women, usually at this time young Fabian girls; philanderings with the wives of friends, usually socialist colleagues; and a consummated love affair with a divorced or separated lady. With Alice Lockett he had tried in a conventional way to combine all his emotional needs in one person, and failing, concluded that it could not be done. On 29 September 1888, more than three years after they had parted, Alice spent the day with Shaw in London. He was more successful now, his life crowded and interesting. 'I sang some of the old *Figaro* bits with Alice, who presently went home,' he noted in his diary, 'overcome, I think, by old associations.'

There was no chance of Shaw being overcome: he overcame. William Archer, who sometimes trailed after him to the Fabian Society, noticed how his friend, though genuinely bent on self-improvement, 'liked to feel himself a triton among the minnows and enjoyed the little thrill of expectancy that always ran through the company when he got onto his feet'. William Rothenstein observed that 'he did not wait until he was famous to behave like a great man . . .' He had plumed himself into a dazzling lecturer, enthralling his audiences with his vitality, humour, and the cadence of his speech. He was marvellously adroit too in debate, retaliating against hecklers with amazing speed, catching their sallies in mid-air like a conjurer and returning them. If he appeared detached from the present, he was passionately involved in the hypothetical future. On the platform he looked like a Jaeger Christ. The expectations he released in many aspiring socialists are beautifully caught by a young Fabian called Grace Black. 'People are so exceedingly miserable in every class, that I should lose hope if I did not know there are many who devote themselves entirely to trying to make things better,' she wrote to him.

'. . . you have a greater power of seeing truth than most people: you can do more than most. It is impossible to help expecting a great deal from you and now is the point – don't fail – please don't. For one thing I don't know how I could bear it – but that is not the point. What I fear is that you do not care for nor believe in people sufficiently, and you won't be able to understand them unless you do, and your socialism must be warped if you don't understand human nature ... do care more for people for that is where you seem to fail.'

Shaw recognized at once a case of Fabian love. He could diagnose love as efficiently as a doctor identifying death. Shaw's objection to it was part of his socialist hatred of private property. The lover who heaped his victim with virtues and blinded himself to everyone else was a deeply conservative person. People said that all the world loved a lover: the truth was that a lover loved all the world, and therein lay his crime. Providing we were in love, the world was a fine place, and we condoned its awfulness. But if Shaw, as Grace Black thought, had a special power of seeing truth, he believed it was because he had resisted this blurred and devouring passion. That we needed to love, he knew. But he represented the *partiality* of romantic love as a perversion of our deepest desire. For it was not to this person, then to that person, but to the whole world that we owed the comprehension of love. The world, however, was not ready for love. True love, for the time being, was best represented by the love of good work and (so he later divined) by the activity of the Life Force – methods of populating and improving the future. To renounce the indulgence of loving was in itself an act of love – the act of deferred love we call faith.

Grace Black had asked for no answer – 'if you sent me one, you might make me unhappy,' she told him. 'If you think it needs an excuse (which I don't) say its because I care for socialism.' But Shaw could not let this alone; it linked sentiment and socialism in a fashion disturbing to him. If such qualities were to be combined, it would have to be in a new metaphysical way. It was enough for him to prove the falsity of Grace Black's argument by accusing her of being in love with him. 'Wrote several letters particularly one to Grace Black,' his diary entry of 28 May 1887 reads. In fact he sent his first letter to her by return of post. Her reply was a rebuke:

'I guessed you would think I was in love with you. So I am, but that has nothing to do with my letter and it is a pity if that thought has clouded my meaning. My personal happiness is certainly connected with your success as a teacher of socialism, & in a less degree with that of Hyndman & Morris, because I care very much for what is implied to me by socialism. But apart from that I do love you, & why do you wish to dissuade me from that and from believing in you? ... You are not right if you are irritated about the matter: there is no cause for it. There is nothing in my attitude, of humility, dependence or expectancy which would give reason for irritation ... You will be really wrong if what I say displeases you. Of course, *of course*, I do not mind whether you care about me or not. I can't imagine you doing so, & if you did I shld be unhappy (not your fault: but it wd be so unsuitable). But it is true that I wish that love were an easier & simpler thing than it is now; but that is to wish for heaven ... You are not much older than me, but all experience is to the bad. I am serious.'

Shaw's experience of love had been 'to the bad', and from Grace Black's feelings he took care to protect himself. When he sees her he notes the fact in his diary; and once, after a lecture on 'The Unemployed', they walk off together, absorbed in each other's company, to the wrong destination. His description of Grace's announcement in 1889 of her marriage is a good example of inverted Shavian romanticism: she 'sent me a note to say what she was going to do,' he wrote, 'adding, by way of apology for throwing me over, that she could never marry a man she loved'. The letter he actually received read as follows:

'You know that the reason I began to love you was because I believed you cared more for truth and would do more to help socialism than any other man ... Long ago I saw that my love for you was a waste of force, because you were so different to me: but it is only lately I have been able to love anyone else. I do now, and am engaged to marry Edwin Human a socialist ... You have a place deep in my heart: my feelings have run through all the personal currents in respect of you and can't go back but have ended as they began in something quite impersonal, rather painful but in a way sacred.

Yrs very sincerely Grace Black'

For Shaw, if not for Grace Black, the inhuman love they shared was rarer and more imaginative than married love: it was *romance*, which the contract of marriage could never be. Meeting Grace some years after her marriage, he records: 'She looked extraordinarily youthful; she has children; her marriage is obviously as happy as it is possible for a marriage to be; her husband no more grudges her her adorations than he grudges her a motor car.' In casting himself as a piece of extra-marital machinery, Shaw re-creates what he hoped were the circumstances of his own Dublin household. There are, he recounts, 'respectable married ladies, who adore me & tell me so, and are no doubt much the better for it, since I take care that they are none the worse, and should lose their adoration if I didnt. And their husbands know it, and bless me for feeding their wives' imaginations & relieving them of the strain of being the family idol.'

One family to have benefited from Shaw's interference had been the Beattys. Among others by now were the Avelings and the Blands. At the head of all three families was a husband notorious for his illicit love affairs. What sort of man was Edward Aveling? According to Shaw, the answer from anyone who knew Aveling was a shriek of laughter and the question: 'How much have you lent him?' Shaw, who was later to place him on the stage as Louis Dubedat in *The Doctor's Dilemma* for all the early Fabians to recognize, enjoyed dramatizing Aveling as the man who, while being spoiled for all social purposes by 'a hopeless and incorrigible deficiency in ordinary moral fibre', would have 'gone to the stake bravely rather than admit that Marx was not infallible or that God existed'. He had no conscience in his private life. 'He seduced every woman he met,' Shaw wrote, 'and borrowed from every man.' But, being a rather charming fellow, he managed to remain popular. He had been particularly popular with Mrs Besant, having shared with her and Charles Bradlaugh the control of the National Secular Society. But as he grew more interested in politics he turned his attention to Karl Marx's youngest daughter, Eleanor. Shaw used to see this clever dark-haired girl at the British Museum, working for eighteen pence an hour as a literary hack, and had also been attracted to her. In June 1884 she decided to go and live with Aveling on the understanding that they would marry if his wife died. For Shaw, who regarded himself as unattractive, here was a revelation. 'Though no woman seemed able to resist him,' he wrote of Aveling, 'he was short, with the face and eyes of a lizard, and no physical charm except a voice like a euphonium.' Like Wilkes, he was only a quarter of an hour behind the handsomest man in Europe. Shaw seemed determined to pursue this mystery. Aveling, who claimed to be an Irishman and an Ibsenite, wrote plays under the name of Alec Nelson. 'Made an attempt to act in a 3rd rate comedy at Notting Hill with the Avelings on the 30th January,' Shaw noted at the beginning of his 1885 diary. Since Aveling worked on the staff of the *Dramatic Review*, Shaw was often able to call at his home, but his diary reveals that it was Eleanor (or 'Mrs Aveling') he came to see. She responded to him, but was not sure what to make of him. 'If you are mad,' she wrote, 'there is marvellous method in your madness & penetration that sanity wd gambol from ... oh, most amiable and sympathetic of cynics.' She would appeal to him to save her 'from a long day and evening of tête-à-tête with myself', and he responded.

'*17 February*   Called on the Avelings ... Talked with Mrs A between 17 and 18 (A went out shortly after I came in).

'*28 February*   Mrs Aveling asked me to call in the afternoon and have a chat. Went at 17 and stayed until 20 nearly. Aveling absent at Crystal Palace concert. Urged her to go on the stage. Chatted about this, death, sex, and a lot of things.

'*9 March*   Wrote article on the future of marriage for *The Commonweal*. Left it at Aveling's and found Mrs A. & Mrs Bland there.

'*12 March*   Corrected article for *Commonweal* as suggested by Mrs Aveling . . . Called on Mrs Aveling. Aveling came in.

'*28 March*   Went to Mrs Aveling and discussed *Love Among the Artists* with her.

'*3 April*   Called on the Avelings in the evening. A[veling] bad with indigestion.

'*14 April*   Called on the Avelings – A[veling] at Ventnor: Eleanor at home: stayed with her from 17 to 19.45.

'*20 June*   After meeting on musical pitch called on Mrs Aveling. Aveling came in later on. Went home and played all the evening.

'*24 August*   Rumour of split between the Avelings mentioned by [ J. M.] Robertson.'

And so on, though much less often. For Shaw had recoiled at the news that the Avelings might separate. His instinct whispered retreat, and it was right. The flare-up of the Avelings' later history exposed everything he most feared about sexual passion. In 1897, following the death of his wife, Aveling secretly married Eva Frye, afterwards blackmailing Eleanor with threats of his intended marriage and of revealing the scandal of Marx's illegitimate son if she did not give him money. Then, following an anonymous letter that told her Aveling had been married, Eleanor poisoned herself. 'My last word to you,' she wrote in her suicide note, 'is the same as I have said during all these long, sad years – love.' But Shaw could not endure the infliction of such love and eliminated it from his tight little note on her death, referring to 'the news of Eleanor Marx's suicide in consequence of Aveling having spent all her money'.

As he began easing out of the Avelings' home, so he had started to infiltrate more deeply the marriage of the Blands. Hubert Bland had been a founder of the Fabian Society, was its first treasurer and responsible for Shaw's recruitment. A precociously ruined brush manufacturer and aspiring journalist, he had the monocled air (though his grandfather was a plumber) of having descended from aristocratic beginnings. No one dared be uncivil to him. He was a man of Norman exterior, imperialist instincts, and huge physical strength, with a tremendous military front and a voice like the scream of an eagle. But to Shaw he seemed 'an affectionate, imaginative sort of person'. In everything except politics he was resolutely Conservative – he was the first of a new breed of 'Tory Socialist'. Like Hyndman, he wore Tory clothes and 'never was seen without an irreproachable frock coat, tall hat, and a single eyeglass which infuriated everybody'.

Bland was uniquely valuable to the Fabians. 'He is always against a foolish proposal, and never against a humane one,' Shaw wrote. 'He knows the suburban Tory through and through; and the suburban Tory is a tremendous factor in English society.' With his different background and personality, he exerted a steadying influence on Fabian policy. But what irritated the Executive was Bland's habit of blackballing recruits on tenuous moral grounds, since they knew him for a virile polygamist. 'Hubert was not a restful husband,' Shaw conceded. He had married his wife, Edith Nesbit, in 1880, when she was twenty-one and seven months pregnant, and subsequently had children by two other women. The first of these women Edith befriended; the second, Alice Hoatson, already was her friend and a part of the Bland household, where, by the tradition of family nicknames she remained 'Mouse' to Edith's 'Cat', and where her daughter Rosamund was brought up by Edith as her own child. The Blands' home in Lee, on the south-east perimeter of London, was a disorganized ménage in the bohemian style, where the conglomeration of parties, charades, music and children formed a refreshing contrast to the sterner Fabian entertainments. Shaw would slip on boxing-gloves and dance round, pawing at the short-sighted, muscle-bound Bland who was incapable of deliberately hurting anyone. 'I was taller by a couple of inches and with longer reach,' Shaw calculated. And Edith watched.

She watched Shaw, observing him to be 'simply irresistible'. According to Edward Pease, Edith was acknowledged as 'the most attractive and vivacious woman of our circle', though burdened with spectacular fainting fits and, at supreme moments of Fabian drama, the habit of calling sensationally for glasses of water. On Shaw's medical advice she took to 'delicious' woollen clothes; she also close-cut her hair, abstained from corsets (a false method of 'girding the loins'), rolled her cigarettes which she smoked from a long holder, and looked every inch an advanced woman. 'On the other hand,' Shaw believed, 'she is excessively conventional; and her ideas are not a woman's ideas, but the ideas which men have foisted, in their own interest, on women.' Her domestic virtues and the indulgent love she gave her blusterous husband, despite many shocks and troubles, kept their home together.

She was soon confiding these shocks and troubles to Shaw. 'Another chat with Mrs Bland,' he noted in his diary, '. . . about children and how to treat them.' Sometimes she would invite him to tea by telegram, but more often she met him at the British Museum, and they would go for long striding walks. 'Mrs Bland came to museum,' ran a typical note on 7 August 1885. 'Walked with her to Charing Cross . . . Missed two trains at

Cannon St. talking.' By the summer of 1886 these meetings had grown longer and more intricate. 'On the whole the day was devoted to Mrs Bland,' Shaw wrote on 26 June 1886. 'We dined together, had tea together, and I went out to Lee with her and played and sang there until Bland came in from his volunteer work. A memorable evening!'

Edith, who was to become famous as a writer of stories for children, appealed to Shaw partly because she retained so much of the child in her. In the 1880s she wrote poetry. 'The faults of the poems are so directly and intimately the faults of the woman,' Shaw wrote in a review of her *Lays and Legends* (1886), '. . . there is too much of the luxury of unreal grief, of getting into the vein by imagining churchyards and jiltings and the like . . . the best of these Lays and Legends plainly owe their quick vitality to the sting of personal experience . . . lightened by an occasional dash of humourous shrewishness.' Shaw knew her verses intimately, since he composed music to some of them, and among the latest were love poems addressed to himself. The necessity for making money obliged her to publish these poems, though not before doctoring them, with Shaw's aid, for the public – changing a reference to his 'white malign face' to 'dark malign face'.

He *was* maddening – 'the grossest flatterer (of men women and children impartially) I ever met,' she called him. '[He] is horribly untrustworthy as he repeats everything he hears, and does not always stick to the truth, and is *very plain* . . . and yet is one of the most fascinating men I ever met.' Having yielded herself to this bewitchment with Shaw, she pursued him to his lair in the British Museum. He would hurry her out to pretty scenes on the river and in the park; give her tea in the Wheatsheaf; see her on to buses and trains. She would versify and he would talk. Then, on their way to Baker Street Station one day, they called in at Shaw's home. Next morning, while he was contemplating breakfast, she returned – but he would not let her in. 'I met her at Portland Rd Station at 10 and we took a walk in Regent's Park for an hour.' From then on it became a struggle for her to get into his house, and for him to keep her walking in the open air. If, on their way to some bus stop or railway station, he needed to leave his books at home, she accompanied him inside and beckoned him upstairs; at other times he went on grimly walking through all weathers, hour after hour, till she dropped exhausted and veered off home at 3.30 a.m. It was an exercising business. On 15 September she won a notable Pyrrhic victory. 'Mrs Bland came to the museum in the afternoon and would not be denied coming here to tea. Drove her to London Bridge and walked back.' For six weeks after this they recovered themselves, getting their breath back until at lunch at the Wheatsheaf on 25 October, having softened him with a visit to her childhood home, Edith boldly challenged Shaw to meet her at King's Cross that evening and walk her off her feet. They met punctually in pouring rain; took trains – he searching for crowded carriages, she for empty ones; went by underground; and walked deep into the night. They got so wet that he felt obliged to buy her hot whisky, but he outlasted her and, by the early hours of the morning, she surrendered her body to a single bed in Pentonville.

Some months that winter it seemed as if Mrs Bland was spending more time in the Reading Room with Shaw than at home with her husband, and it became increasingly difficult to detect in Bland the overflowing gratitude Shaw claimed such husbands lavished on him. 'Mrs Bland at museum,' read Shaw's diary entry for 6 December 1886. 'Bland came in later and looked rather sulky.' Shaw's passport to the Blands was the belief that his influence produced a similar steadying effect on their marriage as Bland produced in the Fabians. His presence was a warning, but not a danger, to Bland. He hoped, by everything short of a sexual relationship, to give Edith compensation for her husband's infidelities. But she protested to him: 'You had no right to write the Preface if you were not going to write the book.' She was anxiously determined – he had made her determined – to bring matters to a climax. On 11 May 1887, finding him hunched over More's *Utopia* in the Reading Room, she marched him out to tea at the Austrian Café and insisted on leading him off to his home. Shaw did not want this but, believing his mother to be there, he agreed. His mother was out. There followed 'an unpleasant scene caused by my telling her that I wished her to go, as I was afraid that a visit to me alone would compromise her'. She went – but the friendship survived this unyielding politeness – and the marriage endured. For Shaw, in his fashion, was a true friend of this marriage, rather than the ally of one partner. In 1914, when Bland was dying and felt troubled as to whether there would be enough money for the education of one of his sons, he told his daughter: 'If there is not enough, ask Shaw' – and indeed it was Shaw who paid for John Bland to go to Cambridge. Anyone who knew Shaw, knew his generosity.

Many people who knew him, and knew something of his flirtations with Eleanor Marx Aveling, Grace Black and Edith Bland, wondered if he were asexual. This, if a Shavian ideal, was not the reality of his life. 'I was, in fact, a born philanderer, a type you don't understand,' he later told Frank Harris. In his play *The Philanderer* he was to portray himself in the part of Leonard Charteris, whom he described as 'the real Don Juan'. With married women and Fabian girls, Shaw still philandered. But Mrs Jane Patterson, an enterprising widow, was to make a Don Juan out of him.

*

'Jenny' Patterson, as she was called, was a particular friend of Shaw's mother from whom she took singing lessons. Some fifteen years older than Shaw, she was closer in age to Mrs Shaw than to her son and may have known the family in Ireland where she had been married to a well-to-do country gentleman. After his death, she moved to London and by 1885 was living in Brompton Square. Mrs Shaw often called on her there and Jenny Patterson regularly returned these visits so that Shaw, coming home from the British Museum, would find the two women together. Sometimes he joined them singing, sometimes he escorted Mrs Patterson to her bus home; but there seems to have been no romantic interest on his part – he had nicknamed her 'Mrs Chatterbox' – until after his father's death on 15 April 1885. Almost at once their relationship changed. On 20 April, finding Mrs Patterson at home when he returned, he 'wasted all the evening' with her – the first entry of this sort in his diary. Seven days later occurs a note of his visiting her alone in Brompton Square: 'Went to Richter concert in the evening, but instead of waiting for the symphony went on to Mrs Patterson. Found her alone, and chatted until past midnight.' Their developing romance was, so Shaw later gave out, a matter of appearances. Up to the time he was twenty-nine, he told Ellen Terry, 'I was too shabby for any woman to tolerate me.'

'I stalked about in a decaying green coat, cuffs trimmed with the scissors, terrible boots, & so on. Then I got a job to do & bought a suit of clothes with the proceeds. A lady immediately invited me to tea, threw her arms round me, and said she adored me. I permitted her to adore, being intensely curious on the subject. Never having regarded myself as an attractive man, I was surprised; but I kept up appearances successfully.'

The clothes with which Shaw tells his story, while fashioning an outline of the truth, also conceal something. At the beginning of his 1885 diary he had written, under the heading 'Fads etc': 'Took to the woollen clothing system, and gave up using sheets in bed.' He had been persuaded to 'rational dress' by an Austrian political refugee and friend of William Morris, Andreas Scheu, an advocate of Dr Gustave Jaeger's sanatory system, who was setting up a Jaeger business in the City. Jaeger expected to regenerate the world by wool. He claimed to have tried out his wool-theories on himself and to have been restored by them from a sick creature – 'fat and scant of breath' with haemorrhoids and tendencies to indigestion – to a man who everywhere inspired affection. It was Jaeger's belief that good health depended upon the disposal of poisons in the body through the exhalations of the skin. He condemned linen, cotton, silk and all dead vegetable fibres for driving these bodily exhalations back on themselves, absorbing noxious vapours and befouling the air. In their place he substituted wool, hair, feathers and ornaments derived from the animal kingdom which orchestrated these fumes into wholesome sweetness. Jaeger was no martinet; he relaxed sufficiently to allow indigo and cochineal dyes, if tested for purity, to be used for Sunday visiting in winter. But those wishing to be hygienically irreproachable had no option but to recognize vegetable and aniline dyes as evil, and replace flannel with unbleached and knitted natural wool worn next to the skin. Shaw, who recognized in Jaeger another Vandeleur Lee, was enthusiastically converted. Twelve years later he was to write to Ellen Terry: 'My much ridiculed Jaegerism is an attempt at cleanliness & porousness: I want my body to breathe. I have long resigned myself to dust & dirt & squalor in external matters . . . but I always have the window wide open night & day; I shun cotton & linen & all fibrous fabrics that collect odors, as far as my person is concerned.'

Shaw ordered his first Jaeger outfit on 19 June 1885 – 'the first new garments I have had for years'. He did not however buy them, as subsequently remembered, with money earned through journalism. 'These will be paid for out of the insurance on my father's life,' he noted in his diary. The reddish-brown Jaeger suit was to become part of his physical personality – 'as if it were a sort of reddish brown fur,' G. K. Chesterton observed, '. . . like the hair and eyebrows, a part of the animal'. The uniform was finished off with correct knee-breeches and stockings after a formula devised by Dr Jaeger to replace the insalubrious tubes of trousers. This was the Shavian equivalent to Oscar Wilde's aesthetic costumes.

Many of Jaeger's most faithful sanatorians and 'Woolleners', as they were called, came from among the Fabians and members of the Fellowship of the New Life, who paid fastidious attention to diet and clothes, eating vegetables and wearing animals. Edward Carpenter, the celebrated apostle of sandals, in his harrowing descriptions of injurious upper-class attire, wrote of 'the pure human heart grown feeble and weary in its isolation and imprisonment, the sexual parts degenerated and ashamed of themselves, the liver diseased, and the lungs straitened down to mere sighs and conventional disconsolate sounds beneath their cerements'. In his writings at least, as Robert Skidelsky has pointed out, Carpenter 'attached more importance to liberating the feet than the sexual parts'. But Shaw advertised his brown woollen combination as being 'the plumes and tunic of Don Juan' and so irresistible to women that almost anyone could knit himself into popularity. In fact it seems to have been less a matter of women regarding him so very favourably in wool as of the woollen Shaw looking at women more confidently. Mrs Patterson, for example, was no longer 'Mrs Chatterbox' but Blanche Sartorius from *Widowers' Houses* – a well-dressed, well-fed, good-looking woman, all the more attractive for being vital and energetic rather than (like Alice Lockett) refined. She had brown hair, black eyes, a 'remarkable bust' and voluptuous temper, the ferocity of which, Shaw sensed, was erotic.

On 30 June, he 'got clothes from Jaeger's and put them on'. Next day he caught a cold but by 4 July was sufficiently recovered to call on Mrs Patterson in the evening. She was out, but he came back later that night and stayed there till one o'clock. 'Vein of conversation decidedly gallant,' he logged in his diary. Over the next three weeks he visited her constantly. She provoked him, taunted him, half-defying and half-inviting him to advance, and he seemed spellbound. 'Supper, music and curious conversation,' he noted on 10 July after another evening in Brompton Square, 'and a declaration of passion. Left at 3. *Virgo intacta* still.' But only just. For these evenings were unlike his visits into other people's love lives. There he had been Vandeleur Lee, the chaste wizard; here, dressed in the clothes from his father's life insurance and with his mother's closest friend, he could re-enact and improve on the romance of George Carr Shaw and Lucinda Elizabeth. The sheer happiness Jenny felt in her love drew him in. On 18 July he bought some contraceptives ('French letters 5/-') which, on examination, 'extraordinarily revolted me' – so much that in the evening at Jenny's there were 'forced caresses' instead of love-making. Much of this must have been known to Lucinda Shaw. She and Jenny had spent most of 25 July together when, in the evening, Shaw came across them walking along the Brompton Road 'looking for a bus, but they were all full,' he noted. 'So, on the corner of Montpelier St. Mother went on by herself, and I returned to the Square with JP, and stayed there until 3 o'clock on my 29th birthday which I celebrated by a new experience. Was watched by an old woman next door, whose evil interpretation of the lateness of my departure greatly alarmed us.'

In his imagination, Shaw seems to have been strongly attracted to the love-making that in practice sometimes disgusted him. He had been starved of sex. 'I was an absolute novice,' he wrote in his diary. 'I did not take the initiative in the matter.' During his 'teens and twenties he had been 'perfectly continent except for the involuntary incontinences of dreamland'. All these years he exercised his imagination in daydreams about women, but not until Jenny Patterson broke through his celibacy did he know the power of sex. He resented this power she had over him which unsteadied his self-sufficiency and exposed his loneliness. 'The spell of your happiness has been potent.' But when the spell evaporated, he was filled with mortification. Love un-Shavianized him, robbed him of his authority and the hard discipline of work through which he was trying to re-create himself. In retrospect his embraces with Jenny became part of a furious wrestling match between her possessiveness and his independence. His diary entries over the next weeks indicate the ambivalence of his feelings, the lassitude, the guilt and the obsession.

'*27 July*    No work done. Went to Museum and wrote a letter to JP . . .

'*2 August*    Did nothing but write a few letters. Went in the evening to JP.

'*3 August*    Wrote full circumstantial account of affair with JP to E. McN[ulty] . . . Spent the evening with Sidney Webb at Colonial Office. He told me about his love affair and disappointment. Wrote a rather fierce letter to JP on my return.

'*4 August*    Did nothing practically. Called on Eleanor Aveling in the afternoon. Resolved to begin new *Pilgrim's Progress* at once . . . Wrote JP in reply to her answer to yesterday's explosion.

'*5 August*    Alice Lockett and Mrs Shenstone here in the morning. Wrote the beginning of *Pilgrim's Progress* . . . to JP to eat and make love until 1.20.

'*7 August* . . . saw May Morris in the window of the Socialist League and went in for a few minutes. JP here when I returned. Hurried off to Mrs Besant's.

'*8 August* . . . Went to JP in the evening.

'*10 August* . . . JP came. To dinner at 16 then to Jaeger's where I ordered a knitted woollen suit. Mother and JP at Jaeger's too. After tea went home with JP & stayed until five minutes before midnight.'

He saw her every week, ending the day with her at Brompton Square and walking back home in the early hours. There would be intervals when she went out of town, usually to her cottage in Broadstairs where she often invited Mrs Shaw. But when she returned, the entries in Shaw's diary would start up again: 'Called on JP'; 'Went to JP in the evening'; 'JP here when I came home. Walked to Brompton Square with her.' He did not always come to her by arrangement – that would admit too much. He turned up whenever he could not stay away – she hardly knew when it might be. Sometimes he came when she would have preferred him not to: 'You will not believe me I know,' she was to write to him, 'but it is absolutely true that often my body has been an unwilling minister to you.' At other times he refused to come when she invited him; or he would arrive so late that she was asleep and he would stand in the square looking up at the unlit windows.

In the shorthand diaries where he listed his expenditure on food and travel, he also noted in code the number of times he and Jenny made love: once on 2 and 10 August; twice on 16 and 22 August – and so on. 'Sexual experience seemed a natural appetite,' G.B.S. wrote forty years later, 'and its satisfaction a completion of human experience necessary for fully qualified authorship.' The author (who would claim, in *Overruled*, to be the first playwright to put sexual intercourse on the stage) learned about the demands and excitements of loving; and he learned the wiles of self-protection. 'Only by intercourse with men and women,' he reasoned, could we learn humanity. 'This involves an active life, not a contemplative one; for unless you do something in the world, you can have no real business to transact with men; and unless you love and are loved, you can have no intimate relations with them. And you must transact business, wirepull politics, discuss religion, give and receive hate, love, and friendship with all sorts of people before you can acquire the sense of humanity.'

'I wanted to love,' he wrote, 'but not to be appropriated . . .' He wanted Jenny to strengthen him by taking the edge off his lust so that he was unassailable in his Fabian flirtations and with those wives into whose marriages he had introduced himself as the favourite son. Whenever he felt restless, he looked to her to settle him; but he forbade her to distract him from his work. 'I was never duped by sex as a basis for permanent relations, nor dreamt of marriage in connection with it,' he insisted. 'I put everything else before it, and never refused or broke an engagement to speak on Socialism to pass a gallant evening.' This was a point of principle with Shaw, and he took some trouble to spell it out to Jenny as honestly as he could. He tried to be unkind – and he succeeded; but then he would relent and afterwards regret it. Feeling too much physical need of her to break off the affair, he aimed at the paradoxical triumph of making her end it, but only provoked her to greater emotional dependence on him. However superior to sex he made himself out to be, once the Fabian meetings were over, he would often find himself, like a sleepwalker, back at her house. 'Went to JP's,' he wrote in his diary on 9 January 1886. 'Revulsion.' But three days later he was there making love to her again. 'Went to JP in the evening and there met T. Tighe Hopkins. He was bent on seduction, and we tried which should outstay the other. Eventually he had to go for his train . . . To bed late.'

'What a fascinating & charming lady your friend Mrs Patterson is!' May Morris told Shaw. 'I wonder why you professed to be reluctant to introduce me to her.' He *was* reluctant – but not to talk about her. 'Are you not a rather disloyal friend?' May questioned him. 'I confess I should hate to be scoffed at behind my back as you profess to scoff at Mrs Patterson.' But Shaw admitted to betraying everybody's confidences in the most exaggerated way. It was a sample, he explained, of Irish tact. Everyone branded him a mischief-maker and thought no worse of the people gossiped over.

Shaw's natural tendency to put Jenny Patterson in a compartment was strengthened by her possessiveness which in turn was naturally increased by this tendency. She accuses him of having 'kissed & mauled about' other girls. She assails him with her forgiveness and need for reassurance. 'Are you thinking of me? Wanting me? ... I wish you were here now! Goodnight my darling Love – when shall I see you?' Then came apologies for her 'awful' rages – 'you know how hard it is to master one self & it is doubly hard for one like myself who has never been educated or controlled, in fact a savage.' She woos him back to Brompton Square with promises of fresh grapes, honey, cocoa, brown bread, strawberries, hand-knitted slippers and a pretty strict pumpkin hour so that they could both be fast asleep by 2 a.m. 'You are absolutely free to do as you please,' she instructs him – but not for long. 'You will run many dangers from my abandoned sex. You will be hardly safe – without Me ... don't fall in love with anyone but me ...'

Early in 1886 Shaw made some effort to end their relationship. '*Do you* indeed really wish never to see me again?' she asks him, and adds, with truth: '*I* could never make you see me if you did not want to ... Be your own man & be mine. I love you well enough for anything. You have done me no harm. Nor have I harmed you ...' But Shaw felt he had harmed her; he had used her body and only he knew what he felt when he did so. His urge to make a confession to McNulty and to start a 'new *Pilgrim's Progress*' were symptoms of a puritan dissatisfaction with himself. 'Be happy,' he had written to her in the first week of their affair, 'for I have not the fortitude enough to bear your misfortunes. Be noble hearted & generous; for all your sins will humiliate me except those which I share.' 'Let me be happy,' she wrote back to him. 'I love you.' But the currency of their love was different, and there could be no exchange between them that seemed fair. He could not make her happy for long; she could not help but sin through sexual jealousy. 'You ask me too much,' she told him, 'when you expect me to look with ... indifference on your attention to other women – such women ... You have treated me very badly. I do not complain ... When a woman does what I have done & expects either consideration or love from her lover she is a fool. I am one for I believed in you & loved you. I alas love you too much now ... You are the one man in all the world to me & this I feel I know after nearly ten months of intimacy.' This letter was written on 8 May and preceded a 'violent scene' between them at Brompton Square the following day. When Shaw got home that night he wrote to tell her that 'our future intercourse must be platonic'. In this letter, which made Jenny 'unutterably unhappy', Shaw tried to explain his own guilt: 'I see plainly that I have played a very poor part for some time past, in fact have done you the only bad turn – & that the worst – that was within my power – I have sacrificed you and am so far the better for it – but you are the worse . . . I had nothing to lose – but I had something to gain and therein lies the rascality of it.'

Jenny was unhappy, but by no means 'unutterably' so. In page after page over the next two days she went through her fears and regrets: 'You make me suffer tortures. Have pity on me. I have some little right to ask it from you. I write in despair . . . oh my love, my love, be good to me . . . do not abandon me . . . Months ago when you taunted me I said leave me but you would not. The parting then would have been less hard for me . . . You tell me to take other lovers as if I took them as easily as a new pair of gloves . . . I deeply deplore Sunday's work – but I am the sufferer. I couldn't help it . . . My grief is for your loss to me. I think my vanity suffers very little, it was not my lover I regretted – but the friend who knew me.'

She feared to open his letters, writing to ask whether they were unkind – and not daring to open the answers. He filled the backs of her envelopes with notes for political speeches. But what he wrote to her was not unkind. '*My thoughts* about you are remorseful and anxious at bottom though I am reckless too at times . . . I do not mean to abandon or desert you – I will not change – but in one thing [sex]. All shall be as before – but that.' Jenny did not read these pages – 'I cannot open your letter. I have longed for it with all my soul.' Knowing she still had some physical influence over him, she decided to go and see him. 'JP called here in the morning distracted about my letter,' Shaw jotted in his diary on 13 May. 'There was a scene and much pathetic petting and kissing, after which she went away comparatively happy', and Shaw, with intense relief, settled down to the economic study of Jevonian curves of indifference. Two days later there was a 'slight scene in consequence of my refusing to budge from our new platonic relations', but after another two days she wrote to him accepting 'all you offer. It will be for you to prove that it [sex] was not "the" one thing that brought you here, that nothing is altered betwixt us really except the thing you hold so cheap.' But, she added, 'I do know this that you are outraging nature.'

Since there is nothing so calculated to generate sexual electricity as the decision to forgo sex, their platonic experiment was not maintained for long. He continued visiting her, but less often; and he left earlier. This had been one of the difficulties between them: whether he should stay the night and neglect his work, or return home at night and neglect her. Fearing that they would drift apart she promised to be 'as good as I possibly can if you will come, not even try to kiss you – unless you wish it'. So he began seeing more of her again, sometimes walking her to the door of her house, sometimes going in. Seven Sundays after their platonic intercourse had begun they made love – twice – and things were calmer. 'My Friend & Lover,' she wrote to him at the end of July 1886, 'I am content that there are no barriers betwixt us – that you have taken me back. I will try to make *you* content with *me*.' But over the next eighteen months, as Shaw struggled to subdue his carnal feelings, they made each other deeply discontented. When she went off to her cottage at Broadstairs, he felt 'much indisposed for her society'; when she returned to London he found himself 'much out of humour with her and things in general'. On 16 December, their relationship exploded in a quarrel that lasted till one o'clock in the morning. 'I *know* my conduct was awful,' she apologized next day. Afterwards he seems to have returned to what she called his 'old games' again – being affectionate and neglectful by turns; arriving faithfully whenever she was out; but at other times outstaying all her other guests and remaining with her till one or two in the morning.

'I can't help wanting to see you,' she had written to him. 'You are so much to me & I am so happy when I am with you. Be as platonic as you will, it is *you* I love beyond any material thing. I can care for you without any sensuality. I am what you want me to be . . .' What he apparently wanted was a platonic experiment with full sexual intercourse. The uncertainty and frustration of her position swept Jenny into a variety of distracted moods. She would demand that he 'sacrifice something or someone for me'; plead with him: 'Where are you? When am I to see you . . . its a million years since I have been in your arms'; cross-examine him: 'Have you been faithful? Absolutely faithful??' The thought of his unfaithfulness, she was constantly reminding him, made her ill. 'I am consumed by all sorts of fancies about you.' Shaw sometimes blatantly provoked these fancies. During platonic intervals, he would drop in on her to change his clothes, plunge into a bath or dash off letters to other women. Once, after she caught him writing to Annie Besant, she followed the two of them next day in the street and was soon plastering him with reproaches. 'You belong to me,' she insisted.

*

'I confess to somewhat doubting her pretensions to the new-acquired name of Socialist,' May Morris wrote of Mrs Patterson. To ensure that G.B.S. would take her seriously, Jenny had interested herself in socialism, turning up at various lectures to keep an eye on him. Nevertheless, his liaison with Annie Besant had been going on for many months before she detected it. At the beginning of his 1886 diary Shaw recorded that 'my work at the Fabian brought me much into contact with Mrs Besant, and towards the end of the year this intimacy became of a very close and personal sort, without, however, going further than a friendship'.

Annie Besant displayed many qualities that appealed to Shaw. She was nine years older than he, a strong, pugnacious, radiantly energetic woman, 'great in impulse and in action'. Though separated from her clergyman-husband she was still legally tied to him and, better still, 'had absolutely no sex appeal'. Like Shaw, she had endured a loveless childhood, but at the age of twenty propelled herself into a painful marriage with Frank Besant, a man resembling Samuel Butler's Theobald Pontifex. She had two children, and from her sense of outrage and disillusionment arose a fascination with celibacy and her conversion to atheism. After she had created a scandal by refusing to take the sacrament, her husband expelled her from their home, and she set out on an extraordinary pilgrimage, leaping from one great cause to another. Each was embodied by a man. The first had been the great secularist saint, Charles Bradlaugh, heroic orator and 'the most muscular man in England'. Side by side with this champion of anti-Christendom, she had 'fought all England in the cause of liberty of conscience'. Then she veered towards the insidious Aveling. But his desertion of scientific secularism for the Socialist League had involved him leaving her for Eleanor Marx. Under the strain of this betrayal, Annie had fallen ill, recovering later in 1884 after persuading a dependable young Scottish secularist, John Mackinnon Robertson, to move from Edinburgh and take Aveling's place on Bradlaugh's *National Reformer* as well as her own new journal *Our Corner*.

Annie had by this time heard of Shaw. She had heard him describe himself as 'a loafer' and had upbraided him in the *National Reformer* – 'for a loafer was my detestation'. They met formally for the first time, together with Robertson, in January 1885 at the Dialectical Society near Oxford Circus where Shaw was to deliver a socialist address. This meeting occasioned a good deal of excitement since it was rumoured that Annie, as the most redoubtable champion of individualist free-thought, had come down to 'destroy me', Shaw recalled, 'and that from the moment she rose to speak my cause was lost'. Public meetings were the elixir of life to her. From the platform her voice, low and thrilling, seemed neither that of a woman nor of a man, but godlike and of irresistible authority. To Shaw's mind she was the greatest orator in England, capable of announcing 'a rose is not a violet' with such mysterious force that her audience would accept it as the revelation of a powerful new truth. Everyone waited for her that night to lead the opposition against Shaw, but she did not rise and the opposition was taken up by another member. 'When he had finished, Annie Besant, to the amazement of the meeting, got up and utterly demolished him,' Shaw remembered. '. . . At the end she asked me to nominate her for election to the Fabian Society and invited me to dine with her.' She was, he concluded, 'a woman of swift decisions'. And he too acted swiftly. On 4 June 1885 he wrote to a fellow Fabian, F. Keddell, informing him that Annie Besant had been proposed for membership by himself and Webb, urging him to remonstrate with 'any person so steeped in bigotry as to object' to her election: otherwise 'I shall finally leave the socialist party and run as a conservative candidate'. Her conversion was partly due to her having discovered that Shaw was 'one of the most brilliant of Socialist writers, and . . . very poor, because he was a writer with principles and preferred starving his body to starving his conscience; that he gave time and earnest work to the spreading of Socialism, spending night after night in workmen's clubs; and that a "loafer" was only an amiable way of describing himself because he did not carry a hod'. For the next three years Shaw became the target for Annie's hero-worship. He described her as an 'incorrigible benefactress'. It was she who was responsible for the long serialization of *The Irrational Knot* and *Love Among the Artists* in *Our Corner*; and it was she who launched him there as an art critic. She had, too, the 'singular habit' of paying her contributors – a device that allowed her to relieve 'necessitous young propagandists without wounding their pride by open alms-giving', and that enabled Shaw to keep modestly alive.

Annie found, as Archer had previously done, that Shaw was extremely difficult to help. He impressed her as one of the most provoking of men, 'with a perfect genius for "aggravating" the enthusiastically earnest, and with a passion for representing himself as a scoundrel'. Shaw himself explained how he would exercise this genius at the expense of her beneficence and pride:

'I would complain, fondly, that I wanted something that I could not afford. She would give it to me. I would pretend that my pride was deeply wounded, and ask her how she dared insult me. In a transport of generous indignation she would throw her present away or destroy it. I would then come and ask for it, barefacedly denying that I had ever repudiated it, and exhibiting myself as a monster of frivolous ingratitude and callousness. But though I succeeded sometimes in making her laugh at me, I never succeeded in making her laugh at herself or check her inveterate largesse.'

Annie shared Shaw's public passion for reform. But when he declared, after her death, that she had had no sex appeal, he meant that she was without a sense of humour. 'Comedy was not her clue to life,' he admitted:

'she had a healthy sense of fun; but no truth came to her first as a joke. Injustice, waste, and the defeat of noble aspirations did not revolt her by way of irony and paradox: they stirred her to direct and powerful indignation and to active resistance . . . the apparently heartless levity with which I spoke and acted in matters which seemed deeply serious, before I had achieved enough to show that I had a perspective in which they really lost their importance, and before she had realised that her own destiny was to be one which would also dwarf them, must have made it very hard for her to work with me at times.'

The aim of Shaw's infuriating little comedies was to awaken in Annie the humorous vision without which there could be no intimacy between them. This treatment was not successful, and each remained merely an episode in the other's life. 'It came to nothing,' Shaw afterwards regretted. 'Nothing *from the inside* ever did come to anything with her: she was a public person first and last.'

At the beginning of his diary for 1887 he noted that by January their intimacy had reached 'a point at which it threatened to become a vulgar intrigue, chiefly through my fault. But I roused myself in time and avoided this'. Such Shavian rousing was signalled from his side by the dispatch of his photograph, and from hers by the composition of a number of fevered poems which, her sympathetic biographer Arthur H. Nethercot comments, 'perhaps fortunately, have not survived'. They did not see each other any less, but orchestrated their incompatibilities (she so downright, he so upstanding) over a series of dreadful piano duets, mostly transcriptions of Haydn's symphonies, on Monday nights. 'Shaw always came in, sat down at the piano, and plunged ahead,' Nethercot records, 'but Mrs Besant whenever possible practised for hours to perfect her parts in advance. The neighbourhood resounded with their efforts to keep in time.'

There is a note in Shaw's diary for 17 April 1887 about discussing 'my relations with Mrs Besant and Robertson, which I explained to them [the Archers] for the first time'. Annie was married and a constant colleague of Robertson's: he therefore treated them as he would a married couple, sparring with Robertson in front of Annie as he did with Pakenham Beatty and Hubert Bland before their wives.

From the Fabian point of view she seemed to borrow everything from other people, adding nothing except the wonder of her voice. Yet Beatrice

Webb, who disliked her, finding her self-deceitful, lacking in candour, and cold, could nevertheless feel that she was 'the most wonderful woman of her century'. To Shaw also she was wonderful, but as someone on stage. 'Like all great public speakers she was a born actress,' he wrote. '. . . There was a different leading man every time.' Shaw tried to repay his debt to her by coaching her, after the duets, in the swift complexities of Shavian economics and making her the best Fabian he could. 'I ought to have done much more for her,' he concluded, 'and she much less for me, than we did.' Annie, too, had hoped for more. In August 1887 she wrote in the *National Reformer*: 'Life had nothing fairer for its favourites than friendship kissed into the passion of love.' Shaw's love had two qualities – extreme levity and extreme tenacity. 'I do not like the proverb "Love me little: love me long",' he wrote; 'but whoever invented it had a very narrow escape of finding its true form, which is, "Love me lightly: love me long." And that is how I loved, and still love, Annie Besant.' But it was not a love she could use.

The most passionate aspect of Shaw's and Annie's relationship appeared in the clouds of suspicion it blew up round Jenny Patterson. 'JP here when I returned,' reads Shaw's diary entry for 15 November 1887. 'Went home with her. Tedious quarrel about Mrs Besant.' After which they made love. With absolute fairness Shaw seemed to have contrived a situation that was almost equally unsatisfactory to all. But while Jenny argued, Annie acted. That December she presented Shaw with a contract setting forth the terms on which they were to live together as man and wife – terms which impressed him as being 'worse than all the vows of all the Churches on earth'. When he refused to sign it ('I had rather be legally married to you ten times over,' he cautiously fulminated) she produced a casket in which she kept all his letters and handed it to him. Next day, 24 December, he returned her side of the correspondence, and on reaching home found that Jenny had been to his room 'and had read my letters to Mrs B. which I had incautiously left on my table'. Some of these letters mentioning herself she had taken with her. 'I make no excuse for taking the letters,' she wrote,

'. . . I should do exactly the same again under the same condition. When I read *her* letters I felt that she must have had great encouragement before she wrote such letters & in a kind of way I excused her because I thought she did not know of me . . . I will not say anything more as to her conduct in doing her best to make me the most miserable woman in London . . . it is most horrible that I have no claim on you or your consideration . . . You have taken advantage of . . . my belief & trust in you . . . I am ill & numb . . . & [my] loneliness [is] almost unbearable. I try to think what is it I have

done to you to deserve this evil . . . What devil came into you to write &
speak of me to this woman as you have . . . I have a thousand memories of
you that I can't forget . . . I feel ashamed beyond telling when I try to
imagine what she must think of me. You have humbled me in the dust . . .
to flatter your own vanity.'

On the morning of Christmas Day, Shaw was woken by a hammering at
the door. It was Jenny Patterson, bristling with letters and complaints.
They argued about it and about, then 'I at last got those she had taken and
destroyed them.' The following evening they passed together, and so far
mended matters that a few days later they saw in the New Year by making
love. Shaw did not arrive home till nearly 3 a.m.

Jenny still engaged his body, but Annie Besant had failed to engage his
mind and faded to a luminous voice in his memory. For her their parting
was a death. Her hair turned white, for several days she thought of suicide
– then flung herself violently for a time into street socialism. Later, in
1890, she was to surrender to the masculine charm of Madame Blavatsky,
'one of the most accomplished impostors in history', and leave the Fabians
to become high priestess of *The Secret Doctrine*. 'Gone to Theosophy,'
Pease noted on his Fabian list, and crossed out her name.

As for Shaw: 'Reading over my letters before destroying them rather
disgusted me with the trifling of the last 2 years with women.'

## [ 4 ]

*The Fabian lecturers are famous throughout the world. Their women*
*are beautiful; their men brave. Their executive council challenges the*
*universe for quality . . . Join the Fabian, and you will find its name a*
*puissant protector. Say to the horseleech, 'I have joined the Fabian,'*
*and he will drop off as though you have overwhelmed him with salt.*

(1887)

'Whatever Society I joined,' Shaw wrote, 'I was immediately placed on the
executive committee.' And he was happy. The Fabians had elected him to
their executive on 2 January 1885, and Hyndman eventually came to
accept that he was lost for ever to the Social Democratic Federation. 'I was
in hope that you had enough regard for the cause in which you are working
to take the course which would most advance it,' he wrote to Shaw later. 'I
am very sorry I was mistaken.'

Over thirty years afterwards, in his last letter to Shaw, Hyndman
observed: 'Of course, we don't agree.' They had agreed only on the

platitudes of socialism and they continued to hold each other in curiously hostile esteem. Hyndman, who claimed to have 'discovered' him, felt that if only Shaw had become his pupil he would have been taken seriously in politics. As it was, his diabolic love of buffoonery blasphemed 'to the very Holy of holies of our great material religion' – he actually boasted of having set back socialism in Great Britain by fully twenty years! Perhaps it was a joke, but Hyndman felt 'downright angry' and would never forgive him for having, as he believed, 'done as much as anyone to prevent the consolidation of a really powerful and united Socialist Party in Great Britain.' Shaw held much the same view of Hyndman and his 'congregation of manual-working pseudo-Marxists'.

'If it had been possible for anyone but a humble satellite to work with Hyndman without a quarrel, the SDF would have enlisted and retained all the important recruits to Socialism instead of antagonizing them, and there might have been no Fabian Society, no Socialist League, no Guild of St Matthew, no Christian Social Union, no Independent Labor Party, nor any other of the sections which placed the British Socialist movement in such striking contrast to the single and solid Social-Democracy of Germany ... As it was, the Federation never federated anybody.'

In selecting a political partner for himself, Shaw was guided by the instinctive motive to discover someone as unlike Hyndman as possible, someone vividly unheroic and unfrockcoated, who would never play at soldiers in the street or represent his own gushing enthusiasms as a public movement. He had already spotted the man: a crushingly plain, poor, earnest clerk from the Colonial Office, with unhealthy skin, a bulky head set on a dumpy body, graceless in movement, in manner complacent, and as a public speaker (he spoke in a cockney mumble) inaudible. According to his future wife, he looked something between a London tradesman and a German professor. 'This was the ablest man in England,' Shaw decided: 'Sidney Webb. Quite the wisest thing I ever did was to force my friendship on him and to keep it; for from that time I was not merely a futile Shaw but a committee of Webb and Shaw.'

He had first met Webb in October 1880 at the Zetetical Society. 'He knew all about the subject of debate,' Shaw recalled; 'knew more than the lecturer; knew more than anybody present; had read everything that had ever been written; and remembered all the facts that bore on the subject. He used notes, read them, ticked them off one by one, threw them away, and finished with a coolness and clearness that seemed to me miraculous.' Though Webb was to laugh away this recollection as romantic, he agreed with Shaw as to the importance of their meeting. Over fifty years later he

172

acknowledged: 'It led to nearly half a century of friendship and companionship, which has been most fruitful to me. I look back on it with wonder at the advantage, and indeed, the beauty of that prolonged friendship. Apart from marriage, it has certainly been the biggest thing in my life.' And Shaw, in his ninetieth year, recalled in a letter to Webb that 'if anyone had asked me what I owed to you I should have said my entire education. The truth is that we complemented one another . . . I can also say that I never met a man who combined your extraordinary ability with your unique simplicity and integrity of character . . . When we met, you knew everything that I didn't know and I knew everything that you didn't know. We had everything to learn from one another and brains enough to do it.'

There was no vanity, competitiveness or sexual rivalry in their long friendship. G.B.S. valued Webb's intelligence which seemed to open up new opportunities for his own talent, and he felt reassured by his emotional limitations. There was something almost comically proper about Webb's selflessness, which appealed to Shaw. Certainly there was nothing to stir his anxieties from a man of such physical and class inferiority – a man who had substituted the public for the private good so wholly as to declare: 'We have no *right* to live our own lives.'

An omnivorous, high-speed reader with a prodigious memory, Webb was indefatigably packed with information. But it was not in their learning alone that he and Shaw complemented each other. In Shaw's opinion, Webb was a political genius; but his simplicity of character acted as a political disadvantage. He was not mean, he had no envy, he was never a Party man; his price was getting things sensibly done, whether by the Right or the Left. He had little humour, was impatient with people less clever than himself, and incapable of dramatizing himself or his subject. 'I did all that for him,' Shaw told Kingsley Martin, and in a letter to Lady Londonderry he explained: 'All I could do for Webb was to beat the big drum in front of his booth, as he would not master that useful instrument himself.' The description he gave of Webb as one who 'never posed, never acted, never courted popular favor or any other favor, and was never in danger of becoming a humbug and a living fiction, not to say a living lie', points to the disgust felt by the fastidious Shaw at the vulgar gyrations G.B.S. went through to gain the attention of a crass world. He forced himself to speak at street corners, set Webb's statistics dancing, produced a fountain of sparkling illustrations to make the dullest subject entertaining. And people listened. For the first time Webb began to command an audience. Shaw had become his loudspeaker. From the other side of a Fabian screen that hid his physical defects, Webb planned to get his ideas implanted in the smart, the powerful, rich and successful figures of the world. Shaw was one of his instruments for achieving this. People who felt chilled by Webb's programme of national efficiency adored Shaw's irrelevancies, his jokes, his acting, and gift for addressing two boys, a woman and a baby in the rain as if they were the greatest demonstration in the world. And behind him, invisible to the public, Webb was whispering the researched facts. But who had really 'permeated' the other was more difficult to know. For when Shaw first met him, Webb was 'no believer in state socialism'. In 1883 Shaw had persuaded him to join the Land Reform Union despite his distrust of land nationalization, and then by May 1885 roped him into the Fabian Society where 'his knowledge, ability, and administrative experience as an upper division civil servant at once swept all the nonsense and Bohemian anarchism out of it, and made it what it finally became'.

Webb and Shaw were the two Supermen of the Fabian Society. According to Webb, the Fabians always expressed Shaw's 'political views and work'. According to Shaw, Webb was 'the real inventor of Fabian Socialism'. Each was a wonder to the other. Their Fabian partnership seemed an example of the miraculous balancing instinct in Nature. Writing in the third person for his biographer Archibald Henderson, Shaw declared that 'they valued and even over-valued one another'. But in overvaluing each other they overlooked one quality, essential in politics, that neither of them possessed: the ability to take action. 'I am not a man of action,' Webb told Pease, and nor was Shaw. Neither of them wanted to go directly into national politics, and it was this side-stepping that gave the Fabians their peculiar obliqueness.

Webb, the man of numbers, gave the Fabians their policy; Shaw, the man of letters, their tone; and the two of them created the Fabian legend. In Webb the Fabians owned the first political computer, programmed with Socialist statistics and designed to do whatever no one else was doing. From this came the distinguished Fabian tradition of research and education at the expense of glamour. But the computer lacked a political instinct. In Shaw, they had a propagandist of astonishing brilliance – a man who could, in the most forthright and amusing terms, fail to speak his mind. His reasons for this were often tactical. He needed to make a family of the Fabians and his loyalty to them was often equivalent to the party loyalty he derided in professional politicians. Beside his passion for reform ran the complementary passion to unify. The wider the Fabian rifts and splits, the greater was Shaw's satisfaction at resolving them. Everything he touched was given a bewilderingly cheerful coherence. 'Keeping together is good business,' he declared. This 'keeping together' of people who were in substantial agreement with one another needed the most gorgeous exercise of Shavian paradoxes, and prompted almost everything he did for the Fabians. He tied up their mutual rivalries in a knot of such rational complexity that no one could unravel it to release his antagonisms. But the tolerance he created amounted to indecisiveness. He used all his theatrical abilities on behalf of the Fabian Shaw – then went on to dramatize his Fabian knowledge for the stage.

Under the joint management of Webb and Shaw, the Fabian Society became a club, a debating chamber, an ideas factory for the Labour movement in Britain, a focus for sociological research and literary-political propaganda. They held together while other organizations came and went because they were so heterogeneous and undoctrinal, and because few of them expected to see their arguments quickly translated into legislation. In place of the old revolutionary notion of attracting recruits until they were numerous enough to defeat capitalism at the barricades, the Fabians substituted the 'staggering novelty' that socialists should join other groups and permeate them with socialist ideas. They took socialism off the streets and sat it down in the drawing-room. They made it respectable by dealing it out as a series of parliamentary measures designed to merge political radicalism with economic collectivism. Shaw offered revolution without tears – you would hardly know it had happened. 'A party informed at all points by men of gentle habits and trained reasoning powers may achieve a complete Revolution without a single act of violence,' he stated. 'A mob of desperate sufferers abandoned by the leadership of exasperated sentimentalists and fanatic theorists may, at vast cost of bloodshed and misery, succeed in removing no single evil, except perhaps the extinction of the human race.'

If Fabianism came to mean anything it was 'permeation'. The Positivists and Radicals had been playing this game for years, but in the political vocabulary it was the Fabians who went on to patent the word. This policy gradually gave the Society its identity. For if they were to survive, they needed to differentiate themselves from the romanticism of William Morris's Socialist League which proclaimed it to be 'a false step for Socialists to attempt to take part in a Parliamentary contest', and from the catastrophist insurrectionary manoeuvres of Hyndman's Social Democratic Federation. The Socialist League had *Commonweal*, a paper that promoted Ruskin's aesthetics and the Utopianism of Morris; the SDF had its paper *Justice*, preaching the Marxist doctrine of the class war; and the Fabians produced their tracts, crammed with facts and linking theoretical socialism to already existing developments of State and municipal enterprise. Shaw and Webb believed in argument on paper. Yet as education spread and more people were to grow literate, the power of words did not increase: it dwindled. The more they became public property, the less the public would take notice of them – their magic would fade in the twentieth century. This was one paradox that Shaw missed.

Other leading Fabians attracted to the Society along the Webb-Shaw axis were also men of paper . Graham Wallas, for example, was a school master and in many respects a perfect representative of the Fabian ethic – a political scientist, high-principled, hard-working, ascetic, impersonal. Like Webb, he had 'the requisite power of attacking blue books, following up newspaper files and worrying out every scrap of information about the historical periods on which he writes and lectures,' Shaw told Havelock Ellis. In this way he had acquired 'a considerable knowledge of Chartism – he probably knows more about it than any man in England'. Wallas was the son of a clergyman and, under the influence of first Darwin, then Butler, had replaced Christianity with socialism. In spite of shabby clothes and slovenly ways, Wallas's aristocratic features and authoritative voice proclaimed him as one of the governing class of public school boys and Oxford Honours men. Perpetually overworked, he seemed a joyless being, an academic gentleman almost callous in manner, who eventually lost his capacity for agreeable companionship in the steady grind of public service. 'I never disagree with what Wallas wrote nor remember it a week later,' Shaw admitted to Sidney Webb. And Beatrice Webb was to echo this opinion in her diary: 'I read and re-read his books with pleasure, but for the life of me I have never been able to remember what they contain . . .'

A more attractive figure was Sydney Olivier who had known Wallas at Oxford and shared with Webb the duty of resident clerk at the Colonial Office. 'He was handsome and strongly sexed,' reported Shaw, 'looking like a Spanish grandee in any sort of clothes, however unconventional . . . I believe he could have carried a cottage piano upstairs; but it would have cracked in his grip.' Shaw recognized in Olivier, largely on account of his romantic appearance, the powerful man needed by the Fabians. 'I have enjoyed (or suffered) much more celebrity,' he was to write, 'or as they call it now, publicity, than this old Fabian colleague of mine, though as a man of action I was not qualified to tie his shoestrings.'

In Fabian terms there was less difference between Sydney Olivier and Sidney Webb than Shaw pictured. Both had come from liberalism to socialism by way of Auguste Comte and the Positivists. Like Webb, Olivier was a bad public speaker. But he had a literary gift, 'which he occasionally uses with more brilliancy than mercy'. He was less the man of action needed by the Fabians than an administrator – someone who saw many moves ahead in an argument. Shaw described him as a man of great distinction who (unlike himself) had not 'suffered the degradation of being generally appreciated. He has an awkward combination of an exceedingly nervous temperament and fine sensibility with a certain stark, stiff strength, the remains of a mastiff-like country-family breed. He writes fine verses occasionally. His fault is a tendency to overelaborate his point in the Meredithian fashion . . . Altogether a very interesting man, whose powers will become effective as he grows older . . .'

Olivier joined the Fabians with Webb in May 1885, and Wallas enrolled the following year. With Webb they became known among Fabians as 'the Three Musketeers', with Shaw taking the role of d'Artagnan. Broken into team work together, this small group directed the affairs of the Society 'as far as what may be called its indoor work was concerned'. Shaw was the only one who took socialism on to the street corners, but the one man of action on the executive was a woman: their celebrity, Annie Besant. She was a 'fifth wheel' on the Musketeers' coach and, in Shaw's words, 'a sort of expeditionary force, always to the front when there was trouble and danger, carrying away audiences for us when the dissensions in the movement brought our policy into conflict with that of the other societies, founding branches for us throughout the country, dashing into the great strikes and free-speech agitations of that time . . . generally leaving the routine to us and taking the fighting on herself.'

With the support of Hubert Bland, Annie Besant urged the Fabians to advance boldly into front-line politics. But Shaw, summoning all his personal fascination, resisted this appeal and persuaded her that such a move would be in the nature of a retreat – no war was conducted from the front line. Bland, who had been deposed as early leader of the Fabians by this politburo of new recruits, 'was hopelessly outmatched', Shaw recalled, 'and it taxed my diplomacy to the utmost to keep the peace between him and the Musketeers . . .' But so successful was he for a time with Annie that the Fabians heard the most convincing exposition of their policy in a speech she gave, insisting that society must be reformed 'by a slow process of evolution, not by revolution and bloodshed'. This was a preliminary to Webb's famous phrase, first uttered in 1923: 'the Inevitability of Gradualness' – a philosophy that, by emphasizing the practical nature of their socialism, surrounded the Fabians with the glow of constitutional power and postponed for many years Shaw's disillusion with the democratic process of politics as practised in Britain.

*

Shaw calculated that the Webb-Shaw machine could replace Marx as the most powerful force in British socialism. Personally he could hold his own with Marxist dialectics and he reckoned Webb too was Marx's equal in the job of marshalling a tremendous battery of official facts. But if the Fabian Society was to become the centre of British socialism then its independence from other groups had to be established not only in tone and tactics, but also in the dismal matter of economic theory.

The job of shifting the Fabians out of the shadow of Marx had begun late in 1884. In the October issue of *To-Day* a criticism of *Das Kapital* had appeared, written by Philip Wicksteed, a Unitarian minister, devoted to the works of Ibsen and the study of economics – in particular the propagation of Stanley Jevons's *Theory of Political Economy*. The socialists had felt bound to answer this attack and, Hyndman having refused on the grounds that Marxian omniscience was unchallengeable, Shaw was reluctantly persuaded to do battle. It was a complicated business. Marx's value theory followed Ricardo in defining the value of a commodity as being determined by the labour involved in producing it. Wicksteed argued that Marxist economists had failed to account for the obvious dependence of prices on supply and demand. Jevons (like Menger in Austria and Walras in France) had abolished this Ricardian confusion by saying that value depended on the utility of the commodity to the consumer. Shaw's qualifications as a Marxist champion had been, to quote his own subsequent words, 'a dextrous pen and a total ignorance of abstract economics'. His article entitled 'The Jevonian Criticism of Marx' appeared in the January issue of *To-Day*, and three months later, in Wicksteed's rejoinder, it earned him the description of someone who had 'renounced mathematical reasoning in favour of the literary method which enables a clever man to follow equally fallacious arguments to equally absurd conclusions without seeing that they are absurd'.

The argument, as was obligatory with Shaw, had been waged in the friendliest spirit and enabled him to gain access to an informal group, meeting every fortnight at the house of a stockbroker, H. R. Beeton, which later grew into the British Economic Association. For four years, from 1885 to 1889, Shaw went to these meetings which, under Wicksteed's leadership, were composed mainly of professional economists and members of the faculty of University College, London. 'It was the closest Shaw had ever come to university education.' Much of the clarifying work he prepared for Fabian propaganda and literature was hatched out over this period of formal economic study, in which he also involved Webb and Wallas. The controversy with Wicksteed had 'ended in my education and conversion by my opponent,' Shaw later concluded, 'and the disappearance of the Marxian theory of value from the articles of faith of British Socialism'.

In fact British socialists took little interest in the Jevonian theory of marginal utility, and when Shaw lectured on it in the Old Kent Road some of his audience fell asleep. Nevertheless, since 'the subject was quite beyond them', he could claim that it aroused no opposition among ordinary socialists, and that it helped to release Webb from the yoke of John Stuart Mill's *Principles of Political Economy*, and himself from the tyranny of that 'innocent old gentleman', Karl Marx. The mechanism of a Jevonian calculus was the first step for Shaw in getting rid of Marx's inevitable class war (which was temperamentally repugnant to him). He moved the Marxist battle lines to a different ground where he, a bustling non-combatant, could dominate the scene. Marx, he insisted, had been a foreigner who, though he could analyse capitalist policy like a god, did not understand the British social system. As someone outside that system, he had lusted after its violent destruction. Those who swallowed Marxism whole – the moral sentimentality of wresting surplus value from the evil exploiting bourgeoisie and handing it to the virtuous victimized proletariat – were possessed by a need for war. Shaw's need was for peace – to an extent where he made war (in *Arms and the Man*, for example, or in his journalism on boxing) unreal by mockery. Instead of a Marxist class war, he saw a conflict of interest between producers and the privileged unemployed – those who earned money and those who lived off rent. Such lines of battle did not run neatly between social classes, he pointed out, but through them. A continual civil war (as to some extent envisaged by Marx) could only come about if the Trade Unions and Employers' Federations were determined to play the capitalist game of labourer versus employer, particularly through free collective bargaining.

The real conflict, Shaw argued, should not be that of capitalist versus worker, but of workers of all classes against such idlers as the aristocracy. 'Socialism, on its aggressive side,' he was to write, 'is, and always has been, an attack on idleness.' The moral link between wealth and virtue forged by the Victorians, who had justified private riches as a 'rent' paid to outstanding individuals for the hire of their wealth-producing capacities, had parted once this system had created an expanding class of unproductive *rentiers* living off past accumulations rather than present efforts, whose existence became a 'tax' on the community. Shaw combined Jevons's theory of value with a compatible extension of Ricardo's theory of rent and produced a Fabian theory of surplus value that could be used to support the economic case for land nationalization. For the time was coming, he believed, to transfer individual riches into common wealth by reversing the capitalist process – that is by converting private property (which was the original sin of the socialist religion) into publicly owned property and equitably redistributing the resultant income among the entire population.

Characteristically, Shaw was soon sharing with Wicksteed the leadership in this circle of economists. On alternate weeks, when they did not meet, he attended another group that, beginning under the name of the Karl Marx Club, soon emerged as the Hampstead Historic Society. They met at Wildwood Farm, a house on the northern edge of Hampstead Heath that belonged to another stockbroker, Arthur Wilson. At the centre of this group was his wife Charlotte Wilson, a firebrand bluestocking from Merton Hall, Cambridge who, disdaining her husband's parasitic earnings, kept chickens at their small comfortably converted farmhouse. Here she ran her discussion club, appointing a novelist, Emma Brooke (whom she had known at Cambridge), as its secretary, and inviting Belfort Bax to take the chair. Bax, who had been the unofficial philosopher of the SDF, and then left with William Morris to found the Socialist League, was a Marxist socialist and Hegelian philosopher whose influence on Shavian thinking Shaw himself took trouble to acknowledge in his Preface to *Major Barbara*. Mrs Wilson, it seems, had chosen him because of his close association with Morris, with whom he edited *Commonweal*. She admired Morris's mixture of near-anarchy with aesthetics, and (though he carefully avoided coming to her house), the décor echoed this admiration. 'The kitchen is an *idealised* farm kitchen,' remembered Edith Bland, 'where of course no cooking is done – but with a cushioned settee – open hearth, polished dresser and benches, and all the household glass and crockery displayed mixed up with aesthetic pots pans curtains chairs and tables – a delightfully incongruous but altogether agreeable effect.'

These arts and crafts, fashionably glittering around them – and even the chickens outside – became the coin of their debates as Shaw, in the course of being converted by Wicksteed ('my master in economics'), saw to it that Marxism was permeated with Fabianism by the characteristic means of arguing, in company with Bax, on behalf of Marx. Mrs Wilson would read out *Das Kapital* in French, Shaw explained,

'until we began to quarrel, which usually occurred before she had gone on long enough to make us feel seriously fatigued. The first chapters were of extraordinary efficacy in setting us by the ears ...

'The controversy raged at Hampstead until Bax shook the dust of the Heath off his boots, and the Historic Club, having had enough of impassioned disputes as to whether the value of Mrs Wilson's vases was fixed by the labour socially necessary to produce them, by their cost of production on the margin of cultivation, or by the "final utility" of the existing stock of vases, insisted on passing to the later chapters and dropping the subject.'

The Hampstead Historic Society became the chief policy-making forum of the Fabian cabinet. D'Artagnan and the Three Musketeers would stride up to Hampstead and argue between themselves so forcefully that other socialists, in particular other socialists' wives, could not believe they would remain friends. For Shaw, the substitution of Marx by Jevons was almost equivalent to the subsequent replacement of Darwin by Lamarck. It did away with the concept of automatic history and admitted human will into political development. The elimination of the traditional class war took this human will from the socialist body and gave it to the socialist head – a transference from the proletariat to the intellectual. If Shaw's and Webb's analyses of capitalism were right, then such men as they were to have the power in the twentieth century. The sense of this power gives Shaw's Fabian writings their lucid tone of authority, and Webb's social investigations their extraordinary persistence.

But there was another battle the Fabian Musketeers needed to win. This was against two anarchist platoons: the Individualist anarchists owing allegiance to Proudhon and Benjamin Tucker, and Communist anarchists led by the Russian geographer, Prince Peter Kropotkin. It was an age of secret agents and bomb makers. Charlotte Wilson, who persuaded the club to turn from Marx to Proudhon, entertained anarchist tendencies, and her farmhouse was sometimes invaded by strange foreign gentlemen, such as Nicolai Tchaykowsky, a revolutionary chemist who, after fleeing from Tsarist Russia and retreating from a Utopian encampment in Kansas, had come to lodge at Harrow-on-the-Hill. Most notorious of all was 'Sergius Stepniak', the Russian nihilist and author of manuals on home-made explosives and guerrilla warfare, dangerously described by Shaw as 'an amiable middleaged gentleman', who had turned up in London after stabbing to death the chief of the Russian secret police in the streets of St Petersburg, but who now entertained girls from Lady Margaret Hall to tea, and was soon to die, ignominiously caught by the heel ('Achilles-like', Shaw suggested) on a suburban level-crossing.

At the beginning of 1885, 'more to shew Mrs Wilson my idea of the line an anarchist paper should take in England than as an expression of my own convictions', Shaw drafted an article favourable to political anarchy that, to his embarrassment, was frequently to be reprinted and cited as evidence of his own anarchist past. Towards the end of the year, Mrs Wilson wrote to Kropotkin, then living in exile in Paris, inviting him to London. He arrived the following spring and soon became co-editor with her of the anarchist fly-sheet *Freedom* – and (it was whispered) her lover.

Containing Mrs Wilson's rising anarchist devotions within the Fabian circle became a sophisticated task. Fabian Tract No. 4, *What Socialism Is*, published in 1886, was an attempt to quarantine this 'influenza of Anarchism' so that all Fabians did not go down with it. But it failed to avert a show-down between Fabian collectivists and anarchists. The instrument of this show-down was Annie Besant, who in September 1886 initiated a meeting at Anderton's Hotel in the Strand of all socialist bodies in London, to debate her motion that, to prevent fragmentation, they should organize themselves into a single political party 'for the purpose of transferring into the hands of the whole working community full control over the soil and the means of production, as well as over the production and distribution of wealth'. Under the management of the Hampstead group this debate was turned into a confrontation with the anarchists.

The question was: how many of the silent Fabians supported Charlotte Wilson? At the end of some high-pitched speeches, a mixed Fabian and SDF team that included Annie Besant, Shaw and John Burns, the Amalgamated Engineer from the SDF executive (and model for Boanerges in *The Apple Cart*), routed by forty-seven votes to nineteen the anarchists, led by William Morris and Mrs Wilson, who had argued that the inevitable compromise and concession of parliamentary politics would poison the well, obscuring socialist principles and hindering socialist education throughout the country. An immediate outcome of this rowdy debate was a notice from the manager of the hotel informing the society that further meetings could not be accommodated there. After an interval in a church, Sydney Olivier arranged for later functions to be held at Willis's Rooms which, decked with silver candelabra and patrolled by liveried footmen, were famous as the least expensive, most aristocratic, meeting-place in London.

After 1887 (when Charlotte Wilson left the executive and the Hampstead group continued their meetings at the local library) the Fabians had no more trouble with anarchists. Tract No. 4, *What Socialism Is*, was never reprinted and Shaw tried to obliterate it in 1890 by bringing out Fabian Tract No. 13, also entitled *What Socialism Is*, that defined socialism exclusively in collectivist terms as 'a plan for securing equal rights and opportunities for all ... in a perfectly constitutional manner through Democratic institutions', by having land and machinery 'made the property of the whole people, in order to do away with idle owners, and to keep the whole product for those whose labor produces it'. Though in Fabian terms there was no further need to mention the subject, Shaw later purged his own past associations with anarchism in a literary spree, entitled *The Impossibilities of Anarchism* (Fabian Tract No. 45), where between the operation of human nature and the theory of economic rent, he sought to grind it into nothing.

*

The way was now clear for Fabianism within the society, but not in the country. For as Shaw admitted: 'The fact is, 1886 and 1887 were not favorable years for drawing-room Socialism and scientific politics.' These were the years in which the Tories, under Lord Salisbury, swept back to power, replacing Gladstone's promise of Home Rule with the continuation of British dominance over Ireland, and replacing Chamberlain's programme of land and housing reform financed by higher taxes on the rich with a policy of expanding the Empire abroad and protecting property at home. The old order had not crumbled but fossilized, and the new order was without authority in Parliament. The trade depression of these years had thrown many out of work. 'They were years of great distress among the working-classes,' Shaw wrote:

' – years for street-corner agitators to marshal columns of hollow-cheeked men with red flags and banners inscribed with Scriptural texts to fashionable churches on Sunday, and to lead desperate deputations from the Holborn Board of Guardians to the Local Government Board office and back again, using stronger language at each official rebuff from pillar to post. These were the days when Mr [H. H.] Champion told a meeting in London Fields that if the whole propertied class had but one throat he would cut it without a second thought, if by doing so he could redress the injustices of our social system; and when Mr Hyndman was expelled from his club for declaring on the Thames Embankment that there would be some attention paid to cases of starvation if a rich man were immolated on every pauper's tomb.'

There was talk of dynamite and the rumour of drill. In many large towns throughout the country stones were thrown, railings uprooted, windows smashed, shops looted. The times seemed to belong to the militants – in particular to Hyndman, who had created in the SDF 'a machine that could mobilize up to twenty thousand demonstrators'. Compared with that, what was this stage army of Fabians – sixty-seven strong in 1886 and with an income of £35 19s. – whose doctrinal differences and peripatetic debates felt so remote from the political excitements seething all around them? In vain did they press advice on the SDF not to confuse hunger with class-consciousness or plot the 'revolt of the empty stomach' as leading to 'the baker's shop'. The Fabian voice, insisting that true socialism was a matter of justice to the poor and not envy of the rich, either jarred or was drowned. For the unemployed had begun to march and the Fabians, protesting their respectability, had no choice but to tag along behind them.

The early demonstrations had promised well. In the autumn of 1885 a police attempt to shut down a traditional 'speaker's corner' in Dod Street had led to a socialist demonstration in which Shaw, as one of the volunteer speakers, had pledged himself to be imprisoned. 'I am in a state of terror about this east end business,' he had admitted. '. . . The prospect is anything but agreeable.' But no arrests were made, the police retreated, and the battle for free speech was won. The following February, the SDF paraded a vast crowd of its supporters in Trafalgar Square. There were incendiary speeches by Hyndman, Burns and Champion from the plinth of Nelson's Column and these led to a 'monstrous riot', as Queen Victoria described it, '. . . a momentary triumph for socialism and a disgrace to the capital'. Once again the police had lost control and London seemed open to a 'French Revolution'. Even the courts were unable to punish the rebel leaders. After the Dod Street affair, William Morris had been acquitted of disorderly conduct; and after Trafalgar Square, Hyndman, Burns and Champion were found not guilty of seditious conspiracy.

The mood of insurrection rose. The SDF which, as William Morris noted, 'must always be getting up some fresh excitement, or else making the thing stale and at last ridiculous', had planned the largest demonstration of all, to take place once more in Trafalgar Square, on Sunday 13 November 1887 – a week after Sir Charles Warren, the new chief of the Metropolitan Police, had closed it for further meetings. Originally a protest against the Government's Irish policy, it became another trial of strength over free speech. Every radical, socialist and anarchist body united to confront the forces of public order. Shaw appealed to these very forces for the dismissal of Warren. 'The right to march in procession to a public meeting is almost as important as the right of meeting itself,' he wrote, 'since it prevents the confusion and disorder of promiscuous massing, minimizes obstruction, and enables the police to ascertain beforehand the nature and route of the traffic which they have to regulate. This right of procession was what Sir Charles Warren attacked . . .'

That day groups from all over London attempted to force their way into the square and were met by 1,500 police, 200 mounted Life Guards and a detachment of Grenadier Guards. Shaw, having studied the Act under which Warren had closed Trafalgar Square and decided that it was being illegally applied, joined the group at Clerkenwell Green. After speeches from William Morris, Annie Besant and Shaw himself, exhorting the people to be orderly and to press on in their irresistible numbers if attacked, the drums rattled, banners nodded, and with polite cries of 'To the Square!' they set off behind Morris. Annie Besant had asked Shaw whether she might march with him. He 'objected strongly to her running the risk of a conflict with the police, and said that if she insisted she must look after herself'. She did insist and they walked on together.

Shaw's various descriptions of what became known as 'Bloody Sunday' are exultant. It was, he wrote, a 'violent farce'. In every avenue leading to Trafalgar Square, the Labour Forces were broken up by squads of police. At High Holborn, Shaw and Mrs Besant were swept aside by the front ranks of their own procession in counter-revolutionary retreat. 'Running hardly expresses our collective action,' he reported. 'We *skedaddled*, and never drew rein until we were safe on Hampstead Heath or thereabouts . . . On the whole, I think it was the most abjectly disgraceful defeat ever suffered by a band of heroes outnumbering their foes a thousand to one.'

Annie Besant now found that Shaw had been speaking no less than the truth about looking after herself. 'You must keep out of this,' he warned her. She made her way independently to the Square and he did not see her again until the evening. But she may have remained long enough to witness his moment of decision in British politics. In the mêlée, a man rushed up to him shouting 'Shaw: give us a lead. What are we to do?' His answer came back firm and unparadoxical. 'Nothing,' he commanded: and went on to suggest that everyone should 'get to the Square as best he can'. Accepting his own advice he melted into the fringe of sightseers, 'the police kindly letting me through in consideration of my genteel appearance'.

The scene at Trafalgar Square was a débâcle. John Burns and Cunninghame Graham, pronounced by Shaw as the two heroes of the day, having failed to penetrate the rampart of policemen, chained themselves to the railings of Morley's Hotel and waved red flags until arrested. Together with Hyndman they received jail sentences – the unretreating Cunninghame Graham (a model for Sergius in *Arms and the Man*) having been sufficiently knocked about to pass his in the prison infirmary. The 'heroine' was Annie Besant who rushed everywhere trying to organize a defence line of carts and wagons against the Foot Guards. The mild-mannered Edward Carpenter was manhandled, he furiously wrote, 'by that crawling thing a policeman'. Stuart-Glennie, a Scottish philosophic historian whose special period was 6000 BC, charged the thin red line of Grenadiers with his raised umbrella as they were fixing bayonets. Shaw arrived unostentatiously with his vegetarian friend Henry Salt who, discovering his watch had been stolen, realized he could not complain to the police since he was there to complain against them. Shaw consulted his own watch and, deciding it was tea time, went home. After tea, he left in search of Annie and they walked to Farringdon Hall where she chaired his evening lecture on 'Practical Socialism'.

According to lurid contemporary reports, the fighting had reached its peak at about five o'clock. But by Shaw's account, which was partly aimed at depriving Sir Charles Warren of his reputation as 'a good soldier', the Square was so empty of insurrectionists that the magistrate-on-horseback who had ridden in to read the Riot Act, found no occasion to do so. 'I am happy to say my skull is intact,' Shaw reported next day to E. T. Cook, assistant editor of the *Pall Mall Gazette*:

'. . . I am an ordinary coward myself, and can sympathize with the white feather; but the cowardice of the people was stupendous. Nobody asked them to stand the charges – only to run away down the side streets and get to the square one by one how they could. But ninety percent of them simply turned tail and fled to the extremity of the four mile radius at the first sign of opposition. There was practically nobody in the square when I got there except sightseers [and] the few hundreds of us who had carried out the plan and come on.'

There were many lessons to be picked up from the ruins of Bloody Sunday. William Morris, who had believed that this might be the start of the Revolution, withdrew from outdoor militancy to the converted stable of his house on the Thames and the gatherings of his Hammersmith Socialist Society. For Hyndman it was the beginning of the end, as popular support hesitated, and veered elsewhere. To Shaw and Webb the retreat seemed a victory, not for capitalism over socialism, but for the Fabian tactics over those of their socialist rivals. Once the Local Government Act of 1888 was passed and the machinery of the London County Council established, they set about turning heroic defeat into prosaic success by pushing forward into municipal politics – a doctrine of reforming local government that was derided by Hyndman as 'gas and water socialism'. Shaw and Webb had looked back from Bloody Sunday to the Paris Commune of 1871 and 'the sanguinary suppression' of socialism. But two people, Annie Besant and John Burns, looked forward and learnt another lesson for the twentieth century.

It is possible that Annie had more humorous subtlety in her character than Shaw credited, and that the 'Contract' she placed before him shortly after Bloody Sunday had been a sympathetic means of replacing him in her life by someone more aggressive – W. T. Stead of the *Pall Mall Gazette*. Amid all the revengeful growlings over their rout in the Square it was she who acted most constructively, forming a Socialist Defence

Association, collecting funds, organizing newspaper support, arranging for the bail and legal defence of prisoners, storming the courts, contradicting witnesses, browbeating the police and overawing magistrates. She was all for returning the following Sunday to the Square, and made an impassioned appeal to the Fabians to do so. But Shaw, speaking in opposition, carried a reluctant meeting with him. 'I object to a defiant policy altogether at present,' he explained to William Morris. 'If we persist in it, we shall be eaten bit by bit like an artichoke. They will provoke; we will defy; they will punish. I do not see the wisdom of that . . .'

Once the agitation had sunk, Annie Besant was left with a conviction that success would have to depend on efficient planning and precisely calculated aims, on influencing public opinion through newspapers and the power of organization through the unions. Her leadership of the match-girls' strike in 1888, which ended with improvements in working conditions and pay and led to the formation of a Matchworkers' Union 'on the most advanced modern model', was recognized as a triumph for these new orderly tactics, and later described by G. M. Trevelyan as the 'first skirmish of the New Unionism'.

Of the many strikes of 1889, the greatest, beginning on 14 August, was the London Dock Strike led by John Burns, which was won with the aid of funds from Australian unions and London demonstrations planned in consultation with the police. Burns, who left the SDF a year before Annie was to leave the Fabians and, like her, was a delegate to the Trades Union Congress, emerged from the Dock Strike victory as a potential leader of British socialism. The future belonged to such people – a working-class man who represented Battersea on the London County Council, went into Parliament in 1892 and became the 'first artisan to reach cabinet rank'. The middle-class Fabians found it difficult to supply candidates for the London County Council because 'some of us are civil servants; some have no qualification; some, like myself, have no money,' Shaw prevaricated. When in March 1889 he was invited to run for Parliament in Battersea, he again pleaded the economic difficulty as he would over emotional crises:

'For the last year I have had to neglect my professional duties so much . . . that my pecuniary position is worse than it was; and I am at present almost wholly dependent on critical work which requires my presence during several evenings in the week at public performances . . . As a political speaker outside Parliament I can just manage to pay my way and so keep myself straight and independent. But you know . . . how a man goes to pieces when he has to let his work go.'

Behind this money difficulty, that 'makes genuine democracy impossible at present', lay Shaw's disinclination to have his talent swallowed up by parliamentary politics; and it was this aversion that largely accounted for the Fabian practice of laying eggs in other people's nests.

The most characteristic 'event' staged by the Fabians in these years of intense struggle was 'the Charing Cross Parliament' on whose mock Cabinet Webb sat as chancellor of the exchequer, Bland as foreign secretary, Olivier as colonial secretary, Wallas as president of the Board of Trade and Shaw as president of the Local Government Board. Such an armchair exhibition of training for public life may have seemed remote from the working-class realities nearby; yet the middle-class revolutionary may be effective with words and it was with words that the Fabians made their greatest success when, in December 1889, they published *Fabian Essays in Socialism*. Shaw had been appointed editor and given the job of preparing the book from a number of Fabian lectures. He was no more successful than he had been in his days as novelist with the publishers who agreed that the book was 'commercially unproducible'. Finally, with misgivings, the Fabians decided to bring out a subscription edition themselves, of a thousand copies at six shillings. It had decorations in dark green by Walter Crane on the front and by May Morris on the spine, and was distributed from Pease's flat. The preface and two of the eight essays were supplied by Shaw, who also compiled the index, chose the paper and type, arranged for the blocks and drafted a handbill announcement. Within a month the entire edition was sold out – 'it went off like smoke'. A year later, in various editions, over twenty thousand had gone and it was still selling at the rate of four hundred copies a week. 'This set of essays is apparently inextinguishable,' claimed Shaw. By becoming a best-seller, socialism was made respectable in capitalist terms; and respectability was Shaw's alternative to revolution – an anaesthetic before the political operation.

*Fabian Essays* became a bible, blending moral peroration with economic theory, with which socialist missionaries went out to convert the natives of England. Suddenly Fabianism was famous. The essays had prompted a call 'for Fabian speakers to come over into Macedonia and tell groups of the discontented and aspiring about Socialism for Britain'. In 1891, 335,000 tracts were distributed; by 1893, the membership, which included many influential figures (Keir Hardie, Ramsay MacDonald, Emmeline Pankhurst, Ben Tillett), rose to over five hundred and, in addition to the metropolitan groups, seventy local societies, with a membership of some two thousand, had sprung up.

This Fabian boom, with its reverberation through the provinces, arose directly from the success of the book. 'In these distinctively English essays,' Shaw wrote, 'there is no trace of Marx or Proudhon or the earlier revolutionary veterans of 1848 ... the transition from Capitalism to Socialism is dealt with as part of the course of ordinary constitutional evolution.' Yet William Clarke in his contribution, 'The Industrial Basis of Socialism', represents Fabianism as an amendment to Marxism; and Hubert Bland, in examining how ordinary constitutional evolution might best be engineered, rejected dreams of permeating the Liberal Party in favour of 'the formation of a definitively Socialist party'. Whereas Shaw, in his early history of the Fabian Society, was to state that: 'We have never advanced the smallest pretension to represent the working classes of this country', Bland, with an eye on future union solidarity, urged the Fabians to make an alignment with the working class. Shaw did some revision work to all the essays (which had begun as lectures before mixed audiences), but he let Bland's opposing pages stand, partly as an example of Fabian catholicity, partly as a precedent for an alternative policy in the future should one be needed, and because he knew that Bland would not agree to have his opposition to Webb tucked away: 'there has been no sacrifice of individuality,' he wrote in his Preface.

One of the reviewers of *Fabian Essays* was William Morris. He regretted that such clear social analysis and exposition of socialist principles, as well as the economic understanding of the Fabians, was no longer at the service of the revolutionary movement. Instead they advocated 'the fantastic and unreal tactic' of permeation which 'could not be carried out in practice; and which, if it could be, would still leave us in a position from which we should have to begin our attack on capitalism over again'. Morris blamed Webb for this 'somewhat disastrous move'. Webb had falsified the class struggle, substituted pieties about state regulation, and, together with Wallas, reduced socialism to the mechanism of a system of property-holding. For Morris himself, socialism remained a 'complete theory of human life, founded indeed on the visible necessities of animal life [which] ... will not indeed enable us to get rid of the tragedy of life ... but will enable us to meet it without fear and without shame'. He absolved Hubert Bland from this Fabian reductionism, and wrote warmly, if regretfully, of Shaw. 'If he could only forget the Sidney-Webbian permeation tactic ... what an advantage it would be to us all! He would encourage his friends thereby; and as to his enemies – could he offend them more than he does now?'

Morris and Webb were more than friends to Shaw: they were his political mentors. Morris was a great man and Webb a great brain; Morris a hero for all time and Webb a man of the times. Shaw wanted to unite the applied arts with the social sciences and use Webb's logic to circumvent Morris's sense of history. But as Morris's review of Webb's essay makes clear, they remained two heralds beckoning Shaw in different directions. So Shaw continued speaking of the Fabians with two voices. His most persistent voice aggrandized the Fabian achievement. The other voice sounded his despair that they had not achieved more. He insisted that 'Webb made no mistake'. But by the 1930s he was also to acknowledge that 'Morris was not right after all'. He turned to one and then to the other: and eventually he turned to Soviet Russia.

# CHAPTER IV

## [ 1 ]

*I attack the current morality because it has come to mean a system of strict observance of certain fixed rules of conduct. Thus, a 'moral' man is one who keeps the ten commandments; and an 'immoral' man is one who breaks them. Among the more thoughtful classes this evil (for such I hold it to be) is intensified by the addition to the ten commandments of sentimental obligations to act up to ideal standards of heroism. Now what Ibsen has done is to call attention to the fact that the moment we begin to worship these commandments and ideals for their own sakes, we actually place them in opposition to the very purpose they were instituted to serve, i.e. human happiness . . . (1890)*

On 7 February 1887, their landlord having gone bankrupt, the Shaws had received less than four weeks' notice to leave their flat at 36 Osnaburgh Street. Shaw, the businessman, immediately went to work, drafting letters to the other tenants and patrolling London for new accommodation. 'Looking for lodgings in Marylebone and Gray's Inn,' he noted in his diary on 26 February, 'where my feelings were somewhat hurt by the brusqueness with which the steward received my question as to whether ladies were permitted to reside within the precincts.' Much of this time was filled making up parcels of his books and moving the furniture out of his bedroom. He was in a helpless and discontented state. 'I can say nothing about Saturday,' he wrote in answer to an invitation from Edith Bland on 15 February. 'If we can find new rooms we must turn out of this on that day or on Friday. If on Saturday, I shall be working like a Billingsgate porter until ten at night. If on Friday, I shall flee from the sordid disorder of our flitting like an angel winging its way from a slum to heaven. But I dont know whether we shall be able to get rooms. I am in mere confusion . . . Yours appalled . . .'

At the beginning of March he retreated to his medical friend Kingston Barton, joining his mother later that month in new lodgings on the third and fourth floors of 29 Fitzroy Square. 'Depressing hall,' he noted on entering the building. He was to remain here for over eleven years until rescued by marriage. A big room overlooking the square became his bedroom, and he turned one of the rooms on the top floor into a study where he could read uninterrupted by the crowds of acquaintances who would come and chat with him in the Reading Room of the British Museum. Here, in grand disorder, he was to write his first seven plays, his finest literary, music and theatre criticism, and carry on his most active political campaigning.

Number 29 Fitzroy Square had a handsome façade, but was in such poor condition that (following complaints from the neighbours) it had to be repaired and redecorated the following year. Shaw, who later bought the lease for his mother, described it as 'a most repulsive house'. There was no bathroom and 'the sanitary arrangements had had no place in the original plans,' he discovered. 'In impressive architecture it is the outside that matters most; and the servants do not matter at all.' It was a fine dung-heap for the flowering of his socialism. After a series of humiliating interviews by the Revising Barrister, he established himself as being not his mother's lodger but head of the household, so that in November 1888 he was able to register 'the first vote I ever gave in my life at an election, though I am over 32 years of age'.

The month he moved in he was proposing a motion at the South Place Ethical Society that 'the welfare of the community necessitates the transfer of the land and existing capital of the country from private owners to the State'. To Shaw's mind the State was a necessary instrument ('a machine to do certain work') for a social revolution. Wherever he spoke he took care to lay down a substratum of political philosophy. His words were 'straight as a ray of light,' wrote H. M. Tomlinson, 'such as we get once or twice in a few centuries, as the result of passionate morality that happens to be gifted with the complete control of full expression'. But it was the seditious style of his utterance that had begun to attract larger audiences. Many who heard this 'tall, thin man with a very pale and gentle face' speaking with deadly playfulness, and denouncing as robbers those usually regarded as the ornaments of society, were convinced that here was a new and powerful figure. Ernest Rhys, who met him at the Hobby Horse Group of writers, artists and rebels, remembered walking 'round and round Fitzroy Square a dozen times, talking of these things, and afterwards I went home with a curious sense of a movement, a revolutionary rising which would upset many of our conventions and bring a new dispensation, political and economic, into the London world'.

In 1887 he delivered sixty-six public lectures; by the end of ten years he had given nearly a thousand. Every Sunday he spoke, usually in the

London area, sometimes against the blaring of brass bands, often at workmen's clubs and coffee houses, to secular societies and radical associations, expounding and arguing from squalid platforms in dens full of tobacco smoke, to a little knot of members whom he had pulled away from their beer and billiards. The 'ubiquitous Mr Shaw', as *The Star* called him, was soon well known as a peculiar feature in their political cabaret: 'a strange and rather startling figure', erect and agile in his serviceable suit of tweed, red scarf, wide-brimmed felt hat and jauntily swinging umbrella – 'a tall, lean, icy man,' reported the *Workman's Times*, 'whitefaced, with a hard, clear, fleshless voice, restless grey-blue eyes, neatly-parted fair hair, big feet, and a reddish, untamed beard'.

He preferred speaking in the open air at all sorts of holes and corners – under lamp-posts, at dock gates, in parks, squares, market places – and in all sorts of weather. He never wrote or read his speeches, but used a series of cards with lists of subjects. By street-corner practice and phonetic study he had learnt to address an audience 'as a man learns to skate or to cycle – by doggedly making a fool of myself until I got used to it'. By the late 1880s he had laboriously perfected his technique 'until I could put a candle out with a consonant'. Though the words were often strong he was never personally abusive. He was known as a 'brilliant and also a merciless theorist', but 'nothing could be less like the conspirator, or fanatical revolutionist, than the freedom with which he poked fun at his own cause or his fellow Socialists,' wrote one Cambridge professor. He stirred the working man and delighted the academics. 'On the platform you must have the smart appearance of the clerk,' he later advised Lady Rhondda, 'the articulation of the telephone girl, the address of the shop assistant, and the knowledge of your wares and of their talking points of the commercial traveller, all in more than Bond Street perfection . . .'

Whether it was 'Capitalism' at the Wolverhampton Trades and Labour Council, 'Communism' at the Dulwich Working Men's Club, 'Socialism' at Plumstead, or 'Food, Death and Civilization' at the headquarters of the London Vegetarian League, he spoke, using his expressive hands, curving and stretching his long pink fingers to reach out to his audience, as if all their lives depended upon it. 'I used to hold big audiences for 110 minutes without turning a hair,' he remembered. Once he continued irrepressibly pouring out socialism for three hours; another time in catapulting rain he gave one of his most hypnotic performances to four policemen at Hyde Park Corner: 'I spoke very well in my effort to convert them.' Conversion to his brand of socialism was perpetually his aim: 'my platform performances are for use, not for ornament.' He packed the halls with crowds of people; he made them listen, made them laugh. Sometimes, to their bewilderment, he made extravagant fun of himself, having ingeniously miscalculated that 'audiences are illnatured enough to enjoy jokes at other people's expense, and goodnatured enough to hate you if you are illnatured. The way to get round this is to be illnatured at your own expense.' The effect, he thought, was homoeopathic: and self-disparagement, even of a paradoxical kind, increased people's respect. In fact it seems to have increased their entertainment but spread a film of incredulity over many of his hearers. Yet it is clear from the text of those lectures he later wrote up for publication that Shaw was passionately serious. His words seemed charged with a new intensity; he was the prophet in a barren land, and socialism a burning fire within his bones:

'. . . your authorised system of medicine is nothing but a debased survival of witchcraft. Your schools are machines for forcing spurious learning on children in order that your universities may stamp them as educated men when they have finally lost all power to think for themselves. The tall silk hats and starched linen fronts which you force me to wear, and without which I cannot successfully practise as a physician, clergyman, schoolmaster, lawyer or merchant, are inconvenient, unsanitary, ugly, pompous and offensive. Your temples are devoted to a God in whom I do not believe; and . . . your popular forms of worship [are] . . . only redeemed from gross superstition by their obvious insincerity . . . Under color of protecting my person and property you forcibly take my money to support an army of soldiers and policemen for the execution of barbarous and detestable laws; for the waging of wars which I abhor; and for the subjection of my person to those legal rights of property which compel me to sell myself for a wage to a class the maintenance of which I hold to be the greatest evil of our time. Your tyranny makes my very individuality a hindrance to me: I am outdone and outbred by the mediocre, the docile, the time-serving. Evolution under such conditions means degeneracy.'

This was the voice of a man who, weary of forbearance, seemed to have burst through a door and raised the torch of revolution. No wonder some of his politer audiences, professors mostly, hurried from the halls with hands held to their ears; no wonder there was sometimes violence – and he had to escape through a window or back door. Lectures with the most respectable titles such as 'The Economic Basis of Socialism' carried fiery diatribes against the consequences of Capitalism:

'. . . your slaves are beyond caring for your cries: they breed like rabbits; and their poverty breeds filth, ugliness, dishonesty, disease, obscenity, drunkenness, and murder. In the midst of the riches which their labor piles up for you, their misery rises up too and stifles you. You withdraw in disgust to the other end of the town from them; you appoint special carriages on your railways and special seats in your churches and theatres for them; you set your life apart from theirs by every class barrier you can devise; and yet they swarm about you still: your face gets stamped with your habitual loathing and suspicion of them: your ears get so filled with the language of the vilest of them that you break into it when you lose your self-control: they poison your life as remorselessly as you have sacrificed theirs heartlessly. You begin to believe intensely in the devil. Then comes the terror of their revolting; the drilling and arming of bodies of them to keep down the rest; the prison, the hospital, paroxysms of frantic coercion, followed by paroxysms of frantic charity. And in the meantime, the population continues to increase!'

Many in his audience were astonished by the effect his words had on them. Henry Sidgwick, Professor of Moral Philosophy at Cambridge, who heard him speak at Bath, noted in his diary that the speaker was 'a live Socialist, redhot "from the Streets"' who

'sketched in a really brilliant address the rapid series of steps by which modern society is to pass peacefully into social democracy ... It is now *urban* ground-rent that the municipal governments will have to seize, to meet the ever-growing necessity of providing work and wages for the unemployed ... There was a peroration rhetorically effective as well as daring, in which he explained that the bliss of perfected socialism would only come by slow degrees, with lingering step and long delays, and claimed our sympathy for the noble-hearted men whose ardent philanthropy had led them to cut these delays short by immediate revolution and spoliation. It was, indeed, a mistake on their part; the laws of social development did not admit of it; but ... we should join him in regretting that this shorter way with property was impossible. Altogether a noteworthy performance:- the man's name is *Bernard Shaw*.'

When advocating physical destruction of the Old Order, Shaw's oratory was like a spur to insurrection, and if he stopped short of calling for the bombardment of the London slums by the new dynamite, it seemed only with reluctance. Gradualness might be inevitable, but it was not welcome: 'if we feel relieved that the change is to be slow enough to avert personal risk to ourselves; if we feel anything less than acute disappointment and bitter humiliation at the discovery that there is yet between us and the promised land a wilderness in which many must perish miserably of want and despair: then I submit to you that our institutions have corrupted us to the most dastardly degree of selfishness.'

For his thousand lectures over these years Shaw received no payment: 'I have never spoken a word in public for money, though I have been offered absurdly large sums to break that rule.' By this rule, since his topics were so spiced with controversy, he secured the freedom to say what he wanted and a safeguard against being identified as a hired political agitator. 'To the propagation of his ideas, he gives up willingly time, labour, the opportunities of self-advancement,' reported *The Star*. 'To such men we can forgive much.' At the election of 1892, while lecturing at the Town Hall in Dover, a man rose and warned his audience not to be taken in by someone whose opinions were purchased: 'I immediately offered to sell him my emoluments for £5,' Shaw recalled. 'He hesitated; and I came down to £4. I offered to make it five shillings – half-a-crown – a shilling – sixpence. When he would not deal even at a penny I claimed that he must know perfectly well that I was there at my own expense. If I had not been able to do this, the meeting, which was a difficult and hostile one . . . would probably have broken up.'

The art of public speaking appealed to the actor in Shaw – 'lecturing takes far more acting,' he advised Irene Vanbrugh, 'than a part on the stage'. His success answered his need for attention, though much of it was 'terrible tongue work'. He had never admired this need in himself and would slowly grow disillusioned with the results of trying to harness it to something he did admire. The development of his public manner had forced brashness on to a nature that was ordinarily sensitive. 'Oratory is a vice,' he complained to the actress Lena Ashwell, and by indulgence in it the orator became 'debauched and repulsive'. He would have accepted this contamination if his oratory had forced a path to something better. But he could not delude himself: the applause that rose through the most gorgeous of his meetings was an empty sound. 'My career as a public speaker was not only futile politically,' he later concluded: 'It was sometimes disgraceful and degrading.'

'I had my platform triumphs, and was vociferously acclaimed a jolly good fellow in town halls crowded with enthusiastic partisans, after which my candidate friends would be duly defeated by opponents who had not a word to say that would have imposed on the giddiest rabbit. But whether my candidate was returned or not I suffered agonies of disgust at the whole business and shame for my part in it.'

He concealed his disgust so effectively as to be accused of glorying in self-advertisement. The success of *Fabian Essays* in 1889 soon led to a train of provincial lectures, particularly in the north of England, and Shaw's flame-coloured beard and illuminated white face were seen in places that had never before borne witness to socialism. His life was hectic with appointments. He worked eighteen hours a day and on the seventh day he worked. 'My hours that make my days, my days that make my years,' he wrote, 'follow one another pell mell into the maw of Socialism.'

*

He had hoped to gain a little money and more self-respect through converting some of this lecture-work into book-work. He had in mind 'a small work on socialism for Sutton's University Series', and a readable volume on modern scientific political economy for a Contemporary Science Series that Havelock Ellis was editing. 'It is quite possible to get into a volume of 200 pages an adequate and bright explanation of the law of rent and the law of value, which really cover the laws of production and of exchange, and so, in a fair sense, cover the whole field of economics,' he explained to Ellis. '. . . I think that the book, if a success, would be worth more than £40, which is somewhat less than the "rent of my ability"'. He had predicted in the middle of 1888 that 'I could produce such a book before the middle of next year', but early in 1889 he wrote to Ellis:

'I never face facts or obtrude them on others sooner than I can possibly help; but the time has come for me to confess that I see about as much prospect of having "Production & Exchange" ready by June as of establishing the millenium . . . I have to keep up my lectures (five this week); and I have to keep myself alive by journalism all the time. This is Production with a vengeance; but it is not "Production & Exchange". There is no use in my pretending to go on at this rate . . .'

Later in 1889 he also abandoned his book on socialism. Then, in the summer of 1890, rather to their dismay, the Fabians found themselves committed to a programme of addresses under the heading 'Socialism in Contemporary Literature'. It was difficult to get speakers but eventually Sydney Olivier consented to talk on Zola; William Morris spoke at the last minute on Gothic architecture; Stepniak tackled the modern Russians, and Hubert Bland 'undertook to read all the Socialist novels of the day, an enterprise the desperate failure of which resulted in the most amusing paper of the series'. Shaw's subject was Ibsen. Between May and July he worked on his paper which was delivered on 18 July at the St James's Restaurant. The minutes record that 'the paper was a long one', nearer two hours than one, but 'the effect on the packed audience was overwhelming'. It had been 'couched in provocative terms', and though Edward Pease noted that it was 'well-received', not all the Fabians were happy. 'It is very clever,' Sidney Webb wrote to Beatrice after the talk, 'and not so bad as I feared ... But his glorification of the Individual Will distresses me.' Shaw had used Ibsen's texts in his case for an adaptable as opposed to doctrinaire socialism, which in its immediate context meant Fabian gradualism and permeation as against the Marxist dogma and revolutionary politics of Hyndman's SDF. *The Star* reported that Shaw had 'made the Fabian flesh creep', but though there was some Fabian uneasiness (particularly from Annie Besant who had been in the Chair) the main attack came from non-Fabian socialists such as Herbert Burrows who denounced the lecture as a 'gospel of egotistic selfishness'.

It was probably the Parnell case that decided Shaw to expand his lecture into a book. This *cause célèbre* had resulted in November 1891 in Captain O'Shea being granted a decree nisi against his wife, naming Charles Stewart Parnell, leader of the Irish Party in the House of Commons, as co-respondent. Both in private letters and letters to *The Star*, Shaw had defended Parnell against the outcry 'Parnell Must GO!' that sounded throughout the country following this flouting of domestic ideals by a public figure. On the same day, 16 December, that he wrote to Sydney Olivier, criticizing the opposition to Parnell from within the Fabian Society, he decided to publish *The Quintessence of Ibsenism*.

The book came out in October the following year, addressed to his own class, the intellectual class, and designed to purge socialism of the flattering sentimentalities that were already becoming encrusted on its reforming body. It is a work of metaphysics and of polemics and, if the glare of the polemics dimmed the argument, this was partly because of Shaw's screen of propaganda. The *Quintessence*, he insisted, had rescued an 'ungrateful generation from Materialism & Rationalism'; it was a 'feminist document', the first four chapters of which (culminating in 'The Womanly Woman') 'broke up homes and made suffragettes in the most unexpected directions'.

Though not, in the academic sense, an Ibsen scholar, Shaw felt an immediate affinity with him. The book was a product of his friendship with Archer through whose early championship of Ibsen Shaw had first got to know his work. Meeting Ibsen in Denmark in 1887, Archer had observed that he 'is essentially a kindred spirit with Shaw – a paradoxist, a sort of Devil's Advocate, who goes about picking holes in every "well-known fact".' It was this similarity that helped to give Shaw such an instinctive insight into Ibsen's plays. 'Your treatment of *Brand* and *Peer Gynt* fills me with envious awe,' Archer wrote to him.

'I have read and re-read these poems until I know them as intimately as Mr Ruskin knows Giotto's Campanile; you, on the other hand, have never read them at all, but have merely picked up a vague, second-hand knowledge of their outlines; yet you have penetrated their mystery (I speak in all seriousness) much more thoroughly than I have.'

Ibsen's plays had more power to move Shaw than the work of any other living dramatist, giving him a 'tremendous sensation in a theatre'. Of a performance of *The Wild Duck*, he was to write:

'To sit there getting deeper and deeper in that Ekdal home, and getting deeper and deeper into your own life all the time, until you forget you are in a theatre; to look on with horror and pity at a profound tragedy, shaking with laughter all the time at an irresistible comedy; to go out, not from a diversion, but from an experience deeper than real life ever brings to most men, or often brings to any man: that is what The Wild Duck was like last Monday at the Globe.'

The joy of his book is that of feeling Shaw's agile and ingenious mind working with such vitality on material so sympathetic to him. His chief critics charged it with being a brilliantly misconceived work that, while helping to gain acceptance for Ibsen on the British stage, put him through a Shavian mincer and served him up to the public as a feast for committed socialists. He had been 'butchered to make a Fabian holiday', one critic commented. Shaw tried to guard against this objection by prefacing his book with the warning that he is not concerned here with Ibsen as a poet or dramatist, but as a teacher; that, though acutely responsive to the poetry and drama, he is not attempting to write literary criticism but 'simply an exposition of Ibsenism' – that is, an examination of the modern philosophy of which Ibsen was an exponent. The *Quintessence* presents Shaw's credentials as a man who was carrying on Ibsen's business of 'changing the mind of Europe'. In seeking a symbolic leader who would unite the contradictory impulses within himself, Shaw leads him immaculately into battle against all those conventional ideals he felt formed the chief obstacle to the advancement of life's purpose. His conversion of Ibsen into a wholesale warrior does involve distortions to some of the plays, though these are partly explained by his not having been able to see all of them performed, and only having heard them in Archer's spontaneous translations.

In January 1886, on the first floor of a Bloomsbury lodging house, while chatting and munching caramels, Shaw had gone through the part of Krogstad in *A Doll's House*, while Eleanor Marx played Nora Helmer; but he had 'a very vague notion of what it was about'. Ibsen's name does not appear in his letters before 1889, and we have Archer's word that he had 'barely heard Ibsen's name' two years before. But by 1891 he has appropriated him. By then, following productions of *A Doll's House* and *Ghosts*, the name of Ibsen (who was sixty-three when the *Quintessence* appeared) had emerged from obscurity into huge contention in Britain as the playwright who was forcing a whole generation to revalue its ideas. Ibsen was by now familiar even to the non-play-going majority, and the critics were battling resoundingly over his reputation. Shaw assumed the generalship of the British campaign as part of that same world struggle he had discovered to be at the centre of Ibsen's plays. In this way Ibsen became for Shaw not just a literary symbol but a tool in the Fabian plan to make things, not as they ought to be (that was utopianism), but as they could be made (that was socialism).

As a model for his argument Shaw had adapted Matthew Arnold and used a threefold division of mankind into philistine, idealist and (pending the word superman) realist. This division required the inversion of the terms realist and idealist which he cleverly justifies in the context of Ibsen's writings. He proposes a hypothetical community of one thousand people in which seven hundred are easygoing philistines, two hundred and ninety-nine dangerous idealists ('the idealist is a more dangerous animal than the philistine just as a man is a more dangerous animal than a sheep'), and there is one realistic pioneer essential to the evolution of the species. The philistine, substituting 'custom for conscience', is satisfied with the social system as it is. The irony of his position is that, though he sees any interference with the social machinery as highly dangerous, the real danger comes from allowing that machinery to grow outdated. The philistine employs the idealist to think for him and to 'idealize' his lack of thought. The idealist, though higher in the ascent of human evolution than the philistine, is a moral coward coerced by the majority into conformity. His instinct is perverted by fear and he uses all his powers of reason to veil the truth, substituting for the human will and spirit a set of abstract ethical principles set hard within the structure of idealized public institutions, laws and creeds. Ideals, in Shavian terminology, are therefore illusions which have their origin in the fear of facts; and they become excuses for doing what we do, which is what we have always done before. So idealism is life by the rule of precedent, and the idealist a pedlar of fancy pictures which advertise this rule. Shaw likens these pictures to beautiful masks which the idealist puts for us on the unbearable faces of truth: the poetic mask of immortality on that king of terrors, death; the mask of eternal romantic happiness, never losing its sweetness within the prison-house of marriage, on the brutalities of the sex instinct; and on his own self-murder the religious concept of self-sacrifice.

But the realist, bolder than the rest, believing in the 'unflinching recognition of facts, and the abandonment of the conspiracy to ignore such of them as do not bolster up the ideals', lays hold of a mask that we have not dared to do without and reveals a new aspect of the disagreeable truth. So he helps to relieve us from useless sacrifice to the tyranny of ideals: for 'the destroyer of ideals, though denounced as an enemy to society, is in fact sweeping the world clear of lies'. This was the Ibsen-impulse: 'to get away from idolatry and get to the truth regardless of shattered ideals'.

Sidney Webb's distress at his friend's 'glorification of the Individual Will' underlines the difference between a man who was by nature a collectivist and another who worked his way from individualism to collectivism, expanding his social consciousness from himself to the nation, partly against the grain of his natural talent. Shaw tried to acknowledge the objection of Webb by admitting that Ibsen was an arch-individualist who 'has not enjoyed this Fabian advantage', since socialism in his day was one of the most outrageously idealistic of all the new '-isms'. But this acknowledgement mocks the cultural philistinism of the Fabians. There were several passages that must have agitated Webb.

'All abstractions invested with collective consciousness or collective authority, set above the individual, and exacting duty from him on pretence of acting or thinking with greater validity than he, are man-eating idols red with human sacrifices . . .'

'The sum of the matter is that unless Woman repudiates her womanliness, her duty to her husband, to her children, to society, to the law, and to everyone but herself, she cannot emancipate herself. But her duty to herself is no duty at all, since a debt is cancelled when the debtor and creditor are the same person. Its payment is simply a fulfilment of the individual will, upon which all duty is a restriction, founded on the conception of the will as naturally malign and devilish.'

But in a number of passages added to the 1913 edition Shaw makes clear that he is enshrining individual will only when it works in harmony with the world-will (or Life Force as it would become known). He is opposed to anarchism and to the aggrandisement of the self. Although society needs to be shocked pretty often, he argues that the 'need for freedom of evolution is the sole basis of toleration, the valid argument against Inquisitions and Censorships, the sole reason for not burning heretics and sending every eccentric person to the madhouse'. So the heretic of today (Galileo, Darwin, Marx and perhaps Shaw himself), striving to realize future possibilities, becomes the pillar of the community tomorrow, and pretence slowly recedes. But pillars of the community are idealists. Only by invading some of those quixotic ideals, which in 1891 he had described as illusions, was Shaw eventually able to reconcile his individual bias to a steady Fabian programme of world-betterment through collectivism:

'Ibsen here [in *Little Eyolf*] explicitly insists for the first time that 'we are all members one of another', and that though the strongest man is he who stands alone, the man who is standing alone for his own sake solely is literally an idiot . . .

'There is no hope in Individualism for egotism. When a man is at last brought face to face with himself by a brave Individualism, he finds himself face to face, not with an individual, but with a species, and knows that to save himself, he must save the race.'

Some of the confusion inhaled by readers of the *Quintessence* arose from Shaw's choice of one word. In the same way as 'superman', with its Nietzschean associations, was to suggest not a symbol of synthesis but a dictatorship, so the word 'Will', with its Schopenhauerian associations, indicated not 'our old friend the soul or spirit' but an assertion of power over others. In neither case did Shaw originally intend this, but the ambiguity of these words points to an impulse that was gradually to gain possession of him.

The philosophy of the *Quintessence* is pragmatism. 'Life is an adventure, not the compounding of a prescription' and we must live it according to circumstances. The golden rule, Shaw tells us, is that 'there are no golden rules'. Human conduct must 'justify itself by its effect on happiness'. By 'happiness' he meant human welfare (a phrase he was to use in a similar sentence in the Preface to *Getting Married*) and for the 1913 edition he changed the word to 'life'. In 1938 he wrote to the editor of *Nordisk Tidende*: 'I have not a word of my *Quintessence* of Ibsenism, written in my early thirties, to withdraw or dilute now that I am in my early eighties.' But in the interval between the first publication and his preparation of the 1913 edition, though he maintained the same apparatus of argument, Shaw's attitude had shifted. Having left his hand-to-mouth existence for a more comfortable married life, and retired from the Fabian executive, he was to grow more involved in the theatre of ideas. In 1891 he had used the word 'idealist' pejoratively to cover all those who inhabited too exclusively the world of ideas, whether they were blinded by illusions or held a fixed vision of a better life. Such people, by preferring fantasy to the actual world, risked being made prisoners of abstractions, he argued, since morality was relative and must be continually tested by experience. His theory had been that theoretical ideals led to pessimism; but his experience as a Fabian would drive him, as a source for optimism, to the ideal collectivist formula of equality of income and a metaphysical creed in the transcendental spirit of Carlyle.

The 1891 *Quintessence*, which aims its ingenious attack at the man he was to become, is a paradoxically prophetic work – and nowhere more so than in the pages about *Emperor and Galilean*, where Shaw begins to explore the synthesis of relations that Ibsen's Maximus called 'the third empire' – 'the empire of Man asserting the eternal validity of his own will,' Shaw wrote.

'He who can see that not on Olympus, not nailed to the cross, but in himself is God: he is the man to build Brand's bridge between the flesh and the spirit, establishing this third empire in which the spirit shall not be unknown, nor the flesh starved, nor the will tortured and baffled.'

Within *Emperor and Galilean* Shaw was to find the theme and dialectical pattern of his middle plays, from *Man and Superman* to *Back to Methuselah*. Yet, despite Shaw's belief in synthesis, the habit of segregation persisted like an hereditary trait, and finally established itself in the flesh-starved Ancients at the end of *Back to Methuselah*. In these almost bodiless fantasies the author of the original *Quintessence* could have seen a dramatic example of the failure of an idealist to accept man as he is.

[ 2 ]

*Some time in the eighties ... The New Journalism was introduced. Lawless young men began to write and print the living English language of their own day ... They split their infinitives, and wrote such phrases as 'a man nobody ever heard of' instead of 'a man of whom nobody had ever heard', or, more classical still, 'a writer hitherto unknown'. Musical critics, instead of reading books about their business and elegantly regurgitating their erudition, began to listen to music and distinguish between sounds; critics of painting began to look at pictures; critics of the drama began to look at something else besides the stage; and descriptive writers actually broke into the House of Commons, elbowing the reporters into the background, and writing about political leaders as if they were mere play-actors. The interview, the illustration and the cross-heading, hitherto looked on as American vulgarities*

> *impossible to English literary gentlemen, invaded all our*
> *papers; and, finally, as the climax and masterpiece of literary*
> *Jacobinism, the Saturday Review appeared with a signed article*
> *in it.* 'Van Amburgh Revived' (1898)

*The Quintessence of Ibsenism* was the most sustained and sophisticated work Shaw wrote before the age of thirty-five. His care in guarding the book against being 'swept into an eddy of mere literary criticism' reflects his own experience of criticism up to this time. It was 'literary criticism' in the form of readers' reports from Morley, Meredith and others, that had blocked his novels and 'put a stop to my life's work'; it was 'literary criticism' – over a hundred anonymous notices for the *Pall Mall Gazette* – on which he had become financially dependent from the spring of 1885 to Christmas 1888.

The *Pall Mall Gazette* was the centre of what Matthew Arnold called 'the New Journalism'. It was edited by W. T. Stead, who used the paper to produce an emotional bond between himself and the public. Together with Frank Harris, who edited the *Evening News*, Stead altered the character of daily journalism in Britain during the mid 1880s. Papers became simpler – as he wished the world to be. He popularized interviews, added illustrations, invented picturesque headlines, pursued virtuous crusades. 'All his indignations did him credit,' Shaw affirmed; but his 'infatuation with his own emotions' made him deeply untrustworthy. His emotions were sacred to him. When he was angry it was obvious to him that everyone shared his anger; when he wept, he took it for granted that the world wept with him. People read his paper to find out what on earth he was up to next. One day he would drop in on General Gordon at Southampton and call for him to be sent to Khartoum; next he was warning Gladstone against declaring war on Russia; then, switching his energies elsewhere, he fell strongly behind Mrs Gordon-Baillie's scheme for establishing fishing settlements in Tasmania for Scottish crofters; and, most extraordinary of all, as part of his campaign against London vice, he had procured five virgins ostensibly for seduction and landed in prison.

Shaw was a contributor to the *Pall Mall* under Stead's editorship, 'but as my department was literature and art, and he was an utter Philistine, no contacts between us were possible,' Shaw wrote. '. . . He had, as far as I could see, no general knowledge of art or history, philosophy or science, with which to co-ordinate his journalistic discoveries; and it was consequently impossible for cultured minds to get into any sort of effective contact with his except on the crudest common human ground.' Yet the *Pall Mall Gazette* had Oscar Wilde, George Moore and William Archer writing on the arts pages, and it was a sign of Stead's journalistic flair that he should also employ there 'a satirical contributor with a turn for prophesy.'

Shaw's exasperation with Stead ('a complete ignoramus') arose mainly from 'the slow murder' of his work. In one of his novel reviews, he wrote of the 'tremendous economic pressure that forces us to do what we can do in this world, instead of what we would like to do'. He had at last begun to earn some money, and at the end of each year would note in his diary what he had made from contributions to papers: £150 in 1888; £197 6s. 10d. in 1889; £252 13s. 2d. in 1890; £281 16s. 10d. for 1891. Much of this money he would hand to his mother, 'asking her for a pound when my pockets were empty'.

Shaw insisted that literature and the arts must not be segregated from politics. Since adding 'a special revolutionist to its staff', the *Pall Mall Gazette* was beginning to be regarded among Socialists 'half incredulously, as a capitalist paper that does not hate the light'. Shaw hoped to illuminate Stead's policy, which he described as 'making at random for righteousness through a dense economic fog'. But it needed every ingenuity to get his voice heard at all since the editorial habit of the literary department was to give 'a page and a half of vapid comment to a book destined to be forgotten without having influenced the conduct or opinions of a single human being; whilst pamphlets that circulate by thousands, dealing with vital questions of national economy and private morals, are tossed aside into the waste-paper basket . . .'

Among the non-fiction works assigned to him were polite journals depicting the genteel life of county families, and the intrepid book-making of tourists bursting with events that might have happened to anybody. He also reviewed biographies whose edifying conclusions added a new terror to other people's deaths, and autobiographies, tasting of pure water, from which he learnt that, unlike himself, 'few men care enough about their past to take the trouble of writing its history'.

To Shaw's mind there was not a gleam of moral responsibility in almost any of these books. They were written in the blinkered English manner that noticed nothing that was not perfectly proper, placid and pleasant – a style that would 'be no worse than ridiculous,' he reasoned, 'if its systematic practice did not unfortunately deceive many innocent people into believing that there is no considerable evil in the world to be fought with, except the existence of a few criminals whose repression may be left to the police'. Shaw's drastic descriptions of these 'cursed parcels of rubbish' reveal the damage done to the art of biography by the social and sexual blight of late nineteenth-century culture. 'The publication of the truth about anything or anyone is attended with considerable risk in English society,' he explained.

'We have agreed to keep up a national pretence that the black spots in human nature are white; and we enforce the convention by treating any person who even betrays his consciousness of them, much less ventures directly to call attention to them and suggest a purifying limewash, as a prurient person and an enemy of public morals ... the convention rigorously exacts – under pretence of not speaking evilly of the dead – that biographers should exhibit great men, not as they were, but as ideal figures in which the Village Blacksmith and Mr Pecksniff are blinded in proportions determined by the degree of sophistication suggested by the social circumstances of the hero subject. That the very worst sort of evil speaking, whether of the living or the dead, is the telling of lies about them, or that the very maddest presumption on the part of a biographer is the taking upon himself to decide how much of the truth it is good for the rest of the world to know is not taken into account in judging biography, as Mr Froude and others have been recently made to feel. The censors will tolerate no offence against hypocrisy, because ... an offence against hypocrisy is an offence against decency, and is punishable as such.'

Shaw's prescription for biography is in the tradition of Dr Johnson's as laid down in *The Rambler*; and his onslaught on Victorian biography coincides with Carlyle's famous jeremiad against the Damocles Sword of Respectability when reviewing Lockhart's *Walter Scott*. The Shavian iconoclasm, which looks forward to the biographical revolution of Lytton Strachey thirty-five years later, is most ironically expressed in his review of a Jubilee chronicle of Queen Victoria:

'With her merits we are familiar ... We know that she has been of all wives the best, of all mothers the fondest, of all widows the most faithful. We have often seen her, despite her lofty station, moved by famines, colliery explosions, shipwrecks, and railway accidents; thereby teaching us that a heart beats in her Royal breast as in the humblest of her subjects. She has proved that she can, when she chooses, put off her state and play the pianoforte, write books, and illustrate them like any common lady novelist. We all remember how she repealed the corn laws, invented the steam locomotive, and introduced railways; devised the penny post, developed telegraphy, and laid the Atlantic cable; how she captured Coomassie and Alexandria, regenerated art by the pre-Raphaelite movement, speculated in Suez Canal stock, extended the franchise, founded the Primrose League, became Empress of India, and, in short, went through such a programme as no previous potentate ever dreamed of. What we need now is a book entitled 'Queen Victoria: by a Personal Acquaintance who dislikes her' . . . The proper person for the work would be some politically indifferent devil's advocate who considers the Queen an over-rated woman, and would take a conscientious delight in disparaging her.

'Such a book, one would think, could not greatly scandalize the nineteenth century. The world is growing out of loyalty . . . That the Queen, if no longer actually hedged with divinity, is yet more than merely human in the eyes of many of us, is made plain by the sacredness which trivial things assume when touched by a Royal hand. What is more *banal* than a pair of boots? What more uninteresting than an umbrella? But the Queen's boots! are they *banal*? The Queen's umbrella! what would you not give for the reversion of it? When a tornado devastates an American province it is chronicled in a quarter of a column. Yet were a gust of wind to blow off our Sovereign's head-gear to-morrow, 'The Queen's Bonnet' would crowd Bulgaria out of the papers.'

Such myths had been fitted out with all those affable ideals against which Shaw directed his torpedo in *The Quintessence of Ibsenism*. But it was through the oceans of Victorian novels that his main warfare was conducted. Readers who felt that George Eliot lacked passion picked up these stories by more recklessly entertaining novelists with the same purpose as others took to drink: to kill time, to be rid of themselves. 'The most dangerous public house in London is at the corner of Oxford St,' Shaw told one of his audiences, 'and is kept by a gentleman named Mudie.' The books in Mudie's Library were uniform, and by recommending any novel as 'very popular at Mudie's' Shaw meant that it was another mammoth romance, encircling us with a false view of human duties and relations. 'Such books,' he concluded, 'are not fair game for the reviewer: they are addressed to children of all ages who are willing to shut their eyes and open their mouths. In this attitude the grown-up children will presently be gratified by some startling flattery.' Second-rate fiction, he concluded, might have become good enough for such adults but 'firstrate fiction is needed for children themselves'.

Though these novels were extravagantly unbelievable, readers persisted in affecting to believe them. Such books were the very honey of false ideals and therein lay their danger. 'Many of our worst habits are acquired in an imaginary world,' Shaw warned.

'. . . For, if bad novels make, as we have seen that they can make, a bad nation, the question remains, what makes bad novels? Clearly, a bad nation: Thus we have got the nation corrupting fiction, and fiction reacting on the nation to make it more corrupt. At the center of this vicious circle, we find the root of all evil – bad economic conditions . . . [producing] a general hypocrisy of the most searching kind, under the influence of which everyone dreads the truth, and agrees to stigmatize all efforts to expose it as indecent. Hence springs up a false morality which seeks to establish dignity, refinement, education, social importance, wealth, power and magnificence, on a hidden foundation of idleness, dishonesty, sensuality, hypocrisy, tyranny, rapacity, cruelty, and scorn. When the novelist comes to build his imaginary castle, he builds on the same foundation, but adds heroism, beauty, romance, and above all, possibility of exquisite happiness to the superstructure, thereby making it more beautiful to the ignorant, and more monstrous to the initiated.'

Looking out from Shaw's imprisonment in this castle, we may catch a splendid view of popular late Victorian fiction. Much of this fiction is in three volumes (a range of *magnum opus* now commandeered by biography) and written in the white heat of self-indulgence. Just as it was the fashion for ladies to wear top hats when out riding, so (in the Brontë and Eliot vein) they called themselves Tom, Dick or Humphry when novel-writing. And what journeys across the torrid desert of fiction they made! Their route lay encumbered by an extraordinary succession of mirages: avalanches, attacks of consumption, unmuzzled dogs, ghosts, lunatics, Chinese executions, runaway trains, fire engines, gunpowder, daggers and much other impedimenta from the locker-room of noveldom. The landscape is infested with fortresses. Outside towers a background of crag, cloud and sea, with green walls of pine and a mountain torrent. Within, aged hounds lie stretched on the carpet, curtains are continually tweaked aside by jewelled fingers and ropes of roses adorn the staircases ascending to the boudoirs. These strongholds, which in the last chapter are all burnt to matchwood, are inhabited by a throng of murderers, bigamists, coquettes, sneaks, paragons and so on, who are never at ease and seldom in safety. Nearly everything takes place at night (to the cry of owls, nightingales and cat-birds), except for a little cockfighting perhaps and the regular afternoon calls which usually carry on the business of the second volume. There are a few old people past love-making, but they have all had prehistoric turns at it and each carries a sorrow to the grave in consequence. The villains, who break out under stress into uncouth scraps of French, are consumed by earthquakes or engulfed in shipwrecks carrying many innocuous travellers down with them. The hero is easily recognized by his faculty for alighting on haystacks when flung from continental expresses, for inheriting fortunes, and for tracking diamond smugglers to their doom. A composite photograph of the heroines at Mudie's would have shown golden tresses, a pair of blue eyes occasionally changing under degrees of emotion to green, hazel or brown, and (for Chapter 1) a plain white dress with a flower at the throat. For three volumes intransigent relatives and designing reprobates block her way to the altar, only to be arbitrarily removed in the last pages by violent Acts of God or the Devil, the sympathetic reader breathing more and more freely as the slaughter proceeds and obstacle after obstacle is removed from the path of true love.

With such caricatures of the love he had once longed for himself, Shaw spent many hours, months, years of his time, first as a book reviewer and subsequently as a theatre critic. After a multitude of such blistering tales, all with the same characters, the same incidents, the same scenery, names and words, Shaw decided it was time to remonstrate. As part of his review of Hall Caine's *A Son of Hager* (three volumes), he proposed a guild of nineteenth-century authors 'with their imaginations out of long-clothes and fairly grown and educated – all sworn to write henceforth according to the following rules:

'1. That the fictitious persons in their books shall not belong to the criminal classes. 2. That their property, parentage, and family relationships shall remain unchanged and unquestioned throughout the story. 3. That no two of them shall resemble each other sufficiently to make a mistake of identity possible. 4.That they shall have lucid and fairly cheerful intervals at least once in every five chapters. 5. That their actions and circumstances, though not necessarily possible, shall always be moderately probable. 6. That they shall bear their disappointments in love with reasonable fortitude, and find something else to talk and think about after a lapse of a week. 7. That none of them shall spend more than a sovereign upon letters, telegrams, advertisements, and railway journeys during one book. 8. That the heroine shall not be subject to fainting fits. 9. That if the hero be incurably addicted to using his hands when irritated, he shall be thrashed by the villain in a fair stand-up fight at least once in the third volume. 10. That persons whom the author does not know how to dispose of otherwise shall be got rid of without railway accidents, colliery disasters, or cataclysms involving the destruction of many innocent persons. 11. That the deceased persons shall not leave ghosts or wills, nor exact solemn oaths from the survivors; and that if they know any important secret they shall out with it at once to save trouble. 12. That nobody, living or dead, shall be capable of inventing, cribbing, or deciphering a cryptogram. 13. That all marriages shall be legal, and not solemnized in Scotland. 14. That books shall not be written at all except under irresistible provocation. 15. That the author shall not seek to mislead, baffle, or excite the reader by the use of plots, or any cognate artifices, but that a straightforward understanding shall be maintained between the two at every step of the narrative. 16. And finally, that the story shall exist for the sake of the characters, and not the characters for the sake of the story.

'Under these conditions a civilized school of novel and drama might be formed, and the lives of reviewers almost indefinitely prolonged.'

In the world of reviewing he needed to fasten his own talent to a stimulating purpose: the creation, by use of irresistible ridicule, of a revolution in the habits of the book-reading, theatre-going public in Britain. He pretended that the first attainment of novelists such as Ouida or Marie Corelli should be a knowledge of political economy. In his 1887 lecture on 'Fiction and Truth' he had spoken of men being 'better or worse morally for going to the theatre or reading a book'. The bookshop or theatre should no longer be an oubliette with its trap-door sealed against reality: it must become a centre for education. The job of the critic was not to act as judge or executioner over single works, but to be a missionary and elucidator whose voice was heard over the whole country: 'Whilst the slums exist and the sewers are out of order, it is better to force them on the attention even of the polite classes than to engage in the manufacture of eau-de-cologne for sprinkling purposes.'

Shaw's voice in the columns of the *Pall Mall Gazette* was one of exasperated geniality, below which moved a current of resentment at being obliged, from financial necessity, to spend his time reading trivial books brought out by publishers who had rejected all his own novels. In the hell of this reviewing he had been fired to a bitterness, always well-concealed, that gave his criticism its sting and point and was to find inspired expression thirty years later in his satire on Arnold Bennett's imagined novelizing of *Macbeth*. It was particularly galling to see that the other Irishmen on the paper were given major writers to review: George Moore wrote on Huysmans and Zola; Oscar Wilde on Dostoevsky, William Morris, Tolstoy, Turgenev and others. Occasionally Shaw was allowed a minor work by an interesting writer: J. M. Barrie's *Better Dead*; Wilkie Collins's *The Evil Genius*; and *A Mere Accident* by George Moore, whose 'commendable reticence' in evading the realities of a rape 'might have been taken further, even to the point of not writing the book'. Usually these were examples of authors, who should have known better, crushing the life out of their books with an artificial plot. 'On the whole, novels are like other works of art,' he wrote: 'uninteresting just so far as they are machine made.'

Shaw's long sojourn in this machine-made world – which was later to enliven his picture of hell in *Man and Superman* – altered his literary perspective. His contempt for *belles lettres* had made him into a Man of Derision. But he was not content to be derisive; whenever possible in his *Pall Mall* reviews, and sometimes refreshingly out of context, he turns from stock-in-trade author to a writer of integrity such as Trollope.

'Society has not yet forgiven that excellent novelist for having worked so many hours a day, like a carpenter or tailor, instead of periodically going mad with inspiration and hewing Barchester Towers at one frenzied stroke out of chaos, that being the only genuinely artistic method. Yet, if we except the giants of the craft, he is entitled to rank among English writers as the first sincerely naturalistic novelist of our day. He delivered us from the marvels, senseless accidents, and cat's-cradle plots of old romance, and gave us, to the best of his ability, a faithful picture of the daily life of the upper and middle classes. If any contemptuously exclaim here, 'Aha! The upper and middle classes! Why did not the snob give us the daily life of the slum and the gutter, on which all society rests to-day?' the answer is simple and convincing. He, as an honest realist, only told what he knew; and, being a middle class man, he did not and could not know the daily life of the slum and gutter.'

Shaw used the stock-in-trade of the novelist and playwright as a block against which to sharpen his own prose style, which was largely formed by his opinions on literary style itself: 'a true original style is never achieved for its own sake,' he wrote. 'Effectiveness of assertion is the Alpha and Omega of style. He who has nothing to assert has no style and can have none: he who has something to assert will go as far in power of style as its momentousness and his conviction will carry him.' What he gave up in texture, he gained in pace and authority. The welding together of many disparate elements into an immediately recognizable and imposing tone was one of Shaw's most outstanding achievements. His writing is luminous with conviction and humour. Though he claims to be writing English and not grammar, there is a vein of pedantry in it. Yet he seldom weeds out the clichés: when in love, his heart is as 'hard as nails'; his longer plays are inevitably 'cut to the bone'. Provided it accurately and speedily expressed what he needed, 'the more familiar the word, the better', he told his translator, Sobieniowski. In a letter to Ernest Newman he is partly thinking of himself when commenting on Mozart: 'If it hadnt been for this cursed dexterity of his, Mozart would have enlarged music more than he did; for when there is no cliché that will serve he produces something new without effort.' Elsewhere, with something of the same thought in mind, he announced: 'I also am a journalist, proud of it, deliberately cutting out of my works all that is not journalism, convinced that nothing that is not journalism will live long as literature, or be of any use whilst it does live.' This was part of a cleansing exercise against his long immersion in pretentious literature. For real literature, despite his inclination to sociologize it, he felt a reverence that calmed the activity of his style. Of Poe's story of the Lady Ligeia, he wrote: 'There is really nothing to be said about it: we others simply take off our hats and let Mr Poe go first.' And after reading D. H. Lawrence's *The Widowing of Mrs Holroyd*, he confided: 'I wish I could write such dialogue – with mine I always hear the sound of the typewriter.'

Yet it was a bright smiling instrument, this typewriter, and he played upon it with wonderful virtuosity. It was also a marvellously efficient machine for turning all the difficulties and despairs of life into an argument – not a bad-tempered argument, but an exchange of point and counterpoint that beats down relentlessly until the rough places are made plane. In his diaries, where Shaw is unprotected by the brilliant shell of this style, we see him several times accidentally coming close to some dreadful event and feeling the shock waves: 'In Wigmore [Street] we saw a young rough beating a girl and I disturbed myself for the rest of the evening by flying at him.' 'Was much upset by having to interfere in an altercation between a young couple and a private watchman who was apparently trying to blackmail them.' Though he attacked the substitution of literature for life, his own battery of words, eliminating all the suffering within range, was in some sense a replacement for action. 'A writer,' he advised Norman Clark, 'must have a gift of intimacy, which is dangerous and offensive without good manners or tact.' Shaw had outrageously good manners, but in place of intimacy he gives us a whirling informality. The effect of his prose is like alcohol upon the nerves: we are exhilarated, intoxicated, breathless and, before the end, exhausted – and still the talkative spirit, the ascending wit, drive on. For it is a style that is always in top gear: emphatic, industrious, omniscient, studded with surprises, and better-trained for shorter distances than the long discursiveness that was to become a feature of his work.

Shaw would suffer anything rather than do his work badly, and his columns in the *Pall Mall Gazette*, though without a byline, were soon making his name notorious in the trade. Two or three times an exceptional book fell his way: the *Rural Rides* of William Cobbett ('probably more dangerous to corrupt Governments than any single man known to English history, excepting only Jonathan Swift'); *A Handbook of the History of Philosophy* by Belfort Bax, and Samuel Butler's *Luck or Cunning*, both of which (as he indicates in his Preface to *Major Barbara*) influenced his thought. He was also allowed to file reports on socialist meetings, provide music notices and contribute his first theatre criticism. But if, for the most part, he was kept to heart-throb fiction, it was because he wrote about it so screamingly well. However trivial the subject, he scrutinized and weighed every word until he had attained the directness as well as the force he needed. He seemed to fill these columns from a magic well that never ran dry or lost its sparkle provided he pumped hard enough. But he chafed against the restriction. In the summer of 1887 he sent Stead a long letter in which he tried to palm a socialist programme on to him. The *Pall Mall Gazette*, he argued, enjoyed a peculiar opportunity; but would it dare, as none of its rivals had dared, 'to tell polite society that it lives by the robbery and murder of the poor'? The plan Shaw tried to smuggle into Stead's mind was one of taking the initiative in radical politics by 'helping to get back the land and the misappropriated capital for the people by such measures as the municipalization of town rents, the nationalization of railways, the sweeping away of our inexpressibly wicked workhouse prisons in favour of state-owned farms and factories ... and the utter repudiation of the claim of the sweater (as the incarnation of enterprise) to be protected from the competition of the whole people organized to secure their own welfare.'

This letter, which had been written in response to one from Ruskin on 'The functions of the P.M.G.', was not intended for publication but for implementation. Stead read it, kept it, and did nothing; its campaign for social reform was too bleak for him. Besides, as an instrument of persuasion, there was a quality in Shaw's letter that was to mar so much of his dazzling propaganda: it was too knowing – everything it said was correct and calculated to be flattering to Stead, but the calculations showed. To act on Shaw's advice so often meant parading one's inferiority to him. His tact was like a brilliant varnish: one saw straight through it.

For a time in 1886 he had been writing in four papers: *The World, Our Corner*, the *Dramatic Review* and *Pall Mall Gazette*. But however much he wrote, since he could not get what he wanted, he still searched for opportunities elsewhere – from the *Manchester Guardian* to the *London Figaro* and the *English Illustrated Magazine* to the *Scots Observer*. His offerings were sometimes mutilated, sometimes rejected, but he persisted. Letters editors of *To-day, Justice*, the *Echo, St James's Gazette, Truth*, were harried with correspondence from George Bunnerd, Shendar Bwra, A. Donis, Redbarn Wash, G. B. S. Larking, Amelia Mackintosh, Horatia Ribbonson and the Revd C. W. Stiggins Jnr, as well as from the 'milkman', an 'English mistress', 'Inveterate Gambler' and 'A Novelist'. Under one name or another, or no name at all, he was everywhere, pleading for the retention of the split infinitive and the abolition of Christmas, protesting against the Russian use of Siberian exile for dissidents and the prosecution of Henry Vizetelly for publishing an English translation of Zola's *La Terre*. As G. Bernard Shaw he even wrote of Jack the Ripper as an 'independent genius' who by 'private enterprise' had succeeded where socialism failed in getting the press to take some sympathetic interest in the conditions of London's East End. When Ernest Parke, proprietor of the *North London Press*, was imprisoned for criminal libel, Shaw stepped in and wrote his leading articles without fee, while drafting unavailing appeals for his release to the Home Secretary. In the summer of 1887, through William Archer's recommendation, he became 'European correspondent' for an American journal called the *Epoch*, but surrendered this when, after two contributions, he was asked by the proprietor for something bright on the incomes of English lords, the performance of Guinness on the London Stock Exchange, and 'why Americans find it so much easier to get into the best English society than the English do themselves'. A couple of years later he agreed to provide the *Penny Illustrated Paper* with a weekly column called 'Asides'. He wrote it under the byline N[o] G[entleman] but it was no good, and when the editor sent back his third contribution (which included a Shavian vindication of burglars), Shaw scribbled across the envelope 'Cant stand any more of it', and cancelled the agreement.

By this time he had also left the *Pall Mall Gazette* after a final vain appeal to its sub-editor: 'Why condemn me to read things that I can't review – that no artistic conscience could long survive the reviewing of! Why don't you begin notices of boots, hats, dogcarts and so on? They would be fifty times as useful and interesting as reviews of the last novel by Miss Braddon, who is a princess among novel manufacturers. There ought to be legislation against this sort of thing – on the lines of the Factory Acts.'

Between 1888 and 1890 Shaw manoeuvred himself from reviewing all the arts into becoming predominantly a critic of music. He had attempted to set himself up as a political correspondent when, in January 1888, a new paper called *The Star* had been founded under the editorship of T. P. O'Connor. But O'Connor, an Irish Catholic, a Liberal and a friend of John Morley, could not accept Shaw's scalding attacks on the Government without pouring into them a lot of tepid water of his own, and Shaw resigned. 'I am not worth my salt to the Star; and you will be more at your ease without having constantly to suppress my articles,' he wrote. '. . . I am no anarchist: I am a practical politician, and, as far as any individual insect can, I know what I want, [and] how to get it . . . If I had energy, eloquence, and physical monumentality, I should bring London up to the mark in one winter's campaign: as it is, I must wait for a better vehicle.'

To H. W. Massingham, O'Connor's deputy, Shaw added: 'I can only relapse into reviewing novels for the P.M.G. and criticising pictures for Yates until I can get a paper of my own.' The power he felt within him seemed everywhere to be blocked. In his diary he confessed to feeling 'rather sulky' about O'Connor. 'I like T.P. immensely,' he insisted to Massingham; but it needed another Irishman, St John Ervine, to interpret this liking – 'G.B.S. felt illimitable contempt . . . [for] his countryman, T. P. O'Connor'. But each knew the worth of the other as a journalist, and when Shaw went into *The Star* offices 'for the last time' on 10 February 1888, he 'arranged with O'Connor to write occasional signed articles and send notes'. This arrangement, with Shaw contributing 'leaderettes', continued until the summer when he accepted Massingham's proposal that he cover occasional musical events that 'Musigena', the paper's regular music critic E. Belfort Bax, could not attend. Towards Massingham Shaw felt lifelong gratitude and respect – he was 'the perfect master journalist,' he wrote. '. . . A first rate editor is a very rare bird indeed: two or three to a generation, in contrast to swarms of authors, is as much as we get; and Massingham was in the first of that very select flight.' When Bax went on holiday in August, Shaw acted as his substitute; after which he carried on as the anonymous second-string critic until, Bax resigning in February 1889, Shaw took his place at two guineas per week.

Something rather similar was to happen on *The World*. Later that year, 'I did a thing that has been in my mind for some time,' he noted in his diary, ' – wrote to Edmund Yates asking him to give the art-criticship of *The World* to Lady Colin Campbell, as it is no longer worth my while to do so much work for so little satisfaction, not to mention money'. Yates replied admitting that Shaw had been 'cavalierly treated', but concluding: 'I have no idea of loosening my hold on you.'

Though he was to return to Yates just over six months later as music critic (having in the interval applied unsuccessfully for the post of art-critic on *Truth* where he wrote a few reviews, and on a new journal *The Speaker*), Shaw had made up his mind to give himself the sack as a poorly paid reviewer of pictures for *The World*. Preparing to bow out of the galleries, he told his readers on 23 October 1889: 'I cannot guarantee my very favourable impression of the Hanover Gallery, as I only saw it by gaslight. This was the fault of Sarasate, who played the Ancient Mariner with me. He fixed me with his violin on my way to Bond Street, and though, like the wedding guest, I tried my best, I could not choose but to hear'.

## [ 3 ]

*The pleasures of the senses I can sympathise with and share;*
*but the substitution of sensuous ecstasy for intellectual activity*
*and honesty is the very devil.* Preface to *Three Plays for Puritans*

Money was one measurement of success. In 1885, his first full year in journalism, Shaw had earned £112; ten years later he was earning almost £800. His training for journalism followed a less literary discipline than for boxing. He bought coloured spectacles, a pair of dumb-bells (five pounds each) and a pendulum alarm clock. He took regular cold baths; he went on spectacular walks (racing against soldiers in the park or against himself for twenty miles or more, and winning); and he gave out so much advice and argument during the day that his contributions to *The World* and the *Pall Mall Gazette* were sometimes not finished until two, three or four o'clock next morning. At night he opened his windows so wide that cats and birds sailed through, interrupting his sleep. He dieted, logged his weight, kept himself at about ten stone ten pounds. To his shelves he added volumes on algebra, Danish and German (though 'men of ordinary capacity can learn Sanscrit in less time than it takes me to buy a German dictionary'); on his desk he stood a modern typewriter bought from H. W. Massingham for £13 and, 'as our rent was reduced and our earnings rather enlarged, we got a new piano on the hire system, and began to live a very little more freely.'

Behind this programme of self-improvement lay a history of backsliding, chronicled in his diaries though seldom obvious to the public. It was as if Sonny were secretly still playing tricks on G.B.S. He sleeps through the alarm clock, or if it wakes him, takes a nap in the British Museum. Despite his diet, he cannot resist a heap of cherries, a few overripe bananas, some indiscreet mushrooms, and sweetmeats from a machine, to which are attributed fits of indigestion, plagues of gumboils, ulcers and terrific nightmares. However icy his baths he breaks out in sweats and into spells of influenza. He increases his walks, but trips and falls; he starts off again, but ends up lame; he bellows out songs 'rather violently' at the piano, 'for the sake of my lungs', and loses his voice; he covers page after page and sees them all swoop and vanish under the wheels of a train.

Despite the grimmest of attempts, he learns no languages, no algebra. His letters to the press are returned, his private correspondence placed in the wrong envelopes. He develops a tendency of 'clean forgetting' to turn up at rallies where he is principal speaker and at meetings where he is chairman; of arriving at theatres without his tickets, mistaking matinées for evening performances, and presenting himself at the Steinway Hall instead of the Princes Hall and vice versa; he believes it to be Thursday when it isn't; he sets his watch at the wrong hour; he goes shopping without money; he calls on people who by arrangement are calling on him and attends At Homes where everyone is abroad. He recklessly gives away money to drunkards and minor poets, crossing-sweepers and 'Street Arabs'. He can admit to delivering one lecture 'with great force – rather unnecessarily', and another that 'was very dull and I felt much discouraged'. Outdoors he watches a squirrel playing in a tree and a huge spider making a web, indoors he dawdles over the piano harmonizing the *Marseillaise* – all when he should have been forming a committee for the municipalization of land. Suddenly unable 'to face more political cackle', he rushes off from an important conference to a performance of *Cymbeline* – 'and enjoyed it much more than I should have enjoyed the meeting'.

More unShavian still are the adventures with his typewriter. Within a month he has mastered the brute and declares himself 'much pleased' with it. Yet his expertise is oddly hypothetical. He knows more than enough to instruct others or to write an impassioned essay on the subject; but much of his knowledge (as with bicycling and photography) has come to him by way of accidents. Despite his technical know-how, the machine won't 'settle'. At last 'to my great annoyance' he is obliged to ask for professional advice, but when he tries to put this advice into practice the typewriter breaks down altogether and he is 'furious over it'. Altogether out of patience, he summons a taxi and carries it to the City, where it is repaired. But six weeks later, 'during the process of oiling', it seizes up. In despair he shows it to Jenny Patterson. Then it works rather better, until in February 1893 he is obliged to trade it in for another.

The diaries become strewn with Johnsonian lamentations over what he calls 'my inveterate laziness and procrastination'. 'Not up till 10 (curse this laziness)', he writes and chides himself for what seems to him his incapacity for doing anything except utter good resolutions. 'Very tired and greatly disposed to curse my fate,' he notes. For Shaw to be off his work has all the pathos of a domestic animal not eating. He loses strength; he loses authority over himself. 'For weeks now I have been going to bed at 2 and not getting up until 11,' he admits. Often he starts

217

towards his desk, only to find himself seated at the piano again. 'Restless and full of work in the morning,' he writes for 9 October 1889; 'but only sat down at the piano after all and played *Parsifal* with a very deep sense of it all'. He is disgusted with this waste of time but goes on playing and singing nonetheless and acknowledges that he feels better for it and that his appetite improves. When he shakes off this idleness and works strictly to timetable, he is overcome by fits of giddiness and nausea. Even his mother notices how his hands shake and his nerves are stretched. Can it be scarlet fever? he wonders. Is his diet insufficiently austere? Perhaps his teeth are at fault. He hurries reluctantly to the dentist and observes (in contrast to the public Shaw who is soothed by the buzzing of the drill) how much his fear exceeds the pain. Finally, he admits: 'Am driving myself too hard,' and tries, unsuccessfully, to take it easy by means of more exercise. Analysing the erosion of his health in 1892, he concludes:

'It is evident that I have been overtaxing myself by working continually for the last few years without having a day of rest every week, and taking no real holiday except for a fortnight at a time when I have gone abroad . . . I vowed repeatedly to make a "Sunday" for myself – that is, a day set aside every week for rest; but I find I cannot carry it out. Circumstances are too strong for me.'

Though it was one of the ways he began to live 'a little more freely' in his thirties, Shaw had no genius for travel. He moved across the North, the Midlands and West Country on many Fabian lecture tours, but anything in the style of a holiday unnerved him. Early in 1888, staying with the Salts, he experimented with a Sunday on the Surrey Hills, and came back with an inventory of its horrors: 'The uneven, ankle-twisting roads; the dusty hedges; the ditch with its dead dogs, rank weeds, and swarms of poisonous flies; the groups of children torturing something; the dull, toil-broken, prematurely old agricultural laborer; the savage tramp; the manure heaps with their horrible odor; the chain of mile-stones from inn to inn, from cemetery to cemetery . . .' And he concluded: 'From the village street into the railway station is a leap across five centuries from the brutalizing torpor of Nature's tyranny over Man into the order and alertness of Man's organized dominion over Nature.'

The following year he went on his first trip to the Continent. Sydney Olivier had suggested they should go to Germany. 'I wonder whether I could manage it . . .' Shaw asked his diary. He did manage, for a week in April, to go to the Netherlands, ostensibly to report on a farcical opera for *The Star*. 'My worst forebodings have been realized,' he assured William

Archer. The *table d'hôte* at Brussels was 'terrible'; Antwerp was 'exactly like Limerick, only duller'; and, as with the Liffey in Dublin, the 'smell of the canal disgusted me with the Hague'. Everywhere the cathedrals looked like 'whitened dogholes' though he was 'greatly delighted' by the galleries in Utrecht. The journey out had been tedious; on the way back he sat on deck all night and was ingloriously sick. 'Nature conspires with you in vain to palm off the Continent on me as a success,' he wrote to Archer.

Three months later *The Star*'s music critic was again sick *en route* for Bayreuth. 'Carried out my program successfully,' he noted in his diary – four articles on Wagner, and such vigorous sight-seeing through Germany that he split his mackintosh 'like a trick coat in a farce'. Returning from a six-day ordeal in Paris the following spring, Shaw's admission of having been 'Very sick crossing...thoroughly wet and cold' was turned by the music critic into a plea for the Channel Tunnel, but for the want of which *The Star* 'would be as great a musical power in Europe as it is in England.'

In August 1890 he attempted a summer holiday with Sidney Webb, the one man whose dislike of all holidaymaking exceeded his own. The climax of their cultural perambulation through Belgium, Germany and France was the Passion Play in a downpour of rain at Oberammergau, where Shaw bounded up the mountainside leaving Webb, seated among trees at its base, apparently 'writing an article on municipal death duties . . .' The result, Shaw hazarded, was that the Fabian 'is getting known in Germany'.

Though he gradually grew bolder, he quickly regretted it. From Italy, where he went on a tour organized by a basketmaker from the Art Workers' Guild in the autumn of 1891, he wrote complaining to William Morris of 'the fearful solitude created by these 27 men, most of whom have taken up art as the last refuge of general incompetence'. This was an untypical rebuke from Shaw, indicating the extent of his irritation with too much co-operative glaring at ornamental architecture, and the inconvenience of having to travel as a devout Catholic under a vow in order to obtain vegetarian meals. 'On reflection,' he added, 'I doubt if this remark will bear examination: I suppose it is in the nature of such an expedition that we should all appear fools to one another . . .'

If there was anything Shaw learnt from bombarding round Europe, it was how travel narrowed the mind. His one weapon, language, broke in his hand and he fell to the conclusion that the only country you could learn more about by going abroad was your own. He also came to recognize how much closer you could feel to those whom you had left behind – and there was an increasing number of people for him to feel close to in this way. He did not leave them impetuously. Among the *jeunes Fabiannes en fleur*, he had, for example, met Grace Gilchrist as early as March 1885, and continued seeing her with considerable infrequency over the next three or four years. 'I have no doubt Miss Gilchrist fell in love with you,' another Fabian, Marjorie Davidson, assured him.

From attentive bachelors in their bearded thirties the Fabian girls secured some serviceable husbands. Shaw's attentions to Grace Gilchrist were much whispered over. He singled her out for long talks; he addressed letters to her and noted each sighting in his diary; he walked her home, sang for her at the piano, wrote music to Browning's 'I go to find my soul' specially for her. What could be clearer? But by 1888 they were joined, not in the marriage many expected, but in a bond of misunderstanding. On Easter Day, Grace's friend the novelist Emma Brooke (author of *The Superfluous Woman* and *Life the Accuser*) called on Shaw and 'heaped abuse on me'. It was like a plot from one of his novels: Shaw embodying the new morality; Grace, struggling unsuccessfully through socialism to escape the morality of the marriage market; and Miss Brooke valuing her friend's happiness above Shaw's lightly worn principles. But instead of arranging it all into another novel he put it into letters – letters to Grace and then letters to Emma, explaining his explanatory letters to her friend. 'Write no more letters,' Emma Brooke instructed him. 'In letters we do not seem able to touch any point of mutual comprehension.' Eventually she infuriated Shaw by returning his letters unopened. But by then, partly as a result of her ardent interference (she would hold him for 'most of the day' in the corridors of the British Museum), he had come to realize that there was 'Great Gossip about Grace Gilchrist'. Even her family, it seemed, had counted on their marriage, and Shaw felt called on to include her brother, a portrait painter, in his explanatory correspondence.

On Hampstead Heath nine months later, Grace and Shaw hurried past each other without a word. Both felt that injustice had been done, Grace to her deep feelings, Shaw to his good intentions, and no words had been able to reconcile such feelings with such intentions. If Shaw treated Grace's unhappiness rather easily, this was partly because, compared with the awful poverty which should be the chief concern of the Fabians, her romantic disappointment seemed almost an indulgence. While he was attempting to wed her to socialism, she had been thinking of wedding him. Perhaps that was unfair; but some unfairness was unavoidable if socialism was to be purged of sentimentality. He had obviously enjoyed Grace's company and he seems to have found her good-looking. But he had never proposed marriage; he had never compromised her sexually; and if he had compromised her socially then it was due to absurd mores which she should have been too intelligent to accept.

'Someday a pair of dark eyes, a fierce temperament and a woman will obtain your body and soul,' Elinor Huddart had written to him. If he was on the lookout for such a creature, it was in order to avoid her. Even while the Gilchrist excitement was babbling to its climax, Shaw was gazing at 'a pretty girl named Geraldine Spooner'. He neither pursued the 'fair and fluffy' Miss Spooner nor ignored her but, after two years and one week of determinedly doing neither, decided that he was 'rather in love with Geraldine' – after which he saw a good deal less of her. Like Alice Lockett, she had taken singing lessons from Mrs Shaw and accepted complimentary tickets from her son for Private Views. Then she had gone to hear him lecture. He seemed to her 'a strange and very wonderful looking man, tall, and thin as a whipping post'. He had walked her to railway stations and together they had eaten lunches at the Wheatsheaf or an Aerated Bread Shop. Each seemed to be presenting the other with opportunities for taking the initiative and neither of them took it – until, Shaw's lack of initiative growing excessive, Geraldine married the philosopher Herbert Wildon Carr. As soon as it was too late Shaw plunged into action, advancing on 'my old love Geraldine', in spite of the desperate fact of her now living in Surrey. He played cricket with her young brothers-in-law, knowledgeably examined her husband's microscope, and penned verses for Geraldine and others:

> If I could truly now declare
> I love but you alone . . .

But he couldn't. The visit had been in the nature of a reconnaissance – to learn whether the Carrs might grow into another of those families where he could act the Sunday husband. They didn't and when Geraldine drove him off to the station in the horse cart, he made straight for the Salts where his Sunday husbandship was by now well-established.

Shaw was a lifelong admirer of Salt, and towards the end of his life declared that his plays had been 'sermons preaching what Salt practised'. They shared many tastes – Ruskin and Shelley, vegetarianism and anti-vivisection – but though Shaw described his Old Etonian socialist colleague as 'a born revolutionist' he seemed more of a born naturalist, armed only with binoculars and eventually 'working all day at my profession which is looking for, and at wildflowers'. He was, as Shaw admitted, 'the mildest-mannered man that ever defied society'. At Eton, to which he returned as an assistant-master, Salt had become a friend of J. L. Joynes, marrying his sister Kate in 1879, and following Joynes in 1885 by resigning his mastership – a decision attributed by Dr Warre, the headmaster, to the incendiary combination of socialism and *légumes*. Leaving Eton, Salt and his wife put on sandals and made for the simple life of the country – in short, Surrey, and the lemonade and potato-digging of Edward Carpenter's world. Salt, who was no politician, belonged more to the Fellowship of the New Life than the Fabian Society (from which he was to resign over the Boer War) and he made a centre for his reforming spirit in the Humanitarian League of which he was a co-founder and whose journals, dedicated to the abolition of blood sports, corporal punishment, the death penalty and the commercial vulgarization of the countryside, he edited for a quarter of a century. Shaw's visits to the Salts were uniquely congenial. 'I took it for granted that some day I should escape from my anything but simple life,' he wrote to Salt years later. '. . . I never did escape and now I never shall.'

Towards Salt himself, 'one of my most intimate and valued friends', he felt an affinity that was to survive more than thirty years of never seeing him; while Mrs Salt, he confessed, 'loved me as far as she could love any male creature'. She was a dark, raven-haired girl 'with large eyes and sensitive, somewhat sad, Dante-like profile', and her company was marvellously calming for Shaw. He was often very tired when he came, and could regain his privacy. 'I have seen him sit at the breakfast-table,' Salt remembered, 'with a forlorn expression, turning perhaps the pages of the Army and Navy Co-operative Society's catalogue, and sadly shaking his head if a remark were made to him. No greater contrast to the G.B.S. on the war-path could have been imagined. We had the real pleasure of seeing that he felt at home.' He bathed, rode on a tandem tricycle, made friends with Cosy 'a cat of fearful passions', put into practice his special theories of bed-making and washing-up, cheated outrageously at an exhibition of table turning, gossiped, sang and played a great quantity of piano duets with Mrs Salt late into the nights; and that was all he did. There was no need for 'gallantries' with Kate Salt since, though intensely emotional, she fell in love with other women. She treated Shaw as a sympathetic asexual confidant but she felt an idealized love for her other Sunday husband, Edward Carpenter, who was homosexual. This preference sometimes riled Shaw. Salt might be a saint, but Carpenter was only 'the ex-clergyman of Millthorpe' and, far from being the genuine 'Noble Savage' they all called him, 'an ultra-civilized impostor'. This teasing, which may have accounted for the 'fearful noise' all three produced at the piano, occasionally misfired: 'Attacked Carpenter rather strongly over his lecture – perhaps too strongly,' he confessed in his diary. 'I believe my nerves are getting too highstrung.' In Shaw's opinion, Carpenter exalted Kate's lesbianism into a cult (she called herself an *Urning*, one of the chosen race). He himself tried to jolly her out of her problems – what were they but time-consuming luxuries that would vanish if she had two or three children to look after? Kate hated this chilling cheeriness of Shaw's. 'Mrs Salt complained considerably of me,' he revealed after a breezy visit in 1896:

'. . . said she believed I had been practising scales (an unheard-of accusation); said I was in a destructively electrical condition and made her feel that she wanted to cry; said that if I undressed in the dark when going to bed, sparks would come out of me; and generally made me conscious of a grinding, destroying energy, and a heart transmuted to adamant . . . I am really only fit for intercourse with sensitive souls when I am broken and weary.'

\*

Shaw counted his friendship with the Salts as one of the most successful of his triangular liaisons. More sinister were the appearances he was concurrently making in the family life of William Morris's daughter, May.

For years he had enveloped May Morris in a romantic haze that emanated from his feelings for what she called 'the father'. 'Great men are fabulous monsters, like unicorns, griffins, dragons, and heraldic lions,' Shaw was to write. '. . . William Morris was great not only among little men but among great ones.' He still saw Morris as a crusader, struggling to make nasty people nice and ugly places beautiful. To Shaw's eyes, the quality 'in which he excelled all his contemporaries was a sense of beauty so far transcending all ordinary endowments of that kind that the things that satisfied him seemed merely queer to the average Philistine.' To go from the barren places of the Fabians to the 'Morris paradise' at their house in Hammersmith was wonderfully refreshing. 'There was an extraordinary absence of vulgarity and ugliness in Morris's house,' he remembered. 'It taught you how much of both there is in ordinary houses.' Shaw went there often and sometimes, he owned, 'to see May Morris'. In his letters to other people he does not often mention May; he keeps her name for his diary. They had been seeing each other fairly regularly since the beginning of 1885. In what was to become a famous passage Shaw tells of a particular incident between them that took place that year.

'One Sunday evening after lecturing and supping, I was on the threshold of the Hammersmith house when I turned to make my farewell, and at this moment she came from the diningroom into the hall. I looked at her, rejoicing in her lovely dress and lovely self; and she looked at me very carefully and quite deliberately made a gesture of assent with her eyes. I was immediately conscious that a Mystic Betrothal was registered in heaven, to be fulfilled when all the material obstacles should melt away, and my own position rescued from the squalors of my poverty and unsuccess . . . I did not think it necessary to say anything. To engage her in any way – to go to Morris and announce that I was taking advantage of the access granted to me as comrade-Communist to commit his beautiful daughter to a desperately insolvent marriage, did not occur to me as a socially possible proceeding. It did not occur to me even that fidelity to the Mystic Betrothal need interfere with the ordinary course of my relations with other women. I made no sign at all: I had no doubt that the thing was written on the skies for both of us.'

Characteristically, this metaphysical evocation both contains and conceals the truth. When Shaw submitted it fifty years later as part of his Introduction to the second volume of May's book on her father, she consented to its publication. 'The Hammersmith Terrace Romance might as well stay,' she wrote to him, 'as people who don't count will view it as an amusing romance in the Shaw manner, and those who count – so few left – will read it understandingly.'

The Shaw manner suggests that he treated May as an ornament in her father's Pre-Raphaelite world. He saw her as someone who had descended from Burne-Jones's *The Golden Stair* and who walked back into the picture whenever he was absent from her. She was also his Dulcinea del Toboso, with 'the divine profile of the most beautiful of women', for he seems to have augmented her beauty and insisted that others do so too. 'She was here yesterday looking as sweet & beautiful as the flower she is called after,' Eleanor Marx wrote to him. 'It was like a breath of fresh air to look at her.'

She was a picture, not real; something to look at and never touch. But there was unintended irony in Shaw's view of May, for she had never occupied the jewelled place he ascribed to her in the William Morris world. Though her tastes were literary and artistic, she had been trained miserably in mathematics as a child by Graham Wallas's sister Kate, and her unhappiness at school was added to at home where her father, passionately fond of her sister Jenny, 'tolerated her with a sort of remorseful tenderness'. Rossetti had wanted to adopt her, but Morris had refused, and May resented this refusal which seemed to bind her to a second-best existence. Shaw, too, who met her so often and liked her so much, yet did not 'think it necessary to say anything', had made her second best. 'Yes, well, of course I'm a remarkable woman,' she later told him, ' – always was, though none of you seemed to think so.' The affair was one of suppers, songs, socialism. He wooed her politically, tried to seduce her from the Socialist League to the Fabians: 'I shall have to overcome my shyness of the Fabians – they are all so gruesomely respectable,' she protested. It was Shaw's respectability that made her shy.

She tried gently to tease 'Comrade Shaw' out of it. But his respectability was like a strait-jacket and he an inspired lunatic, tied hand and foot. Sometimes he made her laugh so much she felt enfeebled the next day; and it was beautiful to hear him lecture so passionately. 'I don't know if you are aware that our audiences love you very much,' she told him; 'their faces broaden with pleasure when we promise them that if they are good Bernard Shaw shall be their next teacher.' But privately his 'insincere compliments' and pretence of being 'utterly shallow' disconcerted her. Did he love her or did he not? It seemed impossible to tell. 'You have succeeded in perplexing *me*. I don't believe I know you a bit better now than when we were first acquainted,' she wrote to him, after they had known each other for more than a year. 'Inscrutable man! I suppose this is *your* form of vanity . . .'

He seems to have been terrified of the unhappiness he would risk if she became real. Instinctively he countered fear with fear, making her feel that, although she wanted to be close to him, 'you keep me in a constant state of terror by your fantastic sarcasms, so I suppose it is impossible'. Sometimes, in her frustration, she was short-tempered: 'I do not know what possesses me to be always so rude when you are invariably kind and courteous to me,' she apologized. In another letter she referred to 'our harmless personal relations'. After a year or more of harmlessness, she turned deliberately elsewhere. The Mystic Betrothal, which Shaw declared did not interfere with 'my relations with other women', had not prevented her starting a relationship with another man. And what a man! Early in April 1886, following a lecture on 'The Unemployed', Shaw wrote in his diary: 'Came back with Sparling, who told me of the love affair between him and May Morris'. Henry Halliday Sparling was a socialist colleague, 'a tall slim immature man,' Shaw decided, 'with a long thin neck on champagne bottle shoulders, and not athletic. He was brave, kind, sincere, and intellectual in his tastes and interests. Having apparently complete confidence in himself he had a quite unconscious pretentiousness which led his audiences and new acquaintances to expect more from him than he was able to give them . . .'

Shaw makes no public mention of this love affair, lasting more than four years, between May and Sparling. But shortly after he had been told of it, May wrote him a wry letter accepting, as it were, his mystic rejection of her the previous year: '. . . your resolution when we became acquainted not to make love was most judicious and worthy of all praise, having, as you say, the most entirely satisfying results: I don't think our intercourse can have caused you more pleasure than it has me.'

Her irony was well-merited. By treating May Morris as a woman-on-a-pedestal, Shaw had exhibited all the sentimental idealism he so vividly attacked in *The Quintessence of Ibsenism*. Though they both agreed to be platonic comrades – 'Let us be comrades by all means,' she agreed, 'I salute you, friend Shaw' – both had by now been wounded by the other. Pakenham Beatty revealed the truth when, a year later, he told Shaw: 'You envy Sparling – you wish you were the happy man.' The insignificance of Sparling amounted almost to an invitation for Shaw to supplant him. But still he could not escape the strait-jacket. 'So nothing happened,' he wrote, 'except that the round of Socialist agitation went on and brought us together from time to time . . .' They spent almost a week together at Kelmscott Manor in August 1888, Shaw rowing and sailing on the river, playing hide and seek, shooting bows and arrows, guessing 'animal, vegetable or mineral' with various children, and feeling very happy. But on 14 June 1890, May married Sparling.

'Suddenly, to my utter stupefaction, and I suspect to that of Morris,' Shaw wrote, 'the beautiful daughter married one of the comrades.'

'This was perfectly natural, and entirely my own fault for taking the Mystical Betrothal for granted; but I regarded it, and still regard it in spite of all reason, as the most monstrous breach of faith in the history of romance. The comrade [Sparling] was even less eligible than I was; for he was no better off financially; and, though he could not be expected to know this, his possibilities of future eminence were more limited . . . there was nothing to be done but accept the situation.'

Yet Shaw, who had accepted the love affair, could not accept the marriage. He presented two reasons for not having proposed or made love to May: his own financial impotence and, 'I had enough sexual satisfaction available elsewhere.' Neither reason, for the period between 1885 and 1890, was wholly true. By 1890 he was earning over £250 a year, and during the late 1880s the sexual satisfaction he enjoyed with Jenny Patterson, then nearing fifty, had grown unsatisfactorily meagre. In fantasy, he saw May as belonging to her father: William Morris was her man. By marrying her, Sparling had violated the idyllic union between father and daughter that Shaw in 'my limitless imagination' had dreamed into existence, with himself understudying the great William Morris and guarding May from the contamination of sexual love.

He continued seeing the Sparlings, singing, playing the piano with May sometimes till past midnight, as if nothing had happened. One evening, in the summer of 1891, after leaving Hammersmith for Jenny Patterson's house in Brompton Square, he noted: 'May only appeared as I was leaving . . . Gloomy evening. Sorry I left Hammersmith.' But was there any need to leave? That autumn he began staying at Hammersmith odd nights; and then having, as it were, placed one foot in the door, he felt obligated to call on the other foot to follow. Fitzroy Square, that 'most repulsive house', seemed 'unbearable' when, late in 1892, the building was being redecorated. To escape the smell of paint, and of the drains, he moved to Hammersmith Terrace for part of November, December and January 1893. This was the nearest he came to impersonating Vandeleur Lee and reproducing the Dublin *ménage à trois*. His description of these months, though revealing the deep satisfaction this arrangement gave him (he even borrowed 'a change of clothes from Sparling'), is skilfully disingenuous. Since he needed 'rest and change very pressingly,' he explained, the 'young couple . . . invited me to stay with them awhile. I accepted, and so found myself most blessedly resting and content in their house . . .'

'. . . Everything went well for a time in that *ménage-à-trois*. She was glad to have me in the house; and he was glad to have me because I kept her in good humour and produced a cuisine that no mere husband could elicit. It was probably the happiest passage in our three lives.

'But the violated Betrothal was avenging itself. It made me from the first the centre of the household; and when I had quite recovered and there was no longer any excuse for staying unless I proposed to do so permanently and parasitically, her legal marriage had dissolved as all illusions do; and the mystic marriage asserted itself irresistibly. I had to consummate it or vanish.'

Reader, he vanished.

Like George Carr Shaw, Sparling had been reduced to nullity in the house, and later blamed the second man (as George Carr Shaw had done) for splitting apart his marriage. Shaw's explanation for what happened went naturally back to his childhood. '. . . my mother was enabled to bear a disappointing marriage by the addition to our household of a musician of genius,' he wrote. '. . . I had therefore, to my own great advantage, been brought up in a *ménage à trois*, and knew that it might be a quite innocent and beneficial arrangement. But when it became evident that the Betrothal would not suffer this to be an innocent arrangement the case became complicated.'

In Shaw's scheme, the music critic of the 1890s must do nothing that the musician of genius had not done in the 1860s. 'I was perfectly content to leave all that to Sparling and go on Platonically,' he added, 'but May was not.' He protested that it would be 'revolting' to make love to May while her husband, the 'irreproachable' comrade-Communist Sparling, remained in the house; and since Sparling could not afford to divorce her and Shaw himself could not afford to marry her, there had been no alternative but to leave.

But Shaw left less convincingly than Sparling. For having gone, he often returned to Hammersmith, trying out his work, admiring her embroidery, reading poetry and 'playing all the evening with May'. Soon she started calling for tea at Fitzroy Square – 'the worst of it was she always wore her heart on her sleeve,' Lucy Shaw remembered, 'and everyone knew about her madness for G[eorge]'. They seemed to go everywhere together – to concerts, lectures, theatres; on long walks and sunburnt siestas in the park; for German lessons, even skating on thin ice in the dark, and sculling along the river together between Chiswick and Barnes ('and got abominably blistered').

Shaw's 1893 diary reveals an intensifying intimacy between them.

'*7 February* . . . went to Sparlings'. May and I played for a while and then had some conversation about old times – rather an emotional one. Stayed the night at the Terrace.

'*28 March* Olivier came down with me in the train [to Oxted] and came into Salts for a while . . . In the evening we did not get to duet playing as usual, Mrs Salt having a great deal to say, chiefly about May Sparling.

'*21 May* . . . rushed off to Hammersmith, not getting there until past 14. May was at the Terrace alone, Sparling being in France . . . May and I walked to Richmond by way of Strand-on-the-Green, Kew Gardens and the towpath. We came back by train and I played *Die Walküre* to her after tea. I slept at the Terrace.

'*23 May* . . . went off to Hammersmith Terrace, but found nobody in. Annie persuaded me to wait; and May came in after a while, Sparling being still in Paris. We played Beethoven's Second Symphony as a duet . . . Emery Walker came in whilst we were playing; but he did not stay long; and after he was gone May and I had a long and rather confidential conversation.

'*8 June* May and I walked along the Embankment from the Temple to Charing Cross on leaving the theatre [*Rosmersholm* at Opera Comique]. Met the Salts . . . Mrs Salt rather mad about May.

'*30 June* After the German class I went to the Terrace with May and slept there.

'*10 July* May came back with me. After tea she and I went for a walk over Primrose Hill where we sat for a while looking at the beautiful sunset. Then to Hampstead Heath all round by the Highgate Ponds. I slept at the Terrace.'

Shaw's conviction that this *ménage à trois* 'was probably the happiest passage in our three lives' has the same Panglossian ring as his description of George Carr Shaw's last years in Dublin after Bessie and the children had left: 'the happiest time of his life'. Sparling apparently believed that Shaw and May had slept together. In the summer of 1893 they had even gone to Zurich – with sixty other members of the British delegation to the International Socialist Workers' Congress. In any event, Shaw had completely captivated May who 'might have been an iceberg so far as her future relations with her husband went'. Sparling, noticeably absent from almost all their meetings over the next six months, finally absented himself completely and went to live in Paris. When rewriting this episode in *Candida* the following year, Shaw made Marchbanks the poet (not Morell the husband) quit the home having realized (as Owen Jack could have told him) that domestic love was not for the artist and that 'life at its noblest leaves happiness far behind'. He originally subtitled *Candida*, his 'modern pre-Raphaelite play', 'A Mystery'; but the mystery was buried not only in this 'secret in the poet's heart', it lay obscurely in that period before the curtain goes up for Act III and discovers Marchbanks and Candida alone, 'curtains . . . drawn', at 'past ten in the evening'.

Shaw's account of what happened during 1893 between May, himself and Sparling is equivalently mysterious. 'The *ménage* which had prospered so pleasantly as a *ménage-à-trois* proved intolerable as a *ménage-à-deux*,' he wrote.

'This marriage which all the mystic powers had forbidden from the first went to pieces when the unlucky parties no longer had me between them. Of the particulars of the rupture I know nothing; but in the upshot he fled to the Continent and eventually submitted chivalrously to being divorced as the guilty party, though the alternative was technically arranged for him . . . he married again, this time I hope more suitably, and lived as happily as he might until his death, which came sooner than an actuary would have predicted.'

Shaw disliked Sparling and made him into a Hardyesque figure pursued by the remorseless Fates. Shaw himself appears as an observer of this retribution; but it is difficult to credit, after his emotional tête-à-têtes with May, that he knew 'nothing' of the particulars of the rupture he had caused. How, for example, did he know that Sparling had legal grounds for obtaining a divorce against May – the 'alternative' that had been 'technically arranged for him' – unless perhaps that technicality had been arranged on one of the nights he slept at her house? May almost certainly looked forward to a love affair and possibly marriage with Shaw. But by the time Sparling left it was at last true that Shaw had 'enough sexual satisfaction elsewhere' – with a woman, also separated from her husband, whom he had met through May. To replace the Sparlings he had also entered into a new complicated triangular liaison, and was left with almost no time for May. In imagination, she had returned to the immortal William Morris and her predestined place for all time. Even Morris's death in 1896 could not alter this: 'You can lose a man like that by your own death,' Shaw wrote, 'but not by his.' But May did not understand. Her divorce (decree nisi) from Sparling on 18 July 1898 was to come just over six weeks after Shaw's marriage. 'May and I discontent one another extremely,' Shaw would admit to his wife two and a half months before their marriage, 'carefully avoiding the subject we are both thinking of. I mount my bike and fly.'

May stayed where she was, reverted to her maiden name, and never remarried. 'I made a mess of things then,' she wrote, 'and always, and [have] only myself to blame for a waste of life . . .' But thirty years later she could accept Shaw's re-creation of their relationship as right because by then it was 'a story out of another world' as it always had been for him.

# [ 4 ]

*Only a musician's appreciation has
any gratification for me.*

The first duty for 'the Star's Own Captious Critic' was to invent a resounding pseudonym. He pondered first on Count di Luna (the baritone villain in Verdi's *Il Trovatore*), then wrapped himself round with the more exotic title Corno di Bassetto – the name of a 'wretched instrument' of the woodwind family long ago made obsolete by the bass clarinet. 'The di Bassettos were known to Mozart, and were of service to him in the production of several of his works,' Shaw wrote on disappearing behind his pseudonym. 'The title was created in 1770. We are a branch of the Reed family . . .'

Few names were less appropriate. The basset horn had been used by Mozart in his Requiem because of its 'peculiar watery melancholy'; Shaw's musical journalism was designed to drive melancholy away – as music itself had driven melancholy from his Dublin home. Lee's music had not unified Shaw's mother and father, but once under its spell Sonny had been able to forget the divisions in the house. If there was love during those years, it was love conveyed by the play of musical instruments and the coming together of voices. Opera in particular, a world of fable and adventure, became a necessity in Shaw's life. He depended upon it: 'music is the brandy of the damned'. What others found in loving relationships, Shaw believed he experienced in music, characterizing himself as a voluptuary rather than an ascetic: 'I . . . never deny myself a Beethoven symphony.' The years of self-tuition from mastering the classics in piano transcription in Dublin to the study of musical treatises in the British Museum, the lessons in harmony and counterpoint, and the long variety of piano duets with everyone's wife, amounted to an unsentimental labour of love. Ever since the Shaws had lodged a piano in their London house, music kept pulling him away from his work. There are occasional entries too in his matter-of-fact diary ('Was moved and excited by the *Don* [Giovanni centenary recital at Crystal Palace]') that indicate the emotional effect good music made on him. As a critic, his friends were those whose skill extracted feelings writers could only describe ('because words are the counters of thinking, not of feeling'). For this reason music was for Shaw 'the sublimest of the arts'. He wanted to segregate it from the rest of his life; but another instinct continually prompted him to override this tendency to segregation by making two connections: the comic connection of what he should have heard with what he actually heard and saw; and the religious connection with what he had experienced as the 'ennobling influence' of music: 'I believe the artistic sense to be the true basis of moral rectitude.'

In the 'Musical Mems' of Corno di Bassetto it was the comic connection Shaw most often used. Between February 1885 and February 1889 he had written some ninety thousand words of music criticism for various magazines: the *Dramatic Review*, the *Magazine of Music*, the *Pall Mall Gazette*. It was in these papers that the spirit of 'Corno di Bassetto' was conceived. Shaw reached his fully precocious style in the spring and summer of 1885. His résumés of the plots of Arthur Goring Thomas's *Nadeshda* and Delibes's *Lakmé* are previews of, for example, his article on Van Milligan's *Brinio* four years later in *The Star*. The readership of *The Star* (which claimed to be the first halfpenny newspaper) was not fastidious. Shaw's musical column was played to an audience from 'the bicycle clubs and the polytechnics, not to the Royal Society of Literature or the Musical Association'. The collaboration he now started between *Star*-writer and *Star*-reader, and the changes he imposed on himself to make this collaboration effective, were part of the human engineering behind his development into a public man. What had begun with almost-an-apology was to become almost-a-boast. In a letter to the conductor August Manns two months before the birth of Bassetto, he had written: '. . . the writer who ventures to criticize you in a public newspaper is . . . a person of no consequence whatever . . . He has no position or reputation which entitle him to the smallest consideration as a writer on music . . . and he was never more astonished and flattered in his life than when he learned that his irresponsible sallies had attracted your attention.'

This, the voice of Shaw's father, appeared to be drowned in later years by a clamour of self-approval, and was only heard again when he confronted people such as Rodin or Einstein, who had not made the sort of public compromise at which G.B.S. excelled. His attitude to this compromise sometimes betrays the self-disgust that was one side of his nature. 'I daresay these articles would seem shabby, vulgar, cheap, silly, vapid enough if they were dug up and exposed to the twentieth century light,' he wrote of his Bassetto pieces in 1906; 'but in those days, and in the context of the topics of that time, they were sufficiently amusing to serve their turn.' In his Preface, written in 1935, to the publication of *London Music in 1888-89 As Heard by Corno di Bassetto*, Shaw's tone has shifted to accommodate the note of justification: 'I cannot deny that Bassetto was occasionally vulgar; but that does not matter if he makes you laugh. Vulgarity is a necessary part of a complete author's equipment; and the clown is sometimes the best part of the circus . . . I purposely vulgarized musical criticism, which was then refined and academic to the point of being unreadable and often nonsensical.'

His extraordinary brilliance in musical journalism made this process easier to accept, and he purified the whole business with a compelling sense of fun. To perform his job of making 'deaf stockbrokers read my two pages on music' it was vital to convince everyone that he knew nothing. 'I now take particular care not to betray my knowledge,' he declared.

'When people hand me a sheet of instrumental music, and ask my opinion of it, I carefully hold it upside down, and pretend to study it in that position with the eye of an expert. When they invite me to try their new grand piano, I attempt to open it at the wrong end; and when the young lady of the house informs me that she is practising the 'cello, I innocently ask her whether the mouthpiece did not cut her lips dreadfully at first.'

This is the voice of the irresistible G.B.S./Bassetto – and Shaw means us not to resist, but to laugh and swallow his words with a sprinkling of salt, and then perhaps discover that what we have assimilated is his burning sense of undervaluation and the resentment he felt at having to overcome it with such imposture. The ancestral title of di Bassetto extended over his real self so that Shaw became merely 'the assumed name under which I conceal my identity in the vulgar business of life'. This Bassetto was a man of modest omniscience, insufficiently ignorant of music to make a professional critic for life. 'Nobody knows better than I do that a musical critic who is always talking about music is quite as odious as an ordinary man who is always talking about himself.' Bassetto muses at length on what he has not heard and portrays himself as careful not to waste much time writing about performances he has been unable to avoid: 'Fifteen minutes after the curtain falls I am at home; in fifteen more the notice is posted, and I am in bed.' Though much laughed at, Bassetto's business 'is not to be funny, but to be accurate'; he explains that 'seriousness is only a small man's affectation of bigness', but that 'there is nothing so serious as great humor'. Though spoken of as severe, Bassetto speaks of himself as 'lenient, almost foolishly goodnatured'. He is scrupulous never to indulge in the cruel practice of giving misleading flattery. Bassetto has his passions: he hates his printers, and the cabal of other music critics, with their free tickets (he calls out 'press' to a street musician who asks for money); he hates the cornet and the banjo ('If it be true that the Prince of Wales banjoizes, then I protest against his succession to the throne'); he hates the interruptions of encores, the habit of bouquet-throwing (the poor artists having to take the same vast bouquet to performance after performance to have it spontaneously hurled at them by one management after another) and he hates the whole machinery of preconcerted orations ('applauding what you dont like is only one out of a great many ways of telling a lie'); he hates the old (Mendelssohn) when used as an obstacle to the new (Wagner); and he hates audiences. Most obvious among the death-watches of the concert room were the practised coughers who, Bassetto suggests, should be removed to Piccadilly where their ailment can be treated 'by gently passing a warm steam-roller over their chests'. More annoying still were the men who beat time – one actually did it by shooting his ears up and down. 'Imagine the sensation of looking at a man with his ears pulsating 116 times per minute in a quick movement from one of Verdi's operas,' Bassetto appealed.

But his chief objection to aristocracy-ridden London audiences was their imposition on music of artificial social standards. A wastefully competitive system obliged managers of opera houses and concert halls to extract money from excessively rich patrons who, far from insisting on having the best of everything on the stage and in the orchestra, converted these places into fashionable post-prandial resorts. Performances began late and intervals, which for many were the main events of the evening, were extended so that part of the audience was still laughing and chattering at full blast while the music was being played. Bassetto, who regularly denounced the stalls, trusted to the gallery and went everywhere waving the democratic flag, did not lack for a solution. The soldiers at present placed for show purposes in the vestibule should be moved into the stalls where they could turn their rifles on anyone who disturbed a performance. He urged other improvements too – such as using convict labour for the chorus and scene-shifting, and the taxing of the stall and private box-holders at twenty shillings in the pound to finance a Public Entertainments Trust under the Chairmanship of Corno di Bassetto. After which, by substituting combination for competition, they could get rid of the sham classical performances that had made the British into a race of cultural humbugs. 'The hypocrisy of culture, like other cast-off fashions, finds its last asylum among the poor,' he wrote. We had produced such a national insensibility to music that 'in this miserable country a man who has seen Die Walküre on the stage is a much greater curiosity than one who has explored the Congo'.

Shaw calculated that the sort of social criticism that T. P. O'Connor had found unendurable on the political pages of *The Star* would be perfectly welcome when dressed up in its musical columns. It was the class mumbo-jumbo of placing theatres and opera houses on the footing of West End drawing-rooms that he attacked in his own dressed-up Bassetto-style. His objections to the tyranny of Evening Dress, though often misrepresented, were famous. Bassetto disliked wearing the uniform of an idealist 'class of gentlemen to which I do not belong, and should be ashamed to belong'. This un-Jaeger-like costume was colourless, characterless and reduced to a formula 'a very vital human habit which should be the subject of constant experiment and active private enterprise'. In Bassetto's eyes, the dress represented an hygienic as well as a social lie, since the starchified whitening process concealed unclean-liness and, in covering up insobriety and bad behaviour, acted as a passport for undesirable persons. 'Next season, I shall purchase a stall for the most important evening I can select,' Shaw threatened Augustus Harris, the cautious manager of Covent Garden Opera House. 'I shall dress in white flannels.'

'I shall then hire for the evening the most repulsive waiter I can find in the lowest oyster shop in London. I shall rub him with bacon crackling, smooth his hair with fried sausages, shower stale gravy upon him, season him with Worcester sauce, and give him just enough drink to make him self-assertive without making him actually drunk. With him I shall present myself at the stalls; explain that he is my brother; and that we have arranged that I am to see the opera unless evening dress is indispensable, in which case my brother, being in evening dress, will take my place.'

Shaw admitted the easy advantages of this compulsory costume. It was cheap, simple, durable. It 'prevents rivalry and extravagance on the part of the male leaders of fashion,' he wrote, 'annihilates class distinctions, and gives men who are poor and doubtful of their social position (that is, the great majority of men) a sense of security and satisfaction . . .' All these arguments applied equally to the regulation of women's clothes: yet they were free to pursue the private enterprise Bassetto recommended – and with horrible consequences:

'At 9 o'clock (the Opera began at 8) a lady came in and sat down very conspicuously in my line of sight. She remained there until the beginning of the last act. I do not complain of her coming late and going early: on the contrary, I wish she had come later and gone earlier. For this lady, who had very black hair, had stuck over her right ear the pitiable corpse of a large white bird, which looked exactly as if someone had killed it by stamping on its breast and then nailed it to the lady's temple, which was presumably of sufficient solidity to bear the operation. I am not, I hope, a morbidly squeamish person, but the spectacle sickened me. I presume that if I had presented myself at the doors with a dead snake round my neck, a collection of blackbeetles pinned to my shirtfront, and a grouse in my hair, I should have been refused admission. Why, then, is a woman to be allowed to commit such a public outrage? . . . I suggest to the Covent Garden authorities that, if they feel bound to protect their subscribers against the danger of my shocking them with a blue tie, they are at least equally bound to protect me against the danger of a woman shocking me with a dead bird.'

Bassetto's 'Musical Mems' were a continual protest against distractions, whether by musicians or audiences, from good musical performance. Whenever the music itself was meretricious he fastened his attention elsewhere. This was a particularly effective technique with opera where he could summon the Shavian literary and dramatic critic to tackle a ludicrous event-plot. *Brinio*, the grand opera in Dutch by S. van Milligan, called for this treatment:

'Rheime sings to a tambourine accompaniment, which indicates that she is distraught. Ada sings then without the tambourine . . . Rheime meanwhile sitting on a stump in a dumb paroxysm of flower and straw mania. Aquilius and Ada then elope, leaving Rheime an easy prey to the two villains, who re-enter and approach her by a series of strategic movements from tree to tree, as if she were a regiment of sharpshooters. At last they bear her off, wrapping her head in a veil, lest they should recognize her and spoil the last Act. Brinio comes in . . . with a host of mistletoe worshippers, and, after declaiming unintelligently at insufferable length in a colorless bass voice, appeals to the heavenly powers, who ring a bell, which causes the limelight man to cast a dazzling ray on Brinio, thus unmistakably pointing him out as the savior of his country . . . Vulpes now announces the advance of the foe, who come charging cautiously over the battlements, preoccupied with the real danger of breaking their necks rather than with the illusory perils of a stage battle. Massa, after a tremendous draught of Dutch courage, takes his sword . . . whereupon most of the Mistletonians fall down dead.'

The worse the music, the more Bassetto diversified. His rich irrelevances, though strategically used, were loved for their own sake. Readers liked to hear of the voice trainer who hit his pupils, declaring that it was the only method to make them produce the vowel *o*; they liked to discover Bassetto himself, after a visit to the ballet, at dawn the next day with a policeman, a postman and a milkman ('who unfortunately broke his leg') attempting *pirouettes* and *entrechats* in Fitzroy Square; they liked, as part of a teetotal campaign, his plea for dancing in Church, which just stopped short of converting Westminster Abbey into a ballroom; they even accepted his rank socialism: 'What we want is not music for the people, but bread for the people, rest for the people, immunity from robbery and scorn for the people, hope for them, enjoyment, equal respect and consideration, life and aspiration, instead of drudgery and despair. When we get that I imagine the people will make tolerable music for themselves . . .'

Part of Bassetto's personality was established by provoking correspondents to accuse him of flippancy or of being no musician ('As well try to prove the earth flat') – then parrying these sometimes violent assaults with outbursts of sweet-temper. Almost the only person not to be diverted by this penplay was T. P. O'Connor. Bassetto had fabricated for the public a very pretty relationship between critic and editor. But the reality was unpleasant. 'I find it impossible to continue as I have been doing lately,' Shaw told Massingham early in 1890. 'This week I have had to attend five concerts; have advanced fourteen shillings from my exhausted exchequer; and have written the Bassetto column, all for two guineas.' But T. P. O'Connor, who in public was to heap apparent encomiums on his fellow Irishman ('There never was such musical criticism on land or flood'), refused to increase Bassetto's salary. He wanted to be rid of him and of his attempts to turn his Liberal paper into a Socialist one. But he had no plausible reason to sack him; to do so would make him one of the most unpopular editors in London and a laughing-stock. So he almost literally starved him out. Bassetto had sometimes made fun of his own resignation – 'this threat never fails to bring Stonecutter Street to its knees,' he told readers; 'though, lest too frequent repetition should blunt it, I am careful not to employ it more than three times in any one week.' In private, Shaw, who was driven by destitution to walk to and from many of the concerts and to wait a year for the repayment of some of his expenses, advised O'Connor that 'the giving up of the Musical Mems will be a gigantic – a Himalayan mistake'. His threat of resignation, however, sounded far sweeter in O'Connor's ears than his promise a month later to 'hold on'.

By the early summer of 1890 their relationship had grown so strained that 'we came to the very grave point of having to exchange assurances that we esteemed one another beyond all created mortals'. Obviously this could not continue. The day O'Connor had been looking forward to arrived in the middle of May 1890, when Bassetto of *The Star* became G.B.S. of *The World*. It was William Archer who persuaded Yates to re-employ Shaw. 'Arranged to take the musical criticship of *The World*,' Shaw wrote in his diary on 14 May, 'if T. P. O'Connor has nothing to say to the contrary.' In his own style, O'Connor had everything to say in its favour. 'I am extremely glad to hear you have got the excellent offer of *The World*,' he congratulated Shaw the next day. '. . . I make large allowance for the latitude in their private relations of those who preach the fraternity of all mankind. Take the offer by all means . . .' Above Corno di Bassetto's last column which appeared on 16 May, O'Connor stuck a discordant adieu: 'The larger salary of a weekly organ of the classes has proved too much for the virtue even of a Fabian . . .' 'After the malediction, the valediction,' Bassetto countered, and went on to show how all grievance (though not forgotten) could be submerged in humour: 'I proposed long ago that not only this column, but the entire paper, political leaders and all, should be conducted on Bassettian lines, and practically dictated by me . . .'

'. . . I had no hesitation in magnanimously admitting that a daily paper requires, in the season at least, a daily and not a weekly chronicle and criticism of musical events. Such a chronicle I am unable to undertake. A man who, like myself, has to rise regularly at eleven o'clock every morning cannot sit up night after night writing opera notices . . . I ask some indulgence for my successor, handicapped as he will be for a time by the inevitable comparison . . . I hope he will never suffer the musical department of The Star to lose that pre-eminence which has distinguished it throughout the administration of "Corno di Bassetto".'

*

Shaw's predecessor on *The World* had been Louis Engel, an extraordinary musical man-about-town who, while acknowledging that there was hardly a composer of eminence among his contemporaries not confessing his influence, had translated *glissando* as a 'sliding scale' – 'one has to be both pianist and trade-unionist,' commented Shaw, 'to catch the full flavour of its exquisite absurdity'. His shrewd, chatty, rather unedifying weekly articles, idolizing favourites and pillorying foes, were society pages which had nothing to say about Wagner other than that he wrote music without melody, drank his coffee from a golden cup and showed ingratitude to Meyerbeer. All this was to be reversed by G.B.S., who made Wagner (as he had Whistler and Ibsen) into a vehicle for enlightenment against the dark forces of London. In fact anti-Wagnerianism had been on the wane since the Wagner Festival at the Albert Hall in 1877; and by the end of the 1880s, according to Corno di Bassetto, the anti-Wagner army was reduced to 'six old gentlemen, more or less like the Duke of Cambridge in personal appearance, who make faces and stop their ears whenever an unprepared major ninth occurs in the harmony'. Except for his agitation to have more of Wagner's music played in Britain, Shaw removed Wagner from an exclusively musical context and, in *The Perfect Wagnerite*, went on to refight the old campaign on extra-musical territory over which he could advance his political beliefs.

The character adopted by G.B.S. was less dramatic than Bassetto whom he later described as 'a mixture of triviality, vulgarity, farce and tomfoolery with genuine criticism'. Though the genuine criticism of Shaw's pages in *The World* was less mixed, G.B.S. still carried on Bassetto's propaganda: 'in this philistine country a musical critic, if he is to be any good, must put off the learned commentator and become a propagandist, versed in all the arts that attract a crowd, and wholly regardless of his personal dignity.'

To attract this crowd, he wrote, 'I yield to no man in the ingenuity and persistence with which I squeeze every opportunity of puffing myself and my affairs.' But, he added, the privilege of joking in public 'should never be granted except to people who know thoroughly what they are joking about – that is, to exceptionally serious and laborious people'. The mental discipline of going to concerts, operas and recitals day after day for a livelihood, making an analysis and delivering his judgement with the knowledge that an oversight or an error may cruelly injure a performer also working for a livelihood, was exceptionally demanding. But the strain was never shown to his readers.

Though G.B.S. often found a use for his humour, he also found it impossible to resist laughter. Anyone who made him laugh melted most of the criticism out of him. Many of his descriptions, such as of the syncopated *corps de ballet* that 'wandered about in the prompt corner as if some vivisector had removed from their heads that portion of the brain which enables us to find our way to the door', or of the German singers at Bayreuth, 'robust as dray horses' who reached 'the prime of their shouting life' at the age of sixty, have all the cruelty carried away on a joyous stream of comedy. By offering the most far-fetched comparisons and analogies as stepping stones to his conclusions – the training of circus horses to compose dance music, for example, or the installation on the site of the prompter's box of a steam crane to hoist despairing critics out of their seats and drop them at the refreshment bar – G.B.S. certainly amused his crowd of deaf stockbrokers, but also encouraged it to overlook what lay behind these fantasies, and to dismiss his 'serious and laborious' recommendations as simply more absurdity. For the first time in his writing a note of exasperated despair sounds over the misreading of his careful statements. He was making himself a master of language, but his readers could not master his language. 'It has taken me nearly twenty years of studied self-restraint, aided by the natural decay of my faculties, to make myself dull enough to be accepted as a serious person by the British public; and I am not sure that I am not still regarded as a suspicious character in some quarters.'

Shaw's method of judging music, he once stated, was to do with his ears what he did with his eyes when he stared. Some critics, perverted by 'the fatal academic habit of studying music otherwise than through one's ears', had imposed on the public by displays of 'scientific analysis'. G.B.S. fiercely resented this fashion for scholarly pretentiousness. Perhaps it was natural, he suggested, that gentlemen who were incapable of criticism should fall back on the sort of musical writing 'which parades silly little musical parsing exercises to impress the laity'. In one of his most effective debunking feats, he parodied this style of criticism with a comparable 'analysis' of Hamlet's soliloquy on death:

'Shakespear, dispensing with the customary exordium, announces his subject at once in the infinitive, in which mood it is presently repeated after a short connecting passage in which, brief as it is, we recognize the alternative and negative forms on which so much of the significance of repetition depends. Here we reach a colon; and a pointed pository phrase, in which the accent falls decisively on the relative pronoun, brings us to the first full stop.'

Shaw believed that literature, drama and poetry had not then been academicized in Britain as had music and painting. When we went to the theatre or read a book we were allowed to judge the work directly by what our sensibilities perceived. But in music (together with painting and sculpture) this natural climate sustaining the art was poisoned by our university factories. Academic preconceptions had warped not only our judgement but also our original composition, G.B.S. argued, and encouraged a ruck of 'barren professors of the art of doing what has been done before and need not be done again'. Using a literary analogy once more, he questioned what would be thought of him if he wrote inane imitations of Milton's *Paradise Lost* and then solicited rapturous comments from his friends over their grammar and scansion. He detected a gentlemanly gang at work in the musical world, and it was with outcast irony that he asked: 'who am I that I should be believed, to the disparagement of eminent musicians?' Commenting on Professor Stanford's hybrid *Eden*, he continued:

'If you doubt that Eden is a masterpiece, ask Dr Parry and Dr Mackenzie, and they will applaud it to the skies. Surely Dr Mackenzie's opinion is conclusive: for is he not the composer of Veni Creator, guaranteed as excellent music by Professor Stanford and Dr Parry? You want to know who Dr Parry is? Why, the composer of Blest Pair of Sirens, as to the merits of which you have only to consult Dr Mackenzie and Professor Stanford.'

Such a round of politeness led to the production of sham classics in imitation of Handel and Mendelssohn. As early as 1885 Shaw made out his historical case against the persisting influence of these composers. 'Our really serious music is no longer recognized as religious,' he wrote, 'whilst our professedly religious music ... is only remarkable as *naïve* blasphemy, wonderfully elaborated, and convinced of its own piety.'

'Doubtless, many of the public are pleased, much as they would be if, on going to church, they found sensational novels bound up in their Bible covers, and were surprised to find Scripture so amusing. The critics are much of the same opinion: Mendelssohn is still their idol; and it was Mendelssohn who popularized the pious romancing which is now called sacred music; in other words, the Bible with the thought left out. M. Gounod proved his capacity in this direction by giving us Faust with all Goethe's thought left out, the result having been so successful (and, it must be confessed, so irresistibly charming), it is natural that he should turn his attention to the Bible, which is worshipped in England so devoutly by people who never open it, that a composer has but to pick a subject, or even a name, from it, to ensure a half-gagged criticism and the gravest attention for his work, however trivial . . .

'If Handel were alive today, his Messiah would wear another guise, which would probably not be recognizable by the Birmingham committee as a sacred one, and which would certainly not be explicitly religious.'

G.B.S. was merciless on the 'flagrant pedantry, imposture, corruption, boredom, and waste of musical funds' which the oratorio market manufactured for the regular English Festivals. His constitution for these pious orgies soon grew famously inadequate. 'I do not know how it is possible to listen to these works without indignation, especially in circumstances implying a parallel between them and the genuine epic stuff of Handel.' The very word oratorio roused in him a tempest of evil passions – even such wild-fowl as Magnificats, Solemn Masses and Tantum Ergos seemed preferable. 'Had oratorio been invented in Dante's time, the seventh circle in his Inferno would have been simply a magnified Albert Hall, with millions of British choristers stolidly singing, All that hath life and breath, sing to the Lord, in the galleries, and the condemned, kept awake by demons, in the arena, clothed in evening dress.'

Shaw's experience as a music critic convinced him that the history of original music in Britain had been broken off by the death of Purcell – and not begun again until the coming of Elgar. He was obliged to listen to a good deal of work by contemporary composers: Sir Frederic Cowen, Sir Alexander Mackenzie, Sir Hubert Parry, Sir Charles Stanford, Sir Arthur Sullivan, and other such knights and bachelors of music, most of whose works he would happily have committed 'to the nearest County Council "destructor"'. To his mind these composers were encouraged to waste their lives, taking themselves too seriously. Sullivan, a musician of care and refinement, who had been trained in the fastidious school of Mendelssohn and spent over twenty years composing for the drawing-room and the Church, managed to fertilize his languishing talent only by plunging into the trivialities of Savoy Opera. His predicament was to have achieved success through a luxurious burlesque of the classics he revered. The organist at 'St Somebody's, Chester-square . . . outdid Offenbach in wickedness,' Shaw wrote, '. . . so that now the first of the Mendelssohn Scholars stands convicted of ten godless mockeries of everything sacred to [John] Goss and [Sterndale] Bennett. They trained him to make Europe yawn; and he took advantage of their teaching to make London and New York laugh and whistle'. In Stanford, one of the few professors of music who had anything to lose, G.B.S. detected a similar division, the healing of which was to become his theme in *John Bull's Other Island*. This division was gigantically exposed to Shaw by the 'somewhat scandalous' success of Stanford's Irish Symphony, into which he read 'a record of fearful conflict between the aboriginal Celt and the Professor'. So often Stanford's native audacity was woodenly checked by what G.B.S. presumed to be his shrinking from the vernacular in music. Shaw, whose musical criticism was soaked in the vernacular, contended that social inhibitions of this kind were out of date. This criticism of his compatriot reflects his own experience over almost twenty years in England; but it is also an indication of his reaction against innate qualities.

Here was a beginning in his quest for a formula that, with its symbol of reconciled England and Ireland, would integrate inherited factors in such deep conflict that they had forced his parents to occupy separate countries and were eventually to neutralize himself as a man without nationality. Much of his advocacy was directed against attitudes he was seen partly to represent himself – a strategy that enabled him as playwright to put convincing argument into the mouths of opposing characters. For who was Shaw to censure Stanford for not displaying his emotions in public? Yet it is partly as self-censure, self-analysis and self-encouragement that we should read such passages:

'The spectacle of a university professor "going Fantee" is indecorous, though to me personally it is delightful. When Professor Stanford is genteel, cultured, classic, pious, and experimentally mixolydian, he is dull beyond belief. His dullness is all the harder to bear because it is the restless, ingenious, trifling, flippant dullness of the Irishman, instead of the stupid, bovine, sleepable-through dullness of the Englishman . . .

'. . . Far from being a respectable oratorio-manufacturing talent, it is, when it gets loose, eccentric, violent, romantic, patriotic, and held in check only by a mortal fear of being found deficient in what are called 'the manners and tone of good society'. This fear, too, is Irish: it is, possibly, the racial consciousness of having missed that four hundred years of Roman civilization which gave England a sort of university education when Ireland was in the hedge school.

'In those periods when nobody questions the superiority of the university to the hedge school, the Irishman, lamed by a sense of inferiority, blusters most intolerably . . . Then the fashion changes; Ruskin leads young Oxford out into the hedge school to dig roads; there is general disparagement in advanced circles of civilization, the university, respectability, law and order . . .

'This reaction is the opportunity of the Irishman in England to rehabilitate his self-respect, since it gives him a standpoint from which he can value himself as a hedge-school man . . . If he seizes the opportunity, he may end in founding a race of cultivated Irishmen whose mission in England will be to teach Englishmen to play with their brains as well as with their bodies; for it is all work and no play in the brain department that makes John Bull such an uncommonly dull boy.'

His few aberrations in judgement usually arise from treating music historically, that is, with a type of academic measuring-rod he scorns. He placed Hermann Goetz 'above all other German composers of the last hundred years, save only Mozart and Beethoven, Weber and Wagner', partly because his Symphony in F was technically and intellectually more symphonic in form than any by Schumann or Schubert. He undervalued Schubert and considered him overplayed because 'I could not see that Schubert added anything to Mozart & Beethoven except sugar: and though the sugar was extraordinarily rich and sweet, I rather jumped over him to Mendelssohn'. Music composed out of the dramatic instinct (such as Goetz's *Taming of the Shrew*) attracted him far more than anything intimate. He had an aversion to reflective, inward-looking music, and was sometimes a poor judge of chamber music because it tended to conflict with his commitment to optimism and the twenty-four-hours-a-day cheerfulness which the public personality of G.B.S. piped forth.

He was deaf to the remorseless exploration of heartbreak by Schubert in his Quintet in C (whose 'melancholy tenderness' he decided went on 'too long'), and with evasive wit he shrugged off the Quartet in D minor, 'Death and the Maiden', as something that did not count for much: 'by the time they came to the variations on Death and the Maiden, I was reconciled to Death and indifferent to the Maiden.' He continually sniped at Brahms, insisting that with all his great powers of utterance he had nothing to say ('Brahms' enormous gift of music is paralleled by nothing on earth but Mr Gladstone's gift of words'). For Shaw, Brahms was an opponent of Wagner and the antithesis of Mozart 'the master of masters', who (he told Busoni) 'taught me how to say profound things and at the same time remain flippant and lively'. It is significant that Shaw's hostility to Brahms focused on his Requiem ('patiently borne only by the corpse'). Earlier he had welcomed his music, as he had that of Dvořák, and in both cases it was these composers' Requiems that drew his fire. In 1936 Shaw was to apologize for Corno di Bassetto's failure to recognize Brahms's unfamiliar idiom; and as late as 1947 he explained that 'the first performances of Brahms's Requiem in London were dreadfully and insincerely mock-solemn and dull. Now that I know the work, its fugal bits and march music amuse me; and its one Mendelssohnic chorus is a favourite of mine'.

But neither apology nor explanation conceal the antipathy of Shaw to all near-contemporary religious music, especially when connected with death

– why, he asked, would anyone (except, in the way of business, an undertaker) want to create at that evolutionary period such sententious celebrations of superstition? Unable to endure melancholy ('black cloth and coffin nails'), he empties these works of poetry and renders them, for the entertainment of his readers, colossal monuments to boredom. He literally cannot listen to them.

But when he listens to other music it is with acute attentiveness. Whenever possible before a performance he studied the score and exposed cuts, interpolations and other textual and interpretative deviations from the composer's aims, as well as derivations from the work of other composers. His descriptions of performers have an exactness that enables us to differentiate one from another precisely: the exuberant hammer-play of Paderewski, a thin flat man with a turban of red hair, and a 'trained athlete of the pianoforte', whose final bow was like the action of a critic falling asleep; the cool muscular strength of another musical gymnast, Slivonski, a prodigiously rapid pianist of the Leschetizky school, toughly knit, free-stepping, spare, whose feathery touch could make the piano sing in transcription of vocal music; the hugely energetic Rubinstein, a player of marvellous manual dexterity, with immense power and spontaneity, limited by his narrowness of intellectual sympathy. Among violinists he discriminates so finely between the judgement of Reményi, the sensitive hand of Sarasate, Joachim's peculiarly thoughtful style and the self-assertiveness of Ysaÿe that we can almost hear their playing. He analyses the strengths, pinpoints the peculiarities of singers, and the varying styles of the conductors from Richard Wagner and Richter, who brought relief to England at a time of musical famine, to Henschel's London Symphony Orchestra, Charles Hallé's Manchester concerts, and the Saturday concerts led by August Manns at the Crystal Palace. He brings us reports from the music halls, and from amateur events in the country such as the brass band of shoemakers playing on a racecourse at Northampton – the sort of place where the music of the country was kept alive. He campaigns against professional conditions which make honest, well-rehearsed, widely heard music so difficult to achieve. His musical manifesto includes the building of a Wagner Theatre on Richmond Hill, an amendment of the Children's Employment Act, stopping the exploitation of children on the stage, the compulsory slimming of singers, and the maintenance of orchestras by municipalities. He argues that public opera houses are as essential to people as public museums and public galleries, and a powerful competition to public houses. He urges thorough rehearsals and daily concerts in London, with permanent engagements and pensions for conductors and players, paid for if necessary by the County Council, which would transform this barren and brainless country 'where you cannot have even a cheap piano provided for the children to march to in a Board School without some mean millionaire or other crying out that the rates will ruin him'. Among his targets for criticism are expensive tickets and programmes; impresarios pandering to that harmless monster the public; a star system that sacrificed the sympathetic comprehension of the whole score to a verbatim report of the solo part; and charity concerts that promoted bad music for well-meaning ends in the belief that music was not worth cultivating for its own sake and that a good orchestra was not as 'important to a town as a good hospital'.

From the pages of Bassetto and G.B.S., and the columns of criticism Shaw scattered anonymously through other papers, the architecture of music in late Victorian England may be recovered. We hear and we watch from among the *prima donna* worshippers, standing three deep in the bird's-eye shilling gallery of the Albert Hall, or sitting at the back against the wall with our legs 'converging straight towards the centre of the dome, and terminating in an inner circumference of boot soles'; we huddle pale-faced in the unbreathable air of St James's Hall in Piccadilly, so cold in winter in our thick shoes and our coats buttoned to the chin that we begin to accompany the music with a castanet from our teeth, in summer so hot that we can hear the violin strings snapping in all directions, while in and out of season we are swamped by odours of shrivelling paint (from the fierce cooking arrangements downstairs), so terrifying as to cause our past lives to career before our minds; year after year our disbelief is revived by an alarmingly tame policy from the Donizettian dark ages at Covent Garden, with its obsolete repertory of expensive traps, visions and makeshifts, its herd of Don Juans swaggering feebly like emancipated billiard-markers to achieve a *succès de rire*; and at lunch-time on Saturday we catch our train from Victoria and shunt eight miles in forty minutes to Sydenham to hear August Manns's orchestra play under the echoing roof of glass and iron in a vast annexe, its platform guarded by white-winged angels on pedestals, while above the arc lights splutter bluely.

The critic who amused stockbrokers in the 1880s and 1890s was to become one of our best guides to the history of music performed in England during the late nineteenth century. He had perfected the Shavian note – assertive, audacious, fantastic, expertly wrapped round with the illusion of intimacy – until he became his own description of the confident journalist-critic: 'magnificently endowed with the superb quality which we dishonor by the ignoble name of Cheek – a quality which has enabled men from time immemorial to fly without wings, and to live sumptuously without incomes.'

In a different style he told a correspondent towards the end of 1893: 'I should starve, myself, but for the fact that I can criticize musical performances rather well.' But in his character of a man of the West End world, accustomed to theatres, concerts, operas, galleries, he was brilliant at diagnosing artistic vanities – apparently aloof, though eventually not immune to some of the symptoms himself. 'The critic who is modest is lost,' he wrote. Because he did not value his past, he could accept the scarring with which Society marks those who seriously attack the status quo. Many passages in Bassetto and G.B.S. celebrate a release from the drill of social deference. But Shaw also knew that damage could be done to those who, to gain the popular ear, force 'vulgarity upon a talent that is naturally quiet and sympathetic'.

[ 5 ]

*. . . very few people in the world have ever had a love affair.*
'Beethoven's Unsterbliche Geliebte' (1893)

Florence Farr, who was to create the roles of Blanche in *Widowers' Houses* and Louka in *Arms and the Man*, was 'an *amiable* woman, with semicircular eyebrows'. Shaw gives a more lingering description of her in his portrait of Grace Tranfield from *The Philanderer*: 'slight of build, delicate of feature, and sensitive in expression . . . but her well closed mouth, proudly set brows, firm chin, and elegant carriage shew plenty of determination and self-respect'. She was four years younger than Shaw and unlike any woman he had met. Yet she seemed to resemble some of the women he had optimistically invented in his novels, in particular Madge Brailsford from *Love Among the Artists* (a copy of which he gave her), who is taught elocution by Owen Jack and, defying her father's throttling morality, follows her true instincts to win success on the stage. This had been one of Shaw's earliest portraits of the New Woman, and in Florence Farr he appeared to have met a New Woman after his own prescription. It was partly her feminism that had brought her to William Morris's house in Hammersmith where she was learning embroidery with May through whom, in about 1890, she met Shaw.

He had seen her act in John Todhunter's *A Sicilian Idyll*, describing it as 'an hour's transparent Arcadian make-believe', much helped by 'Florence Farr's striking and appropriate good looks'. Then, on 4 October 1890, he 'had a long talk' with her at the Private View of an Arts and Crafts exhibition – after which they began seeing each other frequently, 'gadding about' to plays and recitals together, to the Pine Apple, Orange Grove and Wheatsheaf restaurants and, for long teas, to ABC shops where he 'chatted and chatted' and she 'laughed and laughed'. He would turn up out of the night at her lodgings in 123 Dalling Road, only half a mile from May Morris, play a little, sing a little, and take her for walks round Ravenscourt Park. But what was different from his relationship with other women was the excitement of their talk, in which ideas and feelings and laughter swirled together and seemed to carry them off towards new enterprises and experiences. 'First really intimate conversation,' Shaw recorded after an evening with her on 15 November. She told him 'a lot of odd and interesting things about herself'. As the daughter of Dr William Farr, a sanitary reformer who had tried to persuade his countrymen that England was dying of dirt, her Shavian provenance was impeccable. She had been schooled in Shakespeare and tap-dancing but on the last day of what, according to her horoscope, was a 'bad year', had married a handsome undistinguished actor, Edward Emery, who spent much of his time resting. Florence was not an observant woman: it was almost four years later, in 1888, that she noticed that Edward was no longer there. He had woken up and gone to America, leaving her an independent married woman.

Like Jenny Patterson (it was the single quality they seemed to share), Florence took the initiative over Shaw. 'As she was clever, goodnatured, and very goodlooking, all her men friends fell in love with her,' he recalled.

'This had occurred so often that she had lost all patience with the hesitating preliminaries of her less practised adorers. Accordingly, when they clearly longed to kiss her, and she did not dislike them sufficiently to make their gratification too great a strain on her excessive goodnature, she would seize the stammering suitor firmly by the wrists, bring him into her arms by a smart pull, and saying "Let's get it over", allow the startled gentleman to have his kiss, and then proceed to converse with him at her ease . . .'

Before the end of the year they had become lovers. Shaw made no secret of his love for Florence. 'Went over to F.E in the evening,' he wrote in his diary on 30 December 1890: and added uncharacteristically ' – a happy evening'. He told his friends he was in love with her; he told Florence herself she was 'my other self – no, not my other self, but my very self', and 'the happiest of all my great happinesses, the deepest and restfullest of all my tranquillities, the very inmost of all my loves'. It was to Florence that he wrote the shortest and most enchanting of his love letters:

'This is to certify that you are my best and dearest love, the regenerator of my heart, the holiest joy of my soul, my treasure, my salvation, my rest, my reward, my darling youngest child, my secret glimpse of heaven, my angel of the Annunciation, not yet herself awake, but rousing me from a long sleep with the beat of her unconscious wings, and shining upon me with her beautiful eyes that are still blind.

'Also to observe incidentally that Wednesday is the nearest evening that shews blank in my diary.'

He could not always hold on to the self-possession of that last paragraph. She did not oppose him, but sometimes his will-power melted away, and 'when the time came to return I hesitated and was lost'. Whenever he felt incapable of further work by himself and craved for exercise he would leap away from his desk and usually find himself six miles off at Florence's lodgings, where he 'let time slip and lost my train back'. One night he came blustering up to 'find the place in darkness'. He 'wandered about disappointed for a time', then returned to Fitzroy Square, and put down the feelings released in him by her absence, sending them to her as a letter: 'I have fallen in with my boyhood's mistress, Solitude, and wandered aimlessly with her once more ... reminding me of the days when disappointment seemed my inevitable & constant lot.'

Florence promised him a future he had believed to be impossible. 'Women tend to regard love as a fusion of body, spirit and mind,' he later told one of his biographers. 'It has never been so with me.' Yet for a time, perhaps a year, it seemed as if it could be so. Florence had, according to W. B. Yeats, 'three great gifts, a tranquil beauty ... an incomparable sense of rhythm and a beautiful voice'. For Shaw, her attractiveness lay partly in her beauty and partly in her attitude. Though unpuritanical she was fastidious, 'claimed 14 lovers', but was not more drugged by what she called 'the ungraceful antics of love' than he was. 'When a man begins to make love to me,' she admitted, 'I instantly see it as a stage performance.' Though she was far more sexually experienced than Shaw, her opinions about sex were easily reconcilable with his own. 'It gives us every happiness we know on the condition that we never give way to it in our serious relations,' she concluded. 'For heirs certainly. For diversion, yes. As a "hygienic gymnastic", yes.'

Almost before they realized themselves that they were in love, Jenny Patterson knew it. 'JP was angry and jealous about FE,' Shaw wrote on 16 October 1890; 'so the day ended unpleasantly.' 'JP then made a scene,' he noted the following week, ' – jealous as usual.' That winter Jenny Patterson had gone abroad, and for almost four months Shaw and

9 Shaw in his stockinette Jaeger suit, 1886

10 Shaw in Battersea Park, 1888

11 Jenny Patterson

12 Shaw, 1891 (opposite page)

13 Alice Lockett

14 William Morris

15 May Morris

16A Edith Bland, née, Nesbit;   B Eleanor Marx;   C Annie Besant

17 Bloody Sunday, 13 November 1887

18 Beatrice Potter          19 Sidney Webb (opposite page)

20 Mr and Mrs Sidney Webb        21 Sidney Olivier  (opposite page)

22A Janet Achurch and Charles Charrington in 'A Doll's House', 1889;
B Janet Achurch; C Florence Farr

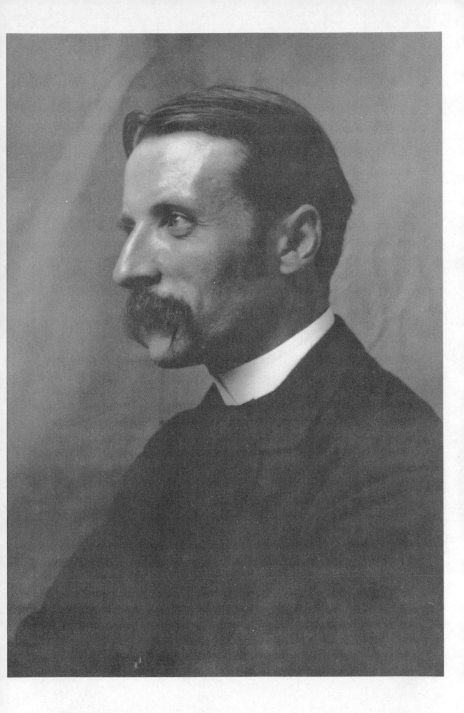

23 William Archer

24 Shaw with Henry Arthur Jones in the early 1890s

Florence saw each other freely. But then, on 27 April 1891, Shaw 'went in to JP's. Fearful scene about FE, this being our first meeting since her return from the East. Did not get home until about 3.' Though these scenes grew fiercer, each time she won a battle she won less – and Shaw promised Florence that: 'Not for forty thousand such relations will I forgo one forty thousandth part of my relation with you. Every grain of cement she [Jenny Patterson] shakes from it falls like a block of granite on her own flimsy castle in the air . . . The silly triumph with which she takes, with the air of a conqueror, that which I have torn out of my own entrails for her, almost brings the lightning down on her . . . Damnation! triple damnation! You must give me back my peace.'

Once Jenny Patterson too had given him peace, but it had been a peace of the body only, as she well understood: 'Any other woman would have brough[t] you the sleep I did.' After the Annie Besant rumpus, she expected their sexual relationship to go on as before: and to some extent it had. Shaw was neglectful, long-suffering, and passionate by turns. 'You are beginning again the old games,' she had warned him in January 1888. But the next month she wrote: 'Be as ardent as you were last week, it is your place to be so – I adore to be made love to like that. It takes my breath away at the time & leaves oh such a memory behind. Your ardor makes me feel not half ardent enough, but I think you find me warm enough?'

Yet she could not conceal from herself that his feelings for her were not what they had been 'when I was dear Mrs Patterson & worth seeing . . . oh les beaux jours'. Her letters, which once glowed with the delight she felt in loving him, had grown increasingly scorch-marked by possessiveness and a resentment at being excluded from so much of his busy life. Her expectations of him seemed to fade. 'How my lover is becoming less my lover every month becoming a wretched common place creature & only just thinking of me as a sucking baby does of its mar when it is hungry!' she had complained on 20 October 1888. '. . . I think I wont bother you with many more letters.' But she bothered him with one more nine days later: 'Adieu most disappointing of men & unsatisfactory of lovers.' She could say goodbye, she could not leave him; and the next month she is begging him to 'write me again so that I may have something to live on until I see you . . . I must have a whole evening & far into the night . . . let nothing come betwixt us – I never loved you better than I do now & you know it'.

But their relationship was static and had become stale to Shaw. He tried not to hurt her – 'You are gentle and good nearly always to me,' she allowed – but increasingly recoiled from the physical centre of their liaison. Nevertheless, though he flirted with Fabian girls and other men's wives during the day, at night he had made love only to Mrs Patterson until he fell in love with Florence. His love affair with Jenny Patterson had separated sex from other interests – but it was not so for Jenny. Lacking an imaginative vocabulary for sex, she repeatedly writes of it as if it were a commodity presented to Shaw like some bargain at a shop. 'I had nothing else to give & I do not hold that gift so cheap that I can give to Hopkins & Co. what I thought good for you.' 'My boy you got all for nothing – it was not to be bought at any price.' Sex was everything she had to give, and through it she gave her whole self. Making love was her language. She loved him to the limits of her being and in a way that he could not love her. He was still the saint of her personal calendar; the important dates were those on which she saw him, and she measured time by their anniversaries (10 July 1887: 'Just this date two years ago!! have you forgotten? much happiness & luck my dear dear boy'). Hers is a small world and her feeling for him so fills it that there is no place for interests or enthusiasms beyond her infatuation. When she writes to him: 'You are my love, my life & all the world to me' there seems no exaggeration.

The tyranny of this love was Shaw's small private hell. Jenny was probably going through the change of life. She weeps, rages, flings a book at his head, provokes quarrels over imaginary offences, breaks off their relationship in high dudgeon, then arranges a luxurious reconciliation. Shaw feels himself to be like Allmers, in Ibsen's *Little Eyolf*, 'a fellow almost damned in a fair wife . . . [who] not only troubles and uncentres him as only a woman can trouble and uncentre a man who is susceptible to her bodily attraction, but is herself furiously and jealously in love with him'. In his chapter called 'The Womanly Woman' from *The Quintessence of Ibsenism*, Shaw is obviously evoking his experiences with Jenny Patterson when he describes 'the infatuation of passionate sexual desire'.

'Everyone who becomes the object of that infatuation shrinks from it instinctively. Love loses its charm when it is not free; and whether the compulsion is that of custom and law, or of infatuation, the effect is the same: it becomes valueless and even abhorrent, like the caresses of a maniac. The desire to give inspires no affection unless there is also the power to withhold; and the successful wooer, in both sexes alike, is the one who can stand out for honorable conditions, and, failing them, go without.'

Only with his New Woman could he achieve these honourable conditions: 'my relations with Florence,' he wrote, 'can be properly described only by someone who does not know too much about them'. In his discretion, Shaw never explained that Florence was infertile. This may help to account for her Leporello list of lovers, and why Shaw entered his name on it so prominently. By implication it may also elucidate a mysterious passage from a letter he wrote in 1930 to Frank Harris and later published in *Sixteen Self Sketches*: 'If you have any doubts as to my normal virility, dismiss them from your mind. I was not impotent; I was not sterile; I was not homosexual; and I was extremely susceptible, though not promiscuously.' There seems no chance that Shaw used the word 'sterile' carelessly, since he was particular to differentiate it from 'impotent'. How then did he know that he was not sterile? The evidence, though meagre, suggests that in the first half of 1886 Jenny Patterson may have had a miscarriage. She had gone to see Shaw's medical friend Kingston Barton early in February. 'I have seen "the" Barton,' she told him and followed this with an enigmatic row of dots. On May 10, in the first of her desperate pleas not to abandon her, she writes of having to hide her predicament from 'Lucy's sharp eyes' and play at being her 'old self' to Shaw's mother: 'I write in despair. I cannot suffer so & I dread being ill it will all come out I fear then'. But it is clear from Shaw's diary that his mother and sister knew of Mrs Patterson's attachment to him. So there must have been something more to come out. During the spring Jenny Patterson had complained of illness, and her letter of 11 May contains a definite allusion to pregnancy. 'You cant help wronging me. I trusted you entirely. Had there been results I should have had to bear that also alone.' So by the second week of May two things were established: that there was now no pregnancy and that they would henceforward experiment with a platonic relationship. The fear of pregnancy and the revulsion caused by a miscarriage could only have been an extra brake to Shaw enjoying sexual intercourse with other women until he met one who was herself sterile. It would also deepen the sexual guilt with which, despite all his freethinking morality, Jenny Patterson had encircled him.

With Florence who could 'go without', there was no tyranny or guilt; and from his gratitude arose a dazzling overestimation of 'the magnetic Miss Farr'. There were times when she could make him feel 'more deeply moved than I could have imagined'. But she also brought him something deeper than the 'revulsion' he had noted against Jenny Patterson's name, and this, as he put in his diary, was 'Disillusion'.

It was said that Florence had two faces: one provocative and tomboyish, the other poetic. After her husband's disappearance she turned her faces simultaneously towards two writers; and the second was W.B. Yeats.

> Great minds have sought you – lacking someone else
> You have been second always . . .

Ezra Pound assured her.

You are a person of some interest, one comes to you
And takes strange gain away:
Trophies fished up: some curious suggestion;
Fact that leads nowhere; and a tale or two,
Pregnant with mandrakes, or with something else
That might prove useful and yet never proves, . . .
No! there is nothing! In the whole and all,
Nothing that's quite your own.
                Yet this is you.

Both Shaw and Yeats were bewitched and fashioned castles in the air with Florence, their amiable Princess, waving airily from them. While Shaw beckoned her towards a bright future, Yeats serenaded her back into a magical past. It was merely the present which was impossible.

To Yeats she could 'tell everything'; from Shaw she heard everything. Like him she had sent herself to school in the Reading Room of the British Museum and absorbed a fine store of facts that led nowhere. 'It is impossible to mention anything she does not know,' Shaw exclaimed in astonishment. He felt a tremendous challenge to discover some purpose within the debris of her knowledge. She even knew about the theatre, had flirted professionally with the stage before her marriage, and was now preparing to float back to it by way of Ibsen's *The Lady from the Sea*. She startled Shaw by inviting him to play the Stranger – after all, he had a red beard and would look capital in the part wearing a pea-green jacket. But Shaw, pleading ineptitude, declined; then, recovering himself, 'delivered to her so powerful a discourse on Rosmersholm that she presently told me that she was resolved to create Rebecca or die'.

Shaw's fascination with the stage had been intensifying during his fifteen years in London. It was a slow-burning fascination, glimmering first in the almost nightly visits of Smith, the hero of *Immaturity*, to the Alhambra; and glimpsed in such moments as Shaw's response ('rather smitten') to the playing of Camille by Ethel Herbert. He had even taken part in the copyright performances of one or two plays, joined in various amateur theatricals such as an 'entertainment' produced by the Socialist League in aid of the Bryant and May Strike, and a '3rd rate comedy' with May Morris. He had been able to express his feelings for May more accurately on the stage than in real life: 'I do not love her – I have too much sense for such follies; but I hate and envy the detestable villain who plays her lover with all my soul.'

Shaw's love of the stage was part boyish-romantic, part a fantasy of the Will. It appealed to him as a place where actions were governed by words. If life could be persuaded to imitate this art then the theatre itself might become a citadel of power, and Shaw's other Parliament. His interest in Florence rapidly concentrated on her acting. 'I have an extraordinary desire to make the most of you – to make effective & visible *all* your artistic potentialities – not seven eighths or nine tenths, but all,' he told her. 'And not, observe, merely as an actress, but as a woman. Your ability to act must only be a mere consequence of your ability to live. You are so real to me as a woman that I cannot think of acting being to you anything more than a technical accomplishment which I want to see carried to a high degree of perfection.'

During February 1891 they went through *Rosmersholm* and from Shaw's diary come whispers of their excitement.

'*6 February*   Went over *Rosmersholm* (first few scenes) with FE. Found it hard to leave . . .

'*11 February*   . . . to FE's. She gave up her intention of going out to dinner and I stayed all the evening. We were playing, singing, trying on *Rosmersholm* dresses, going over the part etc.'

Shaw's influence on Florence was soon obvious to everyone who knew them. 'She spoke of actual things with a cold wit or under the strain of paradox,' observed Yeats. 'Wit and paradox alike sought to pull down whatever had tradition or passion.' The success of *Rosmersholm*, however, was moderate. At the last moment Shaw 'terrified myself at having thrust Florence on such an enterprise'. Her acting 'lacked certainty', though Shaw believed she had 'got through by dint of brains and a certain fascination and dimly visible originality'. In the end 'a sort of dim photograph of the play as it was meant to be was arrived at'. Shaw now redoubled his efforts to make Florence's dim originality blaze forth. 'I am kindling [her conceptions of life] for the purpose of every wile in the Shaw repertory,' he wrote. He became her tutor, calling round at Dalling Road to 'work on her dramatic elocution', and prepare her during the summer of 1892 for playing Beatrice in *The Cenci*. The scenes where Owen Jack coaches Madge Brailsford for the stage in *Love Among the Artists* had invaded life and were to return to fiction in *Pygmalion* (later Shaw was to advise Florence to study phonetics with Beerbohm Tree, the first Professor Higgins, at his school of drama). The name Doolittle irresistibly suggests Florence. She did not lack intelligence or feeling or beauty; she did not lack voice. But there seemed a 'frightful vacuity' at the centre of her life and a purposelessness to much that she did. Shaw strove to plant in this void the seeds of a vigorous and improving energy. She needed willpower, and it was his role to supply this power vicariously from the batteries of his own will. He seemed to believe, so Florence observed, that 'what people say on the stage is real life, and what you see behind the scenes is play-acting'. And she was right. For this was not stage business; this, with intervals for human nature, was Shaw's love: a rigorous, demanding, working love. He preached, pontificated, praised and, after warning her not to shrink from his disparagements, he went on to scold her exorbitantly:

'. . . you are insufferable. You wave your arms about like a fairy in a transformation scene . . . As to the way you tighten your upper lip, and bunch up your back, and stiffen your neck, and hold on by your elbows, that is, I admit, necessary to prevent you falling forward on your nose . . . In the passages of action you manage to make a sort of success. So could anybody, I conclude . . . I wish I could get over tomorrow to go over the part with you, especially the first scene, which is very badly talked . . .'

During rehearsals at the Bedford Park Club on 30 June, Florence fainted but stood up bravely at the opening a fortnight later when 'the white robe and striking beauty of Beatrice' were favourably noticed by the anonymous critic of the *Daily Chronicle*, G. Bernard Shaw. But there were still Himalayas to cross before she could pass as an important leading lady. For Shaw was striving to awaken a slumbering talent that few others could see. Behind the beating of his optimism emerges a bathos whenever he insists too much on the success of their collaboration: 'She actually realized greater possibilities than she had (what a sentence!).'

At the same time he had prudently invested his hopes in another actress. 'Interesting young woman,' he observed on 16 June 1889, after sitting next to Janet Achurch at a dinner in the Novelty Theatre celebrating the English première of *A Doll's House*. 'At 23 we went down from the saloon, where the dinner took place, to the stage,' and Janet had made 'two speeches in a brief and fearless manner' that Corno di Bassetto enjoyed 'far more than I have ever enjoyed Mr. Gladstone's'. Shaw's mother, who accompanied him to this production, had also been struck by Janet, crying out with conviction: 'That one is a *divil*.' But Shaw found himself 'suddenly magnetized, irradiated, transported, fired, rejuvenated, bewitched', and sat up till 2 a.m. the following night writing to his 'wild and glorious young woman' to tell her so. 'I shall always be happy to talk any quantity of insincere nonsense to amuse you,' he assured her, 'yet I, too, have histrionic powers, and can play the serious man on occasion, if no better actor is to be had.'

For Janet Achurch, then twenty-five, the role of Nora was a success 'which seems to be admitted on every hand,' wrote William Archer in *The World*. '. . . In every essential she was the Nora of Ibsen, passing with unfailing sympathy from the childish glee of the opening passages, through the tragic bewilderment and despair of her terrible Christmastide, to the sad, unresentful dignity of the closing scene.'

It was her first triumph in the theatre. She came from a theatrical family, her grandparents (the Achurch Wards) being well-known performers at the Theatre Royal in Manchester. Her mother died at her birth and she had been brought up by a careless, sometimes unkind father. At the age of nineteen she had launched herself upon a stage career and then into marriage. But she soon discarded her first husband, St Aubyn Miller, and, having joined the F. R. Benson Company, married one of its actors, Charles Charrington Martin. Here she played the standard Shakespearean leads – Lady Macbeth, Ophelia, Desdemona – opposite Frank Benson, a splendidly incomprehensible actor whose mission to spread Shakespeare through the country was aided by the widespread belief that he was related to the Archbishop of Canterbury.

There was no conventional prettiness to Janet. She was Amazonian. Shaw could never think of her noble outline 'without imagining myself lost at sea in the night, and turning for refuge toward a distant lighthouse, which, somehow, is you'. Benson wrote of her that she 'was of that fair-haired, voluptuous appearance generally associated with Helen and Guinevere and those Northern beauties who strangled the souls and bodies of heroes in the meshes of their golden tresses'. As an actress she belonged to 'the school of the tragic cadence and the struck brow'.

After an interval with Beerbohm Tree, there followed what Charles Charrington called 'the great event of her career'. The two of them had signed an agreement to tour Australia and New Zealand for two years at twenty-five pounds a week. It was with money borrowed in advance of this salary that they had financed one week's performance of *A Doll's House* at the Novelty Theatre. 'We offered the firm of Williamson, Garner & Musgrove anything in reason to let us stop & confirm our success,' Charrington wrote, 'but they refused.'

That Janet was to leave for the other side of the world in less than three weeks stirred Shaw's feeling magnificently. He saw *A Doll's House* five times, and sent her two of his novels. The serious man was only partly hidden behind the insincere nonsense of his letters. 'The world has vanished,' he wrote: 'the gardens of heaven surround me.'

'I thought I was old – that youth was gone – that I should never be in love again in the starry way of the days before the great Disillusion; and lo! it is all back again, with the added wisdom to know my own happiness. I desire nothing: I hope for nothing: I covet nothing: I possess, enjoy, exult . . . Come: set me some hard, squalid, sordid drudgery – twenty years of it to gain an inch of ground. Away with you to Australia – for ever, if you will. See whether that prospect will dash me one jot! I have drunk the elixir of life – twice – a quarter to nine and a quarter past eleven; and now Time is vanquished. Change, fade, become a mere actress, spoil, wreck yourself, lose yourself, forget yourself: I shall still possess you in your first perfection. I have enjoyed: now let me work for the rest of my life.'

All this, he added (before a long paragraph of technical stage advice), was 'by kind permission of Charles Charrington Esquire, the burden bearer and harvest reaper'.

On the morning of 5 July he went to Charing Cross to see them both off on their Australia tour. He had pledged himself to work in Janet's absence, and over the next two and a half years did so to such purpose that he became 'a mere arguing, committeeing, writing, lecturing machine, constantly going faster and faster'. But once or twice Sonny took advantage of Shaw's 'intoxicated, enamoured will', and G.B.S. would find himself wasting his time with a long letter to Janet. She sent him her photograph and asked for his news. He replied, telling her of all the 'nibblings at Ibsen' in London, of his own *Quintessence* and a short story he had written, 'Still After the Doll's House', in revenge for Walter Besant's sequel to the play. William Archer's criticism was gaining wonderfully in its recklessness, he added. He explained the routine of his Fabian experiments to find a constitutional and parliamentary formula for Socialism. 'I am getting middle-aged and uninteresting,' he wrote. 'Political drudgery has swamped my literary career altogether. Still, as all the follies of love and ambition fall off from me, my soul burns with a brighter flame; and I grow ever more impenetrably conceited.' Then there was the music criticism: Corno di Bassetto of *The Star* was dead – long live (on five pounds a week) G.B.S. of *The World*! 'Since I began to write for the World, revising my work with great labor, and going to great numbers of performances, I have become more and more a slave to art, and can by no means be satisfied with intellectual interest,' he divulged.

'. . . Consequently, my last word tonight shall be said to you, with whom I have no ignoble or unlovely associations. But indeed I have nothing to say: it is only to look at you. And I see you quite distinctly – on the stage of the Novelty, not as Nora, but as Janet Achurch, acknowledging the demonstrations of kind friends in front at the end of the play. This is unusual; for I never think of you with such mildewy surroundings as those of the Great Queen St Upholstery, but always in a vast desert, or walking on the waters of a great Sea, at a great distance from me, but the only other person there besides myself. Take courage then; for if you can cast these magic spells on a man thousands of miles away, after years – centuries – of absence, what can you not do to those only separated from you by a row of footlights, with Ibsen to help you?'

The music, his preoccupation with Ibsen and the spell exercised on his imagination by Janet Achurch, Florence Farr, May Morris, even Jenny Patterson, were all combining to move him towards the theatre. But when 'the fearsome Charringtons', as Henry James called them, returned to England early in 1892 and revived *A Doll's House* at the Avenue Theatre, something had changed. James saw them as being of a 'désespérant' badness, and Shaw heard Janet's voice sounding 'quite Hyde Parkian in its pedal notes'. She exploded into fortissimo, tightened her lower lip 'like an India rubber band' and earned herself the sort of comically blighting letter Shaw had been rehearsing on Florence Farr. But 'though my critical sensibility has been frightfully sharpened by incessant exercise during your absence,' he reassured her, 'my admiration is in nowise abated'. Admiration was the form Shaw's love for Janet was now taking. 'I am actually less enamoured than before,' he told her, 'because my admiration elbows out the commoner sentiment. I speak as a critic, not merely as a miserable two legged man.'

To move his emotions on to the stage was a new experiment for Shaw, but he needed a considerable conviction of love to sustain his critical admiration. All Shaw knew in 1892 was that Janet had been 'cleaned-out and invalided' by her long overseas tour. He still believed her to be 'indomitable'. Then in 1893, turning down an opportunity of producing *Rosmersholm*, Janet and Charrington mounted their own season of plays in London: Richard Voss's *Alexandra*; Brandon Thomas's *Clever Alice*; and Scribe and Legouvé's *Adrienne Lecouvreur*. Shaw was appalled. 'Those old stalking horses are no use: the better you do them the more hopeless do they appear,' he reprimanded Janet. '... You fritter yourself away on clever rubbish ... Alexandra was exquisite rubbish ... Clever Alice was rubbish; and Adrienne was folly.'

Part of the trouble came from Charrington. As Helmer in *A Doll's House* his failure had been complete. Even so, he was more dangerous off the stage where, in addition to being Janet's husband, he played the far more serious role – one obviously intended for Shaw – of her business manager. A man with a considerable knowledge of pawnbrokers, he developed a talent for converting other people's investments into thin air. Shaw, who often insisted that he was 'not fit to be trusted with money', handed him a good deal of his own over the years. 'I have at least the satisfaction of the certainty (as far as one can be certain of anything with so fantastic a man) that the money will be spent on yourself and Janet, and not on your creditors and lawyers. If ever there was a man who lived for others that man is yourself.' Charrington's stupendous borrowings for haphazard purposes eventually established him as 'the most famous bogus manager in England'. This was not exclusively a Shavian opinion: Gilbert Murray declared that he would 'as soon have Mr Micawber' as Dramatic Manager 'or as Manager of anything in the world'. Charrington's determination to promote his wife's career soon threatened to ruin her. He fired her with such reckless anxiety to act that she would jump into any part, however ruinous, rather than abstain, and often resembled an elephant in a troupe of performing dogs. Shaw therefore decided it was time for him to intercede and provide a moral direction to their partnership.

Charrington's debt-collecting was obviously an 'incurable neurosis'; Janet's neurosis took Shaw longer to identify. On their long way back from Australia the Charringtons had toured New Zealand, Tasmania, India and Egypt. In Calcutta and Cairo, Janet felt increasingly ill, getting through her parts only with the help of morphia which the doctors had prescribed after she nearly died in childbirth. Previously she had had a tendency to alcoholism; now she added an addiction to morphia. Her *Doll's House* in 1892 had been sustained 'by brute force and stimulants'. As her condition became clear to Shaw, a method of driving out her disabling addiction by means of a more ingenious drug, distilled upon the stage, began to form in his mind.

The Charringtons appealed to his instinct for turning failure into success. Janet's happy prior attachment obliged Shaw to direct almost all his emotional energy towards her stage life. She could not, like an amoeba, 'split herself up into a dozen of Janets, and satisfy all the men who wanted her'. So: 'I had to be sensible about Janet'. Early in their relationship Shaw explained to her the course it was taking:

'I have two sorts of feeling for you, one valuable to you and the other worthless. The worthless one is an ordinary man-and-woman hankering after you . . . As you know, you are very handsome and clever, and rich in a fine sort of passionate ardor which I enjoy, in an entirely selfish way, like any other man. But I have another feeling for you. As an artist and a trained critic, I have a very strong sense of artistic faculty and its value. I have, as you know, a high opinion of your power as an actress; and just as I want to have my own powers in action and to preserve them from waste or coarsening, so I have sympathetically a strong desire to see your powers in action, and a dislike to see them wasted or coarsened. This is the side on which you may find me useful . . .'

Charrington's rampant impracticality opened the way for Shaw's most romantic role – that of the expert businessman, crackling with exasperated energy. 'Mind you do exactly what I tell you,' he instructed Charrington.

But the Charringtons, while valuing his financial help, did not take the Shavian view of Shaw and tested his instinct for success to its limits. 'Why were you ever born?' he burst out. 'Why did you get married?' And again, echoing his mother: 'Oh Charles and Janet, what a devil of a pair you are!'

They did not rest at dissipating Janet's genius: they conspired to tip the frailer talent of Florence Farr over the precipice, having persuaded her to play the Princess in their production of *Adrienne Lecouvreur*. 'The unspeakable absurdity of that performance is only surpassed by the unparalleled blastedness of the play,' Shaw admonished Florence. '. . . Janet was transcendently bad . . . I thought she was letting you get ahead out of pure consideration for me . . . To her infinite credit, the more she tries to make the play live, the more ghastly & ridiculous becomes its antics. The sooner the play disappears the better for the reputation of the Charringtons & their enterprise. But you rather score off it; and I advise you to make the most of it while it lasts.'

The difference in ability between Janet and Florence was not concealed from Shaw. But he felt committed to Florence and still hoped to produce from that commitment a miraculous transformation. His loyalty to her was intensified by his final break with Jenny Patterson. Between the spring of 1891 and of 1893 the scenes with Jenny had grown worse until both of them looked like caricatures of themselves – he stonily refusing to 'sentimentalize' while Jenny, pretending to open none of his letters to her, scrutinized as many of other people's letters to him as she could put her hands on. In the intervals of remorse they behaved with deliberate kindness to each other. She pasted up all his articles for *The World*; he accompanied her for a few days to Broadstairs – an empty-headed place much recommended for its tedious ozone. 'Before I was ten minutes here,' he had told readers of *The Star*, 'I was bored beyond description.' They got on best while she was away in Australia, Egypt and Ireland – and Shaw could spend more evenings with Florence. 'We read a lot of Walt Whitman and were very happy,' he noted simply in his diary on 26 January 1893. But when Jenny came back all her jealousy revived. She besieged him in his room so that he had to make his way out by physical force, take up asylum in the British Museum and telegraph his mother to clear the house before he returned. But though he tried to bring out the absurdity of these episodes – pretending to throw her out of the window one afternoon – his brief descriptions of them ('terrible scenes all day . . . tempestuous . . . very disagreeable . . . nerves very highly strung') indicate to what extent he could be affected. 'The scene upset me,' he wrote after one row: but still he went to Florence afterwards.

Jenny's hounding of him at Fitzroy Square had probably been an extra inducement for Shaw to go and stay with the Sparlings, so near to Florence's lodgings. Though Jenny would no longer be ruled by his word-power, her emotional influence over him was waning. Something spectacular was needed.

Something spectacular happened on 4 February 1893. 'In the evening,' Shaw wrote in his diary:

'I went to FE; and JP burst in on us very late in the evening. There was a most shocking scene, JP being violent and using atrocious language. At last I sent FE out of the room, having to restrain JP by force from attacking her. I was two hours getting her out of the house and I did not get her home to Brompton Square until near 1, nor could I get away myself until 3. I was horribly tired and shocked and upset; but I kept patience and did not behave badly nor ungently. Did not get to bed until 4; and had but a disturbed night of it. I made JP write a letter to me expressing her regret and promising not to annoy FE again. This was sent to FE to reassure her.'

Next day he wrote letters to both Florence (which he got May Morris to deliver) and to Jenny – but was 'rather put out' when Jenny sent hers back allegedly unread. 'Returned her letter,' he put down in his diary, 'and sent back mine with it'. There was an embattled pause. Then, on 22 February, 'Got a letter from JP, which I burnt at the first glance. Wrote to tell her so, feeling the uselessness of doing anything else'. It was the end. He never spoke to her again, never answered the storm of letters and telegrams that lasted for months afterwards. Jenny never forgave him; and he never forgot her – he even remembered her in his will by leaving her one hundred pounds, though she successfully avoided this by dying first.

They corresponded once more – melodramatically in *The Star* about the case of a police constable condemned to be hanged for the murder of his mistress. This tragedy 'will recur tomorrow or the next day with some other pair,' Shaw predicted. 'We shall never be rid of these butcheries until we make up our minds as to what a woman's claims exactly are upon a man who, having formerly loved her, now wishes to get free from her society. If we find that she has some claims, let us enforce them and protect the man from any molestation that goes beyond them.' In a letter signed E four days later, Jenny Patterson replied: 'I know too well the feeling when a girl knows she is no more loved by the one she has given her all to, but is only a thing to be cast aside like a toy which has been tired of.' Shaw concluded the correspondence by describing this as showing precisely the 'unreason that has got the woman killed and the man hanged.

At the bottom of all the unreason, however, will be found the old theory that an act of sexual intercourse gives the parties a lifelong claim on one another for better or worse.'

Shaw had tried to control Jenny's many tantrums and adapt them for the stage. He had resolved to produce half-a-dozen plays before he was forty. There had been several false beginnings, but by his thirty-seventh birthday in the summer of 1893, two plays were finished, a third started, and the first, *Widowers' Houses*, had already been performed and published.

# CHAPTER V

*In politics, all facts are selected facts . . . This does not mean that one*
*writer is less truthful than another. It means only that one writer*
*notices things that another writer overlooks . . . To put it another*
*way, the very honestest man has an unfair mind.*

While Shaw, between *Parsifal* and the Passion Play, had been leaping up
mountains at Oberammergau, in the heather down below Webb had not
after all been writing on municipal death duties, but pouring out love
letters to a woman called Beatrice Potter. 'I do not see how I can go on
without you,' he implored. 'Do not now desert me.' Shaw, he added, 'does
not suspect my feeling for you'. Though later on G.B.S. would claim to
have sleuthed out the facts from Webb's complexion ('I foresaw the
marriage. Sidney used to come out in spots when he fell in love . . .'), he
was so far unaware of the truth in the summer of 1890 as to discuss with
Webb the Fabian advantages of a match between Beatrice Potter and
Graham Wallas.

Sidney and Beatrice had got to know of each other in 1889 through
their writings. He picked her out as 'the only contributor with any talent'
to the first volume of Booth's *Life and Labour of the People in London*. She
recommended his contribution to *Fabian Essays* as 'by far the most
significant and interesting'. They met early the following year when each
was unusually impressed by the other's presence.

The daughter of a rich *nouveau* middle-class railway promoter, Beatrice
was then in her early thirties and determined, she said, 'to be the old maid
of the family'. Handsome, with huge black eyes, sweeping brown hair
tortured into a knot at the back of her head, a wide rather sensuous mouth,
a voice 'brave and nautical', slender figure, and what was known as a
'beautiful carriage', she did not look an old maid. 'What nonsense is this,'
one of her sisters reprimanded, 'trying to be a bluestocking when you are
meant to be a pretty woman.' Her origins, Beatrice admitted, 'lie in my
sensual nature'. But she had sought to quell this nature, feeling it wicked
to crave from men the love and attention she had missed as a child. 'My
childhood was not on the whole a happy one,' she wrote. She had not been
physically ill-treated but, like Shaw, scrupulously ignored by her mother

who had wanted a son instead of her eighth daughter, and who considered her 'the only one of my children who is below the average in intelligence'. Beatrice inherited from her mother a tendency to melancholia that was deepened by their mutual dislike – once, when very young, she had stolen a bottle of chloroform with the notion of killing herself. As she grew up she turned to the informal warmth of the servants' quarters, curling up among the sheets and tablecloths in the laundry or sitting on the ironing board and confiding to the maids her intention of becoming a nun. Later on, her two mentors were the philosopher Herbert Spencer and Charles Booth, the social investigator who introduced her to the world of politics and philanthropy. But to neither could she give her heart. 'I must pour my poor crooked thoughts into somebody's heart,' she wrote, aged fifteen, at the beginning of her diary, 'even if it be my own.'

To one man she did give her heart – Joseph Chamberlain. He was 'intensely attractive to me,' she confessed, yet she could not overlook his 'personal ambition and desire to dominate'. Sexual passion and the attraction of power divided her – it seemed impossible to reconcile her sensual with her intellectual needs. 'I don't know how it will end,' she wrote. 'Certainly not in *my happiness*.' Chamberlain's rejection of her hit the same spot as her mother's neglect and drove her into suicidal depression. 'If Death comes it will be welcome,' she wrote in her will. '. . . It is curious this feeling of life being ended.'

Another life came to her through social work which numbed the pains of celibacy and rejection, and moved her emotional energies into politics. She brooded over statistics, went (like Major Barbara and somewhat like Epifania Fitzfassenden in *The Millionairess*) 'East Ending' on a study of Sweating in the tailoring trade, kept company with trade unionists and members of the Co-operative movement *en masse*. 'At last I am a Socialist,' she exulted in January 1890.

That month she had met Sidney Webb – 'a London retail tradesman,' as she described him, 'with the aims of a Napoleon.' Though she liked to claim that she was without a sense of beauty, she had an almost voluptuous appreciation of ugliness. 'I am of course very busy,' Sidney had estimated, 'somewhat serious, very analytic and introspective – but, I hope passably honest, sincere, and not obviously hateful or repulsive.' But in this ultimate matter she could not agree. 'His tiny tadpole body, unhealthy skin, lack of manner, Cockney pronunciation, poverty, are all against him,' she noted. His thumbs fixed in his waistcoat, he strutted round the room with an expression of inexhaustible conceit. His 'disproportionate view of his own position is at once repulsive and ludicrous,' she decided. But despite his 'bad habits' she liked him. Beneath the bourgeois black coat, inside the bulky head, lurked an improbable monster of romance who wanted to marry a beauty and to see his ideas command the action of Cabinet Ministers such as Joseph Chamberlain. 'You have it in your hands to make me, in the noblest sense, great,' he informed her. It was as a vehicle of power that Sidney prized her, and Beatrice responded. 'One grasp of the hand,' she recorded, 'and we were soon in a warm discussion on some question of Economics.' He wooed her with charts and equations. A man in love, he acknowledged, is damnably selfish, but his selfishness took the relentless form of altruism. As he lay in bed at night, divinely intoxicated from thinking of her, a vision of her face flashed before him 'in the guise of a co-worker ... between the lines of the despatches.' She had devised a Concordat to hoist their 'camaraderie' from 'the predominance of lower feeling' to the pinnacles of high-mindedness. 'The agony is unendurable,' he assured her. She urged him to consider his health and his clothes, and the string to his pince-nez, but her encouragement was at best tepid. 'Take care of your voice pronunciation,' she commanded: 'it is the chief instrument of influence.' Her heart seemed imprisoned by its past attachment to Chamberlain. 'I am not capable of loving,' she insisted. 'Personal passion has burnt itself out and what little personal feeling still exists haunts the memory of that other man.'

The courtship grew so desperate as to bewilder them both. 'The question is,' Beatrice urgently demanded, 'what is the present position?' Whatever it was, suddenly it changed and ('as an alternative to suicide') she began to brood on matrimony. One day, after Sidney had finally given up all hope of marrying her, she failed to withdraw her hand from his. 'I am still a little in a dream,' he owned. He could not tell what had altered her mind. Though she believed that she had been permeated by Sidney's 'resolute patient affection',. the change had coincided with her advancement – through lectures and the publication of her book *The Co-operative Movement in Great Britain* – into public life, and with her awareness of how much she would need him there.

Marriage, they were agreed, was the waste-paper basket of the emotions. Optimistically he sent her his full-length portrait, but: 'No dear,' she chided him, 'I do not even look at your photograph. It is too hideous ... it is the head only that I am marrying.' 'You have made a splendid beginning,' he responded. Their engagement was cemented, in Sidney's phrase, over the death of Beatrice's father, and on 23 July 1892, in 'a prosaic, almost sordid ceremony', they were married at St Pancras vestry hall, spending their honeymoon in Dublin investigating Irish trade unionism. 'Home Rule is an absolute necessity – in order to depopulate the country of this detestable race,' they instructed Graham Wallas from Lower Baggot Street. 'We are very very happy – far too happy to be reasonable.'

'If all marriages were as happy,' Shaw concluded, 'England, and indeed the civilized world, would be a Fabian paradise.'

*

From the courtship of this super-extraordinary pair Shaw had held aloof. He represented Beatrice as passing in review the two thousand Fabian comrades for marriage, dismissing nineteen hundred and ninety four in her mind before examining the remaining half-dozen personally and selecting Sidney. 'She quite deliberately sampled the Fabians as possible husbands by inviting them down to Gloucester for weekends one after another,' Shaw told Margaret Cole. 'I refused, alleging facetiously that I could not afford the journey, really because I had discovered that Sidney was in love with her and would not take a chance of cutting him out. After that she thoroughly disliked me . . .'

Beatrice initially disliked Shaw not because she felt piqued by his refusal, even by its facetiousness, but because she resented the assumptions behind it. For someone who had been determined to prove an old maid and had only married her 'very small and ugly' husband after an aching struggle, Shaw's gloss on her behaviour was galling – particularly the implication that a sight of himself might have been irresistible to her. He had read her character, then rewritten it after a style that most unsettled her (making the latent part dominant) – and this because he resented her as a rival collaborator with Sidney. Yet it was because of his high opinion of Sidney that she could still welcome him as their joint friend. 'We embarrass each other frightfully when we are alone together,' Shaw observed, 'without some subject of keen and immediate interest to discuss.' His philandering riled her because, not being serious, it seemed to caricature all the agony she had gone through over Chamberlain, and touch an old wound, flippantly. 'His stupid gallantries bar out from him the friendship of women who are either too sensible, too puritanical or too much "otherwise engaged" to care to bandy personal flatteries with him,' she noted contemptuously in her diary. 'One large section of women, comprising some, at any rate, of the finest types, remains hidden from him.' 'Nothing annoyed her so much,' Shaw recognized, 'as being suspected of any sensual attachment to me.' Nor could he resist playing on this until she found a way of neutralizing him. 'Mrs Webb, who is a remarkably shrewd woman, explains her freedom from the fascination to which she sees all the others succumb, by saying "You cannot fall in love with a *sprite*: and Shaw is a sprite in such matters, not a real person",' Shaw himself explained, adding: '. . . It is certainly true.'

They came to understand each other well because of the many 'dry goods' they shared that typified Fabianism. It was after her that Shaw created Vivie Warren in *Mrs Warren's Profession* – an 'attractive . . . sensible . . . self-possessed' woman in whom William Archer (not knowing Beatrice) could see nothing 'but a Shaw in petticoats'. It was Shaw's 'most serious play', Beatrice decided. Both of them had put up an emotional barrier behind which in their different styles they gave themselves orgiastically to public objects. Rejecting personal happiness as an illusion, they devotedly pursued the phantom of service to others. 'We are committed for life to Socialism,' Shaw wrote to her. There was more pain and struggle visible in her commitment than his, but both used the fantasy of literary creation to assuage their disappointments: Shaw in his plays, Beatrice in the diaries, where she came closest to answering her 'longing to create characters and move them to and fro among fictitious circumstances'.

'I think you are in duty bound to join the Fabian Society,' Sidney had advised Beatrice. According to Shaw, she began with an 'intense contempt' for the Fabians as 'a rabble of silly suburban faddists'. Yet this impression did not correspond with her feelings. She delighted in what she called their 'delicious *positivism* . . . their optimistic conclusion that the world is most assuredly going their way, the plausible proof they bring in favour of their confidence, the good temper and the moderation . . .'. As early as the spring of 1890 she had had the feeling that this could be the body of men with whom 'I may sooner or later throw in my lot for good and all'. That her election to membership came three years later, after a period of subscribing rather than joining, she attributed to fears that committed Fabianism might injure her impartiality as a social investigator.

According to the society's secretary, Edward Pease, Beatrice 'took practically no part in the Fabian Society until 1906'. Yet she was behind almost everything that Sidney did, entered strongly into the political discussions of Shaw and Wallas, and affected the régime of all their lives. Each summer the Webbs would take a house in the country for three months – first an enlarged Jacobean mansion called Argoed, at Penallt in the Wye Valley, that had belonged to the Potters; subsequently a rectory in Suffolk or a farm in Surrey – and here they would invite the junta of Sidney's friends on the Fabian Executive. 'The Fabian old gang can only afford a country house for a holiday,' Shaw bluntly put it, 'because one of us has a wife with a thousand a year.' From the common point of view, he

266

admitted, these holidays (from which derived the Fabian Summer Schools) were 'of almost Trappist asceticism'. They passed their mornings, each in separate rooms, doggedly writing; stopped for a ravenous plain meal ('we do not have butter for Sidney's breakfast', Beatrice insisted); strode off on crushing walks during the afternoon and spent the evenings arguing violently over politics. By the mid-1890s they had metamorphosed from walkers into bicyclists. They were not pioneers, never experimented with the boneshaker or pennyfarthing, but were caught up in the boom of bicycles, tricycles, tandems and velocipedes that followed the invention of the 'safety' machine and the Dunlop pneumatic tyre of the late 1880s. 'My new toy is my bicycle,' Shaw proclaimed in 1895. He had already mounted a tandem tricycle with Belfort Bax and experimented with a few humiliating lessons at Goya's school for bicycle riding in Praed Street, Paddington. But that spring, to the convulsions of the coastguards, he started seriously learning to ride this new hobby horse with the Webbs on Beachy Head: 'I will do twenty yards and a destructive fall against any professional in England,' he told Janet Achurch. 'My God, the stiffness, the blisters, the bruises, the pains in every twisted muscle, the crashes against the chalk road that I have endured – and at my age [39] too. But I shall come like gold from the furnace: I will not be beaten by that hellish machine.' Beatrice, who scudded into a wasps' nest but managed to cure herself with whisky, calculated that 'One's "byke" is a great addition to the pleasure of life – we have still to prove that it does not detract from one's desire, if not one's capacity, for work.' To Shaw, lying exhausted in a deep ditch near Argoed, the moonlight faltering on to him through the revolving spokes of the wheels and the laced thorn twigs of a briar, the proof was plain. Yet he concluded: 'Yes: bicycling's a capital thing for a literary man.' On wheels, the Fabians appeared to become schoolboys and girls again. Beatrice, who (until Sidney had one smash too many) rigorously prescribed it during the long Fabian summer afternoons, reckoned that the bicycle added a dimension of 'fun' or 'sport' to their desk-anchored lives; and Shaw hygienically explained: 'Unless I seize every opportunity of bicycling off into the country, if only for a couple of hours, I get beaten by the evil atmosphere in which I have to pass so much of my time.'

For a dozen years, until 1908 when he took dangerously to cars, the bicycle was a prime article of Shavian equipment. Its effect on bodily health he summarized as 'harmless' – a claim that, in view of the extraordinary number of accidents he achieved, sounds impressive. On the mind, he reasoned, its effect was enormous since the bicyclist could extend a day's travel from the pedestrian's few miles to the region of a hundred miles. So, by increasing the efficiency of existence, the bicycle which was popularly attacked as the terror of horses and a temptation to women, became a symbol of modernity. 'Lord de Cresci's sister bicycles in knickerbockers; and the rector's wife advocates dress reform and wears hygienic boots,' Valentine informs the out-of-date twins in *You Never Can Tell*. As such it was wheeled by way of metaphor and analogy into many Shavian arguments – such as his solving of the evolutionary problem of acquired habits in the Preface to *Back to Methuselah*.

The bicycle also established itself as one of Shaw's chief comic props and items of expertise. By 1896 he had enrolled as the 621st member of the Cyclist Touring Club whose Annual General Meeting he considerably lengthened by a forceful plea against improving the tone of the Club's *Gazette* (where fiction, he thought, should be found only among the advertisements). To actresses, parents, schoolboys, he poured out information about nickel plating, solid tyres and the varieties of crack machines. 'Do not expect to improve with practice,' he recommended. 'You wont. The change from hopeless failure to complete success is instantaneous and miraculous.' One miracle was staying alive, though 'if you keep on bicycling long enough,' he promised, 'you will break your leg'.

For someone physically timid, Shaw's experiments by bicycle were extraordinary. 'The infernal machine will be the ruin of me,' he estimated. He would raise his feet to the handlebars and simply *toboggan* down the steep places. Many of his falls, from which he would prance away crying 'I am not hurt,' with black eyes, violet trembling lips and a streaming red almost unrecognizably remodelled face, acted as excellent trials for his optimism. The surgery afterwards was an education in itself and he liked to declare himself 'positively the better for the adventure in nerve'. Each toss he took, smiting the earth like a thunderbolt, was a point scored for one or more of his fads. Was man no more than an omelette? Shaw's untamed spirit showed that he was. After one appalling smash (hills, clouds and farmhouses tumbling around drunkenly), he wrote: 'Still I am not thoroughly convinced yet that I was not killed. Anybody but a vegetarian would have been. Nobody but a teetotaller would have faced a bicycle again for six months.' He enjoyed the elaboration of these exploits for his friends, telling them of the time he tore into Bertrand Russell on the Chepstow Road, demolishing his plus-fours; and another occasion, in the Pall Mall, when he charged an impetuous railway-van horse with his front tyre: 'I hit the dust like the Templar before the lance of Ivanhoe.' After four years of intrepid pedalling, he could claim: 'If I had taken to the ring I should, on the whole, have suffered less than I have, physically.'

*

He saw a good deal of the Webbs during the first half-dozen years of their marriage. The income that Beatrice inherited from her father enabled Sidney to retire from the Colonial Office; and together they planned to give unpaid service to society in return for this unearned income. Beatrice immediately put Sidney to work for the rest of his life, writing what she called their 'solid but unreadable books' on trade unionism, industrial democracy and (for nearly thirty years) English local government. This laborious library, resting heavily on the assumption that political action proceeds from political knowledge, prompted a suspicion in Shaw that his colleagues might be sinking into antiquarianism, and produced spasms of revulsion in Beatrice against 'hideous facts, multitudinous details, exasperating qualifications'. But this work established the Fabian tradition of research. It was complemented by their 'permeation' policy of infiltration and persuasion. Under Beatrice's direction, this was to take a more social turn. 'I am seriously of [the] opinion that what is wanted here is a salon for the social cultivation of the Socialist party in parliament,' Shaw wrote to Sidney. 'Will Madame Potter-Webb undertake it?' Despite a distractingly keen taste for social life, Beatrice was not a good hostess. Like Shaw, her achievement was built on the repression of the body ('one's body becomes less and less of an incubus as the years roll on'). Abstinence (flavoured with prayer) was the way to salvation, she judged, 'for such a one as me'. She grew addicted to fasting, weighing herself regularly at Charing Cross Station and gloating over each little loss of weight. This 'anti-flesh-fish-egg-alcohol-coffee-and-sugar eater', as she described herself, was put in charge of the Fabian kitchens. The frugal diet imposed on herself she extended to the reluctant Sidney and in due course to her dismayed political guests. Her bare lunches and dinners, though feasts of intellect, were parched from lack of wine, and never added an atmosphere of seduction to the austere manipulating activity of permeation. Sometimes, rather wearily, Beatrice would debate 'whether one would not do just as much by cutting the whole business of human intercourse and devoting oneself to thinking . . .' But this regimen became a distinguishing feature of a Society whose executive, at a celebratory soirée, 'agreed that Cecil Sharp's Morris dancers might perform but on a majority voice decided that no ices were to be served'.

Beatrice was to be the *salonnière* of the Fabian Society, with Shaw its instant historian and advertising manager. There was much for him to achieve by way of popularizing their assets and resolving set-backs into tactical advances. His job was to give its fortnightly meetings an intellectual zest. What his audiences heard from him on the platform, what they read by him in their newspapers, kept morale sparkling with the sense that political events were going their way. It also enabled them the more easily to accept decisions in their name that had been made exclusively by the Webbs and Shaw.

Shaw's articles and speeches grew more sophisticated during the 1890s, demonstrating to his audiences how publicly to strip off doctrinaire socialism while getting round awkward issues. Particularly in Scotland and the North of England, politics had risen on a revival of Evangelicism; and socialists wanted to see the Devil Capitalism embodied and then, in the smoke of moral fervour, extinguished by tremendous preaching. This was not Shaw's style. Despite an undiminished Irish voice, several provincial lecture tours, and even a journey in 1893 as far as Zurich for the International Socialist Congress (from the meeting-room of which he would dive out at lunch to make the snow-waters of the lake sizzle with his scalding body) he was classed as a metropolitan Fabian. His socialism was a prescription made up for the working classes: it was not exclusively for them and not prescribed by them. According to Robert Blatchford, the founder-editor of *The Clarion*, Shaw's literary-economic formulas meant nothing to working people who wanted 'horse-sense in tinker's English'. Blatchford, who insisted that socialism 'must be a religion', had caught the revivalist mood of the country with his Utopian *Merrie England*, an enormously successful adaptation of William Morris into tinker's English.

Believing that the Fabian policy of permeation could only 'pick up crumbs' from the Liberal table, he declared that what socialists needed was a self-financed and formidable new party. In 1892, through the columns of *The Workman's Times*, branches of an Independent Labour Party had been established at Bradford, Manchester, Newcastle and other centres, recruiting members from various socialist societies, including the Fabians. Two years earlier, Shaw had called for 'a vigorous campaign' in these cities. 'There is no doubt that the moment has come,' he wrote to Cunninghame Graham, 'for forming bodies in all the big provincial centres to play the same game as the Fabian plays in London.' This opportunity had been missed, but Shaw did not appear worried: the ILP, he told Graham Wallas, was 'nothing but a new S.D.F.O.'. As one of the Fabian representatives at the Foundation Conference of the National Independent Labour Party at Bradford early in 1893, he had determined to 'go uncompromisingly for Permeation,' he told Pease, '. . . and for the bringing up of the country to the London mark by the supplanting of Liberalism by Progressivism.' He began by making fun of the new Independent Labour Party (the success of which, he guaranteed, would come the instant working-class people switched their allegiance from sport to politics), but found himself so unpopular as to be almost voted out of the conference. Dismissed on a technicality from the floor, he 'took up a strong enfilading position in the gallery, from which he bombarded us so violently with his interruptions,' James Sexton recalled, 'that on the following day we admitted him to our deliberations in sheer self-defence'.

This reluctant readmission, by forty-nine votes to forty-seven, was interpreted by Shaw as a victory for Fabian policies and an example of his permeation of the ILP. Behind these tactics lay much face-saving calculation. Only one Socialist, Keir Hardie, had been returned to Parliament at the General Election of 1892. The Fabians had generally supported the Liberals on whom, by means of what was called the Newcastle programme, they believed that they had imposed a detailed plan for constructive social reform. At the beginning of 1893, the future of a Labour Party in Parliament was remote; but implementation by Gladstone's Liberal Government of the Fabian-inspired Newcastle Programme, involving among its measures new factory legislation, the extension of free education, municipal reform, payment of MPs and the 'mending or ending' of the House of Lords, seemed imminent. In the House of Commons that March, Campbell-Bannerman pledged the Government to show itself as the best employers of labour in the country; 'we have ceased,' he said, 'to believe in what are known as competition or starvation wages'. Six months later, it had become clear that, allegedly because of his small majority, Gladstone had abandoned almost all radical reforms and handed Parliament's time over to an Irish Home Rule Bill that would avoid further exacerbation of class conflict. To the Fabians, this was worse than a waste of time (literally so, since the House of Lords halted the Home Rule Bill), it was a betrayal of election promises and an unstitching of Fabian tactics. They had not even picked up crumbs. 'We must,' Shaw wrote to a hesitant Graham Wallas, '... satisfy the legitimate aspirations of the ardent spirits by getting out a furious attack on the Government, rallying labor to put third candidates in the field.'

This furious attack, written by Shaw with Webb's assistance and signed 'By the Fabian Society', appeared in the November *Fortnightly Review* using the Biblical call to revolt, 'To Your Tents, Oh Israel!' Acknowledging that legislative reforms might have been limited by the small Liberal majority, and relying on Webb's knowledge of the Civil Service, Shaw's manifesto examined each of the departments of State and showed what administrative reforms, not subject to this limitation, might have been effected so that individual ministers could redeem some of their Government's pledges. 'Had the will existed,' the manifesto concluded, 'there would have been no difficulty about the way.' This was a triumphant piece of political journalism, which Shaw elaborated in January 1894 into Fabian Tract No. 49, *A Plan of Campaign for Labor*. But as an example of political strategy, it was to prove inept. Far from permeating the ILP with Fabianism, the Society had come, by the beginning of 1894, to echo both Blatchford's *Merrie England* and the 1893 Foundation Conference recommendation in favour of the independent establishment of a labour party in opposition to Liberals and Conservatives. *A Plan of Campaign for Labor* called for the trade unions to raise 'a parliamentary fund of at least £30,000, and the running of fifty *independent* Labor candidates at the next general election'. This manifesto produced two reactions: it alienated the Liberal Party and all those Fabians who still saw in Liberalism a means of introducing a progressive programme into Parliament (some of whom, including Massingham, resigned); and it came too late to kindle sympathy with men of the ILP such as Keir Hardie, who was to lose his seat in the 1895 General Election, and who described the Fabians as 'the worst enemies of the social revolution'. For though *A Plan of Campaign for Labor* proposed similar measures to those of the ILP, Shaw in particular feared that any amalgamation would lead to the extinction of his Fabian family or at best its declension into a backwater debating society. Already by the spring of 1894 the Society, which Shaw was to urge not to 'waste another five minutes on permeation', was drifting back to the idea of grafting collectivism on to Rosebery who had then succeeded Gladstone as Liberal Prime Minister. At the 1895 General Election, 'sitting with their hands in their laps,' the Fabians neutrally committed themselves to the principle of a Collectivist Party, distinct from Liberals, Conservatives and the ILP. The large Conservative victory that summer seemed to mark an end to the socialist resurgence in Britain. The trade-union movement had faltered, the ILP had done badly, and the Fabians had decisively done nothing at all. Though there existed informal co-operation between them, the Fabians went on to cause more hostility among other socialists by once more starting up their wire-pulling tactics, this time with the Conservatives over educational reform. In defence of this manoeuvre, Shaw issued a *Report on Fabian Policy* which, as Tract No. 70, was published in July 1896 and re-established permeation as the Society's electoral philosophy. 'The Fabian Society,' he explained,

'. . . does not seek direct political representation by putting forward Fabian candidates at elections. But it loses no opportunity of influencing elections and inducing constituencies to select Socialists as their candidates. No person, however, can obtain the support of the Fabian Society, or escape its opposition, by merely . . . calling himself a Socialist . . . frivolous candidates give great offence, and discredit the party in whose name they are undertaken, because any third candidate who is not well supported will not only be beaten himself, but may also involve in his defeat the better of the two candidates competing with him. Under such circumstances the Fabian Society throws its weight against the third candidate, whether he calls himself a socialist or not . . .'

Fabian strategy during the 1890s exemplified Shaw's dogma of adaptability, responding to the nuances of political development while insensitive to the magnet of political power. 'You see,' Charlotte Shaw wrote to Pease many years later, 'these ambitious politicians, who want to be successful party men, never have been able to keep with us.' One of the most ambitious members of the Fabian executive, once a supporter of permeation, was Ramsay MacDonald, whose political instinct prompted him in the summer of 1894 to apply for membership of the ILP. 'The time for conciliation has gone by,' he wrote to Keir Hardie, 'and those of us who are in earnest in our professions must definitely declare ourselves.' It was MacDonald, too, who demanded the suppression of Shaw's Tract No. 70 when it appeared two years later.

The Fabians' flexibility was brilliantly exploited on the page by Shaw to keep the specific character of the Society on the political stage and cast it in a theatrical lead. He excelled at seizing the initiative in retrospect. In whichever direction history plunged, there was the ubiquitous Fabian waiting to guide and philosophize. As one of the authors of *A Plan of Campaign for Labor*, he made claim to have been a founder of the Labour Party and a Fabian instrument in driving the Liberals from power; as author of the *Report on Fabian Policy* he was prepared to admit having helped to Fabianize socialism throughout Europe, and initiate the major social advances in the twentieth century. Only occasionally did he privately acknowledge some of this as a 'pose' to be assumed 'whenever advisable'. To some extent these twists and weavings were the natural trials and errors of Shaw's political education. He felt strongly convinced that the humane and reasoned voice of the intellectual must not be lost amid the struggle of professional politicians and the rough and tumble of popular democracy. To be heard, seen, and valued as advocates of progress with safeguards against revolution, the Fabians needed someone to play these political games and command popular appeal – while leaving the central concept of equitable English socialism uncontaminated. It was on such an understanding that Shaw, exploiting all his acting and dialectical skills, had voted himself into exile.

*I go through the world on Mr Winkle's skates, always ridiculously
learning. Widowers' Houses seemed to me better worth printing than
burning; and I have not altered my opinion of it. It is better than
'Love's Labour Lost' in all the qualities which are common to both
plays. I am not burning it: I am just finishing another play, with
which I shall make an ass of myself at the Independent Theatre. Then
I shall write another; and I have no doubt that when I have written
ten or eleven more or less simple and crude plays I shall be able to
write a complex and perhaps powerful one.* (1893)

He had been hovering on the edge of writing plays for a long time. This
fascination with the stage, deriving from those visits in Dublin to the
Theatre Royal and the new Gaiety Theatre, had gradually uncoiled (from
his bloody burlesque about a 'Haunted Winebin' to the unfinished *Passion
Play*) as a succession of verse dramas and then secreted itself in his novels.
Like Beatrice Webb, he seemed to be (so he confessed to readers of the
*Pall Mall Gazette*), 'a sufferer from that strange brain disease which drives
its victims to write long stories that are not true, and to delight in them
more than in any other literature'. He had even turned one of his French
lessons for Ida Beatty into a tiny play. *Un Petit Drame* satirizes his uncle
Walter Gurly's household (as well as the Pakenham Beatty ménage), carries a number of jokes about his family and friends, and demonstrates his
talent for rearranging autobiographical fragments so that they become
absurdly foreign (literally so here) to himself.

In 1884 he had begun his first serious attempt to write for the stage a
full-length play in prose. It was started in collaboration with Archer. That
summer Archer outlined the conspiracy to him: they would borrow a plot
from a 'twaddling cup-and-saucer comedy' by Emile Augier called
*Ceinture Dorée*, Archer doing it into English scene by scene and ladling it
out to Shaw who would set about reconciling it, in sparkling dialogue, with
his Marxist passion for political economy. It was to be called *The Way to a
Woman's Heart*, though they soon began calling it *Rheingold* (later
anglicized to *Rhinegold*). Shaw started on 18 August, using shorthand in a
reporter's notebook, and by 12 September he had completed the first act.
A month later, the second act was also completed; but in mid-November,
after writing twenty-three lines of Act III, he stopped, with the explanation
that he had exhausted all Archer's plot. In fact he was able to find use for
all too little of it. His difficulty lay in matching this contrived Parisian

structure to an analysis of contemporary slum landlordism. Increasingly he was driven away from Augier's story to plunder other sources – *Little Dorrit* and some scenes from his own last novel, *An Unsocial Socialist* (from which he transposed Trefusis into Harry Trench, the twenty-four-year-old 'frank, hasty, rather boyish' doctor). There were Fabian sources too. In the autumn of 1883 a penny pamphlet had appeared, called *The Bitter Cry of Outcast London*. It had been compiled by Congregational Ministers, and presented seventy-two extreme examples of slum tenants. The revelations in this pamphlet had raised a discussion in the press lasting into the following year and eventually leading to a Royal Commission. Shaw had laid hold of many facts and figures made public before this investigation, but by trying to thread them through his play he made the separation between form and content even wider. So he decided to use them elsewhere, to employ himself drafting Fabian Tract No. 3 'To Provident Landlords and Capitalists' (1885) and prepare a number of lectures and articles on the same subject. He 'gave up fiction and took to Socialism,' he explained to Janet Achurch.

There were occasions over the next two or three years when, coming across his notebooks, Shaw would copy out some pages of *Rhinegold* in the hope of regaining his momentum. But the play still lacked direction. The times, which he described as of 'great distress among the working classes', did not seem right for drawing-room socialism; while no other socialism, it appeared, was right for the British theatre. 'Our drama is sinking for want, not of an Augier, but of an Ibsen,' he had written in the summer of 1885 in *The Dramatic Review*.

'Wrote no new fiction,' Shaw noted at the beginning of his 1886 diary. On 22 February that year he made an outline for a new play, 'Plan for St James's Piece', using John Hare and other leading figures from the St James's Theatre, but he did not develop it. He felt the lack of creative writing, and by 14 April 1887 observed himself to be 'hovering on the confines of beginning a novel'. A month later he registered in his diary that he 'began a new novel and sat up till 3 at it. Hooray!' He continued intermittently working on this novel (which transferred the character of Edith Bland into the household of Walter Gurly) for two months; but after 14 June, and for the rest of that year, there is no further mention of it. Instead, between 25 July and 1 August, he had turned to his story 'The Truth about Don Giovanni' – which waited forty-five years for publication – and to his appendix for the poorly selling *An Unsocial Socialist*, wherein he argues that by presenting facts in the guise of fiction we invite readers in our romantic society to judge them in a false light. Despite this argument his 'strange brain disease' persisted, and having put aside the novel he again picked up his play. Early that autumn he made a fair copy in longhand of the first two Acts which he left with Archer on 4 October. 'They are not supposed to be complete,' he told him, 'but they present a series of consecutive dialogues in which your idea is prepared and developed. The central notion is quite perfect . . . but I have no idea of how it is to proceed . . . Will you proceed either to chuck in the remaining acts, or provide me with a skeleton for them?' But it was his next sentence that located their real problem. 'You will perceive that my genius has brought the romantic notion which possessed you, into vivid contact with real life.'

Archer gave his opinion, recorded in Shaw's diary, two days later. 'After tea went up to Archer's and read the unfinished drama. A long argument ensued, Archer having received it with great contempt.' The argument was complicated. Forty years later, in his Preface to Archer's *Three Plays*, Shaw was to expand on this brief note and make fun of the incident.

'He was utterly contemptuous of its construction; but this I did not mind, as I classed constructed plays with artificial flowers, clockwork mice . . . Unfortunately, when I came to the second act, . . . [he] fell into a deep slumber; and I softly put the manuscript away and let him have his sleep out.'

It is a strange scene. Archer, the greatest British advocate of Ibsen at that time, sleeps and argues – almost argues in his sleep – on behalf of the dying traditions of mid-nineteenth-century French Theatre. Shaw, who 'had barely heard of Ibsen's name' in 1887, denounces this sterile artifice of constructed drama and asserts that his play has an organic growth of its own 'like a flowering plant', and can never be 'a manufactured article constructed by an artisan according to plans and specifications supplied by an inventor'. The paradox here is that if Shaw wishes to do without plans and specifications, why has he based his play on a French model, and why was he coming to Archer to ask for more sections of the event-plot or 'skeleton'? What actually happened seems to have been that Archer objected to the disunity of the two acts, in particular to Shaw's breezy, articulate humour (so different from Ibsen's brooding intensity), which broke the coherence of the play. To judge from Archer's account of their argument, Shaw has skilfully borrowed all his lines. For it was Shaw who was asking for more clockwork machinery to be chucked in, and it was Archer himself who resisted this. 'I told him,' Archer wrote, 'that my plot was a rounded and perfect organic whole, and that I could no more eke it out in this fashion than I could provide him or myself with a set of supplementary arms and legs.' In other words, by their own accounts, they were each saying roughly the same thing.

Archer's opinion was important to Shaw. Though he had trained himself to do without encouragement – even to interpret the lack of it as a compliment – he needed the support of this man who had given him so much of his theatrical education. Not receiving it, he was lost, subsequently suggesting to Archer he should give it to Henry Arthur Jones, 'who might borrow a notion from it for a drama touching socialism'.

Once again he laid the play aside: once again he took up his novel, but after adding another six pages to it in January 1888, relinquished it altogether. Coming across the forty-one pages of manuscript towards the end of his life, he wrote:

'. . . it is a complete throwback to the Victorian novel with its triangle of husband wife and lover, who reappear some ten years later in my play called Candida. But in the play marriage is triumphant, with the pair left in an exalted and unassailable union, whilst the lover vanishes into the night, having sanctified their household instead of desecrating it. In the [novel] . . . the convention of George Eliot's supremely famous novel Middlemarch still prevails: the lover is the hero and the husband only the wife's mistake.

'It is not surprising that I found nothing new for me to do in that direction, and abandoned my abortive attempt to return to it so soon . . .'

This is an example of late G.B.S. superimposing himself on the young man who, on 24 December 1890, had 'turned up the beginning of an old novel and was rather pleased with it'. But he could not risk more disappointment: 'the failure has been too heavy,' he told William Sonnenschein, and to an enquiry from another publisher, Fisher Unwin, he replied: 'No thank you: no more novels for me. Five failures are enough to satisfy my appetite for enterprise in fiction.' *An Unfinished Novel* differs from its five predecessors in that it uses more dialogue than narrative. Even so, he explained, 'I could not stand the form: it is too clumsy and unreal.'

He had started on another theatrical collaboration in the autumn of 1888, this time with an Anglo-Norwegian bookseller-journalist, H. L. Braekstad. Their plan called for Shaw to go to the British Museum, copy down, 'without understanding a word of it', sections of Ibsen's *Peer Gynt* and then take them to the Scandinavian Club where Braekstad would give a spontaneous rendering into English, to be in turn converted by Shaw into literary-dramatic shape. 'I am not sure I can write verse at all,' he hesitated. But he took this exercise seriously enough to order for himself a number of Danish lessons, Danish and literary Norwegian being, in effect, the same language in the nineteenth century. He found it 'very slow and difficult work' and, after one or two occasions when he 'clean forgot Braekstad', seems to have abandoned it at the end of the year. 'Braekstad has temporarily relinquished Peer Gynt in order to concentrate all his energies on the family cultivation of measles,' Shaw reported. 'That enterprise therefore is indefinitely postponed . . .'

The following year he tried something new. 'Worked at the plan of the play which has come into my head', he noted in his diary on 29 June 1889. The idea of this play had been stimulated by his meeting with Janet Achurch earlier that month, and by an incident involving her and the Archers. Frances Archer had apparently objected to Shaw having declared his love for Janet, a married woman. Shaw replied that conventional marriage stifled the imagination. He even told Archer that his wife was spoiling him and that he would be 'a lost man' unless he broke free. Archer replied that Shaw must not visit their home while he held views so disparaging to his wife. But the notion that marriage had meant 'checkmate' to Archer as a playwright 'for years to come' persisted in Shaw. Why else had Archer let him down over *Rhinegold*? The idea began to infiltrate a new work. At odd moments, in parks and restaurants, on trains and political platforms – even during the intervals of other people's plays – he would write passages of dialogue for what was turning out to be a comedy of intrigue, called *The Cassone*, with characters based on the Archers, the Charringtons and himself. It was a revenge for *Rhinegold* and a precursor to *Candida*, a battle of the artistic versus the domestic instinct. 'Sometimes in spare moments I write dialogues,' he explained to Tighe Hopkins:

'and these are all working up to a certain end (a sermon, of course) my imagination playing the usual tricks meanwhile of creating visionary persons &c. When I have a few hundred of these dialogues worked up and interlocked, then a drama will be the result – a moral, instructive, suggestive comedy of modern society, guaranteed correct in philosophic & economic detail, and unactably independent of theatrical considerations.'

In January 1890 he had come to feel that 'my next effort in fiction – if I ever have time to make one – will be a play'. But his life was so pell-mell with politics and journalism that during the whole of 1890 he found only part of two days on which to work at *The Cassone*. He appears to have made an attempt to return to it as late as 14 April 1892, but the page with this date on it is blank.

After the failure of his collaboration with Archer, Shaw had despaired of writing an actable play. 'I wish I could write you a real play myself,' he told the actress Alma Murray, 'but unfortunately I have not the faculty. I once wrote two acts of a splendid play, and read them to an eminent dramatic critic. He laughed the first to scorn, and went to sleep in the middle of the second; so I . . . set to work to destroy the society that makes bad plays possible.'

From his other friends over this period he obtained no encouragement. 'I was surprised one day when he told me that he had been trying his hand at a new sort of stuff, some of which he showed me, written lengthwise in a reporter's note-book in his exquisite handwriting, unaffected by the vibration of railway travelling, and which I realized was a dramatic dialogue,' Sydney Olivier remembered.

'. . . I was surprised, because the quality of British play-wrighting, and the deadly artificiality and narrow conventions of native contemporary British Drama were at that time so repellent to me that I could not imagine any man of the intelligence of Shaw . . . conceiving that there was any possibility . . . for expressing himself in that medium.'

What Olivier had missed, and what nerved Shaw to continue, was the example of Ibsen who had demonstrated how serious business (such as the destruction of Victorian ideals and the working out of a new system of social values) could be conducted from the stage. After seeing Archer's translation of *A Doll's House* acted by the Charringtons, he had written:

'I find people enjoying themselves there who have been practically driven from the other theatres by the intolerable emptiness of the ordinary performances. I miss the conventional lies of the stage there; and I do not droop, wither, and protest I am being poisoned for want of them . . . [I] see a vital truth searched out and held up in a light intense enough to dispel all the mists and shadows that obscure it in actual life. I see people silent, attentive, thoughtful, startled – struck to the heart, some of them.'

From the affinity he felt with Ibsen, Shaw emerged with new confidence. 'Never fear,' he assured Tighe Hopkins, 'my comedy will not be unactable when the time comes for it to be acted . . . I have the instinct of an artist; and the impracticable is loathsome to me. But not only has the comedy to be made, but the actors, the manager, the theatre, the audience. Somebody must do these things – somebody whose prodigious conceit towers over all ordinary notions of success . . .'

It was a Dutchman, J. T. Grein, who did this thing by starting what Shaw called 'the most important theatrical enterprise of its time'. Hiring a cheap hall ('the nearest thing to a barn left in Tottenham Court Road'), Grein announced a performance of Ibsen's *Ghosts* in 1891 to inaugurate 'The Independent Theatre', with Thomas Hardy, Henry Arthur Jones,

Meredith, George Moore and Pinero among its members. 'Result – barn too small; performance transferred gloriously' to the Royalty Theatre, and Grein, suddenly the most famous theatrical entrepreneur in Britain, sharing with Ibsen the distinction of being abusively discussed throughout the country.

It was Grein who, the following year, struck the spark of encouragement Shaw needed. While the two of them were walking one autumn night from Hammersmith, Grein mentioned his disappointment at the absence of new British playwrights for his theatre; and Shaw countered this by revealing that he was a new British playwright and that he had written a new British play 'that you'll never have the courage to produce'. Grein answered the challenge by accepting it unread and asking for the manuscript at once. It came, a few days later, 'written partly in a large notebook and for the rest on loose sheets,' Grein recalled, 'and I spent a long and attentive evening in sorting and deciphering it. I had never had a doubt as to my acceptance . . . But I could very well understand how little chance that play would have had [with] . . . the average theatre manager.'

Apart from the odd day's outing in a train, the two acts of *Rhinegold* had lain among Shaw's luggage of discarded manuscripts for over four and a half years until, on 29 July 1892, while attempting to set his papers in order, he came across them again and read them through. Next day he had 'set to work to finish the comedy'. On 31 July he was 'still amusing myself finishing the comedy', and by 2 August he 'began to revise the comedy'. That he was now to solve the problem that had baffled him in the 1880s was due to his education by Ibsen. The hero of the play, Harry Trench, proposes to Blanche Sartorius and is accepted by her in Act I. But in Act II, finding that her money comes from wretched slum properties, he breaks off their engagement. How then was Shaw to bring the lovers together without violating his own and his hero's principles? His solution, by the summer of 1892, was to make the hero more real by making him less 'heroic', and by showing that the slum landlord Sartorius (whose name suggests society in its formal dress) was not a villain but merely the symptom of a wretched social system in which everyone was implicated.

'I think, by the bye, that the title Rheingold ought to be saved for a romantic play,' he had suggested when leaving the first two acts with Archer. 'This is realism.' On 20 October 1892, while working at a new scene near the end of Act II, he decided to replace *Rhinegold* with the 'far-fetched Scriptural title', *Widowers' Houses*. To this he afterwards added the descriptive subtitle: 'An Original Didactic Realistic Play in Three Acts'. From its conception over seven years earlier the play had changed so fundamentally as to make Archer a collaborator only in the sense of having set Shaw's imagination to work. In a letter to him many years later, Shaw explained: 'I distinguish between an idea for a play, and a plot. You made a plot for Widowers' Houses; and you can claim the Rhine scenery of the first act, and the idea of the tainted treasure. I had no difficulty with the Rhine, and no difficulty with the idea; but the plot was no use: the play somehow wouldnt write itself round it.'

The ramshackle rehearsals, scheduled for 14 November, started punctually the following day at a public house, 'the Mona Hotel'; and on 16 November Shaw began cutting. 'Nothing can exceed the devotion of the cast,' he wrote. Sometimes there were not enough actors to carry through a rehearsal at all. When they did turn up they vied anxiously with one another to avoid various parts – in particular Lickcheese, the Dickensian rent collector, who was played by James Welch after entering the pub for a drink. Shaw was there, he was everywhere, helping, until begged to stay away so that the actors could get their words.

*Widowers' Houses* opened at the Royalty Theatre in Dean Street, Soho, on 9 December, the most obvious vocal part that evening being the prompter's. It was a curious example, commented Archer in *The World*, 'of what can be done in art by sheer brainpower'. At the end of the performance, Shaw hurried before the curtain to make a speech and was acclaimed with hisses. This lack-of-indifference seemed so heady that at the second and final performance, a matinée on 13 December, he again climbed on to the stage and, there being no critics present, was applauded.

Shaw sent up all sorts of balloons of publicity for his play, interviewing himself, reviewing reviews, filling columns of *The Era*, *The Speaker* and *The Star* with his correspondence, and claiming for the event the uproar that contemporary notices do not substantiate. 'I *do* read the papers to a reasonable extent,' protested Elinor Huddart, 'yet the only notice of "Widowers' Houses" I came across was in the *Illustrated London News*'. But Shaw insisted that, if it had not achieved success, it had 'made a sensation', and he was suddenly 'infamous as a playwright'. By such methods, after more than eight years, he squeezed out the stimulus he needed. *Widowers' Houses* had been born: its job now was to give birth to him as a professional dramatist.

\*

The novelty of *Widowers' Houses* lay in the anti-romantic use to which Shaw put theatrical cliché. When the father discovers his daughter in the arms of a stranger, he omits to horsewhip him, but pitches into negotiations over the marriage – and these negotiations reveal a naked money-for-social-position bargain. It is the young girl, not the young man, who takes the initiative in the love-scenes, and when her fiancé initially refuses to accept his father-in-law's dowry because it has been acquired from appalling exploitation of the poor, she does not forsake all for love – in fact, she does the opposite. Unlike Augier's hero, who tips his tainted gold into the Rhine, Shaw's hero comes to accept it ('We're all in the same boat it appears'); and the final happy ending is a lustful surrender to corruption. The play's 'didactic' realism, woven into the conventions of romantic comedy, is obtained by parodying and reversing these theatrical conventions, and by dispensing with the fortuitous accident that always in the last act rewarded virtue with unexpected prosperity.

Standing on stage that first night in his dazzling Jaeger wool, Shaw welcomed the turbulent hooting by agreeing that, yes, it was a disgraceful state of affairs they had just witnessed, a true picture of things then going on in middle-class society that he hoped would soon become unintelligible to London audiences. But part of his audience's hostility may have been provoked by the unflatteringly unsympathetic cast of Shaw's characters. 'Everyone is ill-conditioned, quarrelsome, fractious, apt to behave, at a moment's notice, like a badly brought up child,' complained William Archer in *The World*; and in the *Illustrated London News*, H. W. Massingham wrote: 'He gives us love-making without romance, friendship without sincerity, landlordism without pity.' Later on, Shaw would instruct producers that Lickcheese, the reptilian rent-collector, should be played with pathos and sincerity, even geniality. 'There should be absolutely no unpleasantness at all about him . . . The audience should delight in him in a thoroughly friendly way; and he should wallow in their friendliness.' Shaw's point was that Lickcheese, the other characters, and the audience itself, were all incapable of being any better than the world around him: it is a cast of philistines, with Sartorius the idealist at their head. But 'friendly', in the Shavian vocabulary, is a dangerous word. What gives *Widowers' Houses* its power is Shaw's anger. He was writing here from personal experience, as the young man who had 'collected slum rentals weekly with these hands' in Dublin, who in London was immersing himself in municipal politics, and who had felt himself emotionally and sexually bullied by Jenny Patterson. The 'far fetched Scriptural title' of his play is, in truth, a title of retribution: 'Woe unto you, scribes and Pharisees, hypocrites! for ye devour widows' houses, and for a pretence make long prayer: therefore ye shall receive the greater damnation.'

Caught in this spirit of retribution is Shaw's audience, whom he wanted to make 'thoroughly uncomfortable whilst entertaining them artistically' – at which job he reckoned *Widowers' Houses* to have been a promising failure. The philistine audience retaliated through its idealist critics by calling the play 'not a play' (it was a 'topical lecture') and the playwright 'no playwright'. He was a brilliant journalist, they allowed, a fine speaker and would have done well in comic opera or the Church. So began at once Shaw's lifelong battle with the critics in whose schoolroom he was seldom awarded many marks. Even at the height of his career they were generally agreed that, despite wit, intellect and, in a formless way, some excellent fooling, he was (in the words of A. B. Walkley), 'a detestable dramatist', who had started his career with 'a singularly bad piece of work'.

To the criticism that *Widowers' Houses* was 'a dismal, stiff little pamphlet', Shaw responded in his 1893 Preface, first by requesting that 'you will please judge it, not as a pamphlet in dialogue, but as in intention a work of art as much as any comedy of Molière is a work of art . . .'; and then by stating that it 'is deliberately intended to induce people to vote on the Progressive side at the next County Council election in London'. This dual response reflects the two literary styles of the play – a social comedy of manners and a lucid exposition of political economy – that, though matching the needs of the argument, Margery Morgan writes, 'do not fit very well together or fall into any satisfactory dramatic rhythm'. It is realism without naturalism.

*Widowers' Houses* contains the stereotype figures (heavy father, low comedian, walking gentleman, *femme fatale*), but displaced by Shaw from their familiar stage positions. Lickcheese was to develop into Doolittle; the slum landlord Sartorius into the armaments manufacturer, Undershaft; Blanche Sartorius into Ann Whitefield. But they present themselves more crudely here, and without charm, self-mockery or full Shavian guile. In a sense this is Shaw's most human play. Nowhere else is his dislike of the world as it exists more plainly felt. The perfect embodiment of this society is Blanche Sartorius, over whom the pact between aristocratic respectability and financial exploitation is made. 'I see I have made a real lady of you, Blanche,' says her father a little wistfully. She is an enslaving woman, a landlady of the emotions, whose animal sexuality devours men and who betrays, more clearly than anywhere else in Shaw's work, the results of Jenny Patterson's rigorous devotion to him. Here, on paper, was his revenge; and given on the stage an ironic twist by the casting of Florence Farr in the part. The predatory Blanche, with her terrifying temper, prompted Oscar Wilde to congratulate Shaw: 'I admire the horrible flesh and blood of your creatures . . .' But William Archer, who saw only the movement of ingeniously animated puppets, embarrassing in their love-scenes though otherwise as agile as monkeys on a stick, voiced the criticism that was forever to linger round Shaw's plays:

'The fact is that Mr Shaw is himself too utterly unlike the average sensual man to have any sympathetic comprehension of him . . . If Mr Shaw would or could divest his mind of theory, I think he would see that these lovers of his are not human beings at all . . . Truly, for a set of blood-suckers, Mr Shaw's middle-classes are strangely bloodless . . . His world is without atmosphere; no breath of humanity, and least of all any *odor di femmina*, gets over the footlights.'

Though *Widowers' Houses* presents a socialist view of life, there is no socialist in it. Trench is an innocent Conservative who, deciding that he is not called upon to remake the world at his own expense, behaves with all the adaptability and pragmatism that Shaw was urging on the Fabians. But without the vision of socialism, his adaptability to facts becomes merely an acquiescence to corruption and his innocence is lost. To what extent socialism made compromise honourable was a question that was to be tested on Shaw with his next play.

*

With the press-cuttings crammed into his bag and his ears still ringing to the self-induced clamour, Shaw caught a train to join William Morris's Christmas house party at Kelmscott Manor, in Oxfordshire. Over the holiday he began pasting up his scrap-book, pondering his first Preface (to Grein's publication in 1893 of *Widowers' Houses* as Number One of the Independent Theatre Series of Plays), and dreaming of his second play. He foresaw this second play provoking an even franker commotion and making him notorious as a playwright throughout Europe. He would do such things . . . He would handle his Ibsenite critics in the most amazingly disrespectful way; he would sail, all guns smoking, into the topical storm that was engulfing the New Woman; he would demolish the marriage and divorce laws, expose the evil of vivisection, violently assault our modern witch doctors for reducing human beings to chemical machines. It was to be a grand cleaning-up operation, an hygienic whirlwind – the most ambitious thing he had attempted. In his exhilaration he opened a wider window, cracked thicker ice, that winter.

He hardly knew where to begin. For Easter 1893 he went to Oxted to stay with the Salts. His travelling companion on the train was Sydney Olivier who, it seemed, was also writing a play – which was particularly surprising in view of the dismay he had shown over Shaw's writing of *Widowers' Houses*. Olivier even had the nerve to read part of his play to the Salts one day, and was generally 'very full' of it Shaw observed. Here was the pacemaker he needed to get going. His diary entry for the next day, 29

March, reads: 'After breakfast went up to the Common by Rickfield Rd and selected a spot on the West Heath, near the orphanage, where I lay down and got to work on the new play which I have resolved to call *The Philanderer*.'

He had great difficulty with it, squeezing his work in between a heavy programme of journalism, Fabianizing and the important business of letter-writing. Much of the play was written on trains to and from his various lectures and speeches, and (sometimes under an umbrella) in various parks – Hyde Park, the Embankment, Regent's Park, the top of Primrose Hill – whenever he could snatch an hour or two. His progress can be followed through his diary.

'*1 April* . . . did three hours hard work on the play, which tired me enough to induce me to take a nap after dinner.

'*8 April* Worked at the play in the evening here, and in the train; but had a headache and did not get on very well.

'*10 April* Worked at the new play in the train for a couple of hours, getting along famously.'

Then, in May, he suddenly got stuck. On 23 May, he wrote: 'After dinner I went out to Putney and walked by way of Roehampton to Richmond Park, where I tried to get to work on the third act of the play, but could not think of a subject for it.'

It was Sydney Olivier who again acted as catalyst. On 24 May Shaw went to William Archer's house to hear the reading of Olivier's play. Afterwards, on a bus to Shepherd's Bush, 'I hit on the third act of my new play,' he wrote. The idea he had hit on was the marriage question. He continued intermittently working on this act and discussing it with Janet Achurch. On 12 June, in Albemarle Street, he met Beatrice Webb and walked with her across Primrose Hill. 'We had a long discussion about the Woman Question,' he wrote in his diary, and this, he adds, was 'greatly intensified by our meeting Ada Webb in Regent's Park, wheeling her mother about in a bath chair, a striking example of the sacrifice of a young woman to domestic duty.' That evening Shaw went to see a friend of Sydney Olivier's, Hedwig Sonntag, and recorded: 'I read her the play and was horrified to find that it is far too long: it took me three hours to read it.'

Next day he is at the top of Primrose Hill in a high wind, cutting and revising the play. These cuts were mainly in the long second act which had contained a Gilbertian sub-plot involving a long lost dog that belonged to the beautiful Julia Craven. This dog was to have been brought by a professional dog-stealer to the house of her lover, the vivisector Dr Paramore, Julia's hysterics getting her expelled from the Ibsen Club for the crime of 'womanly conduct'. All this Shaw eliminated and on the afternoon of June 17 he read the revised text to Lady Colin Campbell. What then happened changed the content of the play and the course Shaw's work was to follow. Lady Colin Campbell, he explained, 'pointed out to me that the third act at which I have been working ought to be put into the fire. This opened my eyes for the first time to the fact that I have started on quite a new trail and must reserve this act for the beginning of a new play'. A few days later, on 22 June, 'I went up to the top of Primrose Hill and there wrote a new scene for the beginning of the new third act of the play, as suggested by Lady Colin . . .'

Lady Colin Campbell was a formidable woman. She fenced, she rode, she swam, she wrote books on etiquette and, as Q.E.D., Shaw's successor on *The World*, she was 'the most divinely tall of the art critics'. She was also Irish. But she was best known for having obtained, on the grounds of cruelty, a judicial separation from her husband, the youngest son of the eighth Duke of Argyll, in a sensational series of court actions. She was a forthright, practical woman and a sensitive judge of public opinion. What she told Shaw was that no audience in the early 1890s would easily accept the last act as he had written it. He was in his thirty-seventh year. After that tiny taste of success with *Widowers' Houses*, he hungered to have his play produced. But by substituting her suggestion for his original inspiration he was going against much that he claimed for himself as a dramatist. He was picking the artificial flowers, making a pet of the clockwork mouse and preferring her constructed act to his own organic development: in short, he had become an artisan, manufacturing an ending according to plans and specifications laid down by Lady Colin Campbell. This may help to explain the revulsion that sometimes overtook him with this play. 'I am struggling with an almost overpowering temptation to burn The Philanderer,' he wrote to Janet Achurch at the end of 1894 – an interesting choice of phrase in view of Lady Colin Campbell's advice for him to put his first version into the fire. In the event he did not burn his original last act, but simply wrote at the end: 'Cancel all the foregoing.' So it is possible to compare the two versions and describe the nature of the change he made.

In the original act there is one extra character, a comic butler called Spedding. The act takes place at the house of Dr Paramore on his third wedding anniversary to Julia Craven (a cowardly name for the character based on Jenny Patterson). Only a man with the name Paramore and the inventor of a non-existent illness, 'Paramore's Disease', would marry Julia. But now he is a changed man, cynical, as tired of his wife as she is of him, and in love with Grace Tranfield (the character based on Florence Farr).

He is – and this gives a nice symmetry to the play – in very much the same position as the philanderer Charteris in Act I: that is, on with the new love before he is off with the old, but with the additional complication of being married. It is this subject of marriage and of divorce that occupies this act during which they decide to go to South Dakota where the divorce laws have been adapted to human nature. There is one complication. When the ever-jealous Julia discovers that, once he is divorced, Paramore intends to marry Grace, she refuses to consent to the arrangement – until Charteris agrees to accompany her. This act concludes with their plan to visit the Chicago Exhibition.

The fantastical plot (and what plot, stripped to its underwear, is not fantastical?) is carried forward by means of conversation. It is, in fact, Shaw's first discussion drama. There is an interweaving of ideas, an elegance of argument pushed to the point of comic exasperation, and a dissolving of action into talk – all innovations in the theatre that were not actually to reach the stage (through *Getting Married*) for more than another ten years. 'In the abandoned Act III, for the first time one feels that "thought-tension", so typical of Shaw's later work, where ideas in action render physical movement unnecessary: where Stage Directions become fewer page by page: in a word, where Discussive Drama is born,' Brian Tyson has written:

'. . . One cannot but reflect that the new work is feebler dramatically than that which it replaced. It is a collapse again into conformity: simply a tying up of loose ends of this very mutilated play in an unsatisfying fashion. The positive solutions propounded in the original Act III are put aside for a negative restatement of the problem. Retreat is in the air . . . Paramore, momentarily alive in Act III, albeit cynically so, again becomes a puppet: Charteris, for a moment caught in a discussion with his intellectual equal, again becomes patronising; and Julia, for a brief period invested with a mind, loses it again in favour of a bad temper and the habit of crying.'

By the end of June, *The Philanderer* (with Lady Colin Campbell's last act) was finished and early the following month Shaw had his chessmen out and was experimenting with the stage positions of his characters. As the second of what Shaw was to call his 'unpleasant' plays, *The Philanderer* dealt with sex – with the power game of sex that was played in the society of the 1890s, and the vanity, deception and concealed vulnerability of men and women to one another. Charteris, we are meant to understand, has had sexual intercourse with Julia Craven and Grace Tranfield. He is 'making love' to Grace on a sofa before Julia arrives early in Act I. Every woman, Shaw says, belongs to herself or to her work. Grace Tranfield, not

Leonard Charteris, is the hero of *The Philanderer*. Charteris, who reveals some of Shaw's self-dislike, is the victim of over-protection, a champion at the game, who can tell everyone the truth and hear it from no one. His attitude to love is like other people's attitude to death: it is something that may strike at any time, but which should be avoided at all costs.

*The Philanderer* is an extremely advanced comedy that highlights the then fashionable cult of Ibsenism and gives us a glimpse of the New Woman before Mrs Grundy discovered her. The best women, Shaw argues, were breaking loose from the ideal of the womanly woman imposed on them by men; and the worst women were aping them. Grace Tranfield is the authentic New Woman, wedded to self-respect, not self-love. Julia Craven (like Blanche Sartorius) uses her sexual attractiveness to men as a destructive power, and her transports of jealousy are totally without self-respect. Leonard Charteris, despised by Grace because he has been seduced by Julia, is *The Philanderer* of the title and a portrait for which Shaw admitted he was the model. To William Archer he described Charteris as 'the real Don Juan, the man whose blood has gone to his head, and left him with nothing but an appetite which entangles him ridiculously with a woman who is still very violently in the "flesh and blood" stage'. But there is a difference, in Shavian terms, between Don Juanism and philandering. Don Juans (like Tanner in *Man and Superman*) run away and are caught; philanderers (like Charteris) appear to advance, and rush past you. Shaw's Don Juans turn into respectably married gentlemen; philanderers for ever fly away, usually to their work. In a letter to his Swedish translator, Shaw explained:

'A philanderer is a man who is strongly attracted by women. He flirts with them, falls half in love with them, makes them fall in love with him, but will not commit himself to any permanent relation with them, and often retreats at the last moment if his suit is successful – loves them but loves himself more – is too cautious, too fastidious, ever to give himself away.'

Shaw, the romantic businessman, felt there was money in *The Philanderer*. 'When I work it up with a little extra horse play,' he later told Granville Barker, 'it will go like mad.' But it was an unlucky play. In a letter to Ellen Terry he described it as a 'combination of mechanical farce with realistic filth which quite disgusted me'. In the future, the autobiographical element in his plays would be more elaborate and remote. He disapproved of most farce on the grounds of its inhumanity, and only wrote one other, *You Never Can Tell*, among his full-length works, though its originality transcends the genre. In both, the New Woman confronts the Old Adam. But, except for its final sentence, 'Never make a hero of a philanderer', *The*

*Philanderer* is written from the man's point of view and *You Never Can Tell* from the woman's.

Shaw had wanted to include 'everything that is supposed to be hopelessly undramatic, and make them the most amusing part of the piece,' he told Charles Charrington. 'It will be unspeakably improper: so I expect it will only see the light at the Independent Theatre. Grein is already after it eagerly . . .' But Grein was unimpressed. 'I found the play excessively verbose,' he remembered, 'overloaded with side-issues on bacteria and so on . . . Shaw was probably much amused at our lack of appreciation, and took his manuscript away.'

That Grein suspected him to have been 'amused' at this rejection shows how well Shaw could conceal his feelings. At the last moment he had compromised – and his compromise had led nowhere. He put an optimistic face on it, allowing Elizabeth Robins to know that *The Philanderer* was far beyond such acting as the Independent Theatre could command. But the play which he had intended to be so unspeakably improper would not, he confessed some years later, 'shock a convent in Connemara nowadays'. In comparison with the farces that Charles Wyndham was to put on in the West End ten years later, *The Philanderer* was 'a Sunday school tract', but 'the ideas and atmosphere of it belonged to a new world as yet undiscovered at the West End theatres . . .' He had told Archer that *The Philanderer* was to be 'a step nearer to something'. This was true, but at the last moment he had taken a pace back.

\*

After his failure with *The Philanderer*, Shaw returned to the vein he had worked in *Widowers' Houses*, writing a problem play that was to reveal the corruption produced by compromising too readily with society. Once again the theme is one of social inheritance and the profit motive; once again he shadows his audience with guilt as units in a defective social order.

'. . . do you thank God that you are guiltless in this matter? Take care . . . The wages of prostitution are stitched into your button-holes and into your blouse, pasted into your matchboxes and your boxes of pins, stuffed into your mattress, mixed with the paint on your walls and stuck between the joints of your water-pipes . . . you will not cheat the Recording Angel into putting down your debts to the wrong account.'

In having the nerve to go for prostitution, Shaw had chosen the most vicious aspect of capitalism. Writing in 1901 a Note for the end of *Cashel Byron's Profession*, he was to explain that 'the word prostitution should either not be used at all, or else applied impartially to all persons who do things for money that they would not do if they had other assured means of livelihood.' In his play, which he called *Mrs Warren's Profession*, he used the same formula as in *Cashel Byron's Profession* and later in *Major Barbara*, that of taking 'a profession which society officially repudiates as a metaphor for the way in which that larger society is really conducted'. He originally subtitled his play 'A tragic variation on the theme of "Cashel Byron's Profession"'. The theme of his novel had been the improvement of the human species through releasing the sex instinct from restrictions of class and money. But within the capitalist system, which regarded women as property, rewarded vice and penalized virtue, the sex instinct deteriorates into promiscuity and (in the play) near-incest.

For the writing of *Widowers' Houses* Shaw had had personal experience to call on: he learnt about prostitutes from newspapers, and books such as Charles Booth's *Labour and Life of the People in London* (a second edition of which had just been published), and August Bebel's *Women in the Past, Present and Future* which had been serialized in Mrs Besant's *Our Corner* at the same time as *The Irrational Knot*. Ever since the licensing of Continental brothels in the 1870s and the subsequent discovery that British girls were being exported to Brussels and Vienna (where Mrs Warren conducted her business), 'The Great Social Evil', as the Victorians called prostitution, had begun to exceed slum-landlordism as the most controversial topic for the press. In 1885, W. T. Stead had launched his sensational series 'The Maiden Tribute of Modern Babylon' in the *Pall Mall Gazette*, his first article revealing how Mrs Armstrong had sold her daughter for £3. 'I am quite willing to take as many quires of the paper as I can carry and sell them (for a penny) in any thoroughfare in London,' Shaw wrote to Stead. On discovering that Stead had doctored his facts, Shaw felt that he had been betrayed: 'he [Stead] was so stupendously ignorant that he never played the game.' Stead's game had been to force the Criminal Law Amendment Bill (the chief provision of which was to raise the age of consent from thirteen to sixteen) through Parliament.

Shaw's game was not legal but economic. The immense press coverage gave him an insight into the nineteenth century's attitude towards its 'unfortunates'. Victorian domestic virtues were embodied by the middle-class family with its many children and dominating paterfamilias. The wife-and-mother, guardian of the hearth, who ran the household and bore the children, was a submissive and sexless being whose gentility (physicians were agreed) was outward proof of the absence of a female orgasm. For sexual satisfaction, the husband-and-father had to explore the lesser breeds, such as working-class women earning a shilling a day in the sweatshop, for whom prostitution could bring a vital addition to their income. London was honeycombed with houses of assignation illegally maintained through police bribery; but only on the Continent had the brothel become an established social institution operating under government licence. The more superior of these brothels were run as clubs and they offered shrewd businessmen, such as Mrs Warren's Sir George Crofts, opportunities of forming profitable syndicates. These syndicates, which would purchase premises, secure licences and supply girls, provided huge investments similar to those made in the eighteenth century by city merchant houses in the slave trade.

'Prostitution is rightly called White Slavery,' decided Shaw, whose copious writings reveal the extent of his research. In representing prostitution as an economic phenomenon ('Prostitution is not a question of sex: it is a question of money') he was writing from the point of view of women; but he also wrote as a socialist ('Every increase in women's wages produces a decrease in prostitution') who prescribed as his remedy a living wage for women ('a Minimum Wage law and . . . proper provision for the unemployed'); and finally he wrote as a man struggling to supplant the sex instinct in himself.

Shaw began *Mrs Warren's Profession* some six weeks after completing *The Philanderer*. On 16 August he borrowed from Archer a copy, printed for private circulation, of Pinero's *The Second Mrs Tanqueray*. Two days later: 'Went off for a turn into the [Regent's] park with a notion of getting to work on a new play. However, no ideas came' – so he climbed over Primrose Hill towards Finchley 'to look for a swimming bath' where he could cleanse himself of this failure. On August 20, a Sunday, after reading *The Pilgrim's Progress*, 'which still retains its fascination for me', he walked over to the Charringtons and, coming back on the train, 'at last succeeded in beginning a new play' – writing triumphantly next day to Archer, 'pressing him to try his hand at a play'. It had been Janet Achurch who fired the starting gun by telling him the story, dramatizable but ultra-romantic, of a play she was then writing called *Mrs Daintree's Daughter* and based on Maupassant's *Yvette*. The following Tuesday Shaw noted in his diary that he 'had thought of going over to the Charringtons to get from Janet the scenario of the play she wants me to write', having (as he explained later), told her that he would 'work out the real truth about that mother' who was now beginning to take shape as Mrs Warren. On the Saturday he went down to stay with the Webbs at Argoed in the Wye Valley where, after dinner, Sidney 'read us a chapter of his book on Trade Unions'. The following morning Shaw was off along the Monmouth Road, over stiles and descending into a disused quarry, the broken ground of which made an excellent bed of rocks on which to lie down and compose his play. On 30 August he announced to Archer: 'I have finished the first act of my new play, in which I have skilfully blended the plot of The Second Mrs Tanqueray with that of The Cenci. It will be just the thing for the I[ndependent] T[heatre].'

During his three weeks at Argoed, Shaw read through the Webbs' Trade Union manuscript, 'correcting it and suggesting what improvements I could'. He also read out to them the first act of *Mrs Warren's Profession* and Beatrice (who had made a conspicuous contribution to the first volume of Booth's *Life and Labour of the People in London*) suggested that he 'should put on the stage a real modern lady of the governing class – not the sort of thing that theatrical and critical authorities imagine such a lady to be'. To which Shaw added: 'I did so: and the result was Miss Vivie Warren.' Reporting his progress, and enquiring after the progress of her version, on 4 September, he wrote to the woman he hoped would play Vivie, Janet Achurch:

'The play progresses bravely; but it has left the original lines. I have made the daughter the heroine, and the mother a most deplorable old rip (saving your presence). The great scene will be the crushing of the mother by the daughter. I retain the old roué, but keep him restrained by a continual doubt as to whether the heroine may not be his daughter. The young lover's father, an outrageous clergyman, is in the same perplexity, he also being an old flame of the mother's. The lover is an agreeable young spark, wholly good-for-nothing. The girl is a quite original character. The mother, uncertain who the girl's father is, keeps all the old men at bay by telling each one that he is the parent. The second act is half finished and wholly planned.'

Another train journey was needed on which to complete this second act – this time to the Salts, to whom he read both acts on 3 October. The composition of the play, its various sources, trials and development, was similar to that of *Widowers' Houses*. Shaw worked on it between concerts and other people's plays, between visits to the Jaeger Wool Shop and the British Museum. He interrupted the Fabian, the music critic, the student of Danish and German, by setting out for walks with the play in his pocket, camping from time to time on wayside seats to write up the speeches. He called on his friends and, for purposes of revision and casting, delivered his lines. By the time he had finished all four acts on 2 November, he had tried it out on Archer, the Charringtons, Florence Farr, Sydney Olivier, the artist Bernard Partridge (alias the actor Bernard Gould whom he wanted to play Frank), the Salts, the concert pianist Else Sonntag, the Webbs and Mrs Theodore Wright, who being Fabian and London's first Mrs Alving in Ibsen's *Ghosts* would, Shaw hoped, take the title role. He also read it to Lady Colin Campbell who, ironically, was going into collaboration with Janet Achurch over her version which, though licensed the following year, was never professionally performed. After all this preparation *Mrs Warren's Profession* was ready for the Independent Theatre by the second week of December.

The play represents an advance on *Widowers' Houses* in two ways. Vivie Warren, who is of the same generation as Harry Trench and is confronted by a similar discovery, ends by turning her back on a corrupt system, whereas Trench had given way to it. Secondly, in the 'duet' between Vivie and her mother, particularly at the end of Act II where Vivie makes her counter-attack against Mrs Warren's imposition of authority, Shaw achieves a dramatic exposition that excels anything he had so far written for the stage. He was consciously following Ibsen's method by which the action of the play passes chiefly in dialogues, and in the orchestration of numerous conflicting voices the strands of the work are gathered together.

As with *Widowers' Houses*, there were multifarious strands. He had borrowed a chapter from *Cashel Byron's Profession*; he had used Maupassant, Pinero, Shelley. In his criticism of *The Cenci* for Mrs Besant's *Our Corner*, he had written that Shelley, 'groping for the scientific drama which is yet in the future, and which alone could have reconciled his philosophic craving for truth to the unrealities of the stage, certainly got hold of the wrong vehicle when he chose the five-act tragedy in blank verse which had sufficed for Otway and Nicholas Rowe'. But where Shelley imitated Shakespeare in an un-Shakespearian way, Shaw exploited the 'dead machinery and lay figures' of Pinero (and sometimes of W. S. Gilbert) to create the post-Pinero theatre. His criticism of *The Second Mrs Tanqueray* indicates what he set out to do in *Mrs Warren's Profession*. In both plays we have, apparently, innocence confronted by experience. But Shaw found in Pinero's play 'little except a scaffold for the situation of a step-daughter and step-mother finding themselves in the positions respectively of affianced wife and discarded mistress to the same man. Obviously, the only necessary conditions of this situation are that the persons concerned shall be respectable enough to be shocked by it, and that the step-mother shall be an improper person.' Shaw aimed to get above this minimum by means of what Pinero lacked: 'the higher dramatic gift of sympathy with character – of the power of seeing the world from the point of view of others instead of merely describing or judging them from one's own point of view in terms of the conventional systems of morals . . .'

Shaw had accused Shelley of attempting 'to bottle a new wine in an old skin', and Pinero of 'playing the new game according to the safe old rules'. But this was also his own technique. He used the effective stage conventions of the commercial theatre of his day as a vehicle for presenting his theatrically unconventional (or 'unpleasant') facts of life, facts non-romantic and uncommercial. Unlike Maupassant's *Yvette*, Vivie Warren neither attempts to kill herself nor becomes a courtesan like her mother; unlike Mrs Tanqueray, Mrs Warren declines to step into the next room and commit suicide. She is 'a counter-portrait to the general image of the romantic, sentimentally attractive courtesan of the stage'.

*Mrs Warren's Profession* suggests that we all live more or less on immoral earnings. The cast is largely made up of prostitutes and their clients: Sir George Crofts the big-time client; the old vicar who has sold himself for his benefice and turned from rake into sanctimonious humbug; his son Frank, who is the nearest to an authorial presence in the play, almost selling himself in marriage to Vivie; even Liz, the unseen sister of Mrs Warren, who has used sex as the means to respectability in a cathedral town. The incestuous undercurrents that move mysteriously below the talking surface of the play have been met by two critical objections: the first (voiced by Archer) that they have been dragged in unnecessarily; the second (voiced by Eric Bentley) that, having no idea what to do with the incest theme, Shaw had left the situation doubtful. Shaw, however, insisted that 'the case would be incomplete without it'. For he was taking up incest as an Ibsenite theme and reproducing a structural model without breaking away from it at the end.

The incest theme (deriving from *The Cenci* as well as from Ibsen's *Ghosts* and *Rosmersholm*), which was muted after corrections to the first draft, reflects Shaw's own sexual ambivalence. Originally Frank and Vivie were established as half-brother and sister, and Vivie welcomes this fact as saving her from 'the sort of relation my mother's life had tainted for ever for me'. She returns to the moonlight illusion of being 'babes in the wood . . . covered up with leaves'; and as the curtain descends at the end of Act III she 'lifts her face & presses his lips on hers'. The confusing remnants from such incestuous overtures suggest that Shaw felt all sex to be tainted for Vivie. 'I am like you,' Vivie tells her mother. But by focusing his play on the daughter and not (like Pinero and Maupassant) on the mother, Shaw seeks to escape the philosophy of sexual destiny and convert it into work destiny. 'There's no alternative,' says Madame Obardi, the prostitute mother, to Yvette who is shown as unable to avoid her fate in the 'world of gilded prostitution'. But for Vivie Warren there is an alternative: 'my work is not your work,' she tells her mother, 'and my way is not your way'. She gains integrity through sexual isolation – 'away from it all – away from the sentiment of the tie I formed under the spell of that ghastly moonlight, away from the very air breathed by my mother and that man, away from the world they are part of'.

These words of Vivie's Shaw dropped from the published version: but they still lie between the lines and provide an uneasy sub-text to the play. Vivie was partly based on a noted Liberal Feminist, Mrs Orme, who lived in Chancery Lane, practising as an actuary and smoking huge cigars. She is presented with sympathy and detachment, and her choice to separate herself from the world (which may be judged faulty) has the element of tragedy.

Shaw's case is that there are two ways of preventing the present from repeating the errors of the past: love and work. In love we forget, are reborn, speak like infants, and there is hope of doing better. Then the good moment goes, for the world is not lovable. But if what we call love also supplies the future generations, it is work that decides what sort of life those generations will follow. Instinct tells us whether we should love, and what work we should do; and will-power gives us the vitality to carry this work through.

Love had had no shortage of propaganda, so in *Mrs Warren's Profession*, Shaw places his emphasis on the gospel of work and against the religion of love. When Frank sees Vivie with her arm round her mother's waist, he is revolted: 'Dont it make your flesh creep . . .' But when he appeals to the love-instinct in Vivie ('Come and be covered up with leaves again') she gives a 'cry of disgust' and tells him: 'You make my flesh creep.' The audience believes that this is because of the revelation that she is Frank's half-sister and the revelation of how her mother's money is made. But in the next act she says that this 'makes no real difference'. And Frank and she decide that in all probability they are not related after all. That Frank's father had gone through some sexual involvement with Vivie's mother seems certain; in such atmosphere of consanguinity (like the atmosphere of Sonny's home), and among such ordinary people who, beginning as victims, end up as the very organism of corruption, disgust proliferates. Arising from the author's doubts about his parenthood and ambiguous feelings for his mother, incest is made to cover us all, like the leaves. Something of Mrs Shaw can be seen in Mrs Warren, and this may help to account for the uncertainty and aggression of the play, as well as the revulsion Shaw felt for it over thirty years afterwards: 'I can't stand *anybody* as Mrs Warren, because I can't stand the play itself,' he told Gertrude Kingston in 1925. '. . . Ugh!'

When Vivie Warren 'buries herself luxuriously in her actuarial calculations as the curtain falls we are conscious that she has experienced horror and a sense of contamination . . .' This was the reaction, too, of the fastidious Shaw who tried to turn himself from his mother's son to be an immaculate speaking and writing machine. All the characters in the play have names associated with the earth: Gardner, Warren, Crofts, even Praed which, taken from Praed Street, is derived from 'praedial' meaning landed. But Vivie turns her back on nature and goes alone indoors – a step in the direction of a cleansing moral world Shaw associated with *The Pilgrim's Progress*. There is an autobiographical passion, and pathos, in the final stage directions:

*[Mrs Warren goes out, slamming the door behind her. The strain on Vivie's face relaxes; her grave expression breaks up into one of joyous content; her breath goes out in a half sob, half laugh of intense relief. She goes buoyantly to her place at the writing table; pushes the electric lamp out of the way; pulls over a great sheaf of papers; and is in the act of dipping her pen in the ink when she finds Frank's note. She opens it unconcernedly and reads it quickly, giving a little laugh at some quaint turn of expression in it . . . She tears the note up and tosses the pieces into the wastepaper basket without a second thought. Then she goes at her work with a plunge, and soon becomes absorbed in its figures.]*

Shaw's first rejection had come from Mrs Theodore Wright who was so greatly startled when he read it to her that, instead of asking to play Mrs Warren, 'she rose up, declared that not even in her own room could she speak the part to herself, much less in public to a younger woman . . . rushed out of the room in disorder; and came back in ten minutes to hear the rest of the play'. Shaw did not allow this set-back to dent his optimism. 'I do not think there is the least chance of the play being licensed,' he wrote cheerfully to Grein. He had foreseen some little difficulty for Grein's Independent Theatre in finding a place to show the play; he had not foreseen that Grein (who 'is bent on having a play by me'), would feel that *Mrs Warren's Profession* was unfit 'for women's ears' and that, since it might lead even strong men to 'insanity and suicide', he could not sanction a private production. 'I am at my wits end about this unlucky play of mine', Shaw told Elizabeth Robins.

Though it did not take so long as *The Cenci* to reach an audience, *Mrs Warren's Profession* had to wait until 1902 for the first of two private performances by the Stage Society, during what Grein called 'an exceedingly uncomfortable afternoon' at the New Lyric Club, and until 1925 for its first public production in Britain: 'too late,' Shaw remarked. He failed to get a copyright performance in Ireland, and after its world première in America in 1905, it was prosecuted in the Courts, the *New*

*York Dramatic Mirror* deciding: 'Although he is not amenable to the police authorities of this city, BERNARD SHAW should bear the odium of this disgrace.' Even as late as 1955 the play was banned as 'amoral' from the Salle Luxembourg in Paris by the selection committee of the Comédie Française.

Shaw had taken immense trouble to tailor his play to the conventions of the stage. The difficulties preventing its performance produced two strong reactions in him: they thrust him deep into a vigorous campaign against theatre censorship; and they changed his orientation as a dramatist. Slum-landlordism, the marriage laws and prostitution had all proved 'unspeakable' subjects on the Victorian stage, and Shaw made the decision to write no more 'bluebook' plays on current social problems. From a documentary realist issuing plays with a purpose, he sought to become a writer of plays with no purpose 'except the purpose of all poets and dramatists' – that is 'plays of life, character and human destiny'. In order to get his words spoken on the West End stage he moved the emphasis 'from the public institution to the private imagination'; set out to make his audiences laugh rather than feel uncomfortable (though sometimes to laugh at themselves); and resolved to 'sport with human follies, not with crimes'. Having put aside *Mrs Warren's Profession* to wait its opportunity, he went back to the beginning and started again – this time with a nursery play. His diary entry for 26 November 1893 reads: 'spent the evening beginning a new play – a romantic one – for F[lorence] E[mery].'

# [ 3 ]

*I greatly regret that my play, 'Arms and the Man', has wounded the susceptibilities of Bulgarian students in Berlin and Vienna. But I ask them to remember that it is the business of the writer of a comedy to wound the susceptibilities of his audience. The classical definition of his function is 'the chastening of morals by ridicule' . . . When the Bulgarian students, with my sincerely friendly assistance, have developed a sense of humor there will be no more trouble.* (1924)

*I do not yet feel grown-up.* (1904)

By the mid-1890s, despite all his reverses, Shaw had become thoroughly well known. He was well known to the police as a notorious open-air speaker; and he was well known throughout London to musicians, journalists, socialists, artists and actresses. Scurrilous attacks, disguised as interviews, were regularly made on him by sections of the press. Extra-special reporters, athletic rather than intellectual, would force their way into his modest room apparently for no purpose other than to bully and insult him. Keeping control with a terrific effort, Shaw would defend himself in heart-rending tones against these invasions. But why did he stand them? Why didn't he boot these interlopers downstairs? 'I have kept my temper for eighteen years, and have never been uncivil to an interviewer in my life until to-day.' he explained, through grinding teeth, to *The Star*. Many readers hazarded that this 'Shaw' must be an imaginary person, otherwise he would surely have called in the police. Others felt that here was an astonishing example of Christian forbearance. Only a few realized that the interviews had been written by himself.

'I presume, Mr Shaw,' one imaginary reporter asked before the opening of his new play, 'that when the eventful night comes, the most enjoyable part of it will be your speech after ——'. In the event, stepping out before the curtain after the first performance of *Arms and the Man*, Shaw addressed his short speech to the solitary man who in a wildly cheering audience had uttered a loud 'Boo!' 'My dear fellow,' he exclaimed, 'I quite agree with you, but what are we against so many?'

In this Wildean *mot* Shaw placed his true feelings. Writing to his fellow-playwright, Henry Arthur Jones, some eight months later, he explained: 'Like you, I write plays because I like it, and because I cannot remember any period in my life when I could help inventing people and scenes.' But, he went on:

'I am not a storyteller: things occur to me as scenes, with action and dialogue – as moments, developing themselves out of their own vitality . . . my quarrel with the conventional drama is that it is doctrinaire to the uttermost extreme of dogmatism – that the dramatist is so strait-jacketted in theories of conduct that he cannot even state his conventional solution clearly, but leaves it to be vaguely understood, and so for the life of him cannot write a decent last act. I find that when I present a drama of pure feeling, wittily expressed, the effect when read by me to a picked audience of people in a room is excellent. But in a theatre, the mass of the people, too stupid to relish the wit, and too convention-ridden to sympathise with real as distinct from theatrical feeling, simply cannot see any drama or fun there at all, whilst the clever people feel the discrepancy between the real and theatrical feeling only as a Gilbertian satire on the latter, and, appreciating the wit well enough, are eager to shew their cleverness by proclaiming me a monstrously clever sparkler in the cynical line. These clever people predominate in a first night audience; and, accordingly, in 'Arms & the Man', I had the curious experience of witnessing an apparently insane success, with the actors and actresses almost losing their heads with the intoxication of laugh after laugh, and of going before the curtain to tremendous applause, the only person in the theatre who knew that the whole affair was a ghastly failure.'

Part of the 'intelligent misunderstanding' of Shaw's plays, by critics such as Archer and A. B. Walkley, arose from his method of dressing himself in the strait-jacket of theatrical conventions before performing tricks of elastic unconventionality. But it came too from the discrepancy between such sophisticated intellect and emotions that still responded to the adult world from the doorway of the nursery. Of the horrors of war *Arms and the Man* conveyed as little as *Mrs Warren's Profession* did the pleasures of sexual intercourse. But Archer's and Walkley's bewilderment was intensified by the inadequacy of rehearsals and productions of these early plays, as well as by the originality of Shaw's treatment. For *Arms and the Man* the cast had less than a week to prepare.

*Mrs Warren's Profession* had derived from Janet Achurch: *Arms and the Man* revolved round Florence Farr, who had mysteriously received a sum of money via an occult society to promote a theatrical season at the Avenue Theatre in London. Her backer, whose identity was kept secret from Shaw for another dozen years (it came to him, he would claim, in a dream), was Annie Horniman, 'a middle-class, suburban and dissenting spinster' as she called herself, who was to become fairy godmother to the Abbey Theatre in Dublin and innovator at the Gaiety in Manchester of the professional repertory system in Britain. Thin and medieval in appearance (she wore a huge jewelled dragon in oxidized silver round her neck), Annie Horniman rebelliously smoked cigarettes and bicycled in slacks (she had a black eye when Shaw finally met her). She had a passion for cats (being nicknamed Tabby when a Slade student), and for the theatre, which she had to keep hidden from her family. A granddaughter of the original Horniman tea-merchant (a Quaker who made good by selling his tea in packets instead of loose by the pound), she had inherited a substantial sum on the death of her grandmother. 'She was wonderful about the money really,' Florence Farr later told Shaw, '& just gave it me to do anything I liked with in the way of advertising myself.' 'I only gave the money to carry out my idea,' she explained. 'I did nothing else because I feared to do harm.'

Florence asked both Yeats and Shaw to write plays for her. Shaw worked, as usual, in patches – through showers in the park, in intervals at the theatre, at moments between piano duets – and tried out passages of what he had written on his friends. 'I have made a desperate attempt to begin a real romantic play for F. F. in the style of Victor Hugo,' he reported to Janet Achurch. 'The first act is nearly finished; and it is quite the funniest attempt at that style of composition ever made'. But he was too dilatory for Florence who wrote to him at Argoed, 'reproaching me vigorously for not having worked at the play for her. So I set to and wrote 12 pages of it, working up to lunch time, although the Webbs went out for a walk. After lunch I felt rather unwell . . .' Florence also employed more subtle tactics; she read to him from her own novel, *The Dancing Faun* (at the end of which her Shavian cad, George Travers, is most satisfactorily shot by his titled mistress); and she invited him to Dalling Road to hear Yeats read his verse play, *The Land of Heart's Desire*, in which a wife escapes domestic drudgery, through death, into fairyland. Following these goadings, Shaw would surge on energetically at his own play, though soon interrupting himself with more Fabianizing, journalism and singing; and by these methods he began to fall behind.

In its first version, tentatively entitled *Alps and Balkans* (Salt had suggested *Battlefields and Boudoirs*), Shaw had given the play no geography – 'nothing but a war with a machine gun in it' – the names of the places being left blank and the characters simply called the Father, the Daughter, the Heroic Lover, the Stranger and so on. He then went to Sidney Webb and asked him to find a good war for his purpose. Webb 'spent about two minutes in a rapid survey of every war that has ever been waged and then told me that the Servo-Bulgarian was what I wanted,' Shaw remembered. 'I then read the account of the war in the *Annual Register* with a modern railway map of the Balkan peninsula before me, and filled in my blanks, making all the action take place in Servia, in the house of a Servian family.' On 17 March 1894, after missing the Boat Race with Florence Farr, Shaw had also gone round to read his play to the Russian nihilist Stepniak, 'who greatly terrified me by inviting the admiral of the Bulgarian fleet to assist . . . But he fortunately turned out to be a Russian.' In his nervousness, Shaw 'did not catch his name', but later discovered it to have been Admiral Serebryekov, who had commanded the Danube flotilla for the Bulgarians before, being suspected of nihilist sympathies, he escaped to England and became a farmer. This 'horse marine', as Archer called him, gave Shaw a good deal of social and historical information, as a result of which the 'play proved impossible from beginning to end', Shaw told Charles Charrington. 'I have had to shift the scene from Servia to Bulgaria, and to make the most absurd alterations in detail for the sake of local color, which, however, is amusing & will intensify the extravagance of the play & will give it realism at the same time.' He had achieved such a pitch of authenticity, Shaw added, as to 'have given rise to the impression that I have actually been in Bulgaria'.

All this research and rewriting meant that the play, now called *Arms and the Man* from the first line of Dryden's heroic verse translation of Virgil's

*Aeneid* ('*Arma virumque cano*'), was not ready for the opening of Florence Farr's season. Instead, using Yeats's *The Land of Heart's Desire* as a *lever de rideau*, she produced *A Comedy of Sighs* by the Irish physician and pastoral playwright, John Todhunter (whose *Black Cat* had been one of the Independent Theatre's spectacular disasters). Shaw, who attended the first night on 29 March, noted that 'the play at the Avenue Theatre failed rather badly, owing to a lot of unlucky circumstances'. Yeats, in his black sombrero, black silk tie, untidy black trousers and black cloak, in the dress circle with a heavy cold, was to describe the fiasco more voluminously; and in a box sat Todhunter, a sallow, lank, melancholy man, exactly like God in an illustrated Bible, who remained stoically silent to the end. 'For two hours and a half, pit and gallery drowned the voices of the players with boos and jeers that were meant to be bitter to the author who sat visible to all in his box surrounded by his family, and to the actress struggling bravely through her weary part,' Yeats remembered. Todhunter sat on 'listening to the howling of his enemies, while his friends slipped out one by one, till one saw everywhere their empty seats . . .' Archer, who gave thanks that the acoustics were poor enough to make half the dialogue inaudible, described Florence's performance as 'panic-stricken' – not inexcusably so, he added, since she possessed neither the physique nor the art for such acting. 'It is overwhelmingly difficult and one is tempted to add, with Dr Johnson, "Would to heaven, madam, it were impossible".' For Shaw, Florence's acting was the most excruciating part of the evening – 'have you ever seen so horrible a portent on the stage as this transformation of an amiable, clever sort of woman into a nightmare, a Medusa, a cold, loathly, terrifying, grey, callous, sexless devil?' he demanded of Elizabeth Robins.

'What madness led Todhunter to write her a part like that? – what idiocy has led me to do virtually the same thing in the play which I have written to help her in this hellish enterprise? Did you hear those damns and devils, meant to be pretty – did they not sound like the blasphemies of a fiend? Had she been able to give full effect to herself, the audience would have torn her to pieces. I lay under harrows of red hot steel . . .'

The next day Shaw received a telegram 'summoning me to Theatre. Went down and found FE and Hemsley (the acting manager) with *Widowers' Houses* open before them, contemplating its production in despair. I dissuaded them from that and after some discussion took my new play out on to the Embankment Gardens and there and then put the last touches to it before leaving it to be typewritten.'

*Arms and the Man* went into rehearsal on 11 April, three days before Todhunter's play was withdrawn. Alma Murray who had made her name in the celebrated single performance of *The Cenci* at the Grand at Islington, was Raina (the part deriving from Annie Besant); the novelist A. E. W. Mason played Major Plechanoff; the *Punch* draughtsman, Bernard Partridge, sketched Shaw one hand on hip at rehearsal and then, as Bernard Gould, took on the role of Sergius; James Welch, who had earlier been press-ganged into playing Lickcheese, gave an extravagantly funny performance as Petkoff; and Florence Farr, originally intended for Raina, was demoted to the servant Louka, 'a very fine, tragic, passionate, grand-mountain-girl character', Shaw insisted – and, he otherwise calculated, 'the only part that plays itself'. Though the rehearsals were scanty, 'they all took extraordinary interest in it,' he wrote, ' – much more than I could have hoped for in the case of a play which was so bewildering at first sight.'

Shaw exercised as much care over the composition of the audience at the first night as over the cast. Among those adding lustre to the event were Stepniak and the Russian agricultural admiral; and Archer, Henry Arthur Jones, H. W. Massingham, George Moore, Oscar Wilde and W. B. Yeats, whose little play was again used as a curtain raiser. Sidney Webb, who 'might possibly bring a cabinet minister if he has a box,' was joined by Sydney Olivier and Graham Wallas. The Charringtons came, Janet being specially seated 'where her beauty will not be lost'. Mrs Bland, too, Shaw estimated, 'will be worth a thousand posters in Blackheath'. 'Chuckers out' were hired, and the only group Shaw forgot to invite was his family.

Shaw arrived towards the end of Yeats's play. His chocolate cream soldier forced his way into Raina's bedroom some twenty minutes later, in what seemed to be the start of a stereotype military melodrama. '. . . the whole pit and gallery, except certain members of the Fabian Society, started to laugh at the author, and then, discovering that they themselves were being laughed at, sat there not converted – their hatred was too bitter for that – but dumbfounded, while the rest of the house cheered and laughed,' Yeats later recalled. '. . . I listened to *Arms and the Man* with admiration and hatred. It seemed to me inorganic, logical straightness and not the crooked road of life, yet I stood aghast before its energy as to-day before that of the *Stone Drill* by Mr Epstein or of some design by Mr Wyndham Lewis . . . Presently I had a nightmare that I was haunted by a sewing-machine, that clicked and shone, but the incredible thing was that the machine smiled, smiled perpetually.'

No one present forgot this wonderfully entertaining performance of *Arms and the Man*. 'It was applauded,' wrote G. K. Chesterton, 'by that indescribable element in all of us which rejoices to see the genuine thing prevail against the plausible.' Yeats described this venture as 'the first contest between the old commercial school of theatrical folk and the new artistic school.' It ended on a note of expectancy. Like Samuel Butler, Shaw had shown 'that it is possible to write with great effect without music, without style, either good or bad, to eliminate from the mind all emotional implication and to prefer plain water to every vintage . . .' To Shaw himself Yeats's criticism was as deaf-and-blind as that of another dramatic critic, the Prince of Wales (later Edward VII) who, outraged at the violation of military decorum, kept repeating: 'The man is mad, the man is mad.'

Shaw countered such attacks by claiming to be so unoriginal a dramatist as to have been driven 'to take all my dramatic material either from real life at first hand, or from authentic documents . . . all my audacious originalities are simple liftings from stores of evidence which lie ready to everybody's hand'. The inventory of his military authorities includes Lord Wolseley and General Horace Porter; General Marbot's narrative of the Battle of Wagram (from which comes the story of Stolz's death); Zola's *La Débâcle* which had been published in 1892; and as a corrective to Tennyson's 'Charge of the Light Brigade', the eighth volume of Kingslake's *Invasion of the Crimea* (1887). Even Bluntschli's proposal for the hand of Raina (four thousand tablecloths, ten thousand knives and forks, etc.) 'is a paraphrase of an actual proposal made by an Austrian hotel proprietor for the hand of a member of my own family'. And so: 'I created nothing; I invented nothing; I imagined nothing; I perverted nothing; I simply discovered drama in real life.'

The non-fiction argument, which is awkward to refute, does little to convince because Shaw ignores the central viewpoint of *Arms and the Man*: that it is the adult world of warfare seen through the eyes of a child. Shaw contrasted the child's clear-eyed simplicity with the farcical sophistication of parents trying to escape the consequences of their own childhood upbringing. *Arms and the Man* is a 'play' in the sense of its being a childish activity. Every stage trick in its clockwork machinery 'suggests a puppet play for human actors, or a moving toy shop', writes Margery Morgan. '. . . The ease with which Shaw regressed to childishness can be regarded as a sign of psychological weakness and emotional immaturity . . . [but] released within the frame of the play, it is this childishness that constitutes Shaw's genius. He used it as a means of attacking insidiously and openly every form of humbug and pretentiousness, including the unnaturalness of moral virtue that children . . . instinctively detect . . .'

Shaw was particularly exasperated when his deconstruction of heroism – professional soldiers who carry chocolates instead of cartridges and weep when scolded; battles waged mostly by paperwork and won through ludicrously lucky errors – was treated not in the tradition of Cervantes but as mere Gilbertian cynicism. He had used some of the same theatrical devices as W. S. Gilbert, but to a different end. Gilbert was the child who mimicked the adult world; Shaw was the child who saw through it. In a letter to Archer, Shaw explained what he felt was the quintessential difference:

'Gilbert is simply a paradoxically humorous cynic. He accepts the conventional ideals implicitly, but observes that people do not really live up to them. This he regards as a failure on their part at which he mocks bitterly. This position is precisely that of Sergius in the play . . . I do not accept the conventional ideals . . . My whole secret is that I have got clean through the old categories of good & evil, and no longer use them even for dramatic effect. Sergius is ridiculous through the breakdown of his ideals, not odious from his falling short of them. As Gilbert sees, they dont work; but what Gilbert does not see is that there is something else that does work, and that in that something else there is a completely satisfactory asylum for the affections.'

With a confusing paradox for someone presenting a fairy tale to follow Yeats's fairy tale, Shaw defined romanticism as extended immaturity. The beautiful Raina, for instance, had learnt it ('the noble attitude and the thrilling voice') in her nursery. 'I did it when I was a tiny child to my nurse. She believed in it . . . I do it before Sergius. He believes in it.' The contrast between Sergius, the Bulgarian, with the chivalric ideal of personal honour and heroism, and Bluntschli, the capable unaffected Swiss mercenary, had its origin in the different styles of socialism presented by 'the uncompromising Impossibilist and Revolutionary Socialist Cunninghame Graham' and the 'cool, practical, efficient Fabian Socialist Sidney Webb,' Shaw acknowledged. '. . . The scene in which Bluntschli knows all about the forage difficulty, and sits down and settles the business of the regiments off hand, is Sidney Webb to the life'; while Sergius's 'I never withdraw' was uttered by Cunninghame Graham in reply to a request from the Speaker of the House of Commons to take back a 'damn' he had flung at Asquith. In the contest between the two men for Raina's affections, though it is Bluntschli who holds all the winning cards, it is Sergius for whom Shaw has more compassion so that, in theatrical terms, it is always possible on the night for the balance between them to shift. It was essential therefore that Sergius be seen not as a blusterer and humbug, but a man of tortured sensitiveness who lives up to his ideal better than most men: 'a movingly human figure', as Shaw described him, 'whose tragi-comedy is the true theme of the play.' The love-scenes with Raina, both struggling to keep up the high tone, are conducted as if 'they are holding their breath under water'. For Sergius' theory of what a perfect lover, patriot, soldier, gentleman should be is a passion with him; he is straightforwardly sincere in his devotion to heroic ideals. 'But being keen enough, and with a strong sense of ironic humor, he has glimpses of the fact that the world is not built to fit the chivalric ideal,' Shaw wrote to A. B. Walkley.

'He feels more or less consciously that his own conformity to that ideal is forced; and he finds himself dropping into games that are quite incompatible with it. He is conscious of a lack of integrity: he is a hero certainly: the cavalry charge and his scrupulously high minded relations with Raina prove that; but what about the fellow who flirts with Louka behind Raina's back, who says bitter things of other men because he is not promoted, who exclaims 'No, No' by irresistible impulse when Raina asks him has he been flirting, though the truth is 'Yes, Yes,' . . . He is full of doubts about himself; and when Louka's taunt gets home he cries 'Damnation! Oh damnation!! Mockery, mockery everywhere! – everything that I think is mocked by everything that I do' (which is really an injustice to himself). The end is tragic; for when the chivalric ideal proves quite impracticable he takes the Gilbertian, Larochefoucaldian line & denounces life as a farce. He does not see that the error lies in the falsehood of the ideal: he thinks it arises from the inadequacy . . . of human nature. And he dies in the breach, so to speak, marrying Louka sooner than withdraw . . .'

It is Bluntschli who points out that only the romantic ideal of life is farcical: life itself is 'something quite sensible and serious.' When Raina asks him how he found her out, he tells her: 'Instinct, dear young lady. Instinct, and experience of the world.' Though Sergius chides him with having no magnetism ('youre not a man: youre a machine'), Bluntschli continues to have the better of their exchanges until Shaw, with a characteristic volte-face, suddenly reveals him to have been a suppressed romantic all the time. In one area his instinct is blind and he has no experience. This romanticism is more Shavian than Webb-like: he cannot see (because of a secretly low opinion of himself) that Raina is in love with him – a blindness that qualifies him to be, in her words, 'a romantic idiot'. So the virus of romance may spread anywhere and thrive even among those who, in their prosaic way, seem mercifully exempt.

'On my honor it was a serious play,' Shaw protested ' – a play to cry over if you could only have helped laughing.' But the 'tragedy' with which he insisted he had replaced Gilbertian 'heartlessness' was again a nursery view of what is tragic: a petit tragedy – though a delightful comedy. The attempt to show pragmatism and instinct in triumphant league against idealism and rationalism was ingeniously outflanked by the public's instinctive, and the critics' reasoned, misunderstanding. To contend with this Shaw changed the subtitle from 'A Romantic Comedy' to 'An Anti-Romantic Comedy', but the joyous misapprehension continued to swell, finally exploding in Oscar Strauss's comic opera *The Chocolate Soldier* ('that degradation of a decent comedy into a dirty farce', as Shaw called it, in which 'Bluntschli was made a wretched little poltroon, Sergius a coward and a boaster, Petkoff a *vieux marcheur*, and all the women *cocottes*'). From this 'loathsome plagiarism' Shaw struggled to keep legally, financially and explicitly clear for many years, inserting below the title (in lieu of royalties): 'With apologies to Mr BERNARD SHAW for an unauthorized parody on one of his comedies.'

*Arms and the Man* ran for fifty performances between 21 April and 7 July, and was followed by a provincial tour and an acclaimed production in America. But even this, Shaw maintained, was not authentic. The play, he told Edward McNulty, had 'been manufactured into a London success at a net loss of about £4,000. Roughly speaking, it has extracted some £1,500 from the public pocket; and numbers of very clever and distinguished people have come repeatedly (for nothing). The curious thing – to an outsider – is that this is the case with most London successes.'

Shaw had doubts over *Arms and the Man*, telling Alma Murray ten years later it was a 'flimsy', 'fantastic' and 'unsafe' play. Though his claims that it 'taught the public what soldiering is really like' appeared to be vindicated when, during the Boer War, Queen Victoria presented her troops with boxes of chocolates, he cannot have been happy with the use of a stage device such as the rediscovered overcoat. In the contest between 'the old commercial school of theatrical folk and the new artistic school', Shaw the new artist felt he had borrowed too much from the armoury of the old commercial school. It was nearly, but not quite, the masterpiece he needed.

His royalties from *Arms and the Man* at the end of 1894 came to £341 15s. 2d. That autumn, after seven years of continuous musical criticism, he dropped his column in *The World* and immediately gave up going to musical performances: 'I had not before realized the severity of the strain or the attention involved by musical criticism,' he noted in his diary. It seemed as if, in entering his thirty-ninth year, he had at last achieved popularity. 'When you take a theatre of your own,' he told the manager of the Avenue Theatre, 'just bring me pen and ink, a ream of paper, a bottle of ginger beer, and a few beans, and you shall have the most brilliant play of the century to open with.' But privately he knew the quicksand on which he was advancing. 'I have taken the very serious step,' he confided to McNulty, 'of cutting off my income by privately arranging to drop the World business at the end of the season; and now, if I cannot make something out of the theatre, I am a ruined man; for I have not £20 saved; and Lucy and Kate Gurly (my mother's half-sister) are now members of the family. I am about to begin the world at last.'

## [ 4 ]

*I hereby warn mankind to beware of women with large eyes, the crescent eyebrows, and a smile, and a love of miracles and moonshees. I warn them against all who like intellectual pastimes; who prefer liberty, happiness and irresponsibility to care, suffering and life; who live for and in themselves instead of for and in the world; who reject the deep universal material of human relationship and select only the luxuries of love, friendship, and amusing conversation.* (1896)

Using a string of his own words, Shaw had wanted to tie Janet Achurch's theatrical genius to the opportunities and money provided by Florence Farr. But Janet (goaded, Shaw believed, by Charrington) had been greedy, Florence felt slighted, and the knot came apart even as he was tying it. 'Why had you not the handling of that Avenue season?' he upbraided Charrington, '. . . solely because you hated her [Florence], humiliated her, looked at her artistic ambitions with pure murder in your eye . . .' The Charringtons were disillusioning him in their lives; but Florence had disenchanted him on the stage – a more serious business. Her performance in Todhunter's play had been shocking, and Shaw's relegation of her from the part of Raina to that of Louka represented a fall in his estimation, almost a fall from grace. Florence was aware of this. Walking back from the Avenue Theatre in the evenings with Yeats, they would often discuss Shaw: her diabolical mentor and his mechanical man. What feelings lived under that bright surface and, among all that rattle of words, what poetry? Even his laughter was like the shattering of beauty. For all his knowledge, his vitality, his busy politics, there seemed (except for its impenetrable absence) no mystery, no beating of a religious pulse. Florence, like Yeats, had been caught up in the epidemic of occultism overtaking traditional Western religion. She had looked into Egyptology and Babylonish lore, hovered over astral projections, investigated alchemy, covered the walls at Dalling Road with Oriental drapery, practised the hermetic arts; and she was about to be promoted to Praemonstratrix in the ineffable Order of the Golden Dawn. As she ascended in this theosophical hierarchy, the chasm separating her aspirations from her abilities, lit up by the footlights, vanished.

This period had been made more awkward by raids on Shaw's room by Jenny Patterson, who sent pieces of Florence's correspondence to her sister, a married lady living near Worcester, with much anonymous urging of her to intervene. Shaw had meanwhile been pressing Florence to get herself divorced from the ever-absent Edward Emery; and eventually in 1894 she agreed. The procedure, which involved an accusation of adultery, was unpleasant but by February the following year the decree was made absolute. Shaw used the technicality of her freedom to chide Janet Achurch: 'There will be a mail in tomorrow, I suppose: and if I hear nothing then, F. F. shall be Mrs Bernard Shaw at the earliest date thereafter permitted by statute'. But to Florence, as to May Morris, he said nothing. Divorce, which he had urged on her for any number of generously unromantic reasons, was the end of their story. So, two days after this divorce, it was not Shaw but Yeats who travelled to Dalling Road. He came bearing esoteric apparatus and escorted by a mediumistic chemist's assistant. Together they drew the curtains and unwrapped their miracles. It was a relief to turn from the hectic Shavian vocabulary to the less demanding presence of Yeats. In the company of this stooping demonologist, with the cadaverous face and neglected teeth, the matching black sombrero, voluminous tie and trousers, Florence's consonants withered, her phonetics fell away and the athletic articulation drilled into her by Shaw sighed to a stop. Yeats provided for her a single twanging instrument. She began to replace Shaw's elocution with Yeats's cantilla-tory polemics, put down Fabian and picked up magical tracts. She meditated on colours, plucked interesting discords, muttered verse invocations and trance-like intonements that intensified 'ordinary twad-dling,' Shaw protested, 'into a nerve destroying crooning like the maunderings of an idiot-banshee'.

It was now Yeats's turn to see Florence as a 'great success'. Her tranquillity dazzled him. He felt 'a necessity' to 'launch Mrs Emery'. She was a fairy child and would make his poetry a garden for magical thought; for that magical revolution humming within the Chanted Word. 'Cats do the same thing when they are serenading one another,' advised Shaw; and even Yeats (though tone-deaf) spoke of her giving 'the worst performance on the psaltery I have ever heard' – adding: 'There are times when she makes me despair of the whole thing.'

By manipulating occult spells with Shavian relentlessness Florence disenchanted both Shaw (who did not believe these miraculous rituals) and Yeats (who believed that such relentlessness was destructive). In time she dismissed both her Irish champions as 'half-baked' and, as the headmistress of a prim and prosperous boarding school for Hindu girls in Ceylon, went on to end her days in 'the society of the wise'. 'And now you think to undo the work of all these years by a phrase & a shilling's work of exoteric Egyptology,' Shaw had railed at her, continuing in the style of *Candida*'s Marchbanks.

'As for me, I can wait no longer for you: onward must I go; for the evening approaches. To all you flowermaidens I have given more than you gave me, and offered more than any of you would take. My road is the highroad; and your by paths and shortcuts only lead backward . . . Now a great horror & weariness comes on me. I cannot help anyone except by taking help from them; and you cannot help me. You have brains and imagination – the means of deceiving yourself, without faith, honor, heart, holiness – the means of saving yourself. I have the greatest regard for you; but now to be with you is to be in hell: you make me frightfully unhappy . . . Forgive me; but you have driven me to utter desperation . . .'

What had gone wrong? When he called on her he had found her 'busy with somebody over the papers of her Occult Society,' or 'her windows were dark [and] I did not go in'. When they did spend time together 'to my great annoyance I bungled the meeting with FE'. He began sleeping badly – and waking late. He could still outstay Yeats, as he had outstayed Jenny Patterson's suitors, because his plays took longer to read than Yeats's. But in November 1894 they ceased being lovers. Fabian and Occult forces had pulled them as far apart as the North and South Poles. They were still friends. Strolling pleasantly through Richmond Park in the spring of 1895, they chatted about bicycling and literature, but kept what they really cared for to themselves. She lured him with a casual reference to the quarter of a million pounds that Annie Horniman might give her for another theatrical enterprise; but her heart was not in it, and he was not seriously tempted. Their excitement in each other's company had evaporated, leaving a frightful vacuity. 'It must be that she has no religion,' Shaw concluded – which was her conclusion about him. 'I declare before creation,' he wrote to her, as the ashes glowed for a moment in the autumn of 1896, 'that you are an idiot, and that there never has been, never can be, is not now, nor in any yet to be discovered fourth dimension of time ever shall be, so desperate and irreclaimable an idiot, or one whom Destiny has mocked with greater opportunities'. His own sense of loss was painful. He had so little heart, he told another actress, 'that when it kindles for ten minutes once a year I hasten to cry out what I feel, lest I should die without having once done anything to save life from emptiness'.

They continued to see or correspond with each other, amiably and obligingly, but with longer intervals, almost until 1912, when Florence travelled to Ceylon and, at the request of Sir Pannamballam Ramanathan, was appointed the first principal at his College for Girls. There she died in 1917; and thirty years later, after reading her story in the *Ceylon Daily News*, Shaw (then in his nineties) confessed himself astonished. 'I thought that Yeats and I knew her through and through, as far as there was anything to know,' he wrote. 'I now see that we did not know her at all.' To Yeats she had appeared to move 'upwards out of life' to her 'unnoticed end'. From both her Irishmen she had learned little; or else she had mislearned. But Shaw had no doubt that Pannamballam Ramanathan had 'opened her mind and developed the real woman. I should have said that she was the last woman on earth to become the authoritative head of a college, or to break her way out of the little cliques in which she figured in London, and find a spiritual home in philosophic India. I was wrong. I was the wrong man for her, and I am deeply glad that she found the right one after I had passed out of her life.'

[ 5 ]

*It is only the people who have the courage and independence to let themselves go without scruple who discover what a terrifically powerful instinct chastity is . . .*

Shaw's tribute to the unknown knight, Sir Pannamballam Ramanathan, as 'the right man' for Florence who had 'developed the real woman' was grounded in the knowledge and belief that their relationship (unlike those with Yeats and himself) was sexless. In leaving Jenny Patterson for Florence, Shaw had renounced a love that was exclusively sexual; in turning from Florence to Janet Achurch in the mid-1890s he was giving up all sex as an ingredient in love and replacing it with a liaison that sought fulfilment through the planting of his words in the woman he loved so that she could bring his plays to life. Florence had been sterile – but sterile on the stage. 'I renounce spiritual intercourse with you,' he told her. But it was sexual intercourse he was renouncing and spiritual intercourse with Janet he was taking up. 'I have become a sort of sublime monster, to whose disembodied heart the consummation of ordinary lives is a mere anti-climax,' he wrote to Janet early in 1896.

'Do you know who will buy for twopence a body for which I no longer have any use? I have made tolerable love with it in my time; but now I have found nobler instruments – the imagination of a poet, the heart of a child, all discovered through the necessity – the not-to-be denied inmost necessity – of making my way to an innocent love for Janet.'

*

There had been a moment when, quailing before the elephantine challenge of Janet with her interfering husband, her heavy drinking, her drugs, Shaw turned to 'a destroying angel in a bonnet', the Ibsen actress Elizabeth Robins, a woman of prim intensity and devastating stage pathos. Elizabeth was an enigma. For several months, though she took care to see little of him, she had been married to an American actor, George Parks, who (wearing a suit of stage armour) had stepped into the Charles River in Boston, and drowned. It showed how dangerous men were. Dressed in beautiful black weeds, Elizabeth had sailed to England. But even here, she discovered, there were men. How did she know that they were not following her? There seemed no place, not even St Paul's Cathedral, they did not penetrate, staring, standing, breathing . . . It was disgusting! Some of them actually spoke to her; others had helped her across a busy street in broad daylight. She felt safer in the world of Ibsen.

Elizabeth Robins had visited Norway; she had been wonderfully impressed too by Janet Achurch in *A Doll's House*; and in 1891 she had come with her chaperon to see William Archer about a translation of *Hedda Gabler*. Her performance as Hedda that April at the Vaudeville Theatre was described by Archer, reviewing it in *The World*, as 'the finest piece of modern tragedy within my recollection. Sarah Bernhardt could not have done it better.' The anti-Ibsenites had been equally assured. 'It was like a visit to the Morgue,' declared Clement Scott in the *Daily Telegraph*; while the *Pictorial World* described it as a 'hideous nightmare of pessimism'. Shaw, who saw the production two or three times, assured Elizabeth Robins that 'you may safely accept all the compliments you get about the play and the part. I never had a more tremendous sensation in a theatre . . .'

In this battle over Ibsen, Shaw could be in no doubt where his loyalties lay. Yet the army of British Ibsenites, like the army of socialists, was divided and as opposition to Ibsen began to recede so these divisions grew. Elizabeth was Archer's protégée and therefore a rival to Shaw's Janet. Both Archer and Shaw seem to have been attracted to Elizabeth's beauty and talent. Archer's enthusiasm, acting on his Scottish puritan temperament, turned him into a wooden thing – or, as Elizabeth judged, a perfect gentleman. It was like being in the room with a piece of furniture; she

311

could even dismiss her chaperon. But Shaw was a cad. His curdling flattery-and-effrontery revolted her. He implied that Archer was not unaware of her sex appeal; he begged her not to mind his Irish suggestiveness; he boasted that her 'lustrous eyes' would never turn his head; he threatened, before her production of *The Master Builder* in 1893, to call informally at her apartment for the purpose of interviewing her – and he actually came! Very properly she refused to speak to him without the presence of her co-producer. Pointing at a revolver she announced that she would shoot him if he wrote anything, and next day dispatched an icy note regretting 'to have been the occasion of your wasting so much time'. Her lack of humour was irresistible to Shaw. Never had he scored such a professional success, he declared; her offer to shoot him would have made any professional man's fortune. 'Will you just look at this rough sketch of the interview you were good enough to give me on Saturday, and say what you think of it,' he queried.

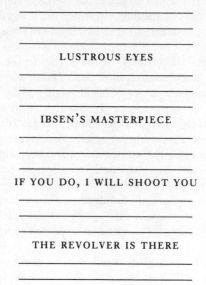

SENSATIONAL HEADINGS ad. lib.

LUSTROUS EYES

IBSEN'S MASTERPIECE

IF YOU DO, I WILL SHOOT YOU

THE REVOLVER IS THERE

&c. &c. &c.

He concluded with the promise not to play more pranks on her if she now gave him the interview with her co-producer. But he had already gone too far.

312

Locked in misunderstanding, they continued to behave to each other with ludicrous obtuseness. Elizabeth felt convinced that all men were potential rapists; Shaw was determined that woman was the huntress and man her prey. Each was a poor specimen of the other's beliefs. Disliking the 'cold stupidity' of her ladylike posture, Shaw enjoyed addressing her as 'Saint Elizabeth' or 'Holy Elizabeth'. Drawing herself up in the character of an American lady, she demanded that he 'use the customary forms of address. My name for you is Miss Robins; and I do not see that the fact of my being an actress entitles anyone to call me by any other name.' Shaw would often campaign for the collective respectability, financial equality and independence of actresses; yet it was hypocritical, he felt, to pretend that the sex instinct did not interfere with individual negotiations between men and women in the theatre. She demanded, as a representative of the modern actress, to be treated as a professional person. He invited her to 'come and play the guitar to me and fascinate and flatter me'; chided her for not having 'petted me, bought me some candy, and wheeled me home in a perambulator'; and accused her of treating him like 'a mere pincushion to stick your inverted commas into'. She drew herself higher, outraged and apprehensive over his appalling lapses in taste. What would happen if his letters were stolen? 'I kiss your beautiful hands and your healing eyes,' he had written: 'you are my wonderful good fortune, my treasure, my one utterly fulfilled desire, my ennobler and my darling. I ask nothing more: it is enough: now let the world work me like a dog until it wears me out: I have had my pay and am content.' Posted out of mischief, such a letter was designed to compromise her. 'I cannot prevent your speaking of me in a misleading fashion behind my back,' she reprimanded him, 'and putting your own interpretation upon my motives and conduct, but if the future should by chance bring us into relation again, either by letter or word of mouth, it is as well you should know the terms upon which I am accessible.'

In their avoidance of sex Elizabeth had glorified the brother-and-sister relationship, and Shaw dreamed of supplanting a wife with a mother. Both wanted to free one sex from the power of the other, to trade women's financial independence for men's sexual immunity. But the only way Shaw could overcome his vulnerability to women who interested him was to envelop their bodies with his words, and then fall in love with his own verbal creation. What attracted him to Elizabeth was that, like his mother, she was at best indifferent to him. She did not believe he would ever succeed as a playwright and when he offered to write a leading part 'especially designed for you & all the other parts about six lines long,' she heard only the voice of the seducer – like an artist offering to do an etching of her. Her apprehensions were confirmed when he sent her *Mrs Warren's*

*Profession*, a play about prostitution. 'It was black ingratitude to try and let you in for this villainous play which is quite unworthy of you,' Shaw admitted. It was a play 'in my most odious vein'; yet, granted that he was odious, that she could not endure him, could they not for stage purposes use each other? 'What has frightened you?' he asked. What had frightened him? This fear was what they shared, and it prevented them from becoming what Ibsen would have called an 'episode' in each other's lives.

*

While Shaw was still involving himself with Florence and hazardously experimenting with Elizabeth Robins, the Charringtons had been sinking. A quintuple bill they presented at Terry's Theatre in 1893 including, besides plays by J. M. Barrie, Conan Doyle and Thomas Hardy, a farce by Lady Colin Campbell, had prompted some critical acclaim; and closed after a week. 'Then smash!' Charrington explained; cheaper lodgings, unsuccessful scripts, smaller parts, shifty deals. 'You dont believe in yourself enough,' Shaw exhorted Janet: 'You are not yet good enough for your own destiny. You will never convince the world except in masterpieces; and you lack severity of taste and thought for them as yet.'

Though Janet had played Nora in *A Doll's House* (after whom she had christened her daughter), unlike Ibsen's Nora she could not slam the door on her husband – and he would ruin her, if she continued to trust in him. But from the practical consequences of his own advice (which he partly concealed in paradox: 'you set yourself to back up Charrington . . . you helped materially to ruin him') Shaw instinctively shrank. He could not enact his beliefs since he was obsessively replaying the old triangular liaison. Until the autumn of 1894 he could find no way of dissolving his sexual attraction for Janet into his admiration for her talent. Then, on 2 October, following another visit to Italy with the Art Workers' Guild – during which he saw the Renaissance sculpture at the Bargello in Florence, particularly admired Raphael's pictures in the Uffizi and the Palazzo Pitti as well as a Botticelli Virgin and Child in Milan, and made a special examination of the Carlo Felice Theatre in Genoa – he began *Candida*, his 'modern pre-Raphaelite play'. 'Titian's Virgin of the Assumption in the Accademia in Venice, and Correggio's in the dome of the cathedral in Parma,' afterwards remembered, 'boiled down into Cockney Candida.' In the Preface he was to write four years later to *Plays Pleasant*, he described it as a religious play. 'Religion was alive again, coming back upon men, even upon clergymen, with such power that not the Church of England itself could keep it out.' Shaw connected this resurgence of religion to socialism; but the religious experience from which his play derived was more subjective.

It was to be their play, his and Janet's. It was to be their salvation together. Candida derived from his mother and was to be replaced by Janet. 'I have been no saint myself – have hunted after one form of happiness occasionally,' he confided to her. 'Janet *recreates* me with an emotion which lifts me high out of that. I become a saint at once and write a drama in which I idealise Janet . . . she rapidly begins to draw on rich stores of life, becomes beautiful, becomes real, becomes almost saintly, looks at me with eyes that have no glamor of morphia in them, and with an affection that is not hysterical . . .' Shaw announced his intention of getting beyond the glamour of Janet's sexual fascination to 'a more human feeling'; a 'heaven, where want is unknown'. *Candida* had been conceived as a spiritual orgasm that was to transport them both to a plane of religious ecstasy. Janet would recreate herself by playing the 'clean dry, strong and straight heroine', the 'true Virgin Mother' Candida, and feel no further need for the stimulants prescribed by Charrington.

In theory, as well as practice, *Candida* contains a curious flaw suggested by the sub-title, 'a mystery', that he later dropped. The Reverend James Mavor Morell, the glib, cocksure Christian Socialist clergyman, is Shaw's pre-Raphaelite; his Raphaelite is Marchbanks, the shy, aristocratic, unconvincing poet. Shaw claimed to have based Marchbanks on De Quincey, though Shelley and Yeats were also to be mentioned as models. 'I certainly never thought of myself as a model,' he objected. Nevertheless, Marchbanks was the vehicle for Shavian beliefs and a silhouette of the almost twenty-year-old Sonny. But by using De Quincey's account of his life as a device behind which to conceal himself, Shaw sentimentalized the part. The rivalry between Marchbanks and Morell over Morell's wife Candida carries echoes from several of Shaw's three-cornered affairs, in particular that of May Morris and Sparling, but was intended as an interpretation of the current drama between himself and the Charringtons. The writing and production of *Candida* was to be a spell, no less magical than the spells of Yeats and Florence Farr, through which Shaw would manifest his will. He had designed the play as *A Doll's House* in reverse, showing the household doll to be the husband. In Candida herself he had written a part at which Janet would excel. Its success, he hoped, would nerve her to separate her interests from Charrington's, emerging from domesticity as an independent actress of genius. That, at any rate, was the play he intended to write; what he actually wrote was something else. 'Candida does not change, as Shaw believed Janet must,' Margot Peters has written.

'She is at the end of the play what she was at the beginning, the mother-sister-nurse-wife of her boy husband Morell, trapped by the very

315

altruism that Shaw was trying to root out of Janet so that she could put herself and her art first. It is Eugene Marchbanks who experiences the metamorphosis from sensuality to spirituality and artistic dedication. Looking upon the suffocating commonplaces of the Morell household, he concludes that domesticity, security, and love are inferior ends compared with the sublime and lonely renunciation of the artist. Shaw thus washed his hands of Janet, leaving her model at home and giving to the poet the exit line he should have given her – and that she had spoken as Nora: "Let me go now. The night outside grows impatient." Shaw the artist closed the door on Janet Achurch with the secret he had meant to tell her unspoken.'

*Candida* is a domestic study in self-deception. Though Shaw suggested it had been written from a 'presentiment' by a 'blind instinct' and that he saw its meaning only after finishing it, he also acknowledged that he might be deceived in what he saw. His meaning was 'no better than anybody else's,' he told Osman Edwards. 'A man may hit out things in fiction that he is not intellectually conscious of and that . . . it may turn out to be something that he himself would have repudiated – also, of course, that his own explanations, if he has offered any, were gross mistakes.'

Nowhere does he confront the implication that his play must have had for Janet, except indirectly when he admitted to W. T. Stead that Marchbanks escaped from the house after discovering that he had 'overrated Candida' and that 'Candida, like the sensible woman she is, knows quite well that Eugene [Marchbanks] is not only too clever for Morell but too clever for *her*, and that in his full maturity he would be far too big a handful for her, both socially & intellectually'. This 'pure' (as her white name indicates) and patronizing Candida was not Janet: she was 'entirely imagined'. But she shares with Janet a sexual charm that she can use to get her own way – and from which Marchbanks disengages himself. But his escape is not a sublimation of lust into admiration; it is rejection – an optimistic re-writing of Lucinda Shaw's rejection of Sonny. For Candida (whom Shaw described on his manuscript as a 'Virgin Mother') was not re-created. She remained, in Beatrice Webb's words, 'a sentimental prostitute'.

The crisis between Candida and Marchbanks comes early in the third act when Candida offers herself ('Do you want anything more?') to Marchbanks. We have been prepared for this and told how to interpret it in her conversation with Morell in the previous act – and the words and situation were as much as the Examiner of Plays would allow. Marchbanks refuses, masking his reason in 'poetic fripperies', optimistically described by Shaw as the instinctive fear of ecstasy descending into domesticity. The poker that Candida holds 'upright in her hand . . . looking intently at the point of it' until it 'must have hypnotised me', and that makes Marchbanks 'horribly uneasy', is converted from an obvious phallic image into an emblem of knightly chastity: 'a flaming sword that turned every way, so that I couldnt go in; for I saw that that was really the gate of Hell'. Morell is led to fear that Marchbanks 'is Candida's "affinity" and that he himself is not,' Shaw explained to W. T. Stead. But the affinity between them is that of mother and son, and the weapon that guards them from Hell is the taboo of incest. It is because the Virgin Mother outlaws sex that she is Shaw's ideal. Candida reduces all men to children by emotional castration. In providing other explanations Shaw falls into the error that he himself had defined so brilliantly in *The Quintessence of Ibsenism* – he idealizes. It is the minor characters who provide the corrective, in particular the secretary 'a brisk little woman of about 30', Miss Proserpine Garnett, nicknamed Prossy. She, as her classical name suggests, represents amorousness unanswered and the physical world in subjugation. She is secretly – though it is an open secret – in love with Morell, and her only expression of love is to make herself his idolizing slave. Others, with whom she is not in love, she can see clearly – such as Candida herself, whose modest qualities she appreciates 'far better than any man can'. But Shaw himself suffered from Prossy's Complaint. He described Candida as being bound by no law and as seducing Marchbanks to exactly the extent she wishes. 'Without brains and strength of mind she would be a wretched slattern & voluptuary', he told James Huneker. 'She is straight for natural reasons, not for conventional ethical ones.' Shaw idealizes these 'natural reasons' – that is to say, her love of Morell – in a way he was far less ready to do after his own marriage. At another level the play opposes the maternal creative force, which may operate through conventional bourgeois marriage, with the artist's need for freedom. Shaw makes Marchbanks's sacrifice of 'happiness for an intenser quality of life' artificial, by cutting poetry off from the complexity of actual life. Sentimental audiences, he said, imagined that Marchbanks flies out of the house broken-hearted, with his excruciating exit lines 'Out, then, into the night with me! . . . The night outside grows impatient'. But the night, he explained, did not mean 'darkness, despair and suicide – an essentially prosaic notion. To the poet the night means the transfiguration of the sordid noonday world by veiling shadows and magical starlight into a poet's world . . .'

But 'night' is an unsatisfactory symbol for poetic maturity. Marchbanks claims to be 'as old as the world now', but he also tells Candida that 'in a hundred years we shall be the same age'. Shaw's afterthought of a 'secret in the poet's heart' may be his acceptance of their eternal incompatibility, of Candida's intellectual and Marchbanks's emotional immaturity, and of Shaw's separation from his mother.

317

Shaw romanticized Marchbanks's chastity, describing him as speaking 'the language of the man recreated by a flash of religion'. But the language of Marchbanks's conversion is the language with which St Joan will choose burning instead of imprisonment: it is the death of 'poetry' through lack of nourishment from the senses and failure in self-knowledge. Marchbanks, not Candida, renounces sex, and it is Shaw's idealism that transfigures this as 'nobler' than happiness. He has not blown away illusions ('free air and holy starlight') but transferred them from people to work ('to do what must be done'), so deferring his disillusion, like Nietzsche's Zarathustra at the end of his discourses: 'Do I seek for *happiness*. I seek for my *work*!' *Candida* was a prophecy rather than the catalyst in Janet Achurch's life Shaw had believed; and that prophecy was to find its fulfilment in the long negotiations over the play's production.

## [ 6 ]

*On the whole, I think I am safer off the stage than on it.*

*Candida* is the most tightly constructed and economical of Shaw's plays, and he hoped it would lead him to the West End. Driven on by the Charringtons' debts, he finished writing it on 7 December 1894, and before the end of the year had tried it out on two leading actor-managers. Charles Wyndham, the most accomplished performer of 'modern' light comedy parts at the Criterion Theatre, had already come to see *Arms and the Man* and agreeably flattered the playwright – only to be sent away with a reading copy of *The Philanderer*. Shaw knew that Wyndham was able to command the perfect balance between caddishness and sensibility for the part of Leonard Charteris, but the sexual content of *The Philanderer* had been too unorthodox. In *Candida*, Shaw now presented him with something apparently more conventional; but Wyndham, wiping his eyes at the end of the final scene, recovered to say that, dear God, it would be a quarter of a century before the London stage was ready for such matter. Shaw also took it to George Alexander, whose St James's Theatre, as the most fashionable playhouse in London, specialized in dramas featuring peers of the realm. One of the handsomest men in England, who had recently caused a sensation with Mrs Patrick Campbell in Pinero's *The Second Mrs Tanqueray*, Alexander offered to play the eighteen-year-old aristocratic Marchbanks if Shaw, to combine an easier disguise with a larger claim for sympathy, would render the poet blind. But, unlike

Shakespeare, Shaw was incapable of such butchery, and had to rest content with Alexander's praise – somewhat mitigated after receiving *The Philanderer*.

Next he pressed it unsuccessfully on Elizabeth Robins; then he read it to Lewis Waller, whose heroic voice had made him a vastly popular stage figure. But Waller, who had just taken over the Haymarket Theatre (opening with Wilde's *An Ideal Husband*), was unrelenting even when Shaw explained that a refusal of *Candida* would inevitably lead to a recital of *The Philanderer*. By reserving the part of Candida for Janet ('no Janet, no Candida'), Shaw had created an extra obstacle for the London actor-managers. But he would not be moved on this, and in February 1895 he decided instead to try the play in America.

There were good reasons for his decision. *Arms and the Man* had been taken the previous year in America by the actor-manager Richard Mansfield who, against Shaw's enthusiastic advice, had played Bluntschli. Mansfield was an Englishman two years older than Shaw who had appeared on the London stage between 1877 and 1882 before emigrating to New York. He was a man who spoke plainly, strongly, though without obvious humour or sometimes meaning. He believed that life was for living, the stage was for actors, and plays were for playing; and he was seldom afraid to say so. Mansfield was not a secretive man. But in the summer of 1894 he had made a secret journey back to England, searching for new exportable talent. The secrecy was forced on him by the rampaging army of creditors he had amassed after his London production of *Richard III*. Like Charles Wyndham, he had slipped one evening into the Avenue Theatre to see *Arms and the Man*; unlike Charles Wyndham he had decided to put it on. Shaw was summoned to see him at the Langham Hotel and, on the strength of having seen him three times before – once as Dr Jekyll-and-Mr Hyde; once in the loss-making *Richard III*; and once on Hampstead Heath in an overcoat and spectacles – he treated him 'with no more respect than if I had been his uncle'. An invigorating antipathy sprang up between them. Each knew better than the other about everything; but each valued the other as a property. A contract, drafted by Shaw, was signed on 9 June 1894 and, some three months later, *Arms and the Man* opened at the Herald Square Theatre in New York where, after sixteen performances, it 'produced reputation, discussion, advertisement', and put Shaw 'to the inconvenience of having a bank account'. By retaining the play in his repertory for the rest of the season and sending it on tour, Mansfield gave Shaw a new theatrical experience: 'It was not an absolute failure.'

It was to Mansfield, on 22 February 1895, that Shaw sent a tantalizing letter about *Candida*, at the same time warning him off that 'dangerous play', *The Philanderer*. 'Now let me ask you whether you can play a boy of eighteen – a strange creature – a poet – a bundle of nerves – a genius – and a rattling good part,' he wrote.

'The actor-managers here can't get down to the age. The play, which is called *Candida*, is the most fascinating work in the world – my latest – in three acts, one cheap scene, and with six characters. The woman's part divides the interest and the necessary genius with the poet's. There are only two people in the world possible for it: Janet Achurch, for whom it was written, and Mrs Kendal. If Janet creates it here, will you pay her fare out and back and give her 300 dollars a week or so for the sake of covering yourself with new and strange fascinations as the poet? By the way, there's probably money in the piece . . .'

Knowing Mansfield's impetuousness, Shaw challenged him to fly straight over to London, play the poet for half a dozen matinées opposite Janet's Candida, and, having set all London buzzing, 'disappear in a flash of blue fire'. There was need for haste. The longer it took *Candida* to achieve success, the less potent would be its spell on Janet. Already she was growing obstreperous; she had made a drunken scene when he took her to the theatre; she had brazenly dyed her hair a heartbreaking yellow; she smoked cigarettes furiously, was 'reckless and invertebrate, out of sorts, sloppy, abandoned in your carriage, quite incapable of exercising any control over yourself'. Despairingly Shaw warned her that 'you will grow fatter; and your flesh instead of being braced and healthy will be slack and open to chills; and you will have heavy sensual eyelids and swimming eyes instead of a clear, open, divine brow; and you will be demonstrative and mendacious and self-indulgent and everything that is damnable. I give you up, indignant with myself for letting my imagination cheat me for the thousandth time with mere germs and potentialities in you which you have not the brute moral strength to realize . . . The fact is, the whole world is incurably addicted to drink . . .'

There was nothing for it, until Janet was reborn in *Candida*, but to wag his finger in this way. His lectures offended her and were a terror to himself lest they ended their relationship. 'But,' he explained, 'all we who are artists are rallied on a narrow ledge about a millionth of an inch broad, which yet makes all the difference between us and the others.'

'A single drop of alcohol will dissolve this ledge away; and once you are past thirty it will not grow again before the next drop comes. I want you to swear off altogether, absolutely and unconditionally. You promised to do it; the doctor told you to do it; and you know yourself you ought to do it . . .

you will go downhill all the rest of your life if you don't do it; and worst of all, you will reduce me to your mere private temperance lecturer if you don't do it . . .

'. . . you will never learn anything from me. In future you may drink and do just as you like: I shall say nothing. When I am really disgusted – genuinely, healthily savage with you – I only annoy you without doing you any good; and when I am not, my remonstrances in spite of myself, are only a long string of flatteries in disguise, the temptation to please you and make you like me being overpowering. You must save yourself: there is no other salvation. And so I step down from the pulpit . . . Forgive this last echo of the for-ever-ended sermon.'

It was Richard Mansfield who, barely in time, thundered to their rescue. He had been intrigued by Shaw's description of *Candida* ('I still play youths of 18. The only trouble is I look too young for the part'), but acting on Shaw's advice stuck in his throat. *The Philanderer*, which he had been sent early in 1895, enabled him to accept Shaw's pleasant play by means of rejecting the unpleasant play as 'not at all pleasant'. In the first week of March he cabled his acceptance to Shaw.

'WILL PLAY CANDIDA WILL ENGAGE JANET WILL COME TO LONDON CONTRACT JANET NOT LESS THAN THREE SEASONS . . . ALL MUST COME NEW YORK QUICK – MANSFIELD'

Shaw had often promised the Charringtons that he would get his plays performed. So now, he confirmed, 'it is all settled and our fortunes are made . . .' The next ten days were hectic. Cablegrams winged continually across the Atlantic, and Shaw was ever by Janet's side, negotiating frantically. She had been fortunate; if Mansfield's wife, the actress Beatrice Cameron, had not injured herself falling on stage, the part of Candida would never have been offered to Janet; and if Shaw had not been her agent she might not have secured a salary of $250 a week. Despite a swirling Fabian programme of meetings and lectures, some travel and several articles on other people's plays, Shaw finished his minutely detailed plan of the stage action ('the full score of Candida and the band parts'), arranged for the prompt copies to be typed and corrected, and had everything ready for the boat on Saturday 16 March. At the station, Janet was so overcome as to take an affectionate farewell of Mansfield's brother Felix (who was travelling with her) under the impression he was her husband Charrington; and Shaw, resembling Bluntschli in the first act of *Arms and the Man*, tottered back shakily to his bed like an exhausted dog, having completed 'a labor which will leave its marks on my constitution until the last trumpet'.

So far as he was concerned, Janet was now on her own. He could no more: 'the time for pupilage is past: you must be left now to your own vigilance and conscience as an artist.' Yet wherever she went Shaw's voice went with her. In his anxiety he pounded her with all the advice on abstinence from which he had himself promised to abstain. Unlike Owen Jack or Professor Higgins he seemed unable to leave his pupil alone. He prescribed the articles of an efficient digestion: distilled water, oatmeal bannocks, walnuts, honey and peaches. 'I urge you to go to church once a day at least to tranquillise your nerves . . . The religious life is the only one possible for you. Read the gospel of St John and the lives of the saints: they will do everything for you that morphia only pretends to do.' He listed all those tricks and habits and vanities that stabbed him in the heart. She must not seek bold type; she must not purr or smoke; she must not place New York at her feet; she must not be fringy or fluffy. He recommended she part her hair in the middle – better still, send for a barber and 'have your hair shaved absolutely bald. Then get a brown wig . . .' So hatted and unsexed she would gain in comely dignity, like the Madonna by Antonio Rosselino he had seen at Santa Croce in Florence, or 'the Virgin Mother in every carpenter's wife'.

Having told her what way to go, he told Mansfield to let her go her own way. 'She comes from Manchester,' he explained, 'she will grab everything you try to keep from her . . . Give her everything she dares ask . . . I hereby authorize you to announce her as the authoress of the play, if that will please her.'

He had condescended to everyone's follies, and now he awaited the results. They came swiftly and with explosive force: a cablegram from Janet telling him and Charrington that well before its production *Candida* had been withdrawn. It seemed that she and Mansfield, far from being transformed by Shaw's words, had never been more themselves. In Mansfield's opinion there were only two things wrong: Shaw's play and Shaw's actress. He was emphatic. *Candida* was 'lacking in all the essential qualities'. Mansfield could see too that Shaw had put a lot of himself into the play, and there, perhaps, lay the fault: it was not a play at all, but simply 'talk-talk-talk'. Now, as Mansfield knew, the world was tired of all this morbid talking and philosophy and womanish whatnot – a bustling, striving, pushing, stirring American audience wouldn't stand for it or sit through it, and Mansfield, who wholeheartedly agreed with them, refused to be sacrificed to their scorn. 'All the world is crying out for deeds – for action!' he informed Shaw.

'When I step upon the stage I want to act – I'm willing to talk a little to oblige a man like you – but I must act – and hugging my ankles for three mortal hours won't satisfy me in this regard . . . people are not satisfied with only the hors d'oeuvres at dinner – where is the soup & the fish & the roast & the game and the salad and the fruit?'

But Mansfield was no corpulent bigot – he could see that *Candida* had charm, so there was no occasion for Shaw to feel unsettled by his words. On the contrary, 'Go on, Shaw,' he urged; 'Beatrice & I are with you – you will be always as welcome as a brother. – We want great work from you. – '

On the subject of Janet, too, Mansfield was obligingly frank. 'I couldn't have made love to your Candida (Miss Janet Achurch) if I had taken ether,' he began.

'I never fall in love with fuzzy-haired persons who purr and are business-like and take a drop when they feel disposed and have weak feminine voices. My ideal is something quite different. I detest an aroma of stale tobacco and gin. I detest intrigue and slyness and sham ambitions. I don't like women who sit on the floor – or kneel by your side and have designs on your shirt-bosom – I don't like women who comb their tawny locks with their fingers, and claw their necks and scratch the air with their chins . . .'

This was rejection for Shaw at every level and in the most galling terms. Mansfield's theatrical instinct represented everything that, as a dramatic critic, Shaw was to pit his strength against over the next three years. The paradox was inescapable: Shaw's success in the theatre, begun with *Arms and the Man* and soon to be established with *The Devil's Disciple*, was achieved by a man with whom he could not even remain on speaking terms. Here was an ironic instance of the stage reconciliation of opposites for which Shaw was always experimenting.

He did not show Mansfield's 'indiscreet' letter to Charrington who, his face swelling alarmingly, was fingering Atlantic time-tables and rehearsing the strangulation of Mansfield in New York. Shaw envied Charrington in that moment. 'If only I could be myself and at the same time be a fool ruining you and myself and everybody else,' he lamented in a letter to Janet.

'Charrington is right because he *is* a fool, Parsifal the incorrigible, hating what he doesn't like and loving what he likes, fighting the one and grudging it its crust, backing up the other in the teeth of all justice . . . Those who hate you make difficulties for you; and you remove them. *I* remove difficulties from your path; and you make them – pile them up faster than I can hurl them away. No matter: I will best you in the long run; the great Boyg does not fight, he conquers.'

But not over *Candida*. Two days later Shaw was conceding defeat. 'I have played my last card, and am beaten, as far as I can see, without remedy,' he told Janet.

'I have done what I could; I have scamped none of the work, stinted none of the minutes or sixpences; I have worked the press; I have privately flattered Mansfield and abused you; I have concentrated every force that I could bring to bear to secure you a good show with Candida. Can I do anything more? And how long must I keep my temper with these rotten levers that break in my hands the moment the dead lift comes?'

For once Shaw's equanimity seemed to falter. 'It is the distance that has defeated me,' he complained. But this was no proper defence for a man who believed in the power of words, of literary style, to influence action (though his fear that words could accomplish nothing had been embodied in Morell). Here was the real defeat, in the horrible obsolescence of words, of letters, even before they could be read. Shaw had urged magnanimity and beauty of thought on Janet: 'and when you shew yourself a capable woman (especially in a matter which I have bungled),' he told her, 'the ocean of my heart is moved by a delightful tidal wave'. For magnanimity and beauty of thoughts were having a hard struggle in his own dealings with Mansfield: 'now that the hour of vengeance is come', he insisted, 'I feel myself in perfect goodhumor, and can do nothing but laugh. I have not the slightest respect left for you; and your acquaintance with my future plays will be acquired in the course of your visits to other people's theatres; but my personal liking for you remains unchanged.'

Mansfield produced an unusual effect on Shaw. 'He drives me out of my senses.' Since this often prevented them from addressing each other, Shaw conducted much of his business with Mrs Mansfield, 'which is much pleasanter'. Besides gaining for him some comic detachment, this device enabled him to drive off ugly thoughts with a ritualistic display of Shavian games. He told Mansfield that his wife had 'made a great mistake in not marrying *me*'; and, by way of explanation, he asked Mrs Mansfield, 'What am I to do? – I must abuse him to somebody, or I shall bust; and you dont want me to abuse him to other people, do you? If you hadnt married him I shouldnt have breathed a word of my sentiments to you; but you *did* marry him, and now you must take the consequences.'

The rivalry that Shaw neutralized with this stratagem had begun to show itself in the two men's struggle over Janet. Mansfield offered to produce *Candida* with her in the leading role 'if I need not appear'. But Shaw, believing that Mansfield was looking to put on the play with a bad cast so as to establish its failure 'and prevent Janet from making a success in New

York', forbade him from producing it 'on any terms whatever'. Despite his dislike of Janet, Mansfield invited her to join his company knowing how hard Shaw would be hit if she accepted. But Shaw's influence persisting, she refused and after a week's engagement playing in *Forget-me-Not* at Hoyt's Theatre in New York, surrounded by many exciting rumours of her plans, she sailed in the second week of June back to London.

# CHAPTER VI

## [ 1 ]

*We all swore by the* Saturday; . . . *Life was not worth living without it; it gave us the latest news from the front. And we craned our necks nightly over the gallery rails to see Shaw our champion take his seat among the well-groomed critics in their 'glad rags'. Shaw played up well to us in the gallery.*
Dan Rider, *Adventures with Bernard Shaw*

'The writer revels in the description of the most atrocious and filthy forms of vice – vice so horrible that probably 99 men out of a 100 are unaware of its existence, even supposing that it *does* exist anywhere except in the writer's putrid imagination.'

This was how, in 1885, the *Evening News* had welcomed W. T. Stead's 'hideous' exposé of child prostitution. The author of this onslaught was the paper's editor, Frank Harris. The *Evening News* was in direct competition with the *Pall Mall Gazette*, all editions of which, during Stead's serialized revelations, had sold out. This had been worrying for Harris, who was subsequently overtaken by a spasm of embarrassment at a denunciation largely prompted by the puritan urge of money-making. For it was a curious feature of the literary and journalistic reaction against Victorian puritanism that it should be led by a new style of puritan – of which the author of *Mrs Warren's Profession* was a choice example.

Puritanism existed on one side of Harris's character as a spur to practical achievement. How, after storming Plevna with Skobeleff and careering as a cowboy through America, he had come at the age of twenty-seven to be editor of the Conservative *Evening News*, has remained a mystery. But the method by which he quadrupled its circulation was unmysterious. He had asked himself whether he should edit the paper 'at the top of my thought as a scholar'. On the whole, he thought not. Instead, he halved his age and edited it according to the tastes of a boy of fourteen. Kissing and fighting, he remembered, had been what he had cared for then. So his New Journalists were sent off to the police courts while Harris laboured at home to improve, often out of recognition, items from other papers. He startled his readers with alluring headlines announcing 'Extraordinary Charge Against a Clergyman'; 'Gross Outrage on a

Female'; 'The Marriage Markets of Belgravia'. It was Harris who had reported in scabrous detail the divorce case of Lady Colin Campbell, receiving an indictment for obscene libel that assisted the paper's Tory proprietor in dismissing him in 1886. From this crisis he quickly recovered, replacing John Morley as editor of *The Fortnightly Review*, a sober literary magazine that (as its title somehow fails to suggest) appeared once a month. For a time respectability descended. The sensationalism of the *Evening News* was unknown to the editor of *The Fortnightly*. 'Every month the review appears regularly,' complained Whistler, 'just what one looks for, a work of high-class English mediocrity: lamentable . . .' Yet from time to time Harris would grow restless and pluck aside the skirts of respectability by printing Verlaine's poems, or Wilde's *The Soul of Man Under Socialism* (written after hearing Walter Crane and Shaw speak at a Fabian meeting in Willis's Rooms), or 'A Modern Idyll', his own first short story – deeply offensive to W. T. Stead – about the adulterous passion of a Baptist Minister for one of his deacons' wives.

It was at this period, too, that Harris had first asked Shaw to write for him: 'have you no article ready you could let me have? Is there no subject on which you would like to unbosom yourself in the Fortnightly?' Intermittently during the early 1890s, as part of his policy of permeation, Shaw would hand him contributions on subjects ranging from Home Rule to 'The Religion of the Pianoforte', including early drafts of Fabian Tracts such as *Socialism and Superior Brains*. None of these could have pleased Frederick Chapman of Chapman & Hall, the proprietor-publisher of the *Fortnightly*, to whom 'Bernard Shaw was anathema'. Worse even than his socialist sympathies were Harris's flirtations with anarchism, reflected in an article by Charles Mulato that praised two bomb throwers, 'the sweetest and noblest of men', and led, in the autumn of 1894, to Harris being fired. 'I had never had such a blow in my life,' he calculated. Brimming with misery he retreated to Maidenhead, to be soothed by lessons in punting from 'Willie Grenfell, now Lord Desborough'. But in next to no time he was back in London and had taken over the editorship of the *Saturday Review*, a moribund magazine that, at £560, was being hawked around for the price of one pound per reader.

Harris's private and public lives had walked exquisitely hand-in-hand. While editor of the sensational *Evening News* he had been torridly in love with 'Laura', the one obsessive passion of his life, though diversified, so as to re-establish 'quiet thought and sanity', by several lesser affairs. As editor of the dignified *Fortnightly* he lived smartly in Park Lane as the husband of a woman of 'high position', often entertaining the Duke of Cambridge. But in 1895 the new editor of the *Saturday Review* was a single man, who had turned his back on social and political advancement through marriage and decided to become immortal through his genius as a man of letters. As a platform for this ambition, he wanted to raise the *Saturday Review*, then known as the *Saturday Reviler*, from a finder of faults to a finder of stars. But the stars he gathered round him irresistibly found fault with other luminaries. Shaw's theatre criticism ('Happy is the nation that has no history, and happy the play that has no criticism in this column') led to some managements withdrawing their free seats; and several of the book reviewers were so severe that publishers cancelled their advertisements, obliging Harris to fill the spaces with publicity for pneumatic tyres and South African mining companies.

'The first man I wrote to was George Bernard Shaw,' Harris recalled. Shaw had been summoned to the *Saturday Review* office in Southampton Street during the late afternoon of 4 December 1894. He was, Harris observed,

'thin as a rail, with a long, bony, bearded face. His untrimmed beard was reddish, though his hair was fairer. He was dressed carelessly in tweeds with the inevitable Jaeger collar. His entrance into the room, his abrupt movements – as jerky as the ever-changing mind – his perfect unconstraint, his devilish look, all showed a man very conscious of his ability, very direct, very sharply decisive . . .'

They were as ill-matched as Don Quixote and Sancho Panza: Shaw so slight and tall and idealistically vegetarian; Harris so short and rumbustious, with his intrepid moustaches. And yet, Shaw decided, Harris was 'the very man for me, and I the very man for him'.

\*

There were several reasons for his succumbing to Harris's offer. Although, following Edmund Yates's death, he had been happy to resign as *The World*'s music critic, Shaw was soon missing the bustle and involvement of weekly journalism, in particular the sense of being heard. During the last five months of 1894 he had sent occasional articles to various magazines, but most of his time was filled with lecturing and local electioneering, for which he received no money; and the writing of *Candida*, which was not to earn him anything for several years. Six days after telling McNulty that 'I have taken the very serious step of cutting off my income', he was letting W. T. Stead know that, 'for an extremely handsome inducement', he was open next winter to offers of employment. That October he turned down an invitation to join the staff of a new periodical, the *New Age*, partly because he had just started work on the play, but also because the remuneration was poor and, as its political correspondent, his life would have been unbalanced by lack of occupation in the arts – he might as well step down altogether into Parliament. Harris's offer came at exactly the right time (as he was finishing *Candida*) and guaranteed him a salary of £6 a week – £1 more than Yates had given him: 'not bad pay in those days'. He would end up 'a ruined man', he had predicted to McNulty, 'if I cannot make something out of the theatre'. But it was as theatre critic rather than playwright that he was to make his basic income over the next three and a half years.

Shaw looked forward to working on the *Saturday Review*. He had long wanted to have a regular theatre column. 'I wish for the sake of Ibsen that I could get a turn at dramatic criticism,' he had told Janet Achurch when still employed by *The World*, 'as I have already left all the foes of musical light as dead as a pen can [k]ill them.' There was one qualm that delayed his acceptance of the job: the question of whether a playwright should also play dramatic critic. 'I am myself a particularly flagrant example of the critic-dramatist,' he was to write. '. . . I am no honester than other people.' Why therefore, apart from pride, did he not feel tempted to offer servile puffery to those actor-managers who might produce his own plays?

'The cardinal guarantee for a critic's integrity is simply the force of the critical instinct itself. To try to prevent me from criticizing by pointing out to me the superior pecuniary advantages of puffing is like trying to keep a young Irving from going on the stage by pointing out the superior pecuniary advantages of stockbroking. If my own father were an actor manager, and his life depended on his getting favorable notices of his performance, I should orphan myself without an instant's hesitation if he acted badly . . . Those who think the things I say severe, or even malicious, should just see the things I do *not* say. I do my best to be partial, to hit out at remediable abuses rather than at accidental shortcomings, and at strong and responsible people rather than weak and helpless ones. And yet all my efforts do not alter the result very much. So stubborn is the critic within me, that with every disposition to be as goodnatured and as popular an authority as the worst enemy of art could desire, I am to all intents and purposes incorruptible.'

While Shaw debated with himself, 'Harris urges me strongly to accept that dramatic criticship', he reported to Janet Achurch on 27 December. Five days later, his diary records, 'I began the year by taking the post of dramatic critic to *The Saturday Review* under the editorship of Frank Harris'. That evening, New Year's Day 1895, he went to the Garrick

Theatre to see a 'new and original' play, out of Wagner and into Sardou, called *Slaves of the Ring*, by Sydney Grundy. Next week, readers of the *Saturday Review* were able to share the experience with him.

'It is not a work of art at all: it is a mere contrivance for filling a theatre bill ... Mr Grundy somehow managed to plunge me into the densest confusion as to who was who, a confusion which almost touched aberration when I saw a double leading lady walk on to the stage, both of her in full wedding dress ... The spectacular effect alone of so much white silk was sufficiently unhingeing. But when the two brides proceeded solemnly to marry one another with a wedding ring, I really did feel for a moment a horrible misgiving that I had at last broken through that "thin partition" which divides great wits from madness ... Unfortunately, though the plot was over, it was too late to begin the play. Further, the scene was in a conservatory, lit with so many lamps that Miss [Kate] Rorke could not have made any particular difference by turning down one of them; so she jumped through a palm-tree instead, and cried, "Aha! I've caught you at last," just as the other lady, though now convalescent and in her right mind, was relapsing into her dream ... let me note gratefully that there is no villain, no hero, a quadrille of lovers instead of a pair, and that Mr Grundy's imagination, stretched and tortured as it is on the Procrustean framework of "the well-made play", yet bursts fitfully into activity ...'

## [ 2 ]

*For him [Archer] there is illusion in the theatre: for me there is none.*
'Mr William Archer's Criticisms' (1895)

*The whole world is ruled by theatrical illusion ... The great critics are those who penetrate and understand the illusion: the great men are those who, as dramatists planning the development of nations, or as actors carrying out the drama, are behind the scenes of the world instead of gaping and gushing in the auditorium after paying their taxes at the door.* 'Toujours Shakespeare' (1896)

*... all the world's a stage, unfortunately.* 'Mrs Tanqueray Plays the Piano' (1893)

'I enjoy a first night,' Shaw wrote, 'as a surgeon enjoys an operation.' Sydney Grundy's *Slaves of the Ring* had been a characteristic first night in the West End: a timid drama, posing as a 'problem play' on the social institution of marriage, full of impossibilities, artificialities, insincerities and put on by a fashionable management to please the smart London person. Through Shaw's eyes, the reader of his remorseless weekly operations can feel seeping through him the monotony of those empty-headed entertainments that made up the stock-in-trade of the late Victorian commercial theatre.

Sometimes the evening would open with a claptrap curtain raiser, 'to keep the gallery amused whilst waiting for the plutocracy to finish their dinners and get down to their reserved seats'. Then came the main play – and it was always the same play, either in the routine of never-ending melodrama or all-conquering farce. Melodramas were equipped with inevitable 'French windows' and misdirected bottles of poison. Hung out on the gallows of a plot, their single situation was kept going with raving soliloquies (stirringly accompanied by harps, horns and violins from the orchestra writhing 'like a heap of trodden worms' in its pit); and with maladroit devices whereby the action was waged immaculately off-stage, being either announced to the audience by telegrams or reported by characters staring wildly through the wings. What the melodrama lacked in reality it tried to make up in verisimilitude. Real water cascaded; a couple of horses were led on for the race or polo match; and some actual magazine guns for the battle in the fourth act. Why not, Shaw eagerly enquired, a mad bull to exercise the hero? Real babies, ostentatiously dandled, were popular; and no drawing-room dared reveal itself without an elaborate display of spirit stands, siphons and decanters, combining 'the charms of the private and the public house'. Between expensive drinks the gentleman-hero, husky with emotion, would alternately have his knuckles imprinted with the kisses of kneeling ladies and his back resoundingly thumped by manly men. The villain, with his accomplice the comic Jew, knew he was performing well if the theatre filled with hisses whenever he presented himself to be thrashed by the hero, and at his arrest in the ballroom before the final curtain.

Farces were not so different from melodramas, though the humour was more sanctimonious, depending usually on the underclothing of the ladies, such 'abject little naughtinesses furtively slipped in under cover of the tamest propriety'. And there, upright and silent in the stalls, sat Shaw, isolated in his boredom from the starched and sweating audience; acutely conscious of the bad smells, bad music, humbug and snobbery playing round him; confronted by preposterous plots that 'I not only do not understand, but I feel that I should go mad if I tried to'; his spirits sinking as the hour grew late until 'at such moments I pull out handfuls of my hair, and sit contemplating them vacantly, asking myself what I am doing in such an absurd place as the British theatre'.

The real question that Shaw was asking himself was how, without abandoning all hope, could such an epidemic of idiocy be explained. Money-making in the theatre was founded on the assumption that it was 'impossible to underrate the taste and intelligence of the British public'. To enter a theatre was to go back two hundred years. Theatrical art had become an 'exploitation of popular superstition and ignorance, as the thrilling of poor bumpkins with ghosts and blood, exciting them with blows and stabs, duping them with tawdry affectations of rank and rhetoric, thriving parasitically on their moral diseases instead of purging their souls and refining their senses: this is the tradition that the theatre finds it so hard to get away from'. And this was called giving the public what pleased and amused it. But audiences did not want to be pleased or amused.

'They want to be excited, and upset, and made miserable, to have their flesh set creeping, to gloat and quake over scenes of misfortune, injustice, violence, and cruelty, with the discomforture and punishment of somebody to make the ending "happy". The only sort of horror they dislike is the horror that they cannot fasten on some individual whom they can hate, dread, and finally torture after revelling in his crimes.'

In a number of devastating passages Shaw's anger overflows and brings forth the misery and disgust he feels with his fellow human beings. This is not sexual disgust – he strongly attacks the secretary of the National Vigilance Association for that form of misanthropy ('Human nature and the human body are to him nasty things. Sex is a scourge. Woman is a walking temptation which should be covered up . . .'). Shaw's horror derives from people's inhumanity, their brutality and silliness exploited for profit by theatre managers. He used all his ingenuity to escape the Shakespearian pessimism to which these reflections naturally led. Desperately he joked himself free. After all, the British public could not stand being given what it wanted for long. The indiscriminate bawling and booing, hissing and hooting of the audiences ('like dogs who had been purposely run over'), the shouts of 'Rats!', even the badly-aimed sausage that had landed in his lap were all evidence of their dissatisfaction. Though he wanted the police called in to suppress the obstreperous interruptions of the actors from the gallery ('Let me tell you that you are acting disgracefully' – 'Hear! Hear!'), and the riots and uproars lasting sometimes up to half an hour, Shaw squeezed some hope out of this 'lust of the rabble to mock, jeer, insult, deride, and yell bestially at their unfortunate fellow-creatures'. The managements and syndicates,

332

continuing to rely on the last decade's formulas for success, deserved their audiences' catcalls.

As another sign of hope he pointed to the advance of the suburban theatres with their four-shilling stalls, early hours and absence of that snobbery-behind-the-scenes. The monopoly of the star system, he exulted, had been broken and only progress was safe. 'Let their flatterer slip, as he always does sooner or later, and they are at his throat mercilessly before he can recover himself,' he gloatingly warned. As with critics so with dramatists: 'there is nothing the public despises so much as an attempt to please it.' Obsequiousness never created beauty, it aped fashion, did not produce drama, but a fuss. 'No great play,' he declared, 'can ever be written by a man who will allow the public to dictate to him.' He assured his readers that the business of the playwright, as of the politician, was 'to strive incessantly with the public; to insist on earnest relations with it, and not merely voluptuous ones; to lead it, nerve it, withstand its constant tendency to relapse into carelessness and vulgar familiarity; in short, to attain to public esteem, authority, and needfulness to the national welfare (things undreamt of in the relations between the theatrical profession and the public today), instead of to the camp-follower's refuge of mere popularity . . .'

This was Shaw bringing the philosophy of his *Quintessence of Ibsenism* to the practical matters of stage business. He tried to persuade theatre managers that there was money in Ibsen and Sudermann; he urged British dramatists to raise their courage in the face of that legendary dragon, the great British donkey of the public. Reviewing a poorly received comic opera, *The King's Sweetheart*, as 'a concession to the vulgarity of certain persons described generally as the British public,' he proceeded to make a masterly discovery: 'The result proves that this mysterious body, to whose demands the self-respect of the rest of the world is habitually sacrificed, has no existence.'

Shaw waved his pen and the philistine brute disappeared. The way was clear for masterpieces – and yet it was not clear after all. One man stood obstructing. For although the British public did not exist, it was represented through the patronage of the Lord Chamberlain in the person of his Examiner of Plays. 'He is the Tsar of the theatres, able to do things that no prime minister dare do,' Shaw explained. Early in 1895 the holder of this office, E. F. Smyth Pigott, died, and the press teemed with tributes to his 'admirable discretion', his 'determination to persist in the path that seemed right to him', his 'kindly blue pencil'. To these plaudits, Shaw added his own feeling citation in the *Saturday Review*:

'The late Mr Pigott is declared on all hands to have been the best reader of plays we have ever had; and yet he was a walking compendium of vulgar insular prejudice, who, after wallowing all his life in the cheapest theatrical sentiment (he was a confirmed playgoer), had at last brought himself to a pitch of incompetence . . . He had French immorality on the brain; he had American indecency on the brain; he had the womanly woman on the brain; he had the Divorce Court on the brain; he had "not before a mixed audience" on the brain; his official career in relation to the higher drama was one long folly and panic . . . It is a frightful thing to see the greatest thinkers, poets, and authors of modern Europe – men like Ibsen, Wagner, Tolstoi, and the leaders of our own literature – delivered helpless into the vulgar hands of such a noodle as this amiable old gentleman – this despised and incapable old official – most notoriously was.'

This Dramatic Opinion, described by Shaw himself as 'the most abusive article ever written on a recently dead man', is quintessentially Shavian – and oddly courageous since, while attracting the charge of being 'a cowardly attack on a dead man', it risked a good deal of unpopularity from among the living. It mixes, too, in characteristic style, a personal and impersonal tone. Shaw relentlessly insists that the late censor, a 'stupendously incompetent' man, uttering bushels of 'immoral balderdash', was invincibly well-intentioned, that his 'personal character' was never in question – indeed that he was 'as excellent a man for all private purposes as Charles I'. Humorously exploited, this contrast between the private and professional man works much better than the division he liked to make in his criticism between structure and content, music and meaning. The division heals: for in defending the 'innocence' of the private man he dramatized his professional ignorance.

Shaw had some personal experience of Pigott on whose account, like all dramatic authors, he had had 'to choose between infanticide and abortion'. It was Pigott who had told the Royal Commission in 1892 that all the characters in Ibsen's plays were 'morally deranged' and that William Archer's praise of Ibsen had been a device to make money out of him. It was Pigott, too, who insisted that Janet Achurch, playing the part of a married woman guilty of an early indiscretion, add the words 'I sinned but in intention' (which, to a hail of applause on her first entrance, she would mutter to the conductor). Pigott it was who had banned the centenary performance of *The Cenci* and refused a licence, in 1894, to Sydney Olivier's *A Freedom in Fetters*. Shaw's 'obituary' was a plea for the appointment of a less despotic censor, prepared to take responsibility for licensing those plays on which the growth and vitality of the theatre depended. It made an excellent impression on Frank Harris – and none at all on the Lord Chamberlain. Pigott's successor as his Examiner of Plays was G. A. Redford, an ex-bank manager, who, during his sixteen years in the post, politely refused licences to *Mrs Warren's Profession*, *The Shewing-up of Blanco Posnet* and the original version of *Press Cuttings*.

Several battles in Shaw's long war against this 'Malvolio of St James's Palace' were fought out in the *Saturday Review*. The results of handing over the drama to be purified by a respectable householder without theatrical qualifications were to prevent all question of sex ('and parentage', Shaw added) being treated honestly on the stage and 'to license their improper and flippant treatment'. Hardly surprising that 'English Literature towers high above English Drama,' he wrote, since 'Literature is subject to no judgment but that of its natural masters, the authors'.

To justify his work in the theatre Shaw needed to feel that 'serious drama is perhaps the most formidable social weapon that a modern reformer can wield'. The duty of the Lord Chamberlain's Examiner of Plays was to prevent the theatre having any effect on public opinion. It was clear to Shaw that if his post were abolished, the theatre would revert to being the social and political power it had been before Walpole instituted censorship, and stopped Fielding's stage exposure of parliamentary corruption. Censorship was the seat of blasphemy for Shaw who believed the theatre to be potentially 'as important as the Church was in the Middle Ages'. Here was a double irony. Almost none of his theatrical colleagues agreed with him, but since the justification for censorship sprang from a belief in the influence of the stage, it was the Lord Chamberlain and his Examiner of Plays who shared Shaw's attitude. From the 'idealistic' point of view, which automatically regarded new opinions as questionable, almost everything written by Shaw, whose instinct was 'to attack every idea which has been full grown for ten years', strengthened the case for censorship. It might have been better to adopt the what-does-it-matter attitude of *The Times* dramatic critic, A. B. Walkley, but Shaw could not. He cared too much. So he was left firing off brilliant salvoes at the eternal enemy – though with the suspicion that he was armed with chocolates rather than real ammunition: 'it is perfectly clear to me that it would pay the nation very well indeed to commute the expectations of the Lord Chamberlain and Mr Redford for a lump sum, buy their office from the Queen, and abolish the whole Censorship as a pestiferous sham which makes the theatre a plague-spot in British art.'

*

The censor became a symbolic figure in Shaw's imagination. In the last few months of his employment by the *Saturday Review*, he was to write optimistically of 'a distinct weakening of the jealous and shameless individualism of the last twenty years, and a movement towards combination and co-operation'. But it had been the insane institution of the censorship that had made 'combination and co-operation' impossible during the time he was dramatic critic. The theatre had been sundered when in 1892 a licence had been refused for *The Cenci*, and the Shelley Society had taken over the Grand Theatre in Islington to give a 'private' performance for its members, headed by Robert Browning. Technically, since no money was taken at the door, no licence was needed for what was in law a meeting of a society rather than the public representation of a play. But the censor was not to be so easily cheated. When the annual licence of the Grand Theatre came to be renewed, the lessee found himself obliged to accept a new clause forbidding performances of unlicensed plays on the premises. This warning had been well understood by other managers. After that, the blockade had been run chiefly by the Independent Theatre, which was technically 'private' like the Shelley Society and which operated mainly by using various halls for its theatrical 'At Homes'.

By the mid-1890s, there were two theatres in London. The miserable commercialization compulsory in the West End relied on costly productions and long runs of entertainments judged to be silly enough to appeal to great multitudes of pleasure-seekers. The managers of these theatres competed with one another as to who should present 'the vulgarest and foolishest play'. Between them they dominated the theatrical world with the old playhouse traditions of crudity, profligacy and 'a promise of as much lewdness as the audience will stand, even with all public sense of responsibility relieved by that sanction which the Lord Chamberlain never seems to withhold from anything that is openly and intentionally vile'.

But Shaw's education as a critic had not been confined to the gutter of the West End. In addition to Grein's Independent Theatre he investigated and reported on such academic-revolutionary bodies as the New Century Theatre, started in 1897 by an aspiring combination of enthusiasts – Archer and Massingham, Alfred Sutro and Elizabeth Robins. The glory of such painfully evolved little organs was their freedom both from actor-managership and censorship. Indifferent to public demand, yet wishing to create a taste for the work of those playwrights who seemed to be the most advanced of the time, these enterprises functioned like laboratories where experiments could be tried out on a particular audience. Their repertory of plays gave playgoers such as Shaw almost their only hope of dramatic nutriment. 'The real history of the drama for the last ten years,' he announced, 'is not the history of the prosperous enterprises of Mr Hare, Mr Irving, and the established West-end theatres, but of the forlorn hopes led by Mr Vernon, Mr Charrington, Mr Grein, Messrs Henley and Stevenson, Miss Achurch, Miss Robins and Miss Lea, Miss Farr, and the rest of the Impossibilists.'

Shaw did not attempt to conceal the slaughterous commercial defeat of these Impossibilists; he did not advocate the suppression of popular entertainment and its substitution by Ibsen, Henry James and Sudermann. He argued for the infiltration of the experimental stage repertory into the repertory of the fashionable theatres. It was useless to appeal to Augustin Daly or Henry Irving, who seemed 'fit for nothing but to be stuffed and mounted under glass to adorn the staircase of the Garrick Club'; but if more imaginative actor-managers – George Alexander, for instance, or Herbert Tree at the magnificent new Her Majesty's Theatre – were to insert a series of matinées of serious plays into their popular farce-and-melodrama seasons, they might lay the foundations of a genuine classic theatre. It was in the context of this need for artistic and financial co-operation that he fashioned his own plays and judged the work of contemporary dramatists. 'The smart nullity of the London person is becoming intolerably tedious,' he wrote, 'and the exhaustion of the novelty of the plays constructed for him has stripped them of their illusion and left their jingling, rickety mechanism patent to a disgusted public.'

Yet Shaw the dramatist continued to make use of the very mechanisms he ridiculed as a critic: *Widowers' Houses* had derived from *Ceinture Dorée*; for *Mrs Warren's Profession* he had borrowed the plot of Pinero's *The Second Mrs Tanqueray*; the mechanics of *Arms and the Man* were Gilbertian; *The Man of Destiny*, which he wrote during his first summer as dramatic critic, was 'an old-fashioned play, as completely pre-Ibsen as Sardou or Scribe'; while *You Never Can Tell* he described as 'a frightful example of the result of trying to write for the *théâtre de nos jours*'. What Shaw objected to was the emotional and intellectual limitations imposed by these theatrical disciplines, but he reluctantly accepted some of this machinery as being temporarily unavoidable for those who, like himself, wanted their plays produced in the West End; and so, dividing form from content, he valued such work by how skilfully it permeated the commercial theatre with social and artistic truth.

337

This method of evaluation is most lucidly exploited in his comparative criticism of Pinero and Henry Arthur Jones. Pinero used his artistry for commercial ends: his 'aptitude for doing what other people have done before that makes him a reactionary force in English dramatic literature,' Shaw asserted. It was to destroy the legend of his mastery of stagecraft that Shaw devastatingly analysed the structure of *The Second Mrs Tanqueray*, concluding that it amounted to little more than 'recklessness in the substitution of dead machinery and lay figures for vital action and real characters'. The purpose of much of Shaw's criticism of Pinero was to combat the popular belief that he embodied a new spirit in the theatre. This popularity derived from his subtle powers of flattery – he was 'no interpreter of character, but simply an adroit describer of people as the ordinary man sees and judges them' – and a bogus reputation for courage: 'he has had no idea beyond that of doing something daring', commented Shaw of *The Notorious Mrs Ebbsmith*, 'and bringing down the house by running away from the consequences'. Only for *The Benefit of the Doubt* did Shaw praise Pinero's honesty of perception: 'Consciously or unconsciously, he has this time seen his world as it really is . . .'

But Pinero was a darling of the drawing-room world Shaw detested, while Henry Arthur Jones merely had one foot in its door – and principally for that reason Shaw affirmed, 'I unhesitatingly class Mr Jones as first, and eminently first, among the surviving fittest of his own generation.' Jones did not have Pinero's gentlemanliness and sophistication; but what he lacked in stage ingenuity he made up for in feeling unsmothered by good taste. There was as much social as dramatic criticism in Shaw's notices, for he saw in Jones's plays, which were regularly produced in the West End, the best available chance of beginning the reformation of that fashionable theatre and making it a force for cultural and social change. Jones, he wrote, was 'the only one of our popular dramatists whose sense of the earnestness of real life has been deep enough to bring him into serious conflict with the limitations and levities of our theatre'. From this and other passages in the *Saturday Review*, Jones is presented as working passionately 'from the real', in contrast to Pinero working decorously from fiction – in particular the fictitious world of Thackeray. Shaw builds from this his most imaginative literary device for matching their work. It is the story of Thackeray and Dickens once again, the insider versus the outsider:

'Mr Jones's pictures of society never seem truthful to those who see ladies and gentlemen as they see themselves. They are restricted to Mr Pinero's plays, recognizing in them alone poetic justice to the charm of good society . . . The pictures of fashionable life in [Pinero's] The Princess and the Butterfly, containing, if we accept the mere kodaking, not one stroke that is objectively lifelike or even plausible, is yet made subjectively appropriate in a most acceptable degree by the veil of sentimental romance which it casts over Mayfair. In [Jones's] The Liars, the "smart" group which carries on the action of the piece is hit off to the life, with the result that the originals will probably feel brutally misrepresented.'

Shaw's support of Jones, which he hoped would reveal a small fissure between smart society and the West End theatre, involved much special pleading. Jones's plays, he told readers, were sometimes disappointing because they were poorly performed by actors who had been taken out of routine parts and, for the first time in their careers, given something original, reflecting his own experience in 1897 with You Never Can Tell. Shaw knew that Jones's heroines were apt to die of 'nothing but the need for making the audience cry'; he recognized the tendency of his last scenes to collapse, and his characters to act as if hypnotized by public opinion. But there was a detachment in Jones – 'he describes Mayfair as an English traveller describes the pygmies' – that Shaw laboured to encourage.

Yet sometimes he would feel a revulsion from all this special pleading. Jones's observation of society, as observed by Shaw, was similar to that of Pinero.

'Those safe old hands Pinero, Grundy, and Jones, cautiously playing the new game according to the safe old rules, fail to retrieve the situation . . . the public are getting tired of the old-fashioned plays faster than the actors are learning to make the new ones effective . . . The managers do not seem to me yet to grasp this feature of the situation. If they did, they would only meddle with the strongest specimens of the new drama, instead of timidly going to the old firms and ordering moderate plays cut in the new style.'

This complaint was written in the same month, July 1895, that he made an abortive attempt, with his first shot at You Never Can Tell, to fashion a moderate play for the West End, cut in its new style. After the experience of having his first five plays turned down by every commercial theatre in London, he had gone to these theatres as a dramatic critic and seen, with deadly repetition, productions of plays more awful than anyone who had not been there would believe. Humiliation and grievance had fuelled his criticisms; he had mocked, goaded, tiraded in the Saturday Review, against the whole scatter-brained institution. As a dramatic critic he was revolutionary; and as a dramatic critic he had represented himself as a revolutionary dramatist. 'Some plays are written to please the author,' he wrote; 'some to please the actor-manager (these are the worst); some to please the public; and some – my own, for instance – to please nobody.' He conceived the motive behind *Widowers' Houses* and *Mrs Warren's Profession* as being similar to that behind Richard Dudgeon's *acte gratuit* in *The Devil's Disciple*. 'The progressive man,' he declared, 'goes through life on the same principle, instinctively making for the focus of struggle and resisting the tendency to edge him out into the place of ease.'

Yet between the author of *Widowers' Houses* and *The Devil's Disciple* (written in 1897), some edging to this position of ease had begun to take place. 'I began my own dramatic career by writing plays in which I faithfully held up the mirror to nature,' he told readers of the *Saturday Review* in the autumn of 1896. 'They are much admired in private readings by social reformers, industrial investigators, and revolted daughters; but on one of them being rashly exhibited behind the footlights, it was received with a paroxysm of execration, whilst the mere perusal of the others induces loathing in every person including myself, in whom the theatrical instinct flourishes in its integrity.' In an article published in *The Humanitarian* in May 1895, Shaw argued that, at periods when political institutions lagged too far behind cultural changes, it was natural for the imagination of dramatists to be set in action on behalf of social reform. But despite this, 'the greatest dramatists shew a preference for the non-political drama . . . for subjects in which the conflict is between man and his apparently inevitable and eternal rather than his political and temporal circumstances'. In writing this, Shaw must have had in mind his own move from 'unpleasant' to 'pleasant' plays. But Pinero also wrote pleasant plays. The greatest dramatists chose subjects that were elementarily natural, Shaw reasoned, out of the comprehensiveness of their philosophy; the minor dramatist, like Pinero, did the same – but for the different reason that, being protected by a vacuous literary environment, he was ignorant of 'the world of politics, business, law, and the platform agitations by which social questions are ventilated'. By such means did Shaw reconcile himself to working in a tradition that he was simultaneously attacking. But how then must the critic differentiate between great drama and merely professional plays? In a passage from the *Saturday Review*, Shaw gave a fine answer.

'. . . vital art work comes always from a cross between art and life: art being one sex only, and quite sterile by itself. Such a cross is always possible; for though the artist may not have the capacity to bring his art into contact with the higher life of his time, fermenting in its religion, its philosophy, its science, and its statesmanship . . . he can at least bring it into contact with the obvious life and common passions of the streets.'

It is this contact that is at the heart of, and makes the heart continue to beat through, Shakespeare's plays. With Pinero, the contact is mainly with social life. But Shaw, by moving the centre of his emotional life on to the stage itself, risked the incestuous conception of a theatrical freak, a living monster born of stage on stage.

As a critic he had banished the bogey of public opinion and invented, not a new theatrical technique, but a new audience to whom he addressed his plays. 'The British public,' he declared, 'likes a sermon, and resents an exhibition of human nature.' If only his early plays had been the dramatized tracts critics had claimed, how popular they would have been! For this mythical public – and bypassing so far as he could the requirements of the censor – he adapted those artificial conventions of the nineteenth-century theatre he had learnt so painfully during his years as dramatic critic, eventually permeating the old traditions of the theatre, as he had urged Henry Arthur Jones to do, with curious new sounds. 'The present transition from romantic to sincerely human drama is a revolutionary one,' he announced: but then he added – 'those who make half-revolutions dig their own graves'. In the *Saturday Review* between 1895 and 1898 there are many passages in which the critic seems to be warning the playwright about the possible dangers of his work: 'Let us have the new ideas in the new style, or the old tricks in the old style; but the new ideas combined with the old tricks in no style at all cannot be borne.'

Shaw's dramatic criticism lies in the classic tradition of Hazlitt and G. H. Lewes. Shaw himself believed that 'Lewes in some respects anticipated me'. He pointed to Lewes's variety of culture, flexibility, fun and particularly 'his free use of vulgarity and impudence whenever they happened to be the proper tools for his job.'

'He had a rare gift of integrity as a critic. When he was at his business, he seldom remembered that he was a gentleman or a scholar. In this he shewed himself a true craftsman, intent on making the measurements and analyses of his criticism as accurate, and their expression as clear and vivid, as possible, instead of allowing himself to be distracted by the vanity of playing the elegant man of letters, or writing with perfect good taste, or hinting in every line that he was above his work.'

Shaw had established a model for himself in Lewes whose 'combination of a laborious criticism with a recklessly flippant manner' reminded him of a certain Corno di Bassetto. Then, almost as an afterthought, he threw in one further trait: Lewes, he added, 'wrote plays of the kind which, as a critic, he particularly disliked'.

341

*I shall never be able to begin a new play until I fall in love with
somebody else.* (1895)

*I have devoted to it [the theatre] far too much of what was meant for
mankind.* 'The Season's Moral' (1895)

The Fabian social critic; the anonymous literary critic of the *Pall Mall
Gazette*; the art critic of *Our Corner* and *The World*; the variously named
musical critics of the *Dramatic Review*, *The Star* and *The World*: all were
given a voice in the dramatic opinions of the *Saturday Review*. It was the
Fabian who called for the establishment both of a National Theatre, 'where
the public can be educated', and of local theatres, supported by a vestry or
municipal corporation, claiming for the drama 'as high a place in the
collectivist program as municipal gas, water and tramways'. It was the
Fabian, too, who campaigned for the respectability of the stage as a method
of achieving better wages for supporting actors and actresses, and who
proposed an academy or Royal College of the Drama 'with scholarships,
and a library scantily furnished with memoirs and reminiscences, and
liberally furnished with technical works, including theatrical instruction
and stage mechanism'.

Shaw would occasionally review such publications – books whose
connection with the stage was as intermittent as Meredith's *An Essay on
Comedy* – rather than fill his column with the convolutions of another
celebrated farce or new and original melodrama. For he had found himself
overtaken by those reckless outpourings, freshly adapted for the theatre, of
Marie Corelli, Rhoda Broughton and other romantic novelists, which he
thought to have left behind with the *Pall Mall Gazette*. 'Great works in
fiction are the arduous victories of great minds over great imaginations,' he
was driven to conclude. '. . . The romantic imagination is the most
unoriginative, uncreative faculty in the world.'

It was Shaw the art critic who felt able to advise (down to the
cane-bottomed seats and unadulterated cushions) on the architecture of
Her Majesty's Theatre; to recommend to George Alexander that he dye his
upholstery and curtains green (a more restful colour than crimson for
entertainments lasting four hours); to review *King Arthur* as if it were
merely an occasion for enjoying the picture-opera of Burne-Jones's sets; or
suddenly to surrender almost all the theatre page to the paintings of Watts
and Ford Madox Brown.

But more persistent than any of these is the voice of Corno di Bassetto. As a dramatist Shaw was to claim that 'my method, my system, my tradition, is founded upon music'. He went back to nineteenth-century opera, which contained its counterpoint of spoken sequences, and concluded that operatic music was essentially a drama of the passions. In a Preface to *Mrs Warren's Profession*, written after his experiences as theatre critic, he judged that the 'drama can do little to delight the senses: all the apparent instances to the contrary are instances of the personal fascination of the performers. The drama of pure feeling is no longer in the hands of the playwright: it has been conquered by the musician, after whose enchantments all the verbal arts seem cold and tame ... there is, flatly, no future now for any drama without music except the drama of thought.'

As a critic Shaw was primarily a listener rather than a watcher. He was not imposed upon by Beerbohm Tree's profusion of stage pageantry, preferring the careful readings of William Poel's Elizabethan Stage Society, assisted by the authentic pipe and tabor of Arnold Dolmetsch, which could do for sixteenth-century blank verse, he believed, what conductors such as Richter and Mottl had successfully done for Beethoven and Wagner. It was to the orchestration of words, 'a rhetorical notation based on musical pitch and dynamics', that Shaw was particularly attentive. Only when these operatic conceptions were lacking did he divert himself by what he saw. But since many actors and actresses seemed little more than walking plates, there was much to divert him – Miss Hope Booth, for example: 'a young lady who cannot sing, act, dance, or speak, but whose appearance suggests that she might profitably spend three or four years in learning these arts, which are useful on the stage.' From Stanley Weyman's *Under the Red Robe* he selected, 'on the score of conciseness', the part of Clon, a servant whose tongue had been cut out. Hardly more audible was Mrs Conover's Lady Macbeth.

'Mrs Conover, perhaps arguing that one must walk before one can run, has learned to whisper before she can speak. Her voiceless "Come, come. To bed: to bed:" is almost her only satisfactorily audible utterance. Tone will develop by-and-bye; but the more distinctly she makes herself heard, the more careful must she be not to call Banquo "Bonco" ...'

Shaw's low self-esteem had led to his need of feeling useful. He saw his job as the practical one of helping audiences get value for money by persuading West End managements to put on well-cast and better plays. His dramatic criticism is itself dramatic writing, supplying cries from the audience and evoking the performances of the players with the attention to detail of a Victorian novelist. He is particularly hilarious over the miscasting of leading actor-managers. Of Beerbohm Tree's Falstaff he concluded that 'Mr Tree might as well try to play Juliet'; George Alexander is seen going through a drunken episode from *The Prisoner of Zenda* 'like a seasoned teetotaller'; and he commiserated with Johnston Forbes Robertson's gentlemanly Romeo on having to engage in the rough-and-tumble of a duel: 'he makes you feel that to do it in that disorderly way, without seconds, without a doctor, shewing temper about it, and actually calling his adversary names, jars unspeakably on him . . . For the rest, Mr Forbes-Robertson is very handsome, very well dressed, very perfectly behaved'.

But Shaw was also expertly observant of the ingredients of good acting, particularly (among the men) in specialist comic parts, where he relished giving contrasting transcriptions of the comedian's vocal and physical tricks – for example, between Coquelin and John Hare in Sydney Grundy's *Mamma*, where the hero discovers that his elaborate labours to murder his mother-in-law have been in vain.

'Coquelin clowned it, even to the length of bounding into the air and throwing forward his arms and legs as if to frighten off some dangerous animal. But he did not produce the electric effect of Mr Hare's white, tense face and appalled stare, conveying somehow a mad speed of emotion and a frightful suspense of action never to be forgotten by any playgoer with the true dramatic memory.'

But Shaw's imagination was most vividly awakened on the stage by women. He mocked himself for this susceptibility, imagining that actresses would themselves mock him if he were not on his guard. 'Woman's greatest art is to lie low, and let the imagination of the male endow her with depths,' he warned. He had transferred into the theatre his struggle to be master of himself in the company of women; and that struggle is mirrored in his dramatic criticism. It was another arduous victory of mind over imagination. He was fond of quoting Robert Buchanan's epigram: 'Thousands of virtuous women on the stage but only six actresses.' And for Shaw the greatest of any six was Eleanora Duse. 'The supreme test of tragic acting,' he wrote, 'is that indescribable disturbance of soul in which the spectator finds himself when the curtain comes down, a sensation from which I have usually found myself perfectly safe in London theatres except when Duse is at large here.'

Duse had no obvious sex-appeal. She was a plain little woman, with genius: 'a most laborious artist hard at work, and not a pretty woman making an exhibition of herself', was how Shaw described her. He refers to her 'exquisite intelligence', and represents her as the finest exponent of the new drama, where emotion existed 'to make thought live and move us'. He uses her acting against which to measure the performances of other actresses – most famously in the beautiful passages comparing her playing of Sudermann's *Magda* with Sarah Bernhardt's. The two crucial words Shaw uses to explain Duse's 'vigilant sense of beauty of thought, feeling and action' are 'integrity' and 'integration'. She did not trade in flattery, solicit applause, manufacture a sham appeal for journalists. She concentrated all her powers on bodily and mental integration. Her acting seemed so spontaneous that it was difficult to persuade her admirers that there was any art in it. But Shaw, describing her as an athlete of the stage, insisted on the years of prodigious industry behind these performances. Most good actresses created themselves, Shaw believed, but were incapable of superimposing another character on top of that creation. 'Duse's greatest work is Duse', he wrote, 'but that does not prevent Césarine, Santuzza, and Camille from being three totally different women, none of them Duses, though Duse is all of them.' And in *Magda*, her face shadowed and lined ('they are the credentials of her humanity'), it seemed to him that she spoke and acted for every woman 'as they are hardly ever able to speak and act for themselves'.

In contrast to Duse stood Mrs Patrick Campbell, a magnificent animal of a woman and perilously bewitching, whose talent depended upon her 'irresistible physical gifts'. It was away from the excitement of Mrs Pat and towards the non-sexual appeal of Duse that Shaw was trying to move Janet Achurch, 'whose playing of Alexandra, in Voss's play,' he wrote, in the same week as Janet was catching the boat back from New York, 'came nearer to Duse's work in subtlety, continuity and variety of detail, and in beauty of execution, than anything I have seen on the English stage'.

'But Duse has been helped to her supremacy by the fortunate sternness of Nature in giving her nothing but her genius. Miss Ellen Terry is a woman of quite peculiar and irresistible personal charm. Miss Achurch has been kept in constant danger of missing the highest distinction in her art by having, as an extra and cheaper string to her bow, an endowment of conventional good looks, and a large share of that power of expressing all the common emotions with extraordinary intensity which makes the vulgar great actress of the Bernhardt school . . . Miss Terry or Miss Achurch, if they had no more skill than can be acquired by any person of ordinary capacity in the course of a few years' experience, would always find a certain degree of favor as pretty leading ladies.'

This was not the first time that Shaw had slipped Ellen Terry's name in next to Janet's. A few months earlier, in his Preface to William Archer's *The Theatrical 'World' of 1894* he had written:

'Miss Ellen Terry's position at the Lyceum Theatre may appear an enviable one; but when I recall the parts to which she has been condemned by her task of "supporting" Mr Irving, I have to admit that Miss Janet Achurch, for instance, who made for herself the opportunity of "creating" Nora Helmer in England by placing herself in the position virtually of actress-manageress, is far more to be envied.'

Since Shaw had written this, Janet had also won – and lost – the opportunity of creating Candida Morell. News of the withdrawal of *Candida* reached him in April 1895. The following month, while Janet still lingered in America, he began to write a new play for Ellen Terry.

*

She was unique; and, when she put forth all her enchantment from the stage, so fascinated him that he warned his own audience in the *Saturday Review* to pay little attention to his response – it was 'sure to be grossly partial'. Her voice was magical: slightly veiled, seeming to enfold herself and those to whom she spoke in a glow of happiness. He described her as 'heartwise', meaning perhaps a little cautious since, nearing fifty, she knew where her tender heart still might lead her. He admired her for her charm and beauty, but most of all for her refusal to trade on them with the sentimental public. He admired her unobtrusive stagecraft, observing how she could hold her audiences with unfailing grip in circumstances that would normally have left them coughing and restless. Her acting 'reminds me of my imaginary violin-playing,' he wrote; 'she seems utterly innocent of it, and yet there it is, all happening infallibly and delightfully.'

Ellen Terry was over nine years older than Shaw and had been brought up 'healthy, happy and wise – theatre-wise at any rate'. By the age of sixteen she had played in forty-five productions round the country, then abruptly left the stage to marry a lukewarm middle-aged gentleman, the painter G. F. Watts. The marriage had failed and she returned to the theatre, but absconded again two years later to live with the man she loved, the architect Edward William Goodwin, by whom she had two children, Gordon and Edy Craig. Much of her vulnerability had circled round these children, and many of her actions were designed to support and protect them. The need for money had impelled her back into the theatre after six years; and in 1877, largely to give them legal status, she had married a sturdy widower, Charles Wardell, 'a manly bulldog sort of man', who had walked in from soldiering on to the boards. Making him her leading man, she had scored a huge success with *New Men and Old Acres* at the Court Theatre in 1878. Shaw, who was in the stalls, dismissed the play as 'piffling'. But the poetry of Ellen Terry had enthralled him: 'I was completely conquered.'

346

The public too was conquered and granted her a place, as its popular darling, set apart from Victorian standards of morality. For her emotional life, though veiled like her voice, had become increasingly unconventional. Before the end of 1878 she had joined Henry Irving at the Lyceum; but her marriage of convenience to Wardell soon began to deteriorate and in 1881 they separated. 'I should have died had I lived one more month with him,' she later told Shaw. 'I gave him three-quarters of all the money I made weekly, and prayed him to go.'

With Irving, Ellen Terry had tried to unite 'the great happiness of occupation' with the great excitement of romance – 'I doted on his looks,' she said. In many ways and for many years she acted as Irving's wife-and-mother, helping to manage the Lyceum cast as if they were a family of children who must not squabble, acting as Irving's hostess at public banquets, touring with him, and leaving the theatre with him at night. But though he bought a house and made it ready, they never lived together: and eventually the house was sold. 'We were terribly in love for awhile,' she said. 'Then, later on, when it didn't matter so much to me, he wanted us to go on, and so I did, because I was very very fond of him and he said he needed me.'

By 1895 he had begun to need her less for romantic roles. In one of his earlier reviews for the *Saturday Review*, Shaw wrote indignantly of Ellen Terry as 'a born actress of real women's parts condemned to figure as a mere artist's model in costume plays which, from the woman's point of view, are foolish flatteries written by gentlemen for gentlemen.' Here, as in other criticism, he was uneasily aware of oversimplifying her contradictory nature: 'I have not the smallest confidence in my own judgment respecting her,' he confessed. In *Captain Brassbound's Conversion* he would claim to have tailor-made for her the part of Lady Cecily Waynflete: a lady of 'cunning simplicity ... of great vitality and humanity' who, by tact, intelligence and the exercise of sympathy, instinctively gets her own way in a man's world. Yet Ellen Terry, who submitted herself to dominant men such as Irving, so far failed to get her own way at the Lyceum that in Shaw's opinion she was never seen 'except in plays that date, in feeling if not in actual composition, from the dark ages before the Married Women's Property Act.' She 'OUGHT to have played in the Lady from the Sea,' he claimed, though at the same time acknowledging that she 'was never called an advanced woman' – perhaps forgetting that he had himself described her in the *Saturday Review* as 'the only real New Woman'. In their *Correspondence*, while parading his feminist credentials ('no male writer born in the nineteenth century outside Norway and Sweden did more to knock Woman off her pedestal and plant her on the solid earth than I'), he

347

called her 'goddesslike' and raised her from the solid earth on to a stage pedestal, explaining: 'I was steeped in the tendency against which I was reacting . . . I did not pause to consider whether this attitude would have earned the approval of Ibsen or Strindberg.' This attitude towards her, which he also termed 'insufferable', reflected the difference between nineteenth-century theatre and life outside it, as well as the unresolved nature of their pen-and-ink attachment.

But in Shaw's mind such contradictions became the accurate reflection of two Ellen Terrys who lived one inside the other. There was *his* Ellen of the 'ultra-modern talent', waiting to be released from Henry Irving's leading actress. For almost twenty years she had lain locked in the ancient dungeons of the Lyceum Theatre, guarded by an ogre called 'His Immensity'. Up to this castle, in the year 1895, Shaw pranced in his newest Ibsenite armour, and flung over the battlements a strange challenge: *The Man of Destiny*.

\*

They had sent each other a few letters haphazardly, almost formally, but it was not until near the end of 1895, when he revealed his 'beautiful little one act play for Napoleon and a strange lady', that their flirtatious correspondence really opened. She demanded to be given the play ('Lord, how attractively tingling it sounds'), and on 28 November he dispatched it with the promise that 'this is not one of my great plays . . . it is only a display of my knowledge of stage tricks – a commercial traveller's sample'.

'I really do love Ellen,' he was to write. They played at love. He loved her for helping to move his romantic feelings from a bruising world on to the stage, from the body to the page. She gave him love without physical life and therefore without threat of death; she gave him consolation in a world where real love was too dangerous. They *acted* love. She drew his imagination out into 'a thousand wild stories and extravagances and adorations' while he sat solitary at his desk 'blarneying audacities'. They protected each other and were safe – but: 'Only the secondrate are safe.'

In *The Man of Destiny* Shaw had written of 'one universal passion: fear'. It was this fear that confined them to an invisible island of enchantment where there was no pain or regret and no growing old. They knew about such things and, when the atmosphere of charm lifted a little, could spy them far off, even mimic them; then go back to their play-acting together.

'Let those who may complain that it was all on paper,' Shaw later cautioned, 'remember that only on paper has humanity yet achieved glory, beauty, truth, knowledge, virtue, and abiding love.' Like soldiers, these strong and rather beautiful words guarded his frightened soul, concealing the truth that we may not put more courage, virtue, love into our words than we practise in our life. It was for this reason that he could not write for Ellen 'one of my great plays', but offered her instead this trifle, *The Man of Destiny*, 'a perfectly idiotic play' that itself revolved around a piece of paper, a supposed love letter.

*The Man of Destiny* was a token, plucked from his involvement with Janet Achurch while she was in America and handed over to Ellen Terry as a symbol of his new engagement. 'If I make money out of my new play I will produce *Candida* at my own expense,' he told her, 'and you & Janet shall play it on alternate nights.' When turning down *Candida* in America, Richard Mansfield had taken the trouble to instruct Shaw that the stage was for romance, for cheering people on their way. 'You'll have to write a play that a *man* can play and about a woman that heroes fought for and a bit of ribbon that a knight tied to his lance.' *The Man of Destiny*, which Shaw began less than a month after receiving Mansfield's letter, is this bit of ribbon – 'not exactly a burlesque: it is more a harlequinade,' he told Janet Achurch, 'in which Napoleon and a strange lady play harlequin & columbine, and a chuckle headed, asinine young sub lieutenant . . . and an innkeeper . . . play clown and pantaloon.' By early September 1895 the play was written. 'Such are the opera bouffe depths to which I have descended,' he wrote, exonerating himself to Janet.

Shaw's joke was that, having written the play 'out of the vacacitude of the densest historical and geographical ignorance', he had fallen back on Richard Mansfield for the character of Napoleon. 'I was much hurt by your contemptuous refusal of "A Man of Destiny",' he would later claim in a letter to Mansfield.

'. . . because Napoleon is nobody else but Richard Mansfield himself. I studied the character from you, and then read up Napoleon and found that I had got him exactly right . . . But you will never get over your difficulties until you become the master and not the slave of your profession. Look at me, enviable man that I am: I act the real part of Bernard Shaw, and get you or anyone else stagestruck enough, to dress up as Bluntschli or any other of my figments and fakements. It is as an organizer of the theatre that you really interest me; and here I find you paralysed by the ridiculous condition that the drama must always be a Mansfield exhibition.'

This teasing for supremacy belongs to *The Man of Destiny*, whose contest between Napoleon and the Strange Lady – a tactical duel between the man of action and a woman of words – was to be parodied by a duel of actor-manager versus playwright. From the first, this contest was implicit. Writing to Janet Achurch while still working on the play, he explained: 'I want to see whether I can write a good curtain raiser. Forbes Robertson ought to play Napoleon in order to forestall Irving in "Madame Sans-Gêne".' But when he had finished 'the wretched thing', he found it was 'impracticable because of its length'. In a letter to the actor-manager, John Martin-Harvey, he praised it as 'the most inconvenient play in the language. It is too long for a sketch; it is too long for a curtain raiser; and it is too short for a whole evening bill.' In these circumstances, it seemed a subtler plan to press this inconvenience on the Lyceum instead of inflicting it on one of Irving's rivals. By such an ingenious route – 'the adroit mixture of flattery and business' he defined it – did Shaw's 'pre-Ibsen' play arrive in the hands of the actress whom he had publicly been urging to play Ellida in *The Lady from the Sea*.

She loved it. 'Just read your play. Delicious,' she telegraphed. She loved Shaw's shrewdly inserted description of herself as the Strange Lady:

'tall and extraordinarily graceful, with a delicately intelligent, apprehensive, questioning face: perception in the brow, sensitiveness in the nostrils, character in the chin: all keen, refined, and original . . . very feminine, but by no means weak: the lithe tender figure is hung on a strong frame . . . her elegance and radiant charm keep the secret of her size and strength . . . She is fair, with golden brown hair and grey eyes.

'She enters with the self-possession of a woman accustomed to the privileges of rank and beauty.'

The Strange Lady had Ellen's appearance; but did she have her character? In the play she succeeds in persuading the twenty-seven-year-old general to let her burn unread a letter that might compromise Josephine and the Director Barras – a letter that early in the play he had been determined to read. Ellen Terry's task, to persuade Irving to read and produce *The Man of Destiny* at the Lyceum with the two of them in its star roles, was hardly less daunting.

She began well. At her request Irving read it and, despite the difficulty of fitting a one-act play into the Lyceum bill, positively did not turn it down. 'H. I. quite loves it,' Ellen translated, 'and will do it finely.' But Shaw was suspicious. What were Irving's real intentions? A production at the Lyceum 'would of course be quite the best thing that could happen to it'. But did he dare hope for this? There seemed only one test. 'As long as I remain a dramatic critic,' he asked Ellen to tell Irving, 'I can neither sell plays nor take advances. I must depend altogether on royalties and percentages on actual performances. Otherwise, you see, I should simply be bribed right and left . . .' And he added: 'I suspect Henry Irving – Oh I suspect him . . . Because everybody *is* corruptible: is not that simple?' This appeared to contradict his *Saturday Review* statement that 'I am to all intents and purposes incorruptible', but followed his familiar tactic of moving to high moral ground from which to cross swords. Here he was fighting two battles: first to get his 'mere stage brutality' produced (why else had he used, almost caricatured, all those stage tricks he was simultaneously deriding in the *Saturday Review*?); and secondly, as a variation of his sparring matches and his Fabian technique of permeation, to win Ellen's allegiance from Irving. Behind these battles, and appearing to justify them, lay the whole warfare he was conducting against the late Victorian theatre.

*

Shaw's objections to Irving's influence over the London theatre of the 1890s were partly personal but on the whole by this time well-merited. 'I am compelled to make the most unjustifiable assaults on Manager Irving and Impresario Harris [of Covent Garden],' Corno di Bassetto had written early in 1891, 'in order to force them to attend to my wants for a night or two at the expense of their contented patrons.' His wants over the following five years had increased with each new play remaining unperformed. So G.B.S. began his theatre criticism, as he later observed, 'with a prejudice against him through the disappointment of a strong fancy for him'.

He had first seen Irving on stage at the Theatre Royal, Dublin, in *The Two Roses*, and 'at once picked him out as the actor for me'. That had been in 1871, and over twenty-five years later he remembered Irving's creation of a character named Digby Grant, 'in a manner which, if applied to an Ibsen play now [1897], would astonish us'. To this opinion Shaw held for the rest of his life, using it partly as the substitution for a more personal vendetta. Irving, he retrospectively concluded, seemed 'born to play ultra-modern parts' – that is to bring to life 'the Shavian drama incipient in me'. Then he saw Ellen Terry in the first glory of her talent and beauty – and 'there I had my leading couple'. Between them, and in combination with the plays of Ibsen and himself, they 'seemed to have been sent by Providence to revive the rotting theatre of that day.'

Beside the terrible power of Sonny's hero, the splendid Barry Sullivan, Irving seemed a meagre presence with spindly legs, a shambling dance for a walk and 'a voice made resonant in his nose which became a whinny when he tried to rant'. Yet with intense perseverance, combining fierce exploitation of his talent with prudent use of his limitations, he had triumphed over these limitations to become for a generation the mesmeric, majestic, unchallengeable leader of the British stage. Even in 1879 he roused in Shaw an interest that, because of the dissimilarity of voice and physique, did not clash with the esteem he felt for Sullivan, who represented 'the grandiose and the violent on its last legs, and could do nothing for the young Irving but mislead him.'

'Irving's mission was to re-establish on the stage the touching, appealing nobility of sentiment and affection – the dignity which only asserts itself when it is wounded; and his early attempts to express these by the traditional methods of the old domineering, self-assertive, ambitious, thundering, superb school led him for a time into a grotesque confusion of style . . . Irving had to find the right expression for a perfectly new dignity and a perfectly new indignity; and it was not until he had done this that he really accomplished his destiny, broke the old tradition, and left Barry Sullivan and Macready half a century behind.'

Ever since coming to London, Shaw had carefully studied Irving's performances. Between April and July 1879, for example, he had seen him as Hamlet, as Claude Melnotte in *Lady of Lyons*, as Cardinal Richelieu and Charles I. 'Richelieu had been incessantly excruciating: Hamlet had only moments of violent ineptitude separated by lengths of dullness,' Shaw reported.

'. . . Before Claude Melnotte had moved his wrist and chin twice, I saw that he had mastered the rhetorical style at last. His virtuosity of execution soon became extraordinary. His Charles I, for instance, became a miracle of the most elaborate class of this sort of acting. It was a hard-earned and well-deserved triumph; and by it his destiny was accomplished . . .'

A man of two destinies, Irving had chosen the misleading one. He had harnessed his new style of acting to no new dramatist of talent. Then he had returned to the much older rhetorical art that, while not itself false, was given over to acting versions that were falsifications of old plays, particularly spurious Shakespeare. In this way he surrendered what Shaw called 'a fundamentally serious social function for a fundamentally nonsensical theatrical accomplishment'. Had he persisted in producing studies of modern life and character such as Digby Grant, 'we should have escaped Lyceum Shakespeares; and we should have had the ablest manager of the day driven by life-or-death necessity to extract from contemporary literature the proper food for the modern side of his talent, and thus to create a new drama instead of galvanizing an old one and cutting himself off from all contact with the dramatic vitality of his time. And what an excellent thing that would have been both for us and for him!'

By the 1890s those 'great possibilities' of Ellen Terry, that Shaw accused Irving of sacrificing, seemed little more than a gallant Shavian hypothesis. The symbolic choice with which Shaw apparently presented Irving – either Sardou's Napoleon, 'the jealous husband of a thousand fashionable dramas' or his own 'baby comediatta' – was never a real one.

For though *The Man of Destiny* was pregnant with a new view of the 'Superman' that would march towards maturity in *Caesar and Cleopatra*, the play relied on rhetorical devices, and largely belonged to the Sardou tradition of historical romance that Shaw had scorned Irving for falling back on.

Shaw claimed to bear Irving 'an ancient grudge which I never quite forgave him . . . So I was never really fair to him . . . for, scrupulously judicial as my criticisms were . . . you can smell a certain grudge in them.' His real grudge lay against Irving's power based partly on something that Shaw himself lacked: money. Money was freedom of action and the power to limit other people's freedom. Money was a substitute for generosity, even for affection. Money was false romance. Over fifty years later, learning that Irving had secretly paid Janet Achurch £100, Shaw still felt sufficiently agitated to declare that 'from anyone else than H.I. it would have been an act of extraordinary generosity and a tribute to Ibsen; and it was very generous of H.I. anyhow.' But

'. . . it was part of H. I.'s mixture of policy with sardonic humor to buy everybody. He liked to see them selling themselves and bought them partly to gratify that taste. He knew he was being robbed; but would not sack the robbers because it put them in his power and at his command. He tried to buy me, and believed I had come to sell myself. But he did not always buy the right people . . .'

\*

What Shaw interpreted as Irving's attempt to 'buy me in the market like a rabbit, wrap me up in brown paper and put me by on his shelf' took place between the summer of 1896 and late spring the following year. Actually, far from wanting to buy Shaw, Irving seemed anxious for him to go away and take his play with him. For over seven months *The Man of Destiny* had lain at the Lyceum: and nothing had happened. Yet Ellen Terry had refused to let go of her confidence and in the first week of July 1896 Irving wilted, indicating that he would 'agree to produce The Man of Destiny next year, or forfeit rights, if that must be an imperative condition', Ellen reported to Shaw. 'He wants the play very much (and so do I want him to have it), and he would like to buy it . . .'

In a sympathetic attempt to permeate the Lyceum, Shaw communicated the following week with Irving, regretting that his play was 'so trivial an affair; but when I wrote it I had no idea it would be so fortunate'. Even now he felt it could be little more than 'a fancy of Miss T's', in which case 'a performance or two on some special occasion' would meet the case. 'I should of course be delighted to license any such without any question of terms.'

Irving countered this effort to establish a virtue out of lack of money with his standard payment of £50 for a year's exclusive option – a proposal Shaw politely described as 'reasonable' but which, he repeated, 'raises a lot of difficulties for me . . . it is impossible for a critic to take money except for actual performances without placing both himself and the manager in a false position'. He therefore suggested that a few performances be given in 1897 without any guarantee as to fees, adding as an apparent 'concession', that: 'If you produce a play by Ibsen . . . then I will not only consent to a postponement of "The Man of Destiny" but will hand over the rights for all the world to you absolutely to do as you like with until your retirement without fee or condition of any kind. But if you will excuse my saying so, I'm hanged if I'll be put off for Shakespeare. Take him away: he lags superfluous.'

With Ellen Terry looking on laughing, there was nothing much Irving could do but (with the deletion of Ibsen) appear to accept the Shavian counter-proposal. Shaw had won a paper victory, though one that must have made any production of Shaw and Ibsen at the Lyceum even more improbable. For Irving could not have taken kindly to being lectured *de haut en bas* on financial ethics, to having his famous Shakespearian repertoire waved aside, or to being upstaged in the matter of Ibsen. In short, he had been ridiculed – what else could Ellen Terry's laughter have meant? Yet he could not afford to look mean, so he grandly did nothing for a further two months. Then, with Shaw in the audience, he announced from the stage that the Lyceum would be producing Sardou's Napoleon show, *Madame Sans-Gêne*, in the spring of 1897. This, the actor's riposte to the writer, was a wonderful provocation to Shaw, who sent an over-polite enquiry as to whether he was 'for the first time' free to submit *The Man of Destiny* elsewhere. Irving's response was to invite him to the Lyceum.

So, at half past twelve on 26 September 1896, the two men met in Irving's office. There was no one with a more imposing presence than Irving; no one bolder with words than Shaw. Both had been provoked. That morning the *Saturday Review* published Shaw's ferocious analysis of Irving's *Cymbeline* production. 'In the true republic of art Sir Henry Irving would ere this have expiated his acting versions on the scaffold,' Shaw had written.

'He does not merely cut plays; he disembowels them . . . This curious want of connoisseurship in literature would disable Sir Henry Irving seriously if he were an interpretative actor. But it is, happily, the fault of a great quality

354

– the creative quality ... The truth is that he has never in his life conceived or interpreted the characters of any author except himself.'

Irving used his creative quality to great effect. There was nothing mean or retaliatory in his attitude. Like royalty, he rose above Shaw's journalism, knew nothing about it, extinguished it. Though Shaw was able to hold to his principle of not accepting money, Irving was magnanimous here too. He tolerated Shaw's eccentricities. Fifty pounds was nothing to him here or there. Of course he would stage *The Man of Destiny* – notwithstanding Sardou's play. He would produce it afterwards, next year ... sometime. The man whom Shaw had that day accused in public of having absolutely no literary judgement was pleased to think highly of *The Man of Destiny*. So the interview, which Shaw was never to describe, ended with what seemed an uneasy truce; and a stage victory for Irving.

\*

The two men had met, but the man and the woman, even after a year of letter writing, had not. Ellen had come to the door where Shaw and Irving were talking, heard their voices, and skedaddled. 'I think I'd rather never meet you – in the flesh,' she had written to him, and he had replied: 'Very well, you shant meet me in the flesh if you'd rather not. There is something deeply touching in that ...' It was lack of confidence that kept them apart. She felt old. Her body ached, sometimes even disgusted her. She could regain her attractiveness only through an illusion. 'They love me, you know!' she wrote. 'Not for what I am, but for what they imagine I am ... because though I may *seem* like myself to others, I never *feel* like myself when I am acting, but some one else, so nice, and so young and so happy, and always in-the-air, light, and bodyless.' She felt he understood. 'How you seem to feel with one!' And he confirmed this understanding: 'Our brains evidently work in the same way.' For he too felt better bodyless. In body he was 'a disagreeably cruel looking middle aged Irishman with a red beard' who, in the *Saturday Review*, turned into a magic Shaw, a phantasm. So they sent out their best imaginary selves to meet each other, she so schoolgirlish, he so cocksure. He entertained her, made her 'fly out laughing', and sometimes with his advice strengthened her stage confidence. 'You have become a habit with me,' she acknowledged. She gave him 'that lost feeling of unfulfilment'. He thought he had found someone like himself, vulnerable yet determined to be self-sufficient: 'you are a fully self-possessed woman and therefore not really the slave of love. You would not delight in it so if it were not entirely subject to your will, if the abandonment were real abandonment, instead of voluntary, artistic, *willed* (and therefore revocable) rapture.' Each enabled the other to keep these illusions, and each was aware of this conspiracy. 'I, too, fear to break the spell,' he wrote; 'remorses, presentiments, all sorts of tendernesses wring my heart at the thought of materialising this beautiful friendship of ours by a meeting.' It was the same for her: 'I love you more every minute,' she owned. 'I cant help it, and I guessed it would be like that! And so we wont meet.'

What he called 'silly longings . . . waves of tenderness' almost broke the spell. He slipped the words 'I love you' into one of his letters, and she admitted not being able to 'cure' herself of him. Sometimes, in bed at night, she felt the need 'to touch you, to put my hand on your arm'. Then he too would grow impatient at the row of footlights separating them and want to hold her in his arms: 'Don't let us break the spell, *do* let us break the spell – don't, do, don't, do, don't, do, don't – ' And the spell did not break.

In place of their bodies they put their work. 'I *must* attach myself to you somehow,' he had written: 'Let me therefore do it as a matter of business.' And she agreed: 'I'm not going to write any more 'cept on business.' His business was to make her 'the greatest actress in the world'. With these letters and in the *Saturday Review* he schooled her, and she responded. 'You bring my name into that article, force it in,' she wrote,

'and now I understand why it is a message to me to tell me I'm in your head and your heart, and that you cant get me out of them and that all your work is for me(!) . . . Such constancy I never knew, and such an example I could never hope to copy.'

Under his tuition her enthusiasm seems sometimes to parallel Beatrice Webb's cephalous passion for Sidney: 'write *for* me, not *to* me,' she instructed. 'We need not waste time with solicitors and deeds and things . . . Quick! I want a bit of you, of your brain – only you can give me that – and you must come . . .' And he came: 'Oh play *me*, Ellen, *me*, ME, *ME*, *ME*, *ME*, *ME*, not Sardou or another. Now go and have a blessed sleep after it all. G.B.S.'

In the intercourse of business 'my secret is that I learn from what you *do*,' he told her, 'knowing that that is the reality of you. The dear silly oldfashioned things *you think you think*: at these I laugh, though never at you . . . My only chance is to awaken your wisdom, which is still asleep . . .' To awaken her wisdom meant closing her eyes to Irving. 'Is H. I. blind, is he deaf?' Shaw demanded. Much of his correspondence is an attempt to undermine Ellen's faith in Irving. 'Has he ever loved you for the millionth fraction of a moment?' he wondered. Or was it simply that 'he is without exception absolutely the stupidest man I ever met'? Such dilemmas worried

Ellen. She had always been in awe of Irving – his beauty, his distinction – but was feeling ever more frustrated in the patriarchy of the Lyceum. Irving was so crafty, so close. 'I wish he were more ingenuous and more direct,' she confided in her diary. '. . . I think it is not quite right in him that he does not care for anybody much.' But to Shaw she wrote: 'I wish you were friends – that *you knew each other* . . . You'd love him. I think everything of him (is that "love"?). He can do everything – except be fond of *people* . . . but that's his great misfortune . . . I wish you knew him to admire him & love him – Love him & be sorry for him.'

*

Ellen's good sense was founded on a simplicity that comprehended the complexities of neither man. They were separated from sympathy towards each other as much by qualities they shared as by their differences. Each had re-created himself through arduous devotion to work from what seemed unlovable human material, Irving's magisterial 'Governor' at the Lyceum being an equivalent self-production to Shaw's phenomenal G.B.S. of the *Saturday Review*. 'I really care deeply for nothing but *fine work*,' Shaw had insisted, and the same was true of Irving who, within a year of his marriage, had affirmatively jumped from a brougham and left his wife in answer to her question (following the sensational opening of *The Bells*): 'Are you going on making a fool of yourself like this all your life?'

Since their work stood opposed they appeared implacable enemies. It is hard not to feel sympathy for Irving. He had stilled his anxieties by creating at the Lyceum a temple of lavish and respectable illusion. 'The artist sacrifices everything to his art, beginning with himself,' Shaw had written of Irving. 'But his art *is* himself; and when the art is the art of acting, the self is both body and soul.' It was Irving's body and soul that Shaw held up to ridicule in the *Saturday Review*. 'Mr Irving must remember that we now applaud him, not critically, but affectionately,' he reminded him.

'. . . we indulge him, every evening at the Lyceum, with a broadsword combat the solemn absurdity of which quite baffles my powers of description. If we treat his orations as lectures, do we not also treat Mr Gladstone's tree-felling exploits as acts of statesmanship? No one can say that we are not indulgent to our favorites.'

It was Shaw's indulgence, his affection, his humorous charity from which Irving had most to fear. His very support diminished Irving's stature as head of the theatre. What could have exasperated him more than the Shavian endorsement of his knighthood conferred on him, *Saturday*

*Review* readers understood, 'by his own peremptory demand, which no mere gentleman would have dared to make lest he should have offended the court and made himself ridiculous'.

Shaw's onslaught on Irving, sometimes in the form of undermining tributes, came from motives partly of principle, partly of power. At the centre was a struggle of author versus actor, dramatist against theatrical manager. Who, in principle, should rule the theatre? Should it be this player who did not 'know literature from penny-a-liner's fustian', worked completely independent of the dramatist, and 'only approaches him in moments of aberration'?

'The history of the Lyceum, with its twenty years' steady cultivation of the actor as a personal force, and its utter neglect of the drama, is the history of the English stage during that period. Those twenty years have raised the social status of the theatrical profession, and culminated in the official recognition of our chief actor as the peer of the President of the Royal Academy, and the figure-heads of the other arts. And now I, being a dramatist and not an actor, want to know when the drama is to have its turn. I do not suggest that G.B.S. should condescend to become K.C.B.; but I do confidently affirm that if the actors think they can do without the drama, they are most prodigiously mistaken.'

Apart from clearing the way for Ibsen and himself, Shaw wanted to advertise his own independence from Irving – particularly in view of the suspended state of *The Man of Destiny*. At the same time, by demonstrating Irving's 'extraordinary insensibility to literature', he was still attempting to transfer Ellen Terry's allegiance to himself. In no other context does Shaw celebrate 'literature' so absolutely. He excelled at making tragic fun of Irving as an actor who, specializing in Shakespeare, did not understand a word of his plays. In the *Saturday Review* he dramatizes the ghastly struggle between Irving and Shakespeare, urging his readers to bear in mind the venerable actor's deep sincerity in preferring his own treasons 'to the unmutilated masterpieces of the genius' on whom he had 'lavished lip-honor'. For this treason Shaw recommended a small penalty: 'my regard for Sir Henry Irving cannot blind me to the fact that it would have been better for us twenty-five years ago to have tied him up in a sack with every existing copy of the works of Shakespeare, and dropped him into the crater of the nearest volcano'. By such tricks did Shaw hope to arrange for Irving's entrances on stage to be greeted with uncontrollable bursts of laughter – a fitting penalty for the actor who (in one sense or another) had played the dramatist off the stage, employed his work simply as a framework for his own creations, and become 'the despair of all authors and true Shakespeareans in consequence'.

Shaw is here classing himself among the true Shakespeareans. He had kept up to date with new textual criticism of Shakespeare, and his attack on the Lyceum's mutilated versions complemented the philological and photographic facsimile scholarship of F. J. Furnivall (whom he had met at the New Shakespere Society), and the austere Elizabethan production methods of William Poel (which he had studied as a dramatic critic). As Sonny, he had lived in Shakespeare's world more vividly than his own, and to the extent that something of Sonny persisted in Shaw, to that extent there lived on in him a legacy of love for Shakespeare. But when Sonny had turned to Dickens, he had taken his first step into the protective sphere of the stage where G.B.S. now enshrined Ellen Terry. His emotional instincts tended to despair; but his mind needed optimism as the oxygen with which to go on breathing. The Shavian theatre became a factory for the manufacture of this life-supporting tonic – while Shakespeare represented death to him. Almost the last work in the official Shavian canon, 'the climax of my eminence', his puppet play *Shakes Versus Shav* (1949), presents the debate as a contest between darkness and light, pain and healing, death and life itself – the same debate in miniature as between the Devil and Don Juan from *Man and Superman*, with Shakespeare now playing the Devil.

SHAKES    Did I not write
          'The heartache and the thousand natural woes
          That flesh is heir to'?

SHAV      You were not the first
          To sing of broken hearts. I was the first
          That taught your faithless Timons how to mend them

SHAKES    Taught what you could not know . . .

SHAV      For a moment suffer
          My glimmering light to shine
                    [A light appears between them]

SHAKES    Out, out, brief candle! [He puffs it out]
                    [Darkness. The play ends.]

In the sense of being a business competitor G.B.S. was also an embattled rival to Irving's Shakespeare, and in the romance of this business war other feelings were obscured. At their best, Shaw's tirades against 'the poor foolish old Swan' were part of theatre politics, and an attempt to cleanse the Victorian theatre of its snobbish bardolatry. But at their worst they dissolve into a stream of puerilities as irrelevant to

Shakespeare's work as anything performed at the Lyceum by Henry Irving; and as self-advertising: 'With the single exception of Homer, there is no eminent writer, not even Sir Walter Scott, whom I can despise so entirely as I despise Shakespeare when I measure my mind against his.' Irving had reduced Shakespeare to a pantomime pet; Shaw fashioned him into a journalistic Aunt Sally whose politics 'would hardly impress the Thames Conservancy Board', let alone a member of the Fabian executive. Whenever this rain of abuse against Shakespeare's 'economics' allows us, Shaw's innate love and scrupulous knowledge of the poetry gleam through. 'It is as though he resented his own susceptibility,' Hilary Spurling was to observe, as though he had to punish him before he could 'admit how deeply he has been moved – overpowered is his own word – by the beauties of the play in question. Time after time he breaks off in the middle of administering the most tremendous wigging to marvel at some mighty line or subtle play of feeling.'

Shaw's attitudes to Shakespeare and Irving reflect his attitudes to sex and power. As there are two Shakespeares in Shaw's world, so there were two Irvings: the dictatorial actor-manager and the man with humours parallel to Shaw's own:

'all attempts to sustain our conduct at a higher level than is natural to us produce violent reactions ... No actor suffers from the tyranny of this grotesque necessity more than Mr Irving. His career, ever since he became a heroic actor, has been studded by relapses into the most impish buffoonery. I remember years ago going into the Lyceum Theatre under the impression that I was about to witness a performance of Richard III. After one act of that tragedy, however, Mr Irving relapsed into an impersonation of Alfred Jingle. He concealed piles of sandwiches in his hat; so that when he afterwards raised it to introduce himself as "Alfred Jingle, Esq., of No Hall, Nowhere," a rain of ham and bread descended on him ... He was simply taking his revenge on Shakespear and himself for months of sustained dignity. Later on ... [as Don Quixote] he makes his own dignity ridiculous to his heart's content ... he tumbles about the stage with his legs in the air; and he has a single combat, on refreshingly indecorous provocation, with a pump. And he is perfectly happy. I am the last person in the world to object; for I, too, have something of that aboriginal need for an occasional carnival in me.'

Irving once complained that Shaw's aim in submitting plays to the Lyceum was to make him appear absurd on stage; and Shaw did not deny it. But this, he pointed out, was not a malevolent endeavour: through absurdity we became human. It was this humanity in Irving that Shaw warmed to whenever he could change their positions and make Irving the clown or outsider. 'Does H .I. really say that you are in love with me?' he asked Ellen. 'For that be all his sins forgiven him! I will go to the Lyceum again & write an article proving him to be the greatest Richard ever dreamed of. I am also touched by his refusing to believe that we have never met. No man of feeling *could* believe such heartlessness.'

*

Shaw's *Saturday Review* article on Irving's *Richard III* had appeared in December 1896, and like a time-bomb exploded four months later under *The Man of Destiny*. The play had seemed fated to bring Shaw and Ellen Terry together. 'So you would like to see me at rehearsals. Well, you soon shall,' he wrote to her on 16 April 1897. '"The Man of Destiny" is due this year: there is no penalty for breach of the agreement: consequently H. I. is on his honor.' The following day he was told that the Lyceum had decided after all not to stage his play.

It was almost a relief. The manuscript had become an entanglement from which both actor and playwright needed to escape. 'I hate failure,' Shaw had once confided to Ellen. So did Irving. It seemed important to each man that he should be judged by Ellen to have acted the better. She was their referee, and in her reaction, even more than in the public's, was success to be sought. For many Saturdays Shaw had been pirouetting round Irving, prodding out his dramatic opinions and trying to goad his opponent into committing some moral foul. But, keeping his guard held high, Irving had waited. Uncowed by accusations of bribing critics, he was simply afraid of making a fool of himself and conceding a Shavian victory-by-default. Also he seems to have felt that Shaw must eventually go too far, trip himself up or dance right out of the ring. For eighteen months they had circled each other while Ellen, believing it actually was a dance and not a fight, looked on.

Irving's sudden action, which Shaw had apparently long expected, took Ellen by surprise. Though involving him in some risk, it was a shrewdly calculated move over which Irving must have brooded in private for almost four months. At first he gave Shaw no reason, allowing the great paradoxer to make a conventional deduction. 'I am in ecstasies. I have been spoiling for a row,' Shaw told Ellen. '. . . Hooray! Kiss me good speed . . .' But far from delighting in what Shaw called 'the fun & chuckle' of it all, Ellen felt irritated. Why were these men quarrelling? They were like schoolboys. 'My dear, this vexes me very much,' she reproved Shaw. 'My friends to fight! And I love both of them, and want each to win.' And then she innocently added what Irving must have passed to her, partly for communication to

Shaw, drawing him deeper into his error.

'Henry has been much vexed lately (I only learned this last evening) by what he calls "your attacks" upon him in the Saturday Review, the Olivia article especially annoying him. For the life of me I cannot realize how it feels, the *pain* for a thing of that kind . . . I said I believed he had another reason than that . . . But he would not "own up". I believe he was ashamed and I felt strangely powerfully sorry for him. I cant bear that he should be ashamed. I didnt bother him about details then . . . he and I are going for a long drive this afternoon, and he shall tell me all then.'

Shaw did not wait to be told more. He felt he knew all. 'Of course I knew all about it,' he complimented himself in his reply to her:

'a good surgeon knows when his knife touches a nerve; a good critic knows the same with his pen. There was a terrible thing in that "Olivia" notice . . . as he does not understand critical points, and treats all intellectual positions as mere matters of feeling . . . he will perhaps think it unfeeling of you not to be angry with me . . . So be kind to him, and if he is clever enough to tell you on that afternoon drive – as I should in his place – that he is giving up the play because he is jealous of me about you, take his part and console him: it is when a man is too much hurt to do the perfectly magnanimous thing that he most needs standing by.'

Shaw had then proceeded to what he assumed must be a quick magnanimous victory. He informed Irving's manager that if the Lyceum broke its pledge on no other grounds than that his *Saturday Review* criticism had been impolite, then the only conclusion to be made was that Irving had used *The Man of Destiny* to purchase good notices. But Irving would find, he added, that he could not deal with him as he did with other dramatists of the younger school. 'I am not likely to put myself in the wrong,' he assured Ellen, 'with you standing between us.'

By the time she read this Ellen had realized it was to be a more complicated business. On their drive that Sunday, Irving had allowed her to know that it was not Shaw's criticism obliging him to reject *The Man of Destiny*, but a libel. The matter of jealousy did not enter into it. Shaw's article on *Richard III*, he indicated, was an accusation of drunkenness on stage, and with someone who used his journalistic position for such scurrilous purposes no gentleman's agreement was binding.

Whether on the night of 19 December 1896 Irving had been 'stimulated artificially' and whether Shaw had intended to convey this information to his readers is difficult to know. But circumstantial evidence seems to indicate there is truth in both suppositions. Irving had fallen later that night, rupturing the ligaments of a knee, and been unable to resume *Richard III* until late in February. Shaw's criticism in the *Saturday Review* contains too many oblique references to drunkenness to be accidental.

'. . . he [Irving] was not, as it seemed to me, answering his helm satisfactorily; and he was occasionally a little out of temper with his own nervous condition. He made some odd slips in the text . . . Once he inadvertently electrified the house by very unexpectedly asking Miss Milton to get further up the stage in the blank verse and penetrating tones of Richard. Finally, the worry of playing against the vein tired him. In the tent and battle scenes his exhaustion was too genuine to be quite acceptable as part of the play. The fight was, perhaps, a relief to his feelings; but to me . . . was neither credible nor impressive . . . If Kean were to return to life and do the combat for us, we should very likely find it as absurd as his habit of lying down on a sofa when he was too tired or too drunk to keep his feet during the final scenes.'

Here was not only an accusation but an opportunity. Irving must have realized that a better one might never turn up before his option on *The Man of Destiny* ran out at the end of the year. It had been no bad thing to wait. Shaw was manoeuvred into attributing everything to his 'brilliant' notice of *Olivia* that February, with its 'indecent relish of Irving's absence'. Also, *Richard III* had opened again to considerable critical acclaim, and most people's memories of that single performance in December had been overlaid by this subsequent success. On 10 April Sardou's rival Napoleon play had opened at the Lyceum, where the box-office manager, making a half-hearted attempt to refuse admission to Shaw, was brushed aside with a threat that the *Saturday Review* critic would enter with a ticket or at the point of a revolver. Shaw's notice, treating *Madame Sans-Gêne* almost as a rehearsal for *The Man of Destiny*, had come out on the same day as he received the Lyceum's rejection.

It had been nicely timed, and was followed up by Irving with a two-fisted initiative. Unofficially, he let his associates in the theatre know of Shaw's monstrous imputation of drunkenness, while allowing the newspapers to report that he had returned the play to Shaw in order to teach him better manners. *The Era* suggested that previous reports of the Lyceum having accepted the play were false; the *Glasgow Herald* announced that Irving, having found Shaw's Napoleon unsuited to him, 'has thought it best to return the manuscript to the author with, it is understood, a handsome compliment and a present'. Suddenly Shaw found himself in a highly flurried situation where his own moral supremacy seemed unclear. It was, he told a friendly journalist, 'enough to make a saint swear'.

Though he had been led into a trap, the battle of words should have suited him perfectly. Yet even here, it seemed, he was obliged to have one hand tied behind his back. '. . . for the first time in all my long long life I am most frightfully dis-spirited,' Ellen wrote to him. 'Oh God, how frightful it is. This last week I've had real courage, to consent to live, being out of love with life . . . Dont quarrel with H[enry]. That would add to my unhappiness.' Ellen's distress immediately clouded Shaw's ecstasies. 'This is at heart a tragic business,' he admitted: 'but we cannot help it. My only anxiety is lest you become involved in it . . . Dont be anxious: I'll behave nicely and nothing particular will happen.' By behaving nicely Shaw meant that instead of going to the press he would try to settle matters privately with Irving. On 29 April he wrote to him in brisk and embattled fashion, camouflaging his note of apology. There had been no imputation of drunkenness, he stated: 'You underrate your immunities . . . I never dreamt of such a thing.' His exasperation with the performance, he assured him, had been found on other, critical grounds. Irving's reply was unaccommodating.

'I had not the privilege of reading your criticism – as you call it – of Richard. I never read a criticism of yours in my life. I have read lots of your droll, amusing, irrelevant and sometimes impertinent pages, but criticism containing judgement and sympathy I have never seen by your pen.'

With journalists clamouring for some riposte, it was becoming increasingly difficult for Shaw to remain silent. 'In a few days, failing any friendly arrangement with Irving, I shall tell the whole story, probably in an interview in the Daily Mail,' he told a friend on 7 May. '. . . [it] will be quite as amusing as a Lyceum performance of the play would have been.' Meanwhile he kept Ellen sweet. A reporter from the *Daily Mail* had arrived three days beforehand, he told her, but 'not being able to tell the man that such a display of my famous marksmanship, though highly delightful to the public, would get me into trouble with my Ellen, I had to shuffle, and finally declined to say anything for publication . . . what is going to happen?'

Though he guessed what would happen, Shaw decided for Ellen's sake to make one more appeal to Irving. On 10 May he wrote to tell him that either he must make a dignified public statement, contradicting the audacious inventions of the press, by announcing the Lyceum's production that year of *The Man of Destiny*; or else they must concoct together an alternative explanation, highly creditable to them both, for the abandonment of the play. For this second course Shaw had ready a scenario involving Mrs Patrick Campbell and Johnston Forbes Robertson as alternative cast, with perhaps a letter composed by Shaw that would appear in the press as having been written to him by Irving. 'If you can think of anything better than this, let me know,' he offered. But for Irving anything was better – even nothing was better. For to accept such a plan would reduce him to a Shavian puppet and allow Shaw's fantasies to flow down from the stage and engulf his life. So he simply arranged for his manager to send back the manuscript of Shaw's play with a brief note of rejection, followed by a more indignant expostulation drafted for him by his secretary.

During this month of manoeuvring Shaw had kept up a magnanimous attitude to Ellen. She had begged him not to quarrel with Irving. Quarrel he would not; but a 'mild tussle', he advised, would clear the blood and enable each to find out the other's value wonderfully quickly. Irving was 'heavily overweighted in the contest, and is making one mistake after another . . .' But, Shaw counselled Ellen, 'Do not be anxious – do not, at all events, betray the least anxiety . . . Don't let it disturb you for a moment: sit quiet and wait patiently.'

To Ellen it appeared that Irving was behaving much the worse. She had not seen his first performance in *Richard III*, and could find nothing wrong with Shaw's notice of it in the *Saturday Review*. His rudeness to her friend and lack of consideration for herself made her feel 'tired and sad and hopeless'. Once again, he was taking her for granted in the knowledge that she would not dare leave the Lyceum. After all those years together, she still did not understand him, could not penetrate the sardonic-sinister, elegant-grotesque veneer of his personality. Shaw had insisted on her magnificent powers of assertion – years afterwards he still believed that she could have settled *The Man of Destiny* squall by bringing Irving and himself 'to heel by mere violence of self-assertion'. But in fact her only implement was tact, and it had been insufficient. For though she felt sympathy for Irving and admired him, her underlying feeling was fear. His secrecy and sensitivity often made her tense. Really, though he might indulge her sometimes and put up with her giggling on stage, he did not much value her, was never close. Sometimes she found herself hating him – and immediately hated herself for doing so. 'H and I are out! A little bit,' she confided to Shaw. For the first time she began to criticize one man to the other.

'I've spoiled him! I was born meek. (Ugh) . . . I do assure you it is *I* all along who wished so hard for the play. He never wishes for anything much outside his own individual effort. I admire him for it, and I hate him for it, that he appreciates NOTHING and NOBODY. . . He wants a good slapping, but *you* must not do that, and *I* wont. I think I'm tired and too indifferent now. It makes me cry to know it . . .'

The men had had their tussle and Shaw, by not going to the newspapers, had behaved the better. The only point at issue was whether *The Man of Destiny* could be saved. Irving, she learnt, had thought of staging it with a translation of Richard Voss's *Schuldig* by Sydney Grundy. Perhaps it might be rescued. She felt ready to give her verdict – which was to be another version of Candida Morell's. The man who had the strength to appear weak in public, who put her private sensibilities before the gratification of his own in front of an audience: that man would win her tribute. But as she turned to Shaw, so he turned to his public.

The Lyceum door had been slammed in his face for all to see; and behind it Ellen had apparently lost her patience with Irving. 'Oh my dear, dear, dearest Ellen, I'm beaten,' he told her, by which he meant he was determined to win a popular Pyrrhic victory. *The Man of Destiny* was no more than a piece of ribbon now ('Damn the play, dearest Ellen: I don't care two straws about *that*.') Ellen, after all, did not seem to be his Strange Lady ('And with you, to you, I shall be just like other people'); Irving, when not acting (like Napoleon when not soldiering) was nobody – and in respect of Shaw's plays would remain nobody. 'Forgive me; but your Henry is not a hero off the stage,' he wrote to Ellen; 'and now that everything is ready to my hand for his discomfiture I find that I cannot bring myself to do any of the things I might do.'

He might have done nothing but he could not. Though he had pretended it was a 'storm in a teacup', this was a bitter cup for him to drink. He had failed to impose a Shavian world around Irving and his work had failed in its invasion of an enemy theatre. He was almost forty-two; he had by now written eight plays; and his career was turning in flight from the stage. There was no disguising the seriousness of this retreat in which *The Man of Destiny* had been one more battle lost. It was essential for morale that his paradoxes sustain him – what else was there? He needed two things as his spoils of defeat: to revenge himself on Irving through Ellen; and to rewrite the whole history of the event through the press.

He felt safe in attacking Irving because Ellen had already begun to criticize him herself. '*You* must not take his part now: I declare him unworthy of my Ellen,' he wrote to her.

'Your career has been sacrificed to the egotism of a fool: he has warmed his wretched hands callously at the embers of nearly twenty of your priceless years; and now they will flame up, scorch his eyes, burn off his rumbathed hair, and finally consume him . . . He tries to hide himself from himself with a rampart of lies; and he got behind it to hide himself from me. That was why he became an actor – to escape from himself . . .'

366

This was sent to Ellen on 13 May, by which day he had already drafted a long interview with himself for the *Daily Mail*. It was characteristic of Shaw to make this the occasion for helping a young office clerk in his ambition to become a journalist; and that this man, Reginald Golding Bright (later to become Shaw's London theatrical agent), should turn out to have been that solitary member of the audience who had heckled *Arms and the Man*. 'Vengeance I leave to Destiny,' Shaw announced to Ellen. What better evidence of this superiority to vengeance could there now be than his helping hand to Golding Bright? Their 'interview' in the *Daily Mail* contained no obvious malice at all, though by describing Irving as 'still obstinately under the spell of my genius' he satisfactorily converts him to a comic Shavian invention.

He was anxious to tell Ellen that he had not let her down. 'You will find nothing quarrelsome in the interview: we all come out of it with haloes of glory round our heads . . . I of course play H. off the stage; but I dress him well and allow him to make a point or two. I promised you not to quarrel, and I won't . . .'

But Ellen wasn't fooled. Though Irving pretended that the whole thing didn't much matter, she could tell from his furtive expression how much he was affected. He would have been happy, he joked, to pay for 'Mr PShaw's' funeral expenses any time. His last letter to Shaw was in effect a cry of 'For God's sake, leave me alone!' How much more human this seemed than all those Shavian acrobatics. Though it might signal surrender to Shaw, this letter helped to turn Ellen's sympathy some way back to Irving. 'My poor Henry!' she exclaimed. Why hadn't Shaw been able to leave him alone – for her sake? She could not hide her disillusionment.

'I CANT take things back (or I would) – for it's always so sweet to remember the sweets. I'd like to say "I hate you and detest you" – but then I'd "remember" THAT *too*. Well, you are quite stupid after all and *not* so unlike other people. You should have given in and said, "Take the play and do it when you can. You'll do it better than anyone else and *nurse* it better than anyone else" . . . I'm angry with you.'

Shaw once told Ellen that sometimes on Sundays he had seen her and Irving driving along Richmond Terrace or thereabouts, 'like two children in a gigantic perambulator, and [I] have longed to seize him, throw him out, get up, take his place, and calmly tell the coachman to proceed.' What Ellen had learnt from this quarrel was that Shaw wanted to seize Irving and throw him out – and then let her proceed alone: a variation of what Irving had done to his own wife after *The Bells*. Ellen knew now that neither man cared for her, loved her, as she had once believed. 'And NOW – well go your ways,' she decided. They were self-centred, curiously impractical men – and they *were* jealous. Irving's jealousy shone plainly through his sardonic reaction to her enjoyment of Shaw's other plays – *The Devil's Disciple* and, later, *Caesar and Cleopatra*. 'Henry will never produce a play by you,' she concluded. And, in his letters to her, what except jealousy kept Shaw piling up execrations upon Irving's head?

'I would pity him, only the thought comes that the crafty wrinkle in his overrated countenance which years of such base exultation have graven there may have been touched by Ellen's lips; and then I stretch my maddened hands to clutch the lightning.'

She could not always remember her lines; she was on the verge of breaking down – and yet at a sound or, most of all, a touch, she could still feel a throb of her heart. 'I fly from "throbs" in these days. It is not becoming. It's absurd.' She flew to her work, which was another sort of love. 'Work hardens and alerts me,' she confirmed in Shavian style. But the discipline of work without a little bit of real love became mechanical. 'If *only* I could be "in love". I cant go on acting like this.' Neither Irving nor Shaw could give her real love; neither would touch her, produce that throb. 'My need has passed,' she pretended. And to Shaw, she confided: 'You see I have no lovers, only loves, and I have as many of those as I want, and you are the only one I dont benefit! You do things for me. I do things for them.'

He did things for her that he wanted to do rather than the things she sometimes might have wanted done for her. Her lack of self-confidence confronted his work-exhaustion and saw in it signs of polite boredom. 'Darling, you are very kind to me,' she ventured.

From the wreckage of those hopes they had placed in each other, kindness persisted. And from that kindness came an honesty; and from honesty a muted revival of hope. Shaw's letters to Ellen tell of his childhood, of his dilemma of loving and the escape from incest into fantasy. Sometimes it is as if J. M. Barrie had taken up his pen.

'I cant in pen and ink rest these bruised brains in your lap & unburden my heart . . . when I can write, then my ideas fly like stones: you can never be sure that one of them will not hurt you – my very love gets knit into an infernal intellectual fabric that wounds when I mean it to caress; . . . When *you* complain, I am terrified another way, thinking that the end has come – for I have only one thing to say to you . . . wanting to sleep, and yet to sleep with you. Only, do you know what the consequences would be? Well, about tomorrow at noon when the sun would be warm & the birds in full song, you would feel an irresistible impulse to fly into the woods. And there, to your great astonishment & scandal, you would be *confined* of a baby that would immediately spread a pair of wings and fly, and before you could rise to catch it it would be followed by another & another and another – hundreds of them, and they would finally catch you up & fly away with you to some heavenly country where they would grow into strong sweetheart sons with whom, in defiance of the prayerbook, you would found a divine race. Would you not like to be the mother of your own grandchildren? If you were my mother, I am sure I should carry you away to the tribe in Central America where – but I have a lot of things to say . . .'

In such passages, and without ever stating openly that the need he felt for his mother's love had set a pattern for his relationships with women, Shaw tried to indicate why he had supplanted the physical act of love with 'a lot of things to say'. In his fashion he loved Ellen; at any rate he wanted to love Ellen; but he could more easily hurt than touch her and felt he must 'get beyond love' to the stage where there was nothing to fear. However much of this Ellen understood, she recognized the integrity and limitation of his feeling for her: 'You are a dear old kind fellow, as well as everything else.'

So they laid the preparations for a second chapter of their love, freed by his theatrical imagination from the actual dominance of his mother, but in another place than the Lyceum. 'Never a play for your Ellen, oh no,' she taunted him. For he had promised her: 'Nevertheless you shall play for me yet; but not with him, not with him, not with him.'

## [ 4 ]

*Here am I, the god who has been happy, among people who say 'I want to be happy just once'. The result, though, is alarming – desiring nothing further, I have become a sublime monster, to whose disembodied heart the consummation of ordinary lives is a mere anti-climax.* (1896)

It had been the end of October 1895 before Janet Achurch found another part. Four months after her return from America, she stepped onto the stage of the Metropole in Camberwell as Mercy Merrick, a man-made angel-woman, in the revival of Wilkie Collins's *The New Magdalen*. Shaw was at the first night to observe it for the *Saturday Review*. It was a fashionably sentimental drama, poorly cast and desperately unprepared, of the sort that had once provoked his 'unpleasant plays'. But he was in the mood to be benevolent. Richard Mansfield having attracted to himself almost all his disappointment over *Candida*, Shaw had felt able to renew his faith in the voluptuous Janet. To his chivalrous imagination she was a 'tigress' on the stage, and in life 'rebel rather than victim'. Describing her as 'the only tragic actress of genius we now possess', he reported that the old play had received powerful acting.

'. . . She reproduced for me an old experience of the days when, as a musical critic, I gained from contact with great works and a living art the knowledge I am now losing and the finely trained sense I am now blunting in our silly and vulgar theatres . . . Miss Achurch [has] taken this innocent old figment of Wilkie Collins's benevolent and chivalrous imagination, and played into it a grim truth that it was never meant to bear – played it against the audience, so that the curious atmosphere of reluctance and remonstrance from which Calvé use to wring the applause of the huge audiences at Covent Garden when the curtain fell on her Carmen, arose more than once when Miss Achurch disturbed and appalled us . . .'

Shaw had designed his notice so as to help re-establish Janet's career. While she was abroad he had kept her name before the public, linking it to Ellen Terry's. Both, it seemed to him, had potential talent enough to compare with his heroine Eleanora Duse. But Irving had often reduced Ellen to a pretty leading lady; and Charrington threatened to plunge Janet into similar second-rate popularity. It was a question of sex appeal versus artistic integrity; and for Shaw it was a question of losing one in the other. Ellen and Janet held twin attractions. Under their spell he was like a child playing at mothers-and-fathers. About business affairs they needed a stream of fatherly advice; and while he chattered out this advice they encircled him with such powerful maternal appeal that, by 1896, he was imagining them performing on alternate nights in *Candida* which he described as 'THE Mother Play'.

'I fear only the character of *the Mother* becomes me,' lamented Ellen Terry. Meanwhile, to the younger Janet, Shaw extended all his father-like protection. Remember, he told her, '*I* will set you right on Saturday . . . and by all that's unmerciful I'll set the others right too. Sit tight, dear Janet; and I will answer for the result . . .'

Janet had talent, but it was not the talent for sitting tight. She was in such an unsmiling hurry to succeed that, as Ellen Terry noticed, she would '*overdo* it'. On this occasion she had barely grasped her words from the prompter than she fell back with an illness diagnosed by herself as pleurisy. This was the moment for Shaw to walk on, prescribing Jaeger innovations, and to implore Charrington to avoid the use of poisonous drugs. But Janet grew worse, and on 10 November Shaw's medical friend Kingston Barton, had diagnosed typhoid fever. Her illness 'occupied me a good deal during the last two months of the year [1895],' Shaw noted in his diary, 'partly because of its bearing on all possible plans for the production of *Candida*, and partly because I have come into relations of intimate friendship with the Charringtons . . .'

He was now under tremendous strain. All his sexual energy was being forced into work which, as *Saturday Review* critic, Fabian pamphleteer and composer of elaborately unperformed plays, was enough to keep him scribbling day and night. 'Life just now is impossible,' he had told Sydney Cockerell: 'there is some confounded performance every night in all sorts of languages . . .' The money he earned from his journalism was absorbed by his family, but whatever small change he could squeeze out he handed over to Charrington; and whatever time he could scratch together, often from his hours of sleep, he spent with Janet at Onslow Square, holding her Wagnerian frame against her pillow. The atmosphere in the house was appalling. Charrington, mentally reduced to the condition of a pair of old slippers, shuffled from room to room. But Shaw, though suffering from hundred-horse-power headaches, refused to admit any pessimism – even when Charrington, rousing himself with a bout of hostility, objected to his closeness to Janet in her bedroom. A nurse was installed, but still Janet grew worse until, her death appearing possible, Shaw was denied her room altogether. Wandering off to the studio of the Fabian artist, Bertha Newcombe, he poured out his feelings. 'He had told me long before how he felt towards death,' she remembered.

'Anxiety, sorrow, and all efforts at prevention would naturally be undertaken, but after the inevitable end he would, as David did, rise, wash & anoint himself and putting death behind him, grasp Life again. He said to me, "Should Janet die, I should *never* forget her." He then characteristically spent a quite cheerful evening with me & even told me that he had had a delightful time and enjoyed himself.'

But Janet did not die: and with her recovery Shaw's irresistible hopes took off again. Perhaps she might play his Strange Lady. From her illness had come health; but after her convalescence she began to slip back into 'your weak wicked old self ', he admonished her, 'your brandy and soda self, your fabling, pretending, promising, company promoting, heavy eyelidded, morphia injecting self '.

'. . . All through your illness you were beautiful and young; now you are beginning to look, not nourished but – steel yourself for another savage word – bloated. Do, for heaven's sake, go back to the innocent diet of the invalid . . . You *can't* drink brandy with wholesome food; and if you take exercise you won't want so much morphia. Eat stewed fruit and hovis . . .'

At least as worrying to Shaw as the effects on Janet's body of morphia and alcohol was the touting for money upon her 'soul'. With his help, Charrington had succeeded J. T. Grein as managing director of the Independent Theatre. It was a calculated gamble, aimed at helping Charrington's chances of achieving a stage career separate from his wife, whom Shaw had once more exhorted to 'live out your own life in your own way, and leave him [Charrington] to do the same'. This was Shaw's way of forbidding Janet's bedroom to her husband. 'The moral of it all is, leave him free and be free yourself,' he told her. But Janet saw here another opportunity: that of fraudulently obtaining a hundred and fifty pounds, and using it to star in *Candida* at the Independent Theatre. Shaw was horrified. This was the very opposite end for which this misconceived play had been designed. Despite her 'gusts of ice and sulphur', he suddenly turned, and forbade her the play he had specifically written for her. It was beginning to seem that, instead of inspiring Janet, he was one of her pieces of ill-luck; that his plays, tempting as they appeared, were not the right vehicle for her genius. Their adventure together was coming to an end.

So *Candida* once more receded and was replaced by the announcement of another Independent enterprise, Ibsen's *Little Eyolf*. The rights of this play had been secured from the publisher William Heinemann by their rival Ibsenite Elizabeth Robins. But she had failed to place it in the West End, and now offered it to the Independent Theatre. Shaw having previously informed Elizabeth Robins that she didn't understand *Little Eyolf* ('I see no signs of it in your handwriting'), urged massive tactfulness on the Charringtons, but then took over the sensitive negotiations himself. 'You see nobody can afford to behave as outrageously as I can in the affair,' he explained to them. '. . . The paramount necessity is to bring you into the most sympathetic possible relation with Heinemann.' He was anxious to replace a beautiful actress, Rhoda Halkett, with Elizabeth Robins herself in the part of Asta. Rhoda Halkett had enough sex appeal to knock a dozen men sideways – and this was why Shaw preferred Miss Robins of 'the beautiful Puritan charm, the "St Elizabeth" sanctity, the pure toned voice'. He had never been easy with her, but that was because she, rather than he, had insisted on the asexuality of their relationship. Besides, she was a protégée of Wilde's. One letter from Shaw ('You dont know your own mind. *Do* pull yourself together and put yourself in some intelligible position'), and Heinemann became immovably opposed to the scheme. By March the Independent Theatre had cancelled *Little Eyolf*.

Shaw's tactics over this incident reveal all his frustration and sense of strain, and may also point to his reluctance to see Janet and Charrington on stage together. In view of his failures, it was remarkable how there still persisted in him 'my growing certainty that I can be a dramatic poet if I concentrate myself on it'. But his confidence in Janet was diminishing as his interest, denied access to Elizabeth Robins, mounted in Ellen Terry. The plot of *Candida* was being enacted in his own life. In a letter he wrote to Janet while Charrington was away in April 1896 can be heard again the accents of Marchbanks at the end of the play. 'The step up to the plains of heaven was made on your bosom, I know; and it was a higher step than those I had previously taken on other bosoms,' he warned her.

'But he who mounts does not take the stairs with him, even though he may dream for the moment that each stair, as he touches it, is a plank on which he will float to the end of his journey. I know that the floating plank image is false and the stair image true; for I have left the lower stairs behind me and must in turn leave you unless you too mount along with me. I cannot change my pace (if I could I would quicken it) or alter my orbit; and if they take me away from you, I must accept the fact and make new combinations and plans based upon it . . . I hope these complaints and disparagements will not make you unhappy. I know myself so fatally well-prone to overrate the powers of the people I like, but, when I once find them out, turning like a shot and accommodating myself to the new estimate of them with appalling and merciless suddenness.'

From Janet's point of view this metaphor was no more convincing than the plot of *Candida* itself. Shaw's appeal was to her ambition. 'During all these years,' he wrote, 'I have acquired a certain power of work, and hardened myself to stand unscraped by many knife edges that cut ordinary folk. But ability does not become genius until it has risen to the point at which its keenest states of perception touch on ecstasy, untainted by mere epileptic or drunken incontinence, or sexual incontinence.' What Shaw had achieved for himself through will-power, he wanted to achieve for Janet vicariously. He wanted to become her guide and the source of her power; he wanted to replace her ordinary husband-and-wife liaison with Charrington by an asexual motherly communion with himself.

Janet gave Shaw her answer the following month by revealing that she had been faithless to his principles 'to the extent of making "Candida" impossible until after next February [1897], when she expects to become once more a mother'. Watching Janet, seeing her beauty (her eyes like moons in a wet fog), Shaw understood what physical joy she took in her pregnancy. It was for her, as it had been for Ellen Terry, a voluptuous confinement. But Ellen was not pregnant and never would be again; while Janet's pregnancy moved the plot of their lives back from the stage into life. In short: she could not act in 'THE Mother Play' because she was to be a mother. That summer he saw and corresponded less with Janet. 'I daren't be devoted now,' he told her in a moment of rare pathos. 'The appeal of your present experience to my sympathy is too strong to be indulged. So don't be angry with Shaw, Limited.'

*

But Shaw had not exhausted his capacity for being surprised by Janet. During this summer Elizabeth Robins had at last found a theatre for *Little Eyolf*. All the British Ibsenites had agreed to join together at the Avenue Theatre to produce a series of matinées of the play in William Archer's translation. Elizabeth Robins herself chose the sympathetic though self-sacrificing part of Asta Allmers that Shaw had originally wanted for her. In the role of Rita Allmers, the sexually jealous husband-devouring wife (in whose greedy love Shaw recognized the passion of Jenny Patterson) was cast the pregnant Janet. And, to thicken the confusion, she had as her understudy Florence Farr. Finally they had somehow serenaded from the West End Mrs Patrick Campbell to play the small but crucial part of the Rat Wife.

The play opened on 23 November 1896 with Shaw stationed in the stalls to report the event for the *Saturday Review*. 'When, in a cast of five, you have the three best yet discovered actresses of their generation,' he wrote, 'you naturally look for something extraordinary.' What he saw was a microcosm of his own life: a disjointed production full of brilliant pieces not carpentered together. Mrs Campbell played the Rat Wife 'once quite enchantingly, and once most disappointingly'; while Elizabeth Robins, he now decided, was not well cast as 'the quiet, affectionate, enduring, reassuring, faithful, domestic' Asta, and, falling back on genteel misery, became 'too atrociously ladylike'. Having placed two of the three best yet discovered actresses in the shade, he shone the lights full on Janet whose role, he declared, was one of the heaviest written for the stage: 'any single act of it would exhaust an actress of no more than ordinary resources.'

'But Miss Achurch was more than equal to the occasion. Her power seemed to grow with its own expenditure. The terrible outburst at the end of the first act did not leave a scrape on her voice (which appears to have the compass of a military band) and threw her into victorious action in that tearing second act instead of wrecking her. She played with all her old originality and success, and with more than her old authority over her audience.'

Shaw's review, almost three thousand words long, was divided into literary and dramatic criticism. First there was this tribute to an actress whose ability (in opposition to Archer's favourite Elizabeth Robins) Shaw believed he alone recognized, and into which he had pumped such a continuous stream of emotional energy. But then there was the other Janet, temperamental and reckless, who had dissipated her talent and his love. So after the celebration comes the comedy, showing the public everything he had had to endure.

'. . . she produced almost every sound that a big human voice can, from a creak like the opening of a rusty canal lock to a melodious-tenor note that the most robust Siegfried might have envied. She looked at one moment like a young, well-dressed, very pretty woman: at another she was like a desperate creature just fished dripping out of the river by the Thames Police. Yet another moment, and she was the incarnation of impetuous, ungovernable strength. Her face was sometimes winsome, sometimes listlessly wretched, sometimes like the head of a statue of Victory, sometimes suffused horrible, threatening, like Bellona or Medusa. She would cross from left to right like a queen, and from right to left with, so to speak, her toes turned in, her hair coming down, and her slippers coming off . . . I very much doubt whether we shall see her often until she comes into the field with a repertory as highly specialized as that of Sir Henry Irving or Duse. For it is so clear that she would act an average London success to pieces and play an average actor-manager off the stage, that we need not expect to see much of her as that useful and pretty auxiliary, a leading lady.

'Being myself a devotee of the beautiful school, I like being enchanted by Mrs Patrick Campbell better than being frightened, harrowed, astonished, conscience-stricken, devastated, and dreadfully delighted in general by Miss Achurch's untamed genius.'

To Ellen Terry four weeks earlier Shaw had admitted that Janet *really* loved him. 'What do *I* do?' Ellen countered; then added 'Goodbye'. Writing his notice of *Little Eyolf* that November, Shaw looked at Janet with the eyes of someone falling out of love. No longer did he feel his future as a playwright to be dedicated to her: 'how is your ship to be of use to me, or I to it,' he asked, 'unless I command the whole fleet?' The genial humour of his review absolved him from disloyalty; he had exposed to the public only those faults in which he had been rubbing Janet's nose privately. But to his disenchanted eye, those faults for the first time appeared insuperable.

Less than six months earlier, reviewing Sudermann's *Magda*, Shaw had described Mrs Campbell's acting as 'the merest baby-play' when compared to Janet at her best. But Janet's best performances were past and the siren voice of Mrs Pat was already beginning to beguile him. Her appearance in the cast of *Little Eyolf* had guaranteed good business, and brought the production to the notice of a theatre syndicate that proposed purchasing the rights from Elizabeth Robins, promoting it 'into a full-blown fashionable theatrical speculation'. Hearing these rumours, Janet went secretly behind Elizabeth Robins's back to negotiate her own terms with the syndicate. But the secret leaked out and Elizabeth Robins quickly passed on the facts and figures to Mrs Pat, enabling her to underbid Janet for the lead. So Elizabeth outscored Janet, and her New Century Theatre, formed to regenerate the British stage, excluded Shaw and the Charringtons with their Independent Theatre. On 6 December, after two weeks in the role of Rita Allmers, Janet was suddenly replaced by Mrs Pat. 'A nice surprise for a woman in her condition, wasn't it?' Shaw fulminated to Ellen Terry. '. . . You can imagine how pleasantly they all get on together under these circumstances.' He propped Janet up over her disappointment, overlooked her deviousness, insisted that everything was best for the unborn baby, bullied her for being upset and enabled her to get through her last two performances 'with sufficient gallantry in the face of the enemy'. The new production, with Florence Farr interrupting her Egyptology to come in (with 'a certain strangeness of effect') for Mrs Pat's old part of the Rat Wife, called forth another two thousand five hundred words from Shaw in the *Saturday Review*. His first notice of *Little Eyolf* had been in part a preview of his coming susceptibility to Mrs Pat. In this second review of the play he summons up all his resistance to her sexual glamour and turns instead to the sublimated attractions of an idealistically remembered Janet.

'. . . Goodness gracious, I thought, what things that evil-minded Miss Achurch did read into this harmless play! And how nicely Mrs Campbell took the drowning of the child! Just a pretty waving of the fingers, a moderate scream as if she had very nearly walked on a tin tack, and it was all over, without tears, without pain, without more fuss than if she had broken the glass of her watch.

'. . . What a contrast to Miss Achurch, who so unnecessarily filled the stage with the terror of death in this passage! This is what comes of exaggeration, of over-acting, of forgetting that people go to the theatre to be amused, and not to be upset! . . . it is these Ibsenite people that create the objections to Ibsen. If Mrs Campbell had played Rita from the first, not a word would have been said of the play; and the whole business would have been quietly over and the theatre closed by this time. But nothing would serve them but their Miss Achurch; and so, instead of a pretty arrangement of the "Eyolf" theme for boudoir pianette, we had it flung to the "Götterdämmerung" orchestra, and blared right into our shrinking souls.'

The ship on which Shaw was here hoisting his colours had to be massively buoyed up if it were not to sink. For a few sentences he seems to be trying out the device he had used in *Love Among the Artists* – but Mrs Pat was not conveniently cast as the well-connected, pseudo-actress blocking the path of Janet's superior talent. So he converts Janet into a symbol of future enterprise – 'some equitable form of theatrical organization' – that was to make its appearance as the Stage Society and in the Court Theatre, breaking free from the star system of the West End so bewitchingly embodied by Mrs Pat. This was adroit footwork, preserving his loyalty to Janet and the Independent Theatre, rescuing himself from sentimentality, and scoring a telling point of theatre politics. It was then Janet's turn once more to surprise him.

*

Later that month Janet seems to have had a miscarriage. 'Poor Janet', Ellen Terry commiserated to Shaw. 'But tell her to wait. One gets everything if one will only wait, and she can. She is young and clever.' Early the next year, 1897, she was already brimming with morphia-bright schemes that would obliterate Shaw's image of her as a symbol of the new theatre. In her home town of Manchester she enjoyed a 'glorious rampage', playing Cleopatra opposite Louis Calvert's 'inexcusably fat' Antony. But Shaw could not share her enjoyment. He had hoped that Janet might establish the Independent Theatre as a successful rival to the commercial West End stage. Instead, she had abandoned the experimental drama for which members of the Independent paid their subscriptions and replaced it with a thirty-year-old acting version of Shakespeare that might be seen any evening at Irving's Lyceum. For his 'nasty' notice in the *Saturday Review*, done in his best 'tomahawking style', Shaw used Janet and Irving 'as bolsters to bang one another with'. For the first time Janet was made an object for the hilarious sarcasm Irving knew so well:

'. . . she is determined that Cleopatra shall have rings on her fingers and bells on her toes, and that she shall have music wherever she goes . . . The lacerating discord of her wailings is in my tormented ears as I write, reconciling me to the grave . . . I am a broken man . . . all Miss Achurch's sins against Shakespear will be forgiven her. I begin to have hopes of a great metropolitan vogue for that lady now, since she has at last done something that is thoroughly wrong from beginning to end.'

Here was a variation on an old tune: the 'nerve destroying crooning' of Florence Farr blending naturally in Janet's 'lacerating discord'. What did he do to these women? What he was trying to do with Janet, and for the last time in public, was to flatter-and-scold her into Shavian word-excellence. Though she appeared in only four fairly minor productions, Shaw mentioned her name on twenty-one occasions in the *Saturday Review*, and supported the Independent Theatre as against Elizabeth Robins's New Century Theatre. He had laughed at Archer's solemn susceptibility to Elizabeth and its effect on his criticism in *The World*, but this was a reflection of his own attitude to Janet. That April Janet agreed to play Ellida in Ibsen's *The Lady from the Sea* (the part Shaw had once earmarked for Ellen Terry), waited for the Independent to issue its prospectus, then changed her mind and suddenly declared for *Candida* again. But with 'iron brutality' Shaw refused.

So Janet fell back once more on *A Doll's House*, enabling Shaw, in his *Saturday Review* column, to compare her performance with the one eight years before that had so hypnotized him. She had lost, he thought, her life-giving naturalness – a loss comparable to that of Alice in Miss Lockett, and matching the disappearance of Sonny within G.B.S. 'Miss Achurch can no longer content herself with a girl's allowance of passion and sympathy,' he wrote.

'She fills the cup and drains it; and consequently, though Nora has all the old vitality and originality, and more than her old hold on the audience, she is less girlish and more sophisticated with the passions of the stage than she was at the Novelty when she first captivated us.'

Their story was ending with a curious reversal. 'At last I am beginning to understand anti-Ibsenism,' Shaw told his *Saturday Review* readers.

'... I understand better what it means to the unhappy wretches who can conceive no other life as possible to them except the Doll's House life... It will be remarked that I no longer dwell on the awakening of the woman, which was once the central point of the drama. Why should I? The play solves that problem just as it is being solved in real life. The woman's eyes are opened; and instantly her doll's dress is thrown off and her husband left staring at her, helpless, bound thenceforth either to do without her (an alternative which makes short work of his independence) or else treat her as a human being like himself, fully recognizing that he is not a creature of one superior species, Man, living with a creature of another and inferior species, Woman, but that Mankind is male and female... We no longer study an object lesson in lord-of-creationism, appealing to our sociological

378

interest only. We see a fellow-creature blindly wrecking his happiness and losing his "love-life", and are touched dramatically.'

In this passage he takes off the mantle of his idealism from Janet – and puts it on Charrington. The sympathy he feels for Helmer reflects a new sympathy for Janet's husband and his own rising fear of being imprisoned himself within a secure and happy marriage. It is Marchbanks out in the night, looking back at the Morells' home and shuddering at having so narrowly escaped from Morell's infatuated domesticity. It is also a preparation for his review of the Independent Theatre's next production, *The Wild Duck*, which, since Janet did not have a part, gave him the opportunity to declare that it had been Charrington (not Janet or Elizabeth) who had struck the decisive blow for Ibsen in England.

'But Mr Charrington, like Mr Kendal and Mr Bancroft, has a wife; and the difference made by Miss Janet Achurch's acting has always been more obvious than that made by her husband's management to a public which has lost all tradition of what stage management really is, apart from lavish expenditure on scenery and furniture . . . Now, however, we have him at last with Miss Janet Achurch out of the bill. The result is conclusive . . . there is not a moment of bewilderment during the development . . . The dialogue, which in any other hands would have been cut to ribbons, is given without the slightest regard to the clock . . . That is a real triumph of management. It may be said that it is a triumph of Ibsen's genius; but of what use is Ibsen's genius if the manager has not the genius to believe in it?'

Shaw still believed that Janet and Charrington ought to part – but now it was for his sake more than hers: Helmer should slam the door; Morell should hurry after Marchbanks. During 1897 Shaw used his *Saturday Review* column to broadcast his conversion and persuade his public to share it. In February he described Charrington as 'the only stage-manager of genius the new movement has produced, and quite its farthest-seeing pioneer'. He followed this up in April by calling him an 'adventurer who explores the new territory at his own risk and is superseded by commercial enterprise the moment he is seen to pick up anything'. This was a complete volte-face for Shaw who, less than four years earlier, had attacked Charrington for frittering away Janet's gifts with his financial and theatrical recklessness. Now he discovers that although all this had 'seemed rash, inexcusable, and senseless at the time; and its disastrous pecuniary failure seemed a salutary check to an otherwise incorrigible desperado . . . today everybody is doing what he did'.

'His view that the only live English fiction is to be found today not in plays but in novels, and his attempt to drag it on to the stage no matter how little playgoers and actors were accustomed to its characteristic atmosphere, cost him several years' income, and would have cost him his reputation for common sense had he possessed one. But since then Trilby has justified her misunderstood predecessor Clever Alice; and the apparently idiotic "quintuple bill" of scenes from stories by Barrie, Conan Doyle, Thackeray, and so on, put up by Mr Charrington at Terry's Theatre, now seems like an epitome of what theatrical enterprise, with its rage for adaptations of novels, has since become. Other more cautious pioneers followed – Mr Grein, Miss Farr, Miss Robins; but nobody foresaw so much and nobody suffered so much as Mr Charrington.'

Here was a handsome apology to Charrington, transformed in Shaw's public imagination from the friend of pawnbrokers, who only cared for 'a pipe, a glass of whisky, a caress from a respectable woman', into a dedicated man-of-the-theatre crippled by obsessive love for his wife. Shaw reinforces his public statement with a private message: 'You are a monster, a moral monster,' he warns Janet.

'How is he [Charrington] to be got out of your clutches: that is what I want to know? It is clear that you are not going to act any more . . . Yes: I note that you will never desert Mr Micawber. Oh, if only he could be induced to desert you!'

\*

Janet *really* loved him, Shaw had told Ellen Terry. Eight months later, in July 1897, he is explaining to Ellen that Janet was 'beginning to dislike me'. So when, having achieved success nowhere else, Shaw finally consented that month to let the Independent Theatre produce *Candida*, it was into the 'capable hands' of Charrington, not to Janet, that he gave it. 'Charrington is taking out a Doll's House tour,' he told Ellen: 'and he's going to try "Candida" on the provincial dog.' In the theatre of human relationships he then introduced some complicated stage directions. Ellen would not act for him: but why should her daughter, Edy Craig, not play Prossy in the Charringtons' production of *Candida* (and Mrs Linden in *A Doll's House*). 'Would she go, do you think?' Shaw asked Ellen. 'It will be a pretty miserable tour,' he promised, '. . . but she might pick up something from Charrington; and Janet would keep her in gossip for a twelve-month to come.' So Shaw proposed; Ellen consented; and Edy was signed up for £20 a week.

Ellen felt tantalized by Shaw's friendship with her daughter. She had sent him a picture of both her children; Shaw had responded with one of himself – but with his eyes averted. Ellen had studied his chin, his ear, his lively nostril; but what of his expression? He had deliberately looked away, he replied. After all, they were not to see each other. Besides, what if Edy, then in her mid-twenties, dark and handsome, had come across a likeness of G.B.S. staring at her. Obviously she would be hypnotized. 'The fatal spell would operate at once: I should have her here by the next underground train, insisting on my flying with her to the ends of the earth, and utterly disregarding my feeble protests that I adore her mother.'

So the photograph had not looked at her; but the man had. Some evenings when Ellen was at the Lyceum, Shaw would call at her home in Barkston Gardens and read his latest play to Edy and her friend Sally Fairchild. By the time Ellen returned, he was gone. They still had not met. She questioned them about him. He was, it seemed, 'the vainest flirt'. 'He'd coquet with a piece of string,' Sally Fairchild volunteered. But they had seen too the dreadful fatigue behind his teasing.

'Oh, I'd love to have a baby every year,' Ellen had written to Shaw. Of course it was a fantasy: all men were babies to her. But to her own children she was not a good mother, spoiling her son, dominating her daughter. She rejected Edy's suitors – but what of Shaw? 'Your sweetheart-Mother,' Ellen signed one of her letters to him. That fantasy would take a step towards reality if he married Edy. In any event Ellen welcomed this tour. The presence of her daughter with those watching eyes, that cool voice, unsettled her.

The rehearsals of *Candida* at Islington were 'inconceivably bad'. Shaw sat there silently as if in pain. It seemed to him he was no longer the author of this play and that his Janet had been an illusion; the reality was *Nicholas Nickleby*'s Mrs Crummles. 'Janet would look, and be, that Candida beautifully,' Ellen had predicted, 'but I could help her I know, to a lot of bottom in it.' Shaw himself could no longer help Janet. 'You have driven a red hot harrow over my heart,' he wrote as the tour started.

*Candida* was first presented to the public for one performance on 30 July 1897 in Aberdeen, to the bewilderment of its Scottish audience. The *Aberdeen Daily Journal* called it a 'risky business', though the drunken scene had been 'much appreciated'. One 'champion criticism' came from the *Northern Figaro*.

'I don't think we'll be much troubled with Mr Shaw's comedy . . . It takes quite a long time to understand what it is all about, and even then it is not very clear . . . I am sorry for Miss Achurch, she had such an uncongenial part to play, she certainly did her best with it, but I don't think she will ever say that "Candida" is her favourite part ... There was not a large audience in the theatre on Friday, and I noticed that they did not even know when they should laugh or keep silent. At the end the actors were cheered for getting through the performance so efficiently.'

Earlier that same month *The Man of Destiny* had had its first presentation to the public by way of three performances at Croydon. 'Picture to yourself the worst you ever feared for it,' Shaw appealed to Ellen:

'raise that worst to nightmare absurdity and horror; multiply it by ten; and then imagine even that result ruined by an attack of utter panic on the part of the company in which each made the other's speeches ...

'But it is not the blundering & incompetence that makes me feel criminal at these performances. As long as people are really *trying* (and they were really trying with pitiable sincerity last night) I have an enormous patience with them. The dreadful thing is the impossibility to them of getting on terms of real intimacy and enjoyment with my stuff ... There was something insane & ghastly about the business ... An agonizing experience for the author, Ellen.'

Ellen tried to encourage him. When the Charringtons' tour reached Eastbourne she went to see it, and told Shaw, 'it comes out on the stage even better than when one reads it. It is absorbingly interesting every second ... Even the audience understood it all.' As for Janet, she would write to her 'about one or two trifling things in her acting, suggestions which she may care, or not care, to try over'.

But Shaw could not bring himself to experience with *Candida* what he had subjected himself to with *The Man of Destiny*. 'I daren't face it,' he told Janet. He was out of love with the theatre, with theatrical people, with Janet. She had tried to borrow money from Ellen Terry and, worse still, from Edy. She had even tried to take advantage of a new friend of Shaw's, a 'public spirited Irish Lady' called Charlotte Payne-Townshend whom he had taken to the disastrous production of *Little Eyolf*. 'You've done it at last,' he exploded. 'I knew you would.' Once he had retreated before the 'moral vacuity' of Florence Farr; now he backed away from Janet, accusing her of being 'a moral void – a vacuum'.

'I would advise you to see Candida before producing it in London,' Ellen Terry had written. Janet had told the press that *Candida* was shortly to start its London run. It was another instance of her mendacity and Shaw instructed Charrington to banish the idea: 'implore her not to bluff about "Candida". You really dont grasp the extent of the mess that has been made of that unhappy play.' Eventually he saw his play when the

Charringtons did one London performance for the Stage Society in the summer of 1900. Edy 'pulled off the typist successfully,' he assured Ellen. But Janet, he decided, 'wasnt the right woman for it at all' and Charrington was 'grotesquely damnable as the parson'.

She still had power to charm him. Calling round one evening at the end of 1897 he had found her as adorable as ever. But soon she grew loud and, after dinner, fuddled – reminding Shaw of his father. With whatever temptations to relent, he knew then what he must do. For too long he had made himself uselessly disagreeable. Now he must walk out into the night. 'Let us drop the subject and say goodbye whilst there is still some Janet left to say goodbye to,' he wrote.

'. . . I held up a mirror in which Janet was beautiful as long as I could, in private and in print: now I've held it up with Janet inarticulate and rowdy. Avoid me now as you would the devil; for from this time I will destroy your self respect if you let me near you . . . I am growing old and cowardly and selfish: it's sufficient that I loved you when I was young. Now I can do nothing but harm unless I say farewell, farewell, farewell, farewell, farewell, farewell, farewell, farewell.'


# [ 5 ]

*My reputation as a dramatist grows with every play of mine that is not performed.* (1897)

We are perpetually moralists, but playwrights only by chance. Between the end of 1895 and the beginning of 1897 Shaw gave the West End stage two more chances of discovering him. In these years of dramatic criticism he described, explained, predicted what was and what should be happening in the theatre. He lectured actor-managers and patiently instructed actresses in their business. And while he was attempting to teach he also learnt, collecting knowledge in the form of images and patterns of drama. But there was a discrepancy between what he taught others and what he was teaching himself.

Both *You Never Can Tell* and *The Devil's Disciple* are apparently good examples of Shaw's skill in writing for a theatre that, in the *Saturday Review*, he was simultaneously campaigning to destroy. The first was farce; the second melodrama. Both were conventional as to form but so unusual in style that readers and actors felt bewildered. 'When I got to the end,' wrote George Alexander returning the text of *You Never Can Tell*, 'I had no more idea what you meant by it than a tom-cat.'

In his Preface to *Plays Pleasant* Shaw described *You Never Can Tell* as an attempt to answer the many requests of managers in search of fashionable comedies for West End theatres. 'I had no difficulty in complying,' he explained,

'as I have always cast my plays in the ordinary practical comedy form in use at all the theatres; and far from taking an unsympathetic view of the popular preference for fun, fashionable dresses, a little music, and even an exhibition of eating and drinking by people with an expensive air, attended by an if-possible-comic waiter, I was more than willing to shew that the drama can humanize these things as easily as they, in the wrong hands, can dehumanize the drama.'

*You Never Can Tell* has all the extravagant materials of those farces Shaw was growing so familiar with as a dramatic critic: lost parents, antiphonal twins, outrageous coincidences, transparent disguises and the crowning emblem of a comic waiter. But despite this parade, he objected to the play being billed as farce, fearing that this label would pack it off to the dehumanized world of mechanical comedy. 'The thing is a poem and a document,' he protested to Archer, 'a sermon and a festival, all in one.' Using dentistry as his metaphor, Shaw was trying under laughing gas (specifically identified in the original manuscript version) to 'pluck from the memory a rooted sorrow', and, at the same time, to modify the stock materials of theatrical comedy.

In his Preface to *The Shewing-up of Blanco Posnet* he was to liken the nation's morals to its teeth ('the more decayed they are the more it hurts to touch them'), and he once wrote to a dentist comparing their professions. 'I spend my life cutting out carious material from people's minds and replacing it with such gold as I possess. It is a painful process and you hear them screaming all through the press. I cannot give anaesthetics, but I do it as amusingly as I can.'

*You Never Can Tell*, which he described as 'the *East Lynne* of my plays', was his attempt to write for, without succumbing to, the theatre of Oscar Wilde's *The Importance of Being Earnest*. He had written about Wilde's comedy for the *Saturday Review* at the end of February 1895 and begun his first attempt at *You Never Can Tell* some four months later. Parts of *The Importance of Being Earnest* he had criticized as being 'almost inhuman enough' to have been conceived by W. S. Gilbert.

'I cannot say that I greatly cared for The Importance of Being Earnest. It amused me, of course; but unless comedy touches me as well as amuses me, it leaves me with a sense of having wasted my evening. I go to the theatre to be moved to laughter, not to be tickled or bustled into it; and that is why, though I laugh as much as anybody at a farcical comedy, I am out of spirits before the end of the second act, and out of temper before the end of the third, my miserable mechanical laughter intensifying these symptoms at every outburst.'

This reaction is so singular that some critics have attributed it to an envy of Wilde. Both men were elaborately respectful yet uneasy with each other. Wilde, coming from a class in Dublin that Shaw abominated, and moving smoothly if precariously on to make his name in London, was a target for envy. But *The Importance of Being Earnest* pressed on a concealed bruise that genuinely seems to have discomforted Shaw.

One morning, before Sonny's first birthday, his father had gone down to the railway station to see his wife as she went through on the train. But 'there you were with your head stuck down into a Book and of course you did not pretend to see me,' he complained. '. . . there is a queer feel over me today, I did not mind it yesterday but I feel so forlorn, forsaken, alone.' Wilde's comedy, involving the identity of a handbagged baby in the cloakroom at Victoria Station, seemed to stir in Shaw the same 'queer feel' experienced by his father, against which G.B.S. had hardened his adult mind. He may also have been affected by Wilde's hostility to the villainous Lady Bracknell (whose husband is kept well out of the way), and later softened this portrait when he came to create Lady Britomart in *Major Barbara*. There are echoes in *You Never Can Tell* of *The Importance of Being Earnest*. The advice of Valentine, the five-shilling dentist, to his patients the young Clandons, that for social respectability they needed 'a father alive or dead', is close to Lady Bracknell's recommendation to Jack Worthing to 'produce at any rate one parent, of either sex, before the season is quite over'. Both plays use that ancient theatrical device of the chance reunion of a separated family.

The long-lost father in *You Never Can Tell* appears to have stepped out of a standard Victorian farce (such as Charles Matthew's *My Awful Dad*). But his crosspatch manner, his drinking, outbursts of temper are seen as deriving from marriage to a woman who did not love him; also, he has most to gain from the affectionate pantomime atmosphere Shaw works up at the end. 'It has always seemed merely a farce written round a waiter,' he wrote to Harley Granville Barker years later. 'It ought to be a very serious comedy, dancing gaily to a happy ending round the grim earnest of Mrs Clandon's marriage & her xixth century George-Eliotism.' This dance from grimness into gaiety represents the humanity Shaw found lacking in Wilde's play. His first title – 'The Terrestrial Twins' – points to another literary source, Sarah Grand's ruthlessly orthodox feminist novel *The Heavenly Twins*, whose elevated themes he brought down to earth and set dancing.

The autobiographical interest in *You Never Can Tell* is never literal, but resides in the reshaping of facts Shaw made while hammering out his philosophy of optimism. In the first version the play was set not in Devon but the Isle of Wight, where he had gone with Lucy and his mother after his sister Agnes had died there. The cast included rewritten versions of his father and mother, Lucy, Agnes ('Yuppy') and himself: they are Fergus Crampton, the unappealing abandoned father with 'an atrociously obstinate ill tempered grasping mouth, and a dogmatic voice'; his wife, now calling herself Mrs Clandon, 'a composite of the advanced woman of the George Eliot period, with certain personal traits of my mother', who rules out 'all attempt at sex attraction', imposes 'respect on frivolous mankind and fashionable womankind' and who is described as 'a woman of cultivated interests rather than passionately developed personal affections'; and the three children she has brought up by herself: Gloria, 'the incarnation of haughty high-mindedness, raging with the impatience of a meddlesome dominative character paralyzed by the inexperience of her youth'; and the twins, a 'darling little creature', Dolly, who is spoilt by her mother, and the 'handsome man in miniature', Philip, whose self-consciousness would be 'insufferable in a less prepossessing youth'. In tandem they are the hermaphrodite ideal, transferred from their Shaw family background into the landscape of Shakespearian romantic comedy, while the imposing and inflexible Finch McComas, who twenty years before fired the imagination of Mrs Clandon, occupies the place of Vandeleur Lee, but is now made an agent for the reunion of the family.

On stage his family is in Shaw's power. He can dress them up and make them move to his music, dissolve their pain in festivity, manhandle them all into pleasant reconciliation; and so, lightly and impersonally, detach himself from his family predicament. His characters all carry the germs of real suffering. Bohun, the lawyer, speaks for everyone when he says: 'It's unwise to be born; it's unwise to be married; it's unwise to live; and it's wise to die.' And his father, the waiter, gives Shaw's answer: 'so much the worse for wisdom!'

But in an unwise world what can human beings do? First, Shaw suggests, they can use their intelligence. Bohun, even in a false nose and goggles, represents the 'terrifying power' of the trained mind, and demonstrates how tragedies may be avoided *in advance* by using intelligence freely; the encouraging presence of the waiter (who is the ideal Fabian and resembles the bust of Shakespeare in Stratford Church) shows how we can avoid giving pain *at the time* by exercising tact, affability, unenvious good manners, and above all the spirit of acceptance recommended by Shakespeare's *As You Like It* and *What You Will (Twelfth Night)*; and in Valentine the dentist we are given an example of how to deal with pain *in retrospect*, extracting it with magical ease. He is the only character without a surname and therefore character without a past.

*You Never Can Tell* is not only a recommendation but also Shaw's attempt to enact Valentine's philosophy. He had criticized Wilde's levity as being cynical in the sense that it sentimentally repressed knowledge and, if taken in earnest (as the title of his play invited), would add to the world's stock of avoidable suffering. Yet there is a sense in which Shaw's lightness of heart shortchanges reality. Mr Crampton acknowledges '*in sudden dread*' that feeling is 'the only thing that can help us'. But the emotions are dangerous. 'Stop. Youre going to tell me about your feelings, Mr Crampton. Dont,' Bohun interrupts. And Gloria too interrupts Valentine: 'Oh, stop telling me what you feel: I can't bear it.' The sea ('You can imagine that the waves are its breathing, and that it is troubled and stirred to its great depths by some emotion that cannot be described') was used by Shaw to indicate the unconscious feelings and is a remnant from the imagery in *The Lady from the Sea*. But he eliminated much of this imagery from the published version of his play and presents us for the most part with a happy seaside spectacle. And for this, he implies, our response should echo the first two words with which Dolly opens the play after her successful operation in the dentist's chair: 'Thank you.' The dentist's anaesthetic at 'five shillings extra' is Shaw's own numbing of emotion ('I have never felt anything since'). 'Where the whole system is one of false good-fellowship,' says the solicitor McComas, '. . . we do unkind things in a kind way: we say bitter things in a sweet voice: we always give our friends chloroform when we tear them to pieces.' That chloroform is Shaw's comedy: the 'heartless' reworking of the Shaw family; and in his final happy pantomime, he raises up another system of good-fellowship.

Shaw gave the atmosphere of *You Never Can Tell* a poetic charm and fizzing humour; but when introducing love he experimented with a new variation of the mechanics he found so distasteful in Victorian farces, replacing their sexual salaciousness with a laboratory demonstration of Nature's production machine. His duel-of-sex between the New Woman Gloria and the Old Adam Valentine moves from the shallow waters of flirtation into the current of creative evolution that sweeps them both into marriage. This is not their choice but a biological imperative and the first try-out in dramatic form of a new creed designed to strengthen Shaw's own platonic ideal. Woman's weapon was her body, which the Shavian theatre treats as an instrument for the manufacture of babies. 'Shaw Limited', he called himself, after Janet told him that year of her pregnancy. His plays were to explore this limitation and eventually place it beyond mortality in a limitless future.

The title, with its Shakespearian associations, summed up most people's reactions to the play. They couldn't tell: and Shaw, perhaps because he flinched from this violation of his own past, was politely unhelpful. It was, he suggested airily, an attempt to show in dramatic form the golden rule that there are no golden rules. Was he not himself a living instance that extraordinary children could proceed from the most unpromising marriages? There was always hope. 'Cheer up, sir, cheer up . . . You never can tell, sir: you never can tell.'

The play, which had been a Mozartian orchestration of 'lightness of heart', was also to prove a test of this commodity. 'I find that the new play is not coming,' he had told Janet in July 1895. He put it aside, returned to it in December, then reported to Janet two days before Christmas that it was 'shaping itself slowly – at least the people are coming to life'. Over the next five months, in spaces between all his other work, he continued writing it, often from a wintry chair in Regent's Park. By the second week of April 1896 he had 'triumphantly' finished the second act and 'if I had the very *faintest* idea of the next act,' he wrote to Janet, 'I should be happy'. By 18 May it was officially finished, though three months later he was still toiling 'to get it ready for the stage'.

This stage was the Haymarket Theatre whose 'exceptionally brilliant' management, he told Ellen Terry, 'appear to be making up their minds to ruin themselves with it'. He had designed it for the West End; and the West End had apparently accepted it – but then postponed its acceptance in order to put on an adaptation of Stanley Weyman's adventure story, *Under the Red Robe*. 'I therefore approach Under the Red Robe full of prejudice against it,' exclaimed the *Saturday Review* critic. 'The very name appears to me a fatuity . . .'

For almost six months matters stayed firmly unsettled, Shaw's spirits rising and sinking. He is determined to be neither surprised nor disappointed if the Haymarket management changes its mind; but he cannot resist playing the lovely game of casting – what about Mrs Patrick Campbell or Elizabeth Robins for Gloria? What about Ellen Terry's son, Gordon Craig, as Philip? Then he reads it to Edy Craig and feels appallingly let down. 'The play's no use: I looked for my gold and found withered leaves. I must try again & again & again.' By the beginning of 1897 he had run up for business purposes a flag of confidence. The play was '*tout ce qu'il y a de plus* Shawesque,' he announced to Richard

Mansfield's wife. 'It requires a brilliant company – eight parts, all immense, the leading man a fine comedian.' On 26 February a memorandum of agreement was at last signed with Frederick Harrison and the actor-manager Cyril Maude (who was to play the waiter) for their production at the Haymarket. Almost at once their troubles multiplied: 'though I shall do all I can at the rehearsals, I feel at present as if nothing could induce me to witness the performance,' Shaw confided to Ellen. He read it to the company on 9 April, and 'it's too long: I shall have to spoil it to suit the fashionable dinner hour'. The rehearsals had started badly and grew worse. 'Oh, if only they *wouldn't* act,' Shaw complained to Ellen. 'They are tolerable until they begin that, but then . . . I could tell you pages of my sufferings.' The actors' sufferings could have filled a library. One of them, Jack Barnes, who was to play McComas, at once withdrew; and shortly afterwards Cyril Maude's wife, Winifred Emery, switched from the part of Dolly to Gloria. Fanny Coleman, as Mrs Clandon, complained that 'there were no laughs and no exits' – then walked out. Patient, persistent, polite, Shaw prowled the theatre dressed in a suit 'which the least self-respecting carpenter would have discarded months before', getting splendidly on everyone's nerves. He was particularly disliked by Alan Aynesworth, a young man who had played Algy in *The Importance of Being Earnest*, and to whom Cyril Maude had been anxious to give the lead. 'They were great friends,' Shaw later explained, 'and Cyril was quite sure he would succeed brilliantly if I would only let him try.' Shaw suspected that the Life Force love scene at the end of Act II, 'the failure of which would mean the failure of the whole', was beyond Aynesworth. But unable to get anyone else, and not feeling justified in denying Aynesworth his opportunity, he had agreed; and now found his suspicions confirmed. At one moment of exasperation Aynesworth turned on Shaw and demanded: 'Let us see you play it yourself.' Shaw sprang up on to the stage and delivered his lines. 'But that,' protested the actor, 'is comedy!' Why had no one told him they were in a comedy? It was too much. Both of them turned to Cyril Maude who seemed affably paralysed, pretending that nothing was wrong – or at least nothing that he and his wife could not pull round by the opening night.

After a fortnight of wretchedness and exhaustion Shaw went to Frederick Harrison, the manager of the Haymarket, telling him he must come to the next rehearsal and judge for himself. 'After the rehearsal,' Shaw later recounted, 'Harrison joined us with such a long face that Maude saw it was all up.'

'It was a miserable moment: they had been a thoroughly happy family; and my confounded play was going to break it up. They had signed the agreement to produce, and could not in any case have thrown me over for the shortcoming of an actor whom I accepted, against my own expressed judgment, to oblige them. I rescued them by saying that 'we' had better withdraw the play and wait for another opportunity. They were enormously relieved, and, I believe, really grateful to me at the moment, though I doubt if Cyril has ever forgiven me for going on as if Harrison was the only adult in the theatre, and for not behaving at least a little badly in common humanity.'

But that was not the end of the affair. There had been one chance of keeping the play alive, and that had been to rewrite the last ten minutes of Act II, eliminating the Life Force. This Shaw refused to do. It had become the most vital section of the work, its centre, and the ingredient that made *You Never Can Tell* into that rare specimen, a religious farce. So at the expense of possible success, he withdrew the play intact, calculating that this would be preferable to having for his West End debut an obvious failure. 'I don't know how to express my appreciation of the way in which you met us over the withdrawal of your play,' Frederick Harrison wrote to him. Shaw, the politician, at once took over the business of stage-managing this change of plans. The press was informed that, due to the increasing popularity of *Under the Red Robe*, rehearsals of *You Never Can Tell* had, for the present, been discontinued.

He was adept at concealing disappointment. His behaviour under depressing circumstances was both impeccable and apparently 'heartless'. He recognized this himself – no wonder Pinero signed one of his letters 'with admiration and detestation'. Apart from the setback to his career, a fear had been planted in him as to whether his plays, in so far as they were original, were unactable. He had blamed Aynesworth whom he disliked – but could any actor play Valentine? 'There is no difficulty about You Never Can Tell,' he told Mrs Mansfield eighteen months later, 'except the difficulty of getting it acted. The end of the second act requires a consummate comedian; and that comedian has never been available.' Only when referring to the play itself ('a whited sepulchre') did he reveal the keenness of his disappointment. It was 'the dullest trash', he exclaimed to Florence Farr, '. . . and has bored me to death.' And to Ellen Terry he burst out: 'It maddens me. I'll have my revenge in the preface by offering it as a frightful example of the result of trying to write for the *théâtre de nos jours*.' In this mood he would have agreed with George Moore's criticism that 'being without any synthesis he cannot pursue a train of thought for more than a few lines and has then to contrive his escape in a joke; and . . . his jokes are vulgar claptrap, the jokes of the clowns in the pantomime'.

*You Never Can Tell* was not presented in public for another three years when it was staged (with James Welch as the waiter) at the Strand Theatre. But Shaw did not see it. Once again 'the rehearsals lacerated my very soul', and he refused to let it proceed beyond six matinées. 'I will be boiled alive,' he wrote to Yorke Stephens who played Valentine, 'sooner than let the play go on again with them.'

Painstakingly he had put aside his arsenal of arguments to produce his least dogmatic, most deliberately pleasant work for the theatre. It was a delightful product of his Mozartian talent; a humorous and humane work of art. If his skill and judgement meant anything, *You Never Can Tell* must be what he later called 'a champion money-maker'. But for eight years it made him almost nothing.

In one respect he was successful. When in 1903 Cyril Maude was writing his history of the Haymarket Theatre, he sent Shaw the chapter dealing with this period and Shaw replied with his own version, written as if from Maude's point of view, which was tipped into the book as Chapter XVI, under the transparent guise of its having been composed by Maude.

'From the first the author showed the perversity of his disposition and his utter want of practical knowledge of the stage. He proposed impossible casts. He forced us into incomprehensible agreements by torturing us with endless talk until we were ready to sign anything rather than argue for another hour . . . I then recognized for the first time that I had to deal with a veritable Svengali . . .

'I can hardly describe the rehearsals that followed. It may well be that my recollection of them is confused; for my nerves soon gave way; sleep became a stranger to me; and there were moments at which I was hardly in possession of my faculties. I had to stage-manage as well as act – to stage manage with that demon sitting beside me casting an evil spell on all our efforts.'

The narrative describes how Svengali-Shaw hypnotized Aynesworth into confusion over the end of Act II; how he almost caused a divorce between Mr and Mrs Maude; how shamelessly he flattered Harrison into submission; how, using 'a certain superficial reasonableness and dexterity of manner to cover an invincible obstinacy', he took over the whole business of stage-managership: and then surveyed the total wreckage he had created 'with that perfidious air of making the best of everything which never deserted him'. Finally, having unnerved them all, he entered the theatre *in a new suit of clothes* bought in anticipation of the play's royalties.

'That this was a calculated *coup de théâtre* I have not the slightest doubt.

That it fulfilled its purpose I cannot deny. With distracted attentions, demented imaginations, and enfeebled reasons we made a bewildered effort to go through the first two acts. I saw with inexpressible aggravation that Harrison's face grew longer and longer . . .

'In concluding this sickening record of a disastrous experience I desire to say that I have the greatest admiration for Mr Shaw's talents and the sincerest esteem for his personal character. In any other walk of life than that of dramatic author I should expect him to achieve a high measure of success. I understand that he has made considerable mark as a vestryman, collecting dust with punctuality and supervising drainage with public-spirited keenness. I do not blame him . . .'

This is paradoxical revenge, parodying himself no less than Cyril Maude and his Haymarket company. The burlesque into which he turned the whole episode was a counterpart of the dramatic pantomime at the end of the play, and proof that he could successfully reassemble facts and dissolve bitterness and grievance into 'lightness of heart'. But to some extent this 'literary lark', as he called it, was evidence of how delightfully he excelled at overcoming rather than confronting truth. For the truth was devastating. 'I sincerely hope that you will bring us another comedy presently,' Frederick Harrison had written to him, 'which we can carry to a successful issue.' But for Shaw, now in his early forties, the time for comedy seemed over. The disappointment was too great. He had finished with the stage.

*

Between the last of Shaw's pleasant plays and the first of his *Three Plays for Puritans* there was much in common. *You Never Can Tell* was a religious farce advocating lightness of heart; *The Devil's Disciple* was a religious melodrama advocating seriousness of instinct. Into both farce and melodrama he had spilled a Shavian ingredient that seemed to contemporary opinion a vast error of taste, making the farce inappropriately solemn and the melodrama so incongruously facetious that *The Times* critic of 1899 complained that its author was 'quite unable to take even his own work seriously'. Shaw had insisted that the seriousness of *You Never Can Tell* needed for its success a consummate comedian; he advised the actors playing *The Devil's Disciple* not to be misled by the laughs: 'It is a full-blooded melodrama, not a farcical comedy.' The Life Force which appears in *You Never Can Tell* as a biological current moving mainly through women, changes its course in *The Devil's Disciple* and works politically through the men.

The form of melodrama was dictated by Shaw's decision to interpret a fanciful suggestion from William Terriss as a commission. Terriss had been a member of Irving's company and then moved to the Adelphi Theatre, which, by the 1890s, had reached the summit of its glory as the home of melodrama. Terriss himself, now in his fiftieth year, invariably played the hero; his mistress, Jessie Millward, was the heroine; and comic relief came from Harry Nichols. On the afternoon of 7 February 1896, Shaw went to the Adelphi where Terriss informed him that he intended to make a world tour and would like to add to his repertoire a play that should contain 'every "surefire" melodramatic situation'. Having staged them all at the Adelphi, he could supply an inventory – from the switched identity to the swooning lady. For Shaw's benefit, he sketched the sort of scenario he had in mind. It involved a succession of hair-raising adventures with, between the acts, miraculously unexplained escapes. These culminated in a hanging that, to preserve the happy ending, turned out to be the nightmare of a sleeping bridegroom shortly before his marriage – the tolling death bell at the hero's execution developing as he woke into a brilliant peal of wedding bells. From Terriss's cupboard of melodramatic ingredients, why should Shaw not cook up a masterpiece?

Shaw's predicament was unfelicitous. He judged the scenario to be not quite 'in my line', but did not wish, through any disparagement of such an ingenious *chef-d'oeuvre*, to make an enemy of Terriss. So, in the letter the following morning, 'I explained to him that what he needed for a tour round the world was not an Adelphi melodrama . . . what would be expected from him as a great wandering star was something like Hamlet – on popular lines.' And here, with the possibility of Shaw himself supplying this popularized Hamlet, negotiations were suspended.

Then, while staying with Graham Wallas over Easter at a Hertfordshire cottage belonging to Mrs Humphry Ward, Shaw had jumped over the head of Act III of *You Never Can Tell* on to the Terriss melodrama. 'You remember a vague idea I had for the first act?' he reminded Janet Achurch. 'Well, I have completed the scenario of not only that act, but the second and third, each of them being dramas in themselves with tremendous catastrophes. I have no longer any doubt of my being able to carry out that project with considerable force.'

The scenario, covering five pages in shorthand and dated 'Aldbury 14/4/96', differs in many respects from the final play. The characters are not named and nor is the place – it is simply 'on the border during warfare'. But it is still what he later described as 'a three-star melodrama and not a one-star Irvingism'. He identifies the stars as:

'A is an Ishmael better than his people and therefore rated as worse, and rating himself so.

'B is a high-minded moralist, the clergyman of the place. He is A's sternest censor and opponent. A hates him and jibes at him; but B steadily refuses to condescend to resentment.

'Z is B's wife. She is very hard on A, and will not forgive him on principle like her husband. She is obsessed with his wickedness and has no suspicion that this obsession is so near love that a touch will reveal her to herself as passionately attached to A.'

These prototypes of Richard Dudgeon, Anthony and Judith Anderson are quintessential examples of the Shavian realist, idealist and philistine.

That autumn Shaw agreed to have his portrait painted by a Slade School artist, Nellie Heath, and turned the sittings to account by scrawling his play in a series of pocket notebooks. 'The play progresses,' he told Ellen Terry on 16 October 1896, '. . . such a melodrama! I sit in a little hole of a room off Euston Road on the corner of a table with an easel propped before me so that I can write and be painted at the same time. This keeps me at work . . .' It was more than melodrama; it seemed composed of all the plots of all the melodramas he had ever sat through for the *Saturday Review* – beginning with a mortgage melodrama and ending with a gallows reprieve.

What he wanted was a simple drama of action and feeling, submerging psychological speculation in bold theatrical effects, with plenty of fun and contrasts of human character. 'The whole character of the piece must be allegorical, idealistic, full of generalisations and moral lessons,' he had written, describing the ideal Adelphi melodrama in the *Saturday Review*; 'and it must represent conduct as producing swiftly and certainly on the individual the results which in actual life it only produces on the race in the course of many centuries'. It was in this last concept that Shaw believed there was room for original ideas within the limitation of the genre. One must go 'straight to the core of humanity to get it,' he wrote, 'and if it is only good enough, why, there you have Lear or Macbeth'. The danger was that, attempting simultaneously to exploit and subvert the stage melodrama, he would get trapped within its conventions, and that however carefully he wrote the speeches, the audience would force its romantic expectations on the play. It was with this in mind that he later boasted that there was not 'a single even passably novel incident. Every old patron of the Adelphi pit would . . . recognize the reading of the Will, the oppressed orphan finding a protector, the arrest, the heroic sacrifice, the court martial, the scaffold, the reprieve at the last moment, as he recognizes beefsteak pudding on the bill of fare at his restaurant.' This image conveys how little these ingredients were naturally to his taste. He was contemptuously familiar with them as a critic but could he use them effectively for his own purposes as a dramatist? 'I finished my play today,' he wrote to Ellen Terry on 30 November, '. . . but I want your opinion; for I have never tried melodrama before; and this thing, with . . . its sobbings & speeches & declamations, may possibly be the most monstrous piece of farcical absurdity that ever made an audience shriek with laughter. And yet I have honestly tried for dramatic effect.'

Though he would later assert its melodramatic full-bloodedness, he was as yet uncertain whether he had not tumbled into burlesque – ascending by the end into Irish pantomime. It had been written round the scene of Dick Dudgeon's arrest 'which had always been floating in my head as a situation for a play'. This scene had probably floated in from Sydney Carton's heroic sacrifice at the end of *A Tale of Two Cities*. Dickens's novel was regularly dramatized for the Victorian stage which, though it dared not exhibit the incidents of sexual love, invariably alleged that love was the motive behind all noble action. Like all theatrical heroes, Sydney Carton went to the gallows for the sake of the heroine. Shaw took this situation and gave it another motive, specifically non-sexual. Judith Anderson, who embodies the love motive, immediately concludes – as any Adelphi audience would – that Dick Dudgeon has taken the place for her husband and let himself be arrested 'for my sake'. But Dick Dudgeon is without such a motive. Like Hamlet, he is a 'tragic figure in black'. 'I had no motive and no interest,' he declares. He denies acting out of love. Everyone, he tells Judith from prison, could 'rise to some sort of goodness and kindness when they were in love [*the word love comes from him with true Puritan scorn*]. That has taught me to set very little store by the goodness that only comes out red hot. What I did last night, I did in cold blood, caring not half so much for your husband, or [*ruthlessly*] for you [*she droops, stricken*] as I do for myself . . . I have been brought up standing by the law of my own nature; and I may not go against it, gallows or no gallows.'

Shaw created in Dick Dudgeon an embryo superman to do battle for him against the power and idolatry of sex. Like Shaw, Dick appears a mountebank, flamboyant, thoroughly misunderstood, mixing instinctive good manners with the desire to shock, and acting *impersonally* for people's good ('my life for the world's') – as Shaw himself acted with the Fabians. That Shaw recognized himself in Dick can be shown by comparing Dick's prison speech to Judith with a letter Shaw himself wrote over ten years later: 'The only aim that is at all peculiar to me is my disregard of *warm* feelings. They are quite well able to take care of themselves. What I want is a race of men who can be kind in cold blood. Anybody can be kind in emotional moments.'

This was the Shavian touch transforming a 'threadbare popular melodrama', without a single novel incident, into a vehicle carrying 'the advanced thought of my day'. Instead of sending the play to Ellen Terry at the beginning of December, he worked on it for a further month. He had decided to place the action during the American Revolution, and he fixed the date in October 1777 with the surrender of General Burgoyne at Saratoga. This, he implied, like the distant background of Madeira in *You Never Can Tell*, was culturally equivalent to modern Ireland. Most of his facts were taken from De Foublanque's biography of Burgoyne, yet Shaw's Burgoyne is a fabricated figure ('a very clever and effective part'), through whom the Shavian comedy works best and who, making his entrance in the last act, often steals the show. Shaw even appears to have invented Burgoyne's nickname 'Gentlemanly Johnny', which historians have copied (it was 'Frosty-faced Fred' in the first draft). In this play (as in his next, *Caesar and Cleopatra*) Shaw rewrote history and set it on course for the future he wanted. 'What will History say?' Major Swindon asks Burgoyne as he contemplates the defeat of Britain by the Americans. 'History, sir, will tell lies as usual,' Burgoyne assures him. For these schoolroom lies Shaw substitutes a series of gentlemanly jests and compliments that eliminate human evil and identify the real enemy of human progress as 'Jobbery and snobbery, incompetence and Red Tape'. The America of 1777 is a man's world full of crude notions that women can see through but do not have the legal or political status to alter. Woman has not grown up; her kingdom is restricted to the home where she is reduced to the life-denying role of practising 'the barren forms and observances of a dead Puritanism' suggested by the name Mrs Dudgeon.

'The Devil's Disciple has, in truth, a genuine novelty in it,' Shaw later wrote. But he was careful not to let this novelty spoil the story. It is, in that sense, one of the least Shavian of his plays, and as deliberate an attempt to reach the West End as the concurrent *You Never Can Tell*. He took it to Terriss even before it was completely finished. But Terriss's dreams of a world tour had failed and he had no recollection of his arrangement with Shaw when 'to his dismay, I turned up again with the Devil's Disciple in my pocket, stuffed with everything from the ragbag of melodrama'. The reading took place at Jessie Millward's flat and was probably, Shaw believed, at her insistence. His account of what happened in some respects resembles his story of reading *Widowers' Houses* to Archer: and it conceals beneath the comedy as ravaging a disappointment. Terriss 'composed himself dismally' as if Jessie Millward 'had taken him to church', listening in deep perplexity as Shaw plunged into his play. At the climax of the first act, he suddenly interrupted to ask whether 'this is an interior?' Then, a short way into the second act, he again apologetically broke in: 'I beg your pardon: but *is* this an interior?' Shaw's answer, he declared, had set him 'completely at rest'. This seemed to be true, for a few minutes later he uttered a long drawn snore. 'We got him into the next room before he was fully awake, and dosed him with tea,' Shaw remembered.

'He was fearfully ashamed of himself, and pleaded that he could read nothing but travels: all other literature sent him to sleep. To console him I assured him that Dr Johnson was just like that; and Miss Millward, radiant, exclaimed, "Oh, Willie: I have been doing you an injustice".
'No further allusion was made to The Devil's Disciple.'

Shaw worked out the stage business early in 1897, had the play typed and undertook to read it to various people including (on 18 February) Forbes Robertson and Mrs Patrick Campbell – for whom he was to write *Caesar and Cleopatra*. But nothing seemed to go right for *The Devil's Disciple*. No one was happy with the ending. 'I think I shall die lonely,' he wrote to Ellen Terry, 'as far as my third acts are concerned.' He still believed that Terriss would be the best person to do it and was again scheming to such an end when, on 16 December 1897, Terriss was motivelessly assassinated on the steps of the Adelphi and died in Jessie Millward's arms. So he became 'only a name and a batch of lies in the newspapers', while the reputation of *The Devil's Disciple*, Shaw told Charrington 'has given me such practice in hardening my heart that I have lost all human sympathy'.

\*

In *The Devil's Disciple* Shaw had tried to show how, by following their true nature, men could find their proper function in life – and in doing so he seemed to have shown that his own function was not that of playwright. 'I have succeeded in baffling all the plans for producing the play here,' he admitted to Mrs Mansfield at the beginning of 1898. After *The Devil's Disciple* he was not to start another play for fifteen months, at which time he gave up his drama criticism for the *Saturday Review*. 'What is the matter with the theatre, that a strong man can die of it?' he was to enquire in his Preface to *Three Plays for Puritans*. He had been attracted to the stage by the opportunities it seemed to offer him of overriding his private life with a public career. He wanted to be reborn through his work and use the theatrical world to develop his new identity, fulfilling what he called 'my instinct . . . to turn failure into success'. But his rejection by the West End hit the same spot made sensitive by all his early neglect – though this was now a well-bandaged wound. He had looked to the stage for another existence but seen that it housed the worst aspects of London society: class snobbery and the snobbery of senseless fame-gone-mad. As Terriss's assassination on the steps of the Adelphi suggested, the insidious illusion of the theatre flowed out and contaminated ordinary life. It propagated lies for commercial ends. Its sentimentalities were dangerously hypocritical: for in the world outside, commented Shaw, 'when we want to read of the deeds that are done for love, whither do we turn? To the murder column: and there we are rarely disappointed.'

There is fury and disgust in Shaw's condemnation. His own compensatory need for fame was deeply implanted, though he had the integrity to dedicate his use of it to ends that seemed to him unegotistical. He had hoped that the theatre might supply a new chapter in his biography. Instead he had entered a paradise of fools where the actor-manager was enthroned as god, the actress as star; and the author merely its word-carpenter. He had wanted power in place of love, but had danced for empty men such as Irving. Everyone, even his friend Archer, insisted that he could not write plays. Yet he persisted. 'Here am I, after 20 years drudging away, at last venturing to tell myself that if I *begin* writing for the stage, I will master the business by the time I am fifty or so,' he wrote to Janet Achurch in the spring of 1896. 'I *know* I will get deeper into it than I now have any idea of, and that I will come to understand the requirements of the art in a way that I do not now.' But the failure of his last two plays seemed to have cracked this confidence. He had risked prostituting his talent, not so much by taking to himself all the standard formulas of the Victorian theatre as by trying to make an effect on an audience he did not admire. Shaw's thought is far more subtle than his orchestration of it for trumpet and big drum suggests. The rhetoric, the overstatement, the ear-catching tricks, jokes to the gallery, all proceeded from his need to be heard; but they masked the precision of what he wanted to say and enabled the public, whose ear he eventually caught, to hear only the voice of an Irish paradoxer who did not mean half of what he said.

Even his sentimental loyalties, it seemed to Shaw, had played him false. He had failed to liberate Ellen Terry from the hypnotic rule of Irving; he had failed to separate Janet Achurch from Charrington or to free her from the dominance of alcohol and morphia; he had failed to make an actress of Florence Farr. In all these endeavours he had sent his plays out to do his work, but the scarcity and poor quality of their performances gave life no chance to imitate the Shavian drama. 'Give up *wanting* to have the plays produced,' he advised another dramatist, 'if you value your happiness as a man and your dignity as an artist.' Early in 1897 he took this advice himself. On being elected a member of the St Pancras Vestry he plunged deeper into local politics, recognizing 'that there is better work to be done in the Vestry than in the theatre'. At about the same time, in another essay at turning failure into success, he decided to publish his plays.

It was not an easy decision. His experience as a novelist had disenchanted him with the publishing profession. 'I object to publishers,' he told Frederick Evans who had proposed bringing out a volume of his musical criticism: 'the one service they have done me is to teach me to do without them.' J. T. Grein's publication of *Widowers' Houses* in 1893 had not been a success. 'His firm never advertised it even once,' Shaw complained, 'and the sale, which was only effected by great perseverance & determination on the part of the purchasers, was 150 copies!' Yet some notion of printing his plays persisted. 'Has your experience with Lady Windermere's Fan &c led you to suppose that publishing plays is worth while?' he questioned John Lane. 'Is there anything to be done with this play of mine [*Arms and the Man*] which is to be produced on Saturday evening by Miss Farr?' John Lane's reply had been discouraging. Only two categories of drama were commonly published as books: non-dramatic plays by poets such as Browning and Tennyson; and acting editions, using a good deal of technical stage business. When, in 1891, American copyright became available, Henry Arthur Jones had brought out his *Saints and Sinners* with a Preface challenging publishers to add English drama to their lists; but the invitation had not been taken up and the book failed.

Yet Shaw was not wholly persuaded: he had also approached William Heinemann, explaining that he particularly wished to see his plays in print because, as a theatre critic, he could not offer them to managers in the usual way. Of this nice point Heinemann disposed very effectually 'by first telling me that nobody bought plays except the people who gave amateur performances of them, and then proving this by shewing me the ledger account of Pinero, whose plays he published at eighteen pence each.'

'And, sure enough, all the items were for little batches of copies consisting of one for each character in the play and one for the prompter, the general reading public being utterly unrepresented, though Pinero was then beyond question the foremost English playwright.

'This was conclusive, as the amateurs of that day never touched plays unless they had seen them performed by fashionable actors and actresses whom they longed to ape. My plays were unperformed; and I could not ask W[illiam] H[einemann] to publish them with an apparent certainty of not selling a single copy.'

Shaw respected Heinemann's businesslike arguments; at the same time he wanted to give the public a new habit of playreading. This notion had grown when, in 1895, the publisher Fisher Unwin approached him; Shaw had had dealings with this firm over several years. It was Fisher Unwin who in 1888 had turned down *Cashel Byron's Profession* and three years later *Love Among the Artists* – good reasons, Shaw pretended to feel, for gratitude. He had been able to behave as scrupulously himself by turning Unwin down as the printer of *Fabian Essays in Socialism* because of the company's involvement in a union wage dispute. These differences had been conducted with politeness and a ripening sense of respect for each other. The more Fisher Unwin read of his journalism, the more he seems to have felt that Shaw would become a good publishing investment. He had shown interest in *The Quintessence of Ibsenism* (which Walter Scott brought out in 1891) and urged him to prepare a volume of Bassetto papers – which Shaw agreed to do only in the most cavalier fashion: 'that is, if I ever again find time to go back on old work.'

Shaw seemed to have experienced a particular pleasure in reversing the old current of rejection. 'It is very good of you to declare your readiness to become my publisher,' he complimented Fisher Unwin, 'but believe me, you deceive yourself.'

'If I sent you anything, you would open it with joyful anticipation, finish reading it with dismay and utter disappointment, and only proceed with it to spare my feelings. I should feel the meanest of mortals if, after nearly sixteen years experience of the effect I produce on publishers . . . I were to take advantage of your personal good nature to involve you in a very doubtful speculation.'

Unwin had been chiefly interested in Shaw as a critic, but continued to interest Shaw as the publisher of a 'Cameo' series of plays by Ibsen, the Spanish playwright José Echegaray, and others: 'is there any public as yet,' Shaw asked, 'which reads plays?' For a few weeks early in 1896 he had thought of giving Unwin *Arms and the Man*. 'It would not make much of a book,' he promised, 'but with a preface by the brilliant author, and a reprint of my article in the New Review (on the military questions raised) by way of appendix, it would make a respectable Cameo.' But to give *Arms and the Man* complete artistic expression as a printed book would take more time than the original composition of the play. 'It is the usual difficulty,' he told Unwin. 'I can make more money by writing articles, and make better provision for the future by writing new plays.'

He had made his decision; and when, towards the end of 1896, one of W. T. Stead's young men, Grant Richards, having set up a new publishing company, offered to become 'publisher in ordinary and publisher extraordinary' of his dramatic works, Shaw was able to tell him categorically that 'the public does not read plays'. But Richards was not put off: 'I went after G.B.S.' He caught up with him after a theatrical first night and together they walked back, Shaw in a baggy Jaeger suit, Richards in evening dress, to Fitzroy Square. They walked fast, Shaw rattling out his sentences in an uninterruptable hail. But he could not shake Richards off.

Shaw had been longing for someone to take no notice of him. All his sensible arguments had been borrowed from others. Richards was the sort of Bohemian gambler who appealed strongly to him. At the age of twenty-four he had borrowed seven hundred pounds from his uncle, Grant Allen, and another seven hundred pounds from his bank, and was now presenting himself to various authors he admired: Wells, Bennett, Chesterton, Masefield, Housman. He was a man of greater artistic than financial conscience, blatantly monocled and with a taste for Monte Carlo, whose charm reconciled friends to his lack of scruples. Shaw's threats of the Bankruptcy Court left Richards amiably unruffled. The struggle between them went on through the winter, Shaw resisting, Richards never tiring; and in the spring of 1897 Shaw suddenly succumbed. 'I am being pressed to publish my plays,' he wrote to Ellen Terry. 'I think I will, and give up troubling the theatre. I only took to it to get closer to somebody; and she is the one person who will not endure my presence.' This decision did in some ways reflect his disenchantment with the stage as a place on which to conduct his love affairs. Fifteen months earlier, in a letter to Janet Achurch, he had predicted that if he could not find beautiful, sober, noble-spirited women to play his roles, 'then I will do what I am often tempted to do – publish my plays and appeal to the imaginations of those who are capable of reading them without wasting myself on trying to have them performed without utter profanation'. That time had now come.

Richards and Shaw combined well. 'You are the most incompetent publisher I ever heard of,' Shaw congratulated him. And Richards, on receiving a certificate of compliance with the Fair Wages Clause, replied: 'You are just about as businesslike a man as I have ever met in my short life.' Shaw seemed to recognize in Richards the sort of 'young villain' that Sonny might have turned into had he remained in Ireland, and he became his most phenomenally Shavian. Richards, he declared, had 'allowed himself to fall in Love with Literature', which was tragic in a publisher. Then he had 'hardly any sense of the kind that one can rely on . . . he'll never come through by himself, though he is an agreeable ruffian somehow.'

Shaw was grateful for this poetic inaptitude. It gave him a chance of playing to his heart's content the 'man of business'. Though Richards had no idea of what he was letting himself in for, he felt little resentment towards the Shavian machine. Shaw, he acknowledged, was 'the born man of affairs'. In fact it was like an affair of love for Shaw; while for Richards it was an education. 'Make yourself pleasant, no matter what provocation you may get,' Shaw later recommended him, 'and you will not only be doing what you do best usually, but you will be pursuing the only possible policy under the circumstances.' This was roughly how their partnership worked. Shaw ordered him to 'sit tight' and 'trust my judgment'; and Richards complied.

There were innumerable matters over which Shaw felt a need to exercise his judgement. He drafted a five-year agreement with Richards, insisted on a union house and assented to R. & R. Clark of Edinburgh becoming his printer. Then he began to knock righteousness into the heads of both printer and publisher. 'I am doing this job in a style that places it far beyond all dependence on publishing seasons,' he told Richards. He issued injunctions on punctuation (which often indicates where the actor shall breathe), demanded narrow margins, made proposals on pagination, introduced experiments with the title page, advised over frontispieces. He established rules for the elimination of 'mutton quads' and played tricks with his text to fill up the trickling 'rivers of white'. He employed lower-case italics in square brackets for stage directions, campaigned vigorously (and ineffectually) against gilt tops, abolished apostrophes from contracted words and substituted spaced letters for italic in underlined words. He ordered specimen pages, selected a green binding and went in search of the blackest printing ink. He let it be known that a single misprint upset him more than the deaths of his father and his sister 'with whom I was on excellent terms'. He threatened proof corrections on the scale of Balzac and Carlyle ('you may charge me for all corrections over and above 95% of the total cost of production'), and prescribed the price and print run. He complained of earning from all this labour far less than a dock worker, and, in short, he enjoyed himself extravagantly. Whenever the docility of Richards (whom he taunted with having 'an india rubber mind') faltered a little, and he dared demur at a comma, Shaw rounded on him, and offered (if 'you still feel suicidal') to take over the whole cost of manufacture himself together with the printer's contract and revert to a commission basis – something he was to do five years later.

Shaw's ideas on book design and elegance of composition derived from William Morris, and he based his page layout and general format on Morris's *Roots of the Mountains*. He looked at a page as a picture and at a book as an ornament that could be admired by a man who could not read a word of it, 'as a XII century chalice or loving cup may be cherished by a heathen or a teetotaller'. 'The only type I like is Caslon's,' he told Holbrook

Jackson, 'and my plan is simple: use no leads, but set solid, taking out the space saved by the omission of leads in the bigness of the fount used.' To Caslon Old Face and hand-set type he remained faithful for over thirty years, after which W. B. Maxwell of R. & R. Clark converted him to Fournier (less 'fat and rich') and he succumbed to mechanical Monotype because, 'as always happens, the machine outdid the hand, and got all the best types on it'.

By the end of August 1897, Shaw reported to Richards that he had sent three plays to the printer 'transmogrified beyond recognition, made more thrilling than any novel'. He had had no idea of the magnitude, he added, of 'your confounded enterprise'. In re-forming these plays for the press Shaw treated the pen and the *viva vox* as different instruments, the one producing a literary language for the eye, the other sounds mainly intelligible to the ear, and each needing separate scoring to blend into an unbroken narrative. To attract the novel-reading public he made it a rule with his stage directions never to mention the stage, proscenium or spectators; to discard all technical expressions and insert plenty of descriptive matter; to give sufficient guidance to the theatre management and information to the actor of *what* but not *how* to act – without spoiling anything for the reader. 'I had to make this rule to get away from the old "Stabs her 2 R C; sees ghost up C (biz); and exit R.U.E." which made plays unreadable and unsaleable . . .'

'But to make this possible and at the same time make my printed versions practicable prompt copies, I have to define positions on the stage by specifications which are quite inessential. For instance, I call a certain chair a Chippendale chair so that when I write "The colonel sits down on the Chippendale chair" the producer may know which chair I mean, and the reader will not be upset by such an absurdity as "sits chair B". But it does not matter two straws whether the chair is Chippendale or Sheraton. The producer must use his common sense . . .'

Shaw took a further step away from the stage with his Prefaces, which 'have practically nothing to do with the plays'. The Shavian Preface was to be a treatise on the social problems with which the plays were connected. 'Every play, every preface I wrote conveys a message,' he told an interviewer. 'I am the messenger boy of the new age. If you piece the various messages together, you will find an astonishing unity of endeavor, often, I admit, disguised and embroidered.'

By adding the publication of his plays to his Fabian activity and theatre reviewing, Shaw filled up each day with sixteen hours of work 'that nobody should ever touch after lunch'. He felt exhausted even in the morning. 'I get out of bed so tired that I am in despair until I have braced myself with tubbing,' he told Ellen Terry. 'When I sit down my back gets tired: when I jump up, I get giddy & have to catch hold of something to save myself from falling.' He gave up all social life and described himself as '15 years in arrear with my afternoon calls'. The plays crept through the press, with Shaw scanning every comma in the proofs. 'I never stop working now,' he wrote Ellen in the first week of 1898. 'I get no exercise. My digestion is beginning simply to stop.'

He had decided to divide the plays into two books, 'Pleasant' and 'Unpleasant'. He began the Unpleasant Plays (*Widowers' Houses, The Philanderer* and *Mrs Warren's Profession*) with a Preface, 'Mainly About Myself', which he continued without further title at the beginning of the Pleasant Plays (*Arms and the Man, Candida, The Man of Destiny* and *You Never Can Tell*). Only *The Devil's Disciple* was laid aside for another volume, *Three Plays for Puritans*, where, on the matter of prefaces, he was to ask: 'Why should I get another man to praise me when I can praise myself?'

Shaw had wanted to fit these plays into one book, printing the 'Unpleasant' on light brown paper with an ugly print face and the 'Pleasant' ones on white paper in the best Kelmscott style. Such a piebald volume, he predicted, 'would make a sensation'. In the event the first two books, with their distinctive typography and grey-green bindings, inaugurated a long series of Shaw's plays in the same format, and changed the fashion in play publishing. 'I was as proud as Punch,' declared Grant Richards. 'The look and feel of it gave me intense pleasure. But it did not make me rich.' He had brought out a first edition of 1,240 sets at a price of five shillings a volume and sold 756 sets in six months (over the same period 734 sets were sold in America by Herbert S. Stone of Chicago). It was a rather slow but not disastrous start.

*Plays Pleasant and Unpleasant* were published in April 1898. The press coverage was wide, but mixed. Archer, in the *Daily Chronicle*, called *Candida* a work of genius, *Mrs Warren's Profession* a masterpiece, *Widowers' Houses* a crude 'prentice work, and *The Philanderer*, 'an outrage upon art and decency, for which even my indignation cannot find a printable term of contumely'. Henry Arthur Jones, whose plays Shaw had consistently overpraised in the *Saturday Review*, wrote that 'much of them is not dramatic and would never be interesting in any circumstances to any possible audience'. But the most devastating response came from Shaw's *Saturday Review*, the tone of polite detachment adding power to the charge that Shaw's lack of human sympathy made him incapable of creating real characters:

'The men are all disputative machines, ingeniously constructed, and the women, who, almost without exception, belong to the strange cult of the fountain-pen, are, if anything, rather more self-conscious than the men . . . Mr Shaw is not, as the truly serious dramatist must be, one who loves to study and depict men and women for their own sake, with or without moral purpose. When Mr Shaw is not morally purposeful, he is fantastic and frivolous, and it is then that his plays are good. In farce, psychological reality is not wanted . . . Flesh and blood are quite invisible to Mr Shaw. He thinks that because he cannot see them they do not exist, and that he is to be accepted as a realist. I need hardly point out to my readers that he is mistaken . . . to all intents and purposes, his serious characters are just so many skeletons, which do but dance and grin and rattle their bones. I can hardly wonder that Mr Shaw has so often hesitated about allowing this or that theatrical manager to produce one of his serious plays. To produce one of them really well would be almost impossible at any ordinary theatre.'

This criticism had been composed by Max Beerbohm, and appeared in the same issue of the *Saturday Review* (21 May 1898) in which Shaw, writing his valedictory as the paper's theatre critic, welcomed his successor 'the incomparable Max'. It was a characteristic example of Frank Harris's editing: lazy but provocative. In the office, where whisky flowed *ad libitum*, Harris had been 'untidy, unpunctual, vociferous, munching biscuits from paper bags'. Each morning he would ride in on a spirited horse and after a hard day's talking, eating and drinking, gallop off into the twilight of Roehampton. His booming voice and dramatic method of delivery (slow as a funeral march) awed his staff, from whom he excited the loyalty due to a sea-rover. But by 1898 the 'little old pirate ship', Max Beerbohm wrote to Shaw, was already 'going down, down, into the waves, with you (Admiral of the Moral Fleet) suddenly perceived standing, in full uniform, with folded arms and steadfast eyes, on the bridge; and with me and other respectable people clinging to the rigging'.

Harris was genuinely puzzled when Shaw called him a buccaneer. 'To himself he is Shelley.' Or Jesus Christ. Early in their relationship, drawing attention to his natural sensitivity, Harris had poured out an inventory of his medical symptoms, and soon seemed on intimate terms with Shaw. Shaw felt envious of, and superior to, Harris who, from a distance, greatly amused him. For all his trenchant articulation, he noted, Harris was 'as weak as a baby in some directions'. He was the hare and Shaw the tortoise in the race for fame. In his lust for success Harris performed all those outrageous and inadvisable acts that Shaw could never permit himself, but which warmed the schoolboy in him. He felt a fondness for Harris similar to his fondness for Grant Richards and, in later life, Gabriel Pascal: they were all irresistible ruffians, appealing to the anarchist lurking apprehensively in Shaw. And what a gloriously poor embodiment Harris became, with his stomach pump and his impotence, of the romantic way of life. In Shavian terms, there was a lot to be said for Harris.

Between Shaw's private and public attitude to Harris, ran a consistent discrepancy. Privately, he admitted to Hesketh Pearson that 'Frank is really a frightful liar'; but in public he defended him as an habitual truth-teller, who used his magazines to scourge iniquities and who, for all his social ambitions, 'understood London society as a bush-ranger would understand it.' When Alfred Douglas later accused him of trumpeting lies all over the place, Shaw replied that he had not 'got the hang of Harris'. He was George Washington. Telling lies was 'exactly what he should have done to establish his place in London society. What he did do was to trumpet the truth all over the place and make himself quite impossible.'

This unusual defence of Harris reveals how 'disguised and embroidered' the truth was becoming within Shaw. At his best, Harris had been an editor of talent and authority. 'The truth is that Harris had the supreme virtue of knowing good literary work from bad and preferring the good,' Shaw explained to Douglas. 'For that I forgave him all his sins, and have always defended him as far as he could be defended.' In fact he defended him further, rubbing away the meaning of words to polish his argument. 'It was this knowledge of the difference between chalk and cheese, and the courage in trumpeting his opinion that made Harris's editorship of The Saturday Review the success it was,' he told Douglas. 'Whatever he was he was neither a liar nor a hypocrite.' In such a statement social tactlessness is elevated into moral courage.

After leaving the *Saturday Review*, Harris was to go into decline; and as this decline deepened, so his advertisements of himself grew louder and more jarring. When, in *Pearson's Magazine*, he announced himself as 'the discoverer and rescuer from poverty of all the men of his day', from Max Beerbohm to H. G. Wells, Shaw realized that he was throwing away the goodwill from these *Saturday Review* years, and decided to take over Harris's public relations. It was himself, Beerbohm, Wells and others, he countered, who had discovered Harris. At the same time, and as part of this exercise, he denied acting from the vile motive of gratitude. He was disinterested. 'I always feel that it is unjust to Harris to suggest that I was grateful to him for giving me the *Saturday Review* job,' he told Hugh Kingsmill. 'I never had any such sentiment. I considered that I was looking about for an editor blackguardly enough to stand my stuff, and, given such a one, that I was a rare catch for him.' Most of those about whom Harris wrote were described by Shaw as 'victims [who] will be furious'. In retrospect, Harris became a Shavian test of how successfully we rise above the vicissitudes of life. '*Don't* blather like all the rest of them about Harris's malicious lies,' Shaw chided Douglas. 'They are imaginary. Put your finger on one of them; and I shall know what grievance you have left.'

Harris was bought out of the *Saturday Review* six months after Shaw left. Over the last year or more the paper had become increasingly given over to matters of finance and such oddments as the promotion of Bovril. Harris's own expenses at gunsmiths, carriage-makers and restaurants were largely paid for by free advertising. There were, too, a number of libel cases and rumours of blackmail – later put down by Shaw to Harris's innocence of English business methods.

But though Shaw was to take this mitigating stance and, long after the curtain had gone down, applaud Harris loyally from the stalls, his description of him as 'neither first-rate, nor second-rate, nor tenth-rate . . . just his horrible unique self ', indicated how much he disliked sharing the stage with him. Harris used to entertain lavishly at the Café Royal, sending out invitations by telegram, each as long as a letter, on the day of the luncheon. 'I attended them for some time,' Shaw noted in his diary.

'. . . Oscar Wilde came once, immediately before the Queensberry trial, with young Douglas. They left in some indignation because Harris refused to appear as a witness – a literary expert witness – to the high artistic character of Wilde's book *Dorian Gray*. These lunches wasted my time and were rather apt to degenerate into bawdy talk.'

In May 1895 Shaw had reviewed *The Home Secretary* by R. C. Carton, taking the opportunity to protest against an attempt in the play to trade on the anarchism bogey, his object being to call attention to some hard features in a recent anarchist trial. But Harris had been alarmed and cut the passage from his article. 'This incident brought my growing impatience with the brag and bawdry of the lunches to a head,' Shaw recorded, 'and I never went again.'

Harris gave as his reason for leaving the *Saturday Review* the need for a little 'nerve-rest'. Following Shaw's recent example, he explained, 'I want to try my hand at books and plays and stuff more enduring than articles.' Harris's move from the paper masqueraded as an advance; there seemed no doubt that Shaw's was a retreat – and he was no more enamoured of failure than he had been over twenty years ago. The work had seriously reduced his health and offered little 'to the enormity of my unconscious ambition'. For all its entertainment, his valedictory shows at what exorbitant human cost he had overcome the poverty, obscurity, ostracism and contempt that infected those Dublin years. 'I have been the slave of the theatre,' he wrote.

'It has tethered me to the mile radius of foul and sooty air which has its centre in the Strand, as a goat is tethered in the little circle of cropped and trampled grass that makes the meadow ashamed. Every week it clamors for its tale of written words; so that I am like a man fighting a windmill: I have hardly time to stagger to my feet from the knock-down blow of one sail, when the next strikes me down ... Do I receive any spontaneous recognition for the prodigies of skill and industry I lavish on an unworthy institution and a stupid public? Not a bit of it: half my time is spent in telling people what a clever man I am. It is no use merely doing clever things in England ... For ten years past, with an unprecedented pertinacity and obstination, I have been dinning into the public head that I am an extraordinarily witty, brilliant, and clever man. That is now part of the public opinion of England ...

'Unfortunately, the building process has been a most painful one to me, because I am congenitally an extremely modest man. Shyness is the form my vanity and self-consciousness take by nature. It is humiliating, too, after making the most dazzling displays of professional ability, to have to tell people how capital it all is. Besides, they get so tired of it, that finally ... they begin to detest it.

'... I can never justify to myself the spending of four years on dramatic criticism. I have sworn an oath to endure no more of it. Never again will I cross the threshold of a theatre. The subject is exhausted; and so am I.'

Even the dapper and incomparable Max would not atone for the absence of that famous harmony in snuff-colour with which G.B.S., like a 'forked raddish in a worsted bifurcated stocking', had enlivened theatre audiences in the 1890s. 'Now the playwrights may sleep in peace,' observed the actor-manager of the Criterion, Charles Wyndham, 'and the actor may take his forty winks without anxiety.'

25 Ellen Terry in the 1880s

27 Shaw at Hammersmith Terrace, 1891
(opposite page)

26 Sir Henry Irving

28 Charlotte Payne-Townshend, 1897

29A & B Shaw and Charlotte, 1898

30 Shaw the music critic

31 Shaw in the 1890s

32 Beardsley poster for 'Arms and the Man', 1894

# CHAPTER VII

## [ 1 ]

*A Vestryman!* You! *You will glory in it.* Ellen Terry (1897)

*People think of me as a theatrical man, but I am really proud of having served six years as a municipal councillor.* (1933)

Fabian progress through the north of England after the success of *Fabian Essays* had been achieved partly through the help of a modestly affluent and elderly Fabian, Henry Hunt Hutchinson. 'Old Hutch' was clerk to the Justices of Derby. Crusty and querulous, exuberantly describing his marriage as a penal servitude, he reminded Shaw of Samuel Butler. 'I liked the man,' he decided. But Hutchinson did not much like Shaw. He had never forgiven him for a singular alphabetical error. 'He sent me a proof of something he had written,' Shaw narrated, 'and on glancing through it superficially my eye caught the word *doable*.'

'This seemed an obvious misprint; and I mechanically corrected it to *double*. But it was not a misprint; the right word was *do-able*, meaning practicable. My correction . . . seemed to prove that I had not understood a word of what I was reading; and I was struck out of his will accordingly.'

Beatrice Webb's diary testifies that Shaw had frequently discomforted Hutchinson. Thriving on imaginary grievances, Hutchinson would alternate with his cheques to the Fabians cantankerous letters complaining of Shaw's rudeness. The Fabian executive, banking the cheques and praising Old Hutch's public spirit, would deplore his advancing age and infirmity. What would happen, they wondered, to Fabian finances when he died?

In the summer of 1894 they had their answer. Old Hutch had shot himself. The Webbs were staying in the Surrey hills and heather, with Shaw and Wallas, when Sidney received a letter informing him that he had been appointed one of Hutchinson's trustees. Old Hutch had been a solicitor and, according to his own lawyer, had made a will that was almost certainly invalid. To his wife he bequeathed one hundred pounds; his two sons and two daughters received smaller bequests; and Fabianism was to benefit, over a period of ten years, by almost ten thousand pounds. This money had been left, not to the Fabian Society, but to trustees (of whom Sidney became first Chairman), to be used for 'the propaganda and other purposes' of the Fabian Society 'and its Socialism', and for promoting Fabian goals 'in any way' that the trustees thought 'advisable'. The legacy was a surprise to the Webbs. Rising early the next morning, however, they were able by breakfast to tell Shaw and Wallas of their decision to found in London a School of Economics and Political Science. They had made some notes. What was needed was not 'a big political splash' but some *hard thinking* and a place, similar to the Massachusetts Institute of Technology or the Ecole Libre des Sciences Politiques, where experts could be specially trained for the purpose of reforming society. Wallas (who was to be an LSE lecturer for twenty-eight years) refused the post of Director; and Shaw, who believed that Hutchinson had 'left his money for Red propaganda by Red vans', would have preferred using it to enliven Fabian campaigns. Yet it was he, over the first few months, who acted as Webb's spokesman and cleverly avoided antagonizing Olivier and Bland, both of whom objected to Webb's plans. 'You cannot treat them as children,' he advised Sidney, 'and now that several thousand pounds are at stake, the slightest attempt at evasion or concealment would destroy our influence at a blow.'

To establish the London School of Economics on a firm base needed skill and energy. Sidney had first to placate the Hutchinson family and then the Fabian executive, which viewed his navigation of money from the Society to a laboratory of sociological research as a violation of the Hutchinson bequest. He had to win support both from the London County Council and from businessmen by representing his school as an institution with commercial courses, though dedicated (despite its socialist propaganda) to disinterested research. Knowing that disinterested research inevitably led to socialist conclusions, Sidney picked out no discrepancy in this – especially since small amounts of the Hutchinson money were to be segregated for the promotion of Fabian lectures and an increase in the secretary's salary. But it was too paradoxical for Shaw. Webb's pains to keep everything 'as quiet as we can' and to protect the Hutchinson Trust accounts from Fabian scrutiny (later diagnosed by Ramsay MacDonald as a symptom of bad faith) seemed alarming evidence of the 'temporary (let us hope) suspension of Webb's wits'. Always scrupulous in financial affairs, Shaw warned Beatrice that Sidney was antagonizing the Fabian executive by what looked like a plan to bribe them with subsidies for provincial lectures in return for permission 'to commit an atrocious malversation of the rest of the bequest'. Sidney, he insisted, must keep faith with his fellow Fabians and avoid shocking them, together with his ILP critics, with talk of academic impartiality. 'Any pretence about having no bias at all, about "pure" or "abstract" research, or the like evasions and unrealities must be kept for the enemy ... the Collectivist flag must be waved, and the Marseillaise played if necessary to attract fresh bequests.' Even if such abstract purity were possible, he concluded, 'its foundation out of Hutchinson's money would be as flagrant a breach of faith as handing it over to the Liberty and Property Defence League, since it was expressly left to endow Socialism'.

As Webb had once frowned on Shaw's individualism, so Shaw now worried over Webb's idealism, fearing that his love for this new invention could cause a break-up in the Fabian family. But partly for reasons of unity, after much discussion, and always a little reluctantly, Shaw supported his friend's dream of a centre for intellectual work and comradeship.

So, by means of a suspect will, at variance with anything Old Hutch could have envisioned, and amid a good deal of Fabian grumbling, one of Webb's lasting achievements was begun. 'It is honestly scientific,' Beatrice pronounced after the school had opened in the summer of 1895. And Shaw was left attributing everything to his innocent proof blunder. 'A good job too,' he commented, 'as Sidney Webb performed miracles with his money which I should never have done.'

*

The London School of Economics was to prove do-able, and fitted perfectly into Webb's Fabian programme of London politics. He was Chairman of the London Technical Education Board, and served on several committees of the London County Council which had come into existence at the end of the 1880s as part of the reform of local government. This reform had created the machinery for social change on an instalment plan, that appealed to the Fabian gradualist temperament far more than the ILP's ambitions of taking over Parliament with apocalyptic national programmes. The London School of Economics was another instrument for long-term permeation (particularly valuable since Lord Salisbury's Tory Government was elected), and for the introduction of collectivism by educationists rather than political partisans. In moving the Fabians into local politics Sidney had been influenced by Beatrice. Before their marriage, she had expressed to him her doubts as to whether he was 'a really big man' like Chamberlain, but assured him that he might be capable of doing 'first-rate work on the London County Council'. After their marriage she supported his refusal to go into Parliament, partly because she believed that 'the finest part of his mind and character' would be unemployed in the House of Commons, and partly because she recognized in a parliamentary career the 'enemy of domesticity'. They had moved at the end of 1893 to an austere ten-room house at 41 Grosvenor Road on the Embankment. 'Sidney says we must work in order to deserve it,' Beatrice observed. It was a short distance from Spring Gardens, where the London County Council held its meetings, and from Adelphi Terrace, where in 1896 the London School of Economics moved. After his meetings and lectures Sidney would return in the evening to Beatrice's simple meat suppers, with cigarettes.

At first sight Shaw's maverick figure does not find a part in the undramatic plans Webb had made for revolution through research. He had refused in 1889 to stand for the London County Council in Deptford – the seat Webb was to win from the Tories three years later. But his experiences in the theatre over the next eight years had reassembled his opinions. It was no longer a grand choice between Parliament and the West End, but a means of combining the limited commitment of municipal politics with a limited success in provincial theatres. National politics he judged to be as hostile to his literary work as it was to the Webbs' domesticity. Early in 1894 he had refused an invitation to put himself up as the parliamentary candidate for Chelsea; but he stood in the School Board elections at the end of that year for the St Pancras Vestry – and was handsomely defeated. Then, letting his name go forward as a Progressive candidate at an uncontested election in May 1897, he was appointed ('by some intriguer or other') to the Vestry Committee of Ward 7 of St Pancras – together with an architect, barrister, builder and tea-dealer. 'I have nothing to do with it,' he pleaded to John Burns. 'I addressed no meetings; I took no steps; I did what I could to provoke the wirepullers to drop me. No use: the Moderates rallied round me; the extra candidates were bullied into withdrawing; and I was elected without a contest on a compromise which enabled both sides to claim me.'

Both sides felt suddenly less eager to claim him a few days later. Acting on his conviction that private charities were pernicious evasions of social duty, he attacked the Princess of Wales's fund ('A ghastly, wicked, wasteful folly'), raised to provide a dinner for 330,000 poor people in celebration of Queen Victoria's Diamond Jubilee. It might, he declared, 'lead to a Moscow catastrophe'. And so 'to stop my mouth they promptly put me on the committee; and now I shall be able to buy up all St Pancras with two-shilling tickets for soup. What a glorious engine of parochial corruption it will be!' He had had his first lesson in the methods of local government.

London local government in the 1890s was an 'archaic patchwork' of vestries. When, in 1888, the County of London had been formed by a union of parts of the counties of Kent, Middlesex and Surrey, the metropolis was placed under the jurisdiction of the London County Council. The LCC was elected for a three-year term by forty-two vestries comprising lay figures, and following the old parish boundaries. The St Pancras Vestry, stretching from Islington to Marylebone and from Holborn to Hampstead and Hornsey, contained almost two hundred thousand inhabitants. Their culture 'may be inferred from the fact that there was not a single bookshop in the entire borough', Shaw recorded. But it clustered with 'houses of ill-fame', especially in the side streets off Tottenham Court Road (one of which was named Warren Street). And there were slums often owned by landlords like Sartorius and managed by rent-collectors such as Lickcheese. 'What we have to do,' Shaw declared, 'is to sit down and try to settle how many people should be let live on an acre of ground, and then pass a Building Act to enforce our conclusions. What maddens me is to see houses cropping up in such a way as to form the beginnings of slums.'

On behalf of their constituents the vestrymen looked after an elastic range of matters from manure receptacles (maintenance of ), horns (blowing of ), graves (purchase of ) and noxious literature (sale of ), to the management of ice cream notices, street cries, the sampling of milk-in-transit and all business involving public baths, lighting, tramways. By Shavian standards, the St Pancras district was 'cheerfully corrupt politically':

'a cheque for £1000, placed in the right quarter, would have secured the return of a baby in arms to Parliament or the County Council for the southern division, where I resided. When cheques were not forthcoming, as at the vestry elections, the little groups of politically-minded local shopkeepers and men of business elected one another for no particular reason except that they seemed likely to keep the rates down to the extreme possible minimum.'

The strength of local government was planted, Shaw believed, in its independence from Parliament. The St Pancras Vestry had a Chairman and one hundred and sixteen vestrymen. Although they all belonged to one of the political parties, they did not operate under the party system. 'Every member can vote as he thinks best without the slightest risk of throwing his party out of power and bringing on a General Election,' Shaw explained. 'If a motion is defeated, nobody resigns: if it is carried, nobody's position is changed.' Reviewing his six years as a vestryman and borough councillor at the age of eighty, he recalled that 'I never had to vote on any question otherwise than on its specific merits . . .'

'in Parliament I should have been a back row chorus man, allowed to amuse the House with a speech occasionally ... [the] perversion of parliament has produced all the modern dictatorships ... The little socialism we have is gas and water Socialism. And it is by extension of Gas & Water Socialism that industry will be socialized.'

Shaw's first meeting took place at the Vestry Hall, Pancras Road, on 26 May 1897. Though he reported himself as being in a minority of one (as anyone may be in a non-party system) this became only half-true the next year, when a young Methodist minister named Ensor Walters joined the Vestry. The two of them sat together at what was supposed to be the Progressive end of the long table on the Mayor's left. Ensor's figure, Shaw noticed, 'and a certain boyishly unconscious authority about him, reminded me of Pope Pius IX,'

'and I at once set him down as likely to end as head of his Church ... The vestry, as far as it knew anything about me, classed me as a Socialist and therefore an atheist, sure to differ with the Methodist minister on every question. What actually happened was that he and I immediately formed a party two strong all to ourselves. And we troubled ourselves about no other party ... He was out to make a little corner for the Kingdom of God in St Pancras; and nothing could have suited me better.'

Shaw served on the Health Committee of which Ensor Walters became Chairman, on the Officers Committee and the Committee for Electricity and Public Lighting. These were three of ten sub-committees which met separately and 'set forth their conclusions as to what the Council ought to do in their departments in a series of resolutions. When the whole Council meets, these strings of resolutions are brought up as the reports of the Committees, and are confirmed or rejected or amended by the general vote.'

This system impressed Shaw as being so sensible that he wondered why Parliamentary business should not be conducted on similar lines. He discovered local government, however, to be undermined by two factors: the inadequacy of the men who were elected and the paralysing poverty of the municipalities. Of the vestry election of 1894 he had written to Pakenham Beatty: 'You should see the candidates! We have to kidnap them in the streets, and daze them into submitting to be brought into the hall and nominated under the impression that they are being pressed for a coroner's jury.' He later acknowledged his fellow-vestrymen to be well-intentioned people but 'absurdly unequal to the magnitude of our task'. The questions with which they were confronted could not be understood, much less answered, by 'councillors without the special knowledge and capacity needed for intelligent dealing with them,' he wrote, nearly fifty years later.

'I was expected to answer them in council with a collection of local shopkeepers, licensed victuallers (publicans), builders, auctioneers, and the like, with an occasional doctor or two and a Methodist minister, I being a playwright. Our ablest leaders were a greengrocer and a bootmaker, both of them much more capable than most members of Parliament; for it needs considerable character and ability to succeed as a shopkeeper, especially as a publican, whereas persons with unearned money enough can easily get into Parliament without having ever succeeded in anything. I found them excellent company, and liked and respected them for their personal qualities . . . but in the effective lump we were as ignorantly helpless politically as the mob of ratepayers who elected us, and who would never have elected me had they had the faintest suspicion of my ultimate political views.'

By their policy of under-rating, these men had by 1900 put the St Pancras Vestry in debt to the bank by £17,000. It was this insolvency that weakened the local authority and made it incapable of exercising its full powers. A weak vestry, Shaw argued, was at the mercy of its officials and of Parliamentary rule. 'He saw in municipal government a valuable decentralizing balance and counter-check to Parliamentary government,' wrote H. M. Geduld. 'It existed to ensure that local necessities were not sacrificed to national interests . . . Unfortunately, Parliamentary government frequently forces its inefficient decisions upon weak municipalities; or, what was even worse, ignored the claims of local governments because they seldom insisted on their rights to be heard and respected.'

The vestrymen deliberately kept the rates down because they themselves, and the people who had voted for them, could not afford a rating figure that would ensure municipal solvency. Shaw strove unsuccessfully to alter the rating system so as to relieve ordinary ratepayers and arrest reckless overdrawing on the bank. 'There is only one remedy,' he wrote, 'and that is to take the burden off the shoulders of the men who do the work & conduct the business of London, & throw it on to those who take enormous sums in rent and interest out of our businesses to squander in idleness.' He proposed to do this by the taxation of ground values ('or, as I want it, taxation of unearned incomes'), with a rating exemption limit and a series of abatement limits as in the case of Income Tax.

Shaw championed the municipality against all classes and other categories of people. He proposed a municipal monopoly on building so that lucrative contracts were no longer secured by privately owned companies, restricting the largely insolvent municipal building projects to dwellings for the poor. With slightly more success he prepared a report recommending the formation of a municipal insurance organization which St Pancras eventually joined, saving the local authorities large sums in premiums. But success was rare. He failed to persuade his colleagues to take action against Lord Mansfield who had annexed part of the public highway by extending his boundary fence even when, the Council having declined to ask for legal advice, Shaw obtained a favourable opinion from his own lawyer. Such support of the public interest against private landowners was predictable; less so perhaps was his championship of the municipality against exclusively working-class interests. He spoke in favour, for example, of moving the costers' market-stalls from the High Street because 'the demands of the traffic compelled it' – though urging the establishment of a market-place for poor people in side streets.

The London Government Act of 1899 replaced the forty-two vestries with twenty-eight Metropolitan Boroughs each with a Mayor and Council. Wards 7 and 8 of the old Vestry were amalgamated into the Southern Division of the new St Pancras Borough and ten candidates stood for the six available seats at the election on 1 November 1900. The result was a triumph for the Progressives, all of whom were elected. For Shaw (who with 704 votes came second only to a clergyman, beating a bootmaker, removal contractor and store proprietor), this was the one successfully contested political election of his career. He campaigned hard, armed himself against failure ('the relief will be enormous'), and described his success as 'a sentence of hard labor'.

He had opposed the London Government Act in that it disqualified women, who had been part of the vestries, from sitting on the Borough Councils – the reason given, during a facetious debate in the House of Lords, being that these Councils would consist of aldermen and a woman could not possibly be an alder*man*. With this 'joke', women vanished for several years from the London municipalities. Using his experiences as a vestryman, Shaw attempted to give publicity to the need for women on public bodies, but *The Times* declined to publish a letter he wrote that threw off 'the customary polite assumption that women are angels'.

'English decency is a rather dirty thing. It is responsible for more indecency than anything else in the world. It is a string of taboos. You must not mention this: you must not appear conscious of that: you must not meddle with the other – at least, not in public. And the consequence is that everything that must not be mentioned in public is mentioned in private as a naughty joke. One day, at a meeting of the Health Committee of the

Borough Council of which I was a member, a doctor rose to bring a case before the Committee. It was the case of a woman. The gravity of the case depended on the fact that the woman was pregnant. No sooner had the doctor mentioned this than the whole Committee burst into a roar of laughter, as if the speaker had made a scandalous but irresistible joke. And please bear in mind that we were not schoolboys. We were grave, mostly elderly men, fathers of families. It was no use being indignant or looking shocked: the only effect of that would have been an impression of ill-natured Puritanism. There is only one absolutely certain and final preventive for such indecency, and that is the presence of women. If there were no other argument for giving women the vote, I would support it myself on no other ground than that men will not behave themselves when women are not present.'

The presence of women cured men from mawkishness in cases involving other women and, by adding new expertise and a differing sensibility to their discussions, assisted them in dealing more comprehensively with numerous social problems. One of these was 'the unmentionable question of sanitary accommodation'. In the Borough of St Pancras women had two special grievances: first, there were so few public lavatories for them; secondly ('which no man ever thought of until it was pointed out to him'), where these had been provided they necessarily consisted not of urinals but separate closets, entrance to which traditionally cost one penny – 'an absolutely prohibitive charge for a poor woman'. The grotesque struggle for free lavatories raged for years, and with particular heat round the site in Camden High Road. Some councillors objected in principle against this 'abomination', reasoning that persons who so far 'forgot their sex' did not deserve a lavatory; one suggested that the water supply would be used by flower girls to wash the violets that he occasionally purchased for his buttonhole – an argument turned by Shaw into another good reason for free access. The site was also assailed as a terror to traffic, an engineering *in*convenience, and a feature so gross as to contaminate the value of all property in the neighbourhood. When a deputation of householders came to protest against even the construction of an underground public lavatory for women in Park Street, Shaw moved that it should not be received 'as this was a woman's question and there was no woman on the deputation'. He was overruled by the Chairman, but proceeded to give the householders' representatives an embarrassingly intimate cross-examination.

It is not easy to chronicle Shaw's activity as a vestryman and borough councillor, partly because it is camouflaged by what he called 'my wily tactics'. Fearing that his own motions and amendments might not be listened to seriously, he often filtered them through other councillors. His participation is further obscured by the Minute Books which, while overflowing through more than two thousand five hundred pages each year, mainly carry tables of population, statistics on infectious diseases, details of tests applied to drains, lists of deaths and their causes, accounts, appointments and charts of temperature, humidity, rainfall and (occasionally) sunshine. Even when they move from figures into words and pass to the selling of sheep's livers 'unfit for the food of man', the laying down of soundless pavements or the improper keeping of fowls, the bureaucratic language smothers everything. Nevertheless, when supplemented by other sources, a pattern to Shaw's municipal work appears. He voted in favour of more free time for workers employed by the council (every other Sunday off instead of every third Sunday for lavatory attendants) and for trams against underground railways in the interests of shopkeepers; and he introduced a motion (4 March 1898) to raise the salaries of the council's clerical staff by means of promotion through independent tests of their qualifications – for example, a certificate of competence from the London School of Economics and Political Science in advanced statistics, English local government and taxation. After St Pancras became a metropolitan borough, the Chairman of the Vestry was translated into a Mayor. The Vestry Chairman had been unpaid, and the first Mayor of St Pancras, Alderman Barnes (whom Shaw accused of making himself 'the representative time after time of the opposition to the sanitary work of the late Vestry'), proposed continuing this magnanimous tradition. Shaw objected, warning the council against making a new precedent:

'It was, of course, very handsome of Mr Barnes to say he would not accept any salary, but at the same time a definite sum of money ought to be placed at his disposal . . . He [Shaw] moved that this question of paying the Mayor be adjourned for further consideration, because it would not be a proper or democratic thing to pass a resolution that might prevent a poor man accepting the office of Mayor.'

Shaw's motion was defeated, but when in 1903 the council appointed, as their second mayor, W. H. Matthews, a greengrocer (and the model for Bill Collins in *Getting Married*), the matter of a salary was again discussed, £200 a year being proposed. Shaw made a strong speech, emphasizing that 'it was quite legal to pay the Mayor, and no other method would place every man there on a footing of absolute equality'.

'But 200 pounds a year was a ridiculous sum; he would multiply it by five. There was no sounder democratic principle than that a man should be paid for public services. At present in that Council when they wanted a man to be Mayor they had first to find out if he could afford it.'

But he was again outvoted and the office of Mayor continued unsalaried.

Shaw's municipal energy took two forms: a passion to cleanse the council from all suspicion of corruption and an obsession with improving the hygiene of the Borough. He feared large business organizations even when they brought gifts to the council; he spoke against municipal profiteering and vested interests within the council (seldom himself taking part in debates on local theatres, libraries and musical halls); and he annoyed all fellow-councillors (including Ensor Walters) by his persistent campaign against badges of office, regalia and robes that converted the St Pancras Aldermen into 'animated pillar boxes'. Sometimes he 'funked' the solemn municipal ceremonies 'not from lack of feeling,' he told Ensor Walters, 'but from excess of it'. When the new mayor was sworn in, Shaw's imagination called up 'the two Mayors, the robes & badges, the attentive assembly of lying tombstones, the long faces, everybody saying the wrong thing, and you receiving infinite sympathy as if you were the unfortunate son of an unlucky mother'. All this his imagination presented to him; and 'I turned back'.

Such an occasion was easily seen by the ratepayer as a misuse of public money. Even on issues he supported Shaw looked carefully at expenditure. When the Mayor proposed spending £40 to send a delegation of councillors rambling into the countryside to come back with a report on the public installation of a crematorium in St Pancras, Shaw intervened to say that he

'sometimes spent his week-ends near Woking, and if they would lend him a councillor for the purposes of cremation (much laughter) he would bring up a report of all that happened (laughter) without cost to anyone (laughter).'

Shaw's advocacy of cremation was part of a campaign for public hygiene he pursued on the Health Committee. He urged that 'if earth-to-earth burial was to be continued, the depth below the surface ought not to be more than a couple of inches, and the coffin of the flimsiest material it was possible to have'. As a member of this committee he visited workhouses, hospitals, sweatshops and the homes of the poor, and witnessed the undernourishment, destitution and disease. 'An appalling number of them live in single-room tenements,' he wrote. 'The districts in which these tenements are most plentiful have been frankly given up by our most energetic sanitary inspectors, who have no time to do anything more than attend to complaints which, I need hardly say, are only made by the people who are enlightened enough to be least in need of attention.'

The slum problem was perpetuated by lack of money on one side and, on the other, by ignorance. After a careful inquiry, the Health Committee had recommended the employment of more sanitary inspectors, but this was rejected as too costly. Many of the tenements were lice-ridden; there were epidemics of smallpox, and occasional cases of typhoid fever, and even bubonic plague. Houses were disinfected with sulphur candles, on the fumes of which pathogenic bacilli actually multiplied. On asking the Medical Officer of Health why ratepayers' money was spent on a useless fumigant, Shaw was told that it was necessary because, though the real disinfectants were soap, water and sunshine, no stripper or cleaner would dare enter an infected house unless it was filled with the superstitious stink of burning sulphur.

Shaw accepted sulphur but not vaccination which, he believed, was seen as a cheap prophylactic and employed as an alternative to a civilized housing programme. During the spread of smallpox in 1901 Shaw battled with the medical advisers in St Pancras, who were urging on the council a compulsory vaccination scheme. 'Are all the leaders of your profession simpletons?' he enquired of Dr Collins, ex-chairman of the London County Council. Their report 'quite took my breath away by the childishness of its calculations'. But he found limited support from the Borough Medical Officer, Dr Sykes. The difference was one of private practice versus socialized medicine. The council paid half-a-crown for each revaccination; 'and children who opened the door in response to a ring or a knock when their parents were out were sometimes seized and re-vaccinated on the spot,' Shaw wrote.

'. . . No doubt the doctors were honestly convinced that vaccination is harmless and prevents smallpox; but the half-crown had more to do with that honest conviction than an unbiased scientific study of the subject . . .'

Dr Sykes's position was dependent on the good health of the district – it was what Shaw called 'the position that one wants Socialism to place all doctors in'. He could not be dismissed by the Borough Councillors with whom he dealt, only by the Local Government Board which judged his efficiency by the health statistics. Compared to the private practitioner his position, Shaw reasoned, was 'independent and responsible'.

'Dr Sykes's income did not get larger when the district got sick. The private practitioners' did. They revelled in an epidemic.

'. . . you could see the private practitioners getting new ties and new hats.

When the death-rate went up they always looked better off and happier. That was not the case with the medical officer of health: he looked more worried: it was a bad time for him.'

Shaw judged it impossible to trust statistics presented by doctors whose income depended upon their interpretation, and he proposed that the figures collected in the Royal Commission's Report of 1896 be analysed by a panel of statistical and actuarial experts ('from which medical men should be rigorously excluded'), under the management of the London School of Economics. Past statistics, he complained, had often been biased by vague medical nomenclature and confused by a deductive fallacy in diagnosing cases of smallpox, syphilis and general vaccinia.

Observing how impressed his fellow-councillors were by puzzling medical terms, Shaw absorbed a good number of them himself. One councillor advised him to leave bacteriology alone and return to his playwrighting; and a doctor calculated that for 'ignorance, conceit and deceit' his anti-vaccination dialectics 'had no parallel'. But what he heard passed in council convinced Shaw that medical opinion was often little more than superstitious masquerade amounting to a conspiracy to exploit public credulity. We had transferred our faith 'from God to the General Medical Council'. To keep the public well-informed and strengthen its democratic representatives, Shaw took his campaign out of the council chambers and into the newspapers. 'We, the councillors, must do our duty at the risk of our seats,' he wrote, 'unless we are vigorously supported by the Press.' Over two years, in a series of what were called 'curious pathological effusions' to *The Times*, the *British Medical Journal*, the *Saturday Review* and *Vaccination Inquirer*, he pressed for a re-examination of statistics, and for a socialized health service as a replacement to the money motive in medicine. Commenting on his lack of success, he later wrote: 'Most of us believe what we wish to believe in the teeth of all evidence.' Shaw believed in the virtue of socialism and the evil of vaccine. Though he knew that vaccination statistics were as worthless as 'figures bandied by meat eaters and vegetarians as to the spread of cancer, by trade unionists and employers' federations, Conservative and Liberal electioneers . . .', he stated in council that 'statistics were everywhere dead against vaccination', and later went on to describe it as 'nothing short of attempted murder'. In the Press, however, as part of his programme of converting the public to socialism and sanitation, he represented himself as professing 'neither vaccinism nor antivaccinism'.

'I am merely a much-perplexed public man . . . when people ask me whether they should get vaccinated or not, I reply that if they have to choose between getting smallpox from the calf and from their neighbors, they had better get it from the calf; but a more excellent way is not to get it at all.'

Shaw treated the Press as a democratic instrument – through which he poured information and advice to the public and from which he hoped to get instructions formed by that advice. The principles by which he tried to reach a workmanlike relationship with voters are revealed by some remarks he made to vestrymen and borough councillors. 'Never do anything for the public that the public would do for themselves,' he told them. And: 'Give the public not what they want but what they ought to want and dont.' It was the responsibility of councillors and Members of Parliament to persuade the public to want what it ought to want.

What Shaw wanted was to command political action without the horror of submerging himself in political life. Exhaustion, absence from London, and the need to earn money from his other work, made it impossible for him to attend all meetings. 'I regret to say,' he wrote as his apology for absence to local ratepayers, 'that the state of my health after eighteen years residence in St Pancras does not permit of my attending your meeting.' Of the possible 321 council and sub-committee meetings he was eligible to attend between November 1900 and September 1903, he turned up at 192.

Failure in the West End theatre had diverted him into local politics; disenchantment with local politics and the sudden success of one of his plays abroad were to pull him back to the stage. 'Just consider my predicament,' he invited a colleague.

'. . . I have a profession which demands the undivided energy of ten men to do it justice . . .

'. . . if I could devote my whole time to the Borough Council work, I should take up the thing seriously; reside in Camden Town; stand for Mayor next year; and organize a municipal party out of the best elements of both the existing parties on the Council. But I have other fish to fry; and I can do no more than I am doing at present . . .'

In public, Shaw's attitude to his municipal duties was one of undisguised optimism – which is to say, disguised pessimism: 'I love the reality of the Vestry and its dustcarts and H'less orators,' he told Ellen Terry, 'after the silly visionary fashion-ridden theatres.' But that had been at the start of his vestry duties and after Irving's refusal to produce *The Man of Destiny*. Already by the next year the vestry had become 'one long exasperation'. An almanac Shaw kept in the early spring of 1898 shows under what strain this municipal work, with its hours of talk (no less fashion-ridden than the theatre) 'about our dignity & respectability', was beginning to place him. 'Vestry beyond all endurance,' he recorded on 30 March, after a meeting as long as a late Shaw play.

'. . . They absolutely refuse the two new sanitary inspectors by 44 to 27. On the other hand the examination proposal is passed without a word as a matter of routine. Too damnable – tea not over till nearly 10. Headache seems imminent, but I have ceased to notice that now: its getting chronic, although somehow my energy is not flagging – rather the contrary.'

But in a letter one month later to the *Daily Chronicle*, he presented these local politicians as true representatives of our society. Despite their absence of courage, they were neither cynical nor in a conventional sense irresponsible. 'On the contrary,' he insisted, 'they are stuffed, every man of them, with good intentions, intense respectability, piety, theoretical humanity and the most exalted ideas of womanly purity.'

'All their finest instincts are jarred unendurably when their minds are dragged down from the contemplation of photographs of princesses to sanitary conveniences for charwomen. Every drop of their blood is so sweetened by charity that they pay starvation wages to their scavengers lest they should be compelled to discharge the worn-out men whom they have employed out of benevolence. At most of their meetings they commit crimes against society for which they would get twenty years' penal servitude if they committed them as individuals against private property instead of as public representatives against the common weal. But they do it from the loftiest, kindliest, most self-sacrificing reasons; and all remonstrance strikes them as being half ludicrous, half cynical, and altogether a breach of good sense and good manners . . .'

From six years of frustrated attempts to impose humanity on St Pancras via this well-intentioned, self-regarding body grew the crust of G.B.S.'s celebrated inhumanity. Looking back from 1938 he concluded that 'everything is interesting in it [St Pancras] except the inhabitants'.

Shaw was to use his experience in local politics as an advertisement for his plays. Of *Man and Superman* he wrote: 'The mornings I gave to it were followed by afternoons & evenings spent in the committee rooms of a London Borough Council, fighting questions of drainage, paving, lighting, rates, clerk's salaries, &c, &c, &c.' Such occupation, he maintained, had developed his business capacities and enabled him to create realistic dramas so unrecognized in the fashionable London theatre that critics believed them to be fantastical – in fact not plays at all. But what are the picturesque tramps and scoundrels of the Sierra Nevada doing at the opening of 'Don Juan in Hell' but holding a St Pancras Vestry meeting? And who are the municipal characters in *Getting Married* but the Aldermen and Borough Councillors with whom Shaw had sat those long unventilated hours? The committee structure of that play derives from his observations of municipal politics; and the conflicting opinions of the medical specialists in *The Doctor's Dilemma* reflect his experiences on the Health Sub-Committee. He was to use this committee work, caricatured in *The Shewing-up of Blanco Posnet*, in much of his non-dramatic writing, specifically in his pamphlet on 'the succulent subject of Municipal Trading', in pages for *The Intelligent Woman's Guide, Everybody's Political What's What*, the volume entitled *Doctors' Delusions* he put together for the Standard Edition of his Works, the Preface to *Major Barbara*, and more generally scattered through many other pages.

All this he took from St Pancras; and if he gave back no dramatic triumphs of municipal legislation, he presented it with a theatre of entertainment. Hygiene itself sprang into an extravaganza when Shaw, proposing a motion for the introduction of fresh air into the St Pancras Town Hall, unfavourably compared its atmosphere, after the full council had been sitting there two hours, with the London Hippodrome, which 'maintains perfect ventilation in the presence of a thousand persons, ten full-grown lions, a dozen horses, several dogs and ponies, and a pack of foxhounds'.

In 1897 Shaw still allowed himself dreams, arising mainly through the mists of permeation, of exercising beneficent political power. But the stultifying party system and elaborate circus of chicanery, by which even local representatives were elected, obstructed much of what he had imagined achieving on the political stage. The theatre, after all, could be a vehicle for social and cultural change better suited to his abilities. Shortly before his fiftieth year, he 'faded out of vestrydom having,' he wrote, 'more important work.'

In a speech supporting Alderman Matthews as Mayor of St Pancras, Shaw gave an oblique notice of his retirement from local politics, in the parentheses of which we may hear that 'universal laughter' drowning Tanner's words at the end of *Man and Superman*.

'Councillor G. Bernard Shaw was glad, speaking from the Progressive part of the chamber, to support the nomination of Alderman Matthews, although it was difficult for them to realize the extent of his (the speaker's) self-sacrifice in taking that course (laughter). He assured them seriously it was very great, indeed (laughter). The first year he served on the old Vestry, the chair was occupied by Mr Matthews. He regarded him as a respectable gentleman (laughter), with little to say and with no political opinions whatever (much laughter). He never was more astonished than when Mr Matthews was out of the chair, because then he found him an active politician with a great deal to say for himself (laughter). In the chair he was most admirable and orderly, out of it he was the most disorderly man he had ever met (laughter). His (the speaker's) self-sacrifice he told them was very great, because he wanted to be the man for Mayor (laughter). He had looked forward to the time very fondly when he would find his life crowned by becoming Mayor of St Pancras (laughter). He had carefully calculated the number of years it would take him to get it, and came to the conclusion that when all the Aldermen of the present Council, all the chairmen of the old Vestry, and some of the more prominent Councillors, had had their turn, that the number of years would be 22 (laughter). That was the prospect before him (laughter), and thus it would come to pass that in the year 1924 an old man, with white hair, dim of sight, and hard of hearing, would be elected Mayor of St Pancras and would pass up the Council chamber to the chair amid encouraging cries of 'Good old Shaw!' and sympathetic murmurs of 'Poor old chap!' (laughter). Having said that, he had now to say that nobody supported the nomination of Alderman Matthews more heartily than himself (applause). He wished it were a better post. He (the speaker) had spent the greater part of the preceding day with Sir James Hoyle, the Lord Mayor of Manchester, who like their out-going Mayor, Councillor Barnes, had become a distinguished public man in connection with education. They had a technical school in connection with the City Council of Manchester, the cellars of which were more splendid than the St Pancras Town Hall (laughter), and on the school was spent 30,000 pounds a year out of the rates. The population was not more than twice as large as St Pancras, where they had not the courage to make sufficient rates to cover their liabilities. As time went on he hoped their ideals would expand, and instead of trying to resist the County Council they should enter into competition with it, and try as far as they could to take this part of London off their hands. In the name of the Progressives he supported the nomination from that intellectual part of the Council chamber (laughter and applause).'

## [ 2 ]

*His sensuality has all drifted into sexual vanity — delight in being the candle to the moths — with a dash of intellectual curiosity to give flavour to his tickled vanity. And he is mistaken if he thinks that it*

425

*does not affect his artistic work. His incompleteness as a thinker, his*
*shallow and vulgar view of many human relationships – the lack of*
*the sterner kind of humour which would show him the dreariness of*
*his farce and the total absence of proportion and inadequateness in*
*some of his ideas – all these defects come largely from the flippant and*
*worthless self-complacency brought about by the worship of rather*
*second-rate women ... Whether I like him, admire him or despise*
*him most I do not know.* Beatrice Webb (1897)

If Shaw could settle down to marriage as she and Sidney had done, Beatrice Webb felt certain she would come to like him better, admire his work more. Already, almost in spite of himself, she was beginning to see 'a sort of affectionateness' beneath his layer of vanity. He was so extraordinarily good-natured, spending days over Sidney's and her books – *Industrial Democracy* or *Problems of Modern Industry*. Any astute reader, she realized, would quickly divine those chapters he had worked over – 'there is a conciseness and crispness in parts subjected to his pruning knife lacking elsewhere'. His fanaticism, which turned everything inside out to see whether the other side wouldn't do as well, gave him a genuine charm. At the various houses where the Fabian junta met, the intellectual vitality and humour he poured out made the company specially agreeable. He was 'the perfect "house friend"', Beatrice observed in her diary, ' – self-sufficient, witty and tolerant, going his own way and yet adapting himself to your ways. If only he would concentrate his really brilliant intellect on some consecutive thought'.

Obviously he needed a good wife. In his fashion he was an honourable man. He would give up all his silly philandering, which so irritated and upset Beatrice, once he was properly married. But would he ever marry? Beatrice decided to find out.

Shaw was seeing a good deal of her and Sidney in the mid-1890s. But this was different from his previous triangular relationships with friends and their wives. He could not flirt with Beatrice and retain his friendship with Sidney; and so he could not flirt. Except in matters of work, he felt painfully excluded watching the Webbs petting each other as if, he noted, they were still honeymooning. At Argoed in the Wye Valley, he had grown used to working in the same room and seeing Beatrice 'every now and then when she felt she needed a refresher (Sidney was tireless) rise from her chair, throw away her pen and hurl herself on her husband in a shower of caresses which lasted until the passion for work resumed its sway; then they wrote or read authorities for their footnotes until it was time for another refresher. Meanwhile I placidly wrote plays ...'

But Shaw was not placid. 'I – I, George Bernard Shaw – have actually suffered from something which in anyone else I should call unhappiness.' His body, which he had done so much through the agency of his plays to displace, ached for 'a moment of really sacred intimacy'. He was physically attracted to Beatrice and sensed that she found him attractive, in much the same hostile way as Judith Anderson in *The Devil's Disciple* is unconsciously drawn to Dick Dudgeon. He had to be constantly on his guard and, feeling her embarrassment, her antipathy, also felt the strain of all that was untried and unspoken between them, rising to 'a perfectly devilish intensity'.

Treading his bicycle up hills on solitary evenings was one relief; confiding many of his emotions by letters to Janet Achurch was another. For what he was witnessing in the Webbs' marriage was the merging of physical passion into a shared obsession for work. That was a marriage he could understand. Had he not been experimenting, in his own style, with similar relationships among actresses? But Beatrice could not consider actresses to be serious women. They were dilettantes among whose gyrations of jealousy and infatuation ('all cordially hating each other') Shaw satisfied his *amour propre*. Of course, with such second-rate people, it was the process, not the unromantic actuality of love, that appealed to him. For that he needed a finer type of woman. As if for a bye-election, Beatrice had already entered a candidate: the Fabian artist Bertha Newcombe.

To Beatrice's eye Bertha Newcombe appeared to enjoy various qualities as a potential wife. She was 'insignificant and undistinguished' and, being devoted to Shaw, would exercise all her energies on his behalf. That she was Fabian was essential; that she was 'lady-like' no disadvantage; and that she was 'not wholly inartistic' an unlooked-for bonus. She was in her thirties and, despite the somewhat unpleasant impression communicated by her aquiline features, thin lips and a figure that put Beatrice in mind of a wizened child, not perhaps lacking absolutely in all attraction. At least she was quite smartly turned out, *petite* and dark, with neat, heavily-fringed, black hair. There was little chance of the philanderer marrying her for the wrong reasons; yet it was not unimaginable that Shaw could put his evolutionary theories of marriage into practice with Bertha.

Shaw had sat to Bertha for his portrait as early as 1892. In February and March that year he had gone for long hours to her Chelsea studio, sometimes spending the whole day there, breaking for tea or a duologue at her piano. She had painted him as the platform spellbinder, full-length, hand-on-hip, his mouth slightly open as if uttering one of his formidable ripostes, his red-gold hair and Irish blue eyes adding to the impression of easy confidence – 'a powerful picture,' Beatrice decided, 'in which the love of the woman had given genius to the artist'.

427

She had painted him as a spellbinder, then fallen under his spell. Later, while he was writing *The Man of Destiny*, lying in a field with his fountain pen and a notebook, she painted him again: *A Snake in the Grass*. He had not deceived her, but he had bewitched her. He was so easy, delightful; almost intimate, though not quite. Not understanding him, she complained that he did not understand her. She doubted whether he had the gift of sympathetic penetration into any woman's nature. Even his kindness had an edge of cruelty. 'He employs his clever detective power and pounces on weaknesses & faults which confirm his preconceived ideas,' she observed shrewdly. 'He imagines he understands. I objected to my emotions being divided into compartments and still retain my opinion that the emotion of love can be a fusion of body, spirit & mind.'

If Shaw was ever emotionally interested in Bertha it had been during the painting of that first portrait, when work and human companionship coincided. After that, though he seems to have liked her, he was protected from any deeper involvement by her obvious obsession with him. But it was an obsession that he had helped to rouse. He told her of his adoration for Ellen Terry; he had kindly introduced her to Janet Achurch so that she could do some drawings of her, and Bertha had been unable to resist meeting 'the siren – the wonderful woman who absorbed Shaw's leisure to an extent of which I was only half-conscious'; and he had joked mercilessly of Beatrice Webb's zeal to see him married. Behind everything he said lay an insistence on his independence. For though he felt the power and pleasure of love, he was determined never to repeat the adventures he had soldiered through with Jenny Patterson. He still wanted some of that power and pleasure, but without emotional risk or undertow of guilt. Therefore he seduced women with his words and personality, not his body. 'Shaw was, I should imagine, by preference a passionless man,' Bertha surmised. She sensed the latent passion that Jenny Patterson had aroused in him, but she could not reach it herself. Her love awoke his apprehensions and he let them out in volleys of apparently unfeeling jokes. 'The sight of a woman deeply in love with him annoyed him,' Bertha commented. '. . . and he found I think those times the pleasantest when I was the appreciative listener.

'Unfortunately on my side there was a deep feeling most injudiciously displayed . . . I realise how exasperating it must have been to him. He had decided I think on a line of honourable conduct – honourable to his thinking. He kept strictly to the letter of it while allowing himself every opportunity of transgressing the spirit. Frequent talking, talking, talking of the pros & cons of marriage, even to my prospects of money or the want of it, his dislike of the sexual relation & so on, would create an atmosphere of love-making without any need for caresses or endearments.'

All this she saw and felt acutely. What she did not see was that his talk, inducing so much pain, was a method of testing her strength. Everyone was recommending him to marry Bertha. But were they really well-matched? If he married it must be to someone who did not swamp him with sentimental demands; someone whose love was meticulously threaded with shared interests, as Beatrice's was for Sidney. His tactics showed that Bertha and he could never be useful partners like the Webbs. Her interest in art and politics was far less embracing than his. She sought in a relationship with him the completeness of her happiness. But he had done with 'happiness'. Bertha was 'neither strong enough nor disorderly enough for a lawless life,' he told Janet, 'nor cold & self-sufficient enough to enjoy a genuinely single one, she ought to marry someone else'.

'She is only wasting her affections on me. I give her nothing; and I do not even take everything – in fact I dont take anything, which makes her most miserable. She has no idea with regard to me except that she would like to tie me like a pet dog to the leg of her easel & have me always to make love to her when she is tired of painting. And she might just as well feel that way to Cleopatra's needle. When I tell her so, it only mortifies & tantalises & attracts her & makes her worse. If you told her so, it would be intolerable. So I wish somebody could come along & marry her before she worries herself into a state of brokenheartedness.'

Shaw's campaign to steer Bertha away from 'this lunacy of hers' employed every means except one: he could not absent himself from her infelicity. He flirted with some of her sitters, teased her with liking him only 'as children like wedding cake, for the sake of the sugar on the top'; explained that all actresses interested him but no women; and was vivisectionally cruel-to-be-kind. 'Heavens! I had forgotten you – totally forgotten you,' he reminded her. He would not let her alone. When he went to Paris to see *Peer Gynt* in the autumn of 1896 he took the trouble to stay in the same lodging-house as her. Revelations of his love-making with another woman had already been eagerly passed on to her by Janet Achurch. But when Bertha accused him of fortune-hunting he cheerfully agreed and topped her second-hand stories with the facetious announcement that he was already engaged to be married to a millionairess and looking forward to a life of luxury. What was she to believe? In desperation she wrote to Beatrice who, on Shaw's instructions, had stopped inviting them together to the Fabian countryside. For five years she had been loyally devoted to Shaw. She had endured rumours of flirtations, largely because she knew that Beatrice was counselling him to marry her. Now she was dismayed to hear that Beatrice was encouraging him to marry someone else. Why?

Beatrice came to the dark wainscoted studio in Cheyne Walk to give her answer. So long as there had seemed a chance of marriage she had been willing to act as Bertha's chaperon. She would have welcomed her as Shaw's wife. But directly she realized he would never marry her she had backed out of the affair. As Beatrice proceeded with her explanation, Bertha's small face seemed to shrink; and, remembering perhaps her own pain over Chamberlain, Beatrice suddenly raged against Shaw. 'You are well out of it, Miss Newcombe,' she said. 'If you had married Shaw he would not have remained faithful to you. You know my opinion of him – as a friend and a colleague, as a critic and literary worker, there are few men for whom I have so warm a liking – but in his relations with women he is vulgar – if not worse – it is a vulgarity which includes cruelty and springs from vanity.'

'It is so horribly lonely,' Bertha answered. 'I daresay it is more peaceful than being kept on the rack – but it is like the peace of death.'

Partly because of the inconclusive nature of their romance, Bertha was never at peace over Shaw. She could not forgive him. She remained at Cheyne Walk and never married. But by 1909, having taken the post of Honorary Secretary of the Civic and Dramatic Guild, she found herself responsible for the private production of *Press Cuttings*. They met; he read her this 'ghastly absurdity', then went home to write her a letter. 'I did not notice any embarrassment; nor did I expect it after such a barefaced assignation.'

'I expected to find a broken hearted, prematurely aged woman: I found an exceedingly smart lady, not an hour older, noting with a triumphant gleam in her eye my white hairs and lined face. When I think that I allowed those brutal letters to hurt me – ME – Bernard Shaw!! Are you not ashamed?'

But Shaw's teasing, even when intended to be complimentary and supportive, never amused Bertha. The following month they were quarrelling over the production of *Press Cuttings* and she was calling him a 'villain'.

'. . . it is far better that I should again efface myself for another 11 years. Possibly we may all die before then. Your letter seems to me rather out of date. Do you still continue to think of yourself as an idol for adoring women? That idol was shattered for me years ago – – – Inadvertently when you mention the care that has been taken of you, you touch upon the lasting grievance.'

And her grievance did last. A World War came and went. Bertha was approaching sixty, approaching seventy; and still it lasted. She became a confidante of Thomas Hardy's wife – at least *she* was married. Her own spinsterhood seemed to be protected by a series of broken appointments, unacceptable or cancelled invitations – assignations that were a 'waste of time. B[ertha] *wont* accept the situation,' Shaw protested to Charrington, who had taken the part of go-between. '. . . Such tomfoolery is beyond human patience.' In his letters he tried to present himself as unappealing, but could not resist the paradoxical flourish, the shattering joke – then would recover himself, too late. 'I am still the same writing speaking machine you know of old,' he assured her in 1922.

'I am in my 66th year; my hair is white, and I am as heartless a brute as ever. Also, again as ever, women adore me more, and are less ashamed of it than when you painted The Snake in the Grass. Hearts can be heard breaking in all directions like china in the hands of a clumsy housemaid. But you need not ask. You have my books – the best of me . . .'

It was not enough, the shattered idol and the broken china. From such debris it had once seemed possible to piece together something valuable. But their correspondence, reviving past expectations, tormented Bertha with these ruined images, and much of it she destroyed. 'Your memories terrify me,' Shaw wrote to her in 1925. 'Thank God there will be no letters.' He had avoided melodrama and fallen into farce. Bertha 'has the most maddening way of giving me impossible invitations at the wrong moment,' he complained to Beatrice Webb, 'and then quarrelling with me for not going. When I *do* offer to go, she trots out an absent servant, or a present sister . . . or something ridiculous to preserve her grievance.'
That was the future.
So Beatrice Webb rose perfunctorily to go. 'Come and see me,' she told Bertha ' – someday.' There seemed nothing else to say. She kissed her on the forehead and escaped downstairs. Would anyone succeed in taming the philanderer? 'I doubt,' Beatrice confided in her diary, 'whether Bernard Shaw could be induced to marry.'

\*

Beatrice had spoken the truth to Bertha; nevertheless it was Beatrice who had inadvertently put an end to Shaw's interest in her. At a luncheon party in the early autumn of 1895 she and Sidney had met an Irish lady named Charlotte Payne-Townshend – wealthy, unmarried, 'a large graceful woman with masses of chocolate brown hair,' Beatrice later described her. 'She dresses well, in flowing white evening robes she approaches beauty. At moments she is plain.'

'By temperament she is an anarchist, feeling any regulation or rule intolerable, a tendency which has been exaggerated by her irresponsible wealth. She is romantic but thinks herself cynical. She is a Socialist and a Radical, not because she understands the Collectivist standpoint, but because she is by nature a rebel. She has no snobbishness and no convention . . . She is fond of men and impatient of most women, bitterly resents her enforced celibacy but thinks she could not tolerate the matter-of-fact side of marriage. Sweet tempered, sympathetic and genuinely anxious to increase the world's enjoyment and diminish the world's pain.'

Beatrice had first made friends with Charlotte 'for the sake of the cause'. Knowing her to be rich, lacking in occupation and socialistic in tendency, she interested her in the London School of Economics, and was rewarded with a subscription of one thousand pounds for the library and the endowment of a woman's scholarship. Charlotte also agreed, at a rent and service charge of £300 a year, to take rooms on the two upper floors above the School when, in October 1896, it moved to 10 Adelphi Terrace. She was not only useful, she was likeable. Beatrice soon began to absorb her 'into our little set of comrades', nominating her for the Fabian Society, with a note to the secretary that the amount of her cheque testified to the degree of her convictions.

Shaw was introduced to her on 29 January 1896. They appear to have made little impression on each other. She noted the event without comment; and he did not go two months later to her At Home at LSE. But he was apparently 'prepared to take my part' in a plan Beatrice had formed to marry Charlotte off to Graham Wallas. In the late summer of 1896 the Webbs rented for six weeks a Spartan rectory at the village of Stratford St Andrew in Suffolk; and Wallas and Charlotte were invited. Shaw was there as a matter of course. 'I was part of the household furniture.' Everything seemed in train for a satisfactory Fabian match.

Within a week, and with Shaw in command, this plan was reshaped. Beatrice had collapsed with a rheumatic cold and Wallas, who left early, arrived four days late. In those four days, as if for the sake of the London School of Economics, Shaw kept Charlotte entertained. He would not have forgotten how, half a dozen years before, he had blindly discussed with Webb the Fabian advantages of marriage between Wallas and Beatrice. Now Beatrice was anxious that, pending Wallas, Charlotte did not become bored. So the pantomime ostrich spread before her his most brilliant plumage. 'I made myself as agreeable as possible.' Charlotte and he were constant companions, pedalling round the country all day, sitting up late at night talking. 'They are, I gather from him, on very confidential terms,'

Beatrice noted anxiously in her diary, 'and have "explained" their relative positions. Though interested I am somewhat uneasy.'

*

'I had a perfectly hellish childhood and youth . . .' There was much in what Charlotte said about herself that appealed to Shaw. She was six months younger than he and her family came from Derry; at least her father's did. Horace Townsend had been 'a marvel of patience'. He liked to hum mildly under his breath and to drum his fingers on the arms of chairs as if waiting for something. There was not much to do in Derry, but Horace was fully occupied with his railway dreams, particularly with the branch line, eight miles long, he would never build (except in dreams). His greatest talent was for politeness. Charlotte, who 'was always attracted to men of action', longed for him to assert himself. It was astonishing how his gentleness provoked everyone – especially his wife, a domineering English lady fretted by social ambitions. It took one to make a quarrel. She filled the house with her lamentations. Humming and drumming he tried to deafen himself, make himself invisible. But she got hold of him, hyphenated and then aspirated his name, dug him up from Derry, extinguished his dreams. 'It was a terrible home,' Charlotte remembered. If only he had quelled her. Instead he submitted, and indulged her moods. 'She could not bear opposition; if it was offered she either became quite violent, or she cried. She constantly cried. She felt (genuinely felt) she had sacrificed her life for us and my father (we were two, my sister and myself ), and she never ceased telling us so. She felt (quite genuinely) that we none of us loved her enough . . .'

The volume of domestic unhappiness rose, submerging her humdrum husband. Early in February 1885 he decided to die. There was nothing much wrong with him – a little rheumatism perhaps – and he was comparatively young. But his patience had given out, and for a polite man there was nothing else to do.

His wife was incredulous, but Charlotte understood. She understood that her mother had killed him – not legally, of course, but in fact. By everything she now did she sought to avenge his death. Her mother had one ambition left: to see her two daughters brilliantly married, if possible into the aristocracy. Charlotte passionately wanted to be free of her family. She could be free through marriage, but she refused to give her mother that satisfaction. A Victorian girl was 'supposed to live at home until she married: and if she didn't marry, to live at home always and "make herself useful". And even in my earliest years I had determined I would never marry.'

Charlotte made herself into the sort of person her mother saw as unmarriageable: a deliberately plain woman, without social wit or grace. She became a bluestocking and a bookworm. Mother and daughter were determined women; and neither would leave the other alone. In a furious dance they struggled across Europe, always circumscribed by 'the best circles' and, except when in the vortex of the London season, seldom anywhere for more than a week. But (as Shaw thought of it) Charlotte had had 'cleverness and character enough to decline the station of life – "great catch for somebody" – to which it pleased God to call her'. Inevitably she blundered into offers of marriage. J. S. Black proposed in 'as few words as I can' in a note from his club; Count Sponnek declared himself in South Kensington and, being rebuffed, rushed off in an emotional state to St Petersbourg; Finch Hutton sent her the skin of a bear shot in Wyoming and twelve dressed beaver skins: but 'I cannot marry you,' Charlotte replied; Herbert Oakley, a barrister, died before completing his case; the wife of Arthur Smith-Barry also died, leaving Arthur Smith-Barry wondering whether Charlotte would take her place. She didn't. And there were others. Majors and Generals and Major-Generals. Mrs Payne-Townshend watched them all, her hopes pumping up and down, until she realized that Charlotte would never marry anyone while she herself remained alive. The hatred between the two women was by now 'almost a tangible thing'. For the first time in her life Mrs Payne-Townshend was not going to get her own way. This did not suit her. She felt ill. A doctor was called but he could find nothing wrong with her except 'nerves'. A few days later she died. 'It is really awful to think how glad I was,' Charlotte admitted. 'I sometimes still wonder whether my constant longing for her death had anything to do with killing her.'

She was thirty-four, affluent, and at last free. For the first time in her life she allowed herself to fall in love. Dr Axel Munthe, hypnotist and story-teller, caught her in the immense web of his vanity and left her there. Extricating herself had been painful, and it was then that she had flown into the Webbs' parlour.

Charlotte appeared to share with Shaw little more than a couple of powerful aversions, to tobacco and marriage. But she had also admired *The Quintessence of Ibsenism* which seemed to give a creative elucidation to her family rebelliousness. For, as Beatrice Webb was discovering, Charlotte was something more than a well-dressed, well-intentioned woman: 'she turns out to be an "original", with considerable personal charm and certain volcanic tendencies.'

Graham Wallas arrived, bored Charlotte with his morality and learning, then left. 'We got on his nerves,' explained Shaw. They resumed their constant companionship. 'I am up to the neck in infidelities and villainies of all kinds,' he promised Janet Achurch.

'If the walls of this simple minded rectory could only describe the games they have witnessed, the parson would move, horror-stricken, to another house . . . Life here is a perfect routine. Breakfast at half past eight; work until half past one (lunch); repair punctures or chat or smoke cigarettes – I wish they wouldn't – until afternoon tea; bicycle until half past seven (dinner); sit round the fire talking or reading plays (as long as my works lasted) until ten; and then to bed. The only variations are that Miss P. T. and I are impatient of wasting the early afternoon, and dont care about tea; so we have made many bicycling expeditions together à deux. Also, instead of going to bed at ten, we go out and stroll about among the trees for a while. She, being also Irish, does not succumb to my arts as the unsuspecting and literal Englishwoman does; but we get on together all the better, repairing bicycles, talking philosophy and religion and Shaw table talk, or, when we are in a mischievous or sentimental humor, philandering shamelessly and outrageously. Such is life at Stratford St Andrew.'

Charlotte had entered Shaw's life at the perfect moment. The loneliness and irritation he had felt at watching the Webbs caressing each other evaporated. Falling out of love with actresses, Shaw was suddenly able to convert them into an audience for his own romantic play-acting opposite this 'Irish lady with the light green eyes and the million of money'. 'I am going to refresh my heart by falling in love with her,' he announced to Ellen Terry, ' – I love falling in love – but, mind, only with her, not with the million; so someone else must marry her if she can stand him after me.' It *was* play-acting. With such a placid, proper, self-possessed person what else could it be? They were so genuinely fond of each other, Shaw reasoned, that anything more would be superfluous. Though sentimental, Charlotte was no slave to romance and 'she doesnt really *love* me'. Kissing in the evening among the trees felt pleasantly unreal. He confided to Ellen what she had told him and what he understood by it. 'The truth is, she is a clever woman, with plenty of romantic imagination . . . She knows the value of her unencumbered independence, having suffered a good deal from family bonds & conventionality before the death of her mother & the marriage of her sister left her free. The idea of tying herself up again by a marriage before she knows anything – before she has exploited her freedom & money power to the utmost – seems to her intellect to be unbearably foolish. Her theory is that she wont do it.'

Here was a challenge and a reassurance. He liked her honesty – she never pretended not to enjoy his company; he liked her involvement with the political side of his life; and he liked her independence. 'You don't love me the least bit in the world,' he informed her. 'But I am all the more grateful.'

Watching them uneasily over these weeks at Stratford St Andrew, Beatrice had reached a different conclusion. Charlotte, she decided, would not be happy without marriage. 'These warmhearted unmarried women of a certain age are audacious and almost childishly reckless of consequences.'

*

The *villeggiatura* in Suffolk came to an end on 17 September. Shaw and Charlotte, Sidney and Beatrice, ascended their machines and wheeled off in quartet to London, which they reached in pouring rain four days later. Shaw was immediately engulfed in business. What with getting the mud off his bicycle, bathing, and changing his clothes, opening his multitude of letters and hurrying down to Camberwell for the first night of a new play, there was time for only the most tantalizing note to Charlotte. 'The enclosed belongs to your [bicycle] pump. I forgot to give it to you. What a lonely evening, and a cold going to bed!' Charlotte, who was staying with the Webbs, had nothing to do but contemplate the past weeks. She missed Shaw – and rather miserably she told him so. 'You look as if you had returned to your old amusement of eating your heart,' he reproved her, remembering Axel Munthe. 'I like it not. Million thunders, you must get something to do: I have a mind to go upstairs & shake you, only then I should lose my train.'

He was determined that she must remain strong, and repeated his directions to her not to become infatuated with him. 'No: you don't love me one little bit. All that is nature, instinct, sex: it proves nothing beyond itself. Don't fall in love: be your own, not mine or anyone else's.'

'From the moment that you can't do without me, you're lost, like Bertha. Never fear: if we want one another we shall find it out. All I know is that you made the autumn very happy, and that I shall always be fond of you for that. About the future I do not concern myself: let us do what lies to our hands & wait for events. My dearest!'

Shaw had called Charlotte a clever woman. Feeling that she was falling in love with him, she suddenly left London for Ireland. Shaw felt nonplussed: he was unused to people taking his advice. The kick of his disappointment took him aback. She had surpassed his expectations. He began by welcoming her journey to Ireland ('I had rather you were well a thousand miles away than ill in my wretched arms'), then complained of her removal ('oh for ten minutes peace in the moonlight at Stratford! . . . keep me deep in your heart . . . why do you choose this time of all others to

436

desert me – just now when you are most wanted? . . . I wish I were with you among those hills'). But his eloquence and even his teasing seemed to dash itself uselessly against the rock of her absence. 'I suppose you won't stay longer than you can help . . . Keep me advised of your address . . . Oh, if I could only talk to you without writing.'

To recover his Shavian poise he turned to his audience of actresses, addressing quantities of indiscreet correspondence in particular to Ellen Terry. His insensitivity affronted Ellen – he had even sent her one of Charlotte's letters. She hesitated to use strong words but really he was *naughty* – 'a little naughty'. She *meant* it. 'I've stormed at you – reviled you – implored you,' she scolded. These letters had not been written by *her* Shaw: she tore them into mince, and scattered them in the fire. For she could recognize (even if he did not) that he was becoming Charlotte's Shaw. But he must stop all this gossip about marriage and money, contain his feelings in silence, find out what they really amounted to and where they led. Ellen's disillusionment was everything Shaw could have expected, and gave him back in nursery style his Mephistophelean fortitude. He had behaved badly to her, but to Charlotte, on the day before her return from Ireland, he had sent an exactly truthful letter. 'I will contrive to see you somehow, at all hazards,' he told her: 'I *must*; and that "must" which "rather alarms" you, TERRIFIES me.'

'If it were possible to run away – if it would do any good – I'd do it; so mortally afraid am I that my trifling & lying and ingrained treachery and levity with women are going to make you miserable when my whole sane desire is to make you hap – I mean strong and self possessed and tranquil. However, we must talk about it . . . My one hope is that you are as treacherous as I am. No matter: let's meet, meet, meet, meet, meet: bless me! how I should like to see you again for pure *liking*; for there is something between us aside and apart from all my villainy.'

He saw her the night she returned. For hours beforehand he had felt curiously agitated. He had missed her – but would her presence make his heart grow less fond? He sent before him a message full of instructions as to how she must keep her distance when they were alone together. Then he arrived and 'I really was happy . . . I am satisfied, satisfied, satisfied deep in my heart.' He had found with Charlotte a real friendliness mixed with some sexual interest. But that sexual interest, as yet not fully realized, extended a faint shadow over his happiness. 'I wish there was nothing to look forward to,' he wrote to her later that night, 'nothing to covet, nothing to gain.' It was, he added, 'mere greediness'. What he actually feared was that there was something to lose; that sex would drive out affection. Charlotte, he had told Ellen Terry, 'knows that what she lacks is physical experience, and that without it she will be in ten years' time an old maid.' Here was the danger, but he could not stay away from Adelphi Terrace. He came – 'and now, dear Ellen,' he confided, 'she sleeps like a child, and her arms will be plump, and she is a free woman, and it has not cost her half a farthing, and she has fancied herself in love, and known secretly that she was only taking a prescription, and been relieved to find the lover at last laughing at her & reading her thoughts and confessing himself a mere bottle of nerve medicine, and riding gaily off.'

Often before Shaw had implored women to *use* him. 'It is only when I am being used that I can feel my own existence, enjoy my own life,' he had claimed. 'All my love affairs end tragically because the women *can't* use me.' Charlotte had used him, not paradoxically, but literally: and 'in the blackest depths' he felt robbed of 'that most blessed of things – unsatisfied desire'. From this desire, so ingeniously provoked and ecstatically unsatisfied, he had conceived the make-believe of his plays. Now, he told Charlotte, 'I have squandered on you all the material out of which my illusions are made'. Once again Charlotte had confounded his expectations. Prim and socially self-effacing, she could take off the mask of proper breeding 'in the most cold blooded way', he discovered, once she selected a man for intimacy. It was one of those 'volcanic tendencies' Beatrice had detected in her. Breaking his vocational vow of chastity, Shaw had given her sleep so that she might never wake up an old maid. But 'now I count what I have discovered, before the illusions return. And I don't find that I have made you feel anything except nervously.'

Shaw had represented Charlotte as wanting physical experience outside marriage. But she had an apprehension of sexual intercourse, deriving from what Shaw later described as 'a morbid horror of maternity'. She was in her fortieth year and 'there was never any question of breeding'. Her nervousness came less from physical revulsion than risk. Over the next eighteen months they seem to have found together a habit of limited sexual experience, diminishing as things improved, reducing for her the risk of conception and preserving for him his subliminal illusions. To such muted sexuality Shaw could give assent. 'ALL CLEAR NOW YES A THOUSAND TIMES,' he had cabled Charlotte in October. That autumn too he started to terminate his relationship with Bertha Newcombe; blew away Ellen Terry's daydreams of becoming his mother-in-law; renounced retrospectively 'spiritual intercourse' with Florence Farr; and, in sympathy with Charlotte's feelings, told Janet Achurch that her maternity had made her 'stark raving mad'. Then, turning back to Charlotte he resumed his intrepid *doubles entendres*: 'Cold much worse – fatal consummation highly probable. Shall see you tonight ... What an exacting woman you are! Is this freedom?'

*

Over the winter, spring and summer of 1897 Charlotte made herself almost indispensable to Shaw. She learnt to read his shorthand and to type, 'amused herself by writing my critical articles at my dictation,' Shaw remembered, and helped him prepare his plays for the press. Her flat above the London School of Economics became 'very convenient for me' – more convenient than Fitzroy Square. There was no question of turning up there at any time in the casual way he had dropped in on Jenny Patterson, Janet Achurch, Florence Farr and others. Charlotte was no 'Bohemian'. He would invite her to theatres, picture galleries and Fabian lectures, and adapt some of his plans to fit in with hers; she invited him to lunch or dinner and saw to it that her cook became expert in vegetarian dishes. 'We got on very well together,' he concluded, 'and soon became close friends.' There were interruptions: his migraines, her neuralgia; his work, her journeys. And there was a momentary crisis when, in response to his demand that she 'get something to do', she threatened to buy a poodle – which drew from him ('Good God, what an idea! DON'T') the panicky suggestion that she 'have (or hire) a baby' instead. In a spirit of compromise she attended lectures at the School of Medicine for Women.

As part of her plan to see as much of Shaw as possible, Charlotte began taking her holidays with the Webbs. Between April and June 1897 she shared with them the expenses of a pretty cottage called Lotus on the North Downs, near Dorking. Shaw went down as frequently as he could. But between his new vestry and continuous Fabian work, his drama criticism for the *Saturday Review* and the varied difficulties over *The Man of Destiny*, *You Never Can Tell* and *The Devil's Disciple*, he had less time and less vitality than at Stratford the previous year – 'tired and careworn' he described himself.

But the Webbs were in excellent working form. The sun streamed through the dancing leaves and they revelled, almost childlike with excitement, in the economic characteristics of Trade Unionism. 'How full and brimming over with happiness human life can be,' Beatrice enthused. The only ruffle (it occasionally woke her at night) was an anxiety lest she were insufficiently astringent over housekeeping. She was to be one of the hundred distinguished women giving a banquet for a hundred distinguished men to celebrate the Queen's Diamond Jubilee. The Fabians had taken a moderate line in these junketings, agreeing to contribute one guinea for decorations in the Strand but refraining from singing the national anthem. The inanities of this frightful festival sickened Shaw but, for political reasons, most socialists were careful not to disassociate themselves from its compulsory conviviality. The drunken sight-seeing and hysterical loyalty had no place in the Webbs' schemes for extending their own paradise, via a task-force of civil servants, to the rest of the country.

While they laboured delightedly at a concept of national efficiency through scientific socialism, Charlotte sat upstairs miserably typewriting *Plays Unpleasant*, while the playwright himself strode the garden vociferating his Dramatic Opinions. Beatrice watched her friends with concern. It was obvious that Charlotte was deeply attached to Shaw, but 'I see no sign on his side of the growth of any genuine and steadfast affection,' she noted. 'He finds it pleasant to be with her in her luxurious surroundings, he has been studying her and all her little ways and amusing himself by dissecting the rich woman brought up without training and drifting about at the beck of impulse.'

'I think he has now exhausted the study, observed all that there is to observe. He has been flattered by her devotion and absorption in him; he is kindly and has a catlike preference for those persons to whom he is accustomed. But there are ominous signs that he is tired of watching the effect of little words of gallantry and personal interest with which he plied her in the first months of the friendship.'

Though she found everything 'very interesting' Charlotte could take only a modest part in what Shaw called 'our eternal political shop'. There was no let up. On Sundays they enlisted a stream of visitors – young radicals, mostly: William Pember Reeves and his wife Maud; Bertrand and Alys Russell; Herbert Samuel; Charles Trevelyan; Graham Wallas – and Charlotte sometimes felt excluded. She hung on, but to Beatrice's eyes her face showed at times 'a blank haggard look'. Without the Fabian habit of hard work or Beatrice's religious sense of intellectual mission, she had nowhere to turn. Beatrice felt that Shaw must share her own irritation at Charlotte's lack of purpose and incapacity for work. 'If she would set to – and do even the smallest and least considerable task of intellectual work – I believe she could retain his interest and perhaps develop his feeling for her.'

Charlotte had struggled to make an occupation out of Shaw's work. On Sundays in London she had made her way to the *terra incognita* of dock gates and street corners to hear him speak on 'The Use of Political Power' or 'The Respectability of Socialism'. But these experiences had mortified her. She hated the roughness of the crowds. 'At first I thought she was bored and tired and incommoded simply,' Shaw told Ellen Terry; 'but now it appears that my demagogic denunciations of the idle rich – my demands for taxation of unearned incomes – lacerate her conscience; for she has great possessions. What am I to do: she won't stay away; and I can't talk Primrose League. Was there ever such a situation?'

It appeared that they were being separated by the very issues – an enthusiasm for socialism and aversion to marriage – that had once seemed to attach them. Only their loathing of tobacco remained intact. Describing himself as 'not a marrying man' Shaw deplored Charlotte's friendship with him as 'a fearful waste of a first rate endowment'. He believed that marriage would soon be modified by an extension of divorce. Therefore it was better at present for 'two people who do not mean to devote themselves to a regular domestic, nursery career to maintain a clandestine connection than to run the risks of marriage.' This had been the theme of the discarded last act of *The Philanderer*. Such views were made puzzling to Charlotte by Shaw's teasing exploitation of them. At first hearing, his personal repugnance to marriage seemed to her quite in line with the 'advanced ideas' that would have made her a member of the Ibsen Club. But she was surprised to find that 'my advice to women was always to insist on marriage, and refuse to compromise themselves with any man on cheaper terms,' Shaw remembered, 'and that I considered the status of a married woman as almost indispensable under existing circumstances to a woman's fullest possible freedom.'

'In short, I prescribed marriage for women, and refused it for myself. I upset her ideas in many directions; for she was prepared for conventional unconventionality, but not for a criticism of it as severe as its own criticism of conventionality.'

Within this argument seem to lie the biological politics that were to vitalize *Man and Superman*. In fact the philosophy of this play was one of the 'illusions' that Shaw substituted for actual experience. For Charlotte did not want marriage in order to breed children; she was beginning to want it as a partnership that, though different from the Webbs', would be no less unique and mysterious in its spiritual consummation. At that level Shaw had nothing to say. Eventually she began to run out of patience with him. 'Miss P. T. has found me out,' he reported to Ellen Terry: 'after about a year of fascination she tells me that I am "the most self-centred man she ever met".'

Charlotte had surprised Shaw before by taking his advice. Now, moving from the general to the particular, she attempted to do so again. If it was her job to marry, she would do so: she would marry him. Since, under present conditions, marriage was more a woman's business than a man's, Shaw would not object to the logical unconventionality of a woman making the proposal. This it seems is what she attempted to do in the second week of July 1897. Shaw, who described the scene as 'a sort of earthquake', realized that she had been cherishing this romantic project 'as a sort of climax to the proofs she was giving me every day of her regard for me'. He received the golden moment, he told Ellen Terry, 'with shuddering horror & wildly asked the fare to Australia'. This description, given a fortnight after the event, is a good example of the replacement of 'Shaw Limited' by 'G.B.S.'. Pain, regret, tenderness are dissolved in the triumphant playing of a Shavian scherzo. A letter he had sent Charlotte the day after her proposal, reads like an early transcription where fact and illusion are in equilibrium. 'I have an iron ring round my chest, which tightens and grips my heart when I remember that you are perhaps still tormented,' he wrote to her.

'Loosen it, oh ever dear to me, by a word to say that you slept well and have never been better than today. Or else lend me my fare to Australia, to Siberia, to the mountains of the moon, to any place where I can torment nobody but myself. I am sorry – not vainly sorry; for I have done a good morning's work, but painfully, wistfully, affectionately sorry that you were hurt; but if you had seen my mind you would not have been hurt. I am so certain of that that I am in violently, brutally high spirits in spite of that iron ring. Write me something happy, but only a few words, and don't sit down to *think* over them. What you think is all wrong.'

But what did Shaw think? Charlotte had not seen his mind, despite his flow of words, because he had not revealed it to her. From his correspondence with Ellen Terry it seems that he had explained to Charlotte that he could not act in private against his public commitments. She was rich, he was poor. Marriage for property, he had written, was prostitution; to sell himself to her would be the act of an adventurer. This financial scruple had the advantage of being kindly; it was not a *personal* rejection. Yet it was a prevarication, and did not protect Charlotte from being 'inexpressibly taken aback'. After all, there was no need for him to have as much money as herself; only that he should be earning enough to keep himself independent of her by his work. Since he was practising his profession successfully it was absurd for him to turn his back on a richer woman simply because people such as Bertha Newcombe might regard him as a fortune-hunter. Or was it that, for all her typing, he feared that, once married, Charlotte would seek to withdraw him from his work and make him dependent on her? It was not flattering.

Politically, Shaw had put his faith in the power of words to inspire action. But in his personal life he employed words to avoid taking action.

His letters to Ellen Terry and others had developed into an oblique device for this avoidance. He talked himself out of emotional danger. Advancing to the front of the stage he liked to put his case mockingly to the audience:

'Oh why won't women be content to leave their stars in the heavens and not want to tear them down and hang them round their necks with a gold ring! Why does their pleasure turn to pain and their love to hate without their knowing that it has happened? I will put an end to it all by marrying. Do you know a reasonably healthy woman of about sixty, accustomed to plain vegetarian cookery, and able to read & write enough to forward letters when her husband is away, but otherwise uneducated? Must be plain featured, and of an easy, unjealous temperament. No relatives, if possible. Must not be a lady. One who has never been in a theatre preferred. Separate rooms.'

Such a monologue, though it floods the auditorium with amusement, does not advance the event-plot of the play, and eliminates (except as the butt of a joke) Shaw's fellow-actor, Charlotte. But does it convince? At least one member of his audience with a shrewd knowledge of such performances thought not. Shaw was protesting far too much. 'Well,' Ellen Terry responded, 'you two will marry.'

\*

Superficially the rupture between Shaw and Charlotte healed quickly with 'Love & blessing'. But added pressure was now being placed on him to marry. Webb had uncharacteristically given him a talking to; and then, at the end of July, Graham Wallas unexpectedly announced his own engagement to a high-principled short-story writer, Ada Radford. With this 'desertion' Shaw was to become the only unmarried member of the Fabian Old Gang. 'They all succumb sooner or later,' he commented: 'I alone remain (and will die) faithful to myself . . .'

That August he had arranged to stay at Argoed with Charlotte and the Webbs. 'I suppose I am going to Wales on Friday,' he announced grudgingly to Ellen. He was more deeply exhausted than ever – too tired to fix up the hammocks Charlotte had brought, too tired to draw rein from writing even for a day, 'Sundays included'. He tried to attend to the 'deliberate poetic beauty' of the country, but even the woodpeckers, 'hammering like leprechaun cobblers all round', helped by their sound to keep him industrious. The days flew past, 'like the telegraph poles on a railway journey', and he worked on. But the work did not give him pleasure. He grew bored; he grew exasperated. 'I am in the most disagreeable humor possible,' he complained to Florence Farr. He had begun by congratulating himself on his handling of Charlotte. The revelation of his self-centredness as a mere artistic machine had come as a shock but she was getting used to him, he fancied. Having failed to take the philanderer she now played up to him with conventional expressions of outrage: 'What a brute you are!' Yet his victory over her disappointed him. They lived an irreproachable life, the writing machine and the typist, in the bosom of the Webb family. It was, to a most dissatisfying degree, everything he had wanted. In his restless mind a dialogue began to develop between G.B.S. and Shaw Limited and was produced in his correspondence. Like Don Juan he confidently occupies centre stage but needs more words to keep his optimism afloat.

'I am fond of women (one in a thousand, say); but I am in earnest about quite other things. To most women one man and one lifetime make a world. I require whole populations and historical epochs to engage my interests seriously ... love is only diversion and recreation to me ... That's why the women who fall in love with me worry me and torment me and make scenes (which they can't act) with me and suffer misery & destroy their health & beauty ... It is also, alas! why I act the lover so diabolically well that even the women who are clever enough to understand that such a person as myself might exist, can't bring themselves to believe that I am that person.'

Shaw Limited, like the Devil, has less to say. He sees the heartless G.B.S. as a bragging emotional bankrupt playing timidly with all the serious things of life and dealing seriously only with the plays. Shaw Limited knows the value of the love he cannot accept as the Devil knows the danger of the loveless superman. His appeal to the audience carries a far-off echo of Sonny's voice:

'It is not the small things that women miss in me, but the big things. My pockets are always full of the small change of love-making; but it is magic money, not real money.'

For his mother's elopement with Vandeleur Lee, G.B.S. had substituted an economic for the emotional necessity; and he had used a financial argument to trick himself out of marrying Charlotte. So now Shaw Limited brings a money metaphor to expose the unreality of G.B.S. If only Charlotte had had the confidence to tear up that ridiculous Shavian balance sheet. Instead, unknown to Shaw, she had committed herself to him on the very terms by which he had rejected her, making a will that (barring a bequest to a cousin) left him her entire fortune. She seemed to have succumbed to a degree that Beatrice described as 'disturbing'.

'Shaw goes on untroubled, working hard at his plays and then going on long rides with her . . . But she is always restless and sometimes unhappy – too anxious to be with him . . . he is getting to feel her a necessary part of his "entourage", and would, I think, object to her breaking away from the relationship. He persuades himself that by keeping her occupied he is doing her good. If it were not for the fact that he is Shaw I should say that he was dishonourable.'

Perhaps Beatrice had a word with Charlotte that September in Wales for, after their return to London at the end of the month, Charlotte's behaviour changed. Suddenly she seemed less anxious to be with Shaw and, as Beatrice had predicted, he began to object. He felt incommoded at having to engage (between piano duets) Kate Salt for some of his typing and dictation. Early in October Charlotte had absconded to Leicester to visit her sister, Mary Cholmondeley, who, Shaw knew, intensely disliked him. 'Where am I to spend my evenings?' he complained. Charlotte returned, but hardly had Shaw unfastened himself from his programme of work than she was off again back to her sister. 'It is most inconvenient having Adelphi Terrace shut up,' he pointed out. 'I have nowhere to go, nobody to talk to.' When Charlotte returned again, she was curiously unavailable. 'I do not know where the devil to go – what the devil to do!' he told her. His nerves were bad; he was positively doing less writing – perhaps it was the weather. When he called one afternoon he was told by the maid that Charlotte was out. She always seemed to be 'out'. But three days later, on his way to dine at the Metropole, he suddenly found 'to my astonishment my legs walked off with me through the railway arches to Adelphi Terrace', where he saw the lights on in Charlotte's bedroom, signalling (he assumed) *her* unhappiness; but hardly had he written triumphantly to tell her so than she had disappeared to Paris. It must, he reasoned, be this hideous weather she was escaping. London was cold. 'I like to think of you germinating in Paris rather than suffering here,' he wrote; 'but I miss you in lots of ways. Shant spare you anything: it is my one virtue with women that I never spare them . . . [But] I wish you could stay in Paris & that I could get there in quarter of an hour. I feel that you are much better & brighter there; but it is damnably inconvenient to have you out of my reach.'

Charlotte came back early in November – but not to London. Instead she went straight to Hertfordshire to stay with some rich Fabian friends, Robert and 'Lion' Phillimore. This was too much for Shaw who pursued her on his bicycle and, travelling back at night, took one of his formidable tosses down a hill. He put the accident to instant use, tying it up into an article for the *Saturday Review*, 'On Pleasure Bent', and extracting tenderness from Charlotte. All the same, she did not return at once and he was driven to inform Ellen Terry that he needed a mistress. 'What rubbish!' she replied, holding to the strict Shavian line. 'We must do without these luxuries. There's so much work, so little time.'

What Shaw really wanted was someone to tell him what he really wanted. Charlotte had merely disconcerted him. When she did get back to London, he was almost cumbersomely tactful. 'I shall not intrude on my secretary tomorrow. If she desires to resume her duties, doubtless she will come to me.' A week later the tone was brisker: 'Secretary required tomorrow, not later than eleven.' But, for Charlotte, typing and shorthand had been a means to an end that seemed to be fading. She wanted to share with him things other than written words, and had invited him to come with her and Lion Phillimore for a day or two that December to Dieppe. Shaw pretended to be horrified by this treat. 'I am to embark in a piercing wind, with lifeboats capsizing and ships foundering in all directions,' he expostulated; 'to go to a watering place in the depth of winter with nothing to do and nowhere to go:'

'I am to be chaperoned by two women, each determined that the other shall seduce me and each determined that I shall not seduce her; I am to sleep in a foreign hotel with the window open and no bedclothes – perhaps without even a lock to the door to protect me . . . No, thank you. I am comfortable as I am.'

But Charlotte was not amused – that was one of her fortitudes. To all the rapids of his 'humor' she was impervious. 'Charlotte can not only resist jokes, but dislikes them,' he once explained to Pinero. 'Hence she was not seduced, as you would have been, by my humorous aberrations.' Having laughed the Dieppe expedition out of existence, he made ready for Charlotte's arrival next morning to continue her secretarial work. His preparations, if simply for a secretary, were exorbitant. He swept the hearth and made the fire; he laid out Charlotte's shawl and footwarmer; and then he waited – and she did not come. She had gone to Dieppe! 'What do you mean by this inconceivable conduct?' he demanded. 'Do you forsake *all* your duties – even those of secretary? Is it not enough that I have returned without a complaint to my stark and joyless life? Must I also go back to writing my own articles, and wasting half hours between the sentences with long trains of reflection? Not a word: not a sign! . . . Is Dieppe China (assuming that you are there)? Are there no stamps? has the post been abolished? have all the channel steamers foundered?'

Shaw had been genuinely put out. So, after making fun of his own discomfort, he turned on Charlotte to accuse her of everything he knew she would most dislike. She was relinquishing what she had found with the

Webbs and himself, and growing into her mother's model daughter. 'Go, then, ungrateful wretch,' he wrote, 'have your heart's desire:'

'find a Master – one who will spend your money, and rule in your house, and order your servants about, and forbid you to ride in hansoms because it's unladylike, and remind you that the honor of his name is in your keeping, and decline in your name further acquaintance with me, and consummate his marriage in the church lest the housemaid should regard his proceedings as clandestine. Protect yourself for ever from freedom, independence, love, unfettered communion with the choice spirits of your day, a lofty path on which to go your own way and keep your own counsel, and all the other blessings which 999 women cry for and the thousandth cries to get away from. But at least tell me when youre *not* coming; and say whether I am to get a new secretary or not.

GBS'

This letter points to one of Charlotte's hidden attractions for Shaw: she was a member of the same family as the 'terribly respectable' land agents, Uniacke Townshend, that had employed him as an office boy twenty-five years ago in Dublin. His attitude seems divided: the socialist responding ironically, the Irishman romantically to this fact. He wanted to raise Charlotte from her antiquated upper-class background on to the modern Fabian plateau – for the sake of Charlotte's emancipation and of the Fabians' political respectability. But there was something more personal too. Shaw knew that, though the Irish might grudgingly admit him to be (in Edith Somerville's words) 'distinctly somebody in a literary way', it was assumed that socially 'he can't be a gentleman'. Marriage to Charlotte would shock some of those who had looked down on the office boy and who (if he ever returned to Ireland) would have to open their doors to him. Such things would of course never influence him; but it was pleasant to speculate on them.

Charlotte's social position was an asset to her in other ways also. It lent her independence. Though he repeatedly insisted on the independence of women, Shaw continued to make them dependent on him, to deprive them of their sexual power over him. He excited interest: then ran. But Charlotte, who had money and the habit of travel, ran first and ran further. She was emotionally dependent but financially independent and had rich friends to carry her away. Though risky, such scorched earth manoeuvres were effective, giving Shaw the appearance of pursuing her. He seemed to win every battle, but could not win the war if Charlotte was never there to sign the unconditional surrender.

The New Year bristled with good intentions. Charlotte was particularly

447

attentive, rubbing vaseline on his bicycle wounds and encouraging him to use Adelphi Terrace as office and convalescent station. Shaw, too, struggled to be reasonable. 'We must adopt some less heart-lacerating way of getting rid of one another than "Good afternoon: shant want you till tomorrow",' he admitted. The duality of Charlotte's role was imposing an increasing strain on them both. Her volcanic tendencies erupted whenever, to her mind, he acted thoughtlessly. 'My nerves are shattered by the scenes of which I have been made the innocent victim,' he claimed. And to Ellen Terry, he confessed: 'my genius for hurting women is extraordinary; and I always do it with the best intentions.'

That March in 1898, the Webbs planned to be off on a ten-month tour round America and the Antipodes, 'seeing Anglo-Saxon democracy'. To rescue her from her unhappy infatuation with Shaw, they invited Charlotte to go with them. 'If she does,' Shaw told Ellen Terry, 'she will be away for about a year, just time enough for a new love affair.' Perhaps because she felt the danger of this herself, Charlotte did not take up the Webbs' invitation, but accepted instead an offer from Lion Phillimore to go for seven weeks to Rome. 'Charlotte deserts me at 11,' Shaw noted in his almanac. He felt 'quite desperate' and put it down to 'lack of exercise'. His friend Wallas was away with his new wife; Sydney Olivier had decided to go to America; his audience of actresses had dispersed and, with the Webbs gone too, Shaw was suddenly alone. 'I live the life of a dog,' he wrote to Sidney Webb, ' – have not spoken to a soul except my mother & the vestry since you left.'

[ 3 ]

*By the way, would you advise me to get married?*
Shaw to Henry Arthur Jones (1898)

*I had always, from my boyhood, had the impression that 38 to 40 was a dangerous age for men of genius, and that I should possibly die like Mozart, Schiller and Mendelssohn at that crisis. It seemed the proper thing for me to do . . .*

'Sisterless men are always afraid of women,' Shaw was to write; yet his own fears proceeded from the women in his family. He had seen their contempt for men – for his father and himself, even for Vandeleur Lee once his usefulness was exhausted. With his mother he had experienced the fear of loving; from his dead sister Yuppy he had gained a didactic apprehension of illness; and through Lucy revived his nervousness of marriage.

448

On 25 November 1886 Lucy had brought home a young man called Harry Butterfield to meet her mother. The purpose of this introduction was to announce her engagement – to Harry's brother, Charles. This curious manoeuvre illustrates by its vicariousness what Lucy intended by marriage. Charles may have been unavailable that evening because he was having an affair with another woman. That Lucy should not have known this until more than twenty years after her marriage – and then by accident – underlines her offhand attitude to her husband.

Charles Butterfield was a bit of a gambler. Besides a couple of 'wives', he had two names. Calling himself 'Cecil Burt' he travelled with a band of unfortunate wanderers called 'Leslie's No 1', as a cherubic tenor. 'He sang with difficulty,' Shaw remembered; 'but . . . his tastes made him quite at home in the theatre.' It was in the theatre that he had met Lucy. The two of them sang together in Alfred Cellier's ever-popular comedy-opera *Dorothy*, which had opened in London late in 1886. Shaw missed the first night; he missed too their wedding ('did not get to the church until the ceremony was over') and the small wedding-party at Fitzroy Square a year later. But (as Corno di Bassetto) he caught up with them at Morton's Theatre, Greenwich, in the autumn of 1889 for the 789th performance of *Dorothy*'s provincial tour. His brother-in-law, Shaw observed, 'originally, I have no doubt, a fine young man, . . . was evidently counting the days until death should release him from the part'. He had the air 'of an energy decayed and a willing spirit crushed' and 'his affability and forbearance were highly creditable to him under the circumstances'. This 'energy decayed' may equally have been attributable to his mistress, 'Constance Barclay', the wife of Eade Montefiore, a theatre manager associated with *Dorothy*. As a singer, Cecil Burt 'had a pleasant speaking voice', but was at his best when muted by applause. 'The G at the end was a vocal earthquake,' Corno di Bassetto declared. 'And yet methought he was not displeased when the inhabitants of Greenwich, coming fresh to the slaughter, encored him.'

This plump couple, Lucy and her tenor husband, were suffering (Shaw informed *Star* readers) from a terminal disease called 'Dorothitis'. Into his description of their illness he spooned the resentment he had accumulated over years of submitting to Lucy's alleged superiority. He knew her mind was commonplace, her talent little more than a trick of facility, her attractions borrowed and superficial. She was a good mimic but a poor actress, wooden on stage. Yet she had the *appearance* of popularity. It had been Lucy whom Bessie had taken with her to London; and Lucy whom Lee had favoured; and Lucy who had been welcome at some of the

London salons where George felt so *gauche*; and again Lucy whom people thought so lovable and entertaining. Great things had been expected of her; great things by the age of thirty-six had led to *Dorothy* at Morton's Theatre, Greenwich. In bread-and-butter terms it was her greatest success. What was it worth?

'. . . she will apparently spend her life in artistic self-murder by induced Dorothitis without a pang of remorse, provided she be praised and paid regularly. Dorothy herself, a beauteous young lady of distinguished mien, with an immense variety of accents ranging from the finest Tunbridge Wells English (for genteel comedy) to the broadest Irish (for repartee and low comedy), sang without the slightest effort and without the slightest point, and was all the more desperately vapid because she suggested artistic gifts wasting in complacent abeyance . . . [Her] voice, a hollow and spectral contralto, betrayed the desolating effect of perpetual Dorothy: her figure alone retains a pleasing plumpness akin to that of the tenor; and her spirits were wonderful, all things considered.

'. . . I never bargained for such a thing as this 789th performance of Dorothy. No: it is a criminal waste of young lives and young talents . . . We exclaim at the dock directors' disregard of laborers' bodies; but what shall we say of the managers' disregard of artists' souls?'

The retributive impulse behind what Lucy called this 'typically fraternal – Irish fraternal – act' was part of the Shaw family feeling from which Lucy had wanted to escape. 'She was more popular outside the family than inside it,' her cousin Judy Gillmore explained, 'and . . . she preferred people who would look up to her to those who would stand up to her: she was too lazy to hold her own among her very critical and argumentative relatives when she could get blind worship from the uncritical.' But inevitably on those who looked up to her she looked down. And on her husband she looked blindly.

Like her brother, Lucy had largely substituted theatre for home life; like him too she tried to replace her own family with another. Shaw had made use of the Fabians; Lucy used her husband's relatives. It was these relatives, pillars of the Irvingite Church, she had married. That was the significance of announcing her engagement in the presence of her future brother-in-law. Both George and Lucy, having grown up in a matriarchal family, instinctively cast about for a mother elsewhere.

Charles Butterfield was not an immediately attractive man – his 'pretty face seemed to be carved on a bladder of lard'. But he had one handsome attribute: an exceptional mother. Mrs Butterfield had gone to bed and was to stay there fifteen years until her death. She had, as St John Ervine observed, 'the discerning eye of the chronic invalid'. She understood Lucy and, understanding her need for financial and emotional reassurance, knitted her into the pattern of the Butterfield family with its comforting social world in the suburbs of Denmark Hill. But the Butterfield family, no less than the Shaws, was matriarchal. After Mrs Butterfield died its centre disintegrated and, by 1894, Lucy had drifted back to Fitzroy Square. 'LOVE,' she wrote, '. . . is dead sea fruit, whether it is parental, fraternal or marital, and anyone who sacrifices their all on its altar plays a game that is lost before it is begun . . . it's a damnable world.' She seemed little more now than a figure of derision to her mother who declared her to be 'going mad'. Much of the money Shaw squeezed out from journalism went towards the maintenance of this unhappy household, which included Bessie's hunchback sister, Kate Gurly (whose 'state of unparalleled inclination' preceded her final plunge into Roman Catholicism), and from time to time her brother Walter Gurly, who would arrive at Fitzroy Square paralytically drunk, threatening to leave his nephew his accumulated debts and heavily mortgaged Carlow property. 'The devil, the devil, the devil!' Shaw cursed. 'Everything is going to hell.'

From this hell, this 'damnable world', with planchette and ouija, Shaw's mother had ridden away to consult with the dead. She found them more congenial company than the living. First there was her favourite child Yuppy; and then even her husband and her father seemed faintly less intolerable since their deaths. But on the whole she preferred chatting with people she had never known, the further remote the better; and eventually she settled for regular intercourse with a sage whose date was approximately 6000 BC.

Bessie's spiritualism was an embarrassment to her son: '[I] held my tongue because I did not like to say anything that could worry my mother'. Yet he did not remain 'reverently mute'. In his diary he had privately dismissed spiritualism as a 'paltry fraud'. At a session of spirit-rapping and table-turning with Belfort Bax and H. W. Massingham, he had cheated from the first and 'as soon as Massingham detected me he became my accomplice and we caused the spirits to rap out long stories, lift the table into the air, and finally drink tumblers of whisky and water, to the complete bewilderment of Bax . . . I have not laughed so much for years.' He released some of this laughter anonymously into the *Pall Mall Gazette*.

'Every Englishman believes that he is entitled to a ghost after death to compensate him for the loss of his body, and to enable him to haunt anybody that may have murdered or otherwise ill-used him in the days when he was solid.'

451

Shaw did more than make sport with the piety, miracles, trances, vigils and the rest of this 'fanciful modern witchcraft'. He attempted to attack it all without attacking his mother. She was 'as sane and shrewd as Sir Oliver Lodge,' he maintained some years later, 'which proves that if a belief in Spiritualism is a craze, it is one which a thoroughly soundheaded person can keep in a thought tight compartment without injury to their general mental health'. As a method of extending our powers of self-deception, this constituted its advantage over alcoholism. To her son, Bessie's wishful writings appeared like a non-malignant growth in an otherwise healthy body. It was not surprising that the conditions of London – in particular the conditions of Fitzroy Square – should have forced up such optimistic illusions. Under cover of anonymity, Shaw supported the work of the 'best ridiculed institution in London,' the Society for Psychical Research, whose volumes of published evidence, he reported, 'justify us in positively refusing to attach any importance to ... a possible regeneration of the human race by a revival of faith in ghost stories'.

Shaw's distaste for his mother's spiritual exercises (as for his father's intoxicating spirits) had made him question his own ambitions as a writer. In one of his reviews for the *Pall Mall Gazette* he had written that 'the existence of a liar is more probable than the existence of a ghost ... [and] the custom of accepting as conclusive the solemn statements of persons of good repute concerning events that are known to be natural does not hold when marvels are in question ... The most intelligent man may be misled by hallucination: the wisest may suddenly go mad; the best may sin against strict veracity.' The pretensions of spiritualism had raised in Shaw's Fabian mind the whole question of the morality of fiction. 'A person who describes events that never happened and persons that never existed is generally classed as a liar – possibly a genial and entertaining liar,' he wrote. 'And what is the business of a novelist if not to describe events that never happened and to repeat conversations that never took place.' To such an uncomfortable conclusion had his failure as a novelist driven him; and his comparative failure as a dramatist was persuading him to look on his plays too as methods of extending his self-deception. 'Physical expression is a subject full of interest in a society like ours,' he wrote.

'When we are young our inordinate fondness for theatrical and novel-writing leads us to simulate and describe emotions which we do not feel. Later, when the struggle for existence becomes too serious for such follies, real emotions come to us in battalions; but we take as much trouble to conceal them as we formerly did to affect them ... [and] Life comes to mean finance.'

In his mother's world there were more liars than ghosts; and in his own the idealists outnumbered realists. He had kept up the appearance of a realist; but who could say whether he too had not been misled by illusions? In later life he was to describe himself as a mystical dramatist. Asking himself why his mother had chosen to practise such an apparently senseless activity as spirit writings, he added another question: 'Why was I doing essentially the same as a playwright?' And answered: 'I do not know. We both got some satisfaction from it or we would not have done it.'

From the chill of Fitzroy Square, Lucy had made a brief escape to America in 1897, playing in Villiers Stanford's *Shamus O'Brien*. This, the last small success of her career, merged with the first large success of his. Over that winter and the spring of 1898 *The Devil's Disciple* was erupting in America into a popular triumph. He had written the play 'with one eye on Terriss and the other on Richard Mansfield in America'; and he encouraged Mansfield by warning him against it – particularly the third act: 'it will probably fail . . . but no matter.' After a furious battle of threats and denunciations over royalties, the play had opened at the Fifth Avenue Theatre on 4 October 1897, running to full houses for sixty-four performances until, early in 1898, Mansfield took it off on a popular mid-western tour. Shaw attributed this success to Mansfield's inability to act. 'I have great faith in Richard's personal fascination,' he explained to Mrs Mansfield, 'in a part which gives him no opportunity of acting, but allows him to be himself to the last inch.'

At a celebration dinner for this production, which established him in the New York theatre, Mansfield hinted that there were drawbacks to his good fortune: 'I go down on my knees at my little bedside every night and thank my Maker for that play. And the last words of my prayer always are "But O God why did it have to be by Shaw?"'

Life, Shaw had written, 'comes to mean finance'. From Mansfield's American production of *The Devil's Disciple* he earned £2,000 and came to be recognized 'as a possible winner in the box office gamble'. This was a turning point of his career. He felt confident, now that his other plays were appearing in book form, that they too would have their turn and that one or two of them, *You Never Can Tell* perhaps or *Arms and the Man*, would charm audiences and make him more money. For more than twenty years in London he had lived from hand to mouth. By the time Charlotte returned from Rome, he was suddenly in easy circumstances and 'with every reason to believe that things would improve'.

One result of this affluence had been his decision to give up drama criticism – 'to hold on to £312 a year for criticism is cowardly, and a fraud to the younger generation,' he wrote to Sidney Webb. 'I have therefore given the Saturday [Review] notice that I shall drop them at the end of the season.' The plunge, he added, 'was inevitable sooner or later' if only because, he told the actress Lena Ashwell, 'I have said all I have to say.'

Another result was his decision to recommence writing plays. He chose Shakespeare's birthday, 23 April, on which to set off and rescue Julius Caesar by composing a puritan prelude to *Antony and Cleopatra*. 'Snatch up my note book & make a start at last on "Caesar & Cleopatra",' he wrote. 'Lifelike scene in the courtyard of the palace at Alexandria among the bodyguard of Cleopatra. Screamingly amusing – will kill the seriousness of the whole play. This enforced inaction is going to save my life.'

Something was needed to save his life, for he was now in his own words 'a fearful wreck'.

*

During Charlotte's absence Shaw struggled to maintain his self-sufficiency, working, in spite of an increasing number of headaches, straight on until 'I got into a sort of superhuman trance in which I made astonishing displays of professional & oratorical brilliancy'. At the theatre he was in 'immense form' and, according to Charrington, a lecture he gave against corporal punishment at the end of March was one of his most belligerent performances. The subject (based on William M. Cooper's *History of the Rod*) revolted him, but it may have suited his temper, which he described as 'ferocious and damnable'. Finding it 'miserably inconvenient' to be his own secretary, a few days after Charlotte left he had again engaged Henry Salt's wife, Kate, to do his typing and dictation. 'I am cross and incommoded to the last degree by having to adapt myself to changed circumstances,' he wrote to Charlotte. '. . . She [Kate Salt] sits down on the floor in the window corner, and begins to write with the screen between her and the fire.'

'For three sentences, I feel resentful, uncomfortable, and quite put out. At the fourth the switch operates and I am on to the new line as if I had never dictated to anybody else. Such is manly fidelity. In the absence of sentimental interruptions we get along famously . . .'

Now that he was alone, he claimed to be 'no longer unhappy, and no longer happy: I am myself'. But though taunting Charlotte with this integration, his moods were veering steeply. Mrs Salt would arrive, carrying a brown paper parcel containing a three-legged stool and a frugal lunch of bananas and biscuits. 'We achieve a phenomenal performance with the arrears of correspondence,' he informed Charlotte. '. . . Your memory is totally obliterated . . . This is indeed a secretary.' Then his temper suddenly changed: Mrs Salt would exasperate him, he would bully her. 'Frightful not to be able to kiss your secretary.'

The longer Charlotte remained in Italy, the harder Shaw worked, and the more unstable he grew. 'After all,' he wrote, 'it is magnificent to be alone, with the ivy stripped off.' A few days later he felt that he was growing old and breaking up. 'I want a woman & a sound sleep,' he exclaimed. '. . . detestably deserted . . . Oh Charlotte, Charlotte: is this a time to be gadding about in Rome!'

He was filled with feelings, but he dared not trust them. He missed her; he felt relieved that she was gone, as if a real crisis had receded. So there must be two Charlottes, as there had been two Alice Locketts. In her absence, he could plant her neatly in his fantasy world. 'You count that I have lost only one Charlotte,' he wrote to her; 'but I have lost two; and one of the losses is a prodigious relief. I may miss "die schöne grünen Augen" occasionally, though the very privation throws me back, brutally great, to my natural dreamland;'

'but then I think of the other Charlotte, the terrible Charlotte, the lier-in-wait, the soul hypochondriac, always watching and dragging me into bondage, always planning nice, sensible, comfortable, selfish destruction for me, wincing at every accent of freedom in my voice, so that at last I get the trick of hiding myself from her, hating me & longing for me with the absorbing passion of the spider for the fly. Now that she is gone, I realize for the first time the infernal tyranny of the past year, which left me the licence of the rebel, not the freedom of the man who stands alone. I will have no more of it . . . *That's* the Charlotte I want to see married. The Charlotte of Iken Heath is another matter; yet I have her in my dreamland, and sometimes doubt whether the other devil ever had anything to do with her.'

This letter shows the extent to which Shaw had been unable to absorb Charlotte into his private mythology. So solid, yet elusive (she wrote little to him from Rome), she occupied his dreamland but threatened him with real daytime experience. His letter seems deliberately hurtful, as if he is trying to rid himself of the strain of their relationship by provoking her to break it off. But she would not; and, while exulting in his 'gigantic recuperation', he continued writing to her every day.

To marry, or not to marry: that was the question: and he answered it differently each hour. 'I probably will marry the lady,' he told the Pakenham Beattys that April. But to Karl Pearson he maintained that he was at this time 'as firmly set against such a step as ever I was in my most inveterate youth and bachelordom'. Walking through the park, bicycling into the country: doing anything that revived his strength or awakened him from the oblivion of his work-addiction, exacerbated the appalling dilemma. Charlotte still lingered in Rome, but her companion Lion Phillimore had returned in April and, seeing Shaw 'on the verge of dissolution', she and her husband invited him to their home for Easter. Once there they started to bully him for his stupidity in not marrying Charlotte. One of the chief delights of married life, they told him, was the avoidance of the pre-nuptial obligation to be constantly paying amorous attentions to one another. Against such a Shavian device, 'I was totally incapable of self-defence,' Shaw declared. But it solved nothing, and left him with another full-force headache.

The length of Charlotte's Italian visit and the infrequency of her letters to him was not due, as Shaw suggested, to 'some Italian doctor'. Though Dr Axel Munthe was then in Rome, Charlotte had avoided seeing him. She was busy, in Fabian fashion, with a study of the municipal services of the city. The Webbs themselves had descanted on the value of such information. She could not return to London until she had completed, and then properly collated, her notes. Shaw, who had so often complained about her incapacity for work, could not now complain over the reason for her extended absence. It was as if everyone had learnt the Shavian game, and was playing it against him.

In the middle of April, while lacing one of his shoes too tightly, Shaw pinched his left instep. He was hardly conscious of it but a week later, when riding to Ealing on his bicycle to see the Beattys, the foot expanded 'to the size of a leg of mutton'. Though he had not the faintest notion of what was the matter he felt confident of curing it 'with hot water', and had just succeeded when, under stress of theatre reviewing in the evenings and vestry meetings during the day, 'I walked on it too soon', and the foot swelled up prodigiously 'to the size of a church bell'. Could it be gout? Some of his friends suggested 'vegetarian gout'; Lucy told him he had a dislocated toe. Despite his repeated hot water operations, walking soon became so excruciating that 'I now simply hop,' he wrote to Charlotte, 'my left foot being no longer of any use'. On 23 April he called in Dr Salisbury Sharpe, Alice Lockett's husband, who told him that his two toe joints had slipped over each other and become inflamed. 'My medical skill is completely vindicated: I have been doing exactly the right thing,' Shaw congratulated himself after the doctor had left. The hot water treatments continued, fortified by a mass of cotton wool swathed in a mackintosh cover, 'to sweat the foot heroically', and these were of great benefit to *Caesar and Cleopatra*. 'Finished whole scene of Cleopatra,' he

456

noted in the almanac he was keeping each day and sending to Charlotte, '. . . quintessence of everything that has most revolted the chivalrous critics Ha! Ha! Julius Caesar as the psychological woman tamer.'

Shaw, as woman tamer, had been letting Charlotte have almost daily reports on his foot with the result that, so he later told Karl Pearson, she came 'back from Italy to nurse me'. His appeals to her had never been direct. His foot was 'positively putrefying', he had told her on 18 April – and continued: 'Air full of reviews of plays etc. Why ain't you back: you'd enjoy it and I'd enjoy *you*.' Four days later he ended another letter: 'I half expected to see you at the [Fabian] meeting tonight: you missed the insane spectacle of my entry on one leg.' The next day, learning that Charlotte had had a headache, he made his appeal vicariously: 'Come back, then. *I* know what your nerves need.'

Charlotte left Rome at the end of April. She was due to arrive in London on the evening of 1 May. Feeling that his troubles would now be over, Shaw limped down Tottenham Court Road, descended at Charing Cross, and limped on slowly to Adelphi Terrace. 'With a long gasp of relief, I lay my two-months burden down & ring the bell.' Martha, the parlourmaid, answered the door. Charlotte was not there! He could do nothing but leave her a note of protest and hobble all the way back to Fitzroy Square.

'Well, I AM Damned!
'Wretch, devil, fiend!
'The train has arrived; & you are not in it? Stopped in Paris, to see Cyrano again, perhaps. No. Satan's own daughter would have telegraphed.'

Travelling from Naples by sea, Charlotte arrived later that night and replied next day on the back of Shaw's note:

'Well, here I am anyway now! Yes, I *might* have telegraphed: it was horrid of me. I am a wreck, mental and physical. Such a journey as it was! I don't believe I shall ever get over it.

'My dear – and your foot? Shall I go up to you or will you come here and when? Only tell me what you would prefer. Of course I am quite free.

Charlotte'

*

'Come when it is most convenient to you . . . the sooner the better (for the first moment at least).'

She came at once to Fitzroy Square and was appalled. His small room with its table, typewriter and wooden-railed chairs, was a shipwreck. Fleets of correspondence and miscellaneous manuscripts, sailing on the wind

457

from his perpetually-open window, lay fluttering among the formations of books and solid debris of cutlery, saucepans, apples, cups of trembling cocoa, plates of half-finished and hardening porridge. Under its drifting surface of smuts and dust, Shaw's programme of work-and-hygiene had filled the place with such chaos that Charlotte could only squeeze in sideways. Unshoe'd, his mobility had 'contracted itself to within hopping distance of my chair'. He was unable to do housework; could no longer look after himself – and no one else there had any interest in him. For over twenty years mother and son had lived under the same roof in London, seldom communicating, and in such conditions. Charlotte's horror turned to a hatred of his mother and his sister.

Something needed to be done at once, so she demanded back the post as his secretary – and he refused. It was a stubborn and ingenious refusal. Kate Salt, he said, was looking after his secretarial needs very well; she was excellent at dictation and eminently bullyable. He did not want to bully Charlotte – he wanted her to bully him. He did not want a replacement for Mrs Salt but for Mrs Shaw. He had given Charlotte no encouragement while she was abroad over her work on the Roman municipality; but now that she had returned with a gigantic collection of documents he interrupted with constructive advice. What form should her book take? 'Her lady-like instincts strongly urge her to a dry official report for the use of students at the school,' he wrote to Sidney Webb. 'I, on the other hand, insist on a thrilling memoir, giving the whole history of a lady of quality suffering from a broken heart (with full particulars) and being rescued from herself by the call of public work.'

'The extent to which the call was reinforced by the renewed activity of the mended heart is to be described, and the whole is to conclude with the voyage to Italy, the adventures there among the old romantic associations, and, incidentally, a complete view, by glimpses, of the municipal humours of Rome.'

Within a week of her return, Shaw believed, reason had resumed her sway and Charlotte was back working on her book. In fact she had done no more than retire to consider how best she might deal with his self-protective, self-destructive perversities. The problems of municipal Rome already seemed unreal when set beside Shaw's cheerfully concealed pain. His foot looked terrible, but though he appeared haggard with strain, he continued desperately joking and working. Ellen Terry had sent them tickets for a new play at the Lyceum on 5 May, and two days later Shaw had teased and flattered his dramatic criticism to its usual fine edge in the *Saturday Review*. Such regular joking-and-working had convinced Frank

Harris and his staff that Shaw did not really mean to retire from the paper at all, and he was obliged to write again, impressing on them 'that there is no question or possibility of hanging on, and that my place must be filled instantly . . . I nearly killed myself last week to keep things going'.

Harris had been persuaded by the Shavian style that Shaw 'was only coquetting'; but Charlotte saw straight through it to the seriousness of his condition. The day after the Lyceum she suddenly took the initiative, calling at Fitzroy Square, collecting G.B.S. and carrying him back to Adelphi Terrace for a long talk. About this talk Charlotte was to reveal nothing ('I am not a public character in any way,' she later explained, '& I have an absolute horror of publicity . . . I just go my own way, & leave curious people to their curiosity.'); and though G.B.S. was to let loose a torrent of protesting bulletins over the events of the next month, there is little record of what he and Charlotte actually said to each other. Three days later he underwent an operation on his left foot. An anaesthetist in the last agonies of influenza, together with nurse Alice Lockett and her physician husband, arrived at Fitzroy Square at half-past eight in the evening. After coming round from the chloroform, Shaw was told by Dr Sharpe that an abscess which had formed on his foot was the result of dead tissue on the middle metatarsus. An attempt had been made to scrape the necrosed bone clean, but until it healed he would be an invalid on crutches and 'in a critical condition'.

Charlotte and the doctor had ascribed the seriousness of his condition (what Shaw called his 'superhuman condition') to undernourishment ('Oh that – vegetarianism!' Charlotte accused); but Shaw attributed everything to overwork, making this the subject next day of his penultimate article, 'G.B.S. Vivisected', for the *Saturday Review*. 'A few weeks ago one of my feet, which had borne me without complaining for forty years, struck work,' he wrote.

'. . . the foot got into such a condition that it literally had to be looked into . . . My doctor's investigation of my interior has disclosed the fact that for many years I have been converting the entire stock of my energy extractable from my food (which I regret to say he disparages) into pure genius. Expecting to find bone and tissue, he has been almost wholly disappointed . . . He has therefore put it bluntly to me that I am already almost an angel and that it rests with myself to complete the process summarily by writing any more articles before I have recovered . . . It is also essential, in order to keep up the sympathy which rages at my bedside, to make the very worst of my exhausted condition.'

This notice of his operation in the theatre pages of the *Saturday Review* was part of the relentless Shavianizing of these strange weeks. He had the critical choice of converting his circumstances into farce or melodrama, and on the whole he directed them as melodramatic farce. Having planted his injured foot in the middle of Frank Harris's paper, he made of it a stage prop – part public property, part the ludicrous substitute for a broken heart. There was nothing pedestrian about Shaw's foot. It was part of the theatrical traffic, a detached and dancing feature in what reads like the scenario for a comic miracle play, helping prepare the public for the extraordinary happening of his marriage. 'I was extinguished by the gas familiar to dentists' patients, and subsequently kept in a state of annihilation with ether,' he wrote. 'My last recollection is a sort of chuckle at being wideawake enough to know when the operator lifted my eyelid and tapped my eyeball to convince himself that he had made an end of me.'

'It was not until I was allowed to recover that the process became publicly interesting. For then a very strange thing happened. *My character did not come back all at once.* Its artistic and sentimental side came first: its morality, its positive elements, its common sense, its incorrigible Protestant respectability, did not return for a long time after. For the first time in my life I tasted the bliss of having no morals to restrain me from lying, and no sense of reality to restrain me from romancing. I overflowed with what people call 'heart'. I acted and lied in the most touchingly sympathetic fashion . . . I carefully composed effective little ravings, and repeated them, and then started again and let my voice die away, without an atom of shame. I called everybody by their Christian names . . .

'At last they quietly extinguished the lights, and stole out of the chamber of the sweet invalid who was now sleeping like a child, but who, noticing that the last person to leave the room was a lady, softly breathed that lady's name in his dreams. Then the effect of the anaesthetic passed away more and more; and in less than an hour I was an honest taxpayer again, with my heart perfectly well in hand. And now comes the great question, Was that a gain or a loss?'

This question is a characteristic device that invites us to see his marriage to Charlotte (which he refers to elsewhere as 'the second operation he has undergone lately') being performed under a bag of ether. How else to account for his surrender? Answering this challenge grew into a game that exercised his finest ingenuity. As with so much of Shaw's fantasy, the starting point was the reversal of a cliché: in this case, that marriage is a fate worse than death. Before his operation someone (perhaps his mother) suggested the possibility of his dying under the anaesthetic. It was almost 'too tempting' to contemplate. 'I found myself,' he told Karl Pearson, 'without the slightest objection to death, and stranger still, with the smallest objection to marriage.' In the initial stages, this connection retains humanity. Though he was perfectly reconciled to dying, he told Philip Wicksteed, 'death did not come; but something which I had always objected to far worse: to wit, Marriage did. I faced it with the calm intrepidity of a man who has left the world behind him, and for a reason I had never anticipated: namely, that I cared more for my wife than for myself.' The following year, in a letter to Mrs Mansfield, he presented the story epigrammatically. Being a wretch on crutches, stifled by chloroform and fully determined to die, 'I proposed to make her [Charlotte] my widow.'

As Dick Dudgeon, in *The Devil's Disciple*, had elected to go to the gallows without a personal motive, so his creator scrupulously purges his own marriage of what he calls any 'corrupt interest in the transaction, either of love or money or happiness or any of the romantic considerations,' he reassured Karl Pearson. 'My inner religious sense was revolted by the general assumption that I was making a bid for happiness. I wasn't: I was signalizing my final redemption from the last taint of that lust. And now the question is: was I mad as a result of my abnormal state of health; and will I, when I have completely recovered, revert to my old state of mind & bachelor existence . . .?'

In eliminating 'such illusions as love interest, happiness interest, & all the rest of the vulgarities,' Shaw did for his marriage what he had accused the fashionable West End dramatists of doing to their plays: he made it mechanical. Charlotte is presented as 'the inevitable & predestined agent, appointed by Destiny', while the Shavian paradox appears with the fact that the union produces not a mother of children but the father of plays.

Some eighteen years later Shaw was still insisting that he had considered the situation, 'from the point of view of a dying man'. In fact he had considered it as a method of prolonging active life. Work was his life; as he lived so he must write. But if he persisted working and writing in Fitzroy Square, 'nailed by one foot to the floor like a doomed Strasburg goose', he would probably become a permanent invalid – that was Charlotte's verdict, and there can be little doubt that she put it to him strongly enough that day at Adelphi Terrace as to convince him of its truth. He had two major works in progress – *Caesar and Cleopatra* and a metaphysical interpretation of the *Ring* cycle, to be called *The Perfect Wagnerite*, which he had begun on 28 April, five days after the play. These, and the sense of having much more work still to do, might attach him to life – but not so tightly as to make the prospect of dying 'in the least disagreeable to me'. Charlotte changed this. The moment for a decision had come; she took it and he acceded. It was agreed between them that he was starved, if not of red meat, then of fresh air and rest. Charlotte proposed renting a house in the country, hiring two nurses and a staff of servants, and superintending his recovery – however long that might take. 'I cannot do much until I can be moved to the country,' Shaw admitted to Grant Richards.

The decision confronted Shaw with more than one moral predicament. Binding Charlotte and him together was the antagonism (subsiding on the side of the Shaws to positive indifference) of their families. Charlotte's sister, Mary Cholmondeley – or 'Mrs Chumly' as Shaw liked to write her name ('I forget the full spelling') – refused to meet her future brother-in-law and, 'as a last kindness to me', requested Charlotte to secure her money. Lucinda Elizabeth Shaw seemed less interested in their news, making no comment beyond saying that it was not unexpected but that it would be difficult to call Miss Payne-Townshend 'Charlotte' since she looked more like a 'Carlotta' – the mockingly glamorous name by which Lucinda and Lucy Shaw were always to know her. After the first few civilities had put them on speaking terms, there was little difficulty in keeping them apart. Shaw knew that 'there was no love lost between them' and that 'Charlotte dreaded and disliked my very unconventional family'. It was necessary for him, however, to demonstrate that while Charlotte was in the right, his mother was not in the wrong. Charlotte had no knowledge, he explained, of how poor people lived. Illness among them was so familiar they seldom made a commotion over it. 'My untidy way of living, and my mother's glorious indifference to it, always shocked her [Charlotte],' he told one of his biographers; 'it seemed to her that it was utter savagery not to make a tremendous fuss and call in no end of doctors and go to bed properly and take the most elaborate diet and wine and so on the very moment anyone was ill. A mother placidly conscious of the vanity of these things, and a drunken looking and shabby medical uncle cracking profane jokes about them, in a lodging with one servant and a charwoman, was outside her conception and experience of life.' No wonder Charlotte wanted to take Shaw away 'and look after me properly,' he added. 'And on the whole that was very much the most sensible arrangement.'

They had spoken that day in Adelphi Terrace of his health and they must have spoken too of her money. The success of Mansfield's American production of *The Devil's Disciple* had removed Shaw's elaborate financial scruple against marriage. 'It did not make me as rich as my wife; but it placed me beyond all suspicion of being a fortune hunter or a parasite.' In 1896 he had earned £589 5s. 1d.; in 1897 his income had risen to £1,098

4s. od. of which £674 8s. 3d. had come from the opening weeks of *The Devil's Disciple*. Since there was no question of his being 'driven into the matrimonial port by the stress of expense,' he explained, 'it appeared to my ordinary prosaically sympathetic sense of economy that she [Charlotte] could not do more conveniently than to marry me . . .' One of the financial matters they seem to have discussed was a marriage settlement to enable 'my mother, if I died, to end her days without having to beg from my widow or from anyone else.' In fact Shaw safeguarded Lucinda, who was now in her sixty-ninth year, by means of an annuity and a private understanding with Charlotte that, if he were unable to meet the payments, she would make them without revealing herself as the source. In May 1899 Charlotte's solicitors drew up a settlement that guaranteed the income from two trust funds (administered by Sidney Webb and Frederick Whelan) to Shaw himself – these funds reverting to Charlotte in the event of his predeceasing her. Two years later, on 1 July 1901, Shaw was to make a will, appointing Charlotte as his sole executrix and trustee, bequeathing her his literary manuscripts and copyrights and all the real and personal estate not otherwise disposed of. Among his specific bequests was an annuity of £600 to be paid to Lucinda Elizabeth Shaw, and, in the event of her death, an alternative annuity of £300 for his sister Lucy.

Between themselves they agreed to share basic expenses, but to keep their unequal incomes mainly apart. 'Her property is a separate property,' Shaw later notified the Special Commissioners of Income Tax, to whom he refused to file a joint income-tax return. 'She keeps a separate banking account at a separate bank.'

'Her solicitor is not my solicitor. I can make a guess at her means from her style of living, exactly as the Surveyor of Income Tax does when he makes a shot at an assessment in the absence of exact information; but beyond that I have no more knowledge of her income than I have of yours.'

This was literally true. 'My wife seems to have a lot of money,' he wrote privately to Philip Wicksteed five months after his marriage, ' – how much I dont know, probably not much according to modern Vanderbillionic notions, but to poor people like you and me, a fortune.'

They had discussed health and money during their long Adelphi Terrace talk. What else was there – except the crucial formality of a proposal of marriage? This was slipped into the agenda by Shaw as an item of social etiquette and accepted by Charlotte 'without comment'. It has the air of 'any other business', agreed to by both parties in spite of their principles, on behalf of the rest of the population.

*Shaw*:   Do you understand that this means our living together in the eyes of the world?
*Charlotte*:   Of course I do: it can't be helped.
*Shaw*:   Go out and buy a ring and a licence.
*Charlotte*:   Shall I have to change my name?
*Shaw*:   Yes.
*Charlotte*:   I can't imagine myself anybody but Miss Payne-Townshend.

This was how, twenty-four years later, Shaw recalled what had passed between them. 'The determining factor was her reputation and dignity,' he added. '. . . It was to preserve that social status for my wife, and for no other reason, that I married her.'

By presenting his marriage contract as a document of social intercourse, Shaw underlined the fact that it was not primarily a sexual arrangement he had entered into with Charlotte. Only with this proposal, he told Beatrice Webb, had the relation between them 'completely lost its inevitable preliminary character of a love affair'. Now, as patient and nurse, they were nearer to being parent and child, and with all the possibility of beginning a new life.

Shaw continued to screen their feelings behind a rattling extravaganza. 'My disabled condition has driven Miss Payne Townshend into the most humiliating experiences,' he exulted in a letter to Graham Wallas. 'I sent in for the man next door to marry us; but he said he only did births and deaths.'

'Miss Payne Townshend then found a place in Henrietta Street, where she had to explain to a boy that she wanted to get married. The boy sent the news up a tube through which shrieks of merriment were exchanged . . . Miss Payne Townshend then had to suffer the final humiliation of buying a ring. The difficulty was to find a West End jeweller's in which she had never been before, but at last she succeeded, and returned with the symbol of slavery . . . of such portentous weight and thickness, that it is impossible for anyone but a professional pianist to wear it; so my mother has presented her with my grandfather's wedding ring for general use.'

He had asked Graham Wallas to act as one of the witnesses and, following a refusal from Kate Salt ('who violently objects to the whole proceeding'), invited as his second witness her husband Henry Salt. CAN YOU MEET US AT FIFTEEN HENRIETTA STREET COVENT GARDEN AT ELEVEN THIRTY TOMORROW WEDNESDAY TO WITNESS A CONTRACT.

Salt and Wallas arrived dressed in their best clothes; Shaw on crutches and in an old jacket with armpits patched with leather that the crutches had badly frayed – and was taken by the registrar for 'the inevitable beggar who completes all wedding processions'.

'Wallas, who is considerably over six feet high, seemed to him the hero of the occasion, and he was proceeding to marry him calmly to my betrothed, when Wallas, thinking the formula rather strong for a mere witness, hesitated at the last moment and left the prize to me.'

They were married in the afternoon of 1 June 1898. A week before, Shaw had written that if 'ever I get married, it will have to be done very secretly'. In fact the newspapers pounced on the event 'as eagerly as the death of Gladstone' – largely because of a report in *The Star* drafted by G.B.S. himself.

'As a lady and gentleman were out driving in Henrietta-st., Covent-garden yesterday, a heavy shower drove them to take shelter in the office of the Superintendent Registrar there, and in the confusion of the moment he married them. The lady was an Irish lady named Miss Payne-Townshend, and the gentleman was George Bernard Shaw.

'. . . Startling as was the liberty undertaken by the Henrietta-st. official, it turns out well. Miss Payne-Townshend is an Irish lady, with an income many times the volume of that which "Corno di Bassetto" used to earn, but to that happy man, being a vegetarian, the circumstance is of no moment. The lady is deeply interested in the London School of Economics, and that is the common ground on which the brilliant couple met. Years of married bliss to them.'

With this procession of Shavian flourishes, G.B.S. started on the 'terrible adventure' that was to turn him into 'a respectable married man'.

# BIBLIOGRAPHICAL NOTE
# AND ACKNOWLEDGEMENTS

I was invited to write this biography in the early 1970s. The most recent Shaw biographies, by St John Ervine, Archibald Henderson, Hesketh Pearson and Stephen Winsten, appeared in or before 1956, Shaw's centenary year. The residuary legatees of the Shaw Estate – the British Museum, the National Gallery of Ireland, and the Royal Academy of Dramatic Art – felt that the time was approaching for an assessment of his life and work to be made for a new generation of readers and by a writer who had not known G.B.S. personally. My nomination was advanced by Shaw's publisher, Max Reinhardt, for whose generous support I owe special thanks. Max Reinhardt's publications of Shaw's plays and non-dramatic works have done much during the past quarter of a century to keep them handsomely before the reading public in Britain. It is particularly appropriate that my biography should be brought out by the publishing group of which his company became a part, and which still publishes Shaw's books.

I did not begin research for this book until after I had finished my previous biography, a life of Augustus John. In 1975 I went to Ireland and started work, polishing up (as the years rolled by) my eloquent explanations as to why the book was not yet completed. It is easy to feel, over such a marathon, that one is wholly alone. In fact there have been many people who have given me aid and comfort on the way.

I remember with gratitude and affection the encouragement of the late Elizabeth Barber, the General Secretary of the Society of Authors (which acts as literary agent for the Shaw Estate), whose work has been most reliably carried on by Roma Woodnutt.

I am especially grateful also to Margery Morgan, a true Shavian scholar, who has rigorously scrutinized my text, recommending improvements and saving me from howlers; to Vivian Elliot, another Shavian expert, who took on the thankless but essential task of checking my quotations and references, and who has further assisted me with the illustrations; and Sarah Johnson, who has miraculously deciphered my handwriting over the years until she can now read it better than I can myself. Her typescript, littered with my revisions and emendations, has then been passed on to Richard Bates, whose magic word processor has enabled me to keep vicariously abreast of technical innovations that came too late in the composition of the book for me to utilize myself. The publication has been prepared from his discs and the savings in costs passed on to the purchaser.

At Chatto & Windus the book has benefited from the commitment of Carmen Callil and her team. I am particularly grateful for the syntactical severities of Hilary Laurie, whose editorial care has been reinforced by that of Joe Fox at Random House.

Shaw himself was determined that his books should be easily accessible to the general reading public, and I have tried to follow this example. I have not added to length or cost by appending a bibliography, since such a listing would merely repeat in part the excellent Soho Bibliography prepared by Dan H. Laurence and published at the Clarendon Press in 1983. A number of books published too late for inclusion in this bibliography have been valuable to me, among them four volumes of Shaw correspondence: *The Playwright and the Pirate. Bernard Shaw and Frank Harris: A Correspondence*, edited, with an introduction, by Stanley Weintraub (Pennsylvania State University Press, 1982); *Bernard Shaw and Alfred Douglas. A Correspondence*, edited by Mary Hyde (John Murray, 1982); *Bernard Shaw. Agitations. Letters to the Press 1875–1950*, edited by Dan H. Laurence and James Rambeau (Frederick Ungar, 1985); and *Bernard Shaw's Letters to Siegfried Trebitsch*, edited by Samuel A. Weiss (Stanford University Press, 1986). *Bernard Shaw: The Diaries* (two volumes), edited and annotated by Stanley Weintraub, were also published in 1986 by the Pennsylvania State University Press. Among recently published books about Shaw that have been useful are: *Bishop of Everywhere and the Life Force* by Warren Sylvester Smith (Pennsylvania State University Press, 1982); *The Unexpected Shaw. Biographical Approaches to G.B.S. and His Work* by Stanley Weintraub (Frederick Ungar, 1982); a two-pamphlet study in the Writers & Their Work Series, *Bernard Shaw* by Margery M. Morgan (Profile Books, 1982), a volume in the Gill's Irish Lives Series *G. B. Shaw* by John O'Donovan (Gill and Macmillan, 1983); and a study in the Macmillan Modern Dramatists Series, *George Bernard Shaw* by Arthur Ganz (Macmillan, 1983); *The Art and Mind of Shaw* by A. M. Gibbs (Gill and Macmillan, 1983); *Bernard Shaw. A Critical View* by Nicholas Grene in the Macmillan Studies in Anglo-Irish Literature; *The Nun, the Infidel and the Superman* by D. Felicitas Corrigan (John Murray, 1985); *Dear Mr Shaw: Selections from Bernard Shaw's Postbag* compiled and edited by Vivian Elliot (Bloomsbury, 1987); and the most valuable *Annual of Bernard Shaw Studies* (Pennsylvania State University Press) with which I have kept up from year to year.

Over these years I have also benefited from reviews and notices of Shaw's plays in performance by a number of theatre critics including Michael Billington, John Cushman, Walter Kerr, Francis King, Benedict Nightingale, John Peter, Michael Ratcliffe, John Simon and Irving Wardle.

Shaw has been posthumously most industrious over the last dozen years or so, and the sources that I have been listing as I wrote often refer to editions that are now superseded or holograph manuscripts that have since appeared in print. In the 1980s Shaw's *Collected Screenplays*, the early texts of his plays in facsimile, and the complete body of his musical criticism have come out in new publications; while the fourth and last volume of his *Collected Letters*, a new edition of his dramatic criticism and the novels in facsimile are all due to appear shortly. I therefore appeared to be confronted with the choice of either providing a list of sources that would (if I were to preserve consistency through the three volumes of this biography) be stupendously out of date, or of delaying publication beyond everyone's endurance including my own. To get round this difficulty I have decided to print my sources separately after the publication of the third volume of my biography. To those Shavian scholars who feel they cannot 'use' my book until these sources are to hand I offer my apologies. But they will know that by not charging general readers for an apparatus they will never use I am acting very much in line with Shaw's own economic practice of making his work fall within the means of as many people as possible. I hope that when my source notes become available, they will appear in a form that is both easier to use and of more lasting use.

I must also record my indebtedness to many people who have helped me in various ways: Ronald Adam, Henry Adler, Sidney P. Albert, Edward Allatt, Gillian Allen-Smith, Antony Alpers, Jean-Claude Amalric, Moira Annand, Jenny Armitage, David Astor, E. Wulston Atkins, M. C. Atkins, Bart Auerbach, Ronald Ayling, Cate

Bailey, Pace Barnes, Robert Becker, Alan Bell, Edward L. Bernays, Pauline Bewick, Molly Bishop, E. E. Bissell, Michael Bloch, R. E. Bodle, Alison M. Bond, Victor Bonham-Carter, Charles J. Boorkman, Clare Boylan, Sarah Bradford, Julia Briggs, Lord Brockway, Harold Brooks, Brigid Brophy, Julia Brown, the late Bernard F. Burgunder, Ada Burlison, Colin Burns, Lady Mairi Bury, Katherine N. Butler, Eric de Candole, D. H. M. Carter, John Casson, J. C. Catford, Molly Cathcart, P. C. Cattle, B. McM. Caven, the late Lord David Cecil, Gwen Cherrell, Susan Chitty, the late Lord Clark, Arthur C. Clarke, John P. Clarke, Margaret Clarke, Dame Frances Clode, Moyra Clough, Tamara Coates, Honor Cobb, Caesar Cohen, the late Dame Margaret Cole, the late John Stewart Collis, Agnes Connely, Alistair Cooke, John Coulter, Philip Coverdale, Nigel Cragg, Jill Craigie, Jonathan Croall, Leigh Crutchley, William H. Davenport, Roy Davids, R. J. Davies, Stan Gébler Davies, John Dawick, Richard Digby Day, Eleanor Deeping, Paul Delaney, Michael De-la-Noy, Gordon Dickerson, Emma Dickinson, Noeleen Dowling, Phyllis Doyle, Rose Doyle, Janet Dunbar, Beanárd ó Dubhthaigh, Bernard F. Dukore, Ellen Smith Dunlap, David Dunn, Alita Dušek, Boris Dvorkovitz, Dorothy Eagle, J. Alex. Edmison, Michael Edmonds, C. H. Edwards, Lord Eliot, the late Richard Ellmann, Jack Emery, T. F. Evans, Victoria Fattorini, John Felstiner, Patrick J. Ferry, W. P. K. Findlay, Kieran Flanagan, C. A. Kyrle Fletcher, Dorothea Flower, Bryan Forbes, Eric Ford, Stephen Foster, Brian Fothergill, Heinrich Fraenkel, Diana Freeman, Charlotte Frieze, Jonathan Fryer, Patrick Garland, G. A. Garreau, F. E. Gaythorpe, Anthony Geikie-Cobb, Ron Genders, Monica George, the late Winifred Gérin, the late Monk Gibbon, A. M. Gibbs, the late Val Gielgud, Martin Gilbert, Brendan Gill, the late Douglas Glass, Victoria Glendinning, R. G. Goodes, Hubert Gregg, Elizabeth Grice, Gareth Griffith, Miron Grindea, John Groser, Phyllis Grosskurth, Pamela Grove, the late Winifred Gwyn-Jeffreys, John Haffenden, Raymond C. Hagel, Norman Hancock, Anthony Hanson, George M. Harper, Rex Harrison, W. L. D. D'Arcy Hart, Walter Hartley, J. Harvey, Leon G. Harvey, Christopher Hawtree, Inez Heron, Jim Herrick, Christopher Hibbert, Frank Hildy, Dame Wendy Hiller, Bevis Hillier, H. M. Hoather, Diana Holman-Hunt, Simon Hornby, A. A. B. Howard, Sheila Huftel, Richard Hugget, N. Hughes, Ida Hughes-Stanton, Michael Hurd, Angela Huth, Graham Hutton, H. Montgomery Hyde, Gill Ingle, Winifred Innes, Norman Inwood, Laurence Irving, Ann M. E. Jackson, Richard Austen Jerrams, Ann Johnson, Dudley Jones, Julia Jones, Michael G. Jordan, Richard Joseph, Maud Karpeles, Jacqueline Kavanagh, Janet Kersley, Daniel J. Kevles, Rowland Knoyle, Paul S. Koda, H. P. Kraus, G. Krishnamurti, Mary Lago, Sally Leach, Monica Lera, Robert Lescher, the late Seymour Leslie, Bernard Levin, Paul Levy, Cecil Lewis, Sarah Lewis, Olivia Lichtenstein, E. J. Linehan, Linda Lloyd Jones, the Countess of Longford, Roger Louis, David Low, John Lucas, Moira Lynd, Arthur Lynnford Smith, H. D. Lyon, Judy Lyons, Jeremy Maas, C. R. McDonald, Leslie Macdonald, Nesta Macdonald, Frederick P. W. McDowell, J. R. Mace, Sue MacGregor, David Machin, the late Jeanne MacKenzie, Norman MacKenzie, A. N. MacKinnon, Joan Margaret Mackinnon, Niall McLaughlin, M. K. C. MacMahon, Tom McNamara, Desmond J. McRory, Rodney Maingot, Raymond Mander, Charles Mann, David Marcus, Jan Marsh, Henry Marshall, T. D. M. Martin, J. I. Mason, Eilis Dillon Mercier, Gabriel Merle, Michael Meyer, P. Blossom Miles, Elaine Mitchell, Joe Mitchenson, Raymond Monk, the late Ivor Montagu, Jerrold Northrop Moore, Elaine Morgan, Arthur B. Morley, Robert Morley, Sybil Morley, Hugh Moxey, William Murphy, John G.

Murray, Maurice Newnes, Nancy Nicholson, Margaret Nickson, Eric Norris, Lucy Norton, Robin Oatridge, Eileen O'Casey, Finstan M. O'Connor, Garry O'Connor, Richard O'Donoghue, the late John O'Donovan, Suzanne O'Farrell, Stanley Olson, Richard Pankhurst, Enid St John Parry, Molly Patterson, Egon Pearson, Steffen Lauge Pedersen, Dorothy Perkins, Margot Peters, Murray T. Pheils, Esmee Phillips, Keith Piercy, A. Pilbeach, the late James Pitman, Ellen Pollock, Reginald Pound, Jean Pownall, Svetlana Prokhorova, Philippa Pullar, M.-E. de Putron, Steve Race, Angela Raspin, Kenneth Reid, Gladys Reynolds, the late I. A. Richards, John Rickard, W. A. Robson, Patricia W. Romero, Adrian Rose, Jim Rose, Abraham Rosenthal, Irving Rosenwater, Anthony Rota, Sir John Rothenstein, Hilary Rubinstein, Cyril Russell, Dora Russell, M. J. Russell, Mary J. Ryan, R. A. Salaman, Leonard Salzedo, E. Michael Salzer, Dorothy Sara, Philip Sargant Florence, John Saumarez Smith, David Schire, the late Hans Schmoller, John L. Scott, the late Martin Secker, Dora Seimons, Margaret Shaw, M. C. Shaw, Dinah Sheean, Russell Sidgwick, the Viscountess Simon, A. Simpson, Geoffrey Sircom, Robert Skidelsky, Martyn Skinner, Arthur Lynnford Smith, W. Roger Smith, Barbara Smoker, Colin Smythe, O. F. Snelling, James Somerset-Sullivan, Ruth Spalding, Peter Stattersfield, Nancy Stone, John Sullivan, Herbert Sumsion, David C. Sutton, Anthony Swerling, Rebecca Swift, Lola Szladits, Arch Tait, Mary Taubman, the late Elizabeth Taylor, J. R. Teggin, Winifred Thomson, Ann Thwaite, Robert Tilling, Claire Tomalin, Peter Tomkins, Feliks Topolski, the late Theodosia Townshend, Geoffrey Trease, A. W. Tuke, Christine Tuke, Brenda Tyler, Grace Usher, H. R. Vallentine, Anita van de Vleet, Betty Vernon, Gillian Vincent, P. Beaumont Wadsworth, Thomas C. Wallace, John Wardrop, Barbara Warner, Nora Warren, Rodelle Weintraub, Stanley Weintraub, Margaret Wheeler, Eric Walter White, Harold White, Terence de Vere White, Alan Wilkes, Mary Wilkinson, Audrey Williamson, Stella Williamson, Colin Wilson, Colin H. Wilson, John Wilson, J. M. Wilson, J. M. Wilson-Wright, Stephen Winsten, Reece Winstone, Joan Winterkorn, J. Howard Woolmer, Gordon Wormald, Eugenia Zilliacus.

The following institutions hold Shaw material or have kindly helped me to locate such material: Abbey Theatre, Dublin; All Soul's College, Oxford (Codrington Library); International Instituut voor Sociale Geschiedenis, Amsterdam; University of Arkansas Library; Society of Authors, London; Leo Baeck Institute, New York; University of Bath Library; University of Birmingham Library; Bodleian Library, Oxford; Book Trust (Book Information Bureau), London; Boston Public Library, Boston, Massachusetts; Boston University (Mugar Memorial Library); Brandeis University Library; British Broadcasting Corporation (Sound Archives, Television and Videotape Library, Written Archives Centre); British Library; British Theatre Institute, London; Bromsgrove Public Library; Bucknell University (Ellen Clarke Bertrand Library); University of Calgary Library (Special Collections Division); University of California, Berkeley (Bancroft Library); University of California Library, Los Angeles; California State University Library, Fullerton; Cambridge University Library; Camden Central Library, London; University of Carbondale, Southern Illinois (Morris Library); University of North Carolina, Chapel Hill (Southern Historical Collection); Lord Chamberlain's Archive, London; Chestnut Hill College (Logue Library), Philadelphia, Pennsylvania; University of Chicago (Joseph Regenstein Library); Christ Church Library, Oxford (Driberg Collection); Christie, Manson & Wood Ltd, London; Churchill College Library, Cambridge; Colby College Library,

Waterville, Maine; University of Colorado Library; Columbia University in the City of New York (Rare Book and Manuscript Library); Library of Congress, Washington; Cornell University Library (Bernard F. Burgunder Collection); Cumbria Record Office, Carlisle; Cyclists' Touring Club; Dallas Public Library (Fine Arts Archives Division); Dartington Hall Trust, Devon; Dartmouth College (Baker Memorial Library), Hanover, New Hampshire; University of Delaware Library; Detroit Public Library; Edward Laurence Doheny Memorial Library (Estelle Doheny Collection), California; Dorset County Museum, Dorchester; Edinburgh University Library; Elgar Foundation; Elgar's Birthplace Museum, Broadheath, Herefordshire; the Trustees of the Sir Edward Elgar Will Trust; the Fabian Society; the Fitzwilliam Museum, Cambridge; Folger Shakespeare Library, Washington; Georgetown University Library; Goldsmith's College (Rachel McMillan Library), London; Gorki Institute, Moscow; Hartwell Brothers, Memphis, Tennessee; Harvard Theater Collection; Harvard University (Houghton Library); County Council of Hereford and Worcester (Record Office); Hertfordshire County Council (Library Service); G. Heywood Hill Ltd; Royal Commission on Historical Manuscripts; Hofstra University Library, Hempstead, New York; University of Hull (Brynmor Jones Library); Huntingdon Library; University of Illinois Library, Urbana-Champaign; Indiana University (Lilly Library); University of Iowa Libraries; Bank of Ireland; National Library of Ireland; Irish Government Record Office, Dublin; Public Record Office of Northern Ireland; Jesus College Library, Oxford; University of Keele Library; King's College Library, Cambridge; the Labour Party, London; University of Liverpool Library; Location Register of Twentieth Century Manuscripts and Letters, Reading; University of London Library; Greater London Record Office; London School of Economics (Passfield Trust Papers; British Library of Political and Economic Science); House of Lords Record Office; Manchester Public Libraries (Central Library); McMaster University (Mills Memorial Library), Ontario; Merton College Library, Oxford; University of Michigan Library; Mills College Library; William Morris Gallery, Walthamstow; National Trust; People's Theatre, Newcastle; University of Newcastle upon Tyne (Pybus Collection); New Jersey Historical Society; State University of New York, Buffalo; New York University (Fales Library); New York Public Libraries (Arent Collection, Astor, Lennox and Tilden Foundations, Berg Collection, Manuscripts and Archives Division, Rare Book Division); New York Public Library, Lincoln Center (Library and Museum of the Performing Arts); Northwestern University Library (Special Collections Department); Nuffield College Library (Fabian Society Archive); University of Oregon Library; Parke-Bernet Galleries Inc.; Penguin Books Ltd; University of Pennsylvania (Charles Petterson Van Pelt Library); Pennsylvania State University (Patee Library, Institute for the Arts and Humanistic Studies); Free Library of Philadelphia (Rare Book Department); International Museum of Photography at George Eastman House; Pierpont Morgan Library, New York; Plunkett Foundation, Oxford; Players' Club; National Portrait Gallery, London; Princeton University (Rare Books and Special Collections, Robert H. Taylor Library); Incorporated Society for Psychical Research, London; University of Reading Library; Kenneth W. Rendell, Inc.; Rhodes House Library, Oxford; Rice University (Fondren Library); London Borough of Richmond-upon-Thames (Central Reference Library); University of Rochester Library; Musée Rodin, Paris; Rosenbach Museum and Library, Philadelphia; Bertram Rota Ltd, London; Ruskin College, Oxford; John Rylands University Library, Manchester; St Pancras Library (Heal Collection), London; National Library of Scotland, Edinburgh; National Register of Archives (Scotland); Scott Polar Research Institute, Cambridge; Scottish Record Office; Scripps College Library; Shaw Festival Theater Foundation, Niagara-on-the-Lake, Ontario; Shaw Society, London; Sheffield Central Library; Somerville College Library, Oxford; Sotheby Parke Bernet & Co.; University of Southern California (Special Collections); Stanbrook Abbey; Stanford University Libraries, California; Kunglika Biblioteket, Stockholm; Royal College of Surgeons Library, London; University of Sussex Library; Royal Swedish Academy, Stockholm; College of Tagore Studies and Research, West Bengal; University of Texas (Harry Ransom Humanities Research Center, T. E. Hanley Collection); The Times Archive, London; Alexander Turnbull Library, Wellington, New Zealand; London Vegetarian Society; Victoria and Albert Museum (British Theatre Museum, Gabrielle Enthoven Collection); University of Victoria, British Columbia; University of Virginia Library; National Library of Wales; Washington University Libraries, St Louis; A. P. Watt Ltd, London; Wellcome Institute for the History of Medicine; Westchester State College Library; Williams College, Massachusetts (Chapin Library); Vaughan Williams Memorial Library (Cecil Sharp House), London; John Wilson (Autographs) Ltd; Yale University (Beinecke Rare Book and Manuscript Library); Zeitlin & Ver Brugge.

I am aware that such lists inadequately record my indebtedness to some of the people and institutions that have assisted me, and that because of the length of time involved I may inadvertently have omitted some names. For this I can only offer my apologies and plead an ageing memory.

Finally, I would like to thank the Shaw Estate for the contributions it has made to my research expenses and for its exemplary patience.

MICHAEL HOLROYD. London. January 1988

## ILLUSTRATION ACKNOWLEDGEMENTS

15, 16B, 16C, 17, 20, 26, 30A and B, 31. Courtesy of the BBC Hulton Picture Library. 1, 3, 4, 5, 7. Courtesy of the British Library. 8. Courtesy of the Trustees of the British Museum. 32. Courtesy of Archibald Henderson, *Bernard Shaw Playboy and Prophet*, D. Appleton and Company, New York, 1932. 2, 28. Courtesy of Archibald Henderson, *Man of the Century*, Appleton, Century, Crofts, New York, 1956. 9. Courtesy of Jaeger. 24. Courtesy of Doris Arthur Jones, *Life and Letters of Henry Arthur Jones*, Victor Gollancz Ltd, London, 1930. 13, 22A and 27. Courtesy of Dan H. Laurence, *Collected Letters Vol. I*, Max Reinhardt Ltd, London, 1965. 29A and B, 30 and 31. Courtesy of Dan. H. Laurence, *Collected Letters Vol. II*, Max Reinhardt Ltd, London, 1970. 11. Courtesy of the Dan H. Laurence collection, University of Guelph Library, Guelph, Ontario. 6. Courtesy of F. E. Lowenstein, *Bernard Shaw Through the Camera*, B. & H. White Publications Ltd, 1948. 16A and 19. Courtesy of Norman and Jeanne Mackenzie, *The First Fabians*, Weidenfeld and Nicolson, London, 1977. 29A and B, 30A and B. Courtesy of the National Trust. 14 and 21. Courtesy of Hesketh Pearson, *Bernard Shaw: his Life and Personality*, Collins, London, 1942. 22B and C. Courtesy of the Victoria and Albert Museum.

# INDEX

474

477

education, 39–40, 42; influenced by
Dickens, 40–1; influenced by
Shakespeare, 41; musical training,
42–3, 51–2, 54, 57, 66; employment at
Uniacke Townshend, 46, 52–3, 58–9,
60; and 'The Calypso Infatuation',
54–5, 106; early works, 56; theatre-
going in Dublin, 56–7; leaves Ireland,
58, 59–60; first summer in London,
61; writes Lee's Hornet criticisms,
62–4; early literary activities (Passion
Play, My Dear Dorothea), 70–3; begins
Immaturity, 73 (see Works); looks for
work, 76; with Edison Telephone
Company, 77–8, 79–80, 81; back in
literary world, 80–1; begins Irrational
Knot, 81 (see Works); self-education at
the British Museum, 84, 98, 102; and
vegetarianism, 84–9, 90, 93; attitude to
alcohol, 89–90; begins Love Among the
Artists, 91 (see Works); gets smallpox,
91–3; campaigns against vaccination,
91–3, 420–2; convalesces, 93; physical
appearance, 93–4, 193; teaches himself
shorthand, 97–8; further attempts to
find work, 98; begins Cashel Byron's
Profession, 98 (see Works); awkwardness
at social gatherings, 99–101; joins
societies, 101, 126; early friendships,
101–2; relationship with the Beattys,
102–4, 105, 114; takes up boxing, 104;
turns to journalism, 104–5; relations
with women, 106–8, 151; affair with
Alice Lockett, 109–13; moves with
mother to Osnaburgh Street, 113;
writes An Unsocial Socialist, 115 (see
Works); interest in socialism awakes,
116, 121, 124, 125–6, 127–9; novels
are published, 120, 121; joins Zetetical
Society, 126; joins literary groups,
126–7; influenced by Henry George,
127–9; goes to meetings of Social
Democratic Federation, 129–30, 131;
introduced to Marxism, 130; joins
Fabian Society, 131, 132–3, 171; edits
Gronlund's Cooperative Commonwealth,
133–4; 'slips into paid journalism', 134;
friendship and collaboration with
Archer (q.v.) 134; on Pall Mall Gazette
(q.v.), 138; on Magazine of Music, 138;
as music critic on Dramatic Review, 138;
refuses Archer's help, 138–40; as art
critic on The World (q.v.), 138–9,
140–4, 147, 149, 213, 215, 216; and
Grace Black, 151–3; infiltration of
Avelings, 153–5; and Blands, 155–8;
affair with Jenny Patterson, 159, 161–6,
170–1, 247, 248–50, 251, 259–61; and
'Jaegerism', 159–61; liaison with Annie

Besant, 167–71; disagreement with
Hyndman, 171–2; meets Sidney Webb
(q.v.), 172; as key figure in Fabian
Society, 174–6, 177–80, 181, 188,
269–73, 275; member of Hampstead
Historic Society, 180–1; in fight against
anarchists, 181–2; takes part in early
demonstrations, 184–6; declines to run
for Parliament, 187–8, 412;
collaborates on Fabian Essays, 188–90;
moves to Fitzroy Square, 191–2; public
lectures, 192–7; brings out The
Quintessence of Ibsenism, 198 (see Works);
his life as chronicled in his diaries, 212,
216–8; as music critic (Corno di
Bassetto) for The Star (q.v.), 214–5;
travels abroad, 218–19; and Grace
Gilchrist, 219–21; and Geraldine
Spooner, 221; 'Sunday husbandry' at
the Salts, 221–3; and May Morris,
223–30; becomes music critic (G.B.S.)
for The World (q.v.), 237; meets
Florence Farr (q.v.), 246; fascination
with the stage, 252, 256, 257, 274; sees
Janet Achurch (q.v.) for the first time,
254; and Beatrice Webb (q.v.), 265;
takes up bicycling, 267–8; collaborates
with Archer on Rhinegold, 274 (see
Widowers' Houses, under Works); works
on unfinished novel, 275, 277;
collaborates with Braekstad, 277–8;
works on The Cassone, 278; and J. T.
Grein, 279–80, 289, 296; Olivier as
catalyst for The Philanderer, 284–5 (see
Works); writes Mrs Warren's Profession,
289–91 (see Works); begins Arms and the
Man, 297 (see Works); and Elizabeth
Robins, 311–14; visits Italy with Art
Workers' Club, 314; begins Candida,
314 (see Works); negotiates with
Mansfield over staging of Candida,
320–25; agrees to write for Harris's
Saturday Review (q.v.), 327–9; and
Eleanora Duse, 344–5; and Ellen
Terry, 346, 355–7, 358, 367–8, 370,
373, 375; writes Man of Destiny for
Terry, 345 (see Works); antagonism for
Irving, 351–3, 357–61, 367, 377; as a
true Shakespearean, 359–60; article on
Irving's Richard III, 360, 361, 362–4;
further involvement with Janet Achurch,
369–83; writes You Never Can Tell, 383
(see Works); writes The Devil's Disciple,
392 (see Works); publishes Plays Pleasant
and Unpleasant, 399–405; attitude to
Frank Harris, 405–7; and establishment
of the London School of Economics,
409–11; elected to St Pancras Vestry,
412; activities as vestryman 413–25;

Beatrice Webb's desire to see married, 426, 427, 428, 429–30, 431; and Bertha Newcombe, 427–31; meets Charlotte Payne-Townshend, 432; and subsequent 'courtship', *see under* Shaw, Charlotte; opposes Bessie Shaw's spiritualism, 451–3; foot injury and operation, 456, 457–8, 459–60, 461; income, 462–3; marriage 464–5

*Shaw on*:

ancestry, 5; art and artists, 140–7, 149–50; his art criticism, 140; Annie Besant, 168–9; his childhood, 17, 18; children, 72, 73; cremation, 419; death, 21–2; Dublin, 16, 27, 49, 59; families, 18–19; his father, 15, 27, 30, 31, 32, 50; his grandfather, 9–10; Walter Gurly, 29–30; Hyndman and the SDF, 172; his Irishness, 3, 5, 22, 28; Keats, 148–9; Lee, 23, 26, 30, 44–5, 49–50, 64–5, 67; London, 61, 68–9, 70; morality, 191; Morris, 147–8, 149; his mother, 11, 16–17, 18, 20, 26, 29; music, 231; novelists and his own novel writing, 121–2; the Press, 104–5, 422; rating system in London, 415; Rationalism, 96–7; relations, 8; religion, 30, 38–9, 72; Ruskin, 142, 143; schooling, 33, 35, 36, 40; sex, 17, 161, 163, 251; society women, 109–10; vaccination, 92, 420–2; vegetarianism, 84–9, 90; Sidney Webb, 172; women on public bodies, 416–17. *See also Pall Mall Gazette; Saturday Review; Star, The; World, The; and the following entry*

*Shaw's letters and communications to*:

Janet Achurch, on bicycling, 267; on taking to socialism, 275; on burning *The Philanderer*, 286; on *Arms and the Man*, 299–300; on wish to 'get a turn at dramatic criticism', 329; on *The Man of Destiny*, 349; on *You Never Can Tell*, 388; on *The Devil's Disciple*, 393; on writing for the stage, 398; on publishing his plays, 401; on Bertha Newcombe, 429; on being with Charlotte at the Webbs, 434–5

William Archer, on Continental travel, 218–19; on *The Philanderer*, 288; on *Mrs Warren's Profession*, 292

Lena Ashwell, on public speaking, 196; on his giving up theatre criticism, 454

Pakenham Beatty, on St Pancras Vestry election (1894), 414; on marrying Charlotte, 455

John Burns, on appointment to St Pancras Vestry, 412

Ferruccio Busoni, on Mozart, 243

Charles Charrington, on *The Philanderer*, 289; on *Arms and the Man*, 300

G. K. Chesterton, on Irishmen, 28

Norman Clark, on writing, 212

Sydney Cockerell, on strain of life, 371

Margaret Cole, on visiting Beatrice Webb, 265

E. T. Cook, on 'Bloody Sunday', 186

Alfred Douglas, on Frank Harris, 406

Osman Edwards, on *Candida*, 316

Havelock Ellis, on Graham Wallas, 176; on writing a book on political economy, 197

St John Ervine, on Lee's religious views, 30; on leaving Ireland, 60

Frederick Evans, on publishers, 399

John Galsworthy, on literary men, 99

Phelan Gibb, on his art criticism, 143

Harley Granville Barker, on *The Philanderer*, 288; on *You Never Can Tell*, 385

Frank Harris, on his mother and Lee, 30; on Lee's buying 13 Park Lane, 65; on being a philanderer, 158; on his sexuality, 251

Archibald Henderson, on his mother, 16; on himself at school, 34; on logic, 96; on *Cashel Byron's Profession*, 115; on art criticism, 142; on Webb, 174

T. Tighe Hopkins, on *Cashel Byron's Profession*, 115; on writing dialogues, 278; on his newly felt confidence in his own ability to write plays, 279

James Huneker, on *Candida*, 317

Holbrook Jackson, on writing an '"Arrows of the Chace" volume', 140; on his favourite type, 402–3

F. Keddell, on Annie Besant and joining the Fabian Society, 168

Hugh Kingsmill, on obtaining *Saturday Review* post, 406

Gertrude Kingston, on *Mrs Warren's Profession*, 295

Lady Londonderry, on Webb, 173

Edith Lyttelton, on death, 22

Charles McEvoy, on his appearance, 94

Margaret Mackail, on childhood, 60

Alexander Macmillan, on *Immaturity*, 75

Beatrice Mansfield, on *You Never Can Tell*, 390; on *The Devil's Disciple*, 397; on Richard Mansfield's acting abilities, 453; on marriage to Charlotte, 461

Kingsley Martin, on Webb, 173

John Martin-Harvey, on *The Man of Destiny*, 349–50

H. W. Massingham, on his work as Corno di Bassetto, 236

Alma Murray, on writing a play, 278–9; on *Arms and the Man*, 306

Gilbert Murray, on dreaming of his mother, 20

482

ABOUT THE AUTHOR

MICHAEL HOLROYD, who was born in 1935, is half Swedish and partly Irish. In 1968 his *Lytton Strachey* was acclaimed as a landmark in contemporary biography and, six years later, his *Augustus John* confirmed his place as one of the most influential modern biographers. He has worked for fifteen years on the research and writing of *Bernard Shaw*. He lives in London and is married to Margaret Drabble.